MAIMONIDES

MISHNEH TORAH

Hilchot Ishut
The Laws of Marriage
הלכות אישות

MAIMONIDES

MISHNEH TORAH

Hilchot Ishut
The Laws of Marriage

A new translation with commentaries and notes

by
Rabbi Eliyahu Touger

MOZNAIM PUBLISHING CORPORATION
NEW YORK / JERUSALEM

רמב"ם
משנה תורה
הלכות אישות

תורגם מחדש לאנגלית
עם מקורות, הערות ודיאגרמות

מאת
הרב אליהו תגר

בית הוצאת ספרים
מאזנים
ירושלים — ניו יארק
תשנ"ה

For information write:
Moznaim Publishing Corporation
4304 12th Avenue
Brooklyn, New York 11219
Tel. (718) 438-7680, 853-0525

ISBN 1-885220-01-4

Printed and bound in Jerusalem, Israel
by Vagshal Ltd.
Typesetting by Vagshal Ltd.
Jerusalem

Printed in Israel

TABLE OF CONTENTS

Hilchot Eruvin

Introduction

Just as a human being represents a fusion of body and soul, so too, the Torah has a body, the laws and practices it ordains, and a soul, the spiritual feelings that these laws and practices propagate.

These two dimensions work hand in hand. For there is no way that the intellectual and emotional att ributes that distinguish our Jewish heritage can be spawned without careful adherence to Torah law. And conversely, there is no way that Torah law can remain a rigid system that promotes observance without appreciating the spiritual goals toward which that observance is directed.

If the above is true of the comprehensive body of Torah law, it is particularly applicable with regard to the laws under discussion in this volume, the laws of marriage. The Jewish home has always been regarded as a model of harmony and tranquil activity. And this atmosphere is a direct outgrowth of the structure of family life mandated by Torah law.

This volume includes a digest of all the laws pertaining to marriage. Although the focus is primarily on the halachic elements of the laws of marriage, by thinking into the laws, one can appreciate the inner dimension towards which they point. And at times the Rambam puts the focus clearly on the inner dimension. Thus at the conclusion of Chapter 15, he states:

> Our Sages commanded that a man honor his wife more than his own person, and love her as he loves his own person. If he has financial resources, he should offer her benefits in accordance with his resources. He should not cast a superfluous measure of fear over her. He should talk with her gently, neither being sad, nor angry.
>
> And similarly, they commanded a woman to honor her husband exceedingly, and to be in awe of him. She should carry out all her deeds according to his directives, considering him as an officer or a king. She should follow the desires of his heart and shun everything which he disdains.
>
> This is the custom of holy and pure Jewish women and men in their marriages. And these ways will make their marriage pleasant and praiseworthy.

* * * *

Give and take, and the synergistic fusion of divergent energies, lies at the core of any successful marriage. These principles are reflected, not only in the content, but also in the composition of this text. It was a team effort, made possible by the combined efforts of many individuals. The full list of all those involved is too long to mention. At the very least, however, recognition must be granted to the following individuals:

Rabbi Moshe Weiner for checking the sources and the accuracy of the translation;

Ira L. Jacobson for his editorial contributions;

Hinda Esther Baruch for proofreading;

Avraham Eisenbach, Dov Schwartz, Michah Witzel, and the entire staff of Moznaim publications for the graphics and layout, which greatly enhance the text;

Finally, my publishers, Rabbis Chanoch and Menachem Wagshall, whose cooperation, support and dedication to the spread of Torah have made working with them a pleasure.

* * *

Every marriage on the earthly plane is an extension of the ultimate marriage bond, the relationship between G-d and the Jewish people. The consummation of this marriage bond will be in the Era of the Redemption, when "with everlasting kindness I will have compassion on you, says G-d your Redeemer" (Isaiah 54:9).

May the printing of this text and its study bring us closer to this ultimate goal.

the 20th of Cheshvan, 5755   *Eliyahu Touger*
Har Nof, Jerusalem

"The instruction of the wise is a source of life, diverting one from deathly pitfalls" (Proverbs 13:14)

The Fourth Book

Sefer Nashim
The Book of [Laws Governing Relations with] Women

It contains five *halachot*. They are, in order:
Hilchot Ishut - The Laws of Marriage
Hilchot Gerushin - The Laws of Divorce
Hilchot Yibbum VaChalitzah - The Laws Pertaining to *Yibbum* and *Chalitzah*
Hilchot Na'arah Betulah - The Laws Pertaining to a Virgin Maiden
Hilchot Sotah - The Laws Pertaining to a *Sotah*

Hilchot Ishut - The Laws of Marriage

They contain four mitzvot: two positive commandments and two negative commandments. They are:

1) To marry a woman, granting her the rights of the formal marriage contract (*ketubah*) and sanctifying the relationship through the rites of *kiddushin*;
2) Not to have relations with a woman unless she has been granted a marriage contract, and the relationship sanctified through the rites of *kiddushin*;
3) Not to deny her food, clothing and marital relations;
4) To be fruitful and multiply.
These mitzvot are explained in the chapters [that follow].

תּוֹרַת חָכָם מְקוֹר חַיִּים, לָסוּר מִמֹּקְשֵׁי מָוֶת:

סֵפֶר נָשִׁים

וְהוּא

סֵפֶר רְבִיעִי

הִלְכוֹתָיו חָמֵשׁ. וְזֶהוּ סִדּוּרָן:

הִלְכוֹת אִישׁוּת
הִלְכוֹת גֵּרוּשִׁין
הִלְכוֹת יִבּוּם וַחֲלִיצָה
הִלְכוֹת נַעֲרָה בְתוּלָה
הִלְכוֹת סוֹטָה

וְהַמִּצְוֹת הַנִּכְלָלִים בָּהֶם מְפֹרָשִׁים בִּשְׁמוֹתָם בִּמְקוֹמוֹתָם.

הִלְכוֹת אִישׁוּת

יֵשׁ בִּכְלָלָן אַרְבַּע מִצְוֹת: שְׁתֵּי מִצְוֹת עֲשֵׂה, וּשְׁתֵּי מִצְוֹת לֹא־תַעֲשֶׂה, וְזֶה הוּא פְּרָטָן:

א) לִשָּׂא אִשָּׁה בִּכְתֻבָּה וְקִדּוּשִׁין.
ב) שֶׁלֹּא תִבָּעֵל אִשָּׁה בְּלֹא כְתֻבָּה וּבְלֹא קִדּוּשִׁין.
ג) שֶׁלֹּא יִמְנַע שְׁאֵר כְּסוּת וְעוֹנָה.
ד) לִפְרוֹת וְלִרְבּוֹת מִמֶּנָּה.

וּבֵאוּר מִצְוֹת אֵלוּ בִּפְרָקִים אֵלוּ:

CHAPTER ONE

1. Before the Torah was given, when a man would meet a woman in the marketplace and he and she decided to marry, he would bring her home, conduct relations in private and thus make her his wife. Once the Torah was given, the Jews were commanded that when a man desires to marry a woman, he must acquire her as a wife in the presence of witnesses. [Only] after this, does she become his wife. This is [alluded to in Deuteronomy 22:13]: "When a man takes a wife and has relations with her...."

2. This process of acquisition fulfills [one of] the Torah's positive commandments.[1] The process of acquiring a wife is formalized in three ways: through [the transfer of] money, through [the transfer of a] formal document and through sexual relations.

[The effectiveness of] sexual relations and [the transfer of a] formal document have their origin in the Torah [itself], while [the effectiveness of transfer of] money is Rabbinic in origin.[2]

This process of acquisition is universally referred to as *erusin* ("betrothal") or *kiddushin* ("consecration"). And a woman who is acquired in any of these three ways is referred to as *mekudeshet* or *me'ureset*.

3. Once this process of acquisition has been formalized and a woman has become *mekudeshet*, she is considered to be married even though the marriage bond has not been consummated and she has not entered her husband's home. Should anyone other than her husband engage in sexual relations with her, he is liable to be executed by the court. If her husband desires to divorce her, he must compose a *get* [a formal bill of divorce].

4. Before the Torah was given, when a man would meet a woman in the marketplace, and he and she desired, he could give her payment, engage in

---

1. *Sefer HaMitzvot* (Positive Commandment 213) and *Sefer HaChinuch* (Mitzvah 552) include this as one of the Torah's 613 commandments.

2. The Ra'avad and others object to this statement, noting that *Kiddushin* 4b derives the concept that the transfer of money is an effective means of formalizing a marriage bond from a *gezerah shavah*, a correlation between two verses in the Torah, indicating that this practice also has its source in the Torah.

The *Maggid Mishneh* and the *Kessef Mishneh* draw attention to the Rambam's statements in *Sefer HaMitzvot* (General Principle 2), which state that any law that is not explicitly stated in the Torah, but rather derived through the Thirteen Principles of Biblical exegesis, is considered to be Rabbinic in origin (*midivrei soferim*). This classification does not, however, in any way diminish the status of this practice, and it is as if it were explicitly stated in the Torah. Thus, a marriage bond formalized through the transfer of money has the same status as one formalized through either of the other means mentioned by the Rambam.

פֶּרֶק רִאשׁוֹן

א קֹדֶם מַתַּן תּוֹרָה הָיָה אָדָם פּוֹגֵעַ אִשָּׁה בַּשּׁוּק, אִם רָצָה הוּא וְהִיא לִשָּׂא לְשָׂא אוֹתָהּ — מַכְנִיסָהּ לְתוֹךְ בֵּיתוֹ וּבוֹעֲלָהּ בֵּינוֹ לְבֵין עַצְמוֹ, וְתִהְיֶה לוֹ לְאִשָּׁה. כֵּיָן שֶׁנִּתְּנָה תּוֹרָה נִצְטַוּוּ יִשְׂרָאֵל, שֶׁאִם יִרְצֶה הָאִישׁ לִשָּׂא אִשָּׁה — יִקְנֶה אוֹתָהּ תְּחִלָּה בִּפְנֵי עֵדִים, וְאַחַר כָּךְ תִּהְיֶה לוֹ לְאִשָּׁה; שֶׁנֶּאֱמַר: כִּי יִקַּח אִישׁ אִשָּׁה וּבָא אֵלֶיהָ.

ב וְלִקּוּחִין אֵלּוּ — מִצְוַת עֲשֵׂה שֶׁל תּוֹרָה הֵם. וּבְאֶחָד מִשְּׁלֹשָׁה דְּבָרִים אֵלּוּ הָאִשָּׁה נִקְנֵית: בְּכֶסֶף, אוֹ בִּשְׁטָר, אוֹ בְּבִיאָה. בְּבִיאָה וּבִשְׁטָר — מֵהַתּוֹרָה, וּבְכֶסֶף — מִדִּבְרֵי סוֹפְרִים. וְלִקּוּחִין אֵלּוּ, הֵן הַנִּקְרָאִין קִדּוּשִׁין אוֹ אֵרוּסִין בְּכָל מָקוֹם. וְאִשָּׁה שֶׁנִּקְנֵת בְּאֶחָד מִשְּׁלֹשָׁה דְּבָרִים אֵלּוּ, הִיא הַנִּקְרֵאת מְקֻדֶּשֶׁת אוֹ מְאֹרֶסֶת.

ג וְכֵיָן שֶׁנִּקְנֵת הָאִשָּׁה וְנַעֲשֵׂת מְקֻדֶּשֶׁת, אַף־עַל־פִּי שֶׁלֹּא נִבְעֲלָה וְלֹא נִכְנְסָה לְבֵית בַּעֲלָהּ — הֲרֵי הִיא אֵשֶׁת אִישׁ. וְהַבָּא עָלֶיהָ חוּץ מִבַּעֲלָהּ — חַיָּב מִיתַת בֵּית דִּין. וְאִם רָצָה לְגָרֵשׁ — צְרִיכָה גֵּט.

ד קֹדֶם מַתַּן תּוֹרָה הָיָה אָדָם פּוֹגֵעַ אִשָּׁה בַּשּׁוּק, אִם רָצָה הוּא וְהִיא — נוֹתֵן לָהּ שְׂכָרָהּ וּבוֹעֵל אוֹתָהּ עַל אִם הַדֶּרֶךְ וְהוֹלֵךְ.

Rav Kapach differs and states that the Rambam altered the text in his later years, and the correct version states, "All three are from the Torah." In explanation, he draws attention to the Rambam's Commentary on the Mishnah (*Kiddushin* 1:1) and to one of the Rambam's responsa, and on this basis differs with the above principle.

He maintains that whenever the Rambam uses the expression *midivrei soferim*, he means that the practice is Rabbinic in origin and does not have the status of Torah law. The only practices that are considered to be ordained by the Torah are those explicitly stated in the Torah or mentioned by the Sages as having the status of Torah law.

In this context, he explains the Rambam's approach. Originally [as evidenced by the Rambam's statements in *Sefer HaMitzvot* (Positive Commandment 213)], the Rambam thought that sexual relations are the only *kiddushin* that are effective according to the Torah. For not only the effectiveness of the transfer of money, but also that of the transfer of a legal document is derived by the Sages only through Biblical exegesis. Afterwards, on the basis of certain passages that state that the effectiveness of the transfer of a legal document has the status of a Torah practice, the Rambam changed his opinion and wrote that the transfer of a document is also effective according to the Torah. This opinion is reflected in the Commentary on the Mishnah and the original version of the *Mishneh Torah*. Even later, the Rambam accepted the opinion that the effectiveness of the transfer of money also stems from the Torah itself. This is reflected in Chapter 3, Halachah 20, and the corrected text mentioned above.

(See *Birkat Avraham*, Responsum 44, in which the Rambam's son, Rabbenu Avraham, substantiates Rav Kapach's version of the *Mishneh Torah*.)

relations with her wherever they desired, and then depart. Such a woman is referred to as a harlot.[3]

When the Torah was given, [relations with] a harlot became forbidden, as [Deuteronomy 23:18] states: "There shall not be a harlot among the children of Israel."[4] Therefore, a person who has relations with a woman for the sake of lust, without *kiddushin*, receives lashes as prescribed by the Torah, because he had relations with a harlot.

5. Whenever it is forbidden to engage in relations from the Torah, and engaging in relations makes one liable for *karet* - i.e., the [forbidden relationships] mentioned in *Parashat Acharei Mot*, such as a person's mother, his sister, his daughter and the like - these relations are called *arayot,* and each particular forbidden relationship is called an *ervah.*[5]

6. There are other women with whom relations are forbidden according to the Oral Tradition; these prohibitions are Rabbinic in origin. These women are called *shniyot* (prohibitions of a secondary nature). There are twenty such women, including:

a) one's maternal grandmother; this prohibition continues upward without interruption: a person's maternal grandmother's maternal grandmother - and also those further removed - are also forbidden;

b) the mother of a person's maternal grandfather; this prohibition applies to her alone [and not her forbears];

c) a person's paternal grandmother; this prohibition continues upward without interruption: a person's paternal grandmother's maternal grandmother - and also those further removed - are also forbidden;

d) the mother of his paternal grandfather; this prohibition applies to her alone [and not her forbears];

e) the wife of his paternal grandfather; this prohibition continues upward without interruption; the wife of our Patriarch Jacob is forbidden to any one of us;

f) the wife of his maternal grandfather; this prohibition applies to her alone;

g) the wife of his father's maternal brother;

h) the wife of his mother's brother, whether a paternal or a maternal brother;

i) his son's daughter-in-law; this prohibition continues downward without interruption; any one of our wives is forbidden to our Patriarch Jacob;

j) the daughter-in-law of one's daughter; this prohibition applies to her alone;

k) the daughter of one's son's daughter; this prohibition applies to her alone;

l) the daughter of one's son's son; this prohibition applies to her alone;

m) the daughter of one's daughter's daughter; this prohibition applies to her alone;

n) the daughter of one's daughter's son; this prohibition applies to her alone;

3. The Ra'avad and others differ and maintain that a woman is not considered to be

וְזוֹ הִיא הַנִּקְרֵאת קְדֵשָׁה.

מִשֶּׁנִּתְּנָה הַתּוֹרָה נֶאֶסְרָה הַקְּדֵשָׁה, שֶׁנֶּאֱמַר: לֹא תִהְיֶה קְדֵשָׁה מִבְּנוֹת יִשְׂרָאֵל.

לְפִיכָךְ, כָּל הַבּוֹעֵל אִשָּׁה לְשֵׁם זְנוּת בְּלֹא קִדּוּשִׁין — לוֹקֶה מִן הַתּוֹרָה, לְפִי שֶׁבָּעַל קְדֵשָׁה.

ה כֹּל שֶׁאֱסַר בִּיאָתוֹ בַּתּוֹרָה, וְחַיָּב עַל בִּיאָתוֹ כָּרֵת — וְהֵם הָאֲמוּרוֹת בְּפָרָשַׁת אַחֲרֵי מוֹת — הֵן הַנִּקְרָאוֹת עֲרָיוֹת.

וְכָל אַחַת מֵהֶן נִקְרֵאת עֶרְוָה. כְּגוֹן אֵם וְאָחוֹת וּבַת וְכַיּוֹצֵא בָּהֶן.

ו וְיֵשׁ נָשִׁים אֲחֵרוֹת, שֶׁהֵן אֲסוּרוֹת מִפִּי הַקַּבָּלָה, וְאִסּוּרָן מִדִּבְרֵי סוֹפְרִים.

וְהֵן הַנִּקְרָאוֹת שְׁנִיּוֹת, מִפְּנֵי שֶׁהֵן שְׁנִיּוֹת לָעֲרָיוֹת. וְכָל אַחַת מֵהֶן נִקְרֵאת שְׁנִיָּה.

וְעֶשְׂרִים נָשִׁים הֵן, וְאֵלּוּ הֵן:

א) אֵם אִמּוֹ. וְזוֹ אֵין לָהּ הֶפְסֵק, אֶלָּא אֲפִלּוּ אֵם אֵם אִמּוֹ אֵם אִמּוֹ עַד מַעְלָה מַעְלָה — אֲסוּרָה.

ב) אֵם אֲבִי אִמּוֹ בִּלְבַד.

ג) אֵם אָבִיו. וְזוֹ אֵין לָהּ הֶפְסֵק, אֶלָּא אֲפִלּוּ אֵם אֵם אֵם אָבִיו עַד לְמַעְלָה — אֲסוּרָה.

ד) אֵם אֲבִי אָבִיו בִּלְבַד.

ה) אֵשֶׁת אֲבִי אָבִיו. וְזוֹ אֵין לָהּ הֶפְסֵק, אֲפִלּוּ אֵשֶׁת יַעֲקֹב אָבִינוּ אֲסוּרָה עַל אֶחָד מִמֶּנּוּ.

ו) אֵשֶׁת אֲבִי אִמּוֹ בִּלְבַד.

ז) אֵשֶׁת אֲחִי הָאָב מִן הָאֵם.

ח) אֵשֶׁת אֲחִי הָאֵם, בֵּין מִן הָאֵם בֵּין מִן הָאָב.

ט) כַּלַּת בְּנוֹ. וְזוֹ אֵין לָהּ הֶפְסֵק, אֲפִלּוּ כַּלַּת בֶּן בֶּן בְּנוֹ עַד סוֹף כָּל הָעוֹלָם — אֲסוּרָה, עַד שֶׁתִּהְיֶה אֵשֶׁת אֶחָד מִמֶּנּוּ שְׁנִיָּה עַל יַעֲקֹב אָבִינוּ.

י) כַּלַּת בִּתּוֹ בִּלְבַד.

יא) בַּת בַּת בְּנוֹ בִּלְבַד.

יב) בַּת בֶּן בְּנוֹ בִּלְבַד.

יג) בַּת בַּת בִּתּוֹ בִּלְבַד.

יד) בַּת בֶּן בִּתּוֹ בִּלְבַד.

a harlot unless she is a professional prostitute. The difference between this approach and the Rambam's involves only the severity of the prohibition. Both agree that sexual relations outside the context of marriage are forbidden. With regard to a *pilegesh*, a woman one designates as a sexual partner but who is not consecrated as a wife, see *Hilchot Melachim* 4:4.

4. *Sefer HaMitzvot* (Negative Commandment 355) and *Sefer HaChinuch* (Mitzvah 570) include this as one of the Torah's 613 commandments.

5. These include incestuous and adulterous relationships as mentioned in Leviticus, Chapter 18. The forbidden relationships that are punishable by execution are discussed in *Hilchot Issurei Bi'ah*, Chapter 1, and those for which one is liable for *karet* and for which lashes are given are discussed in *Hilchot Sanhedrin*, Chapter 19.

o) the daughter of the son of one's wife's son; this prohibition applies to her alone;

p) the daughter of the daughter of one's wife's daughter; this prohibition applies to her alone;

q) the maternal grandmother of one's wife's father; this prohibition applies to her alone;

r) the paternal grandmother of one's wife's mother; this prohibition applies to her alone;

s) the maternal grandmother of one's wife's mother; this prohibition applies to her alone;

t) the paternal grandmother of one's wife's father; this prohibition applies to her alone.

Thus, the categories of *shniyot* that continue without interruption are four: one's maternal grandmother - this continues upward without interruption; one's paternal grandmother - this continues upward without interruption; the wife of one's paternal grandfather - this continues upward without interruption; and the wife of one's son's son - this continues downward without interruption.

7. All relations with women that are forbidden by the Torah, but that are not punishable by *karet*, are referred to as *issurei lavin* (prohibitions forbidden by negative commandments); they are also referred to as *issurei kedushah* (prohibitions [that encourage] holiness).

They are nine: relations between a widow and a High Priest;[6] those between a divorcee, a *zonah*,[7] or a *chalalah*[8] and either a High Priest or an ordinary priest,[9] those between a bastard[10] and a native-born Jewish male or female, those between a native-born Jewish woman and a Moabite or Ammonite convert,[11] those between a man and his divorcee after she has been married to another person,[12] those between a native-born Jewish woman and a man with crushed testicles or a cut member,[13] and those between a *yevamah* and a man other than [one of her deceased husband's brothers] while she is still obligated to them.[14]

According to Rabbinic decree, an equation is established between a divorcee and a woman who undergoes *chalitzah*, and the latter is also forbidden [to engage in relations] with a priest. The Rabbis also placed *netinim* in the same status as bastards. In *Hilchot Issurei Bi'ah*, we will explain who the *netinim* are.[15]

---

6. See Leviticus 21:14.

7. *Hilchot Issurei Bi'ah* 18:1 defines this term as meaning either a woman who is not Jewish, a Jewish woman who has engaged in relations with a man she is forbidden to marry, or one who engages in relations with a *challal* (a male born from relations between a priest and a woman he is forbidden to marry).

טו)   בַּת בֶּן בֶּן אִשְׁתּוֹ בִּלְבַד.

טז)   בַּת בַּת בַּת אִשְׁתּוֹ בִּלְבַד.

יז)   אֵם אֵם אֲבִי אִשְׁתּוֹ בִּלְבַד.

יח)   אֵם אַב אֵם אִשְׁתּוֹ בִּלְבַד.

יט)   אֵם אֵם אֵם אִשְׁתּוֹ בִּלְבַד.

כ)   אֵם אַב אֲבִי אִשְׁתּוֹ בִּלְבַד.

נִמְצְאוּ הַשְּׁנִיּוֹת שֶׁאֵין לָהֶן הֶפְסֵק — אַרְבַּע: אֵם הָאֵם עַד לְמַעְלָה, וְאֵם הָאָב עַד לְמַעְלָה, וְאֵשֶׁת אֲבִי הָאָב עַד לְמַעְלָה, וְאֵשֶׁת בֶּן בְּנוֹ עַד לְמַטָּה.

ז כָּל שֶׁאָסַר בִּיאָתוֹ בַּתּוֹרָה, וְלֹא חַיָּב עָלָיו כָּרֵת — הֵן הַנִּקְרָאִים אִסּוּרֵי לָאוִין. וְעוֹד נִקְרָאִין אִסּוּרֵי קְדֻשָּׁה.

וְתִשְׁעָה הֵן, וְאֵלּוּ הֵן:

אַלְמָנָה לְכֹהֵן גָּדוֹל.

גְּרוּשָׁה אוֹ זוֹנָה אוֹ חֲלָלָה בֵּין לְכֹהֵן גָּדוֹל בֵּין לְכֹהֵן הֶדְיוֹט.

וּמַמְזֶרֶת לְבֶן יִשְׂרָאֵל.

וּבַת יִשְׂרָאֵל לְמַמְזֵר.

וּבַת יִשְׂרָאֵל לְעַמּוֹנִי וּמוֹאָבִי.

וּבַת יִשְׂרָאֵל לִפְצוּעַ דַּכָּא וּכְרוּת שָׁפְכָה.

וּגְרוּשָׁתוֹ אַחַר שֶׁנִּשֵּׂאת לְאַחֵר.

וִיבָמָה שֶׁנִּשֵּׂאת לְזָר וַעֲדַיִן רְשׁוּת הַיָּבָם עָלֶיהָ.

הַחֲלוּצָה — הֲרֵי הִיא כִּגְרוּשָׁה, וְהִיא אֲסוּרָה לְכֹהֵן מִדִּבְרֵי סוֹפְרִים.

וְהַנְּתִינִים — הֲרֵי הֵם כְּמַמְזֵרִים, אֶחָד זְכָרִים וְאֶחָד נְקֵבוֹת, וְאִסּוּרָם מִדִּבְרֵי סוֹפְרִים. וּבְהִלְכוֹת אִסּוּרֵי בִיאָה יִתְבָּאֵר לָךְ מָה הֵם הַנְּתִינִים.

---

8. A woman who engages in relations with a priest despite a prohibition against doing so, or a female born from relations between a priest and a woman he is forbidden to marry (*Hilchot Issurei Bi'ah* 19:1).

9. See Leviticus 21:7, 21:14.

10. A bastard is defined as a person born from any of the forbidden sexual relations that are punishable by execution or *karet*, with the exception of relations with a woman in the *niddah* state. This term does not refer to a child born out of wedlock. Deuteronomy 23:3 forbids a bastard from marrying a native-born Jewish male or female.

11. See Deuteronomy 23:4.

12. See Deuteronomy 24:4.

13. See Deuteronomy 23:2.

14. A *yevamah* is a childless widow, who is obligated to marry one of her deceased husband's brothers or to be discharged of that obligation through the rite of *chalitzah*. Until she and her brother-in-law fulfill this rite, she is forbidden to marry anyone else. (See Deuteronomy 25:5-10.)

15. The *netinim* are the Givonites, who were forbidden to marry into the Jewish people

8. There are certain relationships for which there is a prohibition resulting from a positive commandment [*issurei aseh*], but they are not prohibited by a negative commandment. There are three such prohibitions: the first and second generations of Egyptian or Edomite converts, both men and women [to all native-born Jews and Jewish women], and a woman who is not a virgin to a High Priest.

In these instances, there are no verses that state "He shall not enter [the congregation of God]..." or "he may not take...." The prohibition [against the marriage of the Edomite and Egyptian converts] is instead derived [from Deuteronomy 23:9], which states that "in the third generation they may enter the congregation of God." This implies that the first and second generations may not enter [this marriage group].

Similarly, from [the positive commandment, Leviticus 21:13]: "He [the High Priest] shall marry a virgin," we can derive that he is forbidden to marry a woman who is not a virgin. A prohibition that is derived from a positive commandment has the status of a positive commandment.

CHAPTER TWO

1. From the day of a girl's birth until she becomes twelve years old, she is called a *k'tanah* (minor) and/or a *tinoket* (baby). Even if several [pubic] hairs grow [on her body] during this time, they are [not significant according to Jewish law and are] considered to be merely hairs growing from a mole. If, however, two hairs grow in the pubic area after she becomes twelve years old [her status changes, and] she is considered a *na'arah* (maiden).

2. Growing two pubic hairs at this age is referred to as the lower sign [of physical maturity]. Once a girl manifests this sign [of physical maturity], she is referred to as a maiden for six months. From the last day of these six months and onward, she is referred to as a *bogeret* (mature woman). The difference between the stages of maidenhood and maturity is only six months.

3. From the time a girl reaches the age of twelve years and one day[1] until the age of twenty, if she does not grow two pubic hairs, she is still considered to be a child, even if she manifests the physical signs of barrenness.

If [during this period], she grows two pubic hairs, even if [this occurs] in her twentieth year, she is considered to be a maiden for six months. Only afterwards is she be considered to be a mature woman.

4. Should a woman be less than thirty days below the age of twenty, not have grown two pubic hairs, and have manifested [all] the physical signs of barrenness,[2] she is deemed an *aylonit* (a barren woman).

ח וְיֵשׁ שֶׁאִסּוּר בִּיאָתָן בַּעֲשֵׂה, וְאֵינוֹ מְחַיָּבֵי לָאוִין. וּשְׁלֹשָׁה הֵם:

מִצְרִי וַאֲדוֹמִי, דּוֹר רִאשׁוֹן וְדוֹר שֵׁנִי, אֶחָד זְכָרִים וְאֶחָד נְקֵבוֹת. וּבְעוּלָה לְכֹהֵן גָּדוֹל.

לְפִי שֶׁלֹּא נֶאֱמַר בְּאֵלּוּ 'לֹא יָבוֹא' אוֹ 'לֹא יִקַּח', אֶלָּא מִכְּלָל שֶׁנֶּאֱמַר 'דּוֹר שְׁלִישִׁי יָבֹא לָהֶם בִּקְהַל יְיָ' אַתָּה לָמֵד, שֶׁדּוֹר רִאשׁוֹן וְשֵׁנִי לֹא יָבוֹא;

וּמִכְּלָל שֶׁנֶּאֱמַר 'וְהוּא אִשָּׁה בִבְתוּלֶיהָ יִקַּח' אַתָּה לָמֵד, שֶׁאֵינָהּ בְּתוּלָה לֹא יִקַּח. וְלָאו הַבָּא מִכְּלָל עֲשֵׂה — הֲרֵי הוּא כַּעֲשֵׂה.

פֶּרֶק שֵׁנִי

א הַבַּת מִיּוֹם לֵדָתָהּ עַד שֶׁתִּהְיֶה בַּת שְׁתֵּים עֶשְׂרֵה שָׁנָה גְּמוּרוֹת — הִיא הַנִּקְרֵאת קְטַנָּה, וְנִקְרֵאת תִּינֹקֶת.

וַאֲפִלּוּ הֵבִיאָה כַּמָּה שְׂעָרוֹת בְּתוֹךְ הַזְּמַן הַזֶּה — אֵינָם אֶלָּא כְּשׁוּמָא.

אֲבָל אִם הֵבִיאָה שְׁתֵּי שְׂעָרוֹת לְמַטָּה בַּגּוּף בַּמְּקוֹמוֹת הַיְדוּעוֹת לַהֲבָאַת שֵׂעָר, וְהִיא מִבַּת שְׁתֵּים עֶשְׂרֵה שָׁנָה וְיוֹם אֶחָד וָמַעְלָה — נִקְרֵאת נַעֲרָה.

ב וַהֲבָאַת שְׁתֵּי שְׂעָרוֹת בַּזְּמַן הַזֶּה נִקְרָא סִימָן הַתַּחְתּוֹן.

וּמֵאַחַר שֶׁתָּבִיא סִימָן הַתַּחְתּוֹן תִּקָּרֵא נַעֲרָה עַד שִׁשָּׁה חֳדָשִׁים גְּמוּרִים.

וּמִתְּחִלַּת יוֹם תַּשְׁלוּם הַשִּׁשָּׁה חֳדָשִׁים וָמַעְלָה תִּקָּרֵא בּוֹגֶרֶת.

וְאֵין בֵּין נַעֲרוּת לְבַגְרוּת אֶלָּא שִׁשָּׁה חֳדָשִׁים בִּלְבַד.

ג הִגִּיעָה לִשְׁתֵּים עֶשְׂרֵה שָׁנָה וְיוֹם אֶחָד וְלֹא הֵבִיאָה שְׁתֵּי שְׂעָרוֹת, אַף־עַל־פִּי שֶׁנִּרְאוּ בָּהּ סִימָנֵי אַיְלוֹנִית — עֲדַיִן קְטַנָּה הִיא, עַד עֶשְׂרִים שָׁנָה.

וּכְשֶׁתָּבִיא שְׁתֵּי שְׂעָרוֹת, אֲפִלּוּ בִּשְׁנַת עֶשְׂרִים — תִּהְיֶה נַעֲרָה שִׁשָּׁה חֳדָשִׁים, וְאַחַר כָּךְ תִּקָּרֵא בּוֹגֶרֶת.

ד הָיְתָה בַּת עֶשְׂרִים שָׁנָה פָּחוֹת שְׁלֹשִׁים יוֹם וְלֹא הֵבִיאָה שְׁתֵּי שְׂעָרוֹת, וְנִרְאוּ בָּהּ כָּל סִימָנֵי אַיְלוֹנִית — הֲרֵי הִיא אַיְלוֹנִית.

---

even after their conversion by Joshua. King David reinforced the ban against them. (See *Hilchot Issurei Bi'ah* 12:22-23.)

1. The intent in this halachah, and similarly, whenever the term "...years old and one day" is mentioned, is not that an additional day must pass after the woman's twelfth birthday. Rather, the intent is that she has completed twelve complete years of life and begun the following day.

2. The *Tur* (*Even HaEzer*) differs with the Rambam on two points: a) the girl need only

If she does not manifest all the sign of barrenness, she is still considered to be a child until she grows two pubic hairs or until she reaches the age of 35 years and one day.

5. Should a woman reach this age without growing two pubic hairs, she is deemed barren even though she does not manifest physical signs of barrenness. A barren woman does not [go through the six-month] period of maidenhood. Instead, directly after having been considered a child, she is considered to be a mature woman.

6. The following are the physical signs of barrenness: a) she lacks [protruding] breasts; b) she stiffens during sexual relations; c) her lower abdomen does not resemble a woman's, d) her voice is deep and cannot be differentiated from that of a man.

All three, a maiden, a mature woman and a barren woman, are referred to by the term *gedolah* [adult woman]. [Unlike children, they are held responsible for their conduct.]

7. [In addition to growing pubic hairs,] a woman has signs of physical maturity that are manifest in her upper body. They are referred to as "upper signs." Among them are:
a) when the woman stretches her hand backward, a crease forms in the place of her breast; b) the color of the tip of the breast becomes darker; c) when a person places his hand on the end of the breast and it remains depressed slightly before rising; d) creases form at the end of the breast, and a nipple takes shape; my teachers taught that the formation of creases is sufficient; e) the breasts protrude; f) they become erect; g) the mound of Venus forms above the woman's genitals, below her stomach; h) the flesh of this mound becomes soft and not hard. These are eight signs.

8. If one or even all of these signs of maturity appear in a woman before she becomes twelve years of age, no attention is paid to it. When she becomes twelve years old and one day, and she manifests the lower sign of physical maturity, no attention is paid to [the presence or lack of] these [upper] signs of physical maturity [and she is considered to be a maiden].

If she does not manifest the lower sign of physical maturity, but she does manifest one of these [upper] signs, there is doubt whether she should be considered a child or a maiden, and the more stringent perspective is followed [with regard to all halachic questions] concerning her. If she manifests all these [upper] signs, she is definitely considered to be an adult. For it is impossible for her to manifest all these signs [and yet not have had two pubic hairs grow]. We assume these hairs have grown, but they have dropped off.

be 19 and one month, not 19 and eleven months (Chapter 155) and b) that she need manifest only one, but not all signs of barrenness (Chapter 44, 172).

וְאִם לֹא נִרְאוּ בָּהּ כָּל סִימָנֵי אַיְלוֹנִית — עֲדַיִן קְטַנָּה הִיא, עַד שֶׁתָּבִיא שְׁתֵּי שְׂעָרוֹת אוֹ עַד שֶׁתִּהְיֶה בַּת חָמֵשׁ וּשְׁלֹשִׁים שָׁנָה וְיוֹם אֶחָד.

ה הִגִּיעָה לַזְּמַן הַזֶּה וְלֹא הֵבִיאָה שְׁתֵּי שְׂעָרוֹת — הֲרֵי זוֹ נִקְרֵאת אַיְלוֹנִית, אַף־עַל־פִּי שֶׁלֹּא נִרְאָה בָּהּ סִימָן מִסִּימָנֵי אַיְלוֹנִית.
נִמְצֵאתָ אַתָּה לָמֵד, שֶׁהָאַיְלוֹנִית אֵין לָהּ יְמֵי נַעֲרוּת, אֶלָּא מִקַּטְנוּתָהּ תֵּצֵא לְבַגְרוּת.

ו וְאֵלּוּ הֵן סִימָנֵי אַיְלוֹנִית:
כֹּל שֶׁאֵין לָהּ דַּדִּין,
וּמִתְקַשָּׁה בִּשְׁעַת תַּשְׁמִישׁ,
וְאֵין לָהּ שִׁפּוּלֵי מֵעַיִם כַּנָּשִׁים,
וְקוֹלָהּ עָבֶה וְאֵינָהּ נִכֶּרֶת בֵּין אִישׁ לְאִשָּׁה.
וְהַנַּעֲרָה וְהַבּוֹגֶרֶת וְהָאַיְלוֹנִית — כָּל אַחַת מִשְּׁלָשְׁתָּן נִקְרֵאת גְּדוֹלָה.

ז וְיֵשׁ בְּבַת סִימָנִין מִלְמַעְלָה, וְהֵן הַנִּקְרָאִין סִימָן הָעֶלְיוֹן. וְאֵלּוּ הֵן:
מִשֶּׁתַּחֲזִיר יָדֶיהָ לַאֲחוֹרָהּ וְיֵעָשֶׂה קֶמֶט בִּמְקוֹם הַדַּדִּין.
וּמִשֶּׁיַּשְׁחִיר רֹאשׁ הַדַּד.
וּמִשֶּׁיִּתֵּן אָדָם יָדוֹ עַל עֹקֶץ הַדַּד, וְהוּא שׁוֹקֵעַ וְשׁוֹהֶה לַחֲזֹר.
וּמִשֶּׁיְּפַצֵּל רֹאשׁ חֹטֶם הַדַּד וְיֵעָשֶׂה בְּרֹאשׁוֹ כַּדּוּר קָטָן.
וְרַבּוֹתֵי פֵּרְשׁוּ, מִשֶּׁיְּפַצֵּל הַחֹטֶם עַצְמוֹ.
וְכֵן מִשֶּׁיִּטּוּ הַדַּדִּין.
וּמִשֶּׁיִּתְקַשְׁקְשׁוּ הַדַּדִּין.
וּמִשֶּׁיִּתְקַמֵּט הָעֲטָרָה, שֶׁהוּא מְקוֹם הַבָּשָׂר שֶׁלְּמַעְלָה מִן הָעֶרְוָה לְעֻמַּת הַבֶּטֶן.
וּמִשֶּׁיִּתְמַעֵךְ הַבָּשָׂר הַזֶּה וְלֹא יִהְיֶה קָשֶׁה.

ח כָּל אֵלּוּ הַסִּימָנִין שְׁמוֹנָה.
נִרְאָה בַּבַּת סִימָן אֶחָד מִכָּל אֵלּוּ אוֹ כֻּלָּן, וְהִיא בַּת שְׁתֵּים עֶשְׂרֵה שָׁנָה אוֹ פָּחוֹת — אֵין מַשְׁגִּיחִין בּוֹ, וַהֲרֵי הִיא קְטַנָּה.
נַעֲשֵׂית בַּת שְׁתֵּים עֶשְׂרֵה שָׁנָה וְיוֹם אֶחָד, וְנִרְאָה בָּהּ סִימָן הַתַּחְתּוֹן — אֵין מַשְׁגִּיחִין בְּאֶחָד מִכָּל אֵלּוּ.
וְאִם לֹא נִרְאָה הַתַּחְתּוֹן, וְנִרְאָה בָּהּ אֶחָד מִכָּל אֵלּוּ — הֲרֵי הִיא סָפֵק בֵּין נַעֲרָה לִקְטַנָּה, וְדָנִים בָּהּ לְהַחְמִיר.
וְאִם נִרְאוּ כֻּלָּן, וְלֹא נִרְאָה סִימָן הַתַּחְתּוֹן — הֲרֵי זוֹ גְּדוֹלָה וַדָּאִית;
שֶׁאִי אֶפְשָׁר שֶׁיָּבוֹאוּ כֻּלָּן, אֶלָּא כְּבָר בָּא סִימָן הַתַּחְתּוֹן וְנָשַׁר.

With regard to the first issue, the *Shulchan Aruch* appears to favor the *Tur's* view, although that of the Rambam is also mentioned. With regard to the second issue, the

9. When a woman gives birth after reaching the age of twelve years, she is deemed an adult, even though she did not manifest either upper or lower signs of maturity. [Giving birth to] children is a sign of maturity.

10. A male, from birth until the age of thirteen, is called a *katan* (minor) and/or a *tinok* (baby). Even if several [pubic] hairs grow [on his body] during this time, they are [not significant according to Jewish law] and are considered to be merely hairs growing from a mole. If, however, two hairs grow in the pubic area after he attains the age of thirteen years and one day, [his status changes, and] he is considered a *gadol* (adult male) and/or an *ish* (man).

11. Should a child reach this age without growing two pubic hairs, he is still considered a minor until he reaches the age of twenty years less thirty days, even though he manifests signs of impotency. Should he reach the age [of twenty years less thirty days] and not have grown either pubic hairs or hairs of the beard [the following rules apply]. If he manifests one of the physical signs of impotency, he is considered impotent (a *saris*), and he is considered to be an adult with regard to all matters.

If he does not manifest any of the signs of impotency, he is still considered to be a minor until he grows two pubic hairs or until he reaches the age of thirty five years and one day.

12. If he reaches this age, he is considered impotent, although he did not manifest any of the signs of impotency. If he reached the age of twenty years less thirty days without growing two pubic hairs, but did grow two hairs on his beard, he is not considered to be impotent, even if he manifests one sign of impotency, until he either manifests all the signs of impotency or reaches the age of thirty five years and one day.

13. These are the signs of impotency: a) One lacks a beard, b) his hair grows inadequately, c) his flesh is hairless, d) his urine does not produce vapor, e) his urine does not flow in an arc, f) his semen is off color, g) his urine does not ferment, h) when he washes in the winter, his flesh does not produce steam, and i) his voice is high pitched and cannot be differentiated from that of a woman.

14. An impotent person of this type is referred to as a *s'ris chamah* [one who became impotent because of fever].[3] When, however, the genitals of a male

Shulchan Aruch appears to follow the Rambam's view, while the Ramah cites that of the *Tur*.

ט הַבַּת שֶׁיָּלְדָה אַחַר שְׁתֵּי עֶשְׂרֵה שָׁנָה, אַף־עַל־פִּי שֶׁלֹּא הֵבִיאָה סִימָנִים, לֹא תַחְתּוֹן וְלֹא עֶלְיוֹן — הֲרֵי זוֹ גְדוֹלָה. בָּנִים הֲרֵי הֵם כְּסִימָנִין.

י הַבֵּן מִשֶּׁיִּוָּלֵד עַד שֶׁיִּהְיֶה בֶּן שְׁלֹשׁ עֶשְׂרֵה שָׁנָה — נִקְרָא קָטָן, וְנִקְרָא תִּינוֹק. וַאֲפִלּוּ הֵבִיא כַּמָּה שְׂעָרוֹת בְּתוֹךְ הַזְּמַן הַזֶּה — אֵינוֹ סִימָן, אֶלָּא שׁוּמָא. הֵבִיא שְׁתֵּי שְׂעָרוֹת לְמַטָּה בַּמְּקוֹמוֹת הַיְדוּעוֹת לְשֵׂעָר, וְהוּא מִבֶּן שְׁלֹשׁ עֶשְׂרֵה שָׁנָה וְיוֹם אֶחָד וָמַעְלָה — נִקְרָא גָּדוֹל, וְנִקְרָא אִישׁ.

יא הִגִּיעַ לַזְּמַן הַזֶּה וְלֹא הֵבִיא שְׁתֵּי שְׂעָרוֹת, אַף־עַל־פִּי שֶׁנִּרְאוּ בּוֹ סִימָנֵי סָרִיס — הֲרֵי הוּא קָטָן, עַד שֶׁיִּהְיֶה בֶּן עֶשְׂרִים שָׁנָה פָּחוֹת שְׁלֹשִׁים יוֹם.
הִגִּיעַ לַזְּמַן הַזֶּה וְלֹא הֵבִיא שְׁתֵּי שְׂעָרוֹת לְמַטָּה, וְלֹא הֵבִיא שְׁתֵּי שְׂעָרוֹת בַּזָּקָן:
אִם נִרְאָה בּוֹ אֶחָד מִסִּימָנֵי סָרִיס — הֲרֵי הוּא סָרִיס, וְדִינוֹ דִּין הַגָּדוֹל לְכָל דָּבָר;
וְאִם לֹא נִרְאָה בּוֹ סִימָן מִסִּימָנֵי סָרִיס — עֲדַיִן קָטָן הוּא, עַד שֶׁיָּבִיא שְׁתֵּי שְׂעָרוֹת לְמַטָּה בַּמָּקוֹם הָרָאוּי לָהֶן, אוֹ עַד שֶׁיִּהְיֶה בֶּן חָמֵשׁ וּשְׁלֹשִׁים שָׁנָה וְיוֹם אֶחָד.

יב הִגִּיעַ לַזְּמַן הַזֶּה וְלֹא הֵבִיא — הֲרֵי זֶה סָרִיס, אַף־עַל־פִּי שֶׁלֹּא נִרְאָה בּוֹ אֶחָד מִסִּימָנֵי סָרִיס.
הִגִּיעַ לִשְׁנַת עֶשְׂרִים פָּחוֹת שְׁלֹשִׁים יוֹם וְלֹא הֵבִיא שְׁתֵּי שְׂעָרוֹת לְמַטָּה, וְהֵבִיא שְׁתֵּי שְׂעָרוֹת בַּזָּקָן, אַף־עַל־פִּי שֶׁנּוֹלַד לוֹ אֶחָד מִסִּימָנֵי סָרִיס — אֵינוֹ סָרִיס;
אֶלָּא הֲרֵי הוּא בְּקַטְנוּתוֹ, עַד שֶׁיִּוָּלְדוּ לוֹ כָּל סִימָנֵי סָרִיס, אוֹ עַד שֶׁיִּהְיֶה בֶּן חָמֵשׁ וּשְׁלֹשִׁים שָׁנָה וְיוֹם אֶחָד.

יג וְאֵלּוּ הֵן סִימָנֵי סָרִיס:
כֹּל שֶׁאֵין לוֹ זָקָן,
וּשְׂעָרוֹ לָקוּי,
וּבְשָׂרוֹ מַחֲלִיק,
וְאֵין מֵימֵי רַגְלָיו מַעֲלִים רְתִיחָה,
וּכְשֶׁמֵּטִיל מַיִם אֵינוֹ עוֹשֶׂה כִפָּה,
וְשִׁכְבַת זַרְעוֹ דֵּהָה,
וְאֵין מֵימֵי רַגְלָיו מַחְמִיצִין,
וְרוֹחֵץ בִּימוֹת הַגְּשָׁמִים וְאֵינוֹ מַעֲלֶה בְּשָׂרוֹ הֶבֶל,
וְקוֹלוֹ לָקוּי וְאֵינוֹ נִכָּר בֵּין אִישׁ לְאִשָּׁה.

יד וְסָרִיס זֶה הוּא הַנִּקְרָא סָרִיס חַמָּה בְּכָל מָקוֹם.

3. Our translation follows the interpretation of the *Shulchan Aruch* and the *Aruch*. Yevamot 80a interprets this as meaning, "one who never saw the light of the sun while

have been cut, severed or crushed, as the gentiles do, the person is called a *s'ris adam* [one who became impotent as a result of human activity]. When such a person reaches the age of thirteen and one day, he is considered to be an adult, for he will never manifest signs of maturity.

15. When a male reaches the age of thirteen and one day and does not grow any pubic hairs, but manifests the upper signs of physical maturity,[4] doubt exists whether he is considered to be an adult or a minor. If, however, his pubic area was not inspected, but he manifests signs of physical maturity in his upper body, he is presumed to be an adult.

16. Whenever the term "two pubic hairs" is mentioned with regard to a male or a female, the intent is that the hairs are long enough to be bent in half, with their point touching their base. If they grow to the extent that they can be cut by scissors, but are not [long enough] that they can be bent in half with their point touching their base, [there is doubt regarding the decision], and the more stringent ruling is always followed.

Therefore, when a boy's or girl's pubic hairs have grown to the point that they can be cut by scissors, the individual is considered to be an adult with regard to those matters concerning which the ruling would be more stringent if he or she were so classified. And with regard to those matters concerning which the ruling would be more stringent if he [or she] were classified as a minor, the individual is so classified because the pubic hairs are not long enough to be bent in half with their point touching their base.

17. These two hairs must be located in the pubic area. The entire pubic area is appropriate for the signs to be located. There is no difference whether they are located in the upper area, the lower area or on the sexual organ itself.

The two hairs must be located in a single place, and there must be a follicle at their base. If both of them stem from the same follicle, it is acceptable. If two follicles are located next to each other without hairs growing from them, they are, nevertheless, considered a sign. We follow the presumption that a follicle will not exist without hair. [Surely,] there were hairs [that grew from the follicle], and they fell.

18. As we have explained, when a girl grows two pubic hairs before she is twelve, or a boy grows two pubic hairs before he is thirteen, they are considered to be merely hairs growing from a mole. Even if these hairs remain in their place after the boy reaches the age of thirteen, or the girl reaches the age of twelve, they are not considered signs of physical maturity.

אֲבָל הַבֵּן שֶׁחֲתָכוּ אוֹ נִתְּקוּ אוֹ מֶעֲכוּ גִּידָיו אוֹ בֵּיצָיו, כְּמוֹ שֶׁהָעַכּוּ"ם עוֹשִׂין — הוּא הַנִּקְרָא סָרִיס אָדָם.

וּכְשֶׁיִּהְיֶה בֶּן שָׁלֹשׁ עֶשְׂרֵה שָׁנָה וְיוֹם אֶחָד נִקְרָא גָּדוֹל, שֶׁאֵין זֶה מֵבִיא סִימָן לְעוֹלָם.

טו בֶּן שָׁלֹשׁ עֶשְׂרֵה שָׁנָה וְיוֹם אֶחָד שֶׁלֹּא הֵבִיא סִימָן שֶׁלְּמַטָּה, וְנִרְאוּ בּוֹ כָּל הַסִּימָנִין שֶׁל מַעְלָה — הֲרֵי זֶה סָפֵק בֵּין גָּדוֹל לְקָטָן.

וְאִם לֹא נִבְדַּק מִלְּמַטָּה — כֵּיוָן שֶׁנִּרְאָה בּוֹ סִימָנֵי בַּגְרוּת מִלְמַעְלָה, הֲרֵי זֶה בְּחֶזְקַת גָּדוֹל.

טז שְׁתֵּי שְׂעָרוֹת הָאֲמוּרוֹת בְּבֵן וּבְבַת בְּכָל מָקוֹם, שִׁעוּרָן כְּדֵי לָכֹף רֹאשָׁן לְעִקָּרָן. וּמִשֶּׁיִּצְמְחוּ וְיִהְיוּ יְכוֹלוֹת לְהִנָּטֵל בְּפִי הַזּוּג עַד שֶׁיַּגִּיעוּ לָכֹף רֹאשָׁן לְעִקָּרָן, דָּנִין בָּהֶן לְהַחְמִיר בְּכָל מָקוֹם.

לְפִיכָךְ, בְּבֵן וּבְבַת נַחְשֹׁב אוֹתָם גְּדוֹלִים לְהַחְמִיר, הוֹאִיל וְצָמְחוּ כְּדֵי לְהִנָּטֵל בְּפִי הַזּוּג; וְנַחְשֹׁב אוֹתָם קְטַנִּים לְהַחְמִיר, הוֹאִיל וְלֹא הִגִּיעוּ לָכֹף רֹאשָׁן לְעִקָּרָן.

יז שְׁתֵּי שְׂעָרוֹת אֵלּוּ צְרִיכוֹת שֶׁיִּהְיוּ בִּמְקוֹם הָעֶרְוָה.

וּבֵית הָעֶרְוָה כֻּלּוֹ מְקוֹם סִימָנִין — בֵּין לְמַעְלָה, בֵּין לְמַטָּה, בֵּין עַל אֵיבְרֵי הַזֶּרַע עַצְמָן.

וּצְרִיכוֹת לִהְיוֹת בְּמָקוֹם אֶחָד.

וְשֶׁיִּהְיֶה בְּעִקָּרָן גֻּמּוֹת.

וַאֲפִלּוּ שְׁתֵּיהֶן בְּגֻמָּא אַחַת — הֲרֵי אֵלּוּ סִימָן.

נִמְצְאוּ שְׁתֵּי גֻמּוֹת זוֹ בְּצַד זוֹ, וְאֵין בָּהֶן שֵׂעָר — הֲרֵי אֵלּוּ סִימָן; חֲזָקָה אֵין גֻּמָּא בְּלֹא שֵׂעָר, וּשְׂעָרוֹת הָיוּ בָּהֶן וְנָשְׁרוּ.

יח הַבַּת שֶׁהֵבִיאָה שְׁתֵּי שְׂעָרוֹת בְּתוֹךְ שְׁתֵּים עֶשְׂרֵה שָׁנָה, וְהַבֵּן שֶׁהֵבִיא בְּתוֹךְ שָׁלֹשׁ עֶשְׂרֵה — שְׁנֵיהֶם שׁוּמָא, כְּמוֹ שֶׁבֵּאַרְנוּ. אַף־עַל־פִּי שֶׁאוֹתָן שְׂעָרוֹת בִּמְקוֹמָן הֵם עוֹמְדוֹת אַחַר שָׁלֹשׁ עֶשְׂרֵה לְזָכָר וְאַחַר שְׁתֵּים עֶשְׂרֵה לִנְקֵבָה — אֵינָן סִימָן.

---

fit." A similar interpretation is found in the Jerusalem Talmud (*Yevamot* 8:5). There are several difference in halachah that depend on whether a person's impotence stems from human activity or not. See *Hilchot Issurei Bi'ah* 16:9.
4. I.e., he grows hairs of the beard and in his underarms; his voice changes; his hair grows adequately; and his flesh is not silky (*Ma'aseh Rokeach*). As reflected by the following clause, these signs are sufficient to indicate physical maturity. Nevertheless, because no pubic hairs are detected, the person's status is undetermined.

19. When does the above apply? When the child was inspected [before attaining the age of majority], and the hairs were deemed to be hairs growing from a mole. If, however, no such inspection was made until they reached the age of majority, and afterwards an inspection was made and two hairs were discovered, they are considered acceptable signs of physical maturity. We do not say that perhaps the hairs grew before the child reached majority, and they are merely hairs growing from a mole.

20. Whenever a girl is inspected for [signs of physical maturity] - whether during her twelfth year, after she became twelve or when she is older - the inspection is carried out by trustworthy, ethical women. Even when an inspection has been conducted by one woman, her word is accepted with regard to whether or not [the girl has manifested signs of physical maturity].[5]

21. Whenever the term "years" is mentioned with regard to [the age of] a male or a female, endowment evaluations,[6] or any other matter, the intent is not lunar years, nor solar years, but rather the years as reckoned by the Jewish court to [juxtapose the solar and lunar calendars], whether ordinary years or leap years, as established by the [Jewish] court, as explained in *Hilchot Kiddush HaChodesh*. This is the intent whenever the subject of years is mentioned with regard to religious matters.

22. We do not rely on the testimony of women regarding a child's age, nor on that of relatives. Instead, the matter is determined by the testimony of two men who are fit to testify in court.

23. When a father says, "My son is nine years and one day old," or "My daughter is three years and one day old,"[7] his word is accepted with regard to the obligation of bringing a sacrifice [if sexual relations were carried out without knowledge of the sin involved], but not with regard to administering stripes [for rebellion] or other punishments.

If the father says, "My son is thirteen years and one day old," or "My daughter is twelve years and one day old," his word is accepted with regard to vows, endowment evaluations, property forsworn [and transferred to the priests],[8] or the consecration of property, but not with regard to administering lashes or other punishments.

24. A person who possesses both a male sexual organ and a female sexual organ is called an *androgynous*. There is doubt whether such a person should be classified as a male or as a female; there is no physical sign that can ever enable such a distinction to be made.

25. A person who possesses neither a male sexual organ nor a female sexual organ, but instead, his genital area is a solid mass, is called a *tumtum*. There is

יט בַּמֶּה דְּבָרִים אֲמוּרִים? כְּשֶׁנִּבְדְּקוּ בְּתוֹךְ הַזְּמַן וְנוֹדַע שֶׁהֵן שׁוּמָא; אֲבָל אִם לֹא נִבְדְּקוּ אֶלָּא אַחַר זְמַן, וְנִמְצְאוּ שָׁם שְׁתֵּי שְׂעָרוֹת — הֲרֵי הֵן בְּחֶזְקַת סִימָנִין, וְאֵין אוֹמְרִין: שֶׁמָּא קֹדֶם זְמַן צָמְחוּ, כְּדֵי שֶׁיִּהְיוּ שׁוּמָא.

כ כְּשֶׁבּוֹדְקִין הַבַּת — בֵּין בְּתוֹךְ הַזְּמַן, שֶׁהוּא כָּל שְׁנַת שְׁתֵּים עֶשְׂרֵה, בֵּין קֹדֶם זְמַן זֶה, בֵּין לְאַחַר הַזְּמַן — בּוֹדְקִין עַל פִּי נָשִׁים כְּשֵׁרוֹת וְנֶאֱמָנוֹת. וַאֲפִלּוּ אִשָּׁה אַחַת בּוֹדֶקֶת, וְשׁוֹמְעִין לָהּ אִם הֵבִיאָה וְאִם לֹא הֵבִיאָה.

כא כָּל הַשָּׁנִים הָאֲמוּרוֹת בְּבֵן וּבְבַת וּבְעֲרָכִין וּבְכָל מָקוֹם, אֵינָן לֹא שְׁנֵי הַלְּבָנָה וְלֹא שְׁנֵי הַחַמָּה, אֶלָּא שָׁנִים שֶׁל סֵדֶר הָעִבּוּר, שֶׁהֵן פְּשׁוּטוֹת וּמְעֻבָּרוֹת, עַל פִּי בֵּית דִּין, כְּמוֹ שֶׁהֵם קוֹבְעִין אוֹתָן, כְּמוֹ שֶׁבֵּאַרְנוּ בְּהִלְכוֹת קִדּוּשׁ הַחֹדֶשׁ. וּבְאוֹתָן הַשָּׁנִים מוֹנִין לְכָל דִּבְרֵי הַדָּת.

כב אֵין סוֹמְכִין עַל הַנָּשִׁים בְּמִנְיַן הַשָּׁנִים, וְלֹא עַל הַקְּרוֹבִים, אֶלָּא עַל פִּי שְׁנַיִם אֲנָשִׁים כְּשֵׁרִים לְהָעִיד.

כג הָאָב שֶׁאָמַר: בְּנִי זֶה בֶּן תֵּשַׁע שָׁנִים וְיוֹם אֶחָד, בִּתִּי זוֹ בַּת שָׁלֹשׁ שָׁנִים וְיוֹם אֶחָד — נֶאֱמָן לְקָרְבָּן, אֲבָל לֹא לְמַכּוֹת וְלֹא לַעֲנָשִׁים. בְּנִי זֶה בֶּן שָׁלֹשׁ עֶשְׂרֵה שָׁנָה וְיוֹם אֶחָד, בִּתִּי זוֹ בַּת שְׁתֵּים עֶשְׂרֵה שָׁנָה וְיוֹם אֶחָד — נֶאֱמָן לִנְדָרִים וְלַעֲרָכִין וְלַחֲרָמוֹת וְלַהֶקְדֵּשׁוֹת, אֲבָל לֹא לְמַכּוֹת וְלֹא לַעֲנָשִׁים.

כד מִי שֶׁיֵּשׁ לוֹ אֵיבַר זַכְרוּת וְאֵיבַר נַקְבוּת — הוּא הַנִּקְרָא אַנְדְּרוֹגִינוֹס, וְהוּא סָפֵק אִם זָכָר סָפֵק אִם נְקֵבָה. וְאֵין לוֹ סִימָן שֶׁיִּוָּדַע בּוֹ אִם הוּא זָכָר וַדַּאי אִם הִיא נְקֵבָה וַדָּאִית לְעוֹלָם.

כה וְכָל מִי שֶׁאֵין לוֹ לֹא זַכְרוּת וְלֹא נַקְבוּת, אֶלָּא אָטוּם — הוּא הַנִּקְרָא טֻמְטוּם, וְגַם הוּא סָפֵק.

---

5. Although the testimony of women is not generally accepted in court, an exception is made in this instance because of modesty. The *Shulchan Aruch* (*Even HaEzer* 155:15) quotes the Rambam's wording. Nevertheless, the *Beit Shmuel* 155:23 states that a woman's testimony can be accepted only with regard to making a more stringent ruling, but not a more lenient one.

6. See Leviticus, Chapter 27.

7. If a male is less than nine years old, or a female is less than three years old, they are not fit to engage in sexual relations. Even if they do, in fact, engage in relations, these are of no halachic significance. Hence, if a boy above the age of nine engages in sexual relations with a married woman, the woman is liable. Similarly, if a man engaged in relations with a three-year old girl who was married, the man is liable.

8. See Leviticus, Chapter 27; *Hilchot Arachin* 6:1.

also doubt with regard [to this person's status]. If an operation is carried out and a male [organ is revealed], he is definitely considered to be a male. If a female [organ is revealed], she is definitely considered to be a female.

When a *tumtum* or an *androgynous* reaches the age of twelve years and one day, they are assumed to be adults.[9] Whenever these terms are mentioned, the intent is individuals of this age.

26. Whenever the terms *cheresh* and *chereshet* are used, they refer to a male or female deaf mute, respectively. If, however, a person can speak but cannot hear, or can hear but cannot speak, he is considered to be an ordinary person.[10] A male or a female who is intellectually competent, being neither a deaf mute nor emotionally disturbed, is referred to as a *pike'ach* or a *pikachat*, respectively.

27. We have thus defined twenty terms in these two chapters: *kiddushin, ervah, sh'niyah, issurei lavin, issurei aseh, k'tanah, na'arah, bogeret, aylonit, gedolah,* lower sign of maturity, upper sign of maturity, *katan, s'ris chamah, s'ris adam, gadol, androgynous, tumtum, chershim, pik'chim.* Keep these terms in mind at all times; do not forget their meaning, so that their intent will not have to be explained whenever they are mentioned.

CHAPTER THREE

1. How is the bond of *kiddushin* established with a woman? If the man [desires to establish] the *kiddushin* by [the transfer of] money, [he must give] a *p'rutah*, either in coin or its worth.

[Before giving it], he tells her, "You are consecrated unto me...," "You are betrothed to me...," or "You become my wife through this." He must give her [the money or the item] in the presence of witnesses.

It is the man who makes the statement that implies that he acquires the woman as his wife, and it is he who gives her the money.

2. If she gave him [money] and told him: "Behold, I am consecrated to you," "Behold, I am betrothed to you," "I am your wife," or [she used] any other expression that implied acquisition, the marriage bond is not established. Similarly, if she gave [him money] and he made the statement, the marriage

---

9. The Ra'avad objects to the Rambam's ruling, stating that it is necessary for these individuals to manifest physical signs of maturity before they are classified as adults. The *Maggid Mishneh* states that it appears that the Rambam is saying that there is no need for these individuals to manifest such signs. Needless to say, at the age of twelve these

וְאִם נִקְרַע הַטַּמְטוּם וְנִמְצָא זָכָר — הֲרֵי הוּא כְּזָכָר וַדַּאי;

וְאִם נִמְצָא נְקֵבָה — הֲרֵי הוּא נְקֵבָה.

וְטַמְטוּם וְאַנְדְּרוֹגִינוֹס שֶׁהָיוּ בֶּן שְׁתֵּים עֶשְׂרֵה שָׁנָה וְיוֹם אֶחָד — הֲרֵי הֵן בְּחֶזְקַת גְּדוֹלִים. וְהֵם שֶׁנְּדַבֵּר בָּהֶן בְּכָל מָקוֹם.

כו חֵרֵשׁ וְחֵרֶשֶׁת הָאֲמוּרִים בְּכָל מָקוֹם, הֵן הָאִלְּמִים שֶׁאֵין שׁוֹמְעִין וְלֹא מְדַבְּרִים;

אֲבָל מִי שֶׁמְּדַבֵּר וְאֵינוֹ שׁוֹמֵעַ, אוֹ שׁוֹמֵעַ וְאֵינוֹ מְדַבֵּר — הֲרֵי הוּא כְּכָל אָדָם.

וְאִישׁ וְאִשָּׁה שֶׁהֵן שְׁלֵמִים בְּדַעְתָּן, וְאֵינָן לֹא חֵרְשִׁים וְלֹא שׁוֹטִים — נִקְרָאִין פִּקֵּחַ וּפִקַּחַת.

כז נִמְצְאוּ כָּל הַשֵּׁמוֹת שֶׁבֵּאַרְנוּ עִנְיָנָם בִּשְׁנֵי פְּרָקִים אֵלּוּ — עֶשְׂרִים שֵׁמוֹת.

וְאֵלּוּ הֵן:

קִדּוּשִׁין. עֶרְוָה. שְׁנִיָּה. אִסּוּרֵי לָאוִין. אִסּוּרֵי עֲשֵׂה. קְטַנָּה. נַעֲרָה. בּוֹגֶרֶת. אַיְלוֹנִית. גְּדוֹלָה. סִימָן הַתַּחְתּוֹן. סִימָן הָעֶלְיוֹן. סְרִיס חַמָּה. סְרִיס אָדָם. גָּדוֹל. אַנְדְּרוֹגִינוֹס. טַמְטוּם. חֵרְשִׁים. פִּקְחִים.

שִׂים כָּל הַשֵּׁמוֹת הָאֵלּוּ לְעֻמָּתְךָ תָּמִיד, וְאַל יָלוּזוּ מֵעֵינֶיךָ כָּל עִנְיְנֵיהֶם, כְּדֵי שֶׁלֹּא נִהְיֶה צְרִיכִין לְבָאֵר כָּל שֵׁם מֵהֶן בְּכָל מָקוֹם שֶׁנַּזְכִּיר אוֹתוֹ.

פֶּרֶק שְׁלִישִׁי

א כֵּיצַד הָאִשָּׁה מִתְקַדֶּשֶׁת?

אִם בְּכֶסֶף הוּא מְקַדֵּשׁ — אֵין פָּחוֹת מִפְּרוּטָה כֶּסֶף אוֹ שָׁוֶה פְּרוּטָה.

אוֹמֵר לָהּ: הֲרֵי אַתְּ מְקֻדֶּשֶׁת לִי, אוֹ: הֲרֵי אַתְּ מְאֹרֶסֶת לִי, אוֹ: הֲרֵי אַתְּ לִי לְאִשָּׁה בָּזֶה, וְנוֹתֵן לָהּ בִּפְנֵי עֵדִים.

וְהָאִישׁ הוּא שֶׁאוֹמֵר דְּבָרִים שֶׁמַּשְׁמָעָן שֶׁקּוֹנֶה אוֹתָהּ לוֹ לְאִשָּׁה, וְהוּא שֶׁיִּתֵּן לָהּ הַכֶּסֶף.

ב נָתְנָה הִיא וְאָמְרָה לוֹ: הֲרֵי אֲנִי מְקֻדֶּשֶׁת לָךְ, הֲרֵינִי מְאֹרֶסֶת לָךְ, הֲרֵינִי לְךָ לְאִנְתּוּ, אוֹ בְּכָל לְשׁוֹן הַקִּנְיָן — אֵינָהּ מְקֻדֶּשֶׁת.

וְכֵן אִם נָתְנָה הִיא לוֹ וְאָמַר הוּא — אֵינָהּ מְקֻדֶּשֶׁת.

---

individuals are not considered to be adults with regard to the mitzvot incumbent upon males.

10. Because a deaf mute's ability to communicate and respond is so limited, such a person is considered to be mentally incompetent and is not held responsible for his conduct, nor is he able to enter into a marriage contract, according to Scriptural law.

bond is not established.[1] If he gave [her money] and she made the statement [the matter is unresolved,][2] and the status of the *kiddushin* is in doubt.[3]

3. If the man establishes the marriage bond with [the transfer of] a legal document, [the following rules apply:] He should write on paper, on a shard, on a leaf or on any other article[4] he desires: "You are consecrated unto me...," "You are betrothed to me...," or any similar expression. He must then give her the document in the presence of witnesses.[5]

4. The document must be written for the sake of the woman who is being married, as must a bill of divorce,[6] and it must be written with her consent.[7] If it was not written for her sake, or if it was written for her sake, but was written without her consent, the marriage bond is not established. [This applies] even when he gives her [the document] with her consent in the presence of witnesses.

5. If the man establishes the marriage bond through sexual relations, he should tell the woman, "You are consecrated unto me...," "You are betrothed to me...," or "You become my wife through these relations," or choose a similar statement. He must enter into privacy with her in the presence of witnesses and engage in relations.[8]

When a person establishes a marriage bond through sexual relations, one may assume that his intent is on the conclusion of the relations;[9] when the relations are concluded, the marriage bond is established. Regardless of whether the couple engage in vaginal or anal intercourse, the marriage bond is established.

1. For it is the man's actions that must precipitate the inception of the marriage bond, as implied by Deuteronomy 24:1: "When a man takes a wife." Note, however, Chapter 5, Halachah 22, which mentions an exception to this principle.
2. *Mishneh LaMelech* offers two explanations of the doubt involved: a) We are unsure of his intent. Since he did not specify that he was giving the woman the money for the sake of *kiddushin*, it is possible that he gave her the money for another reason. This interpretation appears to be supported by the rulings of the *Tur* and the *Shulchan Aruch* (*Even HaEzer* 27:8) that in such a circumstance, the marriage bond is established if previously the man and the woman were speaking about getting married, or if the man confirmed the woman's statements. Halachah 8 appears to support this explanation.
b) The second view is that the doubt is one of principle: The Sages did not define whether the obligation that a man precipitate the marriage bond requires merely his giving money, or also making the statement. According to this conception, the doubt would remain even in the two situations mentioned by the *Tur* and the *Shulchan Aruch*.
3. I.e., the woman cannot marry another man until she receives a bill of divorce. Nevertheless, if another man engages in relations with her, he is not executed for adultery.
4. The man may not, however, write the document on a leaf attached to a tree, or any other item that must be severed, for this is unacceptable when writing a bill of divorce. (See the following halachah and notes.)

וְאִם נָתַן הוּא וְאָמְרָה הִיא — הֲרֵי זוֹ מְקֻדֶּשֶׁת מִסָּפֵק.

ג וְאִם קִדֵּשׁ בִּשְׁטָר — כּוֹתֵב עַל הַנְּיָר אוֹ עַל הַחֶרֶס אוֹ עַל הֶעָלֶה אוֹ עַל כָּל דָּבָר שֶׁיִּרְצֶה: הֲרֵי אַתְּ מְקֻדֶּשֶׁת לִי, אוֹ: הֲרֵי אַתְּ מְאֹרֶסֶת לִי, וְכֹל כַּיּוֹצֵא בִּדְבָרִים אֵלּוּ, וְנוֹתְנוֹ לָהּ בִּפְנֵי עֵדִים.

ד וְצָרִיךְ שֶׁיִּכְתֹּב אוֹתוֹ לְשֵׁם הָאִשָּׁה הַמִּתְקַדֶּשֶׁת, כְּגֵט. וְאֵינוֹ כּוֹתְבוֹ אֶלָּא מִדַּעְתָּהּ. כְּתָבוֹ שֶׁלֹּא לִשְׁמָהּ, אוֹ לִשְׁמָהּ שֶׁלֹּא מִדַּעְתָּהּ, אַף־עַל־פִּי שֶׁנְּתָנוֹ לָהּ לְדַעְתָּהּ בִּפְנֵי עֵדִים — אֵינָהּ מְקֻדֶּשֶׁת.

ה וְאִם קִדֵּשׁ בְּבִיאָה — אוֹמֵר לָהּ: הֲרֵי אַתְּ מְקֻדֶּשֶׁת לִי, אוֹ: הֲרֵי אַתְּ מְאֹרֶסֶת לִי, אוֹ: הֲרֵי אַתְּ לִי לְאִשָּׁה בִּבְעִילָה זוֹ, וְכֹל כַּיּוֹצֵא בָּזֶה, וּמִתְיַחֵד עִמָּהּ בִּפְנֵי שְׁנֵי עֵדִים וּבוֹעֲלָהּ. וְהַמְקַדֵּשׁ בְּבִיאָה — מִסְּתָמָא דַּעְתּוֹ עַל גְּמַר בִּיאָה, וּכְשֶׁיִּגְמֹר בִּיאָתוֹ תִּהְיֶה מְקֻדֶּשֶׁת. וּבֵין שֶׁבָּא עָלֶיהָ כְּדַרְכָּהּ וּבֵין שֶׁבָּא עָלֶיהָ שֶׁלֹּא כְּדַרְכָּהּ — הֲרֵי זוֹ מְקֻדֶּשֶׁת.

5. There is a difference of opinion among the Rabbis if it is necessary for the man to make a verbal statement of intent as well. (See *Beit Shmuel* 32:3.) The *Or Sameach* points to Halachah 18 as proof that a statement is required, but *Kin'at Eliyahu* notes that Halachah 7 appears to indicate that a verbal statement is unnecessary.

6. The acceptability of a legal document for the establishment of *kiddushin* from the association between marriage and divorce created by Deuteronomy 24:2: "When she leaves his household, she may go and become [married] to another man." *Kiddushin* 5a states that this verse indicates that just as she "leaves" through a bill of divorce, she can "become" through a bill of *kiddushin*. Hence, all the particulars that apply to a *get* (a bill of divorce) apply to a bill of *kiddushin*.

7. This requirement does not apply with regard to a bill of divorce and is a point of debate in *Kiddushin* 9b. The opinion the Rambam cites maintains that since the woman is being acquired through this document, she must consent to its being written. Because of the debate in the Talmud, the *Shulchan Aruch* (*Even HaEzer* 32:1) differs with the Rambam and maintains that the matter is unresolved, the status of the *kiddushin* is in doubt, and [the stringencies required had] the marriage bond been established [must be followed].

8. Although the man must enter into privacy with the woman in the presence of witnesses, and must make the statement of intent in the presence of witnesses, the relations themselves should be private, as stated in Chapter 14, Halachah 16, and *Hilchot Gerushin* 10:18. It must be noted that this represents a change in the Rambam's thinking. In his Commentary on the Mishnah (*Kiddushin* 1:1), he originally stated that the relations must also be observed by witnesses for the marriage bond to be established. Nevertheless, in the later texts of the Commentary on the Mishnah the Rambam amended the text according to the above conception.

9. The term "the conclusion of sexual relations" (*g'mar bi'ah*) in Hebrew is somewhat of

6. The statements that the man makes when he consecrates [his wife] must imply that he acquires her as a wife, and not that he gives himself to her. What is implied?

Should he tell her, or write in the document he gives her: "I am your husband," "I am your betrothed," "I am your man," or the like, the marriage bond is not established at all. If he tells her or writes to her: "Behold, you are my wife," "Behold, you are my betrothed," "Behold, you are acquired by me," "Behold, you are mine," "Behold, you are my possession," "Behold, you are my designated one,"[10] "Behold, you are within my property," "Behold, you are bound to me," or the like, the marriage bond is established.

7. Should he tell her, or write to her: "You are set aside for me," "You are earmarked for me," "You are my helper," "You are my counterpart," "You are my rib," "You are closed off for me," "You are below me," "You are my captive," "You have been taken by me," [the matter is unresolved, and] the status of the *kiddushin* is in doubt.

The above applies only when the man was [previously] speaking to the woman about establishing a marriage bond. If he was not speaking to the woman about such a matter, these words are of no consequence.

8. A man may consecrate a woman by making statements in any language that she understands, provided that, in that language, his statements mean that he is acquiring her, as explained.

If a man was speaking to a woman about consecrating her and she consented, and he immediately gave her [something] in her hand to consecrate her or engaged in sexual relations [with that intent], without [making a statement] clarifying [his purpose], it is sufficient. Since they were speaking about this matter, it is not necessary for him to be explicit.

Similarly, a man need not tell witnesses who observe *kiddushin* or divorce, "You are my witnesses."[11] As long as he has divorced or consecrated a woman in their presence, she is consecrated or divorced.

9. When a man tells a woman, "Become consecrated to my half," she is consecrated. To what can this be compared? To his saying, "May you become my wife, and also another woman." And so, she has only half a man.

If, however, he said: "Half of you is consecrated to me," she is not consecrated. For a woman cannot be consecrated to two men. Similarly, if he says, "Behold, you are consecrated to me and to him," the woman is not consecrated.

10. If he told her: "Behold, half of you is consecrated to me with a *p'rutah*, and half of you [is consecrated to me with another] *p'rutah*," or if he

ו הַדְּבָרִים שֶׁיֹּאמַר הָאִישׁ כְּשֶׁיְּקַדֵּשׁ, צָרִיךְ שֶׁיִּהְיֶה מַשְׁמָעָם שֶׁהוּא קוֹנֶה הָאִשָּׁה, וְלֹא שֶׁיְּהֵא מַשְׁמַע שֶׁהִקְנָה עַצְמוֹ לָהּ.

כֵּיצַד? הֲרֵי שֶׁאָמַר לָהּ, אוֹ שֶׁכָּתַב בַּשְּׁטָר שֶׁנְּתָנוֹ לָהּ: הֲרֵינִי בַּעֲלִיךְ, הֲרֵינִי אֲרוּסֵיךְ, הֲרֵינִי אִישֵׁךְ, וְכֹל כַּיּוֹצֵא בָּזֶה — אֵין כָּאן קִדּוּשִׁין כְּלָל.

אָמַר לָהּ, אוֹ כָּתַב לָהּ: הֲרֵי אַתְּ אִשְׁתִּי, הֲרֵי אַתְּ אֲרוּסָתִי, אוֹ: הֲרֵי אַתְּ קְנוּיָה לִי, הֲרֵי אַתְּ שֶׁלִּי, הֲרֵי אַתְּ לְקוּחָתִי, הֲרֵי אַתְּ חֲרוּפָתִי, הֲרֵי אַתְּ בִּרְשׁוּתִי, הֲרֵי אַתְּ זְקוּקָה לִי, וְכֹל כַּיּוֹצֵא בָּהֶן — הֲרֵי זוֹ מְקֻדֶּשֶׁת.

ז אָמַר לָהּ, אוֹ כָּתַב לָהּ: הֲרֵי אַתְּ מְיֻחֶדֶת לִי, הֲרֵי אַתְּ מְיֻעֶדֶת לִי, הֲרֵי אַתְּ עֶזְרָתִי, הֲרֵי אַתְּ נֶגְדָּתִי, הֲרֵי אַתְּ צַלְעָתִי, הֲרֵי אַתְּ סְגוּרָתִי, הֲרֵי אַתְּ תַּחְתִּי, הֲרֵי אַתְּ עֲצוּרָתִי, הֲרֵי אַתְּ תְּפוּסָתִי — הֲרֵי זוֹ מְקֻדֶּשֶׁת בְּסָפֵק.

וְהוּא, שֶׁיִּהְיֶה מְדַבֵּר עִמָּהּ תְּחִלָּה עַל עִסְקֵי קִדּוּשִׁין;

אֲבָל אִם אֵינוֹ מְדַבֵּר עִמָּהּ תְּחִלָּה עַל עִסְקֵי קִדּוּשִׁין — אֵין חוֹשְׁשִׁין לְמִלּוֹת אֵלּוּ:

ח וְיֵשׁ לָאִישׁ לְקַדֵּשׁ הָאִשָּׁה בְּכָל לָשׁוֹן שֶׁהִיא מַכֶּרֶת בּוֹ, וְיִהְיֶה מַשְׁמַע הַדְּבָרִים בְּאוֹתָהּ הַלָּשׁוֹן שֶׁקְּנָאָהּ, כְּמוֹ שֶׁבֵּאַרְנוּ.

הָיָה מְדַבֵּר עִם הָאִשָּׁה עַל עִסְקֵי הַקִּדּוּשִׁין וְרָצְתָה, וְעָמַד וְקִדֵּשׁ, וְלֹא פֵּרֵשׁ וְלֹא אָמַר לָהּ כְּלוּם, אֶלָּא נָתַן בְּיָדָהּ אוֹ בָּעַל — הוֹאִיל וְהֵן עֲסוּקִין בָּעִנְיָן — דַּיּוֹ, וְאֵינוֹ צָרִיךְ לְפָרֵשׁ.

וְכֵן עֲדֵי הַקִּדּוּשִׁין וְהַגֵּרוּשִׁין אֵינוֹ צָרִיךְ לוֹמַר לָהֶם: אַתֶּם עֵדַי,

אֶלָּא כֵּיוָן שֶׁגֵּרַשׁ אוֹ קִדֵּשׁ בִּפְנֵיהֶם — הֲרֵי זוֹ מְקֻדֶּשֶׁת אוֹ מְגֹרֶשֶׁת.

ט הָאוֹמֵר לְאִשָּׁה: הִתְקַדְּשִׁי לְחֶצְיִי — הֲרֵי זוֹ מְקֻדֶּשֶׁת.

הָא לְמָה זֶה דוֹמֶה? לְאוֹמֵר לָהּ: תְּהִי אִשְׁתִּי אַתְּ וְאַחֶרֶת, שֶׁנִּמְצָא שֶׁאֵין לָהּ אֶלָּא חֲצִי אִישׁ.

אֲבָל אִם אָמַר: חֶצְיֵךְ מְקֻדֶּשֶׁת לִי — אֵינָהּ מְקֻדֶּשֶׁת, שֶׁאֵין אִשָּׁה אַחַת רְאוּיָה לִשְׁנַיִם.

וְכֵן אִם אוֹמֵר: הֲרֵי אַתְּ מְקֻדֶּשֶׁת לִי וְלָזֶה — אֵינָהּ מְקֻדֶּשֶׁת.

י אָמַר לָהּ: הֲרֵי חֶצְיֵךְ מְקֻדֶּשֶׁת לִי בִּפְרוּטָה, וְחֶצְיֵךְ בִּפְרוּטָה;

---

a misnomer. It refers not to the man's withdrawal from the woman, nor to ejaculation, but to a far earlier stage: the insertion of the penis in its entirety into the vagina (*Hilchot Issurei Bi'ah* 1:10).

10. Leviticus 19:20 associates this term with establishing relations with a maid-servant, as explained in Chapter 4, Halachah 17. Therefore, there is doubt among the Rabbis if it can be used in establishing the marriage bond with an ordinary woman. Thus, the *Shulchan Aruch* (*Even HaEzer* 27:3) states that if this expression is used the matter is unresolved, and the status of the *kiddushin* is in doubt.

11. With regard to the acknowledgement of a debt, such a statement is necessary. (See *Hilchot To'en V'Nit'an* 6:6-8, 7:1-2.)

told her: "Behold, half of you is consecrated to me with half a *p'rutah,* and your other half [is consecrated to me with another] half a *p'rutah,*" she is consecrated.[12]

If he told her: "Behold, half of you is consecrated to me with a *p'rutah* today, and half of you [is consecrated to me with another] *p'rutah* tomorrow," or if he told her: "Your two halves are consecrated to me with a *p'rutah,*"[13] "Your two daughters are consecrated to my two sons with this *p'rutah,*" "Your daughter is consecrated to me, and your cow is sold to me with this *p'rutah,*" or "Your daughter... and your land... with a *p'rutah*" - in all of these circumstances, [the matter is unresolved, and] the status of the *kiddushin* is in doubt.

11. A father may consecrate his daughter without her knowledge while she is a minor. Even when she is a *na'arah,*[14] he still possesses this right, as [implied by Deuteronomy 22:16]: "I gave my daughter to this man."

[The money received as] *kiddushin* belongs to her father. Similarly, he has the right to [any ownerless property] she finds, [the wages she receives for] her labor, and [the money she receives as stipulated in] her *ketubah* if she is divorced or widowed before the marriage bond is consummated. He is entitled to all these until she becomes a *bogeret.*

Therefore, a father is entitled to receive *kiddushin* on behalf of his daughter from the day she was born until she becomes a *bogeret.* Even if she is a deaf mute or intellectually incompetent, if her father consecrates her [to another man], she is his wife.

If a girl is older than three years and one day, she can be consecrated through sexual relations with her father's consent. Should she be below this age, if her father has her consecrated through sexual relations, the marriage bond is not established.[15]

12. After a daughter becomes a *bogeret,* her father has no rights over her; she is like all other women, and she can be consecrated only with her own consent.

Similarly, if her father had her married, the marriage bond was consummated [*nisu'in*],[16] and then she was widowed or divorced, [even] in her father's lifetime, she is considered to be independent, despite the fact that she is still a minor. Once a woman enters *nisu'in,* her father no longer has any authority over her.

13. When a girl receives *kiddushin* without her father's knowledge before she reaches the age of majority, the marriage bond is not established.[17] [This applies] even when the father consents subsequently.[18] Moreover, if she is

---

12. The Ra'avad and similarly, the *Shulchan Aruch* (*Even HaEzer* 31:7) differ and maintain

אוֹ שֶׁאָמַר לָהּ: חֶצְיֵךְ מְקֻדֶּשֶׁת לִי בַּחֲצִי פְרוּטָה, וְחֶצְיֵךְ הָאַחֶרֶת מְקֻדֶּשֶׁת בַּחֲצִי פְּרוּטָה — הֲרֵי זוֹ מְקֻדֶּשֶׁת.

אָמַר לָהּ: חֶצְיֵךְ מְקֻדֶּשֶׁת לִי בִּפְרוּטָה הַיּוֹם, וְחֶצְיֵךְ בִּפְרוּטָה לְמָחָר;

שְׁתֵּי חֲצָיֵיךְ בִּפְרוּטָה;

שְׁתֵּי בְנוֹתֶיךָ לִשְׁנֵי בָנַי בִּפְרוּטָה;

בִּתְּךָ מְקֻדֶּשֶׁת לִי וּפָרָתְךָ מְכוּרָה לִי בִּפְרוּטָה;

אוֹ: בִּתְּךָ וְקַרְקָעָתְךָ לִי בִּפְרוּטָה —

בְּכָל אֵלּוּ מְקֻדֶּשֶׁת בְּסָפֵק.

יא הָאָב מְקַדֵּשׁ אֶת בִּתּוֹ שֶׁלֹּא לְדַעְתָּהּ כָּל זְמַן שֶׁהִיא קְטַנָּה,

וְכֵן כְּשֶׁהִיא נַעֲרָה רְשׁוּתָהּ בְּיָדוֹ, שֶׁנֶּאֱמַר: אֶת בִּתִּי נָתַתִּי לָאִישׁ הַזֶּה לְאִשָּׁה. וְקִדּוּשֶׁיהָ לְאָבִיהָ.

וְכֵן הוּא זַכַּאי בִּמְצִיאָתָהּ וּבְמַעֲשֵׂה יָדֶיהָ וּבִכְתֻבָּתָהּ. אִם נִתְגָּרְשָׁה אוֹ נִתְאַלְמְנָה מִן הָאֵרוּסִין הוּא זַכַּאי בַּכֹּל עַד שֶׁתִּבָּגֵר.

לְפִיכָךְ מְקַבֵּל הָאָב קִדּוּשֵׁי בִּתּוֹ מִיּוֹם שֶׁתִּוָּלֵד עַד שֶׁתִּבָּגֵר.

וַאֲפִלּוּ הָיְתָה חֵרֶשֶׁת אוֹ שׁוֹטָה וְקִדְּשָׁהּ הָאָב — הֲרֵי הִיא אֵשֶׁת אִישׁ גְּמוּרָה.

וְאִם הָיְתָה בַּת שָׁלֹשׁ שָׁנִים וְיוֹם אֶחָד, מִתְקַדֶּשֶׁת בְּבִיאָה מִדַּעַת אָבִיהָ;

פָּחוֹת מִכֵּן, אִם קִדְּשָׁהּ אָבִיהָ בְּבִיאָה — אֵינָהּ מְקֻדֶּשֶׁת.

יב בָּגְרָה הַבַּת — אֵין לְאָבִיהָ בָּהּ רְשׁוּת, וַהֲרֵי הִיא כִּשְׁאָר כָּל הַנָּשִׁים שֶׁאֵינָם מִתְקַדְּשׁוֹת אֶלָּא לְדַעְתָּן.

וְכֵן אִם הִשִּׂיאָהּ אָבִיהָ, וְנִתְאַלְמְנָה אוֹ נִתְגָּרְשָׁה בְּחַיֵּי אָבִיהָ — הֲרֵי הִיא בִּרְשׁוּת עַצְמָהּ וְאַף־עַל־פִּי שֶׁעֲדַיִן הִיא קְטַנָּה.

כֵּיוָן שֶׁנִּשֵּׂאת, אֵין לְאָבִיהָ בָּהּ רְשׁוּת לְעוֹלָם.

יג נִתְקַדְּשָׁה קֹדֶם שֶׁתִּבָּגֵר שֶׁלֹּא לְדַעַת אָבִיהָ — אֵינָהּ מְקֻדֶּשֶׁת, וַאֲפִלּוּ אִם נִתְרַצָּה הָאָב אַחַר שֶׁנִּתְקַדְּשָׁה.

that the status of the *kiddushin* is in doubt. It is only with regard to stringencies that the *kiddushin* are considered to be valid.

13. This clause serves as the basis for the Ra'avad's objection to the Rambam's decisions above.

14. At which time, the girl has the right to accept *kiddushin* from a man herself.

15. For until the age of three, a woman is not considered to be fit for sexual relations.

16. This refers to the second stage of the marriage relationship, as explained in Chapter 11 onward.

17. This and the other laws in this halachah apply when a girl is either a *k'tanah* or a *na'arah* (has reached the age of twelve), but not a *bogeret* (twelve and a half).

18. Since the *kiddushin* were not effective at the time they were given, the father's

widowed or divorced after these *kiddushin*, she is not forbidden [to marry] a priest.[19]

Both she and her father can prevent [the marriage bonds from taking effect].[20] Regardless of whether she was consecrated in the presence of her father or not, she is not consecrated.

14. [The following rules apply when] there is doubt whether or not the girl is a *bogeret*: Whether her father consecrated her without her consent, or she consecrated herself without her father's consent, the status of the *kiddushin* is in doubt. Therefore, [to marry another man,] she must receive a *get* given because of the doubt.

A man may appoint an agent to consecrate a wife for him. [This applies] if he specifies a particular woman, or gives the agent the authority to consecrate any woman. Similarly, a woman past the age of majority[21] may appoint an agent to receive *kiddushin* for her. [This applies] if she specifies [that they be given by] a particular man, or gives the agent the authority to receive them from any man. Similarly, a father may appoint an agent to accept the *kiddushin* of his daughter as long as she is under his authority.

A man may tell his daughter who is below the age of majority, "Go out and receive your *kiddushin*."[22]

15. When an agent is appointed to receive *kiddushin*, he must be appointed in the presence of two witnesses.[23] When, by contrast, a man appoints an agent to consecrate a woman, there is no need for the appointment to be made in the presence of witnesses. For the only purpose witnesses would serve with regard to the agency of the man is to make known the truth of the matter.[24] Therefore, if the agent and the principal acknowledge the appointment, there is no need for witnesses, [as in parallel cases, such as] an agent appointed to bring a *get*[25] or an agent appointed to separate *terumah*.[26]

In all matters, a principal's agent is regarded as the principal himself, and there is no need to appoint witnesses.

---

subsequent consent is of no significance. This point is, however, disputed by some of the later authorities. (See *Shulchan Aruch, Even HaEzer* 37:11.)

19. No priest may marry a divorcee, nor may a High Priest marry a widow. Nevertheless, because these *kiddushin* are not effective, these prohibitions do not apply.

20. According to the *Maharik* (Responsum 30[32]), this applies when the *kiddushin* were given in her father's presence, but he remained silent. In both the *Kessef Mishneh* and the *Shulchan Aruch* (*ibid.*), Rav Yosef Karo differs and explains that according to the Rambam, the father must consent at the time of (or before) the *kiddushin*. If he desires to prevent the *kiddushin* at that time, he may. If he consents, the girl getting married can still prevent the *kiddushin* from taking place. For since her father charged her with this matter, even if he consented to the match it is dependent on her. (See also Chapter 22, Halachah 5, and *Hilchot Terumot* 8:16.)

21. A woman below the age of majority does not have the authority to appoint an agent.

וַאֲפִלּוּ אִם נִתְאַלְמְנָה אוֹ נִתְגָּרְשָׁה מִן אוֹתָן הַקִּדּוּשִׁין — אֵינָהּ אֲסוּרָה לְכֹהֵן. וּבֵין הִיא וּבֵין אָבִיהָ יְכוֹלִין לְעַכֵּב.
בֵּין אִם נִתְקַדְּשָׁה בְּפָנָיו בֵּין שֶׁנִּתְקַדְּשָׁה שֶׁלֹּא בְּפָנָיו — אֵינָהּ מְקֻדֶּשֶׁת.

יד הָיְתָה הַבַּת סָפֵק בּוֹגֶרֶת, בֵּין שֶׁקִּדְּשָׁהּ אָבִיהָ שֶׁלֹּא לְדַעְתָּהּ בֵּין שֶׁקִּדְּשָׁה הִיא עַצְמָהּ שֶׁלֹּא לְדַעַת אָבִיהָ — הֲרֵי זוֹ מְקֻדֶּשֶׁת בְּסָפֵק, לְפִיכָךְ צְרִיכָה גֵּט מִסָּפֵק.
יֵשׁ לְאִישׁ לַעֲשׂוֹת שָׁלִיחַ לְקַדֵּשׁ לוֹ אִשָּׁה, בֵּין אִשָּׁה פְּלוֹנִית בֵּין אִשָּׁה מִשְּׁאָר הַנָּשִׁים.
וְכֵן הָאִשָּׁה הַגְּדוֹלָה עוֹשָׂה שָׁלִיחַ לְקַבֵּל קִדּוּשֶׁיהָ, בֵּין מֵאִישׁ פְּלוֹנִי בֵּין מֵאִישׁ מִשְּׁאָר אֲנָשִׁים.
וְכֵן הָאָב עוֹשֶׂה שָׁלִיחַ לְקַבֵּל קִדּוּשֵׁי בִּתּוֹ כְּשֶׁהִיא בִּרְשׁוּתוֹ.
וְאוֹמֵר הָאָב לְבִתּוֹ הַקְּטַנָּה: צְאִי וְקַבְּלִי קִדּוּשַׁיְךְ.

טו כָּל הָעוֹשֶׂה שָׁלִיחַ לְקַבֵּל הַקִּדּוּשִׁין, צָרִיךְ לַעֲשׂוֹתוֹ בִּפְנֵי עֵדִים.
אֲבָל הָאִישׁ שֶׁעָשָׂה שָׁלִיחַ לְקַדֵּשׁ לוֹ אִשָּׁה, אֵינוֹ צָרִיךְ לַעֲשׂוֹתוֹ בְּעֵדִים.
שֶׁאֵין מָקוֹם לְעֵדִים בִּשְׁלִיחוּת הָאִישׁ אֶלָּא לְהוֹדִיעַ אֲמִתַּת הַדָּבָר, לְפִיכָךְ אִם הוֹדוּ הַשָּׁלִיחַ וְהַמְשַׁלֵּחַ — אֵינָן צְרִיכִין עֵדִים.
כְּמוֹ שָׁלִיחַ הַגֵּט, וּכְמוֹ שָׁלִיחַ שֶׁהִרְשָׁהוּ לְהַפְרִישׁ לוֹ תְּרוּמָה, וְכַיּוֹצֵא בָּהֶן בְּכָל מָקוֹם — שֶׁשְּׁלוּחוֹ שֶׁל אָדָם כְּמוֹתוֹ, וְאֵינוֹ צָרִיךְ עֵדִים.

22. Among the explanations that are given for why this is acceptable: a) If the father had said, "Give an animal food, and my daughter will be consecrated to you," the *kiddushin* would be binding. When he tells the daughter to receive *kiddushin*, it is as if he makes a statement that it is acceptable to him that the man who consecrates her gives her the money (Ra'avad, Ramban).
b) Although a minor may not normally serve as an agent, this instance is an exception. Since the *kiddushin* are being given for her benefit, the girl is entitled to act in this capacity (Rabbenu Asher). The *Beit Shmuel* 37:7 states that the Rambam subscribes to this view.
23. The rationale is that since the marriage bonds are established through the acceptance of the *kiddushin*, witnesses must be present to acknowledge the agent's appointment, for "no matters involving forbidden sexual relations [are established if] fewer than two witnesses are present (*Yevamot* 88a)."
The Ramah (*Even HaEzer* 35:3) quotes the opinion of Rabbenu Asher, who states that if all concerned acknowledge the appointment of the agent, the *kiddushin* are effective. He therefore rules that in such a situation, the woman needs to receive a *get* before she can marry another man.
24. The Rambam's statements are based on the comparison to an agent appointed to bring a woman a *get*. The Ra'avad objects to the comparison, because a *get* is a formal legal document, and possession of it serves to verify the person's agency. The *Shulchan Aruch* (*ibid.*) quotes both opinions, but appears to favor that of the Rambam.
25. *Hilchot Gittin* 6:4. This ruling itself is not accepted by all authorities, as noted in the *Shulchan Aruch* (*Even HaEzer* 141:13).
26. *Hilchot Terumah* 4:1.

16. An agent may serve as a witness. Therefore, if a person appointed two men as agents to consecrate a woman, and they did so, they serve both as agents and as witnesses. Hence, there is no need for them to consecrate her in the presence of two other witnesses.[27]

17. All are fit to serve as agents [in this capacity] except a deaf mute, a mentally incompetent individual and a minor - for they are not responsible - and a gentile, because he is not a member of the covenant. [The latter exclusion is based on Numbers 18:28, which] states: "And so shall you set aside, and you...." [This is interpreted as] including an agent. [Our Sages commented:] Just as you are members of the covenant, your agents must be members of the covenant, thus excluding a gentile.

A [Canaanite] servant, although he is acceptable as an agent with regard to financial matters, is not acceptable as an agent with regard to *kiddushin* and *gittin*, because the laws of marriage and divorce do not apply to him.

18. An agent appointed by a man to consecrate a woman should tell her: "Behold, you are consecrated to so and so by virtue of this money" or "...by virtue of this legal document."

If an agent of the woman receives the *kiddushin*, the [man consecrating her] should tell [the agent]: "So and so who appointed you is consecrated to me," and the agent should reply, "I have consecrated her to you," "I have betrothed her to you," "I have given her to you as a wife," or the like.

Similarly, when a man consecrates a girl by [giving *kiddushin* to] her father, he should tell him, "Behold, your daughter so and so is consecrated to me," and the father should reply: "I have consecrated her to you." If the father or the agent says "yes," or even if he remains silent, it is sufficient. If they were discussing the matter, and the man gave the *kiddushin* to the father or to the agent without making any statement, it is sufficient, and the *kiddushin* are effective.

If the *kiddushin* are established by virtue of [the transfer of] a legal document, he must have the document written with the consent of the father or of the agent. In all matters pertaining to *kiddushin*, the same laws that apply to the man and the woman, apply when [the *kiddushin* are established by] the [man's] agent and [the woman's] agent or [her] father.

19. It is a mitzvah for a man to consecrate his wife by himself, rather than to charge an agent [with this matter]. Similarly, it is a mitzvah for a woman to [receive] *kiddushin* herself rather than to charge an agent with receiving them for her.

Although a father has the option of consecrating his daughter to anyone he desires while she is a minor or while she is a maiden, it is not proper for him to act in this manner. Instead, our Sages enjoined that a person

טז הַשָּׁלִיחַ נַעֲשָׂה עֵד.

לְפִיכָךְ, אִם עָשָׂה שְׁנֵי שְׁלוּחִין לְקַדֵּשׁ לוֹ אִשָּׁה, וְהָלְכוּ וְקִדְּשׁוּ אוֹתָהּ — הֵן הֵן שְׁלוּחָיו וְהֵן הֵן עֵדֵי הַקִּדּוּשִׁין,

וְאֵינָן צְרִיכִין לְקַדְּשָׁהּ לוֹ בִּפְנֵי שְׁנַיִם אֲחֵרִים.

יז הַכֹּל כְּשֵׁרִין לִשְׁלִיחוּת, חוּץ מֵחֵרֵשׁ שׁוֹטֶה וְקָטָן — לְפִי שֶׁאֵינָן בְּנֵי דַעַת,

וְהָעַכּוּ״ם — לְפִי שֶׁאֵינוֹ בֶּן בְּרִית,

וְנֶאֱמַר: כֵּן תָּרִימוּ גַם אַתֶּם — לְרַבּוֹת הַשָּׁלִיחַ; וּמָה אַתֶּם בְּנֵי בְרִית, אַף שְׁלוּחֲכֶם בְּנֵי בְרִית, לְהוֹצִיא אֶת הָעַכּוּ״ם.

אֲבָל הָעֶבֶד, אַף־עַל־פִּי שֶׁהוּא נַעֲשָׂה שָׁלִיחַ לְדָבָר שֶׁבְּמָמוֹן, הֲרֵי הוּא פָּסוּל לִשְׁלִיחוּת הַקִּדּוּשִׁין וְהַגִּטִּין, לְפִי שֶׁאֵינוֹ בְּתוֹרַת גִּטִּין וְקִדּוּשִׁין.

יח שְׁלִיחַ הָאִישׁ שֶׁמְּקַדֵּשׁ אוֹמֵר לָהּ: הֲרֵי אַתְּ מְקֻדֶּשֶׁת לִפְלוֹנִי בְּכֶסֶף זֶה אוֹ בִּשְׁטָר זֶה.

אִם שְׁלִיחַ הָאִשָּׁה הוּא שֶׁמְּקַבֵּל הַקִּדּוּשִׁין, אוֹמֵר לוֹ: הֲרֵי פְּלוֹנִית שֶׁשָּׁלְחָה אוֹתְךָ מְקֻדֶּשֶׁת לִי. וְהוּא אוֹמֵר לוֹ: קִדַּשְׁתִּיהָ לְךָ, אוֹ: אֵרַסְתִּיהָ לְךָ, אוֹ: נְתַתִּיהָ לְךָ לְאִשָּׁה, וְכָל כַּיּוֹצֵא בָּזֶה.

וְכֵן הַמְקַדֵּשׁ עַל יְדֵי הָאָב אוֹמֵר לוֹ: הֲרֵי בִּתְּךָ פְּלוֹנִית מְקֻדֶּשֶׁת לִי. וְהוּא אוֹמֵר לוֹ: קִדַּשְׁתִּיהָ לְךָ.

אִם אָמַר הָאָב אוֹ הַשָּׁלִיחַ: הֵן — דַּיּוֹ. וַאֲפִלּוּ שָׁתַק.

וְאִם הָיוּ עֲסוּקִין בְּאוֹתוֹ עִנְיָן, וְנָתַן לָאָב אוֹ לַשָּׁלִיחַ וְלֹא פֵּרֵשׁ וְלֹא אָמַר דָּבָר — דַּיּוֹ, וְהִיא מְקֻדֶּשֶׁת.

וְאִם קִדֵּשׁ בִּשְׁטָר, אֵינוֹ כּוֹתְבוֹ אֶלָּא מִדַּעַת הָאָב אוֹ מִדַּעַת הַשָּׁלִיחַ.

וְכֵן בְּכָל הַדְּבָרִים כֻּלָּן שֶׁל קִדּוּשִׁין, דִּין הָאִישׁ עִם הָאִשָּׁה כְּדִין שָׁלִיחַ עִם הָאִשָּׁה עִם שָׁלִיחַ אוֹ עִם הָאָב.

יט מִצְוָה שֶׁיְּקַדֵּשׁ אָדָם אֶת אִשְׁתּוֹ בְּעַצְמוֹ יוֹתֵר מֵעַל יְדֵי שְׁלוּחוֹ.

וְכֵן מִצְוָה לְאִשָּׁה שֶׁתִּתְקַדֵּשׁ עַצְמָהּ בְּיָדָהּ יוֹתֵר מֵעַל יְדֵי שְׁלוּחָהּ.

וְאַף־עַל־פִּי שֶׁיֵּשׁ רְשׁוּת לָאָב לְקַדֵּשׁ בִּתּוֹ כְּשֶׁהִיא קְטַנָּה וּכְשֶׁהִיא נַעֲרָה לְכָל מִי שֶׁיִּרְצֶה — אֵין רָאוּי לַעֲשׂוֹת כֵּן.

27. The fundamental principle reflected by this halachah is that despite the fact that the agent is bringing about the *kiddushin*, since he is acting on behalf of the principal, he is not considered as as an involved party. Hence, he may serve as a witness.

As clarified by the *Maggid Mishneh* and the *Shulchan Aruch* (*Even HaEzer* 35:2), this ruling applies only when: a) the *kiddushin* are established by the transfer of a legal document worth less than a *p'rutah*, or b) the *kiddushin* are established by the transfer of money, and the woman admits receiving the money. Otherwise, the agent would not be able to serve as a witness. Since he is responsible for the financial value of the *kiddushin*, he would be considered an involved party.

should not consecrate his daughter while she is a minor until she matures and says, "I would like [to marry] so and so."

Similarly, it is not proper for a man to consecrate a girl below the age of majority. Nor should one consecrate a woman until one sees her and deems her fitting, lest she not find favor in his eyes, and he divorce her, or sleep with her while hating her.

20. *Kiddushin* established by virtue of sexual relations are effective according to Scriptural law. Similarly, *kiddushin* established by virtue [of the transfer] of a legal document are effective according to Scriptural law. Just as [the transfer of a legal document] concludes a divorce, as [Deuteronomy 24;1] states: "And he shall write her a scroll of divorce," so too, [the transfer of a legal document] concludes [the establishment of the marriage bond].

[The effectiveness of the transfer of] money stems from Scriptural law,[28] but its interpretation is based on Rabbinic law. [Deuteronomy, *ibid.*,] states "When a man takes a wife," and our Sages[29] explained: This [process of] acquisition involves [the transfer of] money, as implied by [Genesis 23:13]: "I have given the money for the field; take it from me."

21. Although this is the essence of the principle, it has already become universal Jewish custom to consecrate [a marriage bond] through [the transfer of] money or objects that are worth money. If one desires to consecrate [a woman] by [giving her] a legal document, one may, but at the outset one should not consecrate [a woman] through sexual relations.

If a man consecrates [a woman] through sexual relations, he is given stripes for rebelliousness,[30] so that the Jewish people will not extend beyond the limits of modesty in this manner. Nevertheless, the *kiddushin* are binding.

22. Similarly, a man who consecrates a woman without establishing an engagement previously, or a man who consecrates a woman in the marketplace, is given stripes for rebelliousness, although his *kiddushin* are binding. [This was instituted] lest such a practice accustom people to licentious conduct and invite a comparison to a harlot, as existed before the giving of the Torah.

23. Whenever a man consecrates a woman,[31] whether by himself or via an agent, either he[32] or his agent should recite a blessing before the consecration, as one recites a blessing before performing any of the mitzvot. [After reciting the blessing,] he should consecrate [the woman].

If he consecrates a woman without reciting a blessing, he should not recite the blessing afterwards. It would be a blessing in vain, for the activity has already been performed.[33]

---

28. Our translation follows the Rambam's later emendations to the *Mishneh Torah*. The

אֶלָּא מִצְוַת חֲכָמִים שֶׁלֹּא יְקַדֵּשׁ אָדָם בִּתּוֹ כְּשֶׁהִיא קְטַנָּה, עַד שֶׁתַּגְדִּיל וְתֹאמַר: לִפְלוֹנִי אֲנִי רוֹצָה.

וְכֵן הָאִישׁ אֵין רָאוּי לְקַדֵּשׁ קְטַנָּה.

וְלֹא יְקַדֵּשׁ אִשָּׁה עַד שֶׁיִּרְאֶנָּה וְתִהְיֶה כְּשֵׁרָה בְּעֵינָיו; שֶׁמָּא לֹא תִּמְצָא חֵן בְּעֵינָיו, וְנִמְצָא מְגָרְשָׁהּ אוֹ שׁוֹכֵב עִמָּהּ וְהוּא שׂוֹנְאָהּ.

ב הַמְקַדֵּשׁ בְּבִיאָה — הֲרֵי אֵלּוּ קִדּוּשֵׁי תּוֹרָה.

וְכֵן מִתְקַדֶּשֶׁת בִּשְׁטָר מִן הַתּוֹרָה. כְּשֵׁם שֶׁגּוֹמֵר וּמְגָרֵשׁ, שֶׁנֶּאֱמַר: וְכָתַב לָהּ סֵפֶר כְּרִיתוּת, כָּךְ גּוֹמֵר וּמַכְנִיס.

אֲבָל הַכֶּסֶף מִדִּבְרֵי סוֹפְרִים (וְכֵן דִּין הַכֶּסֶף דִּין תּוֹרָה, וּפֵרוּשׁוֹ מִדִּבְרֵי סוֹפְרִים), שֶׁנֶּאֱמַר: כִּי יִקַּח אִישׁ אִשָּׁה, וְאָמְרוּ חֲכָמִים: לִקּוּחִים אֵלּוּ יִהְיוּ בְּכֶסֶף, שֶׁנֶּאֱמַר: נָתַתִּי כֶּסֶף הַשָּׂדֶה קַח מִמֶּנִּי.

כא אַף־עַל־פִּי שֶׁעִקַּר הַדָּבָר כָּךְ הוּא, כְּבָר נָהֲגוּ כָּל יִשְׂרָאֵל לְקַדֵּשׁ בְּכֶסֶף אוֹ בְּשָׁוֶה כֶּסֶף.

וְכֵן אִם רָצָה לְקַדֵּשׁ בִּשְׁטָר — מְקַדֵּשׁ.

אֲבָל אֵין מְקַדְּשִׁין בְּבִיאָה לְכַתְּחִלָּה.

וְאִם קִדֵּשׁ בְּבִיאָה — מַכִּין אוֹתוֹ מַכַּת מַרְדּוּת, כְּדֵי שֶׁלֹּא יִהְיוּ יִשְׂרָאֵל פְּרוּצִים בְּדָבָר זֶה, אַף־עַל־פִּי שֶׁקִּדּוּשָׁיו קִדּוּשִׁין גְּמוּרִים.

כב וְכֵן הַמְקַדֵּשׁ בְּלֹא שִׁדּוּכִין אוֹ הַמְקַדֵּשׁ בַּשּׁוּק — אַף־עַל־פִּי שֶׁקִּדּוּשָׁיו קִדּוּשִׁין גְּמוּרִין, מַכִּין אוֹתוֹ מַכַּת מַרְדּוּת, כְּדֵי שֶׁלֹּא יְהֵא דָּבָר זֶה הֶרְגֵּל לִזְנוּת, וְיִדְמֶה לְקַדֵּשָׁהּ שֶׁהָיְתָה קֹדֶם מַתַּן תּוֹרָה.

כג כָּל הַמְקַדֵּשׁ אִשָּׁה — בֵּין עַל יְדֵי עַצְמוֹ בֵּין עַל יְדֵי שָׁלִיחַ — צָרִיךְ לְבָרֵךְ קֹדֶם הַקִּדּוּשִׁין, אוֹ הוּא אוֹ שְׁלוּחוֹ, כְּדֶרֶךְ שֶׁמְּבָרְכִין עַל כָּל הַמִּצְוֹת, וְאַחַר כָּךְ מְקַדֵּשׁ. וְאִם קִדֵּשׁ וְלֹא בֵּרַךְ — לֹא יְבָרֵךְ אַחַר הַקִּדּוּשִׁין, שֶׁזּוֹ בְּרָכָה לְבַטָּלָה. מַה שֶּׁנַּעֲשָׂה — כְּבָר נַעֲשָׂה.

---

earlier version of the text states: "The effectiveness of [the transfer of] money stems from Rabbinic law." See the discussion of this concept in the notes on Chapter 1, Halachah 2.
29. *Kiddushin* 4b.
30. The punishment given for transgressing a Rabbinic decree.
31. Today, it is customary for the consecration to be made under the wedding canopy (*chuppah*), and the blessing is recited at this time.
32. The Rambam's wording implies that the blessing should be recited by the groom himself. At present, the current custom in both the Sephardic and Ashkenazic communities is to have the Rabbi conducting the marriage ceremony recite the blessing, lest a groom who does not know how to recite the blessing be embarrassed by his lack of knowledge. (See *Hagahot Maimoniot*.)
33. In *Darchei Moshe* (*Even HaEzer* 34), the Ramah states that one may recite the blessing

24. Which blessing is recited?

Blessed are You, God, our Lord, King of the universe, who has sanctified us with His mitzvot and separated[34] us from illicit relationships, who has forbidden the *arusot* to us, and permitted to us those who are married[35] by [the rites of] *chuppah* and *kiddushin*. Blessed are You, God, who sanctifies Israel.

This is the blessing of *erusin*. The people have established the custom of reciting this blessing over wine or beer. If there is wine available, one should recite the blessing over the wine, recite the blessing of consecration afterwards, and then consecrate the woman.[36] If there is no wine or beer available, one should recite [the blessing of consecration] by itself.

CHAPTER FOUR

1. A woman may be consecrated only voluntarily. If one forces a woman to be consecrated, she is not consecrated. When a man, by contrast, is forced to consecrate [a woman], she is consecrated.[1]

A man may consecrate many women at one time, provided that he does so by [transferring] money, and there is enough money to give each one a *p'rutah*. One of these [women] or another person may accept the money on behalf of them all, [provided] they consent.

2. When a person [desires to] consecrate a woman, and with her consent gives the *kiddushin* to another woman, and tells the latter "And you as well," or uses another similar expression, they are both consecrated.[2]

When, however, the man places [the *kiddushin*] in the hand [of the second woman] and says, "And you," there is doubt whether or not the *kiddushin* are valid. Perhaps his intent was only to clarify her feelings. It was as if he asked her, "What would you say about this?" Therefore, she accepted the *kiddushin*, for she thought he was still asking her about her intent. For this reason, [the question is unresolved,] and the status of the *kiddushin* is in doubt.

---

afterwards as well. Nevertheless, in his gloss on the *Shulchan Aruch*, he does not make such a statement. The current custom in both the Sephardic and Ashkenazic communities is to recite the blessing before the *kiddushin*.

34. The *Shulchan Aruch* (*Even HaEzer* 34:1) states that the blessing should read: "and commanded us concerning," rather than "and separated us from." This is the common practice today.

35. The *Beit Shmuel* 34:3 and others state that the blessing should read "those who are married to us." This is the custom in many communities.

36. At present, the custom is for the officiating Rabbi to recite the blessing over the

כד כֵּיצַד מְבָרֵךְ?

בָּרוּךְ אַתָּה יְיָ אֱלֹהֵינוּ מֶלֶךְ הָעוֹלָם, אֲשֶׁר קִדְּשָׁנוּ בְּמִצְוֹתָיו, וְהִבְדִּילָנוּ מִן הָעֲרָיוֹת, וְאָסַר לָנוּ אֶת הָאֲרוּסוֹת, וְהִתִּיר לָנוּ אֶת הַנְּשׂוּאוֹת עַל יְדֵי חֻפָּה וְקִדּוּשִׁין. בָּרוּךְ אַתָּה יְיָ, מְקַדֵּשׁ יִשְׂרָאֵל.

זוֹ הִיא בִּרְכַּת אֵרוּסִין.

וְנָהֲגוּ הָעָם לְהַסְדִּיר בְּרָכָה זוֹ עַל כּוֹס שֶׁל יַיִן אוֹ שֶׁל שֵׁכָר.

וְאִם יֵשׁ שָׁם יַיִן — מְבָרֵךְ עַל הַיַּיִן תְּחִלָּה, וְאַחַר כָּךְ מְבָרֵךְ בְּרְכַּת אֵרוּסִין, וְאַחַר כָּךְ מְקַדְּשָׁהּ.
וְאִם אֵין לוֹ יַיִן אוֹ שֵׁכָר — מְבָרֵךְ אוֹתָהּ בִּפְנֵי עַצְמָהּ.

פֶּרֶק רְבִיעִי

א אֵין הָאִשָּׁה מִתְקַדֶּשֶׁת אֶלָּא לִרְצוֹנָהּ. וְהַמְקַדֵּשׁ אִשָּׁה בְּעַל כָּרְחָהּ — אֵינָהּ מְקֻדֶּשֶׁת.

אֲבָל הָאִישׁ שֶׁאֲנָסוּהוּ עַד שֶׁקִּדֵּשׁ בְּעַל כָּרְחוֹ — הֲרֵי זוֹ מְקֻדֶּשֶׁת.

וְיֵשׁ לְאִישׁ לְקַדֵּשׁ נָשִׁים רַבּוֹת כְּאַחַת. וְהוּא, שֶׁיִּהְיֶה בַּכֶּסֶף — אִם קִדֵּשׁ בְּכֶסֶף — פְּרוּטָה לְכָל אַחַת וְאַחַת.

וְיֵשׁ לְאַחַת מֵהֶן אוֹ לְאַחֵר לְקַבֵּל הַקִּדּוּשִׁין עַל יְדֵי כֻּלָּן מִדַּעְתָּן.

ב הַמְקַדֵּשׁ אֶת הָאִשָּׁה וְנָתַן הַקִּדּוּשִׁין מִדַּעְתָּהּ בְּיַד חֲבֶרְתָּהּ, וְאָמַר לַחֲבֶרְתָּהּ כְּשֶׁנָּתַן הַקִּדּוּשִׁין בְּיָדָהּ: וְאַתְּ נָמִי, אוֹ: וְכֵן גַּם אַתְּ, וְכַיּוֹצֵא בָּזֶה — הֲרֵי שְׁתֵּיהֶן מְקֻדָּשׁוֹת.

אֲבָל אִם נָתַן בְּיָדָהּ וְאָמַר לָהּ: וְאַתְּ — הֲרֵי זוֹ שֶׁקִּבְּלָה הַקִּדּוּשִׁין מְקֻדֶּשֶׁת בְּסָפֵק; שֶׁמָּא לֹא נִתְכַּוֵּן אֶלָּא לִרְאוֹת מַה בְּלִבָּהּ, וּכְאִלּוּ אָמַר לָהּ: וְאַתְּ מַה תֹּאמְרִי בְּדָבָר זֶה? וּלְפִיכָךְ קִבְּלָה הַקִּדּוּשִׁין הִיא, שֶׁהֲרֵי זֶה עֲדַיִן שׁוֹאֲלָהּ לִרְאוֹת מַה בְּלִבָּהּ, וּמִפְּנֵי זֶה הִיא סָפֵק מְקֻדֶּשֶׁת.

wine and then the blessing of consecration. He then has the groom and bride drink from the wine, and afterwards the groom consecrates the bride.

1. *Bava Batra* 48b states that since it was possible for a man to divorce his wife without her consent (in Talmudic times), there was no need for the Sages to abrogate the man's *kiddushin*. Even if he was forced into consecrating the woman, he could end their relationship at will. With regard to the woman, by contrast, since she cannot initiate a divorce, our Sages abrogated the marriage bond when she was compelled to establish it against her will.

2. The first woman is consecrated based on the principle stated in the following halachah, that a woman may tell a person to give the *kiddushin* to an agent acting on her behalf. The second woman is consecrated, because she accepted the *kiddushin* in silence, which is interpreted as acquiescence.

3. If he told her, "Become consecrated to me with this *dinar*," and she took it and threw it in front of him or to the sea, into a fire or into anything that will cause it to be destroyed, she is not consecrated.[3]

If she told him, "Give it to my father," "...to your father" or "...to so and so," she is not consecrated.[4] If she told him, "Give it to him, so that he will accept it on my behalf,"[5] she is consecrated.

4. [In the above instance, if] the woman told the man, "Place [the *kiddushin*] on [this] rock," she is not consecrated. If the rock belonged to her, she is consecrated. If the rock belonged to both of them, [the question is unresolved, and] the status of the *kiddushin* is in doubt.

If he told her, "Be consecrated to me with this loaf of bread," and she told him, "Give it to a poor person," she is not consecrated. [This applies] even if she supports the poor person in question.

[If she told him,] "Give it to a dog," she is not consecrated.[6] If the dog belonged to her, she is consecrated. If [the dog] was chasing after her and she told him, "Give it to this dog," [the question is unresolved, and] the status of the *kiddushin* is in doubt.

5. [The following laws apply when a man] was selling produce, utensils or the like, and a woman came and asked him: "Give me some of these." If he asked her, "If I give them to you, will you be consecrated to me?" and she said, "Yes," she is consecrated when he gives [the items] to her. If, however, she replied to him: "[Just] give them to me," "Heave them over," or another reply that means "Don't fool around with me regarding such matters, just give me [what I asked for]," she is not consecrated although he gave her [what she asked for].

A similar [decision is rendered] if [a man] was drinking wine and [a woman] asked him, "Give me a cup," and he asks her, "If I do, will you be consecrated to me with it?" If she replies, "[Just] let me drink," "Give me," "Serve me drink," or "Dish it out," she is not consecrated. Her words imply: "Just give me a drink, and don't fool around with me regarding such matters."

6. When [a man] consecrates [a woman] in the presence of a single witness, his *kiddushin*] are of no consequence. [This applies] even when both [the man and the woman] acknowledge [that the *kiddushin* were given].[7] Surely this applies when [a man] consecrates [a woman] without any witnesses at all [observing the act].

---

3. The fact that she discarded the *kiddushin* is a clear indication of her rejection of his proposal.
4. Telling the person to give the *kiddushin* to someone else also indicates that she does not desire them, nor the consequences of accepting them (*Tosafot, Kiddushin* 8b).

ג אָמַר לָהּ: הִתְקַדְּשִׁי לִי בְּדִינָר זֶה, נְטָלַתּוּ וּזְרָקַתּוּ לְפָנָיו אוֹ לַיָּם אוֹ לָאוּר אוֹ לְדָבָר הָאָבֵד — אֵינָהּ מְקֻדֶּשֶׁת.

אָמְרָה לוֹ: תְּנֵהוּ לְאַבָּא, אוֹ לְאָבִיךְ, אוֹ לְאִישׁ פְּלוֹנִי, וְנָתַן — אֵינָהּ מְקֻדֶּשֶׁת.

וְאִם אָמְרָה לוֹ: תְּנֵהוּ לוֹ שֶׁיְּקַבְּלֵהוּ לִי, וְנָתַן — הֲרֵי זוֹ מְקֻדֶּשֶׁת.

ד אָמְרָה: הַנִּיחֵהוּ עַל הַסֶּלַע — אֵינָהּ מְקֻדֶּשֶׁת. וְאִם הָיָה סֶלַע שֶׁלָּהּ — מְקֻדֶּשֶׁת. הָיָה סֶלַע שֶׁל שְׁנֵיהֶם — הֲרֵי זוֹ מְקֻדֶּשֶׁת בְּסָפֵק.

אָמַר לָהּ: הִתְקַדְּשִׁי לִי בְּכִכָּר זֶה, אָמְרָה לוֹ: תְּנֵהוּ לֶעָנִי — אֲפִלּוּ הָיָה עָנִי הַסָּמוּךְ עָלֶיהָ, אֵינָהּ מְקֻדֶּשֶׁת.

תְּנֵהוּ לְכֶלֶב — הֲרֵי זוֹ אֵינָהּ מְקֻדֶּשֶׁת. וְאִם הָיָה הַכֶּלֶב שֶׁלָּהּ — מְקֻדֶּשֶׁת.

וְאִם הָיָה רָץ אַחֲרֶיהָ לְנָשְׁכָהּ, וְאָמְרָה לוֹ: תְּנֵהוּ לְכֶלֶב זֶה — הֲרֵי זוֹ סְפֵק מְקֻדֶּשֶׁת.

ה הָיָה מוֹכֵר פֵּרוֹת אוֹ כֵּלִים וְכַיּוֹצֵא בָּהֶן, בָּאָה אִשָּׁה וְאָמְרָה לוֹ: תֵּן לִי מְעַט מֵאֵלּוּ, וְאָמַר לָהּ: אִם אֶתֵּן לָךְ תְּהִי מְקֻדֶּשֶׁת לִי —

אִם אָמְרָה: הֵן, וְנָתַן לָהּ — הֲרֵי זוֹ מְקֻדֶּשֶׁת;

אֲבָל אִם אָמְרָה לוֹ: תֵּן לִי מֵהֶן, אוֹ: הַשְׁלֵךְ לִי, אוֹ: דְּבָרִים שֶׁעִנְיָנָם: לֹא תִשְׂחַק עִמִּי בִּדְבָרִים אֵלּוּ, אֶלָּא תֵּן לִי בִּלְבַד, וְנָתַן — אֵינָהּ מְקֻדֶּשֶׁת.

וְכֵן אִם הָיָה שׁוֹתֶה יַיִן, וְאָמְרָה לוֹ: תֵּן לִי כּוֹס אֶחָד, וְאָמַר לָהּ: אִם אֶתֵּן לָךְ הֲרֵי אַתְּ מְקֻדֶּשֶׁת לִי בּוֹ, וְאָמְרָה: הַשְׁקֵנִי הַשְׁקוֹת, אוֹ: תֵּן, הַשְׁקֵה, הַשְׁלֵךְ — אֵינָהּ מְקֻדֶּשֶׁת; שֶׁאֵין הַדְּבָרִים נִרְאִין אֶלָּא: הַשְׁקֵנִי בִּלְבַד, וְלֹא תִשְׂחַק עִמִּי בְּדָבָר אַחֵר.

ו הַמְקַדֵּשׁ בְּעֵד אֶחָד — אֵין חוֹשְׁשִׁין לְקִדּוּשָׁיו, וְאַף־עַל־פִּי שֶׁשְּׁנֵיהֶם מוֹדִין. קַל וָחֹמֶר לִמְקַדֵּשׁ בְּלֹא עֵדִים.

---

5. I.e., that the recipient should act as her agent.

6. The Ramah (*Even HaEzer* 30:11) quotes the opinion of the *Tur*, who maintains that if at the outset the woman says, "Put money down in this place and I will be consecrated to you," or "Give food to this dog and I will be consecrated to you," the status of the *kiddushin* is doubtful. Since the man spent money because of her wishes, one might presume that this can be compared to the law stated in the previous halachah. Nevertheless, since the *kiddushin* were not given to a person, it is possible that the comparison is not in place, and the *kiddushin* are not definitely binding. (See also Chapter 5, Halachah 21.)

7. The Ramah (*Orach Chayim* 42:2) quotes an opinion that requires stringency in such an instance, but states that leniency should be granted if following the stringent view will cause a woman great difficulty in getting married.

Although the need for witnesses with regard to marriage and divorce is derived from an analogy (*gezerah shavah*) to claims of monetary law, a difference exists between the two. With regard to a financial claim, no witnesses are necessary if both litigants agree regarding a matter.

When [a man] consecrates [a woman] in the presence of individuals who are disqualified from serving as witnesses by Scriptural law, she is not consecrated. [When he consecrates her in the presence of] individuals who are disqualified from serving as witnesses by Rabbinic law,[8] or in the presence of witnesses regarding whom there is doubt whether or not they are acceptable according to Scriptural law, [the following rules apply]: If he desires to consummate the marriage, he should consecrate the woman again in the presence of acceptable witnesses. If he does not desire to consummate the marriage, the woman must receive a *get* from him [to enable her to marry others], because of the doubt.[9] [This ruling applies] even when the woman denies [the matter], contradicting the witnesses and saying that she was never consecrated.

This ruling applies with regard to all situations in which the status of the *kiddushin* is in doubt. If [the man] desires to consummate the marriage, he should consecrate the woman again in a manner that is unequivocally acceptable. If he does not desire to consummate the marriage, the woman must receive a *get* from him, because of the doubt.

7. When a minor consecrates [a woman], his *kiddushin* are of no consequence. When, by contrast, a male past the age of majority consecrates a girl below the age of majority who is an orphan,[10] or who has left her father's authority,[11] [different rules apply]: If she is below the age of six, even if she is one who shows deep understanding of secret matters,[12] and can differentiate and discern, she is not married, and there is no need for *mi'un*.[13]

If she is more than ten years old, even when she is very foolish, since she willingly accepted the *kiddushin*, she is consecrated [according to Rabbinic law] and [must perform] *mi'un* [should she desire to nullify the marriage]. If she is between the ages of six and ten, [the rabbis] must evaluate her ability to discern. If she is able to differentiate and discern with regard to matters of marriage and *kiddushin*, [the marriage is binding according to Rabbinic law] and *mi'un* is necessary. If she lacks [this degree of discernment], she is not consecrated [at all], and need not perform *mi'un* [to nullify the marriage].

As stated in this halachah, this concept does not apply with regard to the laws of marriage and divorce. Two rationales are given for this matter:

a) When the man and woman agree with regard to the establishment of a marriage bond, they are limiting the privileges of others, for they are unable to consecrate the woman. With regard to financial matters, by contrast, the rights of others are not restricted (Rashba).

b) There is a fundamental difference between the function of witnesses in cases involving financial matters and their function with regard to wedding and divorce. With regard to financial matters, the function of witnesses is to clarify the truth (*eidei berur*). With regard to marriage and divorce, by contrast, the witnesses' function is to notarize the

הַמְקַדֵּשׁ בִּפְסוּלֵי עֵדוּת שֶׁל תּוֹרָה — אֵינָהּ מְקֻדֶּשֶׁת;
בִּפְסוּלֵי עֵדוּת שֶׁל דִּבְרֵי סוֹפְרִים, אוֹ בְּעֵדִים שֶׁהֵן סְפֵק פְּסוּלֵי תּוֹרָה: אִם רָצָה לִכְנֹס — חוֹזֵר
וּמְקַדֵּשׁ בִּכְשֵׁרִים, וְאִם לֹא רָצָה לִכְנֹס — צְרִיכָה גֵט מִמֶּנּוּ מִסָּפֵק.
וַאֲפִלּוּ כָּפְרָה הָאִשָּׁה וְהִכְחִישָׁה אֶת הָעֵדִים וְאָמְרָה: לֹא קִדַּשְׁתַּנִי — כּוֹפִין אוֹתָהּ לְקַח גֵּט.
וְכֵן דִּין כָּל קִדּוּשֵׁי סָפֵק: אִם רָצָה לִכְנֹס — חוֹזֵר וּמְקַדֵּשׁ וַדַּאי, וְאִם לֹא רָצָה לִכְנֹס
— צְרִיכָה גֵט מִמֶּנּוּ מִסָּפֵק.

ז קָטָן שֶׁקִּדֵּשׁ — אֵין קִדּוּשָׁיו קִדּוּשִׁין.
אֲבָל גָּדוֹל שֶׁקִּדֵּשׁ אֶת הַקְּטַנָּה הַיְתוֹמָה, אוֹ קְטַנָּה שֶׁיָּצְאָה מֵרְשׁוּת אָבִיהָ: אִם הָיְתָה
פְּחוּתָה מִבַּת שֵׁשׁ, אַף־עַל־פִּי שֶׁהִיא נְבוֹנַת לַחֲשׁ בְּיוֹתֵר וּמַכֶּרֶת וּמֻבְחֶנֶת — אֵין כָּאן
שָׁם קִדּוּשִׁין, וְאֵינָהּ צְרִיכָה לְמָאֵן;
וְאִם הָיְתָה מִבַּת עֶשֶׂר שָׁנִים וּלְמַעְלָה, אַף־עַל־פִּי שֶׁהִיא סְכָלָה בְּיוֹתֵר — הוֹאִיל וְנִתְקַדְּשָׁה
לְדַעְתָּהּ, הֲרֵי זוֹ מְקֻדֶּשֶׁת לְמָאֵן.
הָיְתָה מִבַּת שֵׁשׁ וְעַד סוֹף עֶשֶׂר — בּוֹדְקִין אֶת יְפִי דַעְתָּהּ:
אִם מַכֶּרֶת וּמֻבְחֶנֶת עִסְקֵי הַנִּשּׂוּאִין וְהַקִּדּוּשִׁין — צְרִיכָה לְמָאֵן, וְאִם לָאו — אֵינָהּ מְקֻדֶּשֶׁת
לְמָאֵן, וְאֵינָהּ צְרִיכָה לְמָאֵן.

event (*eidei kiyyum*). For a marriage bond to be established - or broken - even when the husband and wife agree that the event took place, witnesses must observe the proceedings (*Tumim* 90:14, *Tzaphnat Paneach, Kallei HaTorah*).

8. This ruling sheds light on a theme of larger scope: the interrelation between Rabbinic law and Scriptural law. For the fact that a woman needs a *get* to marry another person appears to indicate that according to Scriptural law, the *kiddushin* are effective.

9. Many of the manuscript copies and early printings of the *Mishneh Torah* state that the obligation to give a *get* is of Rabbinic origin. This view would appear to be supported by the Rambam's ruling in Chapter 5, Halachah 1.

10. If she is not an orphan and has never been married, the right to consecrate her belongs to her father, not to her.

11. I.e., she was married, the marriage was consummated, and then she was either divorced or widowed. In this and the above instance, the girl does not have sufficient authority to create a marriage bond that is binding according to Scriptural law. Nevertheless, a bond that is binding according to Rabbinic law may be established, as the halachah continues to explain.

The Ramah (*Even HaEzer* 155:2) quotes opinions that maintain that the above applies only when the girl's marriage was arranged by her brother or her mother. If she arranged the marriage herself, it is not binding, even according to Rabbinic law. The Ra'avad mentions a third opinion, which states that for a girl between the ages of six and ten, the marriage must be arranged by her family to be binding. After the age of ten, it is binding even if she arranged it herself.

12. Our translation is based on the commentary of *Metzudot* on Isaiah 3:3.

13. The annulment of a marriage that a girl below the age of majority initiates, as explained in the following halachah.

8. What is meant by the statement that she is consecrated [according to Rabbinic law], and [must perform] *mi'un* [should she desire to nullify the marriage]? If she was consecrated but no longer desires to remain with her husband, she must perform *mi'un* in the presence of two witnesses. She should say: "I no longer desire him." Afterwards, she leaves [the relationship] without a divorce, as will be explained in *Hilchot Gerushin*.[14]

Why does she leave [the relationship] without a divorce? Because the consecration is not absolutely binding according to Scriptural law; it is merely a Rabbinic institution. [According to Scriptural law, the outcome] is tentative. If she continues living with her husband until she reaches the age of majority, the *kiddushin* are finalized, and she becomes a married woman in the complete sense of the term.[15] There is no need for [her husband] to consecrate her again after she attains majority. If she does not want [to continue] living with him, she must perform *mi'un*; she then leaves [the relationship] without a divorce.

9. When a male deaf mute marries a mentally competent woman, or a female deaf mute marries a mentally competent man, the marriage bond is not absolutely binding according to Scriptural law; it is merely a Rabbinic institution. Therefore, if a mentally competent man consecrates the wife of a deaf mute man who is herself mentally competent, she is considered to be consecrated to the mentally competent man. He must give her a *get*, and she is permitted to remain married to her deaf mute husband.[16]

When, by contrast, a mentally incompetent man consecrates a mentally competent woman, or a mentally competent man consecrates a mentally incompetent woman, the marriage bond is not at all binding - neither according to Scriptural law nor according to Rabbinic law.[17]

10. When a sexually impotent male - whether a *s'ris chamah* or a *s'ris adam* - consecrates [a woman], and similarly, when [a man] consecrates an *aylonit*, the *kiddushin* are absolutely binding.[18]

When a girl is below the age of six, we assume that she does not have sufficient understanding of the nature of marriage to make a commitment that is binding in any way.

14. Chapter 11, Halachah 8.

15. As the Rambam states in *Hilchot Gerushin* 11:6, if the girl reaches majority before she states that she desires to nullify the marriage bond, Rabbinic law requires her to receive a *get* before she marries another person. If she continues living with her husband and they engage in sexual relations after she attains majority, the marriage bond is binding according to Scriptural law.

ח כֵּיצַד מְקֻדֶּשֶׁת לְמֵאוּן?

שֶׁאִם נִתְקַדְּשָׁה וְלֹא רָצְתָה לֵישֵׁב עִם בַּעֲלָהּ, צְרִיכָה לְמָאֵן בִּפְנֵי שְׁנַיִם וְלוֹמַר: אֵינִי רוֹצָה בּוֹ, וְיוֹצְאָה בְּלֹא גֵט, כְּמוֹ שֶׁיִּתְבָּאֵר בְּהִלְכוֹת גֵּרוּשִׁין.

וְזוֹ הִיא הַנִּקְרֵאת מְמָאֶנֶת.

וְלָמָּה יוֹצְאָה בְּלֹא גֵט? מִפְּנֵי שֶׁאֵין קִדּוּשֶׁיהָ קִדּוּשִׁין גְּמוּרִין מִן הַתּוֹרָה, אֶלָּא מִדִּבְרֵי סוֹפְרִים, וְהֵן תְּלוּיִין:

שֶׁאִם יָשְׁבָה עִם בַּעֲלָהּ עַד שֶׁגָּדְלָה — גָּמְרוּ קִדּוּשֶׁיהָ, וְנַעֲשָׂת אֵשֶׁת אִישׁ גְּמוּרָה, וְאֵינוֹ צָרִיךְ לַחֲזֹר וּלְקַדְּשָׁהּ אַחַר שֶׁגָּדְלָה;

וְאִם לֹא רָצְתָה לֵישֵׁב — צְרִיכָה לְמָאֵן, וְתֵצֵא בְּלֹא גֵט.

ט חֵרֵשׁ שֶׁנָּשָׂא פִּקַּחַת, וְכֵן חֵרֶשֶׁת שֶׁנִּשֵּׂאת לְפִקֵּחַ — אֵין קִדּוּשֵׁיהֶן גְּמוּרִין מִן הַתּוֹרָה, אֶלָּא מִדִּבְרֵי סוֹפְרִים.

לְפִיכָךְ, אִם בָּא פִּקֵּחַ וְקִדֵּשׁ אֵשֶׁת חֵרֵשׁ הַפִּקַּחַת — הֲרֵי זוֹ מְקֻדֶּשֶׁת לַשֵּׁנִי קִדּוּשִׁין גְּמוּרִין. וְנוֹתֵן גֵּט, וְהִיא מֻתֶּרֶת לְבַעֲלָהּ הַחֵרֵשׁ.

אֲבָל הַשּׁוֹטָה שֶׁקִּדֵּשׁ פִּקַּחַת, אוֹ פִּקֵּחַ שֶׁקִּדֵּשׁ שׁוֹטָה — אֵין כָּאן קִדּוּשִׁין כְּלָל, לֹא מִדִּבְרֵי תּוֹרָה וְלֹא מִדִּבְרֵי סוֹפְרִים.

י סָרִיס שֶׁקִּדֵּשׁ, בֵּין סָרִיס חַמָּה בֵּין סְרִיס אָדָם, וְכֵן אַיְלוֹנִית שֶׁנִּתְקַדְּשָׁה — הֲרֵי אֵלּוּ קִדּוּשִׁין גְּמוּרִין.

16. The Ra'avad objects to the Rambam's decision, stating that the woman should not be allowed to remain married to her deaf mute husband. The *Maggid Mishneh* justifies the Rambam's decision, explaining that since the marriage of a deaf mute is a Rabbinic institution, our Sages did not impose the same restrictions that would apply had the marriage been effective according to Scriptural law.

Others state that the Rambam's ruling applies only when the mentally competent man merely consecrated the deaf mute's wife. If he consummated the marriage (*nisu'in*), the deaf mute is forbidden to continue living with her after her divorce.

17. Our Sages differentiated between the marriage of a deaf mute and that of a mentally incompetent person as follows: the marriage of a deaf mute may be harmonious and has the possibility of enduring. The marriage of a mentally incompetent person, by contrast, will surely be plagued by friction and will not endure. For a mentally competent will never be comfortable living with a mentally incompetent person. (See Chapter 11, Halachah 6 and *Yevamot* 112b.)

The Ramah (*Even HaEzer* 44:2) states that this is a sensitive matter, for it is difficult to determine when a person is completely incompetent or not.

18. All the terms mentioned in this halachah are explained in Chapter 2. Although *s'ris adam* (a person who has been castrated) is forbidden to marry, if he violates this prohibition, the marriage bond is binding and a *get* is required for severing the relationship. With regard to an *aylonit*, see Chapter 24, Halachot 1-2, and the accompanying notes.

11. When a *tumtum* or an *androgynous* consecrates a woman, or when either of these individuals has been consecrated by a man, there is doubt whether these *kiddushin* are binding, and because of the doubt, a *get* is required.[19]

12. When a person consecrates one of the women forbidden as *arayot*, his act is of no consequence. For *kiddushin* are not binding with regard to these forbidden relationships, with the exception of [*kiddushin* given] a *niddah*. When a man consecrates a *niddah*, the *kiddushin* are binding absolutely. It is, nevertheless, improper to do so.[20]

13. When a married woman accepts *kiddushin* from another man in the presence of her husband, she is considered to be consecrated to the second man. For a woman's word is accepted when she tells her husband to his face that he had divorced her. We assume it axiomatically that a woman would not act so brazenly in her husband's presence [unless it were true].[21]

If, however, the other person consecrates her outside her husband's presence, these *kiddushin* are not considered to be binding unless she brings proof that she was divorced before she was consecrated. As long as she is outside her husband's presence, it is possible that she will act brazenly.

14. When a man consecrates one of the *shniyot* or a woman forbidden because of a negative commandment [not associated with *karet*] or because of a positive commandment, the *kiddushin* are binding absolutely. [The same ruling applies when] a *yavam* consecrates a woman who was married to the same man as his *yevamah*.[22]

There is one exception to the above principle: when a person other than [the *yavam*] consecrates a *yevamah*, [the question is unresolved, and] the status of the *kiddushin* is in doubt. For our Sages were unsure whether the *kiddushin* of a *yevamah* are valid, like those of others in which the relationship is forbidden by merely a negative commandment, or whether the *kiddushin* are of no consequence, as in the case of an incestuous relationship.

In all the situations mentioned above, although the man who gave the *kiddushin* is forbidden to consummate the marriage, he must terminate it by giving a *get*.

15. [When] a man consecrates a gentile woman or a [Canaanite] maidservant, the *kiddushin* are of no consequence; the woman's status is the same after receiving the *kiddushin* as beforehand. Similarly, when a gentile or a [Canaanite] servant consecrates a Jewish woman, the *kiddushin* are of no consequence.

19. The Ramah (*Even HaEzer* 44:5) quotes the *Tur* as stating that an *androgynous* is considered to be a male, and the *kiddushin* that he gives are binding.
20. This ruling is relevant in the present age, for it is frequent that a woman is a

יא טֻמְטוּם וְאַנְדְּרוֹגִינוֹס שֶׁקִּדְּשׁוּ אִשָּׁה, אוֹ שֶׁקִּדְּשָׁן אִישׁ — הֲרֵי אֵלּוּ קִדּוּשֵׁי סָפֵק, וּצְרִיכִין גֵּט מִסָּפֵק.

יב הַמְקַדֵּשׁ אַחַת מִן הָעֲרָיוֹת — לֹא עָשָׂה כְּלוּם, שֶׁאֵין קִדּוּשִׁין תּוֹפְסִין לְעֶרְוָה; חוּץ מִן הַנִּדָּה, שֶׁהַמְקַדֵּשׁ אֶת הַנִּדָּה — הֲרֵי זוֹ מְקֻדֶּשֶׁת קִדּוּשִׁין גְּמוּרִין. וְאֵין רָאוּי לַעֲשׂוֹת כֵּן.

יג אֵשֶׁת אִישׁ שֶׁפָּשְׁטָה יָדָהּ וְקִבְּלָה קִדּוּשִׁין מֵאַחֵר בִּפְנֵי בַּעְלָהּ — הֲרֵי זוֹ מְקֻדֶּשֶׁת לַשֵּׁנִי; שֶׁהָאִשָּׁה שֶׁאָמְרָה לְבַעְלָהּ בְּפָנָיו: גֵּרַשְׁתַּנִי — נֶאֱמֶנֶת. חֲזָקָה אֵין אִשָּׁה מְעִזָּה פָּנֶיהָ בִּפְנֵי בַּעְלָהּ.

אֲבָל אִם קֻדְּשָׁה אַחֵר שֶׁלֹּא בִּפְנֵי בַּעְלָהּ — אֵין קִדּוּשִׁין תּוֹפְסִין בָּהּ, עַד שֶׁתָּבִיא רְאָיָה שֶׁנִּתְגָּרְשָׁה קֹדֶם שֶׁתְּקַבֵּל הַקִּדּוּשִׁין. כֹּל שֶׁלֹּא בְּפָנָיו — מְעִזָּה.

יד הַמְקַדֵּשׁ אַחַת מִן הַשְּׁנִיּוֹת אוֹ מֵאִסּוּרֵי לָאוִין אוֹ מֵאִסּוּרֵי עֲשֵׂה, וְכֵן יָבָם שֶׁקִּדֵּשׁ צָרַת יְבָמָה — הֲרֵי זוֹ מְקֻדֶּשֶׁת קִדּוּשִׁין גְּמוּרִין;

חוּץ מִיבָמָה שֶׁנִּתְקַדְּשָׁה לְזָר, שֶׁהִיא מְקֻדֶּשֶׁת בְּסָפֵק.

נִסְתַּפֵּק לַחֲכָמִים, אִם הַקִּדּוּשִׁין תּוֹפְסִין בִּיבָמָה כִּשְׁאָר חַיָּבֵי לָאוִין, אוֹ אֵין קִדּוּשִׁין תּוֹפְסִין בָּהּ כְּעֶרְוָה.

וְאַף־עַל־פִּי שֶׁאָסוּר לוֹ לִכְנֹס אַחַת מִכָּל אֵלּוּ, הֲרֵי זֶה מְגָרֵשׁ בְּגֵט.

טו הַמְקַדֵּשׁ כּוּתִית אוֹ שִׁפְחָה — אֵינָן קִדּוּשִׁין, אֶלָּא הֲרֵי הִיא אַחַר הַקִּדּוּשִׁין כְּמוֹ שֶׁהָיְתָה קֹדֶם הַקִּדּוּשִׁין.

וְכֵן עַכּוּ"ם וְעֶבֶד שֶׁקִּדְּשׁוּ בַּת יִשְׂרָאֵל — אֵין קִדּוּשֵׁיהֶן קִדּוּשִׁין.

---

niddah at the time of a marriage. A wedding should never be planned to coincide with the woman's *niddah* state. Nevertheless, since weddings are often planned well in advance, and women's menstrual cycles are flexible, it is possible that the calculations will be in error, and the wedding will be scheduled for the time when the woman is a *niddah*. In such a situation, the commonly accepted ruling is to hold the wedding. Nevertheless, restrictions are placed on the couple's being in private until the woman purifies herself. Needless to say, sexual relations are forbidden.

21. The Ra'avad states that the woman's word should be accepted only insofar as to require her to receive a *get* from the second person. She is not allowed to marry him, nor may she collect her *ketubah* from her first husband unless she proves that she has been divorced. The Ramah (*Even HaEzer* 17:2) states that in the present age, since brazen behavior is more common, the presumption upon which the Rambam's ruling rests is no longer a viable support.

22. The situation is as follows: A man who was married to two women died while childless. As required by Deuteronomy, Chapter 5, one of his brothers (the *yavam*) marries one of his widows (the *yevamah*). Afterwards, neither the *yavam* nor any other of the deceased's brothers is allowed to marry the deceased's second wife. (See *Hilchot Yibbum* 1:12.)

When an apostate Jew consecrates [a woman], his *kiddushin* are absolutely valid, despite the fact that he willingly worships a false deity. The woman must receive a *get* from him.[23]

16. When a man consecrates a woman who is half a maidservant and half a free woman,[24] she is not completely consecrated until she becomes [totally] free. Once she becomes free, the *kiddushin* are [automatically] completed, like the *kiddushin* of a minor who comes of age. There is no need for her to be consecrated again.

If another man consecrates such a woman after she was granted her freedom [before the person who consecrated her originally consummates their marriage], there is doubt regarding the matter,[25] and the status of both their *kiddushin* is in doubt.

17. What then is a *shifchah charufah* [a betrothed maidservant] as described by the Torah [Leviticus 19:20]? A woman who is half a maidservant and half a free woman, who was consecrated by a Hebrew servant.

When a male who is half a servant and half a free man consecrates a woman, [the matter is unresolved, and] the status of the *kiddushin* is in doubt.

18. When a drunk gives [a woman] *kiddushin*, they are valid, even if he is very drunk. If he reaches a state of drunkenness comparable to that of Lot,[26] the *kiddushin* are of no consequence. This matter requires ample deliberation.

19. When a man gives money worth less than a *p'rutah* as *kiddushin*, the *kiddushin* are not valid. When a man consecrates a woman with food or with a utensil worth less than a *p'rutah*, the status of the *kiddushin* is in doubt; perhaps the *kiddushin* are worth a *p'rutah* in another place.

From this one can deduce that whenever a person consecrates a woman with an article worth money, if it is worth a *p'rutah* in that country the *kiddushin* are definitely binding. If it is not worth a *p'rutah* [there], the status of the *kiddushin* is in doubt [as above].[27]

It appears to me that if [a man] consecrated [a woman] with cooked food, a vegetable that will not be preserved or the like, and the item is not worth a *p'rutah* in that place, the *kiddushin* are not binding at all. For by the time this item reaches another place, it will spoil and be worthless. This is a reasonable inference; one may rely on it.

20. When [a man] consecrates a woman with less than a *p'rutah's* worth, or he consecrates two women with a *p'rutah*, the women are not consecrated. [This applies] even when he sends wedding presents [worth more than a *p'rutah*]

יִשְׂרָאֵל מוּמָר שֶׁקִּדֵּשׁ, אַף־עַל־פִּי שֶׁהוּא עוֹבֵד עֲבוֹדַת כּוֹכָבִים וּמַזָּלוֹת בִּרְצוֹנוֹ — הֲרֵי אֵלּוּ קִדּוּשִׁין גְּמוּרִים, וּצְרִיכָה גֵּט מִמֶּנּוּ.

טז הַמְקַדֵּשׁ אִשָּׁה שֶׁחֶצְיָהּ שִׁפְחָה וְחֶצְיָהּ בַּת חֹרִין — אֵינָהּ מְקֻדֶּשֶׁת קִדּוּשִׁין גְּמוּרִין עַד שֶׁתִּשְׁתַּחְרֵר, וְכֵיוָן שֶׁנִּשְׁתַּחְרְרָה — גָּמְרוּ קִדּוּשֶׁיהָ, כְּקִדּוּשֵׁי קְטַנָּה שֶׁגָּדְלָה, וְאֵינוֹ צָרִיךְ לְקַדְּשָׁהּ קִדּוּשִׁין אֲחֵרִים.
בָּא אַחֵר וְקִדְּשָׁהּ אַחַר שֶׁנִּשְׁתַּחְרְרָה — הֲרֵי זוֹ סְפֵק קִדּוּשִׁין לִשְׁנֵיהֶם.

יז וְאֵי זוֹ הִיא שִׁפְחָה חֲרוּפָה הָאֲמוּרָה בַּתּוֹרָה? זוֹ מִי שֶׁחֶצְיָהּ שִׁפְחָה וְחֶצְיָהּ בַּת חֹרִין שֶׁקִּדְּשָׁהּ עֶבֶד עִבְרִי.
וּמִי שֶׁחֶצְיוֹ עֶבֶד וְחֶצְיוֹ בֶּן חֹרִין שֶׁקִּדֵּשׁ בַּת חֹרִין — הֲרֵי זוֹ סְפֵק קִדּוּשִׁין.

יח שִׁכּוֹר שֶׁקִּדֵּשׁ — קִדּוּשָׁיו קִדּוּשִׁין, וְאַף־עַל־פִּי שֶׁנִּשְׁתַּכֵּר הַרְבֵּה.
וְאִם הִגִּיעַ לִשְׁכְרוּתוֹ שֶׁל לוֹט — אֵין קִדּוּשָׁיו קִדּוּשִׁין. וּמִתְיַשְּׁבִין בְּדָבָר זֶה.

יט הַמְקַדֵּשׁ בְּפָחוֹת מִפְּרוּטָה — אֵינָהּ מְקֻדֶּשֶׁת.
קִדְּשָׁהּ בָּאֹכֶל אוֹ בִּכְלִי וְכַיּוֹצֵא בּוֹ שֶׁשָּׁוֶה פָחוֹת מִפְּרוּטָה — הֲרֵי זוֹ מְקֻדֶּשֶׁת בְּסָפֵק, וּצְרִיכָה גֵּט מִסָּפֵק; שֶׁמָּא דָבָר זֶה שָׁוֶה פְּרוּטָה בְּמָקוֹם אַחֵר.
הָא לָמַדְתָּ, שֶׁכָּל הַמְקַדֵּשׁ בְּשָׁוֶה כֶסֶף: אִם הָיָה בְּאוֹתָהּ הַמְּדִינָה שָׁוֶה פְרוּטָה — הֲרֵי אֵלּוּ קִדּוּשֵׁי וַדַּאי, וְאִם אֵינוֹ שָׁוֶה פְּרוּטָה — הֲרֵי אֵלּוּ קִדּוּשֵׁי סָפֵק.
יֵרָאֶה לִי, שֶׁאִם קִדֵּשׁ בְּתַבְשִׁיל אוֹ בְּיָרָק שֶׁאֵינוֹ מִתְקַיֵּם וְכַיּוֹצֵא בָהֶם, אִם לֹא הָיוּ שָׁוֶה פְרוּטָה בְּאוֹתוֹ הַמָּקוֹם — אֵינָהּ מְקֻדֶּשֶׁת כְּלָל;
שֶׁהֲרֵי דָבָר זֶה אֵינוֹ מַגִּיעַ לְמָקוֹם אַחֵר עַד שֶׁיִּפָּסֵד וְיֹאבַד, וְלֹא יְהֵא שָׁוֶה פְרוּטָה.
וְדָבָר שֶׁל טַעַם הוּא זֶה, וְרָאוּי לִסְמֹךְ עָלָיו.

כ הַמְקַדֵּשׁ אִשָּׁה בְּפָחוֹת מִפְּרוּטָה, אוֹ שֶׁקִּדֵּשׁ שְׁתֵּי נָשִׁים בִּפְרוּטָה, אַף־עַל־פִּי שֶׁשָּׁלַח סִבְלוֹנוֹת לְאַחַר מִכֵּן — אֵינָהּ מְקֻדֶּשֶׁת.

---

23. Rav David Cohen (Section 9, Responsum 1) states that the intent is that we are obligated to force the apostate to divorce his wife, lest he cause her to violate Torah law.
24. E.g., a Canaanite maidservant who was owned in partnership by two masters. One granted the woman her freedom, but the other did not.
25. Our translation follows the commentary of the *Maggid Mishneh*, who explains that there is a question whether or not the *kiddushin* of the first person are valid. Nevertheless, if the couple marry and consummate their relationship, this establishes their wedding bond.
26. Who was totally unaware of what he was doing (Genesis, Chapter 19).
27. The commentaries (see *Beit Shmuel* 31:6) debate the status of the *kiddushin* when one

afterwards. Similarly, when a minor consecrates a woman, the *kiddushin* are not valid, despite the fact that he sent marriage presents after he had attained majority. [This ruling was delivered because the presents] were sent because of the original *kiddushin*, which were invalid [and therefore are not considered to be significant in their own right].

21. When [a man] consecrates a woman by [giving her] money or a legal document, he does not have to place the *kiddushin* in her hand. Instead, if she consents that he throw them to her and he does so, she is consecrated, whether he throws them into her hand, her bosom, her courtyard or her field.[28]

If she is standing in a domain belonging to her [prospective] husband, he must place them in her hand or in her bosom. If she is standing in a domain that belongs to both of them, and he threw *kiddushin* to her with her consent, but they did not reach her hand or her bosom, the status of the *kiddushin* is in doubt. Even when she tells him, "Put the *kiddushin* down in this place," if the place belongs to both of them the status of the *kiddushin* is in doubt.[29]

22. [The following rules apply when the two] are standing in the public domain or in a domain that does not belong to either of them, and he throws *kiddushin* to her: If they are closer to him, she is not consecrated. If they are closer to her, she is consecrated. If they are halfway between the two of them, or if there is doubt whether they were closer to him or to her,[30] and they were lost before they reached her hand, there is doubt regarding the status of the *kiddushin*.

What is meant by "closer to him," or "closer to her"? A situation in which he can guard [the *kiddushin*] and she cannot is considered as "closer to him." One in which she can guard them and he cannot is considered to be "closer to her."[31] One in which they can both guard them or neither can guard them is considered to be "halfway between the two of them."

CHAPTER FIVE

1. When a man consecrates a woman with an object from which it is forbidden to derive benefit - e.g., a mixture of milk and meat, *chametz* on Pesach, or other similar objects from which it is prohibited to derive

knows for a fact that they are worth a *p'rutah* in another place. Some maintain that they are absolutely binding, and others maintain that their status remains doubtful.
28. The *Tur* (*Even HaEzer* 30) states that the woman's field or courtyard must be protected. It is possible to state that this is the Rambam's opinion as well, and he relies on the statements he makes in *Hilchot Zechiyah UMatanah* 4:9 regarding giving a present (*Kessef Mishneh*). Nevertheless, it is possible to differentiate between the two

וְכֵן קָטָן שֶׁקִּדֵּשׁ, אַף־עַל־פִּי שֶׁשָּׁלַח סִבְלוֹנוֹת לְאַחַר שֶׁהִגְדִּיל — אֵינָהּ מְקֻדֶּשֶׁת. שֶׁמֵּחֲמַת קִדּוּשִׁין הָרִאשׁוֹנִים שְׁלָחָן, שֶׁהָיוּ קִדּוּשִׁין פְּסוּלִין.

כא הַמְקַדֵּשׁ אֶת הָאִשָּׁה בְּכֶסֶף אוֹ בִּשְׁטָר, אֵינוֹ צָרִיךְ שֶׁיִּתֵּן הַקִּדּוּשִׁין לְתוֹךְ יָדָהּ; אֶלָּא כֵּיוָן שֶׁרְצָתָה לִזְרֹק לָהּ קִדּוּשֶׁיהָ, וּזְרָקָן — בֵּין לְתוֹךְ יָדָהּ בֵּין לְתוֹךְ חֵיקָהּ, אוֹ לְתוֹךְ חֲצֵרָהּ אוֹ לְתוֹךְ שָׂדֶה שֶׁלָּהּ — הֲרֵי זוֹ מְקֻדֶּשֶׁת.
הָיְתָה עוֹמֶדֶת בִּרְשׁוּת הַבַּעַל, צָרִיךְ שֶׁיִּתֵּן לְתוֹךְ יָדָהּ אוֹ לְתוֹךְ חֵיקָהּ.
הָיְתָה עוֹמֶדֶת בִּרְשׁוּת שֶׁהִיא שֶׁל שְׁנֵיהֶן, וְזָרַק לָהּ קִדּוּשֶׁיהָ מִדַּעְתָּהּ, וְלֹא הִגִּיעוּ לְיָדָהּ אוֹ לְחֵיקָהּ הֲרֵי זוֹ מְקֻדֶּשֶׁת קִדּוּשֵׁי סָפֵק.
וַאֲפִלּוּ אָמְרָה לוֹ: הַנַּח קִדּוּשִׁין עַל מָקוֹם זֶה, וְאוֹתוֹ הַמָּקוֹם שֶׁל שְׁנֵיהֶם — הֲרֵי אֵלּוּ קִדּוּשֵׁי סָפֵק.

כב הָיוּ עוֹמְדִים בִּרְשׁוּת הָרַבִּים אוֹ בִּרְשׁוּת שֶׁאֵינוֹ שֶׁל שְׁנֵיהֶם, וְזָרַק לָהּ קִדּוּשֶׁיהָ: קָרוֹב לוֹ — אֵינָהּ מְקֻדֶּשֶׁת; קָרוֹב לָהּ — הֲרֵי זוֹ מְקֻדֶּשֶׁת;
מֶחֱצָה עַל מֶחֱצָה, אוֹ שֶׁהָיוּ סָפֵק קָרוֹב לוֹ סָפֵק קָרוֹב לָהּ, וְאָבְדוּ קֹדֶם שֶׁיַּגִּיעוּ לְיָדָהּ — הֲרֵי זוֹ סָפֵק מְקֻדֶּשֶׁת.
כֵּיצַד הוּא קָרוֹב לוֹ וְקָרוֹב לָהּ? כֹּל שֶׁהוּא יָכוֹל לִשְׁמֹר אוֹתָן, וְהִיא אֵינָהּ יְכוֹלָה — זֶה הוּא קָרוֹב לוֹ.
הִיא יְכוֹלָה לִשְׁמֹר אוֹתָן, וְהוּא אֵינוֹ יָכוֹל — זֶהוּ קָרוֹב לָהּ.
שְׁנֵיהֶן יְכוֹלִין לִשְׁמֹר אוֹתָן, אוֹ שְׁנֵיהֶן אֵין יְכוֹלִים לִשְׁמֹר אוֹתָן — זֶה הוּא מֶחֱצָה עַל מֶחֱצָה.

פֶּרֶק חֲמִישִׁי

א הַמְקַדֵּשׁ בְּדָבָר שֶׁהוּא אָסוּר בַּהֲנָאָה, כְּגוֹן חָמֵץ בְּפֶסַח אוֹ בָשָׂר בְּחָלָב וְכַיּוֹצֵא בָּהֶן מִשְּׁאָר אִסּוּרֵי הֲנָאָה — אֵינָהּ מְקֻדֶּשֶׁת.

and explain that the laws governing *kiddushin* are more lenient. The *Beit Shmuel* 30:3 maintains that this is the view of the *Shulchan Aruch* (*Even HaEzer* 30:1). See *Chelkat Mechokeik* 30:2.

29. Although this would not be acceptable with regard to a business transaction (*Hilchot Mechirah*, Chapter 4), an exception is made here, because of the possibility that the man lent the woman rights to his share of the property.

30. See the *Beit Shmuel* 29:9, which interprets this as meaning that two pairs of witnesses observed the throwing of the *kiddushin*, one maintained that the *kiddushin* were able to be guarded by the man, and one that they were able to be guarded by the woman. If, however, there was only one pair of witnesses, and they were unsure whether the woman could guard them, the *kiddushin* are not effective, because it is as if they were given without being observed by witnesses.

31. The *Makneh* states that the Rambam relies on his statements in *Hilchot Gerushin* 5:13,

benefit - she is not consecrated.[1] [This ruling applies] even if the prohibition against deriving benefit from the object is merely Rabbinic in origin[2] - e.g., *chametz* during the sixth hour on the fourteenth of Nisan.

2. If a man transgresses and sells an article from which it is forbidden to derive benefit, and consecrates [a woman] with the money [he receives] for it, the *kiddushin* are valid. [There is one] exception. If a person consecrates a woman with the money [received] for a false deity, the *kiddushin* are not valid. For it is forbidden to derive benefit from the money received for a false deity, just as [it is forbidden to derive benefit from] the false deity itself.[3]

When [a man] consecrates [a woman] with the dung of cows [consecrated to] a false deity, the *kiddushin* are not valid. For it is forbidden to derive benefit from anything produced by entities [consecrated to] a false deity, as [Deuteronomy 13:18] states: "Let nothing that is condemned cling to your hand."

If, by contrast, [a man] consecrates [a woman] with the dung of an ox condemned to be stoned,[4] the *kiddushin* are binding. Although it is forbidden to derive benefit from an ox condemned to be stoned, this prohibition does not apply to its dung. For the dung is considered of negligible importance when compared to the ox.

3. When [a man] consecrates [a woman] with the produce of the Sabbatical year,[5] with the ashes of the Red Heifer, or with water that was drawn for the purpose of sprinkling [the ashes of the Red Heifer],[6] the *kiddushin* are valid.

which state that the woman must be able to bend over and take the object. Others do not make such a stipulation.

1. Since it is forbidden to derive benefit from the article, according to the Torah, it has no value whatsoever. For a woman to be consecrated, she must receive an article worth a *p'rutah*.
2. The *Maggid Mishneh* and the *Tur* (*Even HaEzer* 28) understand the Rambam as saying that all articles that are forbidden to be used by Rabbinic decree cannot establish a bond of *kiddushin*. Rav Yosef Karo (in the *Kessef Mishneh*) differs and explains that the example given by the Rambam specifies the scope of the ruling. Only when a Rabbinic commandment has its source in a prohibition from the Torah are the *kiddushin* of no effect.

From the Rambam's Commentary on the Mishnah (*Pesachim* 2:1), his view is clearly that even if the prohibition is entirely Rabbinic in origin, the *kiddushin* are not binding.

In the *Shulchan Aruch* (*Even HaEzer* 28:21), Rav Yosef Karo follows the opinion of Rabbenu Asher, who states that if the article is forbidden by force of Rabbinic decree, and that prohibition has no source in the Torah, the *kiddushin* are binding. If the prohibition has its source in the Torah, the status of the *kiddushin* is in doubt.

וַאֲפִלּוּ הָיָה אָסוּר בַּהֲנָאָה מִדִּבְרֵיהֶם, כְּגוֹן חָמֵץ בְּשָׁעָה שִׁשִּׁית מִיּוֹם אַרְבָּעָה עָשָׂר — אֵינָהּ
מְקֻדֶּשֶׁת.

ב עָבַר וּמָכַר דָּבָר הָאָסוּר בַּהֲנָאָה וְקִדֵּשׁ בְּדָמָיו — הֲרֵי זוֹ מְקֻדֶּשֶׁת;
חוּץ מֵעֲבוֹדַת כּוֹכָבִים וּמַזָּלוֹת, שֶׁאִם קִדֵּשׁ קַדְשׁ בְּדָמֶיהָ — אֵינָהּ מְקֻדֶּשֶׁת, מִפְּנֵי שֶׁדְּמֵי עֲבוֹדַת
כּוֹכָבִים וּמַזָּלוֹת אֲסוּרִין בַּהֲנָאָה כָּמוֹהָ.
הַמְקַדֵּשׁ בְּפֶרֶשׁ עֶגְלֵי עֲבוֹדַת כּוֹכָבִים וּמַזָּלוֹת — אֵינָהּ מְקֻדֶּשֶׁת; שֶׁהַכֹּל מֵעֲבוֹדַת כּוֹכָבִים
וּמַזָּלוֹת אָסוּר בַּהֲנָאָה, שֶׁנֶּאֱמַר: וְלֹא יִדְבַּק בְּיָדְךָ מְאוּמָה מִן הַחֵרֶם.
אֲבָל הַמְקַדֵּשׁ בְּפֶרֶשׁ שׁוֹר הַנִּסְקָל — הֲרֵי זוֹ מְקֻדֶּשֶׁת.
אַף־עַל־פִּי שֶׁשּׁוֹר הַנִּסְקָל אָסוּר בַּהֲנָאָה — פִּרְשׁוֹ אֵינוֹ אָסוּר בַּהֲנָאָה, שֶׁאֵינוֹ דָּבָר חָשׁוּב לְגַבֵּי
הַשּׁוֹר.

ג הַמְקַדֵּשׁ בְּפֵרוֹת שְׁבִיעִית אוֹ בְּאֵפֶר פָּרָה אֲדֻמָּה אוֹ בְּמַיִם שֶׁמִּלְאָן לַעֲשׂוֹתָן מֵי נִדָּה — הֲרֵי
זוֹ מְקֻדֶּשֶׁת.

(The rationale for this ruling is that since, according to Scriptural law, the article is worth money, and the woman accepts it as *kiddushin*, the criteria for *kiddushin* have been met.)

The *Beit Shmuel* 28:52 justifies the *Maggid Mishneh's* interpretation of the Rambam's view, explaining that since in practice the article is worthless because of the Rabbinic decree, the woman has not been given an article of value, and the *kiddushin* are not binding. In support, he cites another example: The man must own the article he gives as *kiddushin*. If he acquired that article through a *kinyan* (contractual act) that is Rabbinic in origin and is not accepted by Scriptural law, the *kiddushin* are binding.

Kin'at Eliyahu explains that the difference between these two views can be explained using the concepts of *cheftza* (the article) and *gavra* (the person). The Rambam's perspective puts the emphasis on the person, the woman receiving the *kiddushin*. She must receive an object from which she can derive benefit. Hence, since the Rabbis forbade deriving benefit from such an object, the *kiddushin* are not binding.

Rabbenu Asher, by contrast, puts the emphasis on the article given as *kiddushin*. For *kiddushin* to be effective, an article that is worth a *p'rutah* must be given. Since according to Scriptural law the article has intrinsic worth, the fact that our Sages forbade using it is not relevant in this context.

3. See *Hilchot Avodat Kochavim* 7:9.

4. For goring a person. (See Exodus 21:28.)

5. Although the produce of the Sabbatical year is ownerless, once a person takes possession of it, it becomes his private property and has value. Hence, it can be used to consecrate a woman.

6. As the Rambam states in his Commentary on the Mishnah (*Kiddushin* 2:10, based on *Kiddushin* 58a), it is forbidden to receive money for consecrating or sprinkling the water of the ashes of the Red Heifer. One may, however, take payment for drawing the water and transporting it. Thus, the woman can derive this benefit from the water and/or ashes she is given.

[The following rules apply when a man] consecrates [a woman] with property dedicated to the Temple. If he was unaware [that the property had been dedicated], the *kiddushin* are valid. He must give the value [of the dedicated property] and an [additional fifth] to the Temple treasury and bring a guilt offering, as is required of all those who unwittingly make mundane use of property dedicated to the Temple.[7] If he consecrated the woman knowing [that the property was dedicated], she is not consecrated.[8]

4. When [a man] consecrates [a woman] with the produce of the second tithe - whether unknowingly or knowingly - the *kiddushin* are not valid. For unless a person redeems [this produce], it does not belong to him to use for his other purposes, since with regard to [this] tithe, [Leviticus 27:30] states: "It is God's."[9]

5. When a priest consecrates [a woman] with his share of offerings of the most sacred nature or [his share of] offerings of lesser sanctity, she is not consecrated. For one was permitted merely to eat these sacrifices.

When, by contrast, a priest consecrates [a woman] with the great *terumah*, the *terumah* taken from the tithe or with the first fruits, the *kiddushin* are binding. [This same ruling applies] when a Levite consecrates [a woman] with [produce from] the first tithe, or an Israelite consecrates [a woman] with [produce from] the tithe of the poor.[10]

6. The gifts [required to be separated from produce] that have not been separated are considered as if they have already been separated. Therefore, when an Israelite inherited produce from his maternal grandfather who was a priest, and none of the required gifts had been separated from that produce, he may separate the *terumah* and the tithes [and keep the portions to be given to the priests as his own]. It is as if he inherited the *terumah* and the tithes from his maternal grandfather. Therefore, if he consecrates a woman with them, she is consecrated. Although they are not fit for [the Israelite] to eat, he has the right to sell them to someone for whom they are fit.

When, by contrast, an Israelite consecrates [a woman] with *terumah* that he separates from his grain heap, the *kiddushin* are not effective. For he does not have the right to sell this *terumah*; he possesses merely the privilege of giving it to the priest of his choice. This privilege is not considered to be money.

7. [The following rules apply when] a person consecrates a woman [with property that] he robbed, stole or took against its owner's will. If the owner has despaired of the return of the article,[11] and it is known[12] that [the man] acquired it through the owner's despair, the consecration is effective. If not, it is not valid.

7. See *Hilchot Me'ilah* 1:3.

הַמְקַדֵּשׁ בְּהֶקְדֵּשׁ שֶׁל בֶּדֶק הַבַּיִת בְּשׁוֹגֵג — הֲרֵי זוֹ מְקֻדֶּשֶׁת,
וְהוּא יְשַׁלֵּם קֶרֶן וְחֹמֶשׁ לְהֶקְדֵּשׁ, וְיָבִיא אֲשָׁמוֹ, כְּדִין כָּל מוֹעֵל בִּשְׁגָגָה.
וְאִם קִדֵּשׁ בּוֹ אִשָּׁה בְּמֵזִיד — אֵינָהּ מְקֻדֶּשֶׁת.

ד קִדְּשָׁהּ בְּמַעֲשֵׂר שֵׁנִי, בֵּין בְּשׁוֹגֵג בֵּין בְּמֵזִיד — אֵינָהּ מְקֻדֶּשֶׁת;
לְפִי שֶׁאֵין לוֹ לַעֲשׂוֹת בּוֹ שְׁאָר חֲפָצָיו עַד שֶׁיִּתְחַלֵּל, שֶׁנֶּאֱמַר בְּמַעֲשֵׂר: לַיָי הוּא.

ה כֹּהֵן שֶׁקִּדֵּשׁ בְּחֶלְקוֹ מִקָּדְשֵׁי קָדָשִׁים אוֹ מִקָּדָשִׁים קַלִּים — אֵינָהּ מְקֻדֶּשֶׁת, מִפְּנֵי שֶׁלֹּא
הֻתְּרוּ אֶלָּא לַאֲכִילָה בִּלְבַד.
אֲבָל כֹּהֵן שֶׁקִּדֵּשׁ בִּתְרוּמָה גְדוֹלָה וּבִתְרוּמַת מַעֲשֵׂר וּבְבִכּוּרִים, וְכֵן לֵוִי שֶׁקִּדֵּשׁ בְּמַעֲשֵׂר רִאשׁוֹן,
וְיִשְׂרָאֵל שֶׁקִּדֵּשׁ בְּמַעֲשֵׂר עָנִי — הֲרֵי זוֹ מְקֻדֶּשֶׁת.

ו מַתָּנוֹת שֶׁלֹּא הוּרְמוּ, הֲרֵי הֵם כְּמוֹ שֶׁהוּרְמוּ.
לְפִיכָךְ, יִשְׂרָאֵל שֶׁנָּפְלוּ לוֹ טְבָלִים מִבֵּית אֲבִי אִמּוֹ כֹהֵן, וְהִפְרִישׁ מֵהֶן תְּרוּמָה וּמַעְשְׂרוֹת
— הֲרֵי הֵן כְּתרוּמוֹת וּמַעְשְׂרוֹת שֶׁנָּפְלוּ לוֹ בִּירֻשָׁה מֵאֲבִי אִמּוֹ.
וְאִם קִדֵּשׁ בָּהֶן אִשָּׁה — הֲרֵי זוֹ מְקֻדֶּשֶׁת; שֶׁאַף־עַל־פִּי שֶׁאֵינָן רְאוּיִין לוֹ לַאֲכִילָה, יֵשׁ לוֹ
לִמְכָּרְן לְמִי שֶׁהֵן רְאוּיִין לוֹ.
אֲבָל יִשְׂרָאֵל שֶׁקִּדֵּשׁ בִּתְרוּמָה שֶׁהִפְרִישׁ מִגָּרְנוֹ — אֵינָהּ מְקֻדֶּשֶׁת;
שֶׁהֲרֵי אֵין לוֹ לְמָכְרָהּ, וְאֵין לוֹ בָּהּ אֶלָּא טוֹבַת הֲנָאָה, לְפִי שֶׁנּוּתְנָהּ לְכָל כֹּהֵן שֶׁיִּרְצֶה, וְטוֹבַת
הֲנָאָה אֵינָהּ מָמוֹן.

ז הַמְקַדֵּשׁ אֶת הָאִשָּׁה בְּגָזֵל אוֹ בִּגְנֵבָה אוֹ בְּחָמָס: אִם נִתְיָאֲשׁוּ הַבְּעָלִים וְנוֹדַע שֶׁקָּנָה אוֹתוֹ
דָבָר בְּיֵאוּשׁ — הֲרֵי זוֹ מְקֻדֶּשֶׁת, וְאִם לָאו — אֵינָהּ מְקֻדֶּשֶׁת.

8. For dedicated property that was consciously used for a person's private purposes retains its sacred nature and does not enter the possession of the person to whom it was given. (See *Hilchot Me'ilah* 6:3.)

9. We are required to eat the produce of the second tithe in Jerusalem or redeem it and use the money to buy food to be eaten in Jerusalem. Although one derives personal benefit from eating this produce, it is not considered to be one's own property.

10. In all the latter instances, although the person receives the produce in question because of the Torah's decree - and with regard to *terumah*, it still possesses a dimension of ritual sanctity - once he has received it, it is regarded as his personal property entirely, and he may use it as he pleases. Hence, it is fit to be used to consecrate a woman.

11. A thief or robber cannot normally become the legal owner of an article through the owner's despair alone. The article must be given to a third party or undergo a change before it is considered to have left its original owner's property. Nevertheless, in this instance, since the woman receiving can legally acquire the article - for she is a third party - the *kiddushin* are effective (*Maggid Mishneh*).

12. The Rambam's intent is that if the witnesses to the consecration know that the

8. When a person enters a colleague's home and takes an object, food or the like, and consecrates a woman, she is not consecrated. [This ruling applies] even when the owner comes and says, "Why did you not give her a more valuable article than the one you gave her?" He is making this statement only to prevent the person from being shamed [and it does not reflect his true intent]. Since the man consecrated [a woman] with property belonging to a colleague without the colleague's knowledge, this is robbery, and the woman is not consecrated.

If [the man] consecrated [the woman] with an article that the owner would not object [to its being taken] - e.g., a date or a nut - the status of the *kiddushin* is in doubt.13

9. When a person owns merchandise in partnership with a colleague and divides the merchandise without his colleague's knowledge, using it to consecrate [a woman], the *kiddushin* are not valid. [The rationale is that for the division of a partnership's assets to be effective,] an evaluation by the court is necessary. One [partner] may not take what he wants as his own and leave [the remainder for his colleague].

10. [The following rules apply when] a person robbed or stole an article from a woman or took it without her consent, and afterwards consecrated her with the article that he took from her, saying: "Behold, you are consecrated to me with this." If the two were already engaged, and she took the article in silence, she is consecrated.14 If, however, there was never an engagement between them, she is not consecrated, even if she remained silent when he gave her [the stolen articles] as *kiddushin*.15 If, however, she explicitly agreed [to the *kiddushin*], she is consecrated.

11. Similar [concepts apply when a man] entrusts an article to [a woman] for safekeeping and tells her: "Take care of this article," and afterwards tells her: "Behold, you are consecrated with it." If he told her this before she took [possession of] the article, and she took it in silence, she is consecrated. If, however, he made his second statement after she had accepted the article for the purpose of safekeeping, and she remained silent, [the *kiddushin*] are not valid. For whenever [a woman] remains silent after money has

article was stolen, they must know that the owner of the article has despaired of its return. If they do not have such knowledge, they cannot serve as witnesses. Hence, the *kiddushin* are invalid, for it is as if they were performed without being observed by witnesses (*Noda Biy'hudah, Even HaEzer*, Volume II, Responsum 77).
13. The commentaries have questioned this ruling, for it appears to be the Rambam's own addition. The *Noda Biy'hudah* (*Even HaEzer*, Volume I, Responsum 59) states that it would appear that this refers to a situation in which the owner is present and does not object.

ח הַנִּכְנָס לְבֵית חֲבֵרוֹ וְלָקַח לוֹ כְּלִי אוֹ אֹכֶל וְכַיּוֹצֵא בָהֶן וְקִדֵּשׁ בּוֹ אִשָּׁה, וּבָא בַּעַל הַבַּיִת, אַף־עַל־פִּי שֶׁאָמַר לוֹ: לָמָּה לֹא נָתַתָּ לָהּ דָּבָר זֶה, שֶׁהוּא טוֹב מִמַּה שֶּׁנָּתַתָּ לָהּ? — אֵינָהּ מְקֻדֶּשֶׁת;

שֶׁלֹּא אָמַר לוֹ דָּבָר זֶה אֶלָּא כְּדֵי שֶׁלֹּא לְהִתְבַּיֵּשׁ עִמּוֹ,

וְהוֹאִיל וְקִדֵּשׁ בְּמָמוֹן חֲבֵרוֹ שֶׁלֹּא מִדַּעַת חֲבֵרוֹ — הֲרֵי זֶה גָּזֵל וְאֵינָהּ מְקֻדֶּשֶׁת.

וְאִם קִדְּשָׁהּ בְּדָבָר שֶׁאֵין בַּעַל הַבַּיִת מַקְפִּיד עָלָיו, כְּגוֹן תְּמָרָה אוֹ אֱגוֹז — הֲרֵי זוֹ מְקֻדֶּשֶׁת מִסָּפֵק.

ט הָיְתָה סְחוֹרָה בֵּינוֹ וּבֵין חֲבֵרוֹ, וְחִלְּקָהּ שֶׁלֹּא מִדַּעַת חֲבֵרוֹ, וְקִדֵּשׁ בְּחֶלְקוֹ — הוֹאִיל וּצְרִיכָה שׁוּמַת בֵּית דִּין, אֵינָהּ מְקֻדֶּשֶׁת;

שֶׁאֵין זֶה נוֹטֵל לְעַצְמוֹ מַה שֶּׁיִּרְצֶה וְיַנִּיחַ מַה שֶּׁיִּרְצֶה.

י גָּזַל אֶת הָאִשָּׁה אוֹ גָנַב מִמֶּנָּה אוֹ חֲמָסָהּ, וְחָזַר וְקִדְּשָׁהּ בַּגָּזֵל וּבַגְּנֵבָה וּבֶחָמָס שֶׁלָּהּ, וְאָמַר לָהּ: הֲרֵי אַתְּ מְקֻדֶּשֶׁת בּוֹ —

אִם קָדַם בֵּינֵיהֶן שִׁדּוּכִין, וְנָטְלָה וְשָׁתְקָה — הֲרֵי זוֹ מְקֻדֶּשֶׁת;

וְאִם לֹא שִׁדֵּךְ אוֹתָהּ מֵעוֹלָם, אַף־עַל־פִּי שֶׁשָּׁתְקָה כְּשֶׁנָּתַן לָהּ דְּבָרִים אֵלּוּ בְּתוֹרַת קִדּוּשִׁין — אֵינָהּ מְקֻדֶּשֶׁת;

וְאִם אָמְרָה: הֵן — הֲרֵי זוֹ מְקֻדֶּשֶׁת.

יא וְכֵן אִם נָתַן לָהּ פִּקָּדוֹן, וְאָמַר לָהּ: כְּנִסִי פִּקָּדוֹן זֶה, וְחָזַר וְאָמַר לָהּ: הֲרֵי אַתְּ מְקֻדֶּשֶׁת לִי בּוֹ —

אִם אָמַר לָהּ קֹדֶם שֶׁנְּטָלַתּוּ, וּנְטָלַתּוּ וְשָׁתְקָה — הֲרֵי זוֹ מְקֻדֶּשֶׁת;

וְאִם אַחַר שֶׁנְּטָלַתּוּ בְּתוֹרַת פִּקָּדוֹן אָמַר לָהּ: הֲרֵי אַתְּ מְקֻדֶּשֶׁת בּוֹ, וְשָׁתְקָה — אֵין זֶה כְּלוּם,

Nevertheless, since none of the sages of the earlier generations offered this interpretation, he is not willing to do so.

The *Edut BiY'hosef* (Volume II, Responsum 77) states that this ruling depends on those in the previous halachah. Since *kiddushin* are valid after the owner relinquishes his ownership of stolen property by despairing of its return, they are valid in the present instance. Since the owner does not object to the person's taking the object, he is considered to have relinquished his ownership. A similar interpretation is found in the *Chatam Sofer, Even HaEzer*, Responsum 85.

The *Beit Shmuel* 28:45 states that the doubt is that perhaps the owner indeed objects. The *Chatam Sofer* explains that the doubt concerns the object's worth. Although it is not of significant value in the place of the *kiddushin*, maybe it is valuable in another locale, as stated in Chapter 4, Halachah 19.

14. We interpret her silence as implying that she granted him the stolen object as a present and accepted it as *kiddushin* (Rashi, *Kiddushin* 52b). There is a difference of opinion among the Rabbis whether or not he is obligated to return the value of the stolen property to her. The Rashba maintains that he is not required, while Rabbenu Nissim states that he is. (See the Ramah and commentaries, *Even HaEzer* 28:2.)

15. For she merely accepted her own property.

been given, [the *kiddushin*] are not valid. If, however, she explicitly agreed, she is consecrated, even though she made the statement after accepting the article.[16]

12. [The following rules apply when a man] pays a debt that he owed [a woman] and [upon paying it], says: "You are consecrated with it." If the two were engaged, [the man made the statement] before she accepted the money, and she accepted it in silence, she is consecrated. If they were not engaged, she is not consecrated unless she explicitly agrees.

If he states [his desire to consecrate her] after she accepted payment of the debt, she is not consecrated, even if she explicitly agrees. For nothing has been given her; she merely took what was rightfully hers. The debt he owed was repaid when she took the money, and she cannot demand repayment again.

13. When [a man] consecrates [a woman] with a debt, even with [a debt that is recorded] in a promissory note,[17] she is not consecrated.

What is implied? [The woman] owed [the man] a *dinar*; if he tells her, "Behold, you are consecrated to me with the *dinar* that you owe me," she is not consecrated. [The rationale is that] a loan is given to be spent, and there is nothing that presently exists for her to derive benefit from [and to accept as *kiddushin*]. For she has [- or it is as if she has -][18] already spent that *dinar* and has derived benefit from it already.

14. [A different rule applies when] he has given her a loan [and received] collateral for it. If he consecrates her wi h the loan and returns the collateral,[19] she is consecrated. For she derives benefit from the collateral from that time onward, and thus, [as a result of the *kiddushin*,] she has derived benefit.

15. When [a man] consecrates [a woman] with the benefit [derived from] a loan, the consecration is valid.

What is implied? The consecration is binding if he lends her 200 *zuz* [at the time of the *kiddushin*] and tells her: "Behold, you are consecrated to me through the benefit [you receive] by my extending the length of this loan for you. It may be in your possession for so many days, and I will not demand payment until this date." For she is receiving benefit now [from the opportunity] to use the loan until the end of the time period fixed.

16. Since she acknowledged the *kiddushin*, the situation becomes parallel to that mentioned in Halachah 18.

שֶׁבָּל שְׁתִיקָה שֶׁלְּאַחַר מַתַּן מָעוֹת אֵינָה מוֹעֶלֶת;

אֲבָל אִם אָמְרָה 'הֵן' אַחַר שֶׁנָּטְלָה — הֲרֵי זוֹ מְקֻדֶּשֶׁת.

יב הֶחֱזִיר לָהּ חוֹב שֶׁהָיָה לָהּ אֶצְלוֹ, וְאָמַר לָהּ 'הֲרֵי אַתְּ מְקֻדֶּשֶׁת בּוֹ' קֹדֶם שֶׁתִּטְּלֶנּוּ, וּנְטָלַתּוּ וְשָׁתְקָה:

אִם הָיָה בֵּינֵיהֶן שִׁדּוּכִין — הֲרֵי זוֹ מְקֻדֶּשֶׁת, וְאִם לֹא שִׁדֵּךְ — אֵינָהּ מְקֻדֶּשֶׁת, עַד שֶׁתֹּאמַר 'הֵן'.

וְאִם אָמַר לָהּ אַחַר שֶׁנָּטְלָה הַחוֹב שֶׁלָּהּ 'הֲרֵי אַתְּ מְקֻדֶּשֶׁת בּוֹ' — אֲפִלּוּ אָמְרָה 'הֵן', אֵינָהּ מְקֻדֶּשֶׁת;

שֶׁהֲרֵי לֹא הִגִּיעַ לְיָדָהּ מִמֶּנּוּ כְּלוּם, אֶלָּא שֶׁלָּהּ נָטְלָה, וּכְבָר נִפְרַע חוֹבוֹ מִשָּׁעָה שֶׁנָּטְלָה, וְאֵינָהּ יְכוֹלָה לַחֲזֹר וּלְתָבְעוֹ בַּחוֹב פַּעַם אַחֶרֶת.

יג הַמְקַדֵּשׁ בְּמִלְוָה, אֲפִלּוּ הָיְתָה בִּשְׁטָר — אֵינָהּ מְקֻדֶּשֶׁת.

כֵּיצַד? כְּגוֹן שֶׁהָיָה לוֹ אֶצְלָהּ חוֹב דִּינָר, וְאָמַר לָהּ: הֲרֵי אַתְּ מְקֻדֶּשֶׁת לִי בַּדִּינָר שֶׁיֵּשׁ לִי בְּיָדֵךְ — אֵינָהּ מְקֻדֶּשֶׁת;

מִפְּנֵי שֶׁהַמִּלְוָה לְהוֹצָאָה נִתְּנָה, וְאֵין כָּאן דָּבָר קַיָּם לֵהָנוֹת בּוֹ מֵעַתָּה, שֶׁכְּבָר הוֹצִיאָה אוֹתוֹ דִּינָר וְעָבְרָה הֲנָאָתוֹ.

יד הָיָה לוֹ אֶצְלָהּ מִלְוָה עַל הַמַּשְׁכּוֹן, וְקִדְּשָׁהּ בְּאוֹתָהּ הַמִּלְוָה, וְהֶחֱזִיר לָהּ הַמַּשְׁכּוֹן — הֲרֵי זוֹ מְקֻדֶּשֶׁת;

שֶׁהֲרֵי הִיא נֶהֱנֵית בַּמַּשְׁכּוֹן מֵעַתָּה, וַהֲרֵי הִגִּיעַ הֲנָאָה לְיָדָהּ.

טו הַמְקַדֵּשׁ בַּהֲנָאַת מִלְוָה — הֲרֵי זוֹ מְקֻדֶּשֶׁת.

כֵּיצַד? כְּגוֹן שֶׁהִלְוָה אוֹתָהּ עַתָּה מָאתַיִם זוּז, וְאָמַר לָהּ: הֲרֵי אַתְּ מְקֻדֶּשֶׁת לִי בַּהֲנָאַת זְמַן שֶׁאַרְוִיחַ לָךְ בְּמִלְוָה זוֹ, שֶׁתִּהְיֶה בְּיָדֵךְ כָּךְ וְכָךְ יוֹם, וְאֵינִי תּוֹבְעָה מִמֵּךְ עַד זְמַן פְּלוֹנִי — הֲרֵי זוֹ מְקֻדֶּשֶׁת;

שֶׁהֲרֵי יֵשׁ לָהּ הֲנָאָה מֵעַתָּה לְהִשְׁתַּמֵּשׁ בְּמִלְוָה זוֹ עַד סוֹף זְמַן שֶׁקָּבַע.

---

17. The Ramah (*Even HaEzer* 28:7) notes that if the promissory note is worth a *p'rutah* and he returns it, there are opinions that maintain that the consecration is binding.

18. I.e., even if she has not actually spent the money, from the time she received the loan, the money is hers and not the lender's, and he cannot consecrate her with it (*Beit Yosef, Even HaEzer* 28). See also *Beit Shmuel* 28:19.

19. *Tosafot, Kiddushin* 19a, states that the *kiddushin* are effective even if the collateral is not returned. Although the *Shulchan Aruch* (*Even HaEzer* 28:11) appears to favor the Rambam's view, it also quotes the other opinion.

It is forbidden to make [such a condition], because it is like taking interest.[20] My teachers interpreted the expression "the benefit [derived from] a loan," in a way that is not worthy of mention.[21]

16. If [the man] tells [the woman]: "Behold, you are consecrated to me with this *p'rutah* and with the debt that you owe me," she is consecrated. Similarly, if he tells her, "[Behold, you are consecrated...] with the debt that you owe me and with this *p'rutah*, the consecration is binding.[22]

17. When [a man] is owed a debt by a third party, and he tells [a woman] in the presence of the third party: "Behold, you are consecrated to me by virtue of the debt that I am owed by this person," the consecration is binding.[23]

18. [The following rule applies when a man] consecrates [a woman] with an object that he has entrusted to her for safekeeping or with an article that he has lent her: If the entrusted object or borrowed article is worth a *p'rutah*[24] and it exists within her property, she is consecrated.[25]

19. [The following rule applies when a man] tells [a woman]: "Behold, you are consecrated to me in consideration of my speaking to the ruling authorities on your behalf." Although [the man] indeed spoke to the ruling authorities on her behalf - [and his words had an effect,] causing them to refrain from prosecuting her, she is not consecrated unless he gives her a *p'rutah* of his own.

[The rationale is that] the benefit that she received from his speaking [on her behalf] is regarded as a loan,[26] and when one consecrates [a woman] with a loan, the *kiddushin* are not binding.

20. Since in addition to the eventual repayment of the debt, the person also receives the benefit of consecrating the woman, it is regarded like interest. The Rabbis (Meiri, *Ma'aseh Rokeach*) explain that the Rambam's wording is precise. The expression "like interest" implies that it is not actually considered to be taking interest, as forbidden by Scriptural law.

21. The Rambam is referring to Rabbenu Yitzchak Alfasi, who interprets the passage from *Kiddushin* 6b as referring to a person who extends the length of a loan at the time that payment is due. The Rambam does not accept that interpretation, because it is not logical that extending the length of the loan would be more effective than forfeiting the debt entirely (*Maggid Mishneh*).

Rabbenu Yitzchak Alfasi's view is also followed by Rashi and the Ra'avad. The *Shulchan Aruch* (*Even HaEzer* 28:9) quotes the Rambam's interpretation (for even the opinions that differ agree that such *kiddushin* are binding). In the law that follows, it also quotes the opinion of Rabbenu Yitzchak Alfasi. Although the opinion of the Rambam is mentioned, the other view is favored. The Ramah, however, considers the status of the *kiddushin* to be doubtful because of the Rambam's view.

וְאָסוּר לַעֲשׂוֹת כֵּן, מִפְּנֵי שֶׁהִיא כְּרִבִּית.

וּפֵרְשׁוּ רַבּוֹתַי בַּהֲנָאַת מִלְוָה דְּבָרִים שֶׁאֵין רְאוּי לְשָׁמְעָן.

טז אָמַר לָהּ: הֲרֵי אַתְּ מְקֻדֶּשֶׁת לִי בִּפְרוּטָה זוֹ וּבַחוֹב שֶׁיֵּשׁ לִי אֶצְלֵךְ — הֲרֵי זוֹ מְקֻדֶּשֶׁת.

וְכֵן אִם אָמַר לָהּ: בַּמִּלְוָה שֶׁיֵּשׁ לִי אֶצְלֵךְ וּבִפְרוּטָה זוֹ — הֲרֵי זוֹ מְקֻדֶּשֶׁת.

יז הָיָה לוֹ חוֹב בְּיַד אֲחֵרִים, וְאָמַר לָהּ 'הֲרֵי אַתְּ מְקֻדֶּשֶׁת לִי בַּחוֹב שֶׁיֵּשׁ לִי בְּיַד זֶה' בְּמַעֲמַד שְׁלָשְׁתָּן — הֲרֵי זוֹ מְקֻדֶּשֶׁת.

יח קִדְּשָׁהּ בְּפִקָּדוֹן שֶׁיֵּשׁ לוֹ בְּיָדָהּ אוֹ בִּשְׁאֵלָה שֶׁהִשְׁאִילָהּ,

אִם הָיָה הַפִּקָּדוֹן וְהַשְּׁאֵלָה פְּרוּטָה אוֹ שָׁוֶה פְרוּטָה בְּאֶחָד מֵהֶן קַיָּם בִּרְשׁוּתָהּ — הֲרֵי זוֹ מְקֻדֶּשֶׁת.

יט אָמַר לָהּ: הֲרֵי אַתְּ מְקֻדֶּשֶׁת לִי בִּשְׂכַר שֶׁאֲדַבֵּר עָלַיִךְ לַשִּׁלְטוֹן, וְדִבֵּר עָלֶיהָ לַשִּׁלְטוֹן, וְהִנִּיחַ הַשִּׁלְטוֹן וְלֹא תְּבָעָהּ — אֵינָהּ מְקֻדֶּשֶׁת, אֶלָּא אִם נָתַן לָהּ פְּרוּטָה מִשֶּׁלּוֹ;

שֶׁהֲהֲנָאָה שֶׁבָּאָה לָהּ מִדְּבָרָיו הֲרֵי הִיא כְּמִלְוָה, וְהַמְקַדֵּשׁ בְּמִלְוָה — אֵינָהּ מְקֻדֶּשֶׁת.

22. Although the man mentions the debt, since he also gives her a *p'rutah*, we assume that she considers the money that she actually receives together with the loan. Therefore, the *kiddushin* are binding (*Kiddushin* 46a).

23. As stated in *Hilchot Mechirah* 6:8, when such a statement is made in the presence of all the concerned parties, our Sages accepted it as a formal means of transferring the debt. This law shows that even when money is transferred through means ordained by Rabbinic and not Scriptural law, the *kiddushin* are binding according to Scriptural law.

There are opinions that maintain that the woman is not consecrated. These opinions maintain that even after such a transfer has been made, the original creditor can nullify a debt that has been transferred through such a process. Since there is a possibility that the debt will be nullified, they maintain that the woman will not make the commitment required by *kiddushin*. (See Rabbenu Nissim and the *Shulchan Aruch, Even HaEzer* 28:13 and commentaries.)

24. Our translation is based on the Yemenite manuscripts and early printings of the *Mishneh Torah*. The wording of the standard printed text is somewhat confusing. It could be rendered: "If a *p'rutah's* worth of the article remains..." - i.e., even if the article is lost or stolen, if a *p'rutah's* worth remains - the consecration is binding. See the *Shulchan Aruch* (*Even HaEzer* 28:6) and commentaries.

25. If, however, the entrusted object or borrowed article has been lost, stolen or destroyed, even if the woman is obligated to reimburse the man for its value, that obligation is considered similar to other debts, and the woman cannot be consecrated through it.

Although the entrusted object or borrowed article was located in the woman's property at the time of the *kiddushin*, since she was not the legal owner, she is considered to have received sufficient benefit to make the *kiddushin* effective.

26. Speaking on her behalf is considered equivalent to working for her. Hence, an equation is established between this law and the following halachah.

20. [The following rule applies when a man] tells [a woman]: "Behold, you are consecrated to me [in return] for the work that I will perform on your behalf." Although [the man] indeed performs [the work he promised], she is not consecrated unless he gives her a *p'rutah* of his own.

[The rationale is that] a worker earns his wages [continuously] from [the time he] begins [working] until the end. As he performs a portion of the work, he earns an [equivalent] portion of his wages. Thus, [in the above situation, the man's] wages are considered to be a debt that she [owes him].[27] And when one consecrates [a woman] with a loan, the *kiddushin* are not binding.

21. [The following rule applies when a woman] tells [a man]: "Give so and so a present, and I will be consecrated to you." If he tells her, "Behold, you are consecrated to me for the sake of the present I gave upon your request," the *kiddushin* are binding.[28] Although she [personally] did not receive anything, she derived benefit from the fact that her will was carried out, and the other derived benefit because of her.

Similarly, if she told him, "Give a *dinar* to so and so as a present, and I will be consecrated to him," the *kiddushin* are binding[29] provided the person who receives the present tells [the woman]: "Behold, you are consecrated to me by virtue of the pleasure [you derived] from the present that I received at your request."

22. [To cite a similar instance: A man] tells [a woman]: "Take this *dinar* as a present and become consecrated to so and so"; the *kiddushin* are binding provided that the other person tells her: "Behold, you are consecrated to me by virtue of the benefit you received on my behalf," despite the fact that he himself did not give her anything.[30]

[The following rule applies when a woman] tells [a man]: "Take this *dinar* as a present and I will become consecrated to you"; he receives the present and tells her "Behold, you are consecrated to me by virtue of the pleasure [you received] in my accepting a present from you." If he is an important person, she is consecrated.[31] For she derives satisfaction from the fact that he has benefited from her, and for the sake of this satisfaction, she consecrates herself to him.

23. When [a man] tells a woman: "Become consecrated to me with a *dinar*. [Take this article] as security until I give you the *dinar*," she is not consecrated

---

27. I.e., it is not as if the man's entire wage becomes due at the time he completes his work. Instead, for each moment of work, he earns a corresponding amount of his wages. This money is considered as a loan which is not due until the end of his employment. Thus he is in fact consecrating the women with a loan.
28. *Kiddushin* 7a compares this situation to that of a guarantor who becomes liable to pay a loan if the borrower cannot. In both instances, the benefit received by another person

כ הֲרֵי אַתְּ מְקֻדֶּשֶׁת לִי בִּמְלָאכָה זוֹ שֶׁאֶעֱשֶׂה עִמָּךְ, וְעָשָׂה — אֵינָהּ מְקֻדֶּשֶׁת, אֶלָּא אִם כֵּן נָתַן לָהּ פְּרוּטָה מִשֶּׁלּוֹ;

לְפִי שֶׁהַשָּׂכִירוּת יִזְכֶּה בָּהּ הַפּוֹעֵל מִתְּחִלָּה וְעַד סוֹף, כָּל זְמַן שֶׁיַּעֲשֶׂה מִקְצָת מִן הַמְּלָאכָה זוֹכֶה בְּמִקְצָת מִן הַשָּׂכָר,

וְנִמְצָא הַשָּׂכָר כֻּלּוֹ מִלְוָה אֶצְלָהּ, וְהַמְקַדֵּשׁ בְּמִלְוָה — אֵינָהּ מְקֻדֶּשֶׁת.

כא הָאִשָּׁה שֶׁאָמְרָה: תֵּן דִּינָר לִפְלוֹנִי מַתָּנָה וְאֶתְקַדֵּשׁ אֲנִי לָךְ, וְנָתַן, וְאָמַר לָהּ: הֲרֵי אַתְּ מְקֻדֶּשֶׁת לִי בַּהֲנָאַת מַתָּנָה זוֹ שֶׁנָּתַתִּי עַל פִּיךְ — הֲרֵי זוֹ מְקֻדֶּשֶׁת.

אַף־עַל־פִּי שֶׁלֹּא הִגִּיעַ לָהּ כְּלוּם — הֲרֵי נֶהֱנַת בְּרָצוֹנָהּ שֶׁנַּעֲשָׂה, וְנֶהֱנֶה פְּלוֹנִי בִּגְלָלָהּ.

וְכֵן אִם אָמְרָה לוֹ: תֵּן דִּינָר לִפְלוֹנִי מַתָּנָה וְאֶתְקַדֵּשׁ לוֹ, וְנָתַן לוֹ, וְקִדְּשָׁהּ אוֹתוֹ פְּלוֹנִי וְאָמַר לָהּ: הֲרֵי אַתְּ מְקֻדֶּשֶׁת לִי בַּהֲנָאַת מַתָּנָה זוֹ שֶׁקִּבַּלְתִּי בִּרְצוֹנֵךְ — הֲרֵי זוֹ מְקֻדֶּשֶׁת.

כב אָמַר לָהּ: הֵילָךְ דִּינָר זֶה בְּמַתָּנָה וְהִתְקַדְּשִׁי לִפְלוֹנִי, וְקִדְּשָׁהּ אוֹתוֹ פְּלוֹנִי וְאָמַר לָהּ: הֲרֵי אַתְּ מְקֻדֶּשֶׁת לִי בַּהֲנָאָה זוֹ הַבָּאָה לִיךְ בִּגְלָלִי — הֲרֵי זוֹ מְקֻדֶּשֶׁת, אַף־עַל־פִּי שֶׁלֹּא נָתַן לָהּ הַמְקַדֵּשׁ כְּלוּם.

אָמְרָה לוֹ: הֵילָךְ דִּינָר זֶה מַתָּנָה וְאֶתְקַדֵּשׁ לָךְ, וּלְקָחוֹ, וְאָמַר לָהּ: הֲרֵי אַתְּ מְקֻדֶּשֶׁת לִי בַּהֲנָאָה זוֹ שֶׁקִּבַּלְתִּי מִמֵּךְ מַתָּנָה — אִם אָדָם חָשׁוּב הוּא, הֲרֵי זוֹ מְקֻדֶּשֶׁת;

שֶׁהֲנָאָה יֵשׁ לָהּ בִּהְיוֹתוֹ נֶהֱנֶה מִמֶּנָּה, וּבַהֲנָאָה זוֹ הִקְנַת עַצְמָהּ לוֹ.

כג הָאוֹמֵר לְאִשָּׁה: הִתְקַדְּשִׁי לִי בְּדִינָר, וַהֲרֵי זֶה הַמַּשְׁכּוֹן בְּיָדֵךְ עַד שֶׁאֶתֵּן הַדִּינָר — אֵינָהּ

causes the person who made the commitment (the guarantor or the woman) to incur an obligation.

The *Maggid Mishneh* (4:4) and others compare this law to Chapter 4, Halachah 4, but explain that there is a difference between the two cases. In Chapter 4, the man does not respond to the woman's suggestion, while in this halachah, he makes a clear statement acknowledging the woman's offer of *kiddushin*. The Ramah (*Even HaEzer* 29:2) puts the emphasis on the fact that in this halachah, the woman initially made this suggestion, even before the man proposed the *kiddushin*. In the previous law, by contrast, her statement was made in response to his proposal, and her facetious intent becomes clear.

29. *Kiddushin* 7a derives this law by making a twofold comparison: to a guarantor (as in the law explained in the first portion of the halachah) and to a Canaanite servant. To explain: The servant becomes free when other people give his master money for that purpose, even though he himself gives nothing at all. Similarly, the person receiving the present acquires the woman as a wife even though he did not give anything for that purpose himself. Although there is a difference between the two - because the servant's owner receives money for the sake of freeing him and the woman does not receive any money herself - the comparison to a guarantor resolves that difficulty, as explained above.

30. *Kiddushin, ibid.*, derives this law from a comparison to a Canaanite servant, as explained above.

31. The *Shulchan Aruch* (*Even HaEzer* 27:9) states that clarification is necessary to

to him. For she did not receive the *dinar*, and the security was not given to her for it to be her own.[32]

If the man has in his possession security that he was given for a debt that a third party owes him, and he gives a woman the security as *kiddushin*, the consecration is binding although [the security] does not belong to him. For a creditor has certain rights with regard to the ownership of security.[33]

24. When [a man] tells a woman: "Behold, you are consecrated to me with this *dinar* on condition that you return it to me," she is not consecrated, regardless of whether or not she returns it. For if she does not return it, his condition will not be met. And if she returns it, she will not have derived any benefit, for she will not have received anything.[34]

25. [These rulings were issued with regard to the following instances:] [A man] gave [a woman] a wreath of myrtle or the like and told her: "Behold, you are consecrated to me with this." She accepted it, but [protested], saying: "But it is not worth a *p'rutah*." He responded, "Become consecrated with the four *zuz* that are hidden in the wreath."

If she said yes, she is consecrated. If she remained silent, she is not consecrated with this money, for remaining silent after money has been given is of no consequence.[35] There is nonetheless a doubt: perhaps the *kiddushin* are valid, lest the wreath be worth a *p'rutah* in another place.[36]

26. [The following rules apply when a man] tells a woman: "Become consecrated to me with this date. Become consecrated to me with this one. Become consecrated to me with this one." If one of them is worth a *p'rutah*, she is consecrated. If not, the *kiddushin* are merely of doubtful status,[37] [their viability stemming only from] the possibility that one of the dates would be considered to be worth a *p'rutah* in another place.

determine what is meant by "an important person." Because of the doubt involved, it is proper to require a divorce if the woman desires to become consecrated to another man (*Chelkat Mechokek* 27:21).

32. Thus, it is as if she has received nothing. Therefore, she is not consecrated.

33. The Ramah (*Even HaEzer* 28:12) quotes the *Tur* as stating that this law applies only when the security was taken at the time the loan was given. Otherwise, the *kiddushin* are not binding.

34. From the Rambam's wording, it appears that there is no reason to say that the woman has been consecrated. Rabbenu Asher and others maintain that according to Scriptural law, the consecration is valid, for a present of this nature is considered to be a valid transaction. It is merely that the Rabbis nullified these *kiddushin* lest they resemble *chalifin* (barter).

The difference between these two approaches is that the Rambam puts the emphasis on the benefit the woman receives (or does not receive). Hence in this situation, since

מְקֻדֶּשֶׁת לוֹ;

לְפִי שֶׁלֹּא הִגִּיעַ הַדִּינָר לְיָדָהּ, וְלֹא הַמַּשְׁכּוֹן נָתַן לִהְיוֹתוֹ שֶׁלָּהּ.

הָיָה בְּיָדוֹ מַשְׁכּוֹן עַל חוֹב שֶׁיֵּשׁ לוֹ אֵצֶל אֲחֵרִים, וְקִדֵּשׁ בּוֹ אִשָּׁה — אַף־עַל־פִּי שֶׁאֵינוֹ שֶׁלּוֹ, הֲרֵי זוֹ מְקֻדֶּשֶׁת;

לְפִי שֶׁבַּעַל חוֹב יֵשׁ לוֹ מִקְצָת קִנְיָן בְּגוּפוֹ שֶׁל מַשְׁכּוֹן.

כד הָאוֹמֵר לְאִשָּׁה: הֲרֵי אַתְּ מְקֻדֶּשֶׁת לִי בְּדִינָר זֶה עַל מְנָת שֶׁתַּחֲזִירֵיהוּ לִי — אֵינָהּ מְקֻדֶּשֶׁת, בֵּין הֶחֱזִירָה בֵּין לֹא הֶחֱזִירָה;

שֶׁאִם לֹא הֶחֱזִירַתּוּ — לֹא נִתְקַיֵּם הַתְּנַאי,

וְאִם הֶחֱזִירַתּוּ — הֲרֵי לֹא נֶהֱנַת וְלֹא הִגִּיעַ לְיָדָהּ כְּלוּם.

כה נָתַן לָהּ אֲגֻדָּה שֶׁל הֲדַס וְכַיּוֹצֵא בָהּ וְאָמַר לָהּ: הֲרֵי אַתְּ מְקֻדֶּשֶׁת לִי בָּזוֹ, וְקִבְּלָה אוֹתוֹ, אָמְרוּ לוֹ: וַהֲלֹא אֵין בָּהּ שָׁוֶה פְרוּטָה, וְאָמַר: תִּתְקַדֵּשׁ בְּאַרְבָּעָה זוּזִים הַמֻּחְבָּאִים בְּתוֹךְ הָאֲגֻדָּה —

אִם אָמְרָה 'הֵן' — הֲרֵי זוֹ מְקֻדֶּשֶׁת, וְאִם שָׁתְקָה — אֵינָהּ מְקֻדֶּשֶׁת בְּמָעוֹת אֵלּוּ, שֶׁהַשְּׁתִיקָה שֶׁלְּאַחַר מַתַּן מָעוֹת אֵינָהּ מוֹעֶלֶת כְּלוּם;

וְתִהְיֶה מְקֻדֶּשֶׁת בְּסָפֵק מִפְּנֵי הָאֲגֻדָּה, שֶׁמָּא שָׁוֶה פְרוּטָה בְּמָקוֹם אַחֵר.

כו הָאוֹמֵר לְאִשָּׁה: הִתְקַדְּשִׁי לִי בִּתְמָרָה זוֹ, הִתְקַדְּשִׁי לִי בָּזוֹ, הִתְקַדְּשִׁי לִי בָּזוֹ —

אִם יֵשׁ בְּאַחַת מֵהֶן שָׁוֶה פְרוּטָה — הֲרֵי זוֹ מְקֻדֶּשֶׁת, וְאִם לָאו — אֵינָהּ מְקֻדֶּשֶׁת אֶלָּא מִסָּפֵק, שֶׁמָּא תִשְׁוֶה תְּמָרָה אַחַת פְּרוּטָה בְּמָקוֹם אַחֵר.

---

the woman did not receive any benefit, the *kiddushin* are not binding. Rabbenu Asher, by contrast, puts the emphasis on whether or not the man performed a valid act of transfer. Since he did, the *kiddushin* would be binding, were it not for our Sages' decree (*Or Sameach*).

35. I.e., at the time the money was given, she was not aware of it, and afterwards to be consecrated she must explicitly express her consent. Rabbenu Yitzchak Alfasi differs and maintains that in such an instance there is a doubt whether or not the *kiddushin* are binding, and the more stringent ruling must be followed in every instance. His view is accepted by the *Shulchan Aruch* (*Even HaEzer* 28:5).

36. As stated in Chapter 4, Halachah 19 above.

37. In the *Kessef Mishneh*, Rav Yosef Karo raises a question on this ruling, noting that *Kiddushin* 46a interprets this law as following the reasoning of Rabbi Shimon. In similar instances (see *Hilchot Sh'vuot* 7:10 and *Hilchot Nedarim* 4:11), the Rambam rejects Rabbi Shimon's reasoning.

In his gloss on *Hilchot Nedarim*, the *Kessef Mishneh* resolves that issue, explaining that we find that there is a *mishnah* in the tractate of *Kiddushin* (stated without mentioning the name of the author) that follows Rabbi Shimon's view, and a *mishnah* in the tractate of *Nedarim* that follows the opposing view. One of the principles of Talmudic law

27. [Different rules apply if] he told her: "Become consecrated to me with this one, with this one and with this one." If together, they are all worth a *p'rutah*, she is consecrated. If not, the status of the *kiddushin* is doubtful.

[Different rules apply if] she eats [the dates] one after another as he gives them to her: If the last date is worth a *p'rutah*, she is consecrated. If not, the status of the *kiddushin* is doubtful. For the dates that she ate are considered to be a loan, and when [a man] consecrates [a woman] with a loan, the *kiddushin* are not valid. Thus, the status of the *kiddushin* [depends] solely on [the worth of] the final date.

28. If he tells her: "Behold, you are consecrated with these," the *kiddushin* are binding if all the dates together are worth a *p'rutah*. [This applies] even when she eats [the dates] one after another as he gives them to her. She is consecrated, for she is eating her own property.

29. [The following rules apply when a man] tells a woman: "Behold, you are consecrated to me with this cup." If it is filled with water, the consecration [depends on the combined value of] the cup itself and its contents. If it is filled with wine, the consecration [depends on the value of] the cup itself, but not its contents. If it is filled with oil, the consecration [depends on the value of] the contents, but not of the cup itself.[38]

Therefore, if the oil was not worth a *p'rutah*, the status of the *kiddushin* is doubtful. If the oil is worth a *p'rutah*, she is definitely consecrated; no attention is paid to [the value of] the cup.

CHAPTER SIX

1. [The following rules apply when a man] consecrates [a woman] based on a conditional agreement: If the condition is met, the *kiddushin* are binding. If not, they are of no consequence. This applies regardless of whether the condition was stipulated by the man or by the woman.

Every [valid] conditional agreement whatsoever - whether with regard to *kiddushin*, divorce, commercial transactions or other questions of business law - must conform to the following four rules.[1]

2. These are the four rules governing all conditional agreements:[2]
a) the stipulation must be twofold [with both a positive and negative statement];

is that a *mishnah* is taught without mentioning its author to show that it is accepted by the majority of the Sages. Accordingly, one may presume that since the Rambam saw that the redactor of the *Mishnah* chose to follow Rabbi Shimon's reasoning in one instance and to differ with it in another, the Rambam followed suit.

כז אָמַר לָהּ: הִתְקַדְּשִׁי לִי בָּזוֹ וּבְזוֹ וּבְזוֹ —

אִם יֵשׁ בְּכֻלָּם שָׁוֶה פְּרוּטָה — מְקֻדֶּשֶׁת, וְאִם לָאו — אֵינָהּ מְקֻדֶּשֶׁת אֶלָּא מִסָּפֵק.

הָיְתָה אוֹכֶלֶת רִאשׁוֹנָה רִאשׁוֹנָה: אִם יֵשׁ בָּאַחֲרוֹנָה שָׁוֶה פְּרוּטָה — מְקֻדֶּשֶׁת, וְאִם לָאו — אֵינָהּ מְקֻדֶּשֶׁת אֶלָּא מִסָּפֵק;

שֶׁאוֹתָן תְּמָרִים שֶׁאָכְלָה הֲרֵי הֵן כְּמִלְוָה, וְהַמְקַדֵּשׁ בְּמִלְוָה — אֵינָהּ מְקֻדֶּשֶׁת, וְנִמְצָא שֶׁאֵין הַקִּדּוּשִׁין אֶלָּא בַּתְּמָרָה אַחֲרוֹנָה.

כח אָמַר לָהּ: הֲרֵי אַתְּ מְקֻדֶּשֶׁת לִי בְּאֵלּוּ, אִם יֵשׁ בְּכֻלָּן שָׁוֶה פְּרוּטָה — מְקֻדֶּשֶׁת;

אַף־עַל־פִּי שֶׁהִיא אוֹכֶלֶת רִאשׁוֹנָה רִאשׁוֹנָה — שֶׁלָּהּ הִיא אוֹכֶלֶת, וּמְקֻדֶּשֶׁת.

כט הָאוֹמֵר לְאִשָּׁה: הֲרֵי אַתְּ מְקֻדֶּשֶׁת לִי בְּכוֹס זֶה —

אִם הָיָה מָלֵא מַיִם — הֲרֵי זוֹ מְקֻדֶּשֶׁת בּוֹ וּבְמַה שֶּׁבְּתוֹכוֹ,

וְאִם הָיָה מָלֵא יַיִן — הֲרֵי זוֹ מְקֻדֶּשֶׁת בּוֹ וְלֹא בְּמַה שֶּׁבְּתוֹכוֹ,

וְאִם הָיָה מָלֵא שֶׁמֶן — הֲרֵי זוֹ מְקֻדֶּשֶׁת בְּמַה שֶּׁבְּתוֹכוֹ וְלֹא בּוֹ.

לְפִיכָךְ: אִם לֹא הָיָה בַּשֶּׁמֶן שָׁוֶה פְּרוּטָה — הֲרֵי זוֹ מְקֻדֶּשֶׁת בְּסָפֵק,

וְאִם הָיָה בַּשֶּׁמֶן שָׁוֶה פְּרוּטָה — הֲרֵי זוֹ מְקֻדֶּשֶׁת וַדַּאי.

וְאֵין מַשְׁגִּיחִין עַל הַכּוֹס.

פֶּרֶק שִׁשִּׁי

א הַמְקַדֵּשׁ עַל תְּנַאי: אִם נִתְקַיֵּם הַתְּנַאי — מְקֻדֶּשֶׁת, וְאִם לָאו — אֵינָהּ מְקֻדֶּשֶׁת.

בֵּין שֶׁיִּהְיֶה הַתְּנַאי מִן הָאִישׁ, בֵּין שֶׁיִּהְיֶה מִן הָאִשָּׁה.

וְכָל תְּנַאי שֶׁבָּעוֹלָם — בֵּין בְּקִדּוּשִׁין, בֵּין בְּגֵרוּשִׁין, בֵּין בְּמִקָּח, בֵּין בְּמִמְכָּר, בֵּין בִּשְׁאָר דִּינֵי מָמוֹן — צָרִיךְ לִהְיוֹת בַּתְּנַאי אַרְבָּעָה דְּבָרִים.

ב וְאֵלּוּ הֵן הָאַרְבָּעָה דְּבָרִים שֶׁל כָּל תְּנַאי:

שֶׁיִּהְיֶה כָּפוּל,

---

38. Since the water is of little value, it is considered to have no independent importance. Hence, its value is considered together with that of the cup. The wine is not of negligible value, but - in the Talmudic era - it was worth less than the cup containing it. Hence, the wine is given independent importance and is not considered together with the cup. The oil - in the Talmudic era - was considered to be very valuable, more valuable than the cup containing it. Moreover, oil is not necessarily all used at one time. Therefore, it is apparent that the cup is subservient to the oil, and it is the value of the oil that is the determining factor.

1. See Halachah 14 and notes.
2. We find a conditional agreement in the Torah: Moses' granting the lands of Transjordan

b) the positive aspect must be stated before the negative aspect;
c) the stipulation should be mentioned before the completion of the deed that one desires to make conditional;[3]
d) the stipulation must be something that is possible to comply with.

If one of these rules was not kept when a conditional agreement was made, the stipulation is nullified; it is as if there is no condition at all. Thus, [the woman] is either consecrated or divorced immediately, and the commercial agreement is completed as if no condition had ever been made, for one of the four rules of conditional agreements was not met.

3. What is implied? [When a man] tells a woman: "If you give me 200 *zuz*, you are consecrated to me with this *dinar*. And if you do not give me [that sum], you are not consecrated," and after making this stipulation gives her the *dinar*, the condition is valid, and the *kiddushin* are subject to its terms. If she gives him 200 *zuz*, she is consecrated. If she does not give him, she is not consecrated.

4. If, however, [the man] told [the woman]: "Behold, you are consecrated to me with this *dinar*," gave her the *dinar* in her hand and then made a stipulation, saying: "If you give me 200 *zuz* you are consecrated," and if you do not give me [that sum] you are not consecrated," the stipulation is of no consequence, because he performed the deed first by giving it to her, and then making the stipulation.

[The above applies] even if everything occurred within a brief span of time;[4] she is consecrated immediately and does not have to give [her husband] anything at all.

5. Similarly, when [a man] tells [a woman]: "If you give me 200 *zuz* you are consecrated to me with this *dinar*," and then places the *dinar* in her hand, the stipulation is of no consequence, because the condition was not stated in a twofold manner. He did not tell her: "If you do not give me, you will not be consecrated." [Therefore] she is consecrated immediately without having to give him anything.

6. Similarly, when [a man] tells [a woman]: "If you do not give me 200 *zuz*, you will not be consecrated to me. But if you give me 200 *zuz*, you are consecrated to me with this *dinar*," and then places the *dinar* in her hand, the stipulation is of no consequence, because the negative dimension of the stipulation was stated before the positive one. [Therefore,] she is consecrated immediately without having to give him anything.

to the tribes of Reuven and Gad (Numbers 32:29-30). All these four rules were evident in Moses' phrasing of the stipulation. Accordingly, our Sages (*Kiddushin* 61a) consider this a prototype for all future conditional agreements.

וְשֶׁיִּהְיֶה הֵן שֶׁלּוֹ קֹדֶם לְלָאו,

וְשֶׁיִּהְיֶה הַתְּנַאי קֹדֶם לַמַּעֲשֶׂה,

וְשֶׁיִּהְיֶה הַתְּנַאי דָּבָר שֶׁאֶפְשָׁר לְקַיְּמוֹ.

וְאִם חָסַר הַתְּנַאי אֶחָד מֵהֶן — הֲרֵי הַתְּנַאי בָּטֵל, וּכְאִלּוּ אֵין שָׁם תְּנַאי כְּלָל; אֶלָּא תִּהְיֶה זוֹ מְקֻדֶּשֶׁת אוֹ מְגֹרֶשֶׁת מִיָּד, וְיִתְקַיֵּם הַמִּקָּח אוֹ הַמַּתָּנָה מִיָּד, וּכְאִלּוּ לֹא הִתְנָה כְּלָל, הוֹאִיל וְחָסַר הַתְּנַאי אֶחָד מִן הָאַרְבָּעָה.

ג כֵּיצַד? הָאוֹמֵר לְאִשָּׁה: אִם תִּתְּנִי לִי מָאתַיִם זוּז הֲרֵי אַתְּ מְקֻדֶּשֶׁת לִי בְּדִינָר זֶה, וְאִם לֹא תִּתְּנִי לִי לֹא תִּהְיִי מְקֻדֶּשֶׁת, וְאַחַר שֶׁהִתְנָה תְּנַאי זֶה נָתַן לָהּ הַדִּינָר — הֲרֵי הַתְּנַאי קַיָּם, וַהֲרֵי זוֹ מְקֻדֶּשֶׁת עַל תְּנַאי;

וְאִם נָתְנָה לוֹ מָאתַיִם זוּז — תִּהְיֶה מְקֻדֶּשֶׁת, וְאִם לֹא נָתְנָה לוֹ — אֵינָהּ מְקֻדֶּשֶׁת.

ד אֲבָל אִם אָמַר לָהּ: הֲרֵי אַתְּ מְקֻדֶּשֶׁת לִי בְּדִינָר זֶה, וְנָתַן הַדִּינָר בְּיָדָהּ, וְהִשְׁלִים הַתְּנַאי וְאָמַר: אִם תִּתְּנִי לִי מָאתַיִם זוּז תִּהְיִי מְקֻדֶּשֶׁת, וְאִם לֹא תִּתְּנִי לִי לֹא תִּהְיִי מְקֻדֶּשֶׁת — הֲרֵי הַתְּנַאי בָּטֵל,

מִפְּנֵי שֶׁהִקְדִּים הַמַּעֲשֶׂה וְנָתַן בְּיָדָהּ וְאַחַר כָּךְ הִתְנָה.

וְאַף־עַל־פִּי שֶׁהַכֹּל בְּתוֹךְ כְּדֵי דִבּוּר — הֲרֵי זוֹ מְקֻדֶּשֶׁת מִיָּד, וְאֵינָהּ צְרִיכָה לִתֵּן לוֹ כְּלוּם.

ה וְכֵן אִם אָמַר לָהּ: אִם תִּתְּנִי לִי מָאתַיִם זוּז הֲרֵי אַתְּ מְקֻדֶּשֶׁת לִי בְּדִינָר זֶה, וְאַחַר כָּךְ נָתַן הַדִּינָר בְּיָדָהּ — הֲרֵי הַתְּנַאי בָּטֵל, מִפְּנֵי שֶׁלֹּא כָּפַל תְּנָאוֹ;

שֶׁהֲרֵי לֹא אָמַר לָהּ: וְאִם לֹא תִּתְּנִי לִי לֹא תִּהְיִי מְקֻדֶּשֶׁת.

וַהֲרֵי זוֹ מְקֻדֶּשֶׁת מִיָּד, וְאֵינָהּ צְרִיכָה לִתֵּן לוֹ כְּלוּם.

ו וְכֵן אִם אָמַר לָהּ: אִם לֹא תִּתְּנִי לִי מָאתַיִם זוּז לֹא תִּהְיִי מְקֻדֶּשֶׁת לִי, וְאִם תִּתְּנִי לִי מָאתַיִם זוּז הֲרֵי אַתְּ מְקֻדֶּשֶׁת לִי בְּדִינָר זֶה, וְאַחַר כָּךְ נָתַן הַדִּינָר בְּיָדָהּ — הֲרֵי הַתְּנַאי בָּטֵל, לְפִי שֶׁהִקְדִּים לָאו לְהֵן.

וַהֲרֵי זוֹ מְקֻדֶּשֶׁת מִיָּד, וְאֵינָהּ צְרִיכָה לִתֵּן לוֹ כְּלוּם.

---

3. This is the Rambam's interpretation of the requirement that in its Hebrew original states: שיהיה התנאי קודם למעשה. The Ra'avad (in his gloss on Halachah 4) interprets the phrase differently. He states that in the wording of the person making the stipulation, the stipulation must be stated before the result of its completion: e.g., "If you give me 200 *zuz*, you will be consecrated..., and if you do not give me that sum, you will not be consecrated." The *Beit Shmuel* 38:2 accepts the Ra'avad's interpretation and not that of the Rambam.

4. We have chosen a very loose translation. The Hebrew *toch kedei dibbur* has a precise connotation, meaning the amount of time it takes to say the words *Shalom alecha rabbi umori*.

7. Similarly, when [a man] tells [a woman]: "If you ascend to the heavens or descend to the depths, you are consecrated to me with this *dinar*. But if you do not ascend to the heavens or descend to the depths, you are not consecrated." If he places the *dinar* in her hand afterwards, the stipulation is of no consequence, and the *kiddushin* are effective immediately. For it is well known that she cannot keep this stipulation; he is merely speaking facetiously in a jesting and teasing manner.

8. [The following rules apply when a man] makes a condition with regard to a deed that is possible to be performed, but that is forbidden by the Torah - e.g., he told a woman: "If you eat fat or blood, you are consecrated to me with this *dinar*. But if you do not eat fat or blood, you are not consecrated," or [a man tells his wife]: "If you eat the meat of pigs, this is your *get*. But if you do not eat it, the *get* is not effective." If, after making this stipulation, he placed the *dinar* or the *get* in her hand, the stipulation is valid. If the woman transgresses and eats [the forbidden article as stipulated], she will be either consecrated or divorced [accordingly]. It is not with regard to such a situation that it is said, "the person made a stipulation that contradicts what is written in the Torah." For the woman has the option not to eat and not to be consecrated or divorced.

9. With regard [to which situations] did in fact our Sages say:[5] "Whenever a person makes a stipulation that contradicts what is written in the Torah, his stipulation is nullified, except with regard to financial matters, in which instances his stipulation is binding"?[6]

When a person consecrates, divorces, gives or sells, dependent on a stipulation through which he wants to acquire a right that the Torah did not grant him, but rather prevented him from obtaining, or to use this stipulation to free himself from an obligation for which the Torah made him liable. In such an instance, he is told, "Your stipulation is of no consequence. The deed you have performed is binding. You are not freed from any responsibility for which the Torah obligates you, nor can you acquire any privilege that the Torah does not grant you."

10. What is implied? For example, when a man consecrates a woman on condition that he is not obligated to provide her with her provisions or garments, nor grant her conjugal rights, he is told: "With regard to provisions and garments, your stipulation is binding, for these are financial obligations. With regard to conjugal rights, however, your condition is not binding,[7] for the Torah has obligated you to grant these [to a woman]. Therefore, she is consecrated and you are obligated to grant her conjugal rights. You do not have the potential to free yourself of this responsibility with this stipulation." The same applies in all similar situations.

ז וְכֵן אִם אָמַר לָהּ: אִם תַּעֲלִי לָרָקִיעַ אוֹ תֵרְדִי לַתְּהוֹם הֲרֵי אַתְּ מְקֻדֶּשֶׁת לִי בְּדִינָר זֶה, וְאִם לֹא תַּעֲלִי לָרָקִיעַ וְלֹא תֵרְדִי לַתְּהוֹם לֹא תִּהְיִי מְקֻדֶּשֶׁת, וְאַחַר כָּךְ נָתַן הַדִּינָר בְּיָדָהּ — הֲרֵי הַתְּנַאי בָּטֵל וַהֲרֵי הִיא מְקֻדֶּשֶׁת מִיָּד;

שֶׁהַדָּבָר יָדוּעַ שֶׁאִי אֶפְשָׁר לָהּ לְקַיֵּם תְּנַאי זֶה, וְאֵין זֶה אֶלָּא כְּמַפְלִיגָהּ בִּדְבָרִים דֶּרֶךְ שְׂחוֹק וְהִתּוּל.

ח הֲרֵי שֶׁהִתְנָה בְּדָבָר שֶׁאֶפְשָׁר לַעֲשׂוֹתוֹ אֶלָּא שֶׁהַתּוֹרָה אָסְרָה אוֹתוֹ,

כְּגוֹן שֶׁאָמַר לְאִשָּׁה: אִם תֹּאכְלִי חֵלֶב וָדָם הֲרֵי אַתְּ מְקֻדֶּשֶׁת לִי בְּדִינָר זֶה, וְאִם לֹא תֹּאכְלִי לֹא תִּהְיִי מְקֻדֶּשֶׁת;

אִם תֹּאכְלִי בְּשַׂר חֲזִיר הֲרֵי זֶה גִּטֵּיךְ, וְאִם לֹא תֹּאכְלִי לֹא יְהֵא גֵט;

וְאַחַר שֶׁהִתְנָה נָתַן הַדִּינָר אוֹ הַגֵּט בְּיָדָהּ — הֲרֵי הַתְּנַאי קַיָּם;

וְאִם עָבְרָה וְאָכְלָה — תִּהְיֶה מְקֻדֶּשֶׁת אוֹ מְגֹרֶשֶׁת, וְאִם לֹא אָכְלָה — אֵינָהּ מְקֻדֶּשֶׁת וְאֵינָהּ מְגֹרֶשֶׁת.

וְאֵין אוֹמְרִים בָּזֶה: הֲרֵי הִתְנָה עַל מַה שֶּׁכָּתוּב בַּתּוֹרָה, שֶׁהֲרֵי בְּיָדָהּ שֶׁלֹּא תֹּאכַל וְשֶׁלֹּא תִּתְקַדֵּשׁ וְלֹא תִּתְגָּרֵשׁ.

ט וּבַמֶּה אָמְרוּ חֲכָמִים: כָּל הַמַּתְנֶה עַל מַה שֶּׁכָּתוּב בַּתּוֹרָה — תְּנָאוֹ בָּטֵל, חוּץ מִדָּבָר שֶׁבְּמָמוֹן שֶׁתְּנָאוֹ קַיָּם?

כְּגוֹן שֶׁקִּדֵּשׁ אוֹ גֵרַשׁ אוֹ נָתַן אוֹ מָכַר עַל תְּנַאי, שֶׁהוּא רוֹצֶה בִּתְנָאוֹ שֶׁיִּזְכֶּה עַצְמוֹ בְּדָבָר שֶׁלֹּא זִכְּתָה לוֹ תּוֹרָה וּמָנְעָה מִמֶּנּוּ, אוֹ יִפְטֹר עַצְמוֹ בִּתְנָאוֹ מִדָּבָר שֶׁחִיְּבָה אוֹתוֹ בּוֹ הַתּוֹרָה;

שֶׁאוֹמְרִין לוֹ: תְּנָאֲךָ בָּטֵל, וּכְבָר נִתְקַיְּמוּ מַעֲשֶׂיךָ, וְאֵין אַתָּה נִפְטָר מִדָּבָר שֶׁחִיְּבָה אוֹתְךָ בּוֹ הַתּוֹרָה, וְלֹא תִזְכֶּה בְּדָבָר שֶׁמָּנְעָה אוֹתְךָ מִמֶּנּוּ.

י כֵּיצַד? כְּגוֹן שֶׁקִּדֵּשׁ אִשָּׁה עַל תְּנַאי שֶׁאֵין עָלָיו שְׁאֵר כְּסוּת וְעוֹנָה;

שֶׁאוֹמְרִין לוֹ: בִּכְסוּת וּשְׁאֵר, שֶׁהוּא תְּנַאי שֶׁבְּמָמוֹן — תְּנָאֲךָ קַיָּם, אֲבָל בְּעוֹנָה — תְּנָאֲךָ בָּטֵל, שֶׁהַתּוֹרָה חִיְּבָה אוֹתְךָ בְּעוֹנָה, וַהֲרֵי זוֹ מְקֻדֶּשֶׁת, וְאַתָּה חַיָּב בְּעוֹנָתָהּ, וְאֵין בְּיָדְךָ לִפְטֹר עַצְמְךָ בִּתְנָאֲךָ. וְכֵן כָּל כַּיּוֹצֵא בָזֶה.

---

5. *Kiddushin* 19b.
6. An exception is made with regard to financial matters, because with regard to these matters the Torah grants the person the right to waive monetary privileges that are due him. Privileges that are not monetary in nature may not be waived.
7. Based on the Jerusalem Talmud (*Bava Metzia,* the conclusion of Chapter 7), the Ritba (*Kiddushin* 19a) and the Mordechai (gloss on *Bava Metzia* 93a) maintain that even conjugal rights can be considered to be a financial consideration, for it is a matter of physical pleasure. Nevertheless, this opinion is not accepted as halachah. Instead, withholding conjugal relations is considered a matter of physical anguish. Hence a woman does not have the prerogative of waiving this right.

Similarly, if a man consecrates a woman whom he took as a captive for sexual relations on condition that he may have her perform servile tasks,[8] she is consecrated and he is forbidden to have her perform these tasks, for after he had relations with her this was prohibited by the Torah. His stipulation does not empower him to a privilege that the Torah held back from him. The same applies in all similar situations.

11. If a man established a condition with a woman at the time of *kiddushin* or divorce requiring her to engage in sexual relations with her father, her brother, her son or the like, it is as if he made a stipulation that she ascend to the heavens or descend to the depths, and his condition is of no consequence. For it is not within the woman's capacity to cause others to transgress and to engage in a forbidden sexual relationship. Thus, he has made a stipulation that she is incapable of fulfilling. The same applies with regard to all similar instances.

12. If, however, the man made a stipulation that she [influence] so and so to "give me his courtyard or to have his daughter marry my son," the stipulation is binding. For it is in her capacity to fulfill it, she can give so and so a large amount of money so that he will [consent to] give the man [making the condition] his courtyard or have his daughter marry that man's son. For in this instance, there is no sin involved. The same applies with regard to all similar instances.

13. Have in mind at all times all these guidelines that have been mentioned with regard to conditional agreements. Whenever you hear the expression "A man consecrated [a woman] on the basis of these and these conditions," "gave a divorce on the basis of these and these conditions," or made a sale or gave a present conditionally, you will know that the condition must fit the four rules mentioned. Thus, it will not be necessary to repeat them on every occasion. If one of these rules is not kept, the stipulation is of no consequence.

14. Some of the later *geonim*[9] maintain that a person is required to make a conditional statement twofold only with regard to *kiddushin* and divorce. With regard to financial matters, by contrast, a twofold statement need not be made.

It is not proper to rely on this ruling, for our Sages derived the need to make a twofold statement of the condition, and the other four rules, from the condition made [with] the members [of the tribes] of Gad and Reuven, as [Numbers 38:29-30] states: "If the members [of the tribes] of Gad... cross over. But if they do not cross over...." And this condition involved neither *kiddushin* nor divorce. [My ruling echoes] the decisions of the great *geonim* of the previous eras, and it is fitting to follow it.[10]

וְכֵן הַמְקַדֵּשׁ יְפַת תֹּאַר עַל תְּנַאי שֶׁיִּתְעַמֵּר בָּה — הֲרֵי זוֹ מְקֻדֶּשֶׁת, וְאֵין לוֹ לְהִתְעַמֵּר בָּה; שֶׁהֲרֵי הַתּוֹרָה מָנְעָה אוֹתוֹ מִלְּהִשְׁתַּעְבֵּד בָּה אַחַר שֶׁנִּבְעֲלָה, וְלֹא מִפְּנֵי תְּנָאוֹ יִזְכֶּה בְּדָבָר שֶׁמָּנְעָה אוֹתוֹ תּוֹרָה, אֶלָּא תְּנָאוֹ בָּטֵל. וְכֵן כָּל כַּיּוֹצֵא בָזֶה.

יא הִתְנָה עַל הָאִשָּׁה בִּשְׁעַת קִדּוּשִׁין אוֹ בִּשְׁעַת גֵּרוּשִׁין שֶׁתִּבָּעֵל לְאָבִיהָ וּלְאָחִיהָ אוֹ לִבְנָהּ וְכַיּוֹצֵא בָזֶה — הֲרֵי זֶה כְּמִי שֶׁהִתְנָה עָלֶיהָ שֶׁתַּעֲלֶה לָרָקִיעַ אוֹ שֶׁתֵּרֵד לַתְּהוֹם, וּתְנָאוֹ בָּטֵל;

שֶׁאֵין בְּיָדָהּ שֶׁיַּעַבְרוּ אֲחֵרִים וְיָבוֹאוּ עַל הָעֶרְוָה, וְנִמְצָא שֶׁהִתְנָה עִמָּהּ בְּדָבָר שֶׁאֵינוֹ בְּיָדָהּ לְקַיְּמוֹ. וְכֵן כָּל כַּיּוֹצֵא בָזֶה.

יב אֲבָל אִם הִתְנָה עָלֶיהָ שֶׁיִּתֵּן לִי פְּלוֹנִי חֲצֵרוֹ אוֹ שֶׁיַּשִּׂיא בִּתּוֹ לִבְנִי וְכַיּוֹצֵא בָזֶה — תְּנָאוֹ קַיָּם;

שֶׁהֲרֵי אֶפְשָׁר בְּיָדָהּ לְקַיְּמוֹ, וְתִתֵּן לִפְלוֹנִי מָמוֹן רַב עַד שֶׁיִּתֵּן לוֹ חֲצֵרוֹ וְעַד שֶׁיַּשִּׂיא בִּתּוֹ לִבְנוֹ, שֶׁהֲרֵי אֵין כַּאן עֲבֵרָה. וְכֵן כָּל כַּיּוֹצֵא בָזֶה.

יג שִׂים כָּל אֵלּוּ הַדְּבָרִים שֶׁל תְּנָאִים לְנֶגֶד עֵינֶיךָ תָּמִיד, וְכָל מָקוֹם שֶׁאַתָּה שׁוֹמֵעַ: הַמְקַדֵּשׁ עַל תְּנַאי כָּךְ וָכָךְ, אוֹ הַנּוֹתֵן גֵּט עַל תְּנַאי כָּךְ וָכָךְ, אוֹ הַמּוֹכֵר אוֹ הַנּוֹתֵן עַל תְּנַאי — תֵּדַע, שֶׁהַתְּנַאי יֵשׁ בּוֹ אַרְבָּעָה דְבָרִים אֵלּוּ שֶׁבֵּאַרְנוּ, כְּדֵי שֶׁלֹּא נִהְיֶה צְרִיכִין לְפָרֵשׁ אוֹתָן בְּכָל מָקוֹם, וְאִם חָסֵר אֶחָד מֵהֶן — אֵין כַּאן תְּנַאי.

יד יֵשׁ מִקְצָת גְּאוֹנִים אַחֲרוֹנִים שֶׁאָמְרוּ, שֶׁאֵין צָרִיךְ אָדָם לִכְפֹּל תְּנָאוֹ אֶלָּא בְּגִטִּין וְקִדּוּשִׁין בִּלְבָד, אֲבָל בְּדִינֵי מָמוֹן — אֵינוֹ צָרִיךְ לִכְפֹּל.

וְאֵין רָאוּי לִסְמֹךְ עַל דָּבָר זֶה, שֶׁכְּפִילַת הַתְּנַאי עִם שְׁאָר הָאַרְבָּעָה דְבָרִים מִתְּנָאֵי בְּנֵי גָד וּבְנֵי רְאוּבֵן לָמְדוּ אוֹתָן חֲכָמִים: אִם יַעַבְרוּ בְּנֵי גָד וְגוֹ' וְאִם לֹא יַעַבְרוּ, וּתְנַאי זֶה לֹא הָיָה לֹא בְּגִטִּין וְלֹא בְּקִדּוּשִׁין.

וְכָזֶה הוֹרוּ גְּדוֹלֵי הַגְּאוֹנִים הָרִאשׁוֹנִים, וְכֵן רָאוּי לַעֲשׂוֹת.

8. Deuteronomy 21:11-14 describes the right of a soldier to have relations with a female captive of war whom he desires. Once he has relations with her, he may no longer treat her as a servant.

9. The commentaries have pointed to Rabbenu Yitzchak Alfasi and Rabbenu Shmuel ben Chofni HaCohen.

10. The Ra'avad, the Ramban and the Rashba differ with the Rambam's reasoning. According to the position of these authorities, it is only one Sage, Rabbi Meir, who maintains that the rules regarding conditional agreements were derived from the agreement made between Moses and the tribes of Reuven and Gad. They maintain that the need to repeat the condition applies only with regard to *kiddushin*, and was instituted only because of the severity of the establishment and annulment of the marriage relationship. With regard to other matters, however, there is no such requirement. The *Tur* and the *Shulchan Aruch* (*Choshen Mishpat* 241:9) follow the Rambam's view.

15. When a man consecrates a woman conditionally, the *kiddushin* become effective at the time the stipulation is fulfilled, and not at the time of the [original] *kiddushin*.

What is implied? [For example, a man] tells a woman: "If I give you 200 *zuz* this year, you are consecrated to me with this *dinar*. But if I do not give you, you are not consecrated." If he [made these statements and] gave her the *dinar* in Nisan, but gave her the 200 *zuz* that he stipulated only in Elul, it is in Elul that the consecration takes effect. Therefore, if another person consecrates her before the first completes carrying out his stipulation, she is consecrated to the second.

Similar laws apply with regard to divorce and monetary law. When the stipulation is fulfilled, the divorce is effective or the sale or gift is completed.[11]

16. When does the above apply? When a stipulation was made, and [the person making it did not state that the agreement took effect] from this time onward. If, however, [a man] told [a woman]: "Behold, you are consecrated to me from this time onward with this *dinar* if I give you 200 *zuz*,"[12] when at a later date he gives her the 200 *zuz* she is consecrated. Retroactively, the *kiddushin* are considered to have taken effect at the time they were given, despite the fact that the stipulation was not fulfilled until after much time had passed. Therefore, if a second person consecrates her before the stipulation has been fulfilled, she is not consecrated to that [second] person. Similar laws apply with regard to divorce and monetary law.

17. Whenever a person makes a stipulation and states [that it is effective] "from this time onward," it is not necessary for him to make a twofold statement of the stipulation,[13] nor is it necessary to state the stipulation before performing the deed involved.[14] Even when he performs the deed first, his stipulation is effective. He must, however, make a stipulation that is possible to fulfill. A person who makes a stipulation that is impossible to fulfill is merely speaking facetiously; there is no [intent to make] a [binding] stipulation.

When a person appends a stipulation to an agreement using the wording *al menat* ("on condition that"), the rules that apply when the person states "from this time onward" also apply.[15] It is not necessary for him to make a twofold statement of the stipulation, nor is it necessary to state the stipulation before performing the deed involved.

18. What is implied? When [a man] tells a woman: "Behold, you are consecrated to me on condition that you give me 200 *zuz*," "here is your

---

11. The above applies when the agreement is made verbally. If, however, a conditional sale or a present is recorded in a legal document, it is considered to be effective retroactively

טו הַמְקַדֵּשׁ עַל תְּנַאי — כְּשֶׁיִּתְקַיֵּם הַתְּנַאי, תִּהְיֶה מְקֻדֶּשֶׁת מִשָּׁעָה שֶׁנִּתְקַיֵּם הַתְּנַאי, לֹא מִשָּׁעָה שֶׁנִּתְקַדְּשָׁה.

כֵּיצַד? הָאוֹמֵר לְאִשָּׁה: אִם אֶתֵּן לִיךְ מָאתַיִם זוּז הֲרֵי אַתְּ מְקֻדֶּשֶׁת לִי בְּדִינָר זֶה, וְאִם לֹא אֶתֵּן לִיךְ לֹא תִּהְיִי מְקֻדֶּשֶׁת, וְנָתַן הַדִּינָר לְיָדָהּ בְּנִיסָן, וְנָתַן לָהּ הַמָּאתַיִם זוּז שֶׁהִתְנָה עִמָּהּ בְּאֱלוּל — הֲרֵי זוֹ מְקֻדֶּשֶׁת מֵאֱלוּל.

לְפִיכָךְ, אִם קִדְּשָׁהּ אַחֵר קֹדֶם שֶׁיִּתְקַיֵּם הַתְּנַאי שֶׁל רִאשׁוֹן — הֲרֵי זוֹ מְקֻדֶּשֶׁת לַשֵּׁנִי. וְכֵן הַדִּין בְּגִטִּין וּבְמָמוֹנוֹת: בְּשָׁעָה שֶׁיִּתְקַיֵּם הַתְּנַאי, הוּא שֶׁיִּהְיֶה גֵּט אוֹ יִתְקַיֵּם הַמֶּקַח אוֹ הַמַּתָּנָה.

טז בַּמֶּה דְּבָרִים אֲמוּרִים? בְּשֶׁהָיָה שָׁם תְּנַאי וְלֹא אָמַר 'מֵעַכְשָׁו';

אֲבָל אִם אָמַר לָהּ: הֲרֵי אַתְּ מְקֻדֶּשֶׁת לִי מֵעַכְשָׁו בְּדִינָר זֶה אִם אֶתֵּן לִיךְ מָאתַיִם זוּז, וּלְאַחַר זְמַן נָתַן לָהּ מָאתַיִם זוּז — הֲרֵי זוֹ מְקֻדֶּשֶׁת לְמַפְרֵעַ מִשָּׁעַת הַקִּדּוּשִׁין, אַף־עַל־פִּי שֶׁלֹּא נַעֲשָׂה תְּנָאוֹ אֶלָּא לְאַחַר זְמַן מְרֻבֶּה.

לְפִיכָךְ, אִם קִדְּשָׁהּ הַשֵּׁנִי קֹדֶם שֶׁיַּעֲשֶׂה הַתְּנַאי — אֵינָהּ מְקֻדֶּשֶׁת. וְכֵן הַדִּין בְּגִטִּין וּבְמָמוֹן.

יז כָּל הָאוֹמֵר 'מֵעַכְשָׁו', לֹא יִצְטָרֵךְ לִכְפֹּל תְּנָאוֹ וְלֹא לְהַקְדִּים הַתְּנַאי עַל הַמַּעֲשֶׂה, אֶלָּא אַף־עַל־פִּי שֶׁהִקְדִּים הַמַּעֲשֶׂה — תְּנָאוֹ קַיָּם.

אֲבָל צָרִיךְ לְהַתְנוֹת בְּדָבָר שֶׁאֶפְשָׁר לְקַיְּמוֹ, וְאִם הִתְנָה בְּדָבָר שֶׁאִי אֶפְשָׁר לְקַיְּמוֹ — הֲרֵי זֶה כְּמַפְלִיג בִּדְבָרִים, וְאֵין שָׁם תְּנַאי.

וְכָל הָאוֹמֵר 'עַל מְנָת' — כְּאוֹמֵר 'מֵעַכְשָׁו', וְאֵינוֹ צָרִיךְ לִכְפֹּל הַתְּנַאי וְלֹא לְהַקְדִּימוֹ לַמַּעֲשֶׂה.

יח כֵּיצַד? הָאוֹמֵר לְאִשָּׁה: הֲרֵי אַתְּ מְקֻדֶּשֶׁת לִי עַל מְנָת שֶׁתִּתְּנִי לִי מָאתַיִם זוּז,

from the date stated in the document, although the stipulation is not carried out until much later.

Others maintain that the same principle applies with regard to a *get*, and if a date is included in a conditional bill of divorce, the divorce is retroactively effective from the date of the *get*, even though the stipulation is carried out much later. As stated in *Hilchot Gerushin* 8:1, the Rambam does not follow this approach. (See *Shulchan Aruch, Even HaEzer* 143:2.)

12. In such an instance, the stipulation need not be restated, as mentioned in the following halachah.

13. Since the condition does not have to be restated, there is also no need for the positive statement to precede the negative.

14. This follows the Rambam's interpretation of the Talmud's wording שיהיה התנאי קודם למעשה, as explained in Halachah 2.

15. *Tosafot* and many subsequent Ashkenazic authorities do not accept this ruling. The difference of opinion is noted by the *Shulchan Aruch* (*Even HaEzer* 144:4).

get on condition that you give me 200 *zuz*," or "this courtyard is given to you as a present on condition that you give me 200 *zuz*," the stipulation is binding. She is consecrated or divorced, or she acquires the field, but she must give the 200 *zuz*. If she does not give [the money], she will not be consecrated or divorced, nor will she acquire the field.

[The above applies] even when the man did not make a twofold condition, and even though he performed the deed before stating the condition - i.e., he placed the *kiddushin* or the *get* in her hand or let her take possession of the courtyard, and then completed [the statement of] his stipulation. [The rationale for these leniencies is that] when the stipulation is fulfilled, she retroactively either acquires the field or is consecrated or divorced from the time the deed was performed, as if a stipulation had never been made at all.16

CHAPTER SEVEN

1. [The following rules apply when a man] tells a woman: "Behold, you are consecrated to me on condition that my father will consent." If his father consents, she is consecrated.1 If he does not consent, if he remained silent, or if he died before he heard of the matter, she is not consecrated.2

[If the man tells her: "Behold, you are consecrated to me] on condition that my father does not object." If he hears and objects, she is not consecrated. If he does not object or he dies, she is consecrated. If the son dies, and the father hears afterwards, we instruct the father to say: "I do not consent," so the *kiddushin* will not be effective, and the woman will not be obligated to undergo the rites of *yibbum*.3

2. [The following rules apply when a man] tells a woman: "Behold, you are consecrated to me with this [item] on condition that I possess 200 *zuz* or land on which it is fit to grow a *kor* of grain."4 If there are witnesses

---

16. Among the other rationales offered are that the rules for a conditional agreement are derived from the agreement between Moses and the tribes of Gad and Reuven, and in that instance that condition was phrased using the term "if," rather than "from this time onward" or "on condition that" (Rabbenu Yitzchak Alfasi). The Ra'avad explains that stating a stipulation using the wording "if" nullifies the act the person performs. For a stipulation to have this power, it must be worded precisely. If, however, the wording "on condition that" or "from now onward" is used, the implication is that the act is not nullified, but is merely dependent on the fulfillment of the condition. Since the stipulation is not that powerful, its wording need not be as precise.

הֲרֵי זֶה גִּטֵּךְ עַל מְנָת שֶׁתִּתְּנִי לִי מָאתַיִם זוּז,

הֲרֵי חָצֵר זוֹ נְתוּנָה לִיךְ בְּמַתָּנָה עַל מְנָת שֶׁתִּתְּנִי לִי מָאתַיִם זוּז —

הֲרֵי תְּנָאוֹ קַיָּם, וְנִתְקַדְּשָׁה אוֹ נִתְגָּרְשָׁה וְזָכְתָה זוֹ בֶּחָצֵר, וְהֵם יִתְּנוּ הַמָּאתַיִם זוּז;

וְאִם לֹא נָתְנוּ — לֹא תִּהְיֶה זוֹ מְקֻדֶּשֶׁת וְלֹא מְגֹרֶשֶׁת וְלֹא תִּזְכֶּה זוֹ בֶחָצֵר.

וְאַף־עַל־פִּי שֶׁלֹּא כָּפַל תְּנָאוֹ, וְאַף־עַל־פִּי שֶׁהִקְדִּים הַמַּעֲשֶׂה לַתְּנַאי וְנָתַן הַקִּדּוּשִׁין אוֹ הַגֵּט בְּיָדָהּ וְהֶחֱזִיקָה זוֹ בֶחָצֵר וְאַחַר כָּךְ הִשְׁלִים תְּנָאוֹ;

שֶׁהֲרֵי כְּשֶׁיִּתְקַיְּמוּ הַתְּנַאי, תִּזְכֶּה זוֹ בֶחָצֵר וְתִתְקַדֵּשׁ אוֹ וְתִתְגָּרֵשׁ זוֹ מִשָּׁעָה רִאשׁוֹנָה שֶׁבָּהּ נַעֲשָׂה הַמַּעֲשֶׂה כְּאִלּוּ לֹא הָיָה שָׁם תְּנַאי כְּלָל.

פֶּרֶק שְׁבִיעִי

א הָאוֹמֵר לְאִשָּׁה: הֲרֵי אַתְּ מְקֻדֶּשֶׁת לִי עַל מְנָת שֶׁיִּרְצֶה אָבִי:

רָצָה הָאָב — מְקֻדֶּשֶׁת; לֹא רָצָה, אוֹ שֶׁשָּׁתַק, אוֹ שֶׁמֵּת קֹדֶם שֶׁיִּשְׁמַע הַדָּבָר — אֵינָהּ מְקֻדֶּשֶׁת.

עַל מְנָת שֶׁלֹּא יְמַחֶה אָבִי:

שָׁמַע וּמִחָה — אֵינָהּ מְקֻדֶּשֶׁת; לֹא מִחָה, אוֹ שֶׁמֵּת — הֲרֵי זוֹ מְקֻדֶּשֶׁת.

מֵת הַבֵּן וְאַחַר כָּךְ שָׁמַע הָאָב — מְלַמְּדִין הָאָב שֶׁיֹּאמַר: אֵינִי רוֹצֶה, כְּדֵי שֶׁלֹּא יְהוּ קִדּוּשִׁין וְלֹא תִּפֹּל לִפְנֵי יָבָם.

ב הָאוֹמֵר לְאִשָּׁה: הֲרֵי אַתְּ מְקֻדֶּשֶׁת לִי בָּזֶה עַל מְנָת שֶׁיֵּשׁ לִי מָאתַיִם זוּז אוֹ בֵּית כּוֹר עָפָר:

1. It appears that, according to the Rambam, what is significant is the father's consent (or his objection) the first time he hears of the matter. The Ra'avad and others do not share this view and maintain that the father has the option of consenting (or objecting) at all times. The *Shulchan Aruch* (*Even HaEzer* 38:8) quotes the Rambam's wording.

2. There are two opinions in *Kiddushin* 63a, the source for this halachah, regarding the meaning of "consent": a) to say "yes," b) not to object. The Rambam takes the first view, while the Ra'avad and other authorities favor the second. Both views are mentioned in the *Shulchan Aruch* (*Even HaEzer* 38:9). Significantly, in his Commentary on the Mishnah, the Rambam mentions the second view.

3. Since the *kiddushin* are not effective, the woman will not be under any obligation to marry the brother of her intended husband. Were the father to indeed consent, she would be under obligation either to marry the deceased's brother, or have the obligation removed through *chalitzah*.

4. In his Commentary on the Mishnah (*Kiddushin* 3:2-3), the Rambam writes that it is necessary to mention both land and money, because it is difficult to hide the ownership of land. Were land to be mentioned in the stipulation, one might think that if it were not known that the person did not own land, we would assume that the *kiddushin* would be void.

who say that he possesses these entities, the *kiddushin* are binding. If there are no witnesses, [the *kiddushin* are not nullified entirely; instead,] their status is doubtful. Perhaps he possesses these entities and says he does not own them in order to cause the woman difficulties.[5]

3. [The following rules apply when he tells her:] "Behold, you are consecrated to me with this [item] on condition that I possess 200 *zuz* or land on which it is fit to grow a *kor* of grain in a particular place." If he possesses these entities in that place, the *kiddushin* are binding. If he does not possess these entities in the place he specified, [the *kiddushin* are not nullified entirely; instead,] their status is doubtful. Perhaps he possesses these entities in that place [and says he does not own them] in order to cause the woman difficulties.[6]

4. [The following rules apply when he tells her:] "Behold, you are consecrated to me with this [item] on condition that I show you 200 *zuz* or land on which it is fit to grow a *kor* of grain." When he shows her these entities, she is consecrated. If he shows her money that is possessed by someone else or land on which it is fit to grow a *kor* of grain in a field belonging to someone else, she is not consecrated; he [must] show her what belongs to him.

If he borrowed the money, rented a field or took it on a sharecropping arrangement and showed it to her, she is not consecrated; he [must] show her what belongs to him. For when he says "I will show you," that implies that "I will show you the entity I mentioned that belongs to me and is in my possession."

5. [The following rules apply when] the man owns land on which it is fit to grow a *kor* of grain, but it contains clefts ten handbreadths deep or rocks ten handbreadths high. If the clefts are filled with water, they are considered to be rocks and are not included in the total measure, because they are not fit to be sown.[7] If they are not filled with water, they are included in the total measure, because they are fit to be sown.

6. [The following rules apply when a man] tells a woman: "Behold, you are consecrated to me with this [item] on condition that you are not bound by vows." The *kiddushin* are not binding if she is bound by any of the following three vows: that she may not eat meat, that she may not drink wine, or that she may not wear colored ornaments.[8] If she is bound by any vow other

---

5. I.e., his desire is that she marry another man. He will then show how her original *kiddushin* were valid, causing her to be considered an adulteress and to be forbidden to her second husband.

אִם יֵשׁ שָׁם עֵדִים שֶׁיֵּשׁ לוֹ — הֲרֵי זוֹ מְקֻדֶּשֶׁת; וְאִם אֵין לוֹ — הֲרֵי זוֹ מְקֻדֶּשֶׁת מִסָּפֵק, שֶׁמָּא יֵשׁ לוֹ, וְהוּא אוֹמֵר 'אֵין לִי' כְּדֵי לְקַלְקְלָהּ.

ג הֲרֵי אַתְּ מְקֻדֶּשֶׁת לִי בָּזֶה עַל מְנָת שֶׁיֵּשׁ לִי מָאתַיִם זוּז אוֹ בֵּית כּוֹר עָפָר בְּמָקוֹם פְּלוֹנִי: אִם יֵשׁ לוֹ בְּאוֹתוֹ מָקוֹם — הֲרֵי זוֹ מְקֻדֶּשֶׁת; וְאִם אֵין לוֹ בְּאוֹתוֹ מָקוֹם שֶׁאוֹמֵר — הֲרֵי זוֹ מְקֻדֶּשֶׁת מִסָּפֵק, שֶׁמָּא יֵשׁ לוֹ שָׁם, וְהוּא מִתְכַּוֵּן לְקַלְקְלָהּ.

ד הֲרֵי אַתְּ מְקֻדֶּשֶׁת לִי בָּזֶה עַל מְנָת שֶׁאַרְאֵךְ מָאתַיִם זוּז אוֹ בֵּית כּוֹר עָפָר — הֲרֵי זוֹ מְקֻדֶּשֶׁת, וְיַרְאֶנָּה.

הֶרְאָה הַזּוּזִים בְּיַד אֲחֵרִים, אוֹ שֶׁהֶרְאָה בֵּית כּוֹר עָפָר בְּשָׂדֶה אֲחֵרִים — אֵינָהּ מְקֻדֶּשֶׁת, עַד שֶׁיַּרְאֶנָּה מִשֶּׁלּוֹ.

לָקַח הַמָּעוֹת בְּהַלְוָאָה אוֹ בְּשֻׁתָּפוּת, אוֹ שֶׁשָּׂכַר הַשָּׂדֶה אוֹ לְקָחָהּ בַּאֲרִיסוּת, וְהֶרְאָה — אֵינָהּ מְקֻדֶּשֶׁת, עַד שֶׁיַּרְאֶנָּה מִשֶּׁלּוֹ;

שֶׁמִּשֶּׁמַע 'שֶׁאַרְאֵךְ' — שֶׁאַרְאֵךְ מִשֶּׁל עַצְמִי דָּבָר זֶה שֶׁאָמַרְתִּי לָךְ.

ה הָיָה לוֹ בֵּית כּוֹר עָפָר, וְהָיוּ בּוֹ נְקָעִים עֲמֻקִּים עֲשָׂרָה טְפָחִים, אוֹ סְלָעִים גְּבוֹהִים עֲשָׂרָה טְפָחִים:

אִם הָיוּ הַנְּקָעִים מְלֵאִים מַיִם — הֲרֵי הֵן כִּסְלָעִים, וְאֵין נִמְדָּדִין עִמּוֹ, מִפְּנֵי שֶׁאֵינָן רְאוּיִין לִזְרִיעָה;

וְאִם אֵינָן מְלֵאִין מַיִם — נִמְדָּדִין עִמּוֹ, מִפְּנֵי שֶׁהֵן רְאוּיִין לִזְרִיעָה.

ו הָאוֹמֵר לְאִשָּׁה: הֲרֵי אַתְּ מְקֻדֶּשֶׁת לִי בָּזֶה עַל מְנָת שֶׁאֵין עָלַיִךְ נְדָרִים, וְנִמְצָא עָלֶיהָ אֶחָד מִשְּׁלֹשָׁה נְדָרִים אֵלּוּ:

שֶׁלֹּא תֹּאכַל בָּשָׂר, אוֹ שֶׁלֹּא תִּשְׁתֶּה יַיִן, אוֹ שֶׁלֹּא תִּתְקַשֵּׁט בְּמִינֵי צִבְעוֹנִין — אֵינָהּ מְקֻדֶּשֶׁת.

---

6. Rav Moshe HaCohen and others object to the Rambam's ruling, explaining that in such an instance, it is highly unlikely for a man to possess a field in a particular place without people's knowing about it. Hence, if there are no witnesses, the *kiddushin* are not valid at all; there is no doubt about the matter. The Radbaz (Volume III, Responsum 39) justifies the Rambam's decision, explaining that it is possible that the person temporarily gave the land as a present, or had a deed written in the name of another person to conceal the matter. The *Shulchan Aruch* (*Even HaEzer* 38:20) quotes the Rambam's decision.

7. The *Maggid Mishneh* and the *Shulchan Aruch* (*Even HaEzer* 38:22) differentiate between a cleft filled with water that is not fit to use for irrigation, and a cistern of water that is. The latter is included in the measure of the field, even when it is filled with water, because it enhances the value of the field.

8. The same law applies regarding a vow not to wear any other jewelry, clothing or

than these, she is consecrated, even when [the husband] states: "I object even with regard to these."

If he told her, "[Behold, you are consecrated...] on condition that you are not bound by any vow," even if she has made a vow [as insignificant as] not to eat carobs, she is not consecrated.

7. [The following rules apply when a man tells a woman:] "Behold, you are consecrated to me with this [item] on condition that you do not have any physical blemishes." If she has one of the physical blemishes that cause a woman to be deemed unfit [as a wife], she is not consecrated. If she has a physical blemish other than these, she is consecrated, even though he states, "I object even with regard to these."

What are the physical blemishes that cause a woman to be deemed unfit [as a wife]: All the physical blemishes that cause a priest to be deemed unfit [for service in the Temple] cause a woman to be deemed unfit. In *Hilchot Bi'at HaMikdash*, all the blemishes affecting the priests are explained.[9] In addition, [there are other blemishes that cause] women [to be deemed unfit]. They include: foul body odor, [excessive] sweating, foul breath, deep voice, breasts of abnormal size, being more than a handbreadth larger than those of other women,[10] a distance of more than a handbreadth between one breast and the other, a scar in the place where she was bit by a dog, and a birthmark on her forehead.

This includes even a birthmark that is very small, even if it is close to her hairline, and even if there are no hairs growing from it. This is the birthmark that is mentioned as a disqualifying factor for a woman and not for a priest. If, however, a birthmark has facial hair growing from it, or if it is as large as an *isar*[11] even when no hair grows from it, it is a disqualifying blemish, both for priests and for women.

8. When a man consecrates a woman without making any specific stipulations, and it is discovered that she has one of the physical blemishes that cause a woman to be deemed unfit, or [it is discovered that] she is bound by one of the three vows mentioned above, the status of the *kiddushin* is in doubt.[12]

If [a man] consecrates [a woman] on condition that she is not bound by vows, and she was bound by vows, but [afterwards,] she went to a wise man who nullified them for her,[13] she is consecrated.

cosmetics that women will frequently wear to adorn themselves. (See Chapter 25, Halachah 1.)

Ketubot 72b describes these vows as involving ענוי נפש, "the oppression of the soul" (cf. Numbers 30:14). Simply put, a woman who must live under such restrictions will not be happy, and it will therefore not be pleasant for her husband to live with her.

In the *Beit Yosef* and the *Shulchan Aruch* (*Even HaEzer* 39:1), Rav Yosef Karo mentions that the vows that nullify a relationship have a larger scope than those involving ענוי נפש; it

נִמְצָא עָלֶיהָ נֶדֶר חוּץ מֵאֵלּוּ, אַף־עַל־פִּי שֶׁהוּא אוֹמֵר: מַקְפִּיד אֲנִי אֲפִלּוּ עַל זֶה — הֲרֵי זוֹ מְקֻדֶּשֶׁת.

וְאִם אָמַר לָהּ: עַל מְנָת שֶׁאֵין עָלַיִךְ כָּל נֶדֶר — אֲפִלּוּ נִמְצֵאת שֶׁנָּדְרָה שֶׁלֹּא תֹּאכַל חָרוּבִין, אֵינָהּ מְקֻדֶּשֶׁת.

ז הֲרֵי אַתְּ מְקֻדֶּשֶׁת לִי בָּזֶה עַל מְנָת שֶׁאֵין בָּךְ מוּמִין, וְנִמְצָא בָּהּ אֶחָד מִן הַמּוּמִין הַפּוֹסְלִין בְּנָשִׁים — אֵינָהּ מְקֻדֶּשֶׁת.

נִמְצָא בָּהּ מוּם אֶחָד חוּץ מֵאוֹתָן הַמּוּמִין, אַף־עַל־פִּי שֶׁאָמַר: מַקְפִּיד אֲנִי אֲפִלּוּ עַל זֶה — הֲרֵי זוֹ מְקֻדֶּשֶׁת.

וּמָה הֵן הַמּוּמִין הַפּוֹסְלִין בְּנָשִׁים? כָּל הַמּוּמִין הַפּוֹסְלִין בְּכֹהֲנִים פּוֹסְלִין בְּנָשִׁים. וּבְהִלְכוֹת בִּיאַת מִקְדָּשׁ יִתְבָּאֲרוּ כָּל מוּמִין שֶׁל כֹּהֲנִים.

וְיוֹתֵר עֲלֵיהֶן בְּנָשִׁים: רֵיחַ רַע. וְזֵעָה. וְרֵיחַ הַפֶּה. וְקוֹל עָבֶה. וְדַדִּין גַּסִּין מֵחַבְרוֹתֶיהָ טֶפַח. וְטֶפַח בֵּין דַּד לְדַד. וּנְשִׁיכַת כֶּלֶב וְנַעֲשָׂה הַמָּקוֹם צַלֶּקֶת. וְשׁוּמָא שֶׁעַל הַפַּדַּחַת — אֲפִלּוּ הָיְתָה קְטַנָּה בְּיוֹתֵר, וַאֲפִלּוּ קְרוֹבָה לִשְׂעַר רֹאשָׁהּ, וְאַף־עַל־פִּי שֶׁאֵין בָּהּ שֵׂעָר. וְזוֹ הִיא הַשּׁוּמָא שֶׁיִּתְרָה אִשָּׁה עַל הַכֹּהֲנִים.

אֲבָל אִם הָיְתָה שׁוּמָא שֶׁיֵּשׁ בָּהּ שֵׂעָר בִּשְׁאָר הַפָּנִים, אוֹ שׁוּמָא גְדוֹלָה כְּאִסָּר אַף־עַל־פִּי שֶׁאֵין בָּהּ שֵׂעָר — הֲרֵי זֶה מוּם בֵּין בְּכֹהֲנִים בֵּין בְּנָשִׁים.

ח הַמְקַדֵּשׁ אִשָּׁה סְתָם, וְנִמְצָא עָלֶיהָ אֶחָד מִן הַמּוּמִין הַפּוֹסְלִין בְּנָשִׁים, אוֹ נִמְצָא עָלֶיהָ אֶחָד מִשְּׁלֹשָׁה נְדָרִים — הֲרֵי זוֹ מְקֻדֶּשֶׁת מִסָּפֵק.

קִדְּשָׁהּ עַל מְנָת שֶׁאֵין עָלֶיהָ נְדָרִים, וְהָיוּ עָלֶיהָ נְדָרִים, וְהָלְכָה אֵצֶל חָכָם וְהִתִּיר לָהּ — הֲרֵי זוֹ מְקֻדֶּשֶׁת.

---

also includes those בינו לבינה, affecting the relationship between the husband and wife (cf. Numbers 30:17). (For a more detailed explanation of these types of vows, see *Hilchot Nedarim*, Chapter 12, and *Shulchan Aruch, Yoreh De'ah*, Chapter 234.)

9. Leviticus, Chapter 21, states that a priest who possesses certain physical blemishes may not serve in the Temple. In *Hilchot Bi'at HaMikdash*, Chapters 6-8, these blemishes are listed.

10. Our translation is based on the Rambam's Commentary on the Mishnah (*Ketubot* 7:5).

11. An Italian coin equivalent in weight to four barley corns, with a diameter of 2.7 cm (Rambam's Commentary on the Mishnah, *Kiddushin* 1:1).

12. She cannot marry another man until she receives a divorce, nor may she consummate this marriage unless the husband consecrates her again, stating that he has no objections to her condition.

This ruling is given because we are unsure whether these vows or physical blemishes are disturbing enough to cause a person who did not express concern about the matter to consider himself as having been deceived about the nature of his marriage partner.

13. A wise man has the authority to release people from vows they have taken if they regret having taken them. (See *Hilchot Nedarim*, Chapter 4.)

9. If [a man] consecrates [a woman] on condition that she does not have physical blemishes, and she does have blemishes, she is not consecrated, even if [afterwards,] she goes to a physician who heals these blemishes.[14]

When, by contrast, a man enters into a marriage contract on condition that he is not bound by any vows, and that he does not have any physical blemishes, although he is indeed bound by vows and has physical blemishes, if he goes to a wise man who nullifies the vows, and if he goes to a physician who heals the blemishes, the marriage is valid. [The rationale is that] there is no shame for a man to have had physical blemishes once they have been healed. A woman will not object because of such a thing.[15]

10. [The following rules apply when a man tells a woman:] "Behold, you are consecrated to me with this [item] on condition that I give you 200 *zuz* within 30 days." If he gives her [the money] within 30 days, she is consecrated. If 30 days pass without him giving it to her, she is not consecrated.

[If a man tells a woman,] "Behold, you are consecrated to me with these *zuz* after 30 days," she is consecrated after 30 days, even though she used the money within the 30 days. If either he or she change their minds [and decide to nullify the marriage] within these 30 days, she is not consecrated.

11. If another man comes and consecrates her within these 30 days, she is consecrated to the second man forever. [The rationale is] that at the time the second man consecrated her, she was not consecrated. Therefore, the second man's *kiddushin* are binding and make her a married woman. Thus, after the 30 days pass and the first man's *kiddushin* are fit to take effect, she is already a married woman. It is thus as if the first man consecrated a married woman, in which case the *kiddushin* are not binding.[16]

12. [The following rules apply when a man] tells a woman: "Behold, you are consecrated to me with this *dinar* from this time onward, and after 30 days," and another person consecrates her within the 30 days. [There is doubt regarding the matter,[17] and] both [men] are considered as having established

The *kiddushin* are binding only when the wise man nullifies the vows before the woman's intended husband discovers their existence. Once he discovers that she is bound by vows, the *kiddushin* are nullified even when she has the vows nullified afterwards (*Shulchan Aruch, Even HaEzer* 39:2).

14. The wording used by the man is significant. If he states: "Behold, you are consecrated on condition that you will not have blemishes," the *kiddushin* are binding if a physician is able to heal her (*Shulchan Aruch, Even HaEzer* 39:7).

15. The Rambam appears to be sharing the interpretation of *Tosafot, Ketubot* 74b, that the reason the *kiddushin* are nullified if a woman has blemishes that a physician heals is that even after she is healed, the husband will still be repelled by the fact that at one time she possessed physical blemishes.

ט קְדָשָׁה עַל מְנָת שֶׁאֵין בָּה מוּמִין, וְהָיוּ בָּהּ מוּמִין, וְהָלְכָה אֵצֶל רוֹפֵא וְרִפְּא אוֹתָהּ — אֵינָהּ מְקֻדֶּשֶׁת.

אֲבָל אִם הִתְנָה הָאִישׁ שֶׁאֵין עָלָיו נְדָרִים וְשֶׁאֵין בּוֹ מוּמִין, וְהָיוּ עָלָיו נְדָרִים וְהָיוּ בּוֹ מוּמִין, וְהָלַךְ אֵצֶל חָכָם וְהִתִּירוֹ, אֵצֶל רוֹפֵא וְרִפְּאוֹ — הֲרֵי זוֹ מְקֻדֶּשֶׁת; שֶׁאֵין גְּנַאי לְאִישׁ בְּמוּמִין שֶׁכְּבָר נִרְפְּאוּ, וְהָאִשָּׁה אֵינָהּ מַקְפֶּדֶת עַל זֹאת.

י הָאוֹמֵר לְאִשָּׁה: הֲרֵי אַתְּ מְקֻדֶּשֶׁת לִי בָּזֶה עַל מְנָת שֶׁאֶתֵּן לִיךְ מָאתַיִם זוּז מִכָּן וְעַד שְׁלֹשִׁים יוֹם:

אִם נָתַן לָהּ בְּתוֹךְ שְׁלֹשִׁים יוֹם — מְקֻדֶּשֶׁת, וְאִם עָבְרוּ שְׁלֹשִׁים יוֹם וְלֹא נָתַן לָהּ — אֵינָהּ מְקֻדֶּשֶׁת.

הֲרֵי אַתְּ מְקֻדֶּשֶׁת לִי בְּזוּזִים אֵלּוּ לְאַחַר שְׁלֹשִׁים יוֹם, אַף־עַל־פִּי שֶׁנִּתְאַכְּלוּ הַמָּעוֹת בְּתוֹךְ שְׁלֹשִׁים יוֹם — הֲרֵי זוֹ מְקֻדֶּשֶׁת לְאַחַר שְׁלֹשִׁים יוֹם.

וְאִם חָזַר בּוֹ בְּתוֹךְ הַשְּׁלֹשִׁים אוֹ חָזְרָה הִיא — אֵינָהּ מְקֻדֶּשֶׁת.

יא בָּא שֵׁנִי וְקִדְּשָׁהּ בְּתוֹךְ שְׁלֹשִׁים יוֹם — הֲרֵי זוֹ מְקֻדֶּשֶׁת לַשֵּׁנִי לְעוֹלָם. לְפִי שֶׁבַּשָּׁעָה שֶׁקִּדְּשָׁהּ הַשֵּׁנִי לֹא הָיְתָה מְקֻדֶּשֶׁת, וְתָפְסוּ בָּהּ קִדּוּשֵׁי שֵׁנִי, וְנַעֲשֵׂית אֵשֶׁת אִישׁ; וּלְאַחַר הַשְּׁלֹשִׁים יוֹם, כְּשֶׁיָּבוֹאוּ קִדּוּשֵׁי רִאשׁוֹן, יִמְצְאוּ אוֹתָהּ אֵשֶׁת אִישׁ, וְנִמְצָא הָרִאשׁוֹן כְּמִי שֶׁקִּדֵּשׁ אֵשֶׁת אִישׁ, שֶׁאֵין הַקִּדּוּשִׁין תּוֹפְסִין בָּהּ.

יב הָאוֹמֵר לְאִשָּׁה: הֲרֵי אַתְּ מְקֻדֶּשֶׁת לִי מֵעַכְשָׁו וּלְאַחַר שְׁלֹשִׁים יוֹם בְּדִינָר זֶה, וּבָא אַחֵר וְקִדְּשָׁהּ בְּתוֹךְ הַשְּׁלֹשִׁים יוֹם — הֲרֵי זוֹ מְקֻדֶּשֶׁת מִסָּפֵק לִשְׁנֵיהֶם.

Rashi, by contrast, explains the difference between a wise man's nullification and a physician's healing as follows: The wise man nullifies the vow at its source, causing it to be considered as never having been taken. Thus, retroactively it is as if the woman had not been bound by a vow at the time of the *kiddushin*. A physician, by contrast, can heal a blemish only within the existence of a continuum of time. Thus, at the time of the *kiddushin*, the woman had physical blemishes. Therefore, the *kiddushin* are not binding.

16. From the Rambam's wording, it would appear that if her second husband died or divorced her within the thirty days, the first man's *kiddushin* are binding. The Rashba (in his gloss on *Kiddushin* 59b) does not accept this premise and states that the woman's acceptance of the second *kiddushin* clearly shows a change in her mind with regard to the first *kiddushin*. For this reason, they are nullified and can never be binding again (*Maggid Mishneh*). (See Ramah and *Tur, Even HaEzer* 40:2.)

17. Rashi, *Kiddushin* 59b, explains that the doubt is whether his statement is a conditional statement, and thus, after 30 days pass the original *kiddushin* will retroactively take effect, thus nullifying the *kiddushin* given her by the second man. Or perhaps by saying "after 30 days," the first man withdrew his initial statement, and his intent was that his *kiddushin* would not be effective until after 30 days. If this were so, the second man's *kiddushin* would be binding.

kiddushin that may possibly be binding. Therefore, both are required to divorce her.[18] The divorce may be given within the [original] 30 days[19] or afterwards.

[Should one man tell a woman,] "Behold, you are consecrated to me from this time onward, and after 30 days"; and another man comes and tells her, "Behold, you are consecrated to me from this time onward, and after 20 days," and another man comes and tells her, "Behold, you are consecrated to me from this time onward, and after 10 days," [there is doubt regarding the matter, and] all [the men] are considered as having established *kiddushin* [that may possibly] be binding, and every one must divorce her. [Indeed, these rules apply] even when a hundred men consecrate her in this manner.

13. When [a man] tells a woman, "Behold, you are consecrated to me [and these *kiddushin* apply to everyone] with the exception of so and so" - i.e., that she should not be forbidden to have relations with him - with regard to everyone else she should be considered a married woman, but with regard to him she should be considered to be single - there is doubt regarding the status of the *kiddushin*.[20]

If, however, he tells her, "Behold, you are consecrated to me on condition that you are permitted to so and so," she is consecrated, and she is forbidden to that person as she is forbidden to all others. [The rationale is that] he has made a condition that is impossible to fulfill.[21]

14. When [a man] gives two *p'rutot* to a woman and tells her: "Behold, you are consecrated to me with one today, and with the other after I divorce you," she is consecrated. When he divorces her, she becomes consecrated to him again[22] until he divorces her a second time, because of the *kiddushin* established by the second *p'rutah*.

If, however, [a man] tells a woman: "Behold, you are consecrated to me with this [item] after I convert," "...after you convert," "...after I become freed [from servitude],"[23] "...after you become freed [from servitude]," "...after your husband dies," or "...after your sister dies,"[24] she is not consecrated. [The rationale is] that he cannot consecrate her now.[25]

Significantly, if a person made a similar statement with regard to a sale, the Rambam rules (*Hilchot Mechirah* 2:9) that this is a conditional statement. Thus, it appears that his ruling here is a stringency, accepted because of the severity of the laws of marriage and divorce.

18. The *Tur* (*Even HaEzer* 40) states that this is necessary only when the woman wants to marry a third person. If she wants to marry either of the individuals who consecrated her, she may do so, provided the other divorces her. Although the *Shulchan Aruch* does not quote this ruling, many later authorities do.

לְפִיכָךְ שְׁנֵיהֶם נוֹתְנִין גֵּט, בֵּין בְּתוֹךְ הַשְּׁלֹשִׁים יוֹם בֵּין לְאַחַר הַשְּׁלֹשִׁים יוֹם.

הֲרֵי אַתְּ מְקֻדֶּשֶׁת לִי מֵעַכְשָׁו וּלְאַחַר שְׁלֹשִׁים יוֹם,

וּבָא אַחֵר וְאָמַר: הֲרֵי אַתְּ מְקֻדֶּשֶׁת לִי מֵעַכְשָׁו וּלְאַחַר עֶשְׂרִים יוֹם,

וּבָא אַחֵר וְאָמַר: הֲרֵי אַתְּ מְקֻדֶּשֶׁת לִי מֵעַכְשָׁו וּלְאַחַר עֲשָׂרָה יָמִים,

אֲפִלּוּ הֵן מֵאָה עַל הַסֵּדֶר הַזֶּה — קִדּוּשֵׁי כֻּלָּן תּוֹפְסִין בָּהּ,

וּצְרִיכָה גֵּט מִכָּל אֶחָד וְאֶחָד, מִפְּנֵי שֶׁהִיא סְפֵק מְקֻדֶּשֶׁת לְכֻלָּן.

יג הָאוֹמֵר לְאִשָּׁה: הֲרֵי אַתְּ מְקֻדֶּשֶׁת לִי חוּץ מִפְּלוֹנִי,

כְּלוֹמַר, שֶׁלֹּא תֵאָסֵר עָלָיו, אֶלָּא תִּהְיֶה אֵשֶׁת אִישׁ עַל כָּל הָעוֹלָם וְלִפְלוֹנִי כִּפְנוּיָה — הֲרֵי זוֹ מְקֻדֶּשֶׁת מִסָּפֵק.

אֲבָל אִם אָמַר לָהּ: הֲרֵי אַתְּ מְקֻדֶּשֶׁת לִי עַל מְנָת שֶׁתִּהְיִי מֻתֶּרֶת לִפְלוֹנִי — הֲרֵי זוֹ מְקֻדֶּשֶׁת,

וְתִהְיֶה אֲסוּרָה עָלָיו כִּשְׁאָר הָעָם, מִפְּנֵי שֶׁהִתְנָה בְּדָבָר שֶׁאִי אֶפְשָׁר לְקַיְּמוֹ.

יד הַנּוֹתֵן שְׁתֵּי פְרוּטוֹת לְאִשָּׁה וְאָמַר לָהּ: הֲרֵי אַתְּ מְקֻדֶּשֶׁת לִי הַיּוֹם בְּאַחַת, וּבְאַחַת לְאַחַר שֶׁאֲגָרְשֵׁךְ — הֲרֵי זוֹ מְקֻדֶּשֶׁת,

וּכְשֶׁיְגָרֵשׁ אוֹתָהּ תִּהְיֶה מְקֻדֶּשֶׁת, עַד שֶׁיְגָרֵשׁ אוֹתָהּ פַּעַם שְׁנִיָּה מִן קִדּוּשֵׁי פְּרוּטָה שְׁנִיָּה.

אֲבָל אִם אָמַר לְאִשָּׁה: הֲרֵי אַתְּ מְקֻדֶּשֶׁת לִי בָּזֶה לְאַחַר שֶׁאֶתְגַּיֵּר, לְאַחַר שֶׁתִּתְגַּיְּרִי, לְאַחַר שֶׁאֶשְׁתַּחְרֵר, לְאַחַר שֶׁתִּשְׁתַּחְרְרִי, לְאַחַר שֶׁיָּמוּת בַּעְלֵיךְ, לְאַחַר שֶׁתָּמוּת אֲחוֹתִיךְ — אֵינָהּ מְקֻדֶּשֶׁת, לְפִי שֶׁאֵינוֹ יָכוֹל עַתָּה לְקַדְּשָׁהּ.

19. Although the *kiddushin* given by the first man do not take effect fully until after 30 days, it is possible for him to divorce her before that date. For when the *kiddushin* take effect, she will be consecrated retroactively from the time of the original *kiddushin*, and then these *kiddushin* will be nullified by the divorce.

20. The doubt centers on whether it is possible to establish a bond of *kiddushin* that is incomplete. This is an unresolved issue. The latter clause states that if a person desires to establish a bond of *kiddushin*, but with a proviso, this is definitely unacceptable. As mentioned by the *Beit Shmuel* 38:68, there are authorities who maintain that the *kiddushin* are not binding at all.

21. For the very nature of the marriage bond forbids relations with another man.

22. In the *Kessef Mishneh* and in the *Shulchan Aruch* (*Even HaEzer* 40:7), Rav Yosef Karo rules that the status of these *kiddushin* is doubtful: the woman cannot marry another person until she is divorced, but she must be consecrated again before the marriage can be consummated.

23. This refers to a Canaanite servant, who cannot marry a Jewish woman. Similarly, a male Jew cannot marry a female Canaanite servant.

24. I.e., the man proposing is married to the woman's sister. While his wife (her sister) is alive, he may not marry the woman. Afterwards, he may.

25. *Kiddushin* 62a explains that at the time the *kiddushin* were given, the possibility of marriage is "something that has not come into the world," for it is impossible for them to take effect. Therefore, even when the situation changes afterwards, they are not effective retroactively.

15. When [a man] tells a *yevamah*: "Behold, you are consecrated to me with this [item] after your *yavam* performs *chalitzah* for you,"[26] she is consecrated. [The rationale is] that even if he consecrated her at present, the *kiddushin* would be [at least] of a doubtful status.[27]

16. When a man tells a friend, "If your wife gives birth to a girl, [the girl] is consecrated to me with this [item]," his statements are of no consequence.[28] If the friend's wife is pregnant, and the existence of a fetus has been recognized, [the girl] is consecrated.[29] [Nevertheless,] it appears to me that [the man] must consecrate [his bride] again via her father after she is born, so that she will enter a marriage bond about which there are no questions.

17. When [a man] tells a woman: "Behold, you are consecrated to me with 100 *dinarim*," and gives her at least one *dinar*, she is consecrated, provided he gives her the entire sum. It is as if he told her, "Behold, you are consecrated to me with this *dinar* on condition that I give you 100 *dinarim*." [In such an instance,] the *kiddushin* take effect from [the time he gave her the first *dinar*].

When does the above apply? When he told her "with 100 *dinarim*" without specifying [any particular *dinarim*]. If, however, he is more explicit and tells her, "Behold, you are consecrated to me with these 100 *dinarim*," and begins counting them out into her hand, she is not consecrated until he gives her [all 100].[30] Either of them may retract their consent until the very last *dinar* is given.

Similarly, if one of the *dinarim* was found lacking the standard weight, or one was a *dinar* of brass, she is not consecrated.[31] [The following rules apply when] one of the *dinarim* was inferior: If it would be accepted with difficulty, [the *kiddushin* are valid, provided][32] he exchanges it. If it would not [be accepted], the *kiddushin* are of no consequence.

18. [The following rules apply when a man] tells [a woman]: "Behold, you are consecrated to me with these clothes that are worth 50 *dinarim*." When they are silk or of similar fabrics that a woman would desire,[33] and they are worth

---

26. I.e., when a woman's husband dies childless, she is obligated to marry his brother (referred to as a *yavam*) through the rite of *yibbum*, or be freed of her obligation to him through the rite of *chalitzah*. The Rambam is describing a situation in which another man gives her *kiddushin* with the expectation that *chalitzah* will be performed.

27. See Chapter 4, Halachah 14. Since the *kiddushin* a person gave her now would have some effect, *kiddushin* given with a conditional statement are binding totally.

The *Shulchan Aruch* (*Even HaEzer* 40:6) rules that even when a conditional statement is made, the status of the *kiddushin* is in doubt. There are some manuscripts of the *Mishneh Torah* that indicate that the Rambam also shared that view.

28. For the object of the *kiddushin* does not yet exist.

טו הָאוֹמֵר לִיבָמָה: הֲרֵי אַתְּ מְקֻדֶּשֶׁת לִי בָּזֶה לְאַחַר שֶׁיַּחֲלֹץ לִיךְ יְבָמִיךְ — הֲרֵי זוֹ מְקֻדֶּשֶׁת; הוֹאִיל וְאִלּוּ קִדְּשָׁהּ עַתָּה, הָיוּ קִדּוּשִׁין תּוֹפְסִין בָּהּ מִסָּפֵק.

טז הָאוֹמֵר לַחֲבֵרוֹ: אִם יָלְדָה אִשְׁתְּךָ נְקֵבָה הֲרֵי הִיא מְקֻדֶּשֶׁת לִי בָּזֶה — לֹא אָמַר כְּלוּם. וְאִם הָיְתָה אֵשֶׁת חֲבֵרוֹ מְעֻבֶּרֶת וְהֻכַּר הָעֻבָּר — הֲרֵי זוֹ מְקֻדֶּשֶׁת. וְיֵרָאֶה לִי, שֶׁצָּרִיךְ לַחֲזֹר וּלְקַדֵּשׁ אוֹתָהּ אַחַר שֶׁתֵּלֵד עַל יְדֵי אָבִיהָ, כְּדֵי שֶׁיַּכְנִיס אוֹתָהּ בְּקִדּוּשִׁין שֶׁאֵין בָּהֶן דֹּפִי.

יז הָאוֹמֵר לְאִשָּׁה: הֲרֵי אַתְּ מְקֻדֶּשֶׁת לִי בְּמֵאָה דִינָרִין, וְנָתַן לָהּ אֲפִלּוּ דִּינָר אֶחָד — הֲרֵי זוֹ מְקֻדֶּשֶׁת מִשֶּׁלְּקָחָה הַדִּינָר. וְהוּא, שֶׁיַּשְׁלִים לָהּ הַשְּׁאָר. שֶׁזֶּה כְּמִי שֶׁאָמַר: הֲרֵי אַתְּ מְקֻדֶּשֶׁת לִי בְּדִינָר זֶה עַל מְנָת שֶׁאַשְׁלִים לִיךְ מֵאָה דִינָרִים, שֶׁהִיא מְקֻדֶּשֶׁת לוֹ מֵעַכְשָׁו. בַּמֶּה דְבָרִים אֲמוּרִים? כְּשֶׁאָמַר לָהּ 'בְּמֵאָה דִינָרִים' סְתָם; אֲבָל אִם פֵּרַשׁ וְאָמַר לָהּ: הֲרֵי אַתְּ מְקֻדֶּשֶׁת לִי בְּמֵאָה דִינָרִין אֵלּוּ, וְהִתְחִיל לִמְנוֹת לְתוֹךְ יָדָהּ — אֵינָהּ מְקֻדֶּשֶׁת עַד שֶׁיַּשְׁלִים [לָהּ מֵאָה], וַאֲפִלּוּ בַּדִּינָר הָאַחֲרוֹן שְׁנֵיהֶם יְכוֹלִים לַחֲזֹר זֶה בָּזֶה. וְכֵן אִם נִמְצָא מָנֶה חָסֵר דִּינָר, אוֹ נִמְצָא מֵהֶן דִּינָר נְחֹשֶׁת — אֵינָהּ מְקֻדֶּשֶׁת. נִמְצָא בָהֶם דִּינָר רַע: אִם יְכוֹלָה לְהוֹצִיאוֹ עַל יְדֵי הַדְּחָק — יַחֲלִיפֶנּוּ, וְאִם לָאו — אֵינָהּ מְקֻדֶּשֶׁת.

יח אָמַר לָהּ: הֲרֵי אַתְּ מְקֻדֶּשֶׁת לִי בִּבְגָדִים אֵלּוּ שֶׁהֵן שָׁוִין חֲמִשִּׁים דִּינָרִים, וְהָיוּ שֶׁל מֶשִׁי וְכַיּוֹצֵא בָּהֶן שֶׁהָאִשָּׁה מִתְאַוָּה לָהֶן:

---

29. The Ra'avad, the *Maggid Mishneh* and the *Kessef Mishneh* interpret the Rambam as stating that the *kiddushin* given for the fetus are definitely binding. In his Commentary on the Mishnah (*Kiddushin* 3:5), however, the Rambam explicitly states that this is a Rabbinic stringency, enforced because of the severity of the laws of marriage.
30. Since he began counting them out for her, she is under the impression that she will receive the entire sum, and will not accept less (*Kiddushin* 8a).
31. For she accepted the *kiddushin* under the impression that all 100 *dinarim* were of full value. Nor can he give her a different *dinar*, because he specified that the *kiddushin* would be with the coins he was giving her. Even if neither the man nor the woman retracts, the *kiddushin* are not binding (*Maggid Mishneh*). (See Ramah, *Even HaEzer* 29:7.)
32. The Ra'avad objects to this ruling, explaining that even though the man is obligated to exchange the *dinar*, the *kiddushin* are binding whether or not he does so. The *Shulchan Aruch* (*Even HaEzer* 29:7) quotes the Ra'avad's ruling.
33. The Rambam's wording appears to indicate that the reason no evaluation is necessary is that women usually desire silk, and because of this desire waive the need for evaluation. Implied is that other items that are not that desirable must be evaluated before the *kiddushin* are binding. The *Shulchan Aruch* (*Even HaEzer* 31:1) does not follow this approach. (See *Beit Shmuel* 31:1.)

50 [*dinarim*], the woman is consecrated from the time she took them onward. There is no need that they be evaluated in the market, and only afterwards, when the woman is assured [of their value], will she be consecrated. Instead, since they are worth the amount he states, she is consecrated from the time of the initial [exchange]. If they are not worth [that amount], she is not consecrated.

19. A man and a woman were discussing the subject of their consecration, he saying: "I will consecrate you with 100 *dinarim*," and she saying: "I will not be consecrated for less than 200 [*dinarim*]." [Since they did not agree,] they both went home.

[The following rules apply when] afterwards, [either the man or the woman requested the other [to reconsider], and the man consecrated her without specifying a sum. If the man made the request of the woman, the sum [originally] quoted by the woman is accepted. If the woman made the request of the man, the sum [originally] quoted by the man is accepted.

20. When a man appoints an agent to consecrate a woman, and the agent consecrates her on the basis of a conditional agreement, the *kiddushin* are not valid.[34] Similarly, if [the principal] instructed the agent to consecrate the woman on the basis of a conditional agreement, and he consecrated her without making any stipulation whatsoever, or made another stipulation or changed the stipulation stated by the principal, the *kiddushin* are not valid.

21. When [the principal] tells the agent: "Consecrate her in this and this place," and the agent consecrated her in another place, the *kiddushin* are not valid.[35] [If the principal tells the agent:] "Consecrate her for me. She is in this and this place," and the agent goes and consecrates her in another place, she is consecrated; he is merely suggesting to him the place [where she might be found].

Similarly, if [the woman] tells her agent, "Receive *kiddushin* for me in this and this place," and the agent received them for her in another place, the *kiddushin* are not valid. [If she told her agent: "Receive *kiddushin* for me. My prospective] husband is in this and this place," and [the agent] receives the *kiddushin* in another place, she is consecrated; she is merely suggesting to him the place [where he might be found].

22. When [a man] consecrates a woman, but he or she desires to retract immediately - even if the retraction is made within a very short amount of time[36] - the retraction is of no consequence and the woman is consecrated.[37]

Tosafot, Kiddushin 7b, offer a different rationale for the mention of silk: Most people can make at least a rough evaluation of the value of silk. When, however, an object cannot

אִם הָיוּ שָׁוִין חֲמִשִּׁים — הֲרֵי זוֹ מְקֻדֶּשֶׁת מִשָּׁעַת לְקִיחָה,
וְאֵינָן צְרִיכִין שׁוּמָא בַּשּׁוּק וְאַחַר כָּךְ תִּהְיֶה מְקֻדֶּשֶׁת, כְּדֵי שֶׁתִּסְמֹךְ דַּעְתָּהּ,
אֶלָּא הוֹאִיל וְהֵן שָׁוִין כְּמוֹ שֶׁאָמַר לָהּ — הֲרֵי זוֹ מְקֻדֶּשֶׁת מִשָּׁעָה רִאשׁוֹנָה;
וְאִם אֵינָן שָׁוִין — אֵינָהּ מְקֻדֶּשֶׁת.

יט אִישׁ וְאִשָּׁה שֶׁהָיוּ עֲסוּקִין בְּדִבְרֵי אֵרוּסִין, הוּא אוֹמֵר: בְּמֵאָה דִּינָרִים אֲקַדֵּשׁ אוֹתָךְ,
וְהִיא אוֹמֶרֶת: אֵינִי מִתְקַדֶּשֶׁת לְךָ אֶלָּא בְּמָאתַיִם, וְהָלַךְ זֶה לְבֵיתוֹ וְזוֹ לְבֵיתָהּ, וְאַחַר כָּךְ
תְּבָעוּ זֶה אֶת זֶה וְקִדְּשׁוּ סְתָם:
אִם הָאִישׁ תָּבַע אֶת הָאִשָּׁה — יַעֲשׂוּ דִּבְרֵי הָאִשָּׁה,
וְאִם הָאִשָּׁה תָּבְעָה אֶת הָאִישׁ — יַעֲשׂוּ דִּבְרֵי הָאִישׁ.

כ הָעוֹשֶׂה שָׁלִיחַ לְקַדֵּשׁ לוֹ אִשָּׁה, וְהָלַךְ הַשָּׁלִיחַ וְקִדְּשָׁהּ עַל תְּנַאי — אֵינָהּ מְקֻדֶּשֶׁת.
וְכֵן אִם אָמַר לוֹ לְקַדְּשָׁהּ עַל תְּנַאי, וְהָלַךְ וְקִדְּשָׁהּ סְתָם, אוֹ עַל תְּנַאי אַחֵר, אוֹ שֶׁשִּׁנָּה אֶת
הַתְּנַאי — אֵינָהּ מְקֻדֶּשֶׁת.

כא אָמַר לוֹ: קַדְּשָׁהּ לִי בְּמָקוֹם פְּלוֹנִי, וְהָלַךְ וְקִדְּשָׁהּ בְּמָקוֹם אַחֵר — אֵינָהּ מְקֻדֶּשֶׁת.
קַדְּשָׁהּ לִי וַהֲרֵי הִיא בְּמָקוֹם פְּלוֹנִי, וְהָלַךְ וְקִדְּשָׁהּ בְּמָקוֹם אַחֵר — הֲרֵי זוֹ מְקֻדֶּשֶׁת, מִפְּנֵי
שֶׁמַּרְאֶה מָקוֹם הוּא לוֹ.
וְכֵן הִיא שֶׁאָמְרָה לִשְׁלוּחָהּ: קַבֵּל לִי קִדּוּשַׁי בְּמָקוֹם פְּלוֹנִי, וְקִבְּלָם לָהּ בְּמָקוֹם אַחֵר — אֵינָהּ
מְקֻדֶּשֶׁת.
הֲרֵי הַבַּעַל בְּמָקוֹם פְּלוֹנִי, וְקִבֵּל לָהּ בְּמָקוֹם אַחֵר — הֲרֵי זוֹ מְקֻדֶּשֶׁת, מִפְּנֵי שֶׁמַּרְאָה מָקוֹם
הִיא לוֹ.

כב הַמְקַדֵּשׁ אֶת הָאִשָּׁה וְחָזְרוּ בוֹ מִיָּד הוּא אוֹ הִיא, אַף־עַל־פִּי שֶׁחָזְרוּ בְּתוֹךְ כְּדֵי דִּבּוּר
— אֵין חֲזָרָתָם כְּלוּם, וַהֲרֵי הִיא מְקֻדֶּשֶׁת.

---

be evaluated easily - e.g., a precious stone - a woman is not consecrated, because she is unsure of the value of the gem until she receives an expert's appraisal. This is one of the sources for the custom of consecrating a woman with a wedding ring that does not contain a stone.

34. For by entering into a conditional agreement when he was not instructed to do so by the principal, the agent deviated from the instructions he was given. As such he is acting on his own initiative, and not as the agent of the principal.

35. Here also, the reason is that the agent deviated from the instructions he was given.

36. Here the intent is a specific measure of time, the amount of time it takes to say: *Shalom alecha, rabbi umori.*

37. *Nedarim* 87a states that with the exception of idol worship, marriage and divorce, a retraction made within the abovementioned span of time is reckoned with. Why are these three instances different? In general, a person is not precise with regard to what he says and may make statements, relying on the possibility of retracting them later.

23. When [a man] consecrates [a woman] and attaches a condition [to the *kiddushin*], and after several days changes his mind and nullifies the condition, the condition is of no consequence and it is as if the woman had been consecrated without any condition ever having been made. [This law applies] even when he nullifies the condition in the presence of his intended bride alone, without this being observed by witnesses. Similarly, if the woman was the one who attached a condition to the *kiddushin*, and afterwards nullified it in the presence of her prospective husband alone, the condition is of no consequence.[38]

Therefore, if [a man] consecrated [a woman] and attached a condition [to the *kiddushin*], and afterwards, brought her [to the *chuppah*] without mentioning the condition, or engaged in sexual relations with her without mentioning the condition, she must receive a divorce [before she marries another man][39] even though the condition was never fulfilled. [The rationale is that] perhaps [the man] nullified the condition when he brought her [to the *chuppah*] or when he engaged in sexual relations with her.

Similarly, when [a man] consecrates a woman with [an article] worth less than a *p'rutah* or with a loan, and then engages in sexual relations [with this woman] in the presence of witnesses, without making a statement of intent, the woman must receive a divorce [before she marries another man]. [The rationale is that] perhaps [the man intended to consecrate her through these relations] and relied on them, rather than on the *kiddushin* that are inadequate.

[The principle on which these rulings depend is:] It is an accepted presumption that no virtuous Jewish man will enter into sexual relations that are wanton when he has the potential to engage in these relations in a way that is a mitzvah.[40]

CHAPTER EIGHT

1. When [a man] tells a woman: "Behold, you are consecrated to me with this cup of wine," and the cup is discovered to contain honey [she is not consecrated]. [Similarly, if he tells her: "...Behold, you are consecrated to me with this cup] of honey," and the cup is discovered to contain wine;[1] "...with this *dinar* of silver," and it is discovered to be gold; "...[with this *dinar*] of gold," and it is discovered to be silver; "...on condition that I am a priest," and he was discovered to be a Levite; "[on condition that I am]

In these three instances, however, the severity of the matter is obvious, and a person would not make such statements unless he made them with full presence of mind (Rabbenu Nissim). (See also the Rambam's Commentary on the Mishnah, *Temurah* 5:3, which mentions several other instances in which a person's retraction is of no consequence.)

כג הַמְקַדֵּשׁ עַל תְּנַאי, וְחָזַר אַחַר כַּמָּה יָמִים וּבִטֵּל הַתְּנַאי, אַף־עַל־פִּי שֶׁבִּטְּלוֹ בֵּינוֹ לְבֵינָהּ שֶׁלֹּא בִּפְנֵי עֵדִים — בָּטֵל הַתְּנַאי, וַהֲרֵי הִיא מְקֻדֶּשֶׁת סְתָם.

וְכֵן אִם הָיָה הַתְּנַאי מִן הָאִשָּׁה, וּבִטְּלָה אוֹתוֹ אַחַר כָּךְ בֵּינָהּ וּבֵינוֹ — בָּטֵל הַתְּנַאי.

לְפִיכָךְ, הַמְקַדֵּשׁ עַל תְּנַאי, וְכָנַס סְתָם אוֹ בָּעַל סְתָם — הֲרֵי זוֹ צְרִיכָה גֵּט, אַף־עַל־פִּי שֶׁלֹּא נִתְקַיֵּם הַתְּנַאי;

שֶׁמָּא בִּטֵּל הַתְּנַאי כְּשֶׁבָּעַל אוֹ כְּשֶׁכָּנַס.

וְכֵן הַמְקַדֵּשׁ בְּפָחוֹת מִשָּׁוֶה פְּרוּטָה אוֹ בְּמִלְוֶה, וְחָזַר וּבָעַל סְתָם בִּפְנֵי עֵדִים — צְרִיכָה גֵּט; שֶׁעַל בְּעִילָה זוֹ סָמַךְ, וְלֹא עַל אוֹתָן הַקִּדּוּשִׁין הַפְּסוּלִין.

חֲזָקָה הִיא, שֶׁאֵין אָדָם מִיִּשְׂרָאֵל הַכְּשֵׁרִים עוֹשֶׂה בְּעִילָתוֹ בְּעִילַת זְנוּת, וַהֲרֵי בְּיָדוֹ עַתָּה לַעֲשׂוֹתָהּ בְּעִילַת מִצְוָה.

פֶּרֶק שְׁמִינִי

א הָאוֹמֵר לְאִשָּׁה: הֲרֵי אַתְּ מְקֻדֶּשֶׁת לִי בְּכוֹס זֶה שֶׁל יַיִן, וְנִמְצָא שֶׁל דְּבַשׁ;

שֶׁל דְּבַשׁ, וְנִמְצָא שֶׁל יַיִן;

בְּדִינָר זֶה שֶׁל כֶּסֶף, וְנִמְצָא שֶׁל זָהָב;

שֶׁל זָהָב, וְנִמְצָא שֶׁל כֶּסֶף;

עַל מְנָת שֶׁאֲנִי כֹּהֵן, וְנִמְצָא לֵוִי;

38. The Ra'avad objects to the Rambam's ruling, maintaining that the nullification of the condition must also be made in the presence of witnesses. (He does, however, accept the Rambam's decision that if a man brings the woman to the *chuppah*, without a condition, in the presence of witnesses, the condition is considered to be nullified. For his act is considered equivalent to nullifying the condition.)

The Rashba accepts the Rambam's ruling with regard to conditions involving money - e.g., "Behold, you are consecrated on condition that you give me 200 *zuz*." For a person may waive a debt owed him, and consider it as received. With regard to other conditions - e.g., "Behold, you are consecrated on condition that you are not bound by vows" - he does not accept the Rambam's position. The *Shulchan Aruch* (*Even HaEzer* 38:35) quotes the Rambam's ruling.

39. I.e., the status of the *kiddushin* originally given is doubtful. If the couple want to continue living together, they must establish *kiddushin* that are unquestionably binding. And if a second man consecrates her, she must receive a divorce from both men before marrying a third (Ramah, *Even HaEzer* 38:35).

40. In one of his responsa, the Rambam states that this principle cannot be extended without limit. When a man and a woman engage in sexual relations with a promiscuous intent, we do not say that he intends to consecrate her with these relations. The principle stated above is applied only when there is reason to presume that the man desired to establish a marriage relationship. (See also *Hilchot Gerushin* 10:19.)

1. Even though honey is more valuable than wine, the *kiddushin* are not binding, because the stipulation was not fulfilled, and it is possible that the woman indeed desired wine

a Levite," and he was discovered to be a priest; "...[on condition that I am] a Givonite,"[2] and he was discovered to be a bastard; "...[on condition that I am] a bastard," and he was discovered to be a Givonite; "...[on condition that I am] an inhabitant of a town," and he was discovered to be an inhabitant of a metropolis; "...[on condition that I am] an inhabitant of a metropolis," and he was discovered to be an inhabitant of a town; "...on condition that I am poor," and he was discovered to be rich; "...[on condition that I am] rich," and he was discovered to be poor; "...on condition that my house is close to the bathhouse," and it is discovered to be distant from it; "...[on condition that my house is] distant from the bathhouse," and it is discovered to be close to it; "...on condition that I have a maid," "...a daughter who knows how to braid hair," or "...who bakes," and [it is discovered that] he does not have one; "...on condition that he does not have [one of the above], and [it is discovered that] he does; "...on condition that he has a wife and children," and [it is discovered that] he does not; "...on condition that he does not have [the above], and [it is discovered that] he does - in all these and in any similar instance, the woman is not consecrated. The same rule applies if she [makes a condition based on] false information.

2. In all the above instances, she is not consecrated even though she says: "In my heart, I was willing to be consecrated to him even though he deceived me and gave me wrong information." Similarly, [if she gave him false information,] she is not consecrated even though he says: "In my heart, I was willing to consecrate her even though she deceived me." [The rationale is that] feelings in one's heart are not [the same as explicit] statements.

3. [When a man tells a woman:] "Behold, you are consecrated to me on condition that I am a perfumer," and it is discovered that he is both a perfumer and a leather craftsman;[3] "...on condition that I am an inhabitant of a town," and he was discovered to be an inhabitant of both a town and a metropolis;[4] or "...on condition that my name is Yosef," and it was discovered that his name was Yosef and Shimon; she is consecrated.

If, however, he told her: "[Behold, you are consecrated to me] on condition that my name is only Yosef," and it was discovered that his name was Yosef and Shimon; "...on condition that I am solely a perfumer," and it is discovered that he is both a perfumer and a leather craftsman; or "...on condition that I am solely an inhabitant of a town," and he was discovered to be an inhabitant of both a town and a metropolis; she is not consecrated.

4. When [a man] tells a woman: "Behold, you are consecrated to me on condition that I know how to read," [for the stipulation to be fulfilled] it is necessary that he know how to read from the Torah and translate what he reads according to the translation of Onkelos the convert.

לֵוִי, וְנִמְצָא כֹהֵן;

נָתִין, וְנִמְצָא מַמְזֵר;

מַמְזֵר, וְנִמְצָא נָתִין;

בֶּן עִיר, וְנִמְצָא בֶּן כְּרַךְ;

בֶּן כְּרַךְ, וְנִמְצָא בֶּן עִיר;

עַל מְנָת שֶׁאֲנִי עָנִי, וְנִמְצָא עָשִׁיר;

עָשִׁיר, וְנִמְצָא עָנִי;

עַל מְנָת שֶׁבֵּיתִי קָרוֹב לַמֶּרְחָץ, וְנִמְצָא רָחוֹק;

רָחוֹק, וְנִמְצָא קָרוֹב;

עַל מְנָת שֶׁיֵּשׁ לִי שִׁפְחָה אוֹ בַּת גּוֹדֶלֶת אוֹ אוֹפָה, וְאֵין לוֹ;

עַל מְנָת שֶׁאֵין לוֹ, וְיֵשׁ לוֹ;

עַל מְנָת שֶׁיֵּשׁ לִי אִשָּׁה וּבָנִים, וְאֵין לוֹ;

עַל מְנָת שֶׁאֵין לִי, וְיֵשׁ לוֹ —

בְּכָל אֵלּוּ וְכָל הַדּוֹמֶה לָהֶן אֵינָהּ מְקֻדֶּשֶׁת.

וְכֵן הִיא שֶׁהִטְעַתּוּ.

ב וּבְכֻלָּם, אַף־עַל־פִּי שֶׁאָמְרָה: בְּלִבִּי הָיָה לְהִתְקַדֵּשׁ לוֹ אַף־עַל־פִּי שֶׁהִטְעַנִי וְאֵין הַדָּבָר כְּמוֹ שֶׁאָמַר,

וְכֵן אִם אָמַר הוּא: בְּלִבִּי הָיָה לְקַדְּשָׁהּ אַף־עַל־פִּי שֶׁהִטְעַתְנִי — אֵינָהּ מְקֻדֶּשֶׁת, לְפִי שֶׁהַדְּבָרִים שֶׁבַּלֵּב אֵינָם דְּבָרִים.

ג הֲרֵי אַתְּ מְקֻדֶּשֶׁת לִי עַל מְנָת שֶׁאֲנִי בַּסָּם, וְנִמְצָא בַּסָּם וּבֻרְסִי;

עַל מְנָת שֶׁאֲנִי בֶּן עִיר, וְנִמְצָא בֶּן עִיר וּבֶן כְּרַךְ;

עַל מְנָת שֶׁשְּׁמִי יוֹסֵף, וְנִמְצָא שְׁמוֹ יוֹסֵף וְשִׁמְעוֹן — הֲרֵי זוֹ מְקֻדֶּשֶׁת.

אֲבָל אִם אָמַר לָהּ: עַל מְנָת שֶׁאֵין שְׁמִי אֶלָּא יוֹסֵף, וְנִמְצָא שְׁמוֹ יוֹסֵף וְשִׁמְעוֹן;

שֶׁאֵינִי אֶלָּא בַּסָּם, וְנִמְצָא בַּסָּם וּבֻרְסִי;

שֶׁאֵינִי אֶלָּא בֶּן עִיר, וְנִמְצָא בֶּן כְּרַךְ וּבֶן עִיר — אֵינָהּ מְקֻדֶּשֶׁת.

ד הָאוֹמֵר לְאִשָּׁה: הֲרֵי אַתְּ מְקֻדֶּשֶׁת לִי עַל מְנָת שֶׁאֲנִי יוֹדֵעַ לִקְרוֹת, צָרִיךְ שֶׁיִּקְרָא הַתּוֹרָה וִיתַרְגֵּם אוֹתָהּ תַּרְגּוּם אֻנְקְלוֹס הַגֵּר.

rather than honey. Similarly, with regard to the sets that follow, *Kiddushin* (48b ff) explains reasons why it is possible to say that the woman favored either of the alternatives, and she is therefore not consecrated unless the stipulation that is made is met.

2. Who, like bastards, are forbidden to marry into the Jewish people. (See the notes on Chapter 1, Halachah 7.)

3. Animal feces were used in the processing of leather, and thus leather craftsmen were known for their unpleasant odor.

4. I.e., he maintains two homes.

If he tells her: "...on condition that I am a reader," he must know how to read the Torah, the works of the Prophets and the Holy Writings with proper grammatical precision. [If he tells her:] "...on condition that I know how to study the Mishnah," he must know how to read the Mishnah. "...On condition that I am a sage of the Mishnah," he must know how to read the Mishnah, the *Sifra*,[5] the *Sifre*,[6] and the *Tosefta* of Rabbi Chiyya.[7]

5. [When a man tells a woman: "Behold, you are consecrated to me] on condition that I am a student [of the Torah]," we do not say that [he must be a student] of the caliber of ben Azzai and ben Zoma.[8] Instead, it is sufficient that when one asks him a question regarding his studies, he is able to answer. [This includes] even the laws of the festivals that are studied in public; these are easy matters that are studied close to the festival, so that people at large will be familiar with them.

[When a man tells a woman: "Behold, you are consecrated to me] on condition that I am a wise man," we do not say that [he must be] like Rabbi Akiva and his colleagues. Instead, it is sufficient that when one asks him a point of logic with regard to any subject, he is able to answer. "...On condition that I am mighty," we do not say that [he must be] like Avner ben Ner[9] or Yoav.[10] Rather, it is sufficient that his colleagues fear him because of his might. "...On condition that I am rich," we do not say that [he must be as wealthy] as Rabbi Eleazar ben Azariah.[11] Rather, it is sufficient that the inhabitants of his city honor him because of his wealth.

[When a man tells a woman: "Behold, you are consecrated to me] on condition that I am righteous," even if the person is known to be thoroughly wicked, there is doubt [regarding the status of the *kiddushin*, and] the woman is considered as consecrated. For it is possible that he had thoughts of repentance in his heart at that time.[12]

"...On condition that I am wicked," even if the person is known to be thoroughly righteous, there is doubt [regarding the status of the *kiddushin*, and] the woman is considered as consecrated, since it is possible that he had thoughts of idol worship in his heart at that time. For the sin of idol worship is so great that even when a person thinks of serving [idols] in his heart,[13] he is considered wicked, as [implied by Deuteronomy 11:16, which] states: "lest your hearts be tempted [and you go astray and serve other gods]," and [Ezekiel 14:5, which] states: "that I may detect the House of Israel, [seeing what is] in their hearts [for they are all estranged from Me because of their idols]."

5. A compendium of halachic exegesis of the Book of Leviticus, composed by Rav, a student of Rabbi Yehudah HaNasi, who compiled the Mishnah. Rav was the leader of the first generation of Amoraim in Babylonia.
6. A compendium of the halachic exegesis of the Books of Numbers and Deuteronomy, composed by Rav.

וְאִם אָמַר לָהּ: עַל מְנָת שֶׁאֲנִי קוֹרֵא, צָרִיךְ לִהְיוֹת יוֹדֵעַ לִקְרוֹת תּוֹרָה נְבִיאִים וּכְתוּבִים בְּדִקְדּוּק יָפֶה.

עַל מְנָת שֶׁאֲנִי יוֹדֵעַ לִשְׁנוֹת, צָרִיךְ לִהְיוֹת יוֹדֵעַ לִקְרוֹת הַמִּשְׁנָה.

וְאִם אָמַר: עַל מְנָת שֶׁאֲנִי תַּנָּאָה, צָרִיךְ לִהְיוֹת יוֹדֵעַ לִקְרוֹת הַמִּשְׁנָה וְסִפְרָא וְסִפְרֵי וְתוֹסֶפְתָּא שֶׁל רַבִּי חִיָּא.

ה עַל מְנָת שֶׁאֲנִי תַּלְמִיד — אֵין אוֹמְרִין: כְּבֶן עַזַּאי וּבֶן זוֹמָא, אֶלָּא כֹּל שֶׁשּׁוֹאֲלִין אוֹתוֹ דָּבָר אֶחָד בְּתַלְמוּדוֹ וְאוֹמְרוֹ;

וַאֲפִלּוּ בְּהִלְכוֹת הֶחָג, שֶׁמְּלַמְּדִין אוֹתָן בְּרַבִּים מִדְּבָרִים הַקַּלִּים סָמוּךְ לֶחָג, כְּדֵי שֶׁיִּהְיוּ כָל הָעָם בְּקִיאִין בָּהֶן.

עַל מְנָת שֶׁאֲנִי חָכָם — אֵין אוֹמְרִין: כְּרַבִּי עֲקִיבָא וַחֲבֵרָיו, אֶלָּא כֹּל שֶׁשּׁוֹאֲלִין אוֹתוֹ בְּכָל מָקוֹם דְּבַר חָכְמָה וְאוֹמֵר.

עַל מְנָת שֶׁאֲנִי גִבּוֹר — אֵין אוֹמְרִין: כְּאַבְנֵר בֶּן נֵר וּכְיוֹאָב, אֶלָּא כֹּל שֶׁחֲבֵרָיו מִתְיָרְאִים מִמֶּנּוּ מִפְּנֵי גְבוּרָתוֹ.

עַל מְנָת שֶׁאֲנִי עָשִׁיר — אֵין אוֹמְרִין: [כְּרַבִּי אֶלְעָזָר בֶּן חַרְסוֹם] וּכְרַבִּי אֶלְעָזָר בֶּן עֲזַרְיָה, אֶלָּא כֹּל שֶׁבְּנֵי עִירוֹ מְכַבְּדִין אוֹתוֹ מִפְּנֵי עָשְׁרוֹ.

עַל מְנָת שֶׁאֲנִי צַדִּיק — אֲפִלּוּ רָשָׁע גָּמוּר, הֲרֵי זוֹ מְקֻדֶּשֶׁת מִסָּפֵק, שֶׁמָּא הִרְהֵר תְּשׁוּבָה בְּלִבּוֹ.

עַל מְנָת שֶׁאֲנִי רָשָׁע — אֲפִלּוּ צַדִּיק גָּמוּר, הֲרֵי זוֹ מְקֻדֶּשֶׁת מִסָּפֵק, שֶׁמָּא הִרְהֵר בַּעֲבוֹדַת כּוֹכָבִים וּמַזָּלוֹת בְּלִבּוֹ;

שֶׁעֲוֹן עֲבוֹדַת כּוֹכָבִים וּמַזָּלוֹת גָּדוֹל הוּא, וּמִשֶּׁיְּהַרְהֵר לַעֲבֹד בְּלִבּוֹ נַעֲשֶׂה רָשָׁע, שֶׁנֶּאֱמַר: פֶּן יִפְתֶּה לְבַבְכֶם,

וְכָתוּב: לְמַעַן תְּפֹשׂ אֶת בֵּית יִשְׂרָאֵל בְּלִבָּם.

7. A collection of teachings intended to "explain the Mishnah and expound upon concepts that would require much effort to be derived from the Mishnah." Rabbi Chiyya was one of Rabbi Yehudah HaNasi's primary disciples.

8. Students of Rabbi Akiva, renowned for their scholarship in their youth. Their promising futures were effaced after they entered a mystical experience together with their master. (See *Chaggigah* 14b.)

9. The commander of King Saul's armies.

10. Yoav ben Tz'ruyah, the commander of King David's armies.

11. Who was renowned for his wealth. Each year he would give 12,000 calves as the tithes of his herd (*Shabbat* 54b). Another version of the text also mentions Elazar ben Chersom whose wealth is described in *Yoma* 35b.

12. The doubt exists only because we cannot be aware of what is happening within the person's heart or mind. If we could be sure that he had repented within his heart, he is considered a righteous man, regardless of his previous conduct. This demonstrates the power of *teshuvah*, how one thought of repentance can transform one's spiritual level from one extreme to the other.

13. In general, a person is not punished for a sin unless he commits a deed. The worship of

6. [When a man] consecrates a woman and says, "I thought she was from a priestly family, and instead she is from a family of Levites," "...from a family of Levites, and instead she is from a priestly family," "...poor, and instead she is rich," or "...rich, and instead she is poor," she is consecrated, for she did not cause him to err.[14]

Similarly, if she says, "I thought he was a priest, and instead he is a Levite," "...a Levite, and instead he is a priest," "...poor, and instead he is rich," or "...rich, and instead he is poor," she is consecrated, for he did not cause her to err.

CHAPTER NINE

1. [When a man] consecrates two women whom he is forbidden to marry at the same time, because it creates a prohibited relationship, neither is consecrated. What is implied? When a man consecrates a woman and her daughter or two sisters at the same time, neither of them is consecrated.

2. [The following rule applies when a man] consecrates many women at the same time and says: "Behold, all of you are consecrated to me." If among [these women] were two sisters, a woman and her daughter or the like, none of the women is consecrated.[1]

If [the man] told [the women]: "Those of you who are fit to engage in marital relations with me are consecrated to me," they are all consecrated to him, except the sisters, the mother and her daughter or the like.

Similarly, if [a man] told [a group of women], "Behold, all of you are consecrated to me," and among [these women] was a Canaanite maidservant, a non-Jewish woman or a woman who is forbidden to this man as an *ervah* - e.g., a married woman, his daughter, his sister or the like - none of them is consecrated to him. If he says: "Those of you who are fit to engage in marital relations with me are consecrated to me," they are all consecrated to him, except the women with whom he cannot establish *kiddushin*.

---

false gods is different. (See *Hilchot Avodat Kochavim* 2:6, which states: "Whoever accepts a false god as true, even when he does not actually worship it, disgraces and blasphemes [God's] glorious and awesome name." See also *Hilchot Avodat Kochavim* 2:1,3.)
14. Since he did not explicitly state the matter as a stipulation, his misconception does not cause the *kiddushin* to be nullified.

1. Since all the women were included in the same statement without differentiating between any of them, none is consecrated.
The *Maggid Mishneh* notes that *Kiddushin* 51a equates this law with the following ruling: When one person tells another, "You and this animal will acquire this object," the person

ו הַמְקַדֵּשׁ אֶת הָאִשָּׁה, וְאָמַר: הָיִיתִי סָבוּר שֶׁהִיא כֹהֶנֶת, וַהֲרֵי הִיא לְוִיָּה;

לְוִיָּה, וַהֲרֵי הִיא כֹּהֶנֶת;

עֲנִיָּה, וַהֲרֵי הִיא עֲשִׁירָה;

עֲשִׁירָה, וַהֲרֵי הִיא עֲנִיָּה —

הֲרֵי זוֹ מְקֻדֶּשֶׁת, מִפְּנֵי שֶׁלֹּא הִטְעַתּוּ.

וְכֵן הִיא שֶׁאָמְרָה: סְבוּרָה הָיִיתִי שֶׁהוּא כֹהֵן, וַהֲרֵי הוּא לֵוִי;

לֵוִי, וַהֲרֵי הוּא כֹהֵן;

עָשִׁיר, וַהֲרֵי הוּא עָנִי;

עָנִי, וַהֲרֵי הוּא עָשִׁיר —

הֲרֵי זוֹ מְקֻדֶּשֶׁת, מִפְּנֵי שֶׁלֹּא הִטְעָה אוֹתָהּ.

פֶּרֶק תְּשִׁיעִי

א הַמְקַדֵּשׁ שְׁתֵּי נָשִׁים, שֶׁאָסוּר לָשֵׂא שְׁתֵּיהֶן מִשּׁוּם עֶרְוָה, כְּאַחַת — אֵינָן מְקֻדָּשׁוֹת. כֵּיצַד? כְּגוֹן שֶׁקִּדֵּשׁ אִשָּׁה וּבִתָּהּ אוֹ שְׁתֵּי אֲחָיוֹת כְּאַחַת — אֵין אַחַת מֵהֶן מְקֻדֶּשֶׁת.

ב קִדֵּשׁ נָשִׁים רַבּוֹת כְּאַחַת, וְאָמַר: הֲרֵי כֻּלְּכֶם מְקֻדָּשׁוֹת לִי, וְהָיוּ בָּהֶן שְׁתֵּי אֲחָיוֹת אוֹ אִשָּׁה וּבִתָּהּ וְכַיּוֹצֵא בָּהֶן — אֵין אַחַת מִכֻּלָּן מְקֻדֶּשֶׁת.

וְאִם אָמַר לָהֶן: הָרְאוּיָה מִכֶּם לִי לְבִיאָה מְקֻדֶּשֶׁת לִי — הֲרֵי כֻּלָּן מְקֻדָּשׁוֹת לוֹ, חוּץ מֵאֲחָיוֹת אוֹ אִשָּׁה וּבִתָּהּ וְכַיּוֹצֵא בָּהֶן.

וְכֵן אִם אָמַר לָהֶן: הֲרֵי כֻּלְּכֶם מְקֻדָּשׁוֹת לִי, וְהָיְתָה בָּהֶן שִׁפְחָה אוֹ עַכּוּ״ם אוֹ אִשָּׁה אַחַת עֶרְוָה, כְּגוֹן אֵשֶׁת אִישׁ אוֹ בִּתּוֹ אוֹ אֲחוֹתוֹ וְכַיּוֹצֵא בָּהֶן — אֵין אַחַת מִכֻּלָּם מְקֻדֶּשֶׁת.

וְאִם אָמַר: הָרְאוּיָה מִכֶּם לִי לְבִיאָה תִּהְיֶה מְקֻדֶּשֶׁת לִי — הֲרֵי כֻּלָּן מְקֻדָּשׁוֹת לוֹ, חוּץ מֵאוֹתָהּ אִשָּׁה שֶׁאֵין קִדּוּשִׁין תּוֹפְסִין בָּהּ.

---

acquires half. The correspondence is explained as follows. Although the animal is not fit to acquire the property, the person still acquires the half. Similarly, although some of the women are not fit to be consecrated, the others are, and they should be consecrated.

On this basis, the *Maggid Mishneh* asks: Since in *Hilchot Mechirah* 22:12, the Rambam rules that the person acquires the property although the animal does not, seemingly he should agree that the women who are fit to be married should be consecrated. In resolution, he explains that monetary laws are governed by different principles from marital laws, and therefore there is no contradiction between the two rulings.

Because of this contradiction, although the *Shulchan Aruch* (*Even HaEzer* 41:4) mentions the Rambam's opinion, it also mentions a view that states that the women who are not related are consecrated. It concludes that because of the conflicting opinions, the status of the *kiddushin* is doubtful. The same applies with regard to the law mentioned in the second portion of this halachah.

3. [The following rule applies when] a man tells two sisters: "Behold, one of you is consecrated to me with this [article]," and gives them both a *p'rutah*, or one accepts it on behalf [of herself and] her sister. They both require a divorce from him, and it is forbidden for him to engage in marital relations with either of them, for the *kiddushin* are viable even though he is forbidden to engage in relations with either of them.[2] The same [rule applies] when [a man] tells a father: "One of your daughters is consecrated to me," and the father accepts the *kiddushin*.[3]

4. [The following rule applies when a man] appoints an agent to consecrate a particular woman, the agent went and consecrated her, the principal himself consecrated the woman's mother, daughter or sister, and it is not known which of them was consecrated first: They both require a divorce, and they both are forbidden [to have relations] with him.

A similar [rule applies] if a woman appointed an agent to consecrate her, he [fulfilled her charge], she herself consecrated herself to another man, and it is not known which consecration took place first. Both men are required to divorce her. If they so desire, one may divorce her and one may marry her.[4]

5. When does the above apply? When [the two men who consecrated her] were not related. If, however, they were related, the agent consecrated the woman to a father, and she consecrated herself to his son, to his brother or the like: they both must divorce her, and they both are forbidden [to have relations] with her.

6. [The following rules apply when a man] tells an agent: "Go out and consecrate a woman for me," the agent dies, and it is not known whether or not he consecrated a woman on behalf of the principal. We accept the presumption that he consecrated [on his behalf], for it is an accepted presumption that the agent will carry out the mission with which he was charged.

[Accordingly,] since it is not known which woman he consecrated, the principal is forbidden to marry any woman who has a relative who might be forbidden because of the laws of *ervah* - i.e., a woman who has an [unmarried] daughter, mother, sister or the like.

[The rationale is] that if you say: "Let him marry this one," perhaps the agent had consecrated the woman's mother, sister or daughter. He is permitted [to marry] a woman who does not have relatives like these.[5]

If [the woman the man desires to marry] has a relative like this - e.g., a sister - and that relative was married at the time the agent was appointed,

2. Since the man was not specific as to which of the sisters he was consecrating, there is

ג אָמַר לִשְׁתֵּי אֲחָיוֹת: הֲרֵי אַחַת מִכֶּם מְקֻדֶּשֶׁת לִי בָּזֶה, וְנָתַן לָהֶן פְּרוּטָה אוֹ שֶׁקִּבְּלַתָּה אַחַת עַל יַד חֲבֶרְתָּהּ;

וְכֵן הָאוֹמֵר לָאָב: אַחַת מִבְּנוֹתֶיךָ מְקֻדֶּשֶׁת לִי, וְקִבֵּל הָאָב קִדּוּשֶׁיהָ —

כֻּלָּן צְרִיכוֹת גֵּט מִמֶּנּוּ, וְאָסוּר לוֹ לָבוֹא עַל אַחַת מֵהֶן, מִפְּנֵי שֶׁהַקִּדּוּשִׁין תּוֹפְסִין בָּהֶן אַף־עַל־פִּי שֶׁאִי אֶפְשָׁר לָבוֹא עַל אַחַת מֵהֶן.

ד הָעוֹשֶׂה שָׁלִיחַ לְקַדֵּשׁ לוֹ אִשָּׁה פְּלוֹנִית, וְהָלַךְ וְקִדְּשָׁהּ לוֹ, וְקִדֵּשׁ הַמְשַׁלֵּחַ בְּעַצְמוֹ לְאִמָּהּ אוֹ לְבִתָּהּ אוֹ לַאֲחוֹתָהּ, וְאֵין יָדוּעַ אֵי זוֹ מֵהֶן נִתְקַדְּשָׁה רִאשׁוֹנָה — שְׁתֵּיהֶן צְרִיכוֹת גֵּט, וַאֲסוּרוֹת עָלָיו.

וְכֵן אִשָּׁה שֶׁעֲשָׂתָה שָׁלִיחַ לְקַדְּשָׁהּ, וְהָלַךְ וְקִדְּשָׁהּ, וְהָלְכָה וְקִדְּשָׁה הִיא עַצְמָהּ לְאַחֵר, וְאֵין יָדוּעַ אֵי זוֹ מֵהֶן קוֹדֶם — שְׁנֵיהֶן נוֹתְנִין לָהּ גֵּט.

וְאִם רָצוּ, אֶחָד נוֹתֵן גֵּט וְאֶחָד כּוֹנֵס.

ה בַּמֶּה דְּבָרִים אֲמוּרִים? בִּרְחוֹקִין;

אֲבָל אִם קִדְּשָׁהּ הַשָּׁלִיחַ לָאָב, וְקִדְּשָׁה הִיא עַצְמָהּ לַבֵּן אוֹ לָאָח וְכַיּוֹצֵא בָּהֶן — שְׁנֵיהֶם נוֹתְנִין גֵּט, וְהִיא אֲסוּרָה לִשְׁנֵיהֶם.

ו הָאוֹמֵר לִשְׁלוּחוֹ: צֵא וְקַדֵּשׁ לִי אִשָּׁה, וּמֵת הַשָּׁלִיחַ, וְאֵינוּ יוֹדֵעַ אִם קִדֵּשׁ אִם לֹא קִדֵּשׁ לוֹ אִשָּׁה — הֲרֵי זֶה בְּחֶזְקַת שֶׁקִּדֵּשׁ, שֶׁחֶזְקַת שָׁלִיחַ לַעֲשׂוֹת שְׁלִיחוּתוֹ.

וְהוֹאִיל וְאֵין יָדוּעַ אֵי זוֹ אִשָּׁה קִדֵּשׁ לוֹ — הֲרֵי זֶה אָסוּר בְּכָל אִשָּׁה שֶׁיֵּשׁ לָהּ קְרוֹבוֹת שֶׁהֵן עֶרְוָה עִמָּהּ,

כְּגוֹן אִשָּׁה שֶׁיֵּשׁ לָהּ בַּת אוֹ אֵם אוֹ אָחוֹת וְכַיּוֹצֵא בָּהֶן;

שֶׁאִם תֹּאמַר יִשָּׂא זוֹ, שֶׁמָּא אִמָּהּ קִדֵּשׁ לוֹ שְׁלוּחוֹ אוֹ אֲחוֹתָהּ אוֹ בִתָּהּ.

וּמֻתָּר בְּאִשָּׁה שֶׁאֵין לָהּ קְרוֹבוֹת כְּגוֹן אֵלּוּ.

הָיְתָה לָהּ קְרוֹבָה, כְּגוֹן אֵם אוֹ אָחוֹת וְכַיּוֹצֵא בָּהֶן, וְהָיְתָה הַקְּרוֹבָה אֵשֶׁת אִישׁ בַּשָּׁעָה

---

no way to determine which of them was intended. [Even if the man specifies his intent afterwards, his word is not accepted (Ramah, *Even HaEzer* 37:16).] Therefore, there is doubt as to the status of both of the women.

3. The *Shulchan Aruch* (*Even HaEzer* 37:16) states that this rule applies even when the man consecrating the daughters was engaged to one of them. Since he did not specify his intent at the time of the *kiddushin*, all the daughters require a divorce.

4. In the previous instance, the man was not able to marry either of the women he consecrated, because they were related and it is forbidden to marry one's divorcee's mother, sister or daughter.

5. The Ramah (*Even HaEzer* 35:11) quotes the opinion of Rabbenu Nissim, who maintains that if the relatives state that they were never consecrated and the man marries the woman, they are permitted to remain married.

[the man] is permitted to marry her. [This applies] even if this relative was divorced before the agent died. We do not say that perhaps the agent consecrated her relative after she was divorced. For she was not fit to [marry him] at the time the agent was appointed, and a person does not appoint an agent to consecrate a wife for him if [the intended] is not fit to be consecrated at the time the agent is appointed.

7. [The following rules apply when] a person has five sons, they each appoint their father as an agent to consecrate a wife for them, and the father tells a colleague who has five daughters: "[Each] one of your daughters is consecrated to one of my sons." Should the father [of the girls] accept the *kiddushin*,6 each of the girls must be divorced by each of the five brothers. For they all gave their father the prerogative of consecrating a wife for them [and he did not specify which woman would be the wife for which of his sons].

If one of [the sons] dies, each of the women must be divorced by the four [remaining brothers] and must perform the rite of *chalitzah* with one of them.7

8. [There is, by contrast, no doubt in the following situation:] A father had [two daughters]: one a minor or a *na'arah*8 whom he has the privilege [of consecrating], and one a *bogeret*.9 Even if the *bogeret* gives her father the privilege of consecrating her, when he consecrates one of his daughters without specifying which one, it is assumed that the *bogeret* is not the one intended unless he specifically states [that the *kiddushin* are for] "my older daughter, who is a *bogeret*, who appointed me as [her] agent."10 Therefore, [in such a situation,] the *bogeret* is not consecrated,11 and her sister is consecrated.

9. [The following rules apply with regard to a father] who has two pairs of daughters from two different wives, and he has the prerogative [of consecrating all of them].12 If he consecrated one daughter, and at the time of the *kiddushin* told the husband: "I consecrated my oldest daughter" [there is no confusion with regard to his intent]. Although it is possible to say that perhaps he consecrated the older daughter in the older pair to him, or the older daughter in the younger pair or the younger daughter in the older pair - for she is older than the older daughter in the younger pair [- we do not entertain such doubts]. All [the daughters] are permitted [to marry other men] except the older daughter in the older pair; she alone is considered to be consecrated.

6. If the girls are below the age of *bagrut*, their father has the privilege of consecrating them. If they are above the age of *bagrut*, it is possible that they appointed him as an agent to receive their *kiddushin*. Note, however, the following halachah.

שֶׁעֲשָׂהּ הוּא שָׁלִיחַ, אַף־עַל־פִּי שֶׁנִּתְגָּרְשָׁה קֹדֶם שֶׁיָּמוּת הַשָּׁלִיחַ — הֲרֵי זֶה מֻתָּר
בָּהּ;

וְאֵין אוֹמְרִים: שֶׁמָּא קִדֵּשׁ הַשָּׁלִיחַ אֶת קְרוֹבָתָהּ אַחַר שֶׁנִּתְגָּרְשָׁה,
מִפְּנֵי שֶׁלֹּא הָיְתָה רְאוּיָה בַּשָּׁעָה שֶׁעֲשָׂה הַשָּׁלִיחַ, וְאֵין אָדָם עוֹשֶׂה שָׁלִיחַ לְקַדֵּשׁ לוֹ אֶלָּא אִשָּׁה
שֶׁיָּכוֹל הוּא לְקַדְּשָׁהּ בִּשְׁעַת הַשְּׁלִיחוּת.

ז מִי שֶׁהָיוּ לוֹ חֲמִשָּׁה בָנִים, וְעָשׂוּ כֻלָּן שָׁלִיחַ אֶת אֲבִיהֶם לְקַדֵּשׁ לָהֶם אִשָּׁה,
וְאָמַר אֲבִי הַבָּנִים לְאִישׁ שֶׁיֵּשׁ לוֹ חָמֵשׁ בָּנוֹת: אַחַת מִבְּנוֹתֶיךָ מְקֻדֶּשֶׁת לְאֶחָד מִבָּנַי, וְקִבֵּל
הָאָב הַקִּדּוּשִׁין —

כָּל אַחַת מֵהֶן צְרִיכָה חֲמִשָּׁה גִטִּין מִכָּל הָאַחִין, הוֹאִיל וְכֻלָּן נָתְנוּ רְשׁוּת לָאָב לְקַדֵּשׁ לָהֶן
אִשָּׁה.

מֵת אֶחָד מֵהֶם — כָּל אַחַת מֵהֶן צְרִיכָה אַרְבָּעָה גִטִּין, וַחֲלִיצָה מֵאֶחָד מֵהֶם.

ח הָאָב שֶׁהָיְתָה לוֹ בַּת קְטַנָּה אוֹ נַעֲרָה, שֶׁהִיא בִּרְשׁוּתוֹ, וּבַת בּוֹגֶרֶת, וְנָתְנָה לוֹ הַבּוֹגֶרֶת רְשׁוּת
לְקַדְּשָׁהּ, וְקִדֵּשׁ בִּתּוֹ סְתָם לְאֶחָד —

אֵין הַבּוֹגֶרֶת בַּכְּלָל, עַד שֶׁיְּפָרֵשׁ וְיֹאמַר: בִּתִּי הַבּוֹגֶרֶת שֶׁעֲשָׂאַת אוֹתִי שָׁלִיחַ.
לְפִיכָךְ אֵין הַבּוֹגֶרֶת מְקֻדֶּשֶׁת (וַאֲחוֹתָהּ מְקֻדֶּשֶׁת).

ט מִי שֶׁיֵּשׁ לוֹ שְׁתֵּי בָּנוֹת מִשְׁתֵּי נָשִׁים, וְכֻלָּן בִּרְשׁוּתוֹ, וְקִדֵּשׁ אַחַת מֵהֶן, וּבִשְׁעַת הַקִּדּוּשִׁין
אָמַר לַבַּעַל: קִדַּשְׁתִּי לְךָ אֶת בִּתִּי הַגְּדוֹלָה,
אַף־עַל־פִּי שֶׁיֵּשׁ לוֹמַר: שֶׁמָּא גְדוֹלָה שֶׁבַּגְּדוֹלוֹת קִדֵּשׁ לוֹ אוֹ גְדוֹלָה שֶׁבַּקְּטַנּוֹת, אוֹ קְטַנָּה
שֶׁבַּגְּדוֹלוֹת שֶׁהִיא גְדוֹלָה מִן הַגְּדוֹלָה שֶׁבַּקְּטַנּוֹת —
הֲרֵי כֻלָּן מֻתָּרוֹת חוּץ מִן הַגְּדוֹלָה שֶׁבַּגְּדוֹלוֹת, שֶׁהִיא לְבַדָּהּ הַמְקֻדֶּשֶׁת.

7. For perhaps the brother who died was her betrothed.
8. A girl between the ages of twelve and twelve and a half, who has manifested signs of physical maturity.
9. A girl past the age of twelve and a half, who has manifested signs of physical maturity.
   In the Rambam's Commentary on the Mishnah (*Kiddushin* 3:8), he states that if the man has several daughters below the age of *bagrut*, they all require a divorce, because of the doubt mentioned in the previous halachot, but the daughter above the age of *bagrut* does not require a divorce.
10. *Kiddushin* 51b explains the rationale for this ruling. A person will not abandon a mitzvah for which he is responsible (the consecration of his younger daughter) to fulfill a mitzvah for which he is not responsible (the consecration of his elder daughter).
11. The *Shulchan Aruch* (*Even HaEzer* 37:15) states that this law applies only when the daughter who is above *bagrut* does not specify the identity of a man she desires to marry. If, however, she makes such a specification, and the above situation occurs with regard to this individual, she also requires a divorce.
12. I.e., none of them has reached the age of *bagrut* (*Beit Yosef, Even HaEzer* 37). (See *Beit Shmuel* 37:42.)

Similarly, if [the father says that] he consecrated his youngest daughter: Although it is possible to say that perhaps [he consecrated] the younger daughter in the younger pair to him, or the younger daughter in the older pair or the older daughter in the younger pair - for she is younger than the younger daughter in the older pair [- we do not entertain such doubts]. All [the daughters] are permitted [to marry other men] except the younger daughter in the younger pair; she alone is considered to be consecrated. For the phrase "my oldest daughter" implies the daughter whom none is elder than, and the phrase "my youngest daughter" implies the daughter whom none is younger than.[13]

10. A father's word is accepted with regard to [the status of] his daughter below the age of *bagrut.* [If] he states that she has been consecrated, she is forbidden to marry at all.[14]

11. When a father says, "I consecrated my daughter, but I do not know to whom I consecrated her," she is forbidden [to marry] any man forever unless the father says, "I became aware of the fact that I consecrated her to so and so." He alone must divorce her [before she can marry another person]. [Her father's word is accepted with regard to the identity of the person who consecrated her] even if he becomes aware after she reaches the age of *bagrut.*[15]

12. If a father says, "I don't know to whom I consecrated [my daughter]," and a person comes and says, "I am the one who consecrated her," his word is accepted. [Moreover, he is granted the prerogative of] consummating the marriage.[16] He need not consecrate her a second time.

13. [In the above situation,] if two people come and both claim that they were the ones who consecrated her, they are both required to divorce her. If they desire, one may divorce her, and one may consummate the marriage.[17]

[If the latter option was taken, and] one consummated the marriage,[18] and afterwards a third person came and claimed that he was the one who had consecrated her [originally], his word is not accepted and he does not cause her to be forbidden to her husband.

14. [The following rules apply when] a woman states: "I was consecrated, but I do not know to whom I was consecrated," and a man comes and claims: "I

13. Although the Hebrew words גדולה and קטנה can mean both "older" and "oldest" and "younger" and "youngest" respectively, in this context the man's intent is clear, and the intent is the oldest and the youngest.

וְכֵן אִם קִדֵּשׁ בִּתּוֹ הַקְּטַנָּה, אַף־עַל־פִּי שֶׁיֵּשׁ לוֹמַר: שֶׁמָּא קְטַנָּה שֶׁבַּקְּטַנּוֹת אוֹ קְטַנָּה שֶׁבַּגְּדוֹלוֹת, אוֹ גְדוֹלָה שֶׁבַּקְּטַנּוֹת שֶׁהִיא קְטַנָּה מִן הַקְּטַנָּה שֶׁבַּגְּדוֹלוֹת — הֲרֵי כֻּלָּן מֻתָּרוֹת חוּץ מִן הַקְּטַנָּה שֶׁבַּקְּטַנּוֹת, וְהִיא לְבַדָּהּ הַמְקֻדֶּשֶׁת.

שֶׁמַּשְׁמַע בִּתּוֹ הַגְּדוֹלָה — שֶׁאֵין בִּבְנוֹתָיו גְּדוֹלָה מִמֶּנָּה, וּמַשְׁמַע בִּתּוֹ הַקְּטַנָּה — שֶׁאֵין בָּהֶן קְטַנָּה מִמֶּנָּה.

י נֶאֱמָן הָאָב לוֹמַר עַל בִּתּוֹ קֹדֶם שֶׁתִּבָּגֵר שֶׁהִיא מְקֻדֶּשֶׁת, וְאוֹסְרָהּ עַל הַכֹּל.

יא הָאָב שֶׁאָמַר: קִדַּשְׁתִּי אֶת בִּתִּי וְאֵינִי יוֹדֵעַ לְמִי קִדַּשְׁתִּיהָ — הֲרֵי זוֹ אֲסוּרָה לְעוֹלָם עַל כָּל אָדָם, עַד שֶׁיֹּאמַר הָאָב: נוֹדַע לִי שֶׁלִּפְלוֹנִי קִדַּשְׁתִּיהָ, וְתִהְיֶה צְרִיכָה מִמֶּנּוּ גֵּט בִּלְבַד.

וְאַף־עַל־פִּי שֶׁנּוֹדַע לוֹ אַחַר שֶׁבָּגְרָה.

יב אָמַר הָאָב: אֵינִי יוֹדֵעַ לְמִי קִדַּשְׁתִּיהָ, וּבָא אֶחָד וְאָמַר: אֲנִי הוּא שֶׁקִּדַּשְׁתִּיהָ — נֶאֱמָן אַף לִכְנֹס, וְאֵינוּ צָרִיךְ קִדּוּשִׁין אֲחֵרִים.

יג בָּאוּ שְׁנַיִם, זֶה אוֹמֵר: אֲנִי קִדַּשְׁתִּיהָ, וְזֶה אוֹמֵר: אֲנִי קִדַּשְׁתִּיהָ — שְׁנֵיהֶן נוֹתְנִין גֵּט. וְאִם רָצוּ, אֶחָד נוֹתֵן גֵּט וְאֶחָד כּוֹנֵס.

כְּנָסָהּ, וְאַחַר כָּךְ בָּא אַחֵר וְאָמַר: אֲנִי הוּא שֶׁקִּדַּשְׁתִּיהָ — אֵינוֹ נֶאֱמָן, וְאֵינוּ אוֹסְרָהּ עַל בַּעְלָהּ.

יד הָאִשָּׁה שֶׁאָמְרָה: נִתְקַדַּשְׁתִּי וְאֵינִי יוֹדַעַת לְמִי נִתְקַדַּשְׁתִּי, וּבָא אֶחָד וְאָמַר: אֲנִי הוּא

14. *Kiddushin* 64a derives this concept from Deuteronomy 22:16, "I gave my daughter to this man," the verse that teaches that the father has the prerogative of consecrating his daughter until she becomes a *bogeret*. From "I gave my daughter," we learn that because of her father's words, the woman is forbidden to marry anyone but her intended. From "this man," we learn that he can clarify the identity of the intended.

15. The rationale is that since the prohibition comes on the basis of her father's statements, the license to marry is also granted on that basis.

16. I.e., not only may he free the girl of the prohibition by divorcing her, he may consummate the marriage if he desires. We do not suspect that he is making this statement merely because he is attracted to the woman (*Kiddushin* 63b). The man is given this prerogative because we assume that he would not lie, lest the father protest and deny his claim.

17. He must, however, consecrate the woman again (Rashba, Ramah, *Even HaEzer* 37:22).

18. The Rashba states that this ruling applies even if the marriage was not yet consummated. As long as the license for the marriage was granted, the third person's claims do not cause it to be rescinded. The *Shulchan Aruch* (*Even HaEzer* 37:23) quotes both views, but appears to favor that of the Rambam.

was the one who consecrated her." His word is accepted and he may divorce her [so that] she is permitted to marry others, but not him. He is forbidden to consummate the marriage.[19]

[This restriction was instituted out of suspicion that] perhaps the man's natural inclination overcame him [and he made his statement out of desire for her]. [And we fear that the woman] will encourage [his false statements] so that she will be permitted [to marry].

15. [The following rules apply when a man] tells a woman: "I consecrated you," and the woman denies the matter. He is forbidden [to marry] her close relatives,[20] but she is permitted [to marry] his close relatives.[21] If she says, "You consecrated me," and he denies the matter, he is permitted [to marry] her close relatives, but she is forbidden [to marry] his close relatives.

If he says: "I consecrated you," and the woman says: "It was my daughter, not me, whom you consecrated," he is forbidden [to marry] the close relatives of the mother; the mother is permitted [to marry] his close relatives; he is permitted [to marry] the close relatives of the daughter;[22] and the daughter is permitted [to marry] the man's close relatives.[23]

[The following rules apply when the man says:] "I consecrated your daughter," and the woman says: "It was myself [not my daughter] whom you consecrated." He is forbidden [to marry] the daughter's close relatives; the daughter is permitted [to marry] his close relatives; he is permitted [to marry] the mother's close relatives; and the mother is forbidden [to marry] the man's close relatives.

16. All the claims of *kiddushin* [mentioned in the previous halachah] refer to a situation in which the person making the claim states that the *kiddushin* were given in the presence of witnesses, and the witnesses either journeyed overseas or died. If, however, they acknowledge that the *kiddushin* were given without witnesses observing, the *kiddushin* are of no consequence, as we have explained.[24]

Whenever a woman tells a man, "You consecrated me," and he denies the matter, we ask him to compose a bill of divorce so that she will be permitted to marry others, for [doing this] does not involve any loss to him.[25] If he gives her a divorce on his own volition,[26] we compel him to give her [the monetary settlement, as stated in] the *ketubah*.[27]

19. If, however, he consummates the marriage and the couple live together as man and wife, we do not force them to separate because of the suspicions mentioned (Rashba, *Shulchan Aruch, Even HaEzer* 37:24).

20. I.e., the relatives he would be forbidden to marry if she were his wife. Since according to his statements they are man and wife, he must uphold any prohibitions that such a relationship would bring about.

שֶׁקִּדַּשְׁתִּיךְ — נֶאֱמָן לִתֵּן גֵּט, וְתִהְיֶה מֻתֶּרֶת לְכָל אָדָם חוּץ מִמֶּנּוּ;

אֲבָל אֵינוֹ נֶאֱמָן לִכְנֹס, שֶׁמָּא יִצְרוֹ תְּקָפוֹ וְהִיא תַּרְגִּיל לוֹ כְּדֵי לְהַתִּירָהּ.

טו הָאוֹמֵר לְאִשָּׁה: קִדַּשְׁתִּיךְ, וְהִיא אוֹמֶרֶת: לֹא קִדַּשְׁתַּנִי — הוּא אָסוּר בִּקְרוֹבוֹתֶיהָ, וְהִיא מֻתֶּרֶת בִּקְרוֹבָיו.

קִדַּשְׁתַּנִי, וְהוּא אוֹמֵר: לֹא קִדַּשְׁתִּיךְ — הוּא מֻתָּר בִּקְרוֹבוֹתֶיהָ, וְהִיא אֲסוּרָה בִּקְרוֹבָיו.

קִדַּשְׁתִּיךְ, וְהִיא אוֹמֶרֶת: לֹא קִדַּשְׁתָּ אֶלָּא בִּתִּי — הוּא אָסוּר בִּקְרוֹבוֹת גְּדוֹלָה, וּגְדוֹלָה מֻתֶּרֶת בִּקְרוֹבָיו; וּמֻתָּר בִּקְרוֹבוֹת הַבַּת, וְהַבַּת מֻתֶּרֶת בִּקְרוֹבָיו.

קִדַּשְׁתִּי אֶת בִּתֵּךְ, וְהִיא אוֹמֶרֶת: לֹא קִדַּשְׁתָּ אֶלָּא אוֹתִי — הוּא אָסוּר בִּקְרוֹבוֹת הַבַּת, וְהַבַּת מֻתֶּרֶת בִּקְרוֹבָיו; וּמֻתָּר בִּקְרוֹבוֹת הָאֵם, וְהָאֵם אֲסוּרָה עַל קְרוֹבָיו.

טז וְכָל אֵלּוּ שֶׁטּוֹעֲנִין הַקִּדּוּשִׁין, בִּשְׁטָעַן הַטּוֹעֵן שֶׁהָיוּ שָׁם קִדּוּשִׁין בִּפְנֵי עֵדִים וְהָלְכוּ לִמְדִינָה אַחֶרֶת אוֹ מֵתוּ;

אֲבָל אִם הוֹדוּ שֶׁהָיוּ הַקִּדּוּשִׁין בְּלֹא עֵדִים — אֵין כָּאן קִדּוּשִׁין, כְּמוֹ שֶׁבֵּאַרְנוּ.

וְכָל מָקוֹם שֶׁתֹּאמַר אִשָּׁה לְאִישׁ: קִדַּשְׁתַּנִי, וְהוּא אוֹמֵר: לֹא קִדַּשְׁתִּיךְ — מְבַקְשִׁים מִמֶּנּוּ שֶׁיִּכְתֹּב לָהּ גֵּט לְהַתִּירָהּ לִשְׁאָר הָעָם, שֶׁאֵין לוֹ בָּזֶה הֶפְסֵד.

וְאִם נָתַן לָהּ גֵּט מֵעַצְמוֹ — כּוֹפִין אוֹתוֹ לִתֵּן כְּתֻבָּה.

21. For she denies the matter.
22. I.e., those who are not forbidden to him because of his statements regarding her mother. Since he does not acknowledge the consecration of the daughter, he is not bound by the mother's statements.
23. For the mother's statements are not binding for the daughter. Although Scriptural law gives a father the prerogative to make binding statements regarding his daughter's status, a mother's statements do not have this power even according to Rabbinic law (Rambam's Commentary on the Mishnah, *Kiddushin* 3:11).
24. Chapter 4, Halachah 6.
25. Once the man divorces the woman, he is forbidden to marry her close relatives. Nevertheless, this is not considered a significant loss, since there are many other women he could marry. And yet, because of this factor, he cannot be compelled to divorce the woman (*Maggid Mishneh*; Ramah, *Even HaEzer* 48:6). Others [Rabbenu Eliyahu Mizrachi and the Maharshal (Responsum 25)] differ and maintain that since he divorced the woman only as a favor to her, he is not forbidden to marry her relatives.
26. I.e., without being asked to by others.
27. The *Maggid Mishneh* notes that there are several points that require clarification with regard to the Rambam's statements. As stated in Chapter 10, Halachah 11, a man is not ordinarily obligated to pay a marriage contract until the second stage of the marriage (*nisu'in*). If merely *kiddushin* were given, he is not under such an obligation. It is only when he wrote the woman a *ketubah* and gave it together with the *kiddushin*, that he is obligated.

    This, however, raises a question: If he wrote the woman a *ketubah*, how can he deny the *kiddushin*? The *Maggid Mishneh* explains that this law applies only in a place where it is customary to write the *ketubah* before the *kiddushin* are given. Because in most instances

17. When a man appoints an agent to consecrate a woman for him, and the agent goes and consecrates her for himself, the woman is consecrated to the agent. It is, however, forbidden to do such a thing. Whoever does this or performs a similar act with regard to business matters is considered to be wicked.[28]

18. [The following rules apply when a man] appoints an agent to consecrate a woman for him, the agent consecrates her [but a doubt arises whether the agent consecrated her for himself or for the principal]. When the agent says, "I consecrated [the woman] for myself," and the woman says, "I was consecrated to the principal," [the ruling depends on whether or not the appointment of the agent was made in the presence of witnesses].[29]

If the agent was not appointed in the presence of witnesses, the agent is forbidden to marry the woman's close relatives, and she is permitted to marry [the agent's] close relatives.[30] The woman is forbidden to marry the principal's close relatives, but the principal is permitted to marry her close relatives.[31] If the agent was appointed in the presence of witnesses, she is consecrated to the principal.[32]

19. [The following rules apply when] the woman says, "I do not know to whom I was consecrated, whether to the agent or to the principal." If the agent was not appointed in the presence of witnesses, she is consecrated to the agent. If he was appointed as his agent [in the presence of witnesses], they both are required to divorce her. If they desire, one may divorce her and one may consummate the marriage.

20. [The following rule applies when] a woman appoints an agent to consecrate her, he went and fulfilled his mission, but while he was in the process of doing so, she nullified his agency and rescinded his appointment, and it is not known whether she nullified his agency before he received the *kiddushin* or afterwards. The status of the *kiddushin* is doubtful. [She cannot marry another man without receiving a divorce, nor may the marriage be consummated unless she receives *kiddushin* again.] Similar rules apply when a man appoints an agent and retracts his appointment.

21. [The following rules apply when a man] consecrates one of five women but does not know which of them he has consecrated, and each of them says, "He consecrated me." He is forbidden to marry the [close] relatives of all these women and must divorce each of them. [With regard to the payment of the money due because of the marriage contract,] he should leave [the sum due because of] one marriage contract among all the women and depart.[33]

יז הָעוֹשֶׂה שָׁלִיחַ לְקַדֵּשׁ לוֹ אִשָּׁה, וְהָלַךְ וְקִדְּשָׁהּ לְעַצְמוֹ — הֲרֵי זוֹ מְקֻדֶּשֶׁת לַשָּׁלִיחַ. וְאָסוּר לַעֲשׂוֹת כֵּן. וְכָל הָעוֹשֶׂה דָבָר זֶה וְכַיּוֹצֵא בּוֹ בִּשְׁאָר דִּבְרֵי מִקָּח וּמִמְכָּר — נִקְרָא רָשָׁע.

יח הָעוֹשֶׂה שָׁלִיחַ לְקַדֵּשׁ לוֹ אִשָּׁה, וְהָלַךְ וְקִדְּשָׁהּ, הַשָּׁלִיחַ אוֹמֵר: לְעַצְמִי קִדַּשְׁתִּיהָ, וְהָאִשָּׁה אוֹמֶרֶת: לָרִאשׁוֹן שֶׁשְּׁלָחוֹ נִתְקַדַּשְׁתִּי —

אִם לֹא עָשָׂה הַשָּׁלִיחַ בְּעֵדִים — הֲרֵי הַשָּׁלִיחַ אָסוּר בִּקְרוֹבוֹתֶיהָ, וְהִיא מֻתֶּרֶת בִּקְרוֹבָיו; וְהָאִשָּׁה אֲסוּרָה בִּקְרוֹבֵי הַמְשַׁלֵּחַ, וְהַמְשַׁלֵּחַ מֻתָּר בִּקְרוֹבוֹתֶיהָ;

וְאִם הֻחְזַק הַשָּׁלִיחַ בְּעֵדִים — הֲרֵי זוֹ מְקֻדֶּשֶׁת לָרִאשׁוֹן.

יט אָמְרָה: אֵינִי יוֹדַעַת לְמִי נִתְקַדַּשְׁתִּי, אִם לַשּׁוֹלֵחַ אוֹ לִשְׁלוּחוֹ:

אִם לֹא הֻחְזַק הַשָּׁלִיחַ בְּעֵדִים — הֲרֵי זוֹ מְקֻדֶּשֶׁת לַשֵּׁנִי,

וְאִם הֻחְזַק שֶׁהוּא שְׁלוּחוֹ — שְׁנֵיהֶן נוֹתְנִין גֵּט;

וְאִם רָצוּ, אֶחָד נוֹתֵן גֵּט וְאֶחָד כּוֹנֵס.

כ הָאִשָּׁה שֶׁעֲשָׂתָה שָׁלִיחַ לְקַדְּשָׁהּ, וְהָלַךְ וְקִדְּשָׁהּ, וּבְעֵת הֲלִיכָתוֹ בִּטְּלָה הַשְּׁלִיחוּת וְחָזְרָה בָּהּ, וְאֵין יָדוּעַ אִם קֹדֶם שֶׁקִּבֵּל לָהּ הַקִּדּוּשִׁין חָזְרָה אוֹ אַחַר הַקִּדּוּשִׁין — הֲרֵי זוֹ מְקֻדֶּשֶׁת מִסָּפֵק.

וְכֵן הָאִישׁ שֶׁעֲשָׂה שָׁלִיחַ וְחָזַר בּוֹ.

כא הַמְקַדֵּשׁ אַחַת מֵחָמֵשׁ נָשִׁים וְאֵינוֹ יוֹדֵעַ אֵי זוֹ מֵהֶן קִדֵּשׁ, וְכָל אַחַת וְאַחַת אוֹמֶרֶת: אוֹתִי קִדֵּשׁ — אָסוּר בִּקְרוֹבוֹת כֻּלָּן,

וְנוֹתֵן גֵּט לְכָל אַחַת וְאַחַת, וּמַנִּיחַ כְּתֻבָּה אַחַת בֵּינֵיהֶן וּמִסְתַּלֵּק.

---

there is no obligation to give a *ketubah* after *kiddushin*, the *Shulchan Aruch* does not mention this law at all (*Chelkat Mechokek* 48:2).

28. See *Hilchot Mechirah* 7:10.

29. The Ra'avad maintains that the man must always appoint an agent in the presence of witnesses. He therefore interprets the phrase *huchzak hashaliach* to mean that the appointment of the agent was public knowledge.

30. As in Halachah 15.

31. For his agent states that he did not consecrate the woman on behalf of the principal.

32. The *Maggid Mishneh* states that even though the woman is considered to be consecrated to the principal, the agent is still forbidden to marry the woman's relatives. The Ramah (*Even HaEzer* 35:15) quotes this ruling.

Rabbenu Asher does not accept the Rambam's ruling, stating that if the agent explicitly states that he did not consecrate the woman on behalf of the principal, there is no way that the *kiddushin* can be binding.

33. Because of the doubt, he is not required to pay each of them the sum required by the marriage contract.

If, however, [the man] had consecrated [his intended] through sexual relations, our Sages penalized him[34] [and required him] to give [the sum due because of] the marriage contract to each of the women.[35]

[When could such a situation apply?][36] When it is known that he wrote a marriage contract for one of the women,[37] and the marriage contract was lost, and each of the women claims: "I was the one who was consecrated. He wrote the marriage contract for me and it was lost."

22. When a report is circulated that a woman has been consecrated to a particular man, we operate under the presumption that [the woman] is consecrated although there is no binding evidence to that effect.[38] Whenever a report is not substantiated by a court, no attention is paid to it.[39]

What type of report when substantiated will cause a woman to be considered to be consecrated? Two [men] came [to court] and testified that they saw candles lit, couches spread, people coming in and out of the house, and women celebrating with her, saying "So and so was consecrated today."[40] If the women are heard saying: "So and so will be consecrated today," no attention is paid [to the report]; perhaps they assembled for the purpose of *kiddushin*, but the *kiddushin* were not given. It is only when [the report says that the woman] was [actually] consecrated [that the court considers her as such].

Similarly, if two [men] come and say, "We saw what looked like an *erusin* celebration and we heard sounds [of joy], and we heard from so and so[41] who heard from so and so that this woman was consecrated in the presence of [two witnesses] and the witnesses went to another country or died" - this is a report that could cause a woman to be considered consecrated.

23. When does the above apply? When there is no rationale that offsets the report. If, however, there is a rationale that offsets the report, and that rationale is heard when [the report that] she was consecrated is heard, [the woman] is not considered to be consecrated.

---

34. Because he violated our Sages' instructions not to consecrate with sexual relations.
35. The *Beit Shmuel* 49:2 questions why this ruling differs from the ruling delivered (*Hilchot Gezelot* 4:9) when a man says that he stole from one of five people, and does not know from whom he stole. In such an instance, although the thief is required to reimburse each of the five, this is only when each of the recipients takes an oath that the money was stolen from him. The *Beit Shmuel* leaves the question unresolved.
36. For, as stated in Chapter 10, Halachah 11, a man is not ordinarily required to pay the money due because of a marriage contract until *nisu'in*, the second stage of the

וְאִם קִדֵּשׁ בְּבִיאָה — קָנְסוּ אוֹתוֹ חֲכָמִים, שֶׁיִּתֵּן כְּתֻבָּה לְכָל אַחַת וְאַחַת.
וְהַדָּבָר יָדוּעַ שֶׁכְּתֻבָּה שֶׁכָּתַב לְאַחַת מֵהֶן אָבְדָה, וְכָל אַחַת וְאַחַת אוֹמֶרֶת: אֲנִי הִיא שֶׁקִּדַּשְׁתַּנִי וְכָתַבְתָּ לִי כְּתֻבָּה וְאָבְדָה כְּתֻבָּתִי.

כב הָאִשָּׁה שֶׁיָּצָא עָלֶיהָ קוֹל שֶׁהִיא מְקֻדֶּשֶׁת לִפְלוֹנִי — הֲרֵי זוֹ בְּחֶזְקַת מְקֻדֶּשֶׁת, אַף-עַל-פִּי שֶׁאֵין שָׁם רְאָיָה בְּרוּרָה.

וְכָל קוֹל שֶׁלֹּא הֻחְזַק בְּבֵית דִּין, אֵין חוֹשְׁשִׁין לוֹ.

וְכֵיצַד הוּא הַקּוֹל שֶׁתִּחְזַק זוֹ בּוֹ שֶׁהִיא מְקֻדֶּשֶׁת? כְּגוֹן שֶׁבָּאוּ שְׁנַיִם וְהֵעִידוּ, שֶׁרָאוּ הַנֵּרוֹת דּוֹלְקוֹת, וּמִטּוֹת מֻצָּעוֹת, וּבְנֵי אָדָם נִכְנָסִין וְיוֹצְאִין, וְנָשִׁים שְׂמֵחוֹת לָהּ וְאוֹמְרוֹת: נִתְקַדְּשָׁה פְּלוֹנִית הַיּוֹם.

שָׁמְעוּ אוֹתָן אוֹמְרוֹת: פְּלוֹנִית תִּתְקַדֵּשׁ הַיּוֹם — אֵין חוֹשְׁשִׁין לָהּ, שֶׁמָּא נִזְדַּמְּנוּ לְקַדֵּשׁ וְלֹא נִתְקַדְּשָׁה, עַד שֶׁיִּשְׁמְעוּ שֶׁנִּתְקַדְּשָׁה.

וְכֵן אִם בָּאוּ שְׁנַיִם וְאָמְרוּ: רָאִינוּ כְּמוֹ שִׂמְחַת אֵרוּסִין, וְשָׁמַעְנוּ קוֹל הֲבָרָה, וְשָׁמַעְנוּ מִפְּלוֹנִי שֶׁשָּׁמַע מִפְּלוֹנִי שֶׁנִּתְקַדְּשָׁה פְּלוֹנִית בִּפְנֵי פְּלוֹנִי וּפְלוֹנִי, וְהָלְכוּ לָהֶם הָעֵדִים לִמְדִינָה אַחֶרֶת אוֹ מֵתוּ — הֲרֵי זֶה קוֹל שֶׁמַּחֲזִיק אוֹתָהּ מְקֻדֶּשֶׁת.

כג בַּמֶּה דְּבָרִים אֲמוּרִים? שֶׁלֹּא הָיְתָה שָׁם אֲמַתְלָא;
אֲבָל אִם הָיְתָה שָׁם אֲמַתְלָא, וְשָׁמְעוּ הָאֲמַתְלָא כְּשֶׁשָּׁמְעוּ שֶׁנִּתְקַדְּשָׁה — לֹא הֻחְזְקָה מְקֻדֶּשֶׁת.

---

marriage relationship. If the woman has merely been consecrated, this obligation is not incumbent upon him unless he wrote a marriage contract for her.

37. The Ra'avad states that there is no need for the marriage contract to have been written. If the man made a verbal agreement to that effect when consecrating the woman, he is obligated. The *Maggid Mishneh* explains that the Rambam would also accept the Ra'avad's law, and was merely giving one of several possible settings in which the law stated could be applied.

38. As the *Shulchan Aruch* (*Even HaEzer* 46:1) states, the woman is bound by the same rules as all those whose status of their *kiddushin* is in doubt. She may not marry any one other than the man to whom the report says she is consecrated, but before she may consummate the marriage with him, she must be consecrated again.

39. I.e., it is possible for many rumors to be spread. When is credence given to a rumor? When it can be substantiated in court with testimony, as mentioned below. (See Rashi, *Gittin* 99b.)

40. In this part of the halachah (in contrast to its beginning), the Rambam does not mention that the witnesses state to whom the woman was consecrated. The later authorities (*Chelkat Mechokek* 46:1; *Beit Shmuel* 46:1) maintain that this information must also be stated; otherwise the woman is not considered to be consecrated.

41. I.e., according to the Rambam, it is sufficient for two witnesses to hear from one person who originally heard the report from another person. The Rashba and Rabbenu Asher maintain that unless a report is spread by at least two individuals, it cannot be substantiated in court. The *Shulchan Aruch* (*Even HaEzer* 46:2) quotes the Rambam's view and the Ramah quotes the other opinions.

What is [an example] of a rationale that offsets a report? "So and so was consecrated with a stipulation attached," or "[So and so was given] *kiddushin* whose status is in doubt."[42] [In such instances,] the woman is not considered [consecrated]. Instead, we ask her [for an account of the circumstances] and rely on her word, since there is no clear evidence nor firm report.

24. [The following rules apply when at first] a report spreads that [a woman] was consecrated to a particular man, and after a few days a rationale that offsets the report is stated. If it appears to the court that the rationale is true, they rely on it, and [the woman] is not considered to be consecrated. If not, since the rationale was not heard at the time the report of the *kiddushin* was heard, we do not take it into consideration.

25. An incident once occurred involving a report that a particular woman was consecrated to the son of so and so. After time passed, they asked [the husband's] father, who said, "There was a stipulation attached when she was consecrated to him, and the stipulation was not fulfilled." The Sages did not rely on his words. Instead, they ruled that the status of the *kiddushin* was in doubt, as if there were no rationale that offsets [the original report].

26. [The following rules apply when] a report is spread that [a woman] was consecrated to a particular man, and a second man came and consecrated her in our presence. We attempt to verify the report of the *kiddushin* of the first man. If witnesses come and give clear testimony that [the woman] was consecrated to the first man, the *kiddushin* given by the second are of no consequence.

If not, the first man, for whom there is merely a report of his *kiddushin*, must divorce the woman, and the second man, who definitely consecrated her, is allowed to consummate the marriage.[43] If the second man divorces her, the first should not consummate the marriage, lest people at large say, "He remarried the woman he divorced after consecrating her, after she had been consecrated by another man."[44]

27. When a report is spread that a woman was consecrated to one man, and a second report is later spread that she was consecrated to another, one of the men should write her a bill of divorce, and the other - either the first or the last - may consummate the marriage.

28. In a place where it is customary for [a prospective groom] to send gifts to his [prospective] bride after consecrating her, and witnesses who had seen presents being brought to [a woman] come [and testify to that effect], we suspect that she has been consecrated.[45] [Because of this] suspicion, she

כֵּיצַד הִיא הָאֲמַתְלָא? פְּלוֹנִית נִתְקַדְּשָׁה עַל תְּנַאי, אוֹ קִדּוּשֵׁי סָפֵק — לֹא הָחֱזְקָה,
אֶלָּא שׁוֹאֲלִין אוֹתָהּ, וְסוֹמְכִין עַל דְּבָרֶיהָ, הוֹאִיל וְאֵין שָׁם רְאָיָה בְּרוּרָה וְלֹא קוֹל חָזָק.

כד יָצָא עָלֶיהָ קוֹל שֶׁנִּתְקַדְּשָׁה לִפְלוֹנִי, וּלְאַחַר יָמִים אָמְרוּ אֲמַתְלָא:
אִם נִרְאִין הַדְּבָרִים לְבֵית דִּין שֶׁהוּא כֵן — סוֹמְכִין עַל הָאֲמַתְלָא, וְלֹא תֵחָזֵק מְקֻדֶּשֶׁת;
וְאִם לָאו — הוֹאִיל וְלֹא נִשְׁמְעָה הָאֲמַתְלָא בְּעֵת שֶׁנִּשְׁמְעוּ הַקִּדּוּשִׁין, אֵין חוֹשְׁשִׁין לָאֲמַתְלָא.

כה מַעֲשֶׂה בְּאַחַת, שֶׁיָּצָא עָלֶיהָ קוֹל שֶׁנִּתְקַדְּשָׁה לִבְנוֹ שֶׁל פְּלוֹנִי, וּלְאַחַר זְמַן שָׁאֲלוּ לְאָבִיו
וְאָמַר: עַל תְּנַאי כָּךְ נִתְקַדְּשָׁה לוֹ וְלֹא נִתְקַיֵּם הַתְּנַאי. וְלֹא סָמְכוּ חֲכָמִים עַל דְּבָרָיו,
אֶלָּא אָמְרוּ: הֲרֵי זוֹ סְפֵק מְקֻדֶּשֶׁת, וּכְאִלּוּ אֵין שָׁם אֲמַתְלָא.

כו יָצָא עָלֶיהָ קוֹל שֶׁהִיא מְקֻדֶּשֶׁת לִפְלוֹנִי, וּבָא שֵׁנִי וְקִדְּשָׁה בְּפָנֵינוּ — בּוֹדְקִין עַל קִדּוּשֵׁי
רִאשׁוֹן שֶׁהֵן בְּקוֹל:
אִם בָּאוּ עֵדִים בִּרְאָיָה בְּרוּרָה שֶׁהִיא מְקֻדֶּשֶׁת לָרִאשׁוֹן — אֵין קִדּוּשֵׁי שֵׁנִי כְּלוּם;
וְאִם לָאו — מְגָרֵשׁ רִאשׁוֹן שֶׁקִּדּוּשָׁיו בְּקוֹל, וְנוֹשֵׂא הַשֵּׁנִי שֶׁקִּדּוּשָׁיו וַדַּאי.
וְאִם גֵּרֵשׁ הַשֵּׁנִי — לֹא יִכְנֹס הָרִאשׁוֹן,
שֶׁמָּא יֹאמְרוּ: הֶחֱזִיר גְּרוּשָׁתוֹ מִן הָאֵרוּסִין אַחַר שֶׁנִּתְאָרְסָה לְאַחֵר.

כז יָצָא עָלֶיהָ קוֹל שֶׁהִיא מְקֻדֶּשֶׁת לִפְלוֹנִי, וְיָצָא קוֹל אַחֵר כְּמוֹתוֹ שֶׁהִיא מְקֻדֶּשֶׁת לְאַחֵר —
אֶחָד כּוֹתֵב גֵּט וְאֶחָד כּוֹנֵס, בֵּין רִאשׁוֹן בֵּין אַחֲרוֹן.

כח מָקוֹם שֶׁנָּהֲגוּ לִשְׁלֹחַ סִבְלוֹנוֹת לָאֲרוּסָה אַחַר שֶׁתִּתְאָרֵס, וּבָאוּ עֵדִים שֶׁרָאוּ סִבְלוֹנוֹת
שֶׁהוּבְלוּ לָהּ — חוֹשְׁשִׁין לָהּ שֶׁמָּא נִתְקַדְּשָׁה, וּצְרִיכָה גֵּט מִסָּפֵק,

---

42. I.e., there is a question whether the *kiddushin* were worth a *p'rutah*, or the youth consecrating her had reached the age of majority (*Gittin* 9:9; *Shulchan Aruch, Even HaEzer* 46:3).
43. If the first man does not divorce her, the second is not allowed to consummate the marriage. If he does not heed this ruling and marries her before she receives a divorce, the Rabbis ruled that the woman is forbidden to him, and he is required to divorce her (*Shulchan Aruch, Even HaEzer* 46:5).
44. This is forbidden, as explained in *Hilchot Gerushin* 11:12. If the first man does not heed this ruling and marries her, the Rabbis are unresolved whether or not the marriage is allowed to stand (*Chelkat Mechokek* 46:13).
45. I.e., although the presents are worth more than a *p'rutah*, they themselves do not establish a bond of *kiddushin*, because they are not given with that intent. Nevertheless, the fact that the presents were given indicates that there is a possibility that *kiddushin* had been given previously.

must be divorced. [This ruling applies] even when the majority of the men in the city send presents before consecrating [their prospective brides].[46]

In a place where it is customary for all the men [of the locale] to send presents first and then consecrate, [the fact that witnesses] saw presents [being sent] is not a cause for suspicion.

29. [The following rules apply when] it was established that a marriage contract had been composed [for a specific woman]: If it is common for some of the people in that place to consecrate and then have [a marriage contract] composed, we suspect [that the woman was consecrated].[47] [This law applies] even when there is no scribe in the locale. We do not say that because a scribe happened to be found [in the locale], [the man had the marriage contract] written before [he consecrated the woman].

If all the men in a locale have marriage contracts composed before consecrating [their wives], [the existence of a marriage contract] is not a cause for suspicion [that a woman has been consecrated].

30. [The following rule applies when there is a dispute between two pairs of witnesses:] two [witnesses] say: "We saw [a woman] consecrated on this particular day," and two [witnesses] say: "We did not see [this happen]." Although they are all neighbors, living in the same courtyard, [the woman] is considered to be consecrated; the claim "We did not see [this happen]" is of no consequence, for it is common for [a man] to consecrate [a woman] in private.

31. When one witness says, "This [woman] has been consecrated," and [the woman] herself says, "I have not been consecrated," she is permitted [to marry without restriction].[48]

When one [witness] says, "[This woman] has been consecrated," and another [witness] says, "she has not been consecrated," she should not marry[49] [anyone other than the person to whom the witness says she has been consecrated]. If she, nevertheless, marries another person, [there is no necessity to] terminate [the marriage], for she says, "I was not consecrated."

[The following rules apply when a woman herself] says, "I have been consecrated," and afterwards she accepts *kiddushin* [a second time]. If she can offer a rationale that explains her previous statements, explaining why she said she was consecrated, and the reason appears substantial [to the court],[50] she

---

46. Since there are a number of men who send presents after consecrating, we suspect that perhaps this person also followed that practice. Although rulings of Torah law are ordinarily determined by the practice of the majority, an exception is made in this case, because of the severity of the laws of marriage and divorce (*Tosafot, Kiddushin* 50b), or because this majority practice is not fixed and may change at the whim of the people (Rabbenu Nissim).

אַף־עַל־פִּי שֶׁרֹב אַנְשֵׁי הָעִיר אֵין מְשַׁלְּחִין סִבְלוֹנוֹת אֶלָּא קֹדֶם הָאֵרוּסִין.
וּמָקוֹם שֶׁנָּהֲגוּ כֻּלָּן לִשְׁלֹחַ סִבְלוֹנוֹת בַּתְּחִלָּה וְאַחַר כָּךְ מְקַדְּשִׁין, וְרָאוּ סִבְלוֹנוֹת — אֵין
חוֹשְׁשִׁין לָהּ.

כט הֶחְזִק שְׁטַר כְּתֻבָּתָהּ: אִם דֶּרֶךְ מִקְצָת אַנְשֵׁי הַמָּקוֹם שֶׁמְּקַדְּשִׁין וְאַחַר כָּךְ כּוֹתְבִין
— חוֹשְׁשִׁין לָהּ;
וְאַף־עַל־פִּי שֶׁאֵין שָׁם סוֹפֵר, אֵין אוֹמְרִין: שֶׁמָּא מִפְּנֵי הַסּוֹפֵר שֶׁמָּצָא הִקְדִּים וְכָתַב;
וְאִם דֶּרֶךְ כָּל אַנְשֵׁי הַמָּקוֹם שֶׁכּוֹתְבִין הַכְּתֻבָּה קֹדֶם הַקִּדּוּשִׁין — אֵין חוֹשְׁשִׁין לָהּ.

ל שְׁנַיִם אוֹמְרִין: רְאִינוּהָ שֶׁנִּתְקַדְּשָׁה בְּיוֹם פְּלוֹנִי, וּשְׁנַיִם אוֹמְרִין: לֹא רְאִינוּהָ — אַף־עַל־פִּי
שֶׁכֻּלָּם שְׁכֵנִים בְּחָצֵר אַחַת, הֲרֵי זוֹ מְקֻדֶּשֶׁת;
שֶׁאֵין [טַעֲנַת] 'לֹא רְאִינוּהָ' רְאָיָה, שֶׁדֶּרֶךְ הָעָם לְקַדֵּשׁ בְּצִנְעָה.

לא אָמַר עֵד אֶחָד: מְקֻדֶּשֶׁת הִיא זוֹ, וְהִיא אוֹמֶרֶת: לֹא נִתְקַדַּשְׁתִּי — הֲרֵי זוֹ מֻתֶּרֶת.
אֶחָד אוֹמֵר: מְקֻדֶּשֶׁת, וְאֶחָד אוֹמֵר: אֵינָהּ מְקֻדֶּשֶׁת — לֹא תִּנָּשֵׂא;
וְאִם נִשֵּׂאת — לֹא תֵּצֵא, שֶׁהֲרֵי הִיא אוֹמֶרֶת: לֹא נִתְקַדַּשְׁתִּי.
אָמְרָה: מְקֻדֶּשֶׁת אֲנִי, וּלְאַחַר זְמַן עָמְדָה וְקִדְּשָׁה עַצְמָהּ:
אִם נָתְנָה אֲמַתְלָא לִדְבָרֶיהָ, וְאָמְרָה: מִפְּנֵי כָּךְ וָכָךְ אָמַרְתִּי בַּתְּחִלָּה שֶׁאֲנִי מְקֻדֶּשֶׁת, וְרָאִינוּ
בִּדְבָרֶיהָ מַמָּשׁ — הֲרֵי זוֹ מֻתֶּרֶת לַשֵּׁנִי;

---

47. I.e., the marriage contract, like the gifts mentioned in the previous halachah, are a sign that perhaps the woman was consecrated (*Maggid Mishneh*).

48. In this instance, the testimony of one witness is not accepted when the woman denies his statements. If her words were not true, she would not dare to contradict the witness's testimony (*Maggid Mishneh*).

49. The Rambam's ruling appears to be based on the rationale that since the woman has a witness who supports her, we suspect that she might contradict the other witness even when she is not telling the truth (*Maggid Mishneh*).

This rationale is not accepted by the Ra'avad and other authorities, who object to the Rambam's ruling. They maintain that since the woman's statements are accepted when she has no support, surely they should be accepted when they are supported by another witness. They explain that *Ketubot* 23a, the source for this halachah, is referring to an instance when a man threw *kiddushin* to a woman, one witness claims that the *kiddushin* were closer to the woman (and hence, she was consecrated), the other claims that they were closer to the man (and thus she was not consecrated), and the woman herself does not know. This is the view accepted by the *Shulchan Aruch* (*Even HaEzer* 47:3).

50. *Ketubot* 22a gives an example of a rationale that the Sages accepted. A very attractive woman at first said that she was consecrated, and afterwards accepted *kiddushin*. When asked to account for her behavior, she explained that her suitors were originally not worthy people, and she therefore wanted nothing to do with them. When a worthy suitor came, she was happy to accept his offer.

is permitted to [marry] the second man.[51] If she cannot offer an explanation, or she offers one but it does not appear substantial, she is forbidden [to marry]. [Nevertheless, we also give certain consideration to] the *kiddushin* given by the second man, and [require] him to divorce her. She is forbidden to [marry] him or anyone else until the person who first consecrated her comes.

Similar [rules apply with regard to] a woman who comes [to a new community] and says that she is a married woman, and afterwards says that she is unmarried. If she gives a rationale that explains her statements, and it [appears] substantial, her word is accepted.

CHAPTER TEN

1. According to Rabbinic law, a woman who has been consecrated (i.e., an *arusah*) is forbidden to engage in sexual relations[1] with her husband as long as she is living in her father's home.[2] A man who has relations with his *arusah* in his father-in-law's home is punished with "stripes for rebelliousness."

Even when [the husband] consecrated [his *arusah*] by having sexual relations with her, he is forbidden to engage in sexual relations with her again until he brings her to his home, enters into privacy with her, and thus singles her out as his [wife].

[Their entry into] privacy is referred to as entry into the *chuppah*,[3] and it is universally referred to as *nisu'in*.[4]

When a man has relations with his *arusah* for the sake of [establishing] *nisu'in* after he has consecrated her, the relationship is established at the beginning of sexual relations. This causes her to be considered his wife with regard to all matters.[5]

2. Once an *arusah* has entered the *chuppah*, her husband is allowed to have relations with her at any time he desires, and she is considered to be his wife with regard to all matters. Once she enters the *chuppah*, she is called a *nesu'ah*, although [the couple] has not engaged in sexual relations.

51. Note the ruling of the Ramah (*Even HaEzer* 47:4), who states that this law applies only when the woman says "I was consecrated," but does not state to whom. If she mentions the name of a person who she claims to have consecrated her, her retraction is not accepted even when the rationale she offers appears to have substance.

1. Indeed, the two are forbidden to remain in privacy together. For the prohibition against *yichud*, being alone with a woman other than one's wife, applies until the marriage is consummated (Ramah, *Even HaEzer* 55:1).

וְאִם לֹא נָתְנָה אַמַתְלָא, אוֹ שֶׁנָּתְנָה וְאֵין בָּהֶן מַמָּשׁ — הֲרֵי זוֹ אֲסוּרָה, וְקִדּוּשֵׁי שֵׁנִי קִדּוּשֵׁי סָפֵק.

לְפִיכָךְ נוֹתֵן לָהּ גֵּט, וְתִהְיֶה אֲסוּרָה עָלָיו וְעַל הַכֹּל עַד שֶׁיָּבוֹא עַד אֲרוּסָהּ.

וְכֵן הָאִשָּׁה שֶׁבָּאת וְאָמְרָה: אֵשֶׁת אִישׁ אֲנִי, וְחָזְרָה וְאָמְרָה: פְּנוּיָה אֲנִי — אִם נָתְנָה אַמַתְלָא לִדְבָרֶיהָ וְיֵשׁ בִּדְבָרֶיהָ מַמָּשׁ, הֲרֵי זוֹ נֶאֱמֶנֶת.

פֶּרֶק עֲשִׂירִי

א הָאֲרוּסָה אֲסוּרָה לְבַעְלָהּ מִדִּבְרֵי סוֹפְרִים כָּל זְמַן שֶׁהִיא בְּבֵית אָבִיהָ.

וְהַבָּא עַל אֲרוּסָתוֹ בְּבֵית חָמִיו — מַכִּין אוֹתוֹ מַכַּת מַרְדּוּת.

וַאֲפִלּוּ אִם קִדְּשָׁהּ בְּבִיאָה — אָסוּר לוֹ לָבוֹא עָלֶיהָ בִּיאָה שְׁנִיָּה בְּבֵית אָבִיהָ, עַד שֶׁיָּבִיא אוֹתָהּ לְתוֹךְ בֵּיתוֹ וְיִתְיַחֵד עִמָּהּ וְיַפְרִישֶׁנָּה לוֹ.

וְיִחוּד זֶה הוּא הַנִּקְרָא כְּנִיסָה לְחֻפָּה וְהוּא הַנִּקְרָא נִשּׂוּאִין בְּכָל מָקוֹם.

וְהַבָּא עַל אֲרוּסָתוֹ לְשֵׁם נִשּׂוּאִין אַחַר שֶׁקִּדְּשָׁהּ — מִשֶּׁיַּעֲרֶה בָּהּ קְנָאָהּ, וְנַעֲשָׂת נְשׂוּאָה, וַהֲרֵי הִיא אִשְׁתּוֹ לְכָל דָּבָר.

ב כֵּיוָן שֶׁנִּכְנְסָה הָאֲרוּסָה לְחֻפָּה — הֲרֵי זוֹ מֻתֶּרֶת לָבוֹא עָלֶיהָ בְּכָל עֵת שֶׁיִּרְצֶה, וַהֲרֵי הִיא אִשְׁתּוֹ גְּמוּרָה לְכָל דָּבָר.

וּמִשֶּׁתִּכָּנֵס לְחֻפָּה נִקְרֵאת נְשׂוּאָה, אַף-עַל-פִּי שֶׁלֹּא נִבְעֲלָה.

2. This is alluded to by the wording of the blessing recited before consecrating a woman (Chapter 3, Halachah 24), which praises God "who has forbidden the *arusot* to us, and permitted to us those who are married by [the rites of] *chuppah* and *kiddushin*" (*Kessef Mishneh*).

3. Popularly, the term *chuppah* is understood to refer to the wedding canopy. There are also sources for this definition (see *Sotah* 49b and Rashi's commentary; for other definitions, see the notes of the Ramah, *Even HaEzer* 55:1). Nevertheless, the common practice is to follow the Rambam's view as well. For this reason, after the ceremony under the wedding canopy, the bride and groom go to a private room, the *cheder yichud*. This constitutes the halachic definition of *chuppah*.

4. As mentioned previously, in Jewish law, marriage is a two-stage process involving *erusin* and *nisu'in*. *Erusin* (also referred to as *kiddushin*) is the stage described in the previous chapters, that causes a woman to be designated as a man's wife and causes her to be forbidden to other men. It is not until *nisu'in*, however, that the couple begins living together as man and wife. At present, *nisu'in* follows directly after *erusin*; under the wedding canopy the groom consecrates the bride, and afterwards they go to a private room.

5. I.e., all the privileges and obligations of the *ketubah* (marriage contract) apply. He alone nullifies her vows, and if he is a priest, should his wife die, he must become impure when burying her.

[The above applies when] it is fitting to engage in relations with the woman. If, however, the woman is in the *niddah* state [when relations are forbidden], the marriage bond is not completed and she is still considered to be an *arusah* although she entered the *chuppah* and remained in privacy [with her husband].[6]

3. The marriage blessings must be recited in the groom's home[7] before the marriage takes place. There are six blessings; they are:

Blessed are You, God, our Lord, King of the universe, who has created all things for His glory.

Blessed are You, God, our Lord, King of the universe, Creator of man.[8]

Blessed are You, God, our Lord, King of the universe,[9] who created man in His image, in an image reflecting His likeness; [He brought forth] his form and prepared for him from His own Self a structure that will last for all time.[10] Blessed are You, God, Creator of man.

May the barren one rejoice and exult as her children are gathered to her with joy. Blessed are You, God, who makes Zion rejoice in her children.[11]

Grant joy to these loving companions, as You granted joy to Your creation in the Garden of Eden long ago. Blessed are You, God, who grants joy to the groom and the bride.[12]

Blessed are You, God, our Lord, King of the universe, who created joy and happiness, bride and groom, gladness, song, cheer and delight, love and harmony, peace and friendship. Soon, God, our Lord, may there be heard in the cities of Judah and the outskirts of Jerusalem, a voice of joy and a voice of happiness, a voice of a groom and a voice of a bride, a voice of grooms rejoicing from their wedding canopies and youths from their songfests.[13] Blessed are You, God, who grants joy to the groom together with the bride.[14]

---

6. This ruling is not accepted by Rabbenu Asher and other authorities. They maintain that a *chuppah* conducted with a *niddah* is binding, despite the fact that the couple are forbidden to engage in sexual relations. (See *Tur* and *Shulchan Aruch* 61:1.) At present, every effort is made to schedule a wedding so that the woman will not be in the *niddah* state at that time. If, however, that is not possible, the wedding is held and is considered binding, despite the woman's condition.

7. This applied when the wedding celebrations were held in the groom's home. The intent is that the blessings be recited before the complete establishment of the marriage bond. Therefore, at present, these blessings are recited under the marriage canopy, before the couple goes to their private room.

8. Rashi (*Ketubot* 7b) explains that this blessing is in praise of the creation of Adam, the first man.

In *Hilchot Berachot* 10:11, where the text of the wedding blessings is mentioned, this blessing precedes the blessing "who has created all things for His glory." The order mentioned in these halachot is the sequence in which these blessings are recited today.

וְהוּא, שֶׁתִּהְיֶה רְאוּיָה לִבְעִילָה; אֲבָל אִם הָיְתָה נִדָּה, אַף־עַל־פִּי שֶׁנִּכְנְסָה לַחֻפָּה וְנִתְיַחֵד עִמָּה — לֹא גָמְרוּ הַנִּשּׂוּאִין, וַהֲרֵי הִיא כַּאֲרוּסָה עֲדַיִן.

ג וְצָרִיךְ לְבָרֵךְ בִּרְכַּת חֲתָנִים בְּבֵית הֶחָתָן קֹדֶם הַנִּשּׂוּאִין.

וְהֵן שֵׁשׁ בְּרָכוֹת, וְאֵלּוּ הֵן:

בָּרוּךְ אַתָּה יְיָ אֱלֹהֵינוּ מֶלֶךְ הָעוֹלָם, שֶׁהַכֹּל בָּרָא לִכְבוֹדוֹ.

בָּרוּךְ אַתָּה יְיָ אֱלֹהֵינוּ מֶלֶךְ הָעוֹלָם, יוֹצֵר הָאָדָם.

בָּרוּךְ אַתָּה יְיָ אֱלֹהֵינוּ מֶלֶךְ הָעוֹלָם, אֲשֶׁר יָצַר אֶת הָאָדָם בְּצַלְמוֹ, בְּצֶלֶם דְּמוּת תַּבְנִיתוֹ, וְהִתְקִין לוֹ מִמֶּנּוּ בִּנְיַן עֲדֵי עַד. בָּרוּךְ אַתָּה יְיָ, יוֹצֵר הָאָדָם.

שׂוֹשׂ תָּשִׂישׂ וְתָגֵל עֲקָרָה בְּקִבּוּץ בָּנֶיהָ לְתוֹכָהּ בְּשִׂמְחָה. בָּרוּךְ אַתָּה יְיָ, מְשַׂמֵּחַ צִיּוֹן בְּבָנֶיהָ.

שַׂמֵּחַ תְּשַׂמַּח רֵעִים הָאֲהוּבִים, כְּשַׂמֵּחֲךָ יְצִירְךָ בְּגַן עֵדֶן מִקֶּדֶם. בָּרוּךְ אַתָּה יְיָ, מְשַׂמֵּחַ חָתָן וְכַלָּה.

בָּרוּךְ אַתָּה יְיָ אֱלֹהֵינוּ מֶלֶךְ הָעוֹלָם, אֲשֶׁר בָּרָא שָׂשׂוֹן וְשִׂמְחָה, חָתָן וְכַלָּה, גִּילָה רִנָּה דִּיצָה וְחֶדְוָה, אַהֲבָה אַחֲוָה שָׁלוֹם וְרֵעוּת. מְהֵרָה יְיָ אֱלֹהֵינוּ יִשָּׁמַע בְּעָרֵי יְהוּדָה וּבְחוּצוֹת יְרוּשָׁלַיִם קוֹל שָׂשׂוֹן קוֹל שִׂמְחָה קוֹל חָתָן וְקוֹל כַּלָּה, קוֹל מִצְהֲלוֹת חֲתָנִים מֵחֻפָּתָם וּנְעָרִים מִמִּשְׁתֵּה נְגִינָתָם. בָּרוּךְ אַתָּה יְיָ, מְשַׂמֵּחַ הֶחָתָן עִם הַכַּלָּה.

It appears more appropriate, particularly according to Rashi's commentary (*ibid.*), which explains that the blessing "who has created all things..." is not directly connected to the wedding itself, but rather is recited in appreciation of the guests who have come to celebrate together with the new couple.

9. Despite the fact that this blessing follows two (or three) blessings that begin with "Blessed..." it also begins with "Blessed...." Among the explanations offered is that the first blessings are short, and if the phrase "Blessed..." were not mentioned, they would appear to be a single blessing (*Tosafot, Ketubot, ibid.*).

10. Rashi (*ibid.*) interprets this as a reference to the creation of woman, who was created from man ("his own self"), and gives him the potential for reproduction ("a structure that will last for all time").

11. "The barren one" refers to Jerusalem. Psalms 137:6 states: "Let my tongue cleave to my palate if I do not place Jerusalem above my highest joy." Thus, at the height of the wedding celebration, we recall the holy city and pray that it be rebuilt.

12. This is a prayer that the bride and groom enjoy the happiness experienced by Adam and Eve before the first sin.

13. Cf. Jeremiah 33:11. This blessing joins our wishes for the happiness of the particular couple with our hope for the Messianic redemption and the rebuilding of Jerusalem. The ultimate marriage relationship is the bond between God and the Jewish people, which will be realized in the Messianic age. Thus, the two themes, marriage and redemption, share an intrinsic link.

14. Rashi, *Ketubot* 8a, explains the difference between the last two blessings. The fifth of the blessings concludes with a request that the bride and groom enjoy a lifetime of happiness and success together. The sixth and final blessing concludes with a request that

4. If wine is available, a cup of wine should be brought, and the blessing over wine recited first. Afterwards, all the above blessings should be recited over the cup of wine; thus, one recites seven blessings.[15]

In certain places, it is customary to bring a myrtle [branch] together with the wine. The blessing over the myrtle is recited after [the blessing over] the wine, and then the six blessings [mentioned above] are recited.

5. The wedding blessings are recited only in the presence of a quorum of ten adult free men.[16] The groom is counted as part of the quorum.

6. When a man consecrates a woman, recites the wedding blessings, but does not enter into privacy with her in his home, she is still considered to be [merely] an *arusah*. For *nisu'in* are not established by the recitation of the wedding blessings, but rather by [the couple's] entry into the *chuppah*.

When [a man] consecrates [a woman] and [the two] enter a *chuppah*, but do not have the wedding blessings recited, the woman is considered to be married with regard to all matters. The wedding blessings may be recited even after several days have passed.

A woman in the *niddah* state should not marry until she is purified. The marriage blessings are not recited for her until she is purified.[17] If a person transgresses, marries [a woman in this state] and has the blessings recited, they should not be recited again afterwards.

7. [A man] must write a marriage contract (a *ketubah*) [for his wife] before their entry into the *chuppah*; only afterwards is he permitted to live with his wife. The groom pays the scribe's fee.

How much does [the marriage contract require him to promise to have paid to her in the event of his death or his divorcing her]? If the bride is a virgin, no less than 200 *dinarim*. If she is not a virgin, no less than 100 *dinarim*.[18] This amount is called the fundamental requirement of the *ketubah*.

If the groom desires to add to this amount he may, [promising any sum,] even a talent of gold. The laws pertaining to this addition and to the fundamental requirement of the *ketubah* are the same with regard to most matters. Therefore, every time the term *ketubah* is used without any additional explanation, it should be understood to include the fundamental requirement of the *ketubah* together with the additional amount [promised by the groom].

they find happiness in each other, that their wedding joy be extended throughout their lives. Alternatively, the final blessing is a blessing for the Jewish people as a whole, who find fulfillment in married life.

ד וְאִם יִהְיֶה שָׁם יַיִן — מֵבִיא כּוֹס שֶׁל יַיִן, וּמְבָרֵךְ עַל הַיַּיִן תְּחִלָּה, וּמְסַדֵּר אֶת כֻּלָּן עַל הַכּוֹס, וְנִמְצָא מְבָרֵךְ שֶׁבַע בְּרָכוֹת.

וְיֵשׁ מְקוֹמוֹת, שֶׁנָּהֲגוּ לְהָבִיא הֲדַס עִם הַיַּיִן, וּמְבָרֵךְ עַל הַהֲדַס אַחַר הַיַּיִן, וְאַחַר כָּךְ מְבָרֵךְ הַשֵּׁשׁ.

ה וְאֵין מְבָרְכִין בִּרְכַּת חֲתָנִים אֶלָּא בַּעֲשָׂרָה גְדוֹלִים וּבְנֵי חוֹרִין, וְחָתָן מִן הַמִּנְיָן.

ו הַמְאָרֵס אֶת הָאִשָּׁה וּבֵרֵךְ בִּרְכַּת חֲתָנִים וְלֹא נִתְיַחֵד עִמָּהּ בְּבֵיתוֹ — עֲדַיִן אֲרוּסָה הִיא; שֶׁאֵין בִּרְכַּת חֲתָנִים עוֹשָׂה הַנִּשּׂוּאִין, אֶלָּא כְּנִיסָה לְחֻפָּה.

אֵרֵס וְכָנַס לְחֻפָּה וְלֹא בֵּרֵךְ בִּרְכַּת חֲתָנִים — הֲרֵי זוֹ נְשׂוּאָה גְמוּרָה, וְחוֹזֵר וּמְבָרֵךְ אֲפִלּוּ אַחַר כַּמָּה יָמִים.

וְלֹא תִּנָּשֵׂא נִדָּה עַד שֶׁתִּטְהַר, וְאֵין מְבָרְכִין לָהּ בִּרְכַּת חֲתָנִים עַד שֶׁתִּטְהַר. וְאִם עָבַר וְנָשָׂא וּבֵרֵךְ — אֵינוֹ חוֹזֵר וּמְבָרֵךְ.

ז וְצָרִיךְ לִכְתֹּב כְּתֻבָּה קֹדֶם כְּנִיסָה לְחֻפָּה, וְאַחַר כָּךְ יִהְיֶה מֻתָּר בְּאִשְׁתּוֹ. וְהֶחָתָן נוֹתֵן שְׂכַר הַסּוֹפֵר.

וְכַמָּה הוּא כּוֹתֵב לָהּ?

אִם הָיְתָה בְּתוּלָה — אֵין כּוֹתְבִין לָהּ פָּחוֹת מִמָּאתַיִם דִּינָרִים; וְאִם בְּעוּלָה — אֵין כּוֹתְבִין לָהּ פָּחוֹת מִמֵּאָה דִּינָרִים.

וְזֶה הוּא הַנִּקְרָא עִקַּר כְּתֻבָּה.

וְאִם רָצָה לְהוֹסִיף לָהּ, אֲפִלּוּ כִּכַּר זָהָב — מוֹסִיף.

וְדִין הַתּוֹסֶפֶת וְדִין הָעִקָּר אֶחָד הוּא לְרֹב הַדְּבָרִים.

לְפִיכָךְ, כָּל מָקוֹם שֶׁנֶּאֱמַר בּוֹ כְּתֻבָּה סְתָם, הוּא הָעִקָּר וְהַתּוֹסֶפֶת כְּאֶחָד.

---

15. These seven blessings are also recited after grace at the festive meals held during the seven days of celebration after a couple's marriage. (See *Hilchot Berachot* 2:9-11.)

16. *Ketubot* 7b derives this from Ruth 4:2, "And he took ten men from the elders of the city," which is interpreted to refer to the marriage between Boaz and Ruth.

In the Guide for the Perplexed, Vol. III, Chapter 49, the Rambam explains that our Sages required ten men to be present to publicize all weddings, so that a man will live together with a woman only after their marriage has become public knowledge. Their intent was to make it socially unacceptable for couples to live together without marriage.

17. As mentioned in the notes on Halachah 2, although all efforts are made not to schedule a marriage when the woman is in the *niddah* state, if this is unavoidable the wedding may be held and the blessings recited. Nevertheless, the consummation of the marriage is possible only when the woman is purified.

18. Rav Ovadiah of Bertinoro (*Pe'ah* 8:8) states that this is the sum of money required for a person to support himself for one year.

It was our Sages[19] who ordained the requirement of [writing] a *ketubah* for a woman. [They instituted this obligation] so that it would not be a casual matter for [her husband] to divorce her.[20]

8. [Our Sages] did not require that these *dinarim* be of pure silver. Instead, [their intent was] the coin [commonly used] in the [Talmudic] period, which was seven parts copper and one part silver. Thus, a *sela* (a coin worth four *dinarim*) contained half a *zuz* of [pure] silver.[21] And the 200 *dinarim* to be paid a virgin were equivalent to 25 *zuz* of pure silver, while the 100 *dinarim* to be paid to a woman who had previously engaged in sexual relations was 12 and a half *zuz* [of pure silver].

The weight of each *zuz* is 96 barley corns, as explained at the beginning of *[Hilchot] Eruvin*.[22] A *dinar* is universally referred to as a *zuz*, regardless of whether it was of pure silver or of the coins used in the [Talmudic] period.

9. [A marriage contract] for a virgin may not be less than 200 [*zuz*], nor less than 100 [*zuz*] for a woman who is not a virgin. Whenever anyone [composes a marriage contract for] a lesser sum, the sexual relations [he conducts with his wife] are considered promiscuous.

[Marital relations] are permitted whether the husband composes a legal document [recording] the *ketubah*, or whether he has witnesses observe him making a commitment for either 100 or 200 [*zuz*] and [reaffirms that] commitment with a contractual act.[23] Similarly, if [a man] gives his wife possessions equivalent to the value of her *ketubah* [as security], he is permitted to engage in relations with her until he has the opportunity to [have the document] composed.[24]

10. When a man brings a woman [into a *chuppah*] without writing a *ketubah* for her, or he has written her a *ketubah* but it was lost, or the woman waived the *ketubah* in favor of her husband, or she sold her *ketubah* to him, he

19. This point is a matter of debate, for there are certain opinions (among them that of Rabbenu Tam) that maintain that the obligation to pay the fundamental requirement of the *ketubah* stems from the Torah. Support for the latter opinion may be drawn from the wording commonly used in most Ashkenazic *ketubot* "200 silver *zuz* that are rightfully yours [as required by] the Torah." [Significantly, even the text of the *ketubah* in the standard printed texts of the *Mishneh Torah* (*Hilchot Yibbum VaChalitzah* 4:34) includes this phrase. Nevertheless, many authorities maintain that this is a printer's addition and not the Rambam's own words.]

Most authorities (including Rabbenu Asher) agree that the obligation to pay the fundamental requirement of the *Ketubah* is Rabbinic in origin. Nevertheless, the abovementioned phrase is traditionally included in the *ketubah* to teach us the value of the silver to which we are referring, as is explained in the notes on the following halachah.

וַחֲכָמִים הֵם שֶׁתִּקְּנוּ כְּתֻבָּה לְאִשָּׁה, כְּדֵי שֶׁלֹּא תִהְיֶה קַלָּה בְּעֵינָיו לְהוֹצִיאָהּ.

ח דִּינָרִים אֵלּוּ לֹא תִקְּנוּ אוֹתָם מִן הַכֶּסֶף הַטָּהוֹר, אֶלָּא מִמַּטְבֵּעַ שֶׁהָיָה בְּאוֹתָן הַיָּמִים, שֶׁהָיָה שִׁבְעָה חֲלָקִים נְחשֶׁת וְאֶחָד כֶּסֶף, עַד שֶׁיִּהְיֶה בְּסֶלַע חֲצִי זוּז כֶּסֶף. וְנִמְצָא מָאתַיִם דִּינָרִים שֶׁל בְּתוּלָה — חֲמִשָּׁה וְעֶשְׂרִים זוּזִין שֶׁל כֶּסֶף טָהוֹר, וּמֵאָה דִּינָרִים שֶׁל בְּעוּלָה — שְׁנֵים עָשָׂר זוּזִים וּמֶחֱצָה.

וּמִשְׁקַל כָּל זוּז — שֵׁשׁ וְתִשְׁעִים שְׂעוֹרוֹת, כְּמוֹ שֶׁבֵּאַרְנוּ בִּתְחִלַּת עֵרוּבִין.

וְהַדִּינָר הוּא הַנִּקְרָא זוּז בְּכָל מָקוֹם, בֵּין שֶׁיִּהְיֶה מִן הַכֶּסֶף הַטָּהוֹר בֵּין שֶׁיִּהְיֶה מִמַּטְבֵּעַ אוֹתָן הַיָּמִים.

ט אֵין פּוֹחֲתִין לִבְתוּלָה מִמָּאתַיִם וְלִבְעוּלָה מִמֵּאָה, וְכָל הַפּוֹחֵת — בְּעִילָתוֹ בְּעִילַת זְנוּת. אֶחָד הַכּוֹתֵב אֶת הַכְּתֻבָּה בִּשְׁטָר וְאֶחָד שֶׁהֶעִידוּ עָלָיו עֵדִים וְקָנוּ מִיָּדוֹ שֶׁהוּא חַיָּב לָהּ מֵאָה אוֹ מָאתַיִם — הֲרֵי זֶה מֻתָּר.

וְכֵן אִם נָתַן לָהּ מִטַּלְטְלִין כְּנֶגֶד כְּתֻבָּתָהּ — הֲרֵי זֶה מֻתָּר לַבַּעַל עַד שֶׁיִּהְיֶה לוֹ פְּנַאי לִכְתֹּב.

י הַכּוֹנֵס אֶת הָאִשָּׁה וְלֹא כָתַב לָהּ כְּתֻבָּה,

אוֹ שֶׁכָּתַב וְאָבַד שְׁטַר הַכְּתֻבָּה,

אוֹ שֶׁמָּחֲלָה כְּתֻבָּתָהּ לְבַעְלָהּ,

אוֹ שֶׁמְּכָרָה לוֹ כְּתֻבָּתָהּ —

20. I.e., when the man understands that divorcing his wife will cost him a significant sum of money, he will think twice before doing so.
21. The Ashkenazic authorities (even those who agree with the Rambam with regard to the Rabbinic origin of the fundamental requirement of the *ketubah*) differ with him regarding the value the man is required to pay [*Tur*, Ramah (*Even HaEzer* 66:6)]. According to these authorities, our Sages ordained that a man pay his virgin bride 200 *zuz* of pure silver. With regard to a bride who is not a virgin, however, they differ and maintain that the obligation is 100 *zuz* of the Talmudic period. In practice, however, the custom is to give such a bride half the sum given to a virgin (*Beit Shmuel* 66:14).
22. Chapter 1, Halachah 12. According to most authorities, the equivalent of a *dinar* in contemporary measure is 4.8 grams. According to Rabbi Shneur Zalman of Liadi (*Piskei Siddur*), it is 5.1 grams.
23. I.e., a *kinyan chalifin*, in which the recipient gives the seller a handkerchief and thus reaffirms his commitment. After this act, the transaction is binding. (See *Hilchot Mechirah* 5:5.)
Once a person reaffirms his commitment by performing a contractual act in the presence of witnesses, the witnesses have the right to draw up a document attesting to the obligation he accepted upon himself. They need not consult him before doing so (*Ketubot* 55a).
24. Implied by the Rambam's wording is that this is only a temporary measure, and that a *ketubah* must be composed at the earliest possible opportunity. (See Ramah, *Even HaEzer* 66:2.)

must compose a document [obligating himself] for [at least] the fundamental requirement of the *ketubah*[25] if he desires to continue living with his wife. For it is forbidden for a man to continue living with his wife for even a single moment without [her having] a *ketubah*.

When, however, a woman sells her *ketubah* to others for the possible benefit,[26] [her husband] does not have to write another *ketubah* for her. For the *ketubah* was instituted solely so that it would not be a casual matter for [a man] to divorce [his wife]. In this instance, if [the woman's husband] divorces her, he must pay her *ketubah* to the purchaser in the same way that he would pay her if she had not sold it.

11. When [a man] consecrates a woman and writes her a *ketubah*, but does not enter into a *chuppah* with her, her status is that of an *arusah* and not that of a *nesu'ah*. For a *ketubah* does not bring about *nisu'in*. If [the husband] dies or divorces her, she may collect the fundamental requirement of the *ketubah* from property possessed by the man or his estate.[27] She does not collect the additional sum [that he attached to the *ketubah*] at all, for they did not enter [a *chuppah*].[28]

If, by contrast, a man consecrates a woman and does not write a *ketubah* for her, and he dies or divorces her while she is still an *arusah*, she has no claim against him, not even for the fundamental [requirement of the *ketubah*]. For our Sages did not grant [a woman] the fundamental requirement of the *ketubah* until the marriage is consummated or until the husband writes a document for her.[29]

When a man consecrates his daughter, and [her intended husband] writes her a *ketubah* and dies or divorces her while she is a *na'arah*, her father receives [payment for] her *ketubah*, as explained in Chapter Three[30] above.

12. Similarly, our Sages ordained that whoever weds a virgin should celebrate with her for seven days.[31] He should not pursue his occupation, nor should he involve himself in commercial dealings; he should eat, drink and celebrate.[32] [This ruling applies] regardless of whether the groom had been married before or not.

---

25. I.e., he does not have to give her the full value of her original *ketubah*. He must, however, give her a *ketubah* in which he obligates himself for the minimal amount required by our Sages. Note the *Beit Shmuel* 66:10, who questions whether he must write the *ketubah* for 100 or 200 *zuz*.

The *Beit Shmuel* (*op. cit.*) and the *Chelkat Mechokek* 66:14 state that the man is obligated for the minimal amount only in the latter two instances mentioned by the Rambam. When the woman loses her *ketubah*, her husband must write her a new *ketubah* for the initial amount.

26. I.e., she sells the rights to her *ketubah* to a purchaser for a price below its face

חוֹזֵר וְכוֹתֵב לָהּ עִקַּר כְּתֻבָּה, אִם רָצָה לְקַיְּמָהּ,

לְפִי שֶׁאָסוּר לוֹ לְאָדָם לִשְׁהוֹת עִם אִשְׁתּוֹ אֲפִלּוּ שָׁעָה אַחַת בְּלֹא כְּתֻבָּה.

אֲבָל הַמּוֹכֶרֶת כְּתֻבָּתָהּ לַאֲחֵרִים בְּטוֹבַת הֲנָאָה — אֵינוֹ צָרִיךְ לִכְתֹּב לָהּ כְּתֻבָּה אַחֶרֶת;

שֶׁלֹּא תִקְנוּ כְּתֻבָּה אֶלָּא כְּדֵי שֶׁלֹּא תְהֵא קַלָּה בְּעֵינָיו לְהוֹצִיאָהּ,

וְאִם הוֹצִיא זֶה — מְשַׁלֵּם כְּתֻבָּתָהּ לַלּוֹקֵחַ כְּדֶרֶךְ שֶׁהָיָה מְשַׁלֵּם לָהּ אִם לֹא מָכְרָה.

יא הַמְאָרֵס אֶת הָאִשָּׁה, וְכָתַב לָהּ כְּתֻבָּה, וְלֹא נִכְנְסָה לַחֻפָּה — עֲדַיִן אֲרוּסָה הִיא, וְאֵינָהּ נְשׂוּאָה; שֶׁאֵין הַכְּתֻבָּה עוֹשָׂה נִשּׂוּאִין.

וְאִם מֵת אוֹ גֵּרְשָׁהּ — גּוֹבָה עִקַּר כְּתֻבָּתָהּ מִבְּנֵי חֹרִין, וְאֵינָהּ גּוֹבָה תּוֹסֶפֶת כְּלָל, הוֹאִיל וְלֹא כָנְסָהּ.

אֲבָל אִם אֵרַס אִשָּׁה וְלֹא כָתַב לָהּ כְּתֻבָּה, וּמֵת אוֹ גֵּרְשָׁהּ וְהִיא אֲרוּסָה — אֵין לָהּ כְּלוּם, וַאֲפִלּוּ הָעִקָּר;

שֶׁלֹּא תִקְנוּ לָהּ עִקַּר כְּתֻבָּה עַד שֶׁתִּנָּשֵׂא אוֹ עַד שֶׁיִּכְתֹּב.

וְהַמְאָרֵס אֶת בִּתּוֹ, וְכָתַב לָהּ כְּתֻבָּה, וּמֵת אוֹ גֵּרְשָׁהּ כְּשֶׁהָיְתָה נַעֲרָה — כְּתֻבָּתָהּ לְאָבִיהָ, כְּמוֹ שֶׁבֵּאַרְנוּ [לְמַעְלָה בְּפֶרֶק שְׁלִישִׁי].

יב וְכֵן תִּקְנוּ חֲכָמִים, שֶׁכָּל הַנּוֹשֵׂא בְּתוּלָה יִהְיֶה שָׂמֵחַ עִמָּהּ שִׁבְעַת יָמִים. אֵינוֹ עוֹסֵק בִּמְלַאכְתּוֹ, וְלֹא נוֹשֵׂא וְנוֹתֵן בַּשּׁוּק, אֶלָּא אוֹכֵל וְשׁוֹתֶה וְשָׂמֵחַ. בֵּין שֶׁהָיָה בָּחוּר, בֵּין שֶׁהָיָה אַלְמוֹן.

value. Should her husband die or divorce her, the purchaser receives the full value of the *ketubah*. If the woman dies before her husband, the purchaser does not receive anything.

27. I.e., after a marriage has been consummated, a woman may collect her due even from property that has been sold, for all her husband's property is on lien to her *ketubah*. Before the marriage bond is consummated, however, she does not have this right (*Ketubot* 43b).

Rabbenu Asher and Rabbenu Nissim differ with the Rambam in this regard and maintain that the woman should be able to collect her *ketubah* from property that has been sold as well. The *Shulchan Aruch* (*Even HaEzer* 55:6) follows the Rambam's view.

28. *Ketubot* 54b explains that the additional amount was granted the woman in consideration of the couple's sexual relationship.

29. In this matter as well, Rabbenu Asher differs with the Rambam and maintains that a woman is entitled to a *ketubah* from *erusin* onward. The *Shulchan Aruch* (*ibid.*) quotes the Rambam's view. Although the Ramah mentions Rabbenu Asher's opinion, he states that it is customary to follow the Rambam's ruling.

30. Halachah 11.

31. *Hilchot Eivel* 1:1 states that Moses ordained the seven days of mourning and the seven days of wedding celebrations for the Jewish people.

32. During these days, it is customary for the friends and family of the bride and groom to host them at celebrations referred to as *sheva berachot* ("seven blessings") for the seven wedding blessings recited after the meal at these celebrations, as explained in *Hilchot Berachot*, Chapter 2.

If the bride is not a virgin, [he should celebrate with her] for no less than three days. For it is an ordinance of our Sages that a husband - regardless of whether he was married before or not - should celebrate with a non-virgin bride for three days.[33]

13. A man may wed several women at one time on one day and recite the marriage blessings for all of them at the same time. With regard to the celebrations, however, he must rejoice with each bride the time allotted to her: seven days for a virgin, three days for a non-virgin. One celebration should not be allowed to overlap with another.[34]

14. It is permitted to consecrate a woman on any weekday,[35] even on Tish'ah B'Av,[36] whether during the day or during the night. With regard to weddings, by contrast, a wedding is not conducted on a Friday[37] or a Sunday. [This is] a decree, [ordained] lest conducting the wedding feast lead to the desecration of the Sabbath, for a groom is preoccupied with the wedding feast. Needless to say, a wedding is not conducted on the Sabbath.[38]

Even on Chol HaMo'ed weddings are not held, as we have explained,[39] for one celebration should not be mixed with another, as [implied by Genesis 29:27]: "Complete the week [of celebration] of this one and then I will give you this other one."

On other days, it is permitted to wed a woman on any day one desires, provided one spends three days preparing for the wedding feast.

15. In a locale where the court holds session only on Monday and Thursday, a virgin bride should be wed on Wednesday. Thus, if her husband has a claim with regard to her virginity,[40] he can take it to the court early the next morning.[41]

It is the custom of the Sages that a man who weds a non-virgin bride should wed her on Thursday, so that he will celebrate with her on Thursday, Friday and the Sabbath.[42] On Sunday, he will go back to work.

---

33. The *Maggid Mishneh* states that if the groom was not married previously, he should celebrate with his bride for seven days even when she had been married before. He draws support from *Hilchot Berachot* 2:9, which states that in such an instance the seven wedding blessings are recited for the week following the wedding.

34. See Halachah 14, which explains the source for this ruling.

35. Even during Chol Hamo'ed (*Hilchot Sh'vitat Yom Tov* 7:16).

36. The mourning customs of that day do not prevent one from consecrating a wife. The rationale: another man may consecrate the woman instead of him (Jerusalem Talmud, *Ketubot* 1:1).

37. Although many of the early Sephardi authorities object, the *Shulchan Aruch* (*Even HaEzer* 64:3, based on the ruling of the *Tur*) states that in the present age, it is customary

וְאִם הָיְתָה בְּעוּלָה — אֵין פָּחוֹת מִשְּׁלֹשָׁה יָמִים.

שֶׁתַּקָּנַת חֲכָמִים הִיא לִבְנוֹת יִשְׂרָאֵל, שֶׁיִּהְיֶה עִם הַבְּעוּלָה שְׁלֹשָׁה יָמִים, בֵּין בָּחוּר בֵּין אַלְמוֹן.

יג יֵשׁ לוֹ לְאָדָם לִשָּׂא נָשִׁים רַבּוֹת כְּאַחַת בְּיוֹם אֶחָד, וּמְבָרֵךְ בִּרְכַּת חֲתָנִים לְכֻלָּן כְּאַחַת. אֲבָל לְשִׂמְחָה — צָרִיךְ לִשְׂמֹחַ עִם כָּל אַחַת שִׂמְחָה הָרְאוּיָה לָהּ: עִם בְּתוּלָה — שִׁבְעָה, עִם בְּעוּלָה — שְׁלֹשָׁה; וְאֵין מְעָרְבִין שִׂמְחָה בְּשִׂמְחָה.

יד מֻתָּר לָאָרֵס בְּכָל יוֹם חֹל, אֲפִלּוּ בְּתִשְׁעָה בְּאָב, בֵּין בַּיּוֹם בֵּין בַּלַּיְלָה. אֲבָל אֵין נוֹשְׂאִין נָשִׁים לֹא בְּעֶרֶב שַׁבָּת וְלֹא בְּאֶחָד בְּשַׁבָּת, גְּזֵרָה שֶׁמָּא יָבוֹא לִידֵי חִלּוּל שַׁבָּת בְּתִקּוּן הַסְּעֻדָּה, שֶׁהֶחָתָן טָרוּד בַּסְּעֻדָּה. וְאֵין צָרִיךְ לוֹמַר שֶׁאָסוּר לִשָּׂא אִשָּׁה בְּשַׁבָּת. וַאֲפִלּוּ בְּחֻלּוֹ שֶׁל מוֹעֵד אֵין נוֹשְׂאִין נָשִׁים, כְּמוֹ שֶׁבֵּאַרְנוּ, לְפִי שֶׁאֵין מְעָרְבִין שִׂמְחָה בְּשִׂמְחָה, שֶׁנֶּאֱמַר: מַלֵּא שְׁבַע זֹאת וְנִתְּנָה לְךָ גַּם אֶת זֹאת. וּשְׁאָר הַיָּמִים מֻתָּר לִשָּׂא אִשָּׁה בְּכָל יוֹם שֶׁיִּרְצֶה. וְהוּא, שֶׁיִּטְרַח בִּסְעֻדַּת נִשּׂוּאִין שְׁלֹשָׁה יָמִים קֹדֶם הַנִּשּׂוּאִין.

טו מָקוֹם שֶׁאֵין בֵּית דִּין בּוֹ יוֹשְׁבִין אֶלָּא בְּשֵׁנִי וּבַחֲמִישִׁי בִּלְבַד, בְּתוּלָה נִשֵּׂאת בְּיוֹם רְבִיעִי; שֶׁאִם הָיְתָה לוֹ טַעֲנַת בְּתוּלִים, יַשְׁכִּים לְבֵית דִּין. וּמִנְהַג חֲכָמִים, שֶׁהַנּוֹשֵׂא אֶת הַבְּעוּלָה יִשָּׂאֶנָּה בַּחֲמִישִׁי, כְּדֵי שֶׁיִּהְיֶה שָׂמֵחַ עִמָּהּ חֲמִישִׁי וְעֶרֶב שַׁבָּת וְשַׁבָּת, וְיוֹצֵא לִמְלַאכְתּוֹ יוֹם רִאשׁוֹן.

---

to hold weddings on Friday, provided the groom spends three days preparing for the wedding feast.

(A wedding may be held on Sunday or Monday. The fact that the Sabbath is interposed in between does not mean that three days were not spent in preparation for the wedding.)
38. With regard to weddings on the Sabbath, there is an additional reason for the prohibition. A wedding involves a *kinyan*, the acquisition of the rights of the marriage contract, and it is forbidden to make a *kinyan* on the Sabbath (*Hilchot Shabbat* 23:14).
39. *Hilchot Sh'vitat Yom Tov, loc. cit.*
40. This subject is discussed in detail in the following chapter.
41. Our Sages desired that he take the matter to court so the matter be investigated, lest the bride had in fact committed adultery (for in the Talmudic age, *erusin* preceded *nisu'in*). If the wedding were held on another day, our Sages feared that in the time the husband was waiting for the court to hold sessions, his wife would soothe his anger (Rashi, *Ketubot* 2a).
42. Since the wedding blessings are recited for only one day when both the bride and the groom have been married before, our Sages feared that the man would ignore his wife on the day following their wedding and immediately return to work. To prevent this, they

16. When a man consecrates his daughter while she is below the age of majority, both she and her father may object and delay the wedding until she comes of age and becomes a *na'arah*. If [the husband] desires to wed her, he may.[43] It is not proper, however, to do so.[44]

17. If a man consecrated [a girl], delayed several years, and seeks to wed her while she is a *na'arah*, the girl is given twelve months from the day he makes his request, to outfit herself[45] and prepare what she needs for him. Only afterwards, must she wed.

If he makes his request after she becomes a *bogeret*, she is given twelve months from the day she becomes a *bogeret*. Similarly, if he consecrates her on the day on which she becomes a *bogeret*, she is given twelve months from the day of the *kiddushin* - i.e., the day on which she became a *bogeret*.

When he consecrates her after she has become a *bogeret*, if more than twelve months have passed from the time she became a *bogeret* until he consecrates her, she is given only 30 days from the day he requests to wed her [to prepare]. Similarly, when a man consecrates a non-virgin bride,[46] she is given 30 days [to prepare] from the day he requests to wed her.

18. Just as a woman is given time to outfit herself after her groom requests to wed her and then the wedding is held, so too, time is granted to the man to prepare himself[47] if the woman requests the wedding to be held.

How much time is granted him? The same as is granted her. If [she would be granted] twelve months, [he is granted] twelve months. If [she would be granted] thirty days, [he is granted] thirty days.[48]

19. When the time allotted to the man passes and he still has not wed his *arusah*, he is obligated to provide her livelihood, although they have not wed. [Nevertheless,] if [the final day in] the time allotted him falls on Sunday or Friday, he is not liable for her livelihood on that day, for the wedding cannot be held then.[49] Similarly, if he or she falls ill or she enters the *niddah* state at the conclusion of the time allotted him, he is not obligated to

suggested that the wedding be held on Thursday. For the husband will not consider going to work on Friday and the Sabbath (*Ibid.*).

43. I.e., if the husband forces the bride to agree, the wedding is binding. The *Drishah* (*Even HaEzer* 56) interprets the Rambam's wording to mean that the father desires to have his daughter wed before she comes of age. Some maintain that there is a slight printing error in the standard text of the *Mishneh Torah*, and the proper version is "if they desire" - i.e., the bride and her father. (See *Chelkat Mechokek* 56:6.)

44. Instead, the father should wait until his daughter comes of age and willingly agrees to marry her spouse. (See Chapter 3, Halachah 19.)

45. I.e., to buy garments and jewelry (*Ketubot* 57b).

טז הַמְאָרֵס אֶת בִּתּוֹ קְטַנָּה, וּתְבָעָהּ הַבַּעַל לְנִשּׂוּאִין —
בֵּין הִיא בֵּין אָבִיהָ יְכוֹלִין לְעַכֵּב לְעַצְמָהּ שֶׁלֹּא תִנָּשֵׂא עַד שֶׁתַּגְדִּיל וְתֵעָשֶׂה נַעֲרָה.
וְאִם רָצָה לְכָנְסָהּ — כּוֹנֵס. וְאֵין רָאוּי לַעֲשׂוֹת כֵּן.

יז אֵרְסָהּ וְשָׁהָה כַּמָּה שָׁנִים וּתְבָעָהּ לְנִשּׂוּאִין וַהֲרֵי הִיא נַעֲרָה —
נוֹתְנִין לָהּ שְׁנֵים עָשָׂר חֹדֶשׁ מִיּוֹם הַתְּבִיעָה לְפַרְנֵס אֶת עַצְמָהּ וּלְתַקֵּן מַה שֶּׁהִיא צְרִיכָה לָהּ,
וְאַחַר כָּךְ תִּנָּשֵׂא.
תְּבָעָהּ אַחַר שֶׁבָּגְרָה — נוֹתְנִין לָהּ שְׁנֵים עָשָׂר חֹדֶשׁ מִיּוֹם הַבֶּגֶר.
וְכֵן אִם קָדְשָׁהּ בְּיוֹם הַבֶּגֶר — נוֹתְנִין לָהּ שְׁנֵים עָשָׂר חֹדֶשׁ מִיּוֹם הַקִּדּוּשִׁין, שֶׁהוּא יוֹם הַבֶּגֶר.
קִדְּשָׁהּ אַחַר שֶׁבָּגְרָה, אִם עָבְרוּ עָלֶיהָ שְׁנֵים עָשָׂר חֹדֶשׁ בְּבַגְרוּתָהּ וּלְאַחַר כֵּן נִתְקַדְּשָׁה — אֵין
נוֹתְנִין לָהּ אֶלָּא שְׁלֹשִׁים יוֹם מִיּוֹם הַתְּבִיעָה.
וְכֵן הַמְאָרֵס אֶת הַבְּעוּלָה — נוֹתְנִין לָהּ שְׁלֹשִׁים יוֹם מִיּוֹם הַתְּבִיעָה.

יח כְּשֵׁם שֶׁנּוֹתְנִין זְמַן לָאִשָּׁה מִשֶּׁתְּבָעָהּ הַבַּעַל לְפַרְנֵס אֶת עַצְמָהּ וְאַחַר כָּךְ תִּנָּשֵׂא, כָּךְ נוֹתְנִין
זְמַן לָאִישׁ לְפַרְנֵס אֶת עַצְמוֹ מִשֶּׁתְּבָעָה הָאִשָּׁה אוֹתוֹ.
וְכַמָּה נוֹתְנִין לוֹ? כְּמוֹ שֶׁנּוֹתְנִין לָהּ: אִם שְׁנֵים עָשָׂר חֹדֶשׁ — שְׁנֵים עָשָׂר חֹדֶשׁ, וְאִם שְׁלֹשִׁים
יוֹם — שְׁלֹשִׁים יוֹם.

יט הִגִּיעַ זְמַן שֶׁנָּתְנוּ לָאִישׁ וְלֹא נָשָׂא — נִתְחַיֵּב בִּמְזוֹנוֹתֶיהָ, אַף־עַל־פִּי שֶׁלֹּא כָנַס.
וְאִם הִגִּיעַ הַזְּמַן בְּאֶחָד בְּשַׁבָּת אוֹ בְּעֶרֶב שַׁבָּת — אֵינוֹ מַעֲלֶה לָהּ מְזוֹנוֹת בְּאוֹתוֹ הַיּוֹם, מִפְּנֵי
שֶׁאֵינוֹ יָכוֹל לִכְנֹס.
וְכֵן אִם חָלָה הוּא אוֹ הִיא אוֹ שֶׁפֵּרְסָה נִדָּה כְּשֶׁהִגִּיעַ הַזְּמַן — אֵינוֹ מַעֲלֶה לָהּ מְזוֹנוֹת;

---

46. I.e., even if she is not yet a *bogeret*. The *Maggid Mishneh* and others explain that the Rambam is referring to a widow who is consecrated. (Therefore, she is given only 30 days, for she had already prepared herself for her first marriage.) He uses the term "non-virgin" to exclude a bride who had previously been widowed after consecration, but had never wed.

47. I.e., to prepare for the wedding celebrations and to prepare a home and furnishings.

48. The *Maggid Mishneh* states that the Rambam's wording implies that everything depends on the woman's status. If she would be given twelve months to prepare herself, her husband is given that amount of time. The Jerusalem Talmud (*Ketubot* 5:3) states that it is his status that is the determining factor: if he has never been married, he is given twelve months. If he is a widower, he is given thirty days. The *Tur* (*Even HaEzer* 56) follows that position.

49. See Halachah 14. With regard to this and the other examples that follow, the rationale is that since he is prevented by forces beyond his control from wedding her, he is not liable. Note the Ramah (*Even HaEzer* 56:3), who states that if the man voluntarily delays the wedding and thus, becomes obligated to support his *arusah*, he must continue to support her even if she falls ill, and the wedding must be postponed because of her illness.

provide her with her livelihood. For she is not fit to wed until she purifies herself,[50] or until she becomes healthy. Similarly, he is not able to wed a woman until he regains his health.

CHAPTER ELEVEN

1. [The following laws apply when a man] weds a virgin who was widowed or divorced or who underwent the rite of *chalitzah*.[1] If she was widowed or divorced or underwent the rite of *chalitzah* after *erusin* alone, the *ketubah* [to which she is entitled from her second husband] is 200 *zuz*. If, however, she had been wed, the *ketubah* [to which she is entitled from her second husband] is 100 *zuz*. Once she is wed, she is considered to be a non-virgin.[2]

Similar [rules apply when a man] weds a virgin [bride] who is [a Canaanite maidservant] who has been freed, who is a convert, or who was held captive [by gentiles and freed]. If the maidservant had been freed, the convert had converted, or the women held captive had been redeemed before they reached the age of three years and one day,[3] they are entitled to a *ketubah* of 200 *zuz*. If [this took place after they reached that age, their *ketubah* is [only] 100 [*zuz*].

2. Why did our Sages ordain that these women receive a *ketubah* of [only] 100 [*zuz*] even though they are virgins? Because it is a presumption that can be accepted as fact that a woman who is wed will engage in marital relations, and similarly, that a maidservant, a gentile woman and a woman held captive by gentiles will have engaged in relations. Hence, they ordained that such women would be entitled to [only] 100 [*zuz*], whether they engaged in relations or not. With regard to all matters, they are considered to be non-virgins.

3. A *mukat etz*[4] [is granted] a *ketubah* of 100 [*zuz*]. Even if [her husband] wed her under the presumption that she was a virgin and then he discovered that she was a *mukat etz*, she is entitled to a *ketubah* of 100 [*zuz*].[5]

When a girl of less than three years of age engages in sexual relations, even when her partner is an adult male, she [is entitled to] a *ketubah* of 200 [*zuz*]. Ultimately, she will heal and be a virgin like all others.

Similarly, when a boy below the age of nine engages in sexual relations with an adult woman, she [is entitled to] a *ketubah* of 200 [*zuz*], as if she had never engaged in relations.[6] For it is only after a boy reaches the age of nine years and one day that relations with him are of consequence. Before that age, they are of no consequence.

50. See Halachah 2.

שֶׁהֲרֵי אֵינָהּ רְאוּיָה לְהִנָּשֵׂא עַד שֶׁתִּטְהַר אוֹ עַד שֶׁתַּבְרִיא, וְכֵן הוּא אֵינוֹ יָכוֹל לִשָּׂא אִשָּׁה עַד שֶׁיַּבְרִיא.

פֶּרֶק אַחַד עָשָׂר

א הַנּוֹשֵׂא בְּתוּלָה שֶׁנִּתְאַלְמְנָה אוֹ שֶׁנִּתְגָּרְשָׁה אוֹ נֶחְלְצָה:

אִם מִן הָאֵרוּסִין נִתְאַלְמְנָה אוֹ נִתְגָּרְשָׁה אוֹ נֶחְלְצָה — כְּתֻבָּתָהּ מָאתַיִם,

וְאִם מִן הַנִּשּׂוּאִין — כְּתֻבָּתָהּ מֵאָה, שֶׁמִּשֶּׁנִּשֵּׂאת הֲרֵי הִיא כִּבְעוּלָה.

וְכֵן הַנּוֹשֵׂא בְּתוּלָה מְשֻׁחְרֶרֶת אוֹ גִּיֹּרֶת אוֹ שְׁבוּיָה:

אִם נִשְׁתַּחְרְרָה הַשִּׁפְחָה וְנִתְגַּיְּרָה הַכּוּתִית וְנִפְדָּת הַשְּׁבוּיָה וְהֵן פְּחוּתוֹת מִבַּת שָׁלֹשׁ שָׁנִים וְיוֹם אֶחָד — כְּתֻבָּתָן מָאתַיִם,

וְאִם הָיוּ בְּנוֹת שָׁלֹשׁ שָׁנִים וְיוֹם אֶחָד וָמַעְלָה — כְּתֻבָּתָן מֵאָה.

ב וּמִפְּנֵי מָה תִּקְּנוּ חֲכָמִים לְאֵלּוּ כְּתֻבָּה מֵאָה וְאַף־עַל־פִּי שֶׁהֵן בְּתוּלוֹת?

הוֹאִיל וְחֶזְקַת הַנְּשׂוּאָה שֶׁתִּבָּעֵל, וְחֶזְקַת הַשִּׁפְחָה וְהַכּוּתִית וְהַשְּׁבוּיָה שֶׁתִּבָּעֵל, תִּקְּנוּ לְאֵלּוּ מֵאָה בֵּין נִבְעֲלוּ בֵּין לֹא נִבְעֲלוּ, וַהֲרֵי הֵן כִּבְעוּלוֹת לְכָל דָּבָר.

ג מַכַּת עֵץ — כְּתֻבָּתָהּ מֵאָה.

אֲפִלּוּ נָשָׂא עַל מְנָת שֶׁהִיא בְּתוּלָה שְׁלֵמָה, וְנִמְצֵאת מַכַּת עֵץ — כְּתֻבָּתָהּ מֵאָה.

קְטַנָּה מִבַּת שָׁלֹשׁ שָׁנִים וּלְמַטָּה שֶׁנִּבְעֲלָה, אֲפִלּוּ בָּא עָלֶיהָ אָדָם גָּדוֹל — כְּתֻבָּתָהּ מָאתַיִם; סוֹפָהּ שֶׁתַּחְזוֹר בְּתוּלָה כִּשְׁאָר הַבְּתוּלוֹת.

וְכֵן גְּדוֹלָה שֶׁבָּא עָלֶיהָ קָטָן מִבֶּן תֵּשַׁע שָׁנִים וּלְמַטָּה — כְּתֻבָּתָהּ מָאתַיִם, כְּאִלּוּ לֹא נִבְעֲלָה כְּלָל;

שֶׁבִּיאַת בֶּן תֵּשַׁע שָׁנִים וְיוֹם אֶחָד — בִּיאָתוֹ בִּיאָה, פָּחוֹת מִזֶּה — אֵין בִּיאָתוֹ בִּיאָה.

---

1. I.e., the woman had been consecrated or wed, but before she and her husband engaged in marital relations, she was either widowed or divorced.
2. Even if there are witnesses to the fact that her husband died directly after they entered the *chuppah* (*Ketubot* 11a).
3. The rationale is that even if a woman engaged in sexual relations before the age of three, her hymen will grow back, as stated in Halachah 3, based on *Ketubot* 11b.
4. Literally, "one struck by a piece of wood," a woman who claims that she did not have hymenal bleeding at the time of her first sexual experience, because she had previously been "struck by a piece of wood" and caused to bleed at that time. As mentioned in Halachah 10, the term is used to refer to any woman who claims that her failure to have hymenal bleeding resulted from causes other than intercourse.
5. Although one might think that the marriage would be annulled, because the husband was operating under a misconception (מקח טעות), *Ketubot* 11b rules that this is not so. As long as she had not engaged in sexual relations previously, their marriage is binding.
6. The *Shulchan Aruch* (*Even HaEzer* 67:4) follows the ruling of *Tosafot, Ketubot* 11b, who

4. Whether a virgin is a *bogeret*,[7] blind,[8] or an *aylonit*,[9] she [is entitled to] a *ketubah* of 200 [*zuz*]. By contrast, no provision was made for a *ketubah* for a woman who is a deaf mute or mentally incompetent. [The rationale is] that no provision has been made for the marriage of a mentally incompetent woman at all.

With regard to a woman who is a deaf mute, although our Sages made provision for her marriage, they did not entitle her to a *ketubah*, so that a man would not refrain from marrying her. Just as she is not entitled to a *ketubah*, so too, [her husband] is not [obligated to provide] her with her livelihood or grant her any other [of the ordinary] conditions of the marriage contract.

If one wed a woman who was a deaf mute and her difficulty was remedied, she is entitled to a *ketubah* and to the other conditions of the marriage contract. [The amount of] her *ketubah* is 100 *zuz*.[10]

5. When a man marries a woman who is a deaf mute or mentally incompetent and writes her a *ketubah* for 10,000 [*zuz*], the obligation is binding; it was he who desired to diminish his assets.

6. [The following rules apply when] a deaf mute or a mentally incompetent man married a woman who was mentally competent. Even if afterwards the deaf mute's disability disappears and the mentally incompetent person gains stability, they are under no obligation to their wives. If, however, [the men] desire to remain [married] to [the women] after their own wellbeing has been restored, [the wives] are entitled to a *ketubah*, and its value should be 100 *zuz*.

If the deaf mute's marriage was made by the court, and they write [his wife] a *ketubah* against his assets, she is entitled to everything that the court has prescribed for her. A court will not arrange a marriage for a mentally incompetent person at all. Since our Sages' injunction will not be maintained in his instance,[11] they did not ordain marriage for him at all.

Similarly, our Sages did not ordain marriage for a male below the age of majority; [the rationale is that] ultimately he will gain the potential to enter into a comprehensive marriage bond.

Why then did they ordain marriage for a girl below the age of majority[12] although she too will ultimately gain the potential for a comprehensive marriage bond? So that she will not be treated in a wanton manner.[13]

A youth should not be [allowed to] marry until he has been examined, and it has been determined that he has manifested signs of physical maturity.

explain that this law applies only when the woman's hymen remains intact despite these relations.
7. This point is necessary to mention because of the factors stated in Halachah 12.

ד בְּתוּלָה שֶׁהִיא בּוֹגֶרֶת אוֹ סוֹמָא אוֹ אַיְלוֹנִית — כְּתֻבָּתָן מָאתַיִם.
אֲבָל הַחֵרֶשֶׁת וְהַשּׁוֹטָה לֹא תִקְּנוּ לָהֶן כְּתֻבָּה.
הַשּׁוֹטָה — לֹא תִקְּנוּ לָהּ נִשּׂוּאִין כְּלָל;
וְהַחֵרֶשֶׁת, אַף־עַל־פִּי שֶׁיֵּשׁ לָהּ נִשּׂוּאִין מִדִּבְרֵיהֶם — לֹא תִקְּנוּ לָהּ כְּתֻבָּה, כְּדֵי שֶׁלֹּא יִמָּנְעוּ מִלָּשֵׂאת אוֹתָהּ.
וּכְשֵׁם שֶׁאֵין לָהּ כְּתֻבָּה, כָּךְ אֵין לָהּ מְזוֹנוֹת וְלֹא תְנַאי מִתְּנָאֵי כְּתֻבָּה.
וְאִם כָּנַס הַחֵרֶשֶׁת וְנִתְפַּקְחָה — יֵשׁ לָהּ כְּתֻבָּה וּתְנָאֵי כְּתֻבָּה, וּכְתֻבָּתָהּ מֵאָה.

ה נָשָׂא חֵרֶשֶׁת אוֹ שׁוֹטָה וְכָתַב לָהֶן מֵאָה מָנֶה — כְּתֻבָּתָן קַיֶּמֶת, מִפְּנֵי שֶׁרָצָה לְהַזִּיק נְכָסָיו.

ו חֵרֵשׁ אוֹ שׁוֹטֶה שֶׁנָּשְׂאוּ נָשִׁים פְּקְחִיוֹת, אַף־עַל־פִּי שֶׁנִּתְפַּקַּח הַחֵרֵשׁ וְנִשְׁתַּפָּה הַשּׁוֹטֶה — אֵין לִנְשֵׁיהֶם עֲלֵיהֶם כְּלוּם.
רָצוּ לְקַיְּמָן אַחַר שֶׁהִבְרִיאוּ — יֵשׁ לָהֶן כְּתֻבָּה, וּכְתֻבָּתָן מֵאָה.
וְאִם בֵּית דִּין הֵם שֶׁהִשִּׂיאוּ הַחֵרֵשׁ וְכָתְבוּ לָהּ כְּתֻבָּתָהּ עַל נְכָסָיו — נוֹטֶלֶת כָּל מַה שֶׁכָּתְבוּ לָהּ בֵּית דִּין.
אֲבָל הַשּׁוֹטָה אֵין בֵּית דִּין מַשִּׂיאִין אוֹתוֹ בְּכָל מָקוֹם.
וּמִפְּנֵי שֶׁאֵין תַּקָּנַת חֲכָמִים עוֹמֶדֶת בּוֹ, לֹא תִקְּנוּ לוֹ נִשּׂוּאִין.
וְכֵן הַקָּטָן לֹא תִקְּנוּ לוֹ חֲכָמִים נִשּׂוּאִין, הוֹאִיל וְסוֹפוֹ לָבוֹא לִידֵי נִשּׂוּאִין גְּמוּרִין.
וּמִפְּנֵי מָה תִּקְּנוּ נִשּׂוּאִין לִקְטַנָּה וְאַף־עַל־פִּי שֶׁהִיא בָּאָה לִידֵי נִשּׂוּאִין גְּמוּרִין?
כְּדֵי שֶׁלֹּא יִנְהֲגוּ בָהּ מִנְהַג הֶפְקֵר.
וְאֵין מַשִּׂיאִין אֶת הַקָּטָן עַד שֶׁבּוֹדְקִין אוֹתוֹ וְיוֹדְעִים שֶׁהֵבִיא סִימָנִין.

---

8. *Ketubot* 36b explains that we are afraid that such a woman might have suffered hymenal bleeding from causes other than intercourse, but will not have noticed the fact.
9. Rashi (*Ketubot* 36a) explains that since an *aylonit* is considered a *bogeret*, this point must be clarified, as it must with regard to a *bogeret*. The above ruling applies only when the husband was aware that the woman was an *aylonit*. If he was not aware of that fact, the woman is not entitled to a *ketubah* at all, as explained in Chapter 24, Halachah 2.
10. Even if she was a virgin at the time of their original marriage, at present she is not a virgin.
11. I.e., a marriage between a mentally incompetent man and an ordinary woman will constantly be pained by strife and will not last. In contrast, a deaf mute is more passive, and his household will not necessarily be characterized by friction (*Yevamot* 112b).
12. This refers to a girl who has been orphaned of her father, or who was divorced after being wed. The Torah - and not our Sages - gives a father the right to consecrate his daughter before she becomes a *na'arah*.
13. If the girl remains unmarried, the prohibitions against relations with her are not as severe, and the Sages feared that they would not be upheld. If she were allowed to marry, the prohibition against adultery would be respected, and she would be treated differently. Moreover, her husband will guard against her association with other men.

7. When a male below the age of majority marries a woman, she is not entitled to a *ketubah*, even if he is already nine years and one day old. If he attains majority and remains [married] to her, she is entitled to the fundamental requirement of the *ketubah*.[14]

Similarly, when a man converts together with his wife, she is entitled to a *ketubah* [of 100 *zuz*]. It was with this intent that he maintained their marriage.[15]

8. Whenever a virgin bride is entitled to a *ketubah* of 200 [*zuz*], there is [the possibility of issuing] a claim against her, [denying] her virginity. Whenever, by contrast, a bride is entitled to a *ketubah* of [only] 100 [*zuz*],[16] or the Sages did not entitle her to a *ketubah* at all,[17] there is no [possibility of issuing] a claim against her [denying] her virginity. [Similarly,] if [a groom] enters into privacy with his *arusah* before their wedding, there is no [possibility of issuing] a claim against her [denying] her virginity.[18]

9. What is meant by a claim [denying a woman's] virginity? [A man] married a woman on the assumption that she was a virgin, and [after the wedding] claims that he did not find signs of virginity. For there are two signs of virginity: a) [hymenal] bleeding at the conclusion of her first sexual experience; b) tightness that is felt during sexual relations at that time.[19]

10. When [a man] weds a virgin who is granted a *ketubah* of 200 [*zuz*], and claims that he did not discover signs of her virginity, the woman is questioned [regarding the matter]. If she says, "It is true that he did not find me a virgin, but this is because I fell, and I was struck by a piece of wood or the ground, and my hymen was damaged," her word is accepted and she is entitled to a *ketubah* of [100 *zuz*].[20]

---

14. I.e., only the fundamental requirements of the *ketubah*, but not any additional amount that the youth added to the marriage contract, unless he renews that commitment after he reaches majority. Otherwise, that commitment - like any commitment made by a minor - is of no substance. Moreover, he is obligated for the fundamental requirement of the *ketubah* only when he engaged in marital relations with his wife after he attained majority. If not, the marriage - and thus the marriage contract - is of no consequence.

With regard to the fundamental requirements of the *ketubah*, the Rambam writes in his Commentary on the Mishnah (*Ketubot* 9:8) that she is entitled to either 200 or 100 *zuz*, depending on her status at the time of the wedding.

15. Rabbenu Asher differs and maintains that the laws applying to a convert are the same as those applying to a minor. Both opinions are alluded to by the *Shulchan Aruch* (*Even HaEzer* 67:11). (See the *Beit Shmuel* 67:12, which explains the Rambam's position: Even if a convert made a commitment of more than 100 *zuz* to his wife, any sum above 100 *zuz* is considered to be an addition to the *ketubah* and is therefore no longer binding when the convert accepts his new status as a Jew.)

ז קָטָן, אֲפִלּוּ בֶּן תֵּשַׁע שָׁנִים וְיוֹם אֶחָד, שֶׁנָּשָׂא אִשָּׁה — אֵין לָהּ כְּתֻבָּה.

וְאִם הִגְדִּיל וְקִיְּמָהּ אַחַר שֶׁהִגְדִּיל — יֵשׁ לָהּ עִקַּר כְּתֻבָּה.

וְכֵן גֵּר שֶׁנִּתְגַּיֵּר הוּא וְאִשְׁתּוֹ — כְּתֻבָּתָהּ מָנֶה, שֶׁעַל מְנָת כֵּן קִיְּמָהּ.

ח כָּל בְּתוּלָה שֶׁכְּתֻבָּתָהּ מָאתַיִם — יֵשׁ לָהּ טַעֲנַת בְּתוּלִים;

וְכֹל שֶׁכְּתֻבָּתָהּ מֵאָה, אוֹ שֶׁלֹּא תִּקְּנוּ לָהּ חֲכָמִים כְּתֻבָּה — אֵין לָהּ טַעֲנַת בְּתוּלִים.

וְהַמִּתְיַחֵד עִם אֲרוּסָתוֹ קֹדֶם נִשּׂוּאִין — אֵין לָהּ טַעֲנַת בְּתוּלִים.

ט וּמַה הִיא טַעֲנַת בְּתוּלִים?

זֶה שֶׁנָּשָׂא אִשָּׁה שֶׁחֶזְקָתָהּ שֶׁהִיא בְתוּלָה, וְטוֹעֵן וְאוֹמֵר: לֹא מְצָאתִיהָ בְתוּלָה.

וּשְׁנֵי סִימָנִין הֵן לִבְתוּלָה:

הָאֶחָד — דָּמִים שֶׁשּׁוֹתְתִין מִמֶּנָּה בְּסוֹף בִּיאָה רִאשׁוֹנָה.

וְהַשֵּׁנִי — הַדֹּחַק שֶׁיִּמָּצֵא בָּהּ בְּבִיאָה רִאשׁוֹנָה בִּשְׁעַת תַּשְׁמִישׁ.

י הַנּוֹשֵׂא אֶת הַבְּתוּלָה שֶׁכְּתֻבָּתָהּ מָאתַיִם, וְטָעַן וְאָמַר: לֹא מְצָאתִיהָ בְּתוּלָה — שׁוֹאֲלִין אוֹתָהּ:

אִם אָמְרָה: אֱמֶת הוּא, לֹא מְצָאַנִי בְתוּלָה, מִפְּנֵי שֶׁנָּפַלְתִּי וְהֻכַּנִי עֵץ אוֹ קַרְקַע וְהָלְכוּ בְתוּלַי — הֲרֵי זוֹ נֶאֱמֶנֶת, וְתַחֲזֹר כְּתֻבָּתָהּ לְמָנֶה.

16. I.e., even a woman who was widowed after the wedding, before engaging in relations with her husband. Even though her second husband marries her under the impression that she is a virgin, there is no possibility of issuing such a claim against her.

17. The obligation to grant a virgin bride a *ketubah* of 200 *zuz* is Rabbinic in origin. At the same time that our Sages instituted that obligation, they granted the husband a safeguard: that his word would be accepted with regard to a claim denying the woman's virginity. In these instances, since the woman was not granted the additional money, the safeguard provided by the Sages also does not apply (*Maggid Mishneh*).

18. We suspect that the groom had relations with her and later forgot the matter (Rashi, *Ketubot* 9b). See also note 30.

19. As stated in the following halachot, unless there are other factors that support the woman's position, as will be explained, the husband's claim is accepted. We assume that the husband would not go to the time and expense of preparing a wedding feast and then mar the celebration by denying his wife's virginity unless the claim were true (*Ketubot* 10a).

20. Unless there are witnesses who can testify that the woman engaged in relations previously, the only question before the court is the amount of the woman's *ketubah*. She is permitted to remain married to her husband, because there is no proof that she willingly engaged in sexual relations with another person after she was consecrated. (See *Hilchot Issurei Bi'ah* 18:10.)

An exception to the above is a woman married to a priest. Issuing a claim questioning her virginity places the entire foundation of their marriage in doubt.

Although [her husband] claims: "Perhaps you engaged in intercourse, and I am under no obligation to you,"[21] his claim is not accepted, for his claim is not absolute.[22] He may, however, have a ban of ostracism issued, conditional on her having engaged in relations with another man.

11. If [the woman] says, "It is true that he did not find me a virgin, for another man raped me after I had been consecrated by him," her word is accepted, and she is entitled to a *ketubah* of 200 [*zuz*] as before.[23]

If [her husband] claims: "Perhaps you were raped before you were consecrated, and the agreement I entered was based on false premises. Or perhaps you willingly engaged in relations after you were consecrated" [his claim is not accepted]. He may, however, have a ban of ostracism issued conditionally against anyone who makes a false claim to have him incur a financial obligation for which he is not liable.

12. If he claims, "I did not find her a virgin," and she claims, "He has not had intercourse with me and I am still a virgin," she should be examined. Alternatively, he should have relations with her under the surveillance of witnesses [and the truth will be clarified].[24]

If she claims, "He had relations with me and he found me a virgin like all others, and his claim is false," he is questioned [and asked to clarify his statements]. We ask him: "Why do you say that she was not a virgin?" If he answers: "Because she did not have hymenal bleeding," we check her family [history]. Perhaps [the women of] this [family] are known not to have [vaginal] bleeding at all: neither menstrual bleeding nor hymenal bleeding. If this was found to be true, we presume [that she was a virgin, and she is entitled to a *ketubah* of 200 *zuz*].

If the women in her family are not known to have such a condition, we check her [physical state]; perhaps she is afflicted by a serious infirmity that has parched her body's natural fluids, or [perhaps] she was afflicted by hunger. Therefore, we have her bathe, eat and drink until she becomes healthy. At which point, [the couple] engage in relations again to see if she manifests hymenal bleeding or not.

If she is not hampered by sickness, hunger or the like, the [husband's] claim that she was not a virgin [is accepted]. [This applies] even if he felt tightness during relations. Since there was no hymenal bleeding, her hymen was not intact. For every virgin will manifest hymenal bleeding, whether she is a minor or above the age of majority, whether a *na'arah* or a *bogeret*, unless [this is prevented by an external factor,] illness or the like, as explained.

21. I.e., the husband claims that he has entered into a *mekach ta'ut*, an agreement based on false premises. He had desired to marry a virgin, and he was not prepared to marry a woman who had had relations with another man. Therefore, he desires to have the marriage annulled entirely.

אַף־עַל־פִּי שֶׁהוּא טוֹעֵן וְאוֹמֵר: שֶׁמָּא אִישׁ בָּא עָלַיִךְ וְאֵין לָךְ כְּלוּם — אֵין מַשְׁגִּיחִין בְּטַעֲנָתוֹ.

וְיֵשׁ לוֹ לְהַחֲרִים סְתָם שֶׁלֹּא בָא עָלֶיהָ אִישׁ, שֶׁאֵין הַדָּבָר וַדַּאי לוֹ.

יא אָמְרָה הִיא: אֱמֶת אָמַר, שֶׁלֹּא מְצָאַנִי בְתוּלָה, וְאִישׁ בָּא עָלַי בְּאֹנֶס אַחַר שֶׁנִּתְאָרַסְתִּי לוֹ —

הֲרֵי זוֹ נֶאֱמֶנֶת, וּכְתֻבָּתָהּ מָאתַיִם כְּמוֹ שֶׁהָיְתָה.

וְאִם טָעַן וְאָמַר: שֶׁמָּא עַד שֶׁלֹּא אֲרַסְתִּיךְ נֶאֱנַסְתְּ וּמִקָּחִי מְקַח טָעוּת, אוֹ אַחַר שֶׁאֵרַסְתִּיךְ נִבְעַלְתְּ בִּרְצוֹנֵךְ —

הֲרֵי זֶה מַחֲרִים סְתָם עַל מִי שֶׁטּוֹעֵן שֶׁקֶר כְּדֵי לְחַיְּבֵנִי מָמוֹן שֶׁאֵינִי חַיָּב בּוֹ.

יב טָעַן וְאָמַר: לֹא מְצָאתִיהָ בְתוּלָה, וְהִיא אוֹמֶרֶת: לֹא בָּא עָלַי וַעֲדַיִן אֲנִי בְתוּלָה — בּוֹדְקִין אוֹתָהּ, אוֹ חוֹזֵר וּבוֹעֵל בִּפְנֵי עֵדִים.

אָמְרָה: בָּא עָלַי וּבְתוּלָה מְצָאַנִי כְּכָל הַבְּתוּלוֹת, וְשֶׁקֶר הוּא טוֹעֵן — שׁוֹאֲלִין אוֹתוֹ וְאוֹמְרִין לוֹ: מֶה הָיָה הַדָּבָר עַד שֶׁאָמַרְתָּ עַד שֶׁאֵינָהּ בְּתוּלָה?

אִם אָמַר: מִפְּנֵי שֶׁלֹּא מָצָאתִי לָהּ דָּם — בּוֹדְקִין בְּמִשְׁפַּחְתָּהּ, שֶׁמָּא אֵין לָהֶם דָּם כְּלָל, לֹא דַם נִדָּה וְלֹא דַם בְּתוּלִים.

אִם נִמְצְאוּ כֻּלָּן כֵּן — הֲרֵי זוֹ בְּחֶזְקָתָהּ;

לֹא נִמְצְאוּ בְּנוֹת מִשְׁפַּחְתָּהּ כֵּן — בּוֹדְקִין אוֹתָהּ, שֶׁמָּא חֳלִי גָדוֹל יֵשׁ בָּהּ שֶׁיִּבֵּשׁ לַחְלוּחִית הָאֵיבָרִים, אוֹ שֶׁהָיְתָה מִתְעַנִּית בְּרָעָב.

מַרְטִיבִין אוֹתָהּ וּמַאֲכִילִין אוֹתָהּ וּמַשְׁקִין אוֹתָהּ עַד שֶׁתַּבְרִיא, וְתִבָּעֵל שֵׁנִית, וְנִרְאֶה אִם תּוֹצִיא דָם אִם לָאו.

וְאִם אֵין שָׁם חֳלִי וְלֹא רָעָב וְלֹא כַּיּוֹצֵא בּוֹ — הֲרֵי זוֹ טַעֲנַת בְּתוּלִים.

וְאַף־עַל־פִּי שֶׁמָּצָא דֹחַק בְּעֵת תַּשְׁמִישׁ — הוֹאִיל וְלֹא יָצָא דָם, אֵין כָּאן בְּתוּלִים;

שֶׁכָּל בְּתוּלָה יֵשׁ לָהּ דָּם — בֵּין קְטַנָּה בֵּין גְּדוֹלָה, בֵּין נַעֲרָה בֵּין בּוֹגֶרֶת — אֶלָּא מִפְּנֵי הַחֳלִי, כְּמוֹ שֶׁבֵּאַרְנוּ.

22. I.e., he is not certain that she had engaged in relations with another man. In all matters of Torah law, whenever one person has a claim that is absolute (*bari*, in this instance the woman's claim that her hymen was damaged by factors other than intercourse) and one that is not absolute (*shema*, the man's claim), the claim that is absolute is accepted.
23. Since she was raped against her will, she is not forced to suffer a loss and is entitled to the full amount of the *ketubah*.
24. The intent is not that witnesses should observe the couple engaging in relations. This is forbidden, as stated in Chapter 14, Halachah 16. Instead, the intent is that they should inspect the sheet before and after the couple engage in relations for signs of hymenal bleeding.

If [the husband] said: "[I claim that she was not a virgin,] because I did not feel tightness [during intercourse]. Instead, I found an open passageway," we inquire with regard to [the woman's] age. Perhaps she is a *bogeret*, and most *bogrot* do not have tightness that can be felt substantially [during intercourse], for as she grew older [the adhesion of] her limbs lessened, and the virginal [tightness] disappeared.

If she had not become a *bogeret* yet, we ask him: "Perhaps you leaned on the side or [entered] gently[25] during intercourse, and therefore you did not feel any tightness?" If he replies: "No. I found an open passageway," [his] claim that she was not a virgin [is accepted] with regard to any woman who has not reached the age of *bagrut*, regardless of whether she was a minor or a *na'arah*, or whether she was healthy or sick. For the vaginal channel of every virgin is closed. Even if she manifests hymenal bleeding, she is not considered to be a virgin, because the vaginal channel was open.[26]

13. There are *geonim* who rule that for a *bogeret*, the claim that she did not have hymenal bleeding is not valid, but the claim that her vaginal channel was open is valid. This does not appear [to be based on the proper text of] the Talmud. They had inaccurate versions of the text. I have investigated many texts, including those of an early era,[27] and I have discovered the version to be as I ruled. For a *bogeret*, the only valid claim is [that she did not manifest] hymenal bleeding.[28]

14. Our Sages were those who instituted the fundamental requirement of a marriage contract for a woman and they also instituted [the following consideration]: Whenever [a man] makes a claim that his wife was not a virgin, and the woman disputes his claim, [the husband's claim] is accepted. It is the woman's responsibility to bring support for her claim, not the man's. [The rationale is] that we assume that a man will not labor to prepare a [wedding] feast and then mar it, turning his celebration into mourning.[29]

15. Until when may a husband issue a claim denying his wife's virginity? If [the couple] went into privacy, only immediately [thereafter].[30] If they did not enter into privacy, he has this option even after 30 days.

---

25. Other authorities (and their opinion is quoted in the *Shulchan Aruch, Even HaEzer* 68:6) state: "Maybe you did not enter gently?" - i.e., because of the husband's hurry to complete the sexual act, he did not feel the tightness.

The Ramah (*loc. cit.*) quotes the opinion of Rabbenu Asher, who states that the claim: "I discovered an open passageway," can be made only by a man who has been married before. If he was not married before, he would not have the experience to know the difference between virginal tightness and a non-virgin's state.

וְאִם אָמַר: מִפְּנֵי שֶׁלֹּא מָצָאתִי דֹחַק, אֶלָּא פֶּתַח פָּתוּחַ מָצָאתִי — שׁוֹאֲלִין עַל שְׁנוֹתֶיהָ, שֶׁמָּא בּוֹגֶרֶת הִיא;

שֶׁרֹב הַבּוֹגָרוֹת אֵין לָהֶן דֹּחַק שֶׁמַּרְגִּישִׁין בּוֹ הָרֻבֶּה, שֶׁהֲרֵי גָדְלָה וְנִתְרַפּוּ אֵיבָרֶיהָ וְכָלוּ בְּתוּלֶיהָ. וְאִם לֹא בָּגְרָה עֲדַיִן — אוֹמְרִין לוֹ: שֶׁמָּא הִטֵּיתָה אוֹ בְּעַלְתָּהּ בְּנַחַת וּלְפִיכָךְ לֹא הִרְגַּשְׁתָּ בַּדֹּחַק?

אִם אָמַר: לֹא כִי, אֶלָּא וַדַּאי פֶּתַח פָּתוּחַ הָיָה — הֲרֵי זוֹ טַעֲנַת בְּתוּלִים לְכָל בְּתוּלָה שֶׁלֹּא בָּגְרָה: בֵּין קְטַנָּה בֵּין נַעֲרָה, בֵּין בְּרִיאָה בֵּין חוֹלָה;

שֶׁכָּל נַעֲרָה בְּתוּלָה — פִּתְחָהּ סָתוּם הוּא.

וְאַף־עַל־פִּי שֶׁיָּצָא הַדָּם — הוֹאִיל וּמָצָא פֶּתַח פָּתוּחַ, אֵין כָּאן בְּתוּלִים.

יג יֵשׁ גְּאוֹנִים שֶׁהוֹרוּ, שֶׁהַבּוֹגֶרֶת אֵין לָהּ טַעֲנַת דָּמִים וְיֵשׁ לָהּ טַעֲנַת פֶּתַח פָּתוּחַ. וְאֵין דֶּרֶךְ הַגְּמָרָא מַרְאֶה דָּבָר זֶה, וְטָעוּת הָיָה בַּנֻּסְחָאוֹת שֶׁלָּהֶם.

וּכְבָר בָּדַקְתִּי עַל סְפָרִים רַבִּים וְקַדְמוֹנִים, וּמָצָאתִי שֶׁהַדָּבָר כְּמוֹ שֶׁבֵּאַרְנוּ, שֶׁאֵין לַבּוֹגֶרֶת אֶלָּא טַעֲנַת דָּמִים בִּלְבַד.

יד חֲכָמִים הֵם שֶׁתִּקְּנוּ עִקַר כְּתֻבָּה לָאִשָּׁה,

וְהֵם הִתְקִינוּ וְאָמְרוּ, שֶׁכָּל הַטּוֹעֵן טַעֲנַת בְּתוּלִים וְהָאִשָּׁה מַכְחֶשֶׁת אוֹתוֹ — נֶאֱמָן, וְעָלֶיהָ לְהָבִיא רְאָיָה, לֹא עַל הָאִישׁ;

שֶׁחֲזָקָה הִיא, שֶׁאֵין אָדָם טוֹרֵחַ בִּסְעֻדָה וּמַפְסִידָהּ, וְהוֹפֵךְ שִׂמְחָתוֹ אֵבֶל.

טו וְעַד מָתַי יֵשׁ לוֹ לִטְעֹן טַעֲנַת בְּתוּלִים?

אִם נִסְתְּרָה — מִיָּד,

וְאִם לֹא נִסְתְּרָה — אֲפִלּוּ לְאַחַר שְׁלֹשִׁים יוֹם.

---

26. The Ramban and the Rashba state that the claim that the woman's vaginal channel was open can be made only in an instance in which the sheet on which the couple had relations was lost. If, however, the sheet is available, it should be inspected. If it has signs of blood, she is considered a virgin; and if not, she is not. This opinion is mentioned in the *Shulchan Aruch* (*loc. cit.*), but does not appear to have been accepted.

27. See *Hilchot Malveh V'Loveh* 15:2, where the Rambam states that he had available texts of the Talmud that were almost 500 years old. These would have been written approximately 200 years after the time of the Talmud's composition.

28. The Rambam's ruling is substantiated by our text of the Talmud (*Ketubot* 36b) and the ruling of the *Shulchan Aruch* (*Even HaEzer* 68:3). The differing opinion mentioned by the Rambam is that of Rabbenu Chanan'el.

29. Based on this rationale, the *Maggid Mishneh* mentions opinions that state that the man's word is accepted only when he prepared the wedding feast. If he did not, the woman's word is accepted.

30. We assume that the couple had relations and he discovered her to be a virgin. The fact that he issued a claim against her afterwards stemmed from discontent for other reasons, without any connection to her personal state.

16. All the *geonim* have ruled that our Sages' statement that the husband's statements are accepted even though his wife disputes his claim applies only with regard to nullifying the obligation for the fundamental requirement of the marriage contract. Nevertheless, the woman is entitled to the additional amount [to which her husband committed himself][31] unless there is clear proof that she was not a virgin, or she admitted that she was not a virgin before she was consecrated and that she deceived him.

Therefore, [the husband] may require her to take an oath while holding a sacred article,[32] as must be done by all others who must take oaths before they collect [the money due them].[33] Afterwards, she may collect the additional sum.

She, by contrast, does not have the option of requiring him to take an oath that he did not discover her to be a virgin, before she must forfeit the fundamental requirement of the marriage contract, for it is a presumption accepted as fact that a person will not labor to prepare a [wedding] feast and then mar it. She may, however, have a ban of ostracism issued conditionally, applying to anyone who lodges false claims against her.

17. If [the husband] desires to remain married to [his wife] after causing her to forfeit the fundamental requirement of the marriage contract, he must write her [a new *ketubah* for] 100 [*zuz*]. For it is forbidden for a man to live with his wife for even one moment without a *ketubah*, as we have explained.[34]

CHAPTER TWELVE

1. When a man marries a woman, whether she is a virgin or a non-virgin, whether she is above the age of majority or a minor, and whether she was born Jewish, is a convert or a freed slave, he incurs ten responsibilities toward her and receives four privileges.[1]

2. With regard to his ten responsibilities: three stem from the Torah. They include *sha'arah, kesutah v'onatah.*[2] *Sha'arah* means providing her with subsistence.[3] *Kesutah* means supplying her with garments, and *onatah* refers to conjugal rights.

31. Although there are authorities (among them Rabbenu Asher) who offer reasons why the husband's word should be accepted in this instance as well, the prevailing view (and the ruling of the *Shulchan Aruch, Even HaEzer* 68:8) follows the Rambam's decision. The rationale is that the fundamental requirement of the marriage contract is a Rabbinic injunction, and the same authority that obligated the husband to meet this requirement rescinded it when he lodged a claim denying her virginity. The additional amount,

טז הוֹרוּ כָּל הַגְּאוֹנִים, שֶׁזֶּה שֶׁאָמְרוּ חֲכָמִים שֶׁהוּא נֶאֱמָן אִם הִכְחִישַׁתּוּ אִשְׁתּוֹ — לְהַפְסִידָהּ עִקַּר הַכְּתֻבָּה, אֲבָל הַתּוֹסֶפֶת — יֵשׁ לָהּ;

אֶלָּא אִם כֵּן נוֹדַע בִּרְאָיָה בְּרוּרָה שֶׁהָיְתָה בְּעוּלָה, אוֹ שֶׁהוֹדֵת לוֹ שֶׁהִיא בְּעוּלָה קֹדֶם שֶׁתִּתְאָרֵס וְהִטְעַתּוּ.

לְפִיכָךְ יֵשׁ לוֹ לְהַשְׁבִּיעָהּ בִּנְקִיטַת חֵפֶץ, כְּדִין כָּל הַנִּשְׁבָּעִין וְנוֹטְלִין, וְאַחַר כָּךְ תִּגְבֶּה הַתּוֹסֶפֶת. וְאֵין לָהּ לְהַשְׁבִּיעוֹ שֶׁלֹּא מְצָאָהּ בְּתוּלָה וְאַחַר כָּךְ תַּפְסִיד עִקַּר כְּתֻבָּה, שֶׁחֶזְקָה הִיא שֶׁאֵין אָדָם טוֹרֵחַ בִּסְעֻדָּה וּמַפְסִידָהּ;

וְיֵשׁ לָהּ לְהַחֲרִים סְתָם עַל מִי שֶׁטּוֹעֵן עָלֶיהָ שֶׁקֶר.

יז הֲרֵי שֶׁרָצָה לְקַיְּמָהּ אַחַר שֶׁהִפְסִידָה עִקַּר הַכְּתֻבָּה — חוֹזֵר וְכוֹתֵב לָהּ מֵאָה, לְפִי שֶׁאָסוּר לְאָדָם לִשְׁהוֹת עִם אִשְׁתּוֹ שָׁעָה אַחַת בְּלֹא כְּתֻבָּה, כְּמוֹ שֶׁבֵּאַרְנוּ.

פֶּרֶק שְׁנֵים עָשָׂר

א כְּשֶׁנּוֹשֵׂא אָדָם אִשָּׁה — בֵּין בְּתוּלָה בֵּין בְּעוּלָה, בֵּין גְּדוֹלָה בֵּין קְטַנָּה, אַחַת בַּת יִשְׂרָאֵל וְאַחַת הַגִּיֹּרֶת אוֹ הַמְשֻׁחְרֶרֶת — יִתְחַיֵּב לָהּ בַּעֲשָׂרָה דְבָרִים, וְיִזְכֶּה בְּאַרְבָּעָה דְבָרִים.

ב וְהָעֲשָׂרָה — שְׁלֹשָׁה מֵהֶן מִן הַתּוֹרָה, וְאֵלּוּ הֵן:
שְׁאֵרָהּ, כְּסוּתָהּ, וְעוֹנָתָהּ.
שְׁאֵרָהּ — אֵלּוּ מְזוֹנוֹתֶיהָ.
כְּסוּתָהּ — כְּמַשְׁמָעוֹ.
עוֹנָתָהּ — לָבוֹא עָלֶיהָ כְּדֶרֶךְ כָּל הָאָרֶץ.

by contrast, is a present to which the husband voluntarily obligated himself, and that obligation may be nullified only if it is proven that it was made under false premises.
32. See *Hilchot Sh'vuot* 11:8, which states that such an oath is administered while the person is holding a Torah scroll. Significantly, the Rambam's ruling here represents a change of mind from his statements in his Commentary on the Mishnah (*Ketubot* 1:3), where he states that in such a situation the woman is required to take merely a *sh'vuat hesset*, a less severe oath.
33. I.e., the situation is analogous to a person who holds a promissory note and may be asked to take an oath that it is valid before he can collect it, as explained in *Hilchot Malveh V'Loveh* 14:2-3.
34. Chapter 10, Halachah 10.

1. These ten responsibilities and four privileges are all explained in detail in the chapters that follow, through Chapter 23.
2. These requirements are mentioned in Exodus 21:10. The verse forbids a husband from denying his wife these rights. *Sefer HaMitzvot* (Negative Commandment 262) and *Sefer HaChinuch* (Mitzvah 46) consider this to be one of the 613 mitzvot of the Torah.
3. Note the commentary of the Ramban on Exodus (loc. cit.), which interprets *sha'arah* and

The seven responsibilities ordained by the Rabbis are all conditions [of the marriage contract] established by the court. The first is the fundamental requirement of the marriage contract. The others are referred to as *t'na'ei ketubah*, the conditions of the marriage contract. They are:

a) to provide medical treatment if she becomes sick;

b) to redeem her if she is held captive:

c) to bury her if she dies;

d) the right for her to continue living in his home after his death as long as she remains a widow;

e) the right for her daughters to receive their subsistence from his estate after his death until they become consecrated;

f) the right for her sons to inherit her *ketubah* in addition to their share in her husband's estate together with their brothers [borne by other wives, if she dies before her husband does].

3. The four privileges that the husband is granted are all Rabbinic in origin. They are:

a) the right to the fruits of her labor;

b) the right to any ownerless object she discovers;

c) the right to benefit from the profits of her property during her lifetime;

d) the right to inherit her [property] if she dies during his lifetime. His rights to her property supersede [the rights of] all others.[4]

4. Our Sages also ordained that the fruits of a wife's labor should parallel her subsistence, [the obligation to] redeem her should parallel [the right to] the benefit from her property, and [the obligation to] bury her should parallel [the right to] inherit [the property mentioned in] her *ketubah*.

Therefore, if a woman says: "I will not [hold you obligated for] my subsistence, but I will not work,"[5] she is given this option, and she cannot be compelled to work.[6] If, however, her husband says: "I will not provide for your subsistence, and I will not receive the right to the fruits of your labor," he is not given this option, lest the woman be unable to earn her subsistence.[7] Because of this institution, [the obligation to provide for a woman's] subsistence is considered to be one of the *t'na'ei ketubah*.[8]

---

kesutah as also referring to conjugal rights and maintains that the obligation to provide a wife with her subsistence and with garments is Rabbinic. Most authorities, however, follow the Rambam's understanding.

4. The Ra'avad and others maintain that the husband's right to inherit his wife's property stems from the Torah itself. The matter is the subject of a difference of opinion between our Sages (*Ketubot* 83b), and there is no explicit resolution of the question in the Talmud. Rav Kapach maintains that the early manuscripts of the Rambam's Commentary on the Mishnah (*Ketubot* 9:1; *Bava Batra* 8:1) indicate that the Rambam himself originally

וְהַשְּׁבָעָה מִדִּבְרֵי סוֹפְרִים. וְכֻלָּן תְּנָאֵי בֵּית דִּין הֵם.
הָאֶחָד מֵהֶם — עִקַּר כְּתֻבָּה,
וְהַשְּׁאָר — הֵם הַנִּקְרָאִין תְּנָאֵי כְּתֻבָּה, וְאֵלּוּ הֵן:
לִרְפֹּאתָהּ אִם חָלְתָה,
וְלִפְדּוֹתָהּ אִם נִשְׁבֵּת,
לְקָבְרָהּ אִם מֵתָה,
וְלִהְיוֹת נִזּוֹנֶת מִן נְכָסָיו וְיוֹשֶׁבֶת בְּבֵיתוֹ אַחַר מוֹתוֹ כָּל זְמַן אַלְמְנוּתָהּ,
וְלִהְיוֹת בְּנוֹתֶיהָ מִמֶּנּוּ נִזּוֹנוֹת מִנְּכָסָיו אַחֲרֵי מוֹתוֹ עַד שֶׁתִּתְאָרַסְנָה,
וְלִהְיוֹת בָּנֶיהָ הַזְּכָרִים מִמֶּנּוּ יוֹרְשִׁין כְּתֻבָּתָהּ יוֹתֵר עַל חֶלְקָם בַּיְרֻשָּׁה שֶׁעִם אֲחֵיהֶם.

ג וְהָאַרְבָּעָה שֶׁזּוֹכֶה בָּהֶן — כֻּלָּם מִדִּבְרֵי סוֹפְרִים, וְאֵלּוּ הֵן:
לִהְיוֹת מַעֲשֵׂה יָדֶיהָ שֶׁלּוֹ,
וְלִהְיוֹת מְצִיאָתָהּ שֶׁלּוֹ,
וְשֶׁיִּהְיֶה אוֹכֵל כָּל פֵּרוֹת נְכָסֶיהָ בְּחַיֶּיהָ,
וְאִם מֵתָה בְּחַיָּיו — יִירָשֶׁנָּה, וְהוּא קוֹדֵם לְכָל אָדָם בַּיְרֻשָּׁה.

ד וְעוֹד תִּקְּנוּ חֲכָמִים, שֶׁיִּהְיוּ מַעֲשֵׂה יְדֵי הָאִשָּׁה כְּנֶגֶד מְזוֹנוֹתֶיהָ,
וּפִדְיוֹנָהּ — כְּנֶגֶד אֲכִילַת פֵּרוֹת נְכָסֶיהָ,
וּקְבוּרָתָהּ — כְּנֶגֶד יְרֻשָּׁתוֹ לִכְתֻבָּתָהּ.
לְפִיכָךְ, אִם אָמְרָה הָאִשָּׁה: אֵינִי נִזּוֹנֶת וְאֵינִי עוֹשָׂה — שׁוֹמְעִין לָהּ, וְאֵין כּוֹפִין אוֹתָהּ.
אֲבָל אִם אָמַר הַבַּעַל: אֵינִי זָנֵךְ וְאֵינִי נוֹטֵל כְּלוּם מִמַּעֲשֵׂה יָדַיִךְ — אֵין שׁוֹמְעִין לוֹ, שֶׁמָּא לֹא יַסְפִּיקוּ לָהּ מַעֲשֵׂה יָדֶיהָ בִּמְזוֹנוֹתֶיהָ.
וּמִפְּנֵי תַּקָּנָה זוֹ יֵחָשְׁבוּ הַמְּזוֹנוֹת מִתְּנָאֵי הַכְּתֻבָּה.

subscribed to the view mentioned by the Ra'avad and changed his mind later in life. (See also Halachah 9.)

5. With regard to the other two matters that are linked the husband's obligation to redeem her and to bury her, the woman does not have this option. Although this arrangement was instituted for the woman's benefit, our Sages did not give her a choice regarding these matters, because they desired to ensure that the woman would not be forced to remain in captivity among the gentiles and that she would be buried (*Shulchan Aruch* and Ramah, *Even HaEzer* 69:5).

6. Our Sages instituted this arrangement for the woman's benefit, since a woman's income could not ordinarily provide for her subsistence. Accordingly, the option of whether or not to forego the arrangement is in the woman's hands. If a woman can earn more than her subsistence, she is also entitled to forego the above arrangement.

Even in such a situation, the woman is still responsible for taking care of the household tasks (*Maggid Mishneh*).

7. The husband may, however, tell his wife: "Endeavor to earn your subsistence, and I will compensate for whatever deficiency remains" (Ramah, *Even HaEzer* 69:4).

8. I.e., although the *t'na'ei ketubah* are rabbinic in origin, and the obligation to provide

5. Whether or not these matters were written in the marriage contract - indeed, even if a marriage contract was not written and the couple merely married - once they marry, the husband is granted the four privileges mentioned, and the woman is granted the ten rights mentioned. There is no need to state them explicitly.[9]

6. If the husband made a stipulation that he would not be responsible for one of these obligations - or the wife made a stipulation that [her husband] would not be granted one of these privileges - [and the other party agreed,] the stipulation is binding,[10] with the exception of three matters with regard to which it is impossible for a stipulation to be made. Indeed, if a stipulation is made with regard to these three matters, it is of no consequence. These [three] are: [the woman's] conjugal rights, the fundamental requirement of the marriage contract and [the husband's right] to inherit [his wife's property].

7. What is implied? If [the groom] made a stipulation with his bride that he is not obligated to give her conjugal rights, his stipulation is of no substance. For he has made a stipulation against what is written in the Torah, and the stipulation does not concern financial matters.[11]

8. When a man makes a stipulation to reduce the amount of the fundamental requirement of the marriage contract - or he writes a *ketubah* for either 200 or 100 [*zuz*], but she writes that she has already received a portion of the sum, when in fact she did not[12] - his stipulation is of no substance.[13] For whenever a person establishes a marriage contract with a virgin for less than 200 [*zuz*] or with a non-virgin for less than 100 [*zuz*], the sexual relations [he conducts with his wife] are considered promiscuous.[14]

9. If he makes a stipulation after he weds her[15] that he will not inherit her property, his stipulation is of no consequence. Although the husband's [right to] inherit [his wife's property] is a rabbinic institution, [our Sages] reinforced their edict, [giving it the power of a statute of] the Torah.

With regard to [the Torah's statutes of] inheritance, all stipulations that are made are of no consequence, despite the fact that financial matters are concerned, as [derived from Numbers 27:11]: "the statutes of judgment."[16]

---

for the woman's subsistence is from the Torah, since the linkage of it with her wages is rabbinic, the obligation is considered to be part of the *t'na'ei ketubah.*

9. I.e., they are obligations that apply universally and are not dependent on the consent of a particular couple.

10. The principle upon which this statement is based is that any stipulation to which both parties agree that concerns monetary rights - even those that are granted to a person by the Torah - is binding (*Kiddushin* 19b). For a person has the option to waive his right

ה כָּל הַדְּבָרִים הָאֵלוּ, אַף־עַל־פִּי שֶׁלֹּא נִכְתְּבוּ בִּשְׁטַר הַכְּתֻבָּה, וַאֲפִלּוּ לֹא כָּתְבוּ כְּתֻבָּה אֶלָּא נָשָׂא סְתָם — כֵּיוָן שֶׁנְּשָׂאָהּ, זָכָה בְּאַרְבָּעָה דְּבָרִים שֶׁלּוֹ, וְזָכְתָה הָאִשָּׁה בַּעֲשָׂרָה דְּבָרִים שֶׁלָּהּ, וְאֵינָן צְרִיכִין לְפָרֵשׁ.

ו הִתְנָה הַבַּעַל שֶׁלֹּא יִתְחַיֵּב בְּאֶחָד מִן הַדְּבָרִים שֶׁהוּא חַיָּב בָּהֶן, אוֹ שֶׁהִתְנַת הָאִשָּׁה שֶׁלֹּא יִזְכֶּה הַבַּעַל בְּאֶחָד מִן הַדְּבָרִים שֶׁהוּא זוֹכֶה בָּהֶם — הַתְּנַאי קַיָּם; חוּץ מִשְּׁלֹשָׁה דְּבָרִים, שֶׁאֵין הַתְּנַאי מוֹעִיל בָּהֶן, וְכָל הַמַּתְנֶה עֲלֵיהֶן — תְּנָאוֹ בָּטֵל. וְאֵלּוּ הֵן: עוֹנָתָהּ, וְעִקַּר כְּתֻבָּתָהּ, וִירֻשָּׁתָהּ.

ז כֵּיצַד? הִתְנָה עִם הָאִשָּׁה שֶׁאֵין לָהּ עָלָיו עוֹנָה — תְּנָאוֹ בָּטֵל, וְחַיָּב בְּעוֹנָתָהּ; שֶׁהֲרֵי הִתְנָה עַל מַה שֶּׁכָּתוּב בַּתּוֹרָה, וְאֵינוֹ תְּנַאי מָמוֹן.

ח הִתְנָה עִמָּהּ לִפְחֹת מֵעִקַּר כְּתֻבָּה, אוֹ שֶׁכָּתַב לָהּ מָאתַיִם אוֹ מֵאָה עִקָּר כְּתֻבָּה, וְכָתְבָה לוֹ שֶׁנִּתְקַבְּלָה מֶהֶן כָּךְ וְכָךְ, וְהִיא לֹא נִתְקַבְּלָה — תְּנָאוֹ בָּטֵל; שֶׁכָּל הַפּוֹחֵת לִבְתוּלָה מִמָּאתַיִם וּלְאַלְמָנָה מִמֵּאָה — הֲרֵי בְּעִילָתוֹ בְּעִילַת זְנוּת.

ט הִתְנָה עִמָּהּ אַחַר שֶׁנְּשָׂאָהּ שֶׁלֹּא יִירָשֶׁנָּה — תְּנָאוֹ בָּטֵל. וְאַף־עַל־פִּי שֶׁיְּרֻשַּׁת הַבַּעַל מִדִּבְרֵי סוֹפְרִים, עָשׂוּ חִזּוּק לְדִבְרֵיהֶם כְּשֶׁל תּוֹרָה. וְכָל תְּנַאי שֶׁבִּירֻשָּׁה בָּטֵל וְאַף־עַל־פִּי שֶׁהוּא מָמוֹן, שֶׁנֶּאֱמַר בָּהּ: לְחֻקַּת מִשְׁפָּט.

to property or privileges that justly belong to him (Rashi, *loc. cit.*). Therefore, a woman may waive even the rights to her subsistence or clothing that the Torah itself grants her.
11. Instead, the failure to provide a woman with conjugal rights is considered to cause her physical anguish (Rashi, *loc. cit.*). Although the Mordechai maintains that conjugal rights can also be considered monetary matters, for it is possible to give a woman enough money that she would be willing to forego her rights, the Rambam's view is accepted by most authorities.
12. I.e., the woman writes a receipt for part of the sum on her *ketubah*.
With regard to this instance, the *Tur* (*Even HaEzer* 66) differs and maintains that the man is not obligated to pay her the full sum.
13. Although this is a situation that concerns financial matters, our Sages desired that the fundamental requirement of the marriage contract be a binding institution, and therefore did not allow any modification of this obligation. Hence, the stipulation is nullified.
Note the *Maggid Mishneh*, who mentions views that differ with that of the Rambam and maintains that if the man desires to divorce the woman, he is not obligated to give her the sum for which the Sages obligated him. It is only when he wants to remain married to her that our Sages enforced their requirement.
14. The *Shulchan Aruch* (*Even HaEzer* 66:9) states that even though the man's stipulations are of no consequence, the sexual relations he conducts with his wife are considered promiscuous, because she may be unaware of the law and not know the amount due her.
15. A different ruling applies if the stipulation is made between *erusin* and *nisu'in*, as explained in Chapter 23, Halachah 6.
16. See *Hilchot Nachalot* 6:1.

With regard to other [aspects of the marriage contract], a stipulation [made by the husband and accepted by his wife] is binding. For example, if he made a stipulation that he is not obligated to supply her with her subsistence or with clothing, or that he would not receive the benefits from her property, his stipulation is binding.

10. What is the amount that is designated for a woman's subsistence? We allot her bread for two meals every day, according to the norm of the people of her town, for a person who is neither sick nor a glutton.

The allotment is also made according to the type of bread eaten as a staple in that locale, be it wheat or barley, or rice, millet, or other grains, as is customary [in that locale]. Similarly, she is allotted other foods that are eaten together with bread - i.e., legumes, vegetables and the like. [She is also allotted] oil for food and to light a lamp and also fruit. She is also [allotted] a small amount of wine, if it is the local custom for women to drink wine.

On the Sabbath, she is allotted three meals,[17] and meat or fish according to the local custom. And she is given a *me'ah*[18] of silver for her private needs - e.g., a *p'rutah* for laundry, or for the bath and the like.

11. To whom does the above apply? To a poor Jewish man. But if the husband is wealthy, [the support he is required to provide his wife is apportioned] according to his wealth. If he is wealthy enough to provide her with several dishes of meat each day, he is compelled to do so, and she is allotted [subsistence] commensurate with his wealth.

If he is extremely poor and is unable to provide his wife with even the bread that she requires,[19] he is compelled to divorce her.[20] He remains indebted for her *ketubah* until he finds the means to provide payment for it.

12. When a husband desires to provide his wife with subsistence as befits her, on condition that she should eat and drink alone,[21] and that he should eat and drink alone, he is given this prerogative, provided he eats together with her on Friday night.[22]

---

17. For a woman is obligated to eat three meals on the Sabbath as a man is (*Shulchan Aruch, Orach Chayim* 291:6).
   Note the slight difference between the Rambam's statements here and those in *Hilchot Matnot Aniyim* 9:13.
18. A *me'ah* is one sixth of a *dinar* (*Kiddushin* 12a). Based on the Rambam's statements in *Hilchot Shekalim*, ch. 1, it is evident that this is a coin of relatively small value, approximately 1.5 grams of pure silver.
19. The *Beit Shmuel* 70:7 states that if he can provide her with bread, even if he cannot provide her with other food, he is not obligated to divorce her. (See, however, *Chelkat Mechokek* 70:12.)

וּבִשְׁאָר הַדְּבָרִים — תְּנָאוֹ קַיָּם.

כְּגוֹן שֶׁהִתְנָה עִמָּהּ שֶׁאֵין לָהּ שְׁאֵר וּכְסוּת, עַל מְנָת שֶׁלֹּא יֹאכַל פֵּרוֹת נְכָסֶיהָ, וְכֹל כַּיּוֹצֵא בָּזֶה — תְּנָאוֹ קַיָּם.

י כַּמָּה מְזוֹנוֹת פּוֹסְקִין לְאִשָּׁה?

פּוֹסְקִין לָהּ לֶחֶם שְׁתֵּי סְעֻדּוֹת בְּכָל יוֹם. סְעֻדָּה בֵּינוֹנִית שֶׁל כָּל אָדָם בְּאוֹתָהּ הָעִיר, כְּאָדָם שֶׁאֵינוּ לֹא חוֹלֶה וְלֹא גַרְגְּרָן.

וּמֵאוֹתוֹ מַאֲכָל שֶׁל אַנְשֵׁי אוֹתָהּ הָעִיר: אִם חִטִּים — חִטִּים, וְאִם שְׂעוֹרִים — שְׂעוֹרִים, וְכֵן אֹרֶז וְדֹחַן אוֹ מִשְׁאָר מִינִין שֶׁנָּהֲגוּ בָּהֶן.

וּפוֹסְקִין לָהּ פַּרְפֶּרֶת לֶאֱכֹל בָּהּ אֶת הַפַּת, כְּגוֹן קִטְנִית אוֹ יְרָקוֹת וְכַיּוֹצֵא בָּהֶן.

וְשֶׁמֶן לַאֲכִילָה, וְשֶׁמֶן לְהַדְלָקַת הַנֵּר, וּפֵרוֹת, וּמְעַט יַיִן לִשְׁתּוֹת, אִם הָיָה מִנְהַג הַמָּקוֹם שֶׁיִּשְׁתּוּ הַנָּשִׁים יַיִן.

וּפוֹסְקִין לָהּ שָׁלֹשׁ סְעֻדּוֹת בְּשַׁבָּת, וּבָשָׂר אוֹ דָגִים כְּמִנְהַג הַמָּקוֹם.

וְנוֹתֵן לָהּ בְּכָל שַׁבָּת וְשַׁבָּת מָעָה כֶּסֶף לְצָרְכֶיהָ, כְּגוֹן פְּרוּטָה לִכְבּוּס אוֹ לְמֶרְחָץ וְכַיּוֹצֵא בָּהֶן.

יא בַּמֶּה דְּבָרִים אֲמוּרִים? בְּעָנִי שֶׁבְּיִשְׂרָאֵל;

אֲבָל אִם הָיָה עָשִׁיר — הַכֹּל לְפִי עָשְׁרוֹ.

אֲפִלּוּ הָיָה מָמוֹנוֹ רָאוּי לַעֲשׂוֹת לָהּ כַּמָּה תַבְשִׁילֵי בָשָׂר בְּכָל יוֹם — כּוֹפִין אוֹתוֹ וּפוֹסְקִין לָהּ מְזוֹנוֹת כְּפִי מָמוֹנוֹ.

וְאִם הָיָה עָנִי בְּיוֹתֵר וְאֵינוּ יָכוֹל לִתֵּן לָהּ אֲפִלּוּ לֶחֶם שֶׁהִיא צְרִיכָה לוֹ — כּוֹפִין אוֹתוֹ לְהוֹצִיא, וְתִהְיֶה כְּתֻבָּתָהּ חוֹב עָלָיו עַד שֶׁתִּמְצָא יָדוֹ וְיִתֵּן.

יב בַּעַל שֶׁרָצָה לִתֵּן לְאִשְׁתּוֹ מְזוֹנוֹתֶיהָ הָרְאוּיוֹת לָהּ, וְתִהְיֶה אוֹכֶלֶת וְשׁוֹתָה לְעַצְמָהּ, וְהוּא שׁוֹתֶה וְאוֹכֵל לְעַצְמוֹ — הָרְשׁוּת בְּיָדוֹ;

וּבִלְבַד שֶׁיֹּאכַל עִמָּהּ מִלֵּילֵי שַׁבָּת לְלֵילֵי שַׁבָּת.

The *Chatam Sofer* (*Even HaEzer*, Responsum 131) states that the Rambam's words imply that if the husband cannot support his wife from his own earnings, he is compelled to divorce her, even if she herself has the means to provide herself with subsistence.
20. The rationale is that since he cannot provide her with subsistence, he is obligated to give her the opportunity to find another husband who can.

The *Hagahot Maimoniot* question whether the husband can be compelled to seek to hire himself out as a laborer, or the court's only resort is to compel him to divorce his wife. Although that text does not favor either approach, the latter opinion is quoted by the Ramah (*Even HaEzer* 70:3). The Ramah also mentions the opinion of *Tosafot* (*Ketubot* 63a), which states that a husband who has no resources is not compelled to divorce his wife.

21. I.e., even in a separate dwelling (Rambam's Commentary on the Mishnah, *Ketubot* 5:9).
22. In his Commentary on the Mishnah (*loc. cit.*), the Rambam states that this prerogative may in no way infringe on the husband's obligation to provide his wife with conjugal rights.

13. When a woman has been allotted subsistence, and [the entire allotment was not used], the remainder belongs to her husband.[23]

If her husband is a priest, he is not entitled to provide her with all her provisions from *terumah*. [He is not given this option] because it is very difficult for her to protect [the *terumah*] from contacting ritual impurity, and to eat it while ritually pure [herself].[24] Instead, he should give her half her provisions from ordinary [food] and half from *terumah*.

14. Just as a man is required to provide his wife with her subsistence, he is required to provide for the maintenance of his children, both male and female, until they reach the age of six.[25] Afterwards, he should continue to provide for their maintenance until they reach majority, as ordained by our Sages.[26]

If, however, he does not, he should be rebuked and embarrassed publicly, and appeals should be made to him. If he [persists in his] refusal, a public announcement is made with regard to him: "So and so is cruel and does not desire to provide for the maintenance of his children. He is worse than an impure bird, which does provide for its chicks." Nevertheless, he should not be compelled to provide for the maintenance [of children] six and older.

15. To what does the above apply? To a person who is not known to have resources, and it is not known whether or not he is capable of giving charity. If, however, he has resources and he possesses the means to give an amount to charity that would provide for [his children's] needs, his property is expropriated against his will[27] for the purposes of charity,[28] and [his children's] needs are provided for until they reach majority.

16. When a person travels to another country [and leaves his wife behind], [the following rules apply] should his wife come to court to place a claim [against her husband] for her subsistence. For the first three months from the day her husband departed, she is not given an allotment for her subsistence.

In addition, he must share the Friday night meal with her, implying that this is for the sake of communication, not only as preparation for marital relations, as understood by some commentaries.

Note the Ramah (*Even HaEzer* 70:2), who objects to the Rambam's ruling, and states that a man is given this prerogative only if his wife consents.

23. Note *Mishneh LaMelech* and the *Dagul MeRevavah* (*Even HaEzer* 70), which state that this applies only when the woman purchased her food at a lower price than was originally estimated. If, however, she starved herself and consumed less than was allotted her, she, and not her husband, is entitled to the remainder.

24. Food that is *terumah* may not be eaten if it contracts ritual impurity, nor may it be eaten by a person who is himself ritually impure.

25. Rabbenu Nissim maintains that this obligation is incumbent on a father from the

יג הָאִשָּׁה שֶׁפָּסְקוּ לָהּ מְזוֹנוֹת, וְהוֹתִירוּ — הַמּוֹתָר לַבַּעַל.
הָיָה בַּעְלָהּ כֹּהֵן — אֵינוֹ נוֹתֵן לָהּ כָּל מְזוֹנוֹתֶיהָ תְּרוּמָה, מִפְּנֵי שֶׁטֹּרַח גָּדוֹל הוּא לָהּ לְשָׁמְרָן מִדְּבָרִים הַמְטַמְּאִין וּלְאָכְלָן בְּטָהֳרָה;
אֶלָּא נוֹתֵן לָהּ מֶחֱצָה חֻלִּין וּמֶחֱצָה תְּרוּמָה.

יד כְּשֵׁם שֶׁאָדָם חַיָּב בִּמְזוֹנוֹת אִשְׁתּוֹ, כָּךְ הוּא חַיָּב בִּמְזוֹנוֹת בָּנָיו וּבְנוֹתָיו הַקְּטַנִּים, עַד שֶׁיִּהְיוּ בְּנֵי שֵׁשׁ שָׁנִים;
מִכָּאן וְאֵילָךְ — מַאֲכִילָן עַד שֶׁיִּגְדְּלוּ, כְּתַקָּנַת חֲכָמִים.
וְאִם לֹא רָצָה — גּוֹעֲרִין בּוֹ, וּמַכְלִימִין אוֹתוֹ, וּפוֹצְרִין בּוֹ.
וְאִם לֹא רָצָה — מַכְרִיזִין עָלָיו בַּצִּבּוּר וְאוֹמְרִים: פְּלוֹנִי אַכְזָרִי הוּא, וְאֵינוֹ רוֹצֶה לָזוּן בָּנָיו,
וַהֲרֵי פָּחוּת הוּא מֵעוֹף טָמֵא שֶׁהוּא זָן אֶת אֶפְרוֹחָיו.
וְאֵין כּוֹפִין אוֹתוֹ לְזוּנָם אַחַר שֵׁשׁ.

טו בַּמֶּה דְּבָרִים אֲמוּרִים? בְּאִישׁ שֶׁאֵינוֹ אָמוּד, וְאֵין יָדוּעַ אִם רָאוּי לִתֵּן צְדָקָה אוֹ אֵינוֹ רָאוּי;
אֲבָל אִם הָיָה אָמוּד שֶׁיֵּשׁ לוֹ מָמוֹן הָרָאוּי לִתֵּן מִמֶּנּוּ צְדָקָה הַמַּסְפֶּקֶת לָהֶן — מוֹצִיאִין מִמֶּנּוּ בְּעַל כָּרְחוֹ מִשּׁוּם צְדָקָה, וְזָנִין אוֹתָן עַד שֶׁיִּגְדְּלוּ.

טז מִי שֶׁהָלַךְ לִמְדִינָה אַחֶרֶת, וּבָאָה אִשְׁתּוֹ לְבֵית דִּין לִתְבֹּעַ מְזוֹנוֹת:
שְׁלֹשָׁה חֳדָשִׁים הָרִאשׁוֹנִים מִיּוֹם הֲלִיכָתוֹ — אֵין פּוֹסְקִין לָהּ בָּהֶן מְזוֹנוֹת, שֶׁחֲזָקָה שֶׁאֵין אָדָם

Torah itself, as an extension of his obligation to provide for his wife. Rabbenu Asher, however, maintains that the father's obligation is independent of the marriage bond. Even if he fathers children outside marriage, he is liable for their support.

26. The obligation to provide for one's children's subsistence until majority was one of the enactments instituted by the *Sanhedrin* after this body was relocated in Usha in the Galilee after the destruction of Jerusalem. At that time, several enactments were passed to direct the functioning of the Jewish community in this new phase. (See *Ketubot* 49b.)

Today, most rabbinic authorities maintain that because of changes in the socio-economic system, it is proper for a father to continue supporting his children well past the age of Bar or Bat Mitzvah.

27. As evident from Halachah 17, this applies only when the father is present. The Rambam maintains that a person's property may not be expropriated for this purpose outside his presence.

28. See *Hilchot Matnot Aniyim* 10:16, which states:

> Although he is not obligated, when a person provides subsistence for his older sons and daughters, so that the males can study the Torah and the females will follow the straight path,... it is an act of charity, and indeed, a great act of charity.

And Chapter 7, Halachah 10, of that source, states:

> When a person does not desire to give charity,... the court compels him, and administers stripes for rebelliousness until he meets the assessment made for him. [Moreover,] when he is present, his property is expropriated [for this purpose].

[The rationale is that] it is an accepted assumption that a person does not depart without leaving provisions for his household.[29]

Afterwards,[30] an allotment is made for her subsistence. If her husband owns property, the court expropriates his property and sells it to provide for his wife's subsistence. [When doing so,] no account is made for his wife's earnings until her husband comes.[31] If it is discovered that she earned [money during the time that he was away], he is granted that sum.

Moreover, even if the matter is not taken to court, and instead the woman sells [her husband's property] on her own[32] in order to pay for her subsistence, the sale is binding. There is no need for a public announcement [regarding the sale of the property].[33] Similarly, the woman is not required to take an oath [that her husband did not leave her money] until her husband comes and lodges a claim [against her], or until she comes to claim [the money due her, as stated in her] ketubah in the event of her husband's death. [In the latter instance, together with the oaths she is required to take to collect her ketubah,][34] on the basis of the principle of gilgul shevu'ah,[35] [she is also required to take an oath] that she did not sell [any more of her husband's property than] was necessary for her subsistence.

17. Just as the court [expropriates and] sells [the property of] a husband who travelled [to another country to provide for] the subsistence of [his] wife, so too, it [expropriates and] sells property to provide for the subsistence of his sons and daughters who are six years old or less. If, however, they are more than six [years old], [the court] does not provide for their subsistence from his property when he is not present, even when he is reputed to have means.[36]

Similarly, when a person loses his mental faculties, the court expropriates his property and sells it to provide subsistence and other necessities for his wife and his children below the age of six.[37]

29. The Ramah (*Even HaEzer* 70:5) quotes opinions that state that this ruling applies only when the husband left home in an atmosphere of peace. In such a situation, we can be sure that he has provided for his family. If, however, he left home annoyed with his wife, it is plausible to assume that he did not provide for her needs.

30. I.e., after three months, or after she approaches the court. If she waits longer than three months, she is not given any payment for the previous period (Ramah, *ibid.*).

31. Rabbenu Asher differs and maintains that the court should consider the amount the woman can earn when deciding on the size of her allotment. His rationale is that before expropriating a person's property, we should try to act in his interests. Although many authorities speak in favor of Rabbenu Asher's logic, they rule according to the Rambam's decision. (See *Chelkat Mechokek* 70:20.)

The *Avnei Milu'im* 70:3 explains the Rambam's position, stating that the husband is granted the right to his wife's earnings only when he provides for her subsistence willingly. When he forces her to approach the court to receive her subsistence, he has no claim on her earnings.

מַנִּיחַ בֵּיתוֹ רֵיקָן;

מִכָּאן וְאֵילַךְ — פּוֹסְקִין לָהּ מְזוֹנוֹת. וְאִם הָיוּ לוֹ נְכָסִים — בֵּית דִּין יוֹרְדִין לִנְכָסָיו וּמוֹכְרִין לִמְזוֹנוֹתֶיהָ.

וְאֵין מְחַשְּׁבִין עִמָּהּ עַל מַעֲשֵׂה יָדֶיהָ, עַד שֶׁיָּבוֹא בַּעְלָהּ; אִם מָצָאָה שֶׁעָשְׂתָה — הֲרֵי אֵלּוּ שֶׁלּוֹ.

וְכֵן אִם לֹא עָמְדָה בַּדִּין, אֶלָּא מָכְרָה לְעַצְמָהּ לִמְזוֹנוֹת — מִכְרָהּ קַיָּם.

וְאֵינָהּ צְרִיכָה הַכְרָזָה וְלֹא שְׁבוּעָה, עַד שֶׁיָּבוֹא בַּעְלָהּ וְיִטְעַן,

אוֹ עַד שֶׁתָּבוֹא לִגְבּוֹת כְּתֻבָּתָהּ אַחַר מוֹתוֹ — מְגַלְגְּלִין עָלֶיהָ שֶׁלֹּא מָכְרָה אֶלָּא לִמְזוֹנוֹת שֶׁהִיא צְרִיכָה לָהֶן.

יז וּכְשֵׁם שֶׁבֵּית דִּין מוֹכְרִין לִמְזוֹן הָאִשָּׁה שֶׁהָלַךְ בַּעְלָהּ, כָּךְ מוֹכְרִין לִמְזוֹן בָּנָיו וּבְנוֹתָיו כְּשֶׁהֵן בְּנֵי שֵׁשׁ שָׁנִים אוֹ פָּחוֹת;

אֲבָל יָתֵר עַל שֵׁשׁ — אֵינָן זָנִין אוֹתָן מִנְּכָסָיו שֶׁלֹּא בְּפָנָיו, אַף־עַל־פִּי שֶׁהוּא אָמוּד.

וְכֵן מִי שֶׁנִּשְׁתַּטָּה — בֵּית דִּין יוֹרְדִין לִנְכָסָיו וּמוֹכְרִים, וְזָנִין אִשְׁתּוֹ וּבָנָיו וּבְנוֹתָיו שֶׁהֵן בְּנֵי שֵׁשׁ שָׁנִים אוֹ פָּחוֹת, וּמְפַרְנְסִין אוֹתָן.

32. There is a debate among the authorities whether or not she must consult experts with regard to the evaluation of the object. (See *Chelkat Mechokek* 70:21.)

33. Generally, when property is sold by the court, it is necessary that a public announcement be made informing people of the sale, to attract customers and assure competitive bidding. (See *Hilchot Malveh V'Loveh* 22:6.) In this instance, no such requirement is made, in order that the woman will not have to wait to receive the funds she requires.

34. See Chapter 16, Halachah 4.

35. Whenever a person is required to take an oath, the plaintiff can obligate him to take an oath on another claim. In this instance, since the woman is obligated to take an oath to her husband's heirs to collect the money due her for her *ketubah*, she can be required to take an additional oath regarding the sale of his property for her subsistence.

36. We do not expropriate his property and provide for his children as an act of charity, because it is possible that he is giving charity in the place to which he has journeyed.

The Ramah (*Even HaEzer* 71:2) states that if the person had supported his older children before leaving on his journey, provisions should be made for his children while he is away. It can be assumed that this would be his desire. The Ramah also mentions the opinion of Rabbenu Nissim, which states that if he possesses means, support should be provided for his children from his property as an act of charity. This view is not, however, accepted by most later authorities.

37. The *Maggid Mishneh* states that the Rambam's wording appears to imply that no provision is made for his older children, even when he has the means to support them. The *Maggid Mishneh*, however, refers to *Hilchot Nachalot* 11:11, which states that when a person who has means loses control of his faculties, the court levels an assessment for charity on his estate. Accordingly, it would appear that if the man has the means to give charity, his property is expropriated to pay for his children's subsistence, even if they are over six.

The *Tur* (*Even HaEzer* 71) states that in such an instance, the court should expropriate

18. Some *geonim* ruled that an assessment should not be made for the subsistence of a woman whose husband journeyed overseas, or who died, unless she evinces possession of her *ketubah* document. If she does not evince possession of her *ketubah*, she is not entitled to subsistence. Perhaps she has already received payment for her *ketubah* from her husband, or perhaps she forfeited her *ketubah* in his favor, as will be explained.[38] Others maintain that an assessment is made on her behalf for her subsistence, for we accept it as a presumption that she neither received payment for nor forfeited [her *ketubah*]. Hence, she is not required to show her *ketubah* [when presenting her claim].

I favor [the latter view] with regard to [a woman] whose husband has departed,[39] since her claim to her subsistence stems from the Torah itself.[40] With regard to a woman whose husband died, however, she is not entitled to her subsistence until she brings her *ketubah*, for she [derives her subsistence] by virtue of a rabbinic enactment. Furthermore, her subsistence is paid from property belonging to [her husband's] heirs, and [the court] always advances claims in support of the interests of an heir.[41]

19. If [a woman's] husband departed on a journey, and she borrowed money for her subsistence, [her husband] is required to pay [the debt] when he returns.[42]

If a person voluntarily took the initiative of providing for her subsistence, when [her husband] returns the husband is not required to pay [that person]. The other person forfeited his money, [the rationale being] that [the husband] did not instruct him to provide for her, nor did she [request the assistance] as a loan.[43]

20. When a husband [who plans to] depart on a journey tells his wife: "Use your earnings to purchase your subsistence," she has no [right to demand] her subsistence [from him afterwards]. For if she had not accepted this agreement, and she had not felt confident, she could have issued a claim against him, or told him, "My earnings are not sufficient for me."[44]

21. [The following rule applies if] the woman took the matter to court and was awarded an assessment for her subsistence, the court sold [her husband's landed property] and gave her [the proceeds] - or she sold [the property] herself - and afterwards, the husband came and claimed that he left provisions for her. She is required to take an oath, while holding a sacred article, that he did not make provisions for her [and then she is not held liable].

funds for the subsistence of the person's older children even if the person's estate is not large enough for an assessment for charity to be leveled against it. The rationale is that we assume that, like the majority of people, this person would also desire to support his

יח יֵשׁ מִן הַגְּאוֹנִים שֶׁהוֹרָה, שֶׁאֵין פּוֹסְקִין מְזוֹנוֹת לָאִשָּׁה שֶׁהָלַךְ בַּעְלָהּ לִמְדִינַת הַיָּם אוֹ שֶׁמֵּת בַּעְלָהּ, עַד שֶׁיְּהֵא שְׁטַר כְּתֻבָּה יוֹצֵא מִתַּחַת יָדָהּ, וְאִם לֹא תוֹצִיא שְׁטַר כְּתֻבָּה — אֵין לָהּ מְזוֹנוֹת;

שֶׁמָּא נָטְלָה כְּתֻבָּתָהּ מִבַּעְלָהּ אוֹ מָחֲלָה לוֹ כְּתֻבָּתָהּ, שֶׁאֵין לָהּ מְזוֹנוֹת, כְּמוֹ שֶׁיִּתְבָּאֵר.

וְיֵשׁ מִי שֶׁהוֹרָה, שֶׁפּוֹסְקִין לָהּ מְזוֹנוֹת בְּחֶזְקַת שֶׁלֹּא נָטְלָה וְלֹא מָחֲלָה, וְאֵין מַצְרִיכִין אוֹתָהּ לְהָבִיא כְּתֻבָּה.

וְדַעְתִּי נוֹטָה לָזֶה בְּמִי שֶׁהָלַךְ בַּעְלָהּ, הוֹאִיל וְיֵשׁ לָהּ מְזוֹנוֹת מִן הַתּוֹרָה;

אֲבָל אִם מֵת בַּעְלָהּ — אֵין לָהּ מְזוֹנוֹת עַד שֶׁתָּבִיא כְּתֻבָּה, מִפְּנֵי שֶׁהִיא אוֹכֶלֶת בְּתַקָּנַת חֲכָמִים.

וְעוֹד, שֶׁנִּזּוֹנֶת מִנִּכְסֵי יוֹרְשִׁים, וּלְעוֹלָם טוֹעֲנִין לְיוֹרֵשׁ.

יט הָלַךְ בַּעְלָהּ, וְלָוְתָה וְאָכְלָה — כְּשֶׁיָּבוֹא חַיָּב לְשַׁלֵּם.

עָמַד אֶחָד מִדַּעַת עַצְמוֹ וְזָנָהּ מִשֶּׁלּוֹ — אִם יָבוֹא הַבַּעַל, אֵינוּ חַיָּב לְשַׁלֵּם לוֹ; וַהֲרֵי זֶה אִבֵּד אֶת מְעוֹתָיו, מִפְּנֵי שֶׁלֹּא צִוָּהוּ לְזוּנָהּ וְהִיא לֹא לָוְתָה מִמֶּנּוּ.

כ הַבַּעַל שֶׁאָמַר לְאִשְׁתּוֹ בְּשָׁעָה שֶׁהָלַךְ: טְלִי מַעֲשֵׂה יָדַיִךְ בִּמְזוֹנוֹתַיִךְ — אֵין לָהּ מְזוֹנוֹת; שֶׁאִלּוּ לֹא רָצְתָה בְּדָבָר זֶה וְלֹא סָמְכָה דַעְתָּהּ — הָיָה לָהּ לִתָּבְעוֹ, אוֹ לוֹמַר לוֹ: אֵין מַעֲשֵׂה יָדַי מַסְפִּיקִין לִי.

כא הֲרֵי שֶׁעָמְדָה בַּדִּין וּפָסְקוּ לָהּ מְזוֹנוֹת, וּמָכְרוּ בֵּית דִּין וְנָתְנוּ לָהּ, אוֹ שֶׁמָּכְרָה הִיא לְעַצְמָהּ, וּבָא הַבַּעַל וְאָמַר: הִנַּחְתִּי לָהּ מְזוֹנוֹת — הֲרֵי זוֹ נִשְׁבַּעַת בִּנְקִיטַת חֵפֶץ שֶׁלֹּא הִנִּיחַ לָהּ.

children. The *Chelkat Mechokek* 71:6 maintains that the *Shulchan Aruch* follows this view, and not that of the Rambam.

38. See Chapter 17, Halachah 19.

39. Rabbenu Asher and others do not accept the Rambam's distinction, and maintain that the court should also protect the interests of a person who is in another country and cannot defend himself. Nevertheless, in his *Kessef Mishneh*, Rav Yosef Karo defends the Rambam's decision, explaining that in contrast to an heir, the husband has the potential to take his claim to court when he returns. In his *Shulchan Aruch* (*Even HaEzer* 70:5), he quotes the Rambam's ruling. This ruling is also accepted by the later authorities.

40. See Halachah 2.

41. Since the heir himself was not aware of the details of his benefactor's affairs, he cannot necessarily advance claims in his own interests. Therefore, the court acts to protect them. (See *Bava Batra* 23a.)

42. The Ramah (*Even HaEzer* 70:8) states that the benefactor must lodge a claim against the wife, who in turn must lodge a claim against her husband.

43. Although the husband is obligated to pay for his wife's subsistence, our Sages rule that when a person pays a debt on behalf of a colleague without being instructed to do so, the debtor is not at all obligated to his patron.

44. Although our Sages associated a woman's earnings with her subsistence, they made

[The following rule applies when a husband departed on a journey, and the woman] did not take the matter to court, nor sell his property, but instead waited until he returned. [If upon his return there is a dispute,] he claims: "I made [provisions for you]," while she claims, "You did not make provisions. Instead, I borrowed money from this person to provide for myself," he is required to take a rabbinic oath[45] that he left provisions for her, and then he is not held liable. She remains responsible for the debt.[46]

22. [In the above instance,] if she sold movable property, claiming that she sold it to provide for her subsistence, and her husband claimed that he had left provisions for her, she is required to take a rabbinic oath that he did not leave her any provisions.[47]

If she did not issue a claim against him, did not borrow money, and she did not sell his property, but instead strained herself during the day and during the night and earned her livelihood, she is not entitled to any recompense.[48]

23. [The following rules apply when] a man takes a vow that his wife should not derive any benefit from him [or his property]. Whether he specified the span of the vow or did not specify the span of the vow, we grant him an interval of thirty days.[49] If the span of his vow is concluded, or even though it is not concluded, but he has his vow annulled, this is acceptable. If not, he must divorce his wife,[50] and pay her [the money due her because of] her *ketubah*.

During those thirty days, she should work and [attempt to] sustain herself [through her labor]. One of [her husband's] friends should provide her[51] with those things she needs that she cannot purchase through the fruits of her labor, if the fruits of her labor are not sufficient for her.

24. When a person makes a vow [preventing] his wife from tasting one of the species of produce,[52] he should be given an interval of thirty days. [If he prolongs the situation] beyond this time, he is required to divorce [his wife] and pay [her the money due her by virtue of her] *ketubah*. [This ruling

---

this association for the woman's sake and gave her the prerogative of accepting or declining such a request. In a responsum, the Rambam writes that if it is not logical to assume that she could earn the funds required for her subsistence, for her to forfeit her rights, she must explicitly consent to her husband's stipulation.

45. I.e., a less severe oath instituted by the Rabbis. (See *Hilchot To'en V'Nit'an* 1:3.)

46. She, however, does not have the opportunity of paying the debt until she is divorced or becomes widowed, because all her property is under lien to her husband, and he is entitled to her earnings.

47. Since it was movable property and not landed property that was sold, the oath that the woman is required to take is more lenient than that mentioned in the previous halachah.

לֹא תָבְעָה וְלֹא מָכְרָה, אֶלָּא שָׁהֲתָה עַד שֶׁבָּא, הוּא אוֹמֵר: הַנַּחְתִּי, וְהִיא אוֹמֶרֶת: לֹא הַנַּחְתָּ, אֶלָּא לָוִיתִי מִזֶּה וְנִתְפַּרְנַסְתִּי —
נִשְׁבַּע שְׁבוּעַת הֶסֵּת שֶׁהִנִּיחַ לָהּ וְנִפְטָר, וְיִשָּׁאֵר הַחוֹב עָלֶיהָ.

כב מָכְרָה מִטַּלְטְלִין וְאָמְרָה: לִמְזוֹנוֹת מָכַרְתִּי, וְהוּא טוֹעֵן וְאוֹמֵר: מְזוֹנוֹתַיִךְ הִנַּחְתִּי — נִשְׁבַּעַת שְׁבוּעַת הֶסֵּת שֶׁלֹּא הִנִּיחַ.
הֲרֵי שֶׁלֹּא תָבְעָה וְלֹא לָוְתָה וְלֹא מָכְרָה, אֶלָּא דָחֲקָה עַצְמָהּ בַּיּוֹם וּבַלַּיְלָה וְעָשְׂתָה וְאָכְלָה — אֵין לָהּ כְּלוּם.

כג הַמַּדִּיר אֶת אִשְׁתּוֹ מֵהֲנָאוֹת לוֹ — בֵּין שֶׁפֵּרֵשׁ עַד זְמַן פְּלוֹנִי, בֵּין שֶׁלֹּא פֵרֵשׁ אֶלָּא סָתַם — מַמְתִּינִין לוֹ שְׁלֹשִׁים יוֹם:
אִם תַּמּוּ יְמֵי נִדְרוֹ אוֹ שֶׁלֹּא תַּמּוּ וְהִתִּיר נִדְרוֹ — הֲרֵי זֶה מוּטָב, וְאִם לָאו — יוֹצִיא וְיִתֵּן כְּתֻבָּה.
וּבְאוֹתָן הַשְּׁלֹשִׁים יוֹם תִּהְיֶה הִיא עוֹשָׂה וְאוֹכֶלֶת, וְיִהְיֶה אֶחָד מֵחֲבֵרָיו מְפַרְנֵס אוֹתָהּ דְּבָרִים שֶׁהִיא צְרִיכָה לָהֶן יָתֵר עַל מַעֲשֵׂה יָדֶיהָ, אִם אֵין מַעֲשֵׂה יָדֶיהָ מַסְפִּיקִין לַכֹּל.

כד הַמַּדִּיר אֶת אִשְׁתּוֹ שֶׁלֹּא תִּטְעַם אֶחָד מִכָּל הַפֵּרוֹת — מַמְתִּינִין לוֹ עַד שְׁלֹשִׁים יוֹם; יָתֵר עַל כֵּן — יוֹצִיא וְיִתֵּן כְּתֻבָּה.

The rationale is that had she desired to lie, she could have claimed that the goods were stolen or lost.

48. I.e., she cannot demand reimbursement for the difference between her earnings and the amount she would ordinarily be entitled to for her subsistence (*Chelkat Mechokek* 70:41). If she earned more than her subsistence, the additional funds belong to her, not to her husband (*Shulchan Aruch, Even HaEzer* 70:11).

49. Based on *Ketubot* 59b, Rabbenu Asher and Rabbenu Nissim object to the Rambam's ruling. Since the husband is liable to provide for his wife's subsistence, the vow he takes cannot override that obligation, except in specific instances. In both the *Kessef Mishneh*, and the *Shulchan Aruch* (*Yoreh De'ah* 235:2), Rav Yosef Karo follows these views.

50. After thirty days, the matter will become public knowledge and the woman will suffer ridicule. Therefore, her husband is obligated to divorce (Rambam's Commentary on the Mishnah, *Ketubot* 7:1).

51. The Mishnah (*Ketubot, op. cit.*) states that her husband should appoint a person to provide for her. As the Talmud explains (*Ketubot* 71a), this does not mean that he should appoint this person as an agent, for this is forbidden by his vow. Instead, he should say, "Whoever provides for my wife will not suffer a loss."

52. As the *Maggid Mishneh* explains, this refers to a situation in which the husband took a vow that if his wife partakes of a particular species of produce, she will be forbidden to benefit from his property (or according to the *Shulchan Aruch, Yoreh De'ah* 235:3, that sexual relations between them will be forbidden). If, however, the husband takes a vow that his wife may not eat a particular type of produce, that vow is nullified. For a person cannot take a vow to restrict the actions of another person.

applies] even when his vow prevents her from eating undesirable food, or a species that she has never tasted in her life.

[The following rules apply when a woman] took a vow not to partake of a particular species of produce, and [her husband] allowed the vow to stand, or she took a Nazarite vow and he did not annul it.[53] If he desires to remain married to her and for her not to partake of this species or to be a Nazarite, he may.[54] If, however, he says: "I do not desire a woman with vows," he may divorce her, but he is required to pay her the money due her because of her *ketubah*. [The rationale is that] he had the option to nullify [her vow], and instead, he willingly allowed the vow to stand.

CHAPTER THIRTEEN

1. To what extent is he required to provide her with garments? Annually, he must purchase for her clothes that were worth 50 *zuz* in the coinage prevalent [in the Talmudic period], these being worth six and one fourth *dinarim* of pure silver.[1]

He should provide her with new [garments] during the rainy season. After these garments become worn, she should wear them in the summer. Frayed garments - that which remains from her garments from the previous year - belong to her; she should wear them while she is in the *niddah* state.

She is granted a belt for her loins, a cap for her head and new shoes on each festival.

2. When does the above apply? In [the Talmudic period,] and in *Eretz Yisrael*, but in other ages or in other countries, there is no fixed amount of money [determined for this purpose]. For there are some places where garments are very expensive, and others where they are inexpensive.

The fundamental principle is[2] that he is obligated to provide her with appropriate clothes for the winter and the summer, the minimal that are worn by a married woman in that country.

3. Included in the [obligation to provide her with] garments is the requirement to provide her with household goods and a dwelling place.[3]

With which household goods is he obligated to provide her? With a bed and its spreads, a reed or woven rug to sit on, and utensils with which to eat and drink - e.g., a pot, a plate, a cup, a bottle and the like.

With regard to her dwelling? He must rent a dwelling at least four cubits by four cubits. It must have a yard outside for her use and a latrine [nearby].

---

53. For, as Numbers 30:8-9 relates, a husband has the right to nullify or uphold the vows his wife takes.

אֲפִלּוּ הַדִּירָהּ שֶׁלֹּא תֹּאכַל מַאֲכַל רַע, אֲפִלּוּ הַדִּירָהּ מִמִּין שֶׁלֹּא אֲכָלַּה מִיָּמֶיהָ — יוֹצִיא
אַחַר שְׁלֹשִׁים יוֹם וְיִתֵּן כְּתֻבָּה.

נָדְרָה הִיא שֶׁלֹּא תֹּאכַל אֶחָד מִכָּל הַפֵּרוֹת, וְקִיֵּם לָהּ הוּא אֶת נִדְרָהּ, אוֹ נָדְרָה בְּנָזִיר וְלֹא הֵפֵר
לָהּ:

אִם רָצָה שֶׁתֵּשֵׁב תַּחְתָּיו וְלֹא תֹּאכַל פֵּרוֹת אוֹ תִּהְיֶה נְזִירָה — תֵּשֵׁב,
וְאִם אָמַר: אֵינִי רוֹצֶה בְּאִשָּׁה נַדְרָנִית — יוֹצִיא וְיִתֵּן כְּתֻבָּה;
שֶׁהֲרֵי הָיָה בְּיָדוֹ לְהָפֵר, וְהוּא קִיֵּם לָהּ בִּרְצוֹנוֹ.

פֶּרֶק שְׁלֹשָׁה עָשָׂר

א כַּמָּה הַכְּסוּת שֶׁהוּא חַיָּב לִתֵּן לָהּ?
בְּגָדִים שֶׁל חֲמִשִּׁים זוּז מִשָּׁנָה לְשָׁנָה, מִמַּטְבֵּעַ אוֹתָן הַיָּמִים, שֶׁנִּמְצְאוּ הַחֲמִשִּׁים — שִׁשָּׁה
דִּינָרִין וּרְבִיעַ דִּינָר כֶּסֶף.
נוֹתְנִין לָהּ חֲדָשִׁים בִּימוֹת הַגְּשָׁמִים, וְלוֹבֶשֶׁת בְּלָאוֹתֵיהֶן בִּימוֹת הַחַמָּה.
וְהַשְּׁחָקִים, וְהֵם מוֹתַר הַכְּסוּת — הֲרֵי הֵן שֶׁלָּהּ, כְּדֵי שֶׁתִּתְכַּסֶּה בָּהֶם בִּימֵי נִדָּתָהּ.
וְנוֹתְנִין לָהּ חֲגוֹרָה לְמָתְנֶיהָ וְכִפָּה לְרֹאשָׁהּ וּמִנְעָל מִמּוֹעֵד לְמוֹעֵד.

ב בַּמֶּה דְּבָרִים אֲמוּרִים? בְּאוֹתָן הַיָּמִים וּבְאֶרֶץ יִשְׂרָאֵל; אֲבָל בִּשְׁאָר זְמַנִּים וּשְׁאָר הַמְּקוֹמוֹת
— אֵין הַדָּמִים עִקָּר.
יֵשׁ מְקוֹמוֹת שֶׁיִּהְיוּ שָׁם הַבְּגָדִים בְּיֹקֶר הַרְבֵּה אוֹ בְּזוֹל הַרְבֵּה.
אֶלָּא הָעִקָּר שֶׁסּוֹמְכִין עָלָיו, שֶׁמְּחַיְּבִין אוֹתוֹ לִתֵּן לָהּ בְּגָדִים הָרְאוּיִים בִּימוֹת הַגְּשָׁמִים וּבִימוֹת
הַחַמָּה, בְּפָחוֹת שֶׁלּוֹבֶשֶׁת כָּל אִשָּׁה בַּעֲלַת בַּיִת שֶׁבְּאוֹתָהּ הַמְּדִינָה.

ג וּבִכְלַל הַכְּסוּת — שֶׁהוּא חַיָּב לִתֵּן לָהּ כְּלֵי בַיִת, וּמָדוֹר שֶׁיּוֹשֶׁבֶת בּוֹ.
וּמָה הֵן כְּלֵי בַיִת? מִטָּה מַצַּעַת, וּמַפָּץ אוֹ מַחְצֶלֶת לֵישֵׁב עָלֶיהָ,
וּכְלֵי אֲכִילָה וּשְׁתִיָּה, כְּגוֹן קְדֵרָה וּקְעָרָה וְכוֹס וּבַקְבּוּק וְכַיּוֹצֵא בָּהֶן.
וְהַמָּדוֹר? שֶׁשּׂוֹכֵר לָהּ בַּיִת שֶׁל אַרְבַּע אַמּוֹת עַל אַרְבַּע אַמּוֹת, וְתִהְיֶה רְחָבָה חוּצָה לוֹ כְּדֵי
לְהִשְׁתַּמֵּשׁ בּוֹ,
וְיִהְיֶה לוֹ בֵּית הַכִּסֵּא חוּץ מִמֶּנּוּ.

---

54. As Rav Yosef Karo mentions in both the *Kessef Mishneh* and the *Shulchan Aruch* (*loc. cit.*), other opinions require the husband to divorce his wife in such a situation.

1. For a *zuz* was only one eighth pure silver.
2. See Halachah 5.
3. I.e., the obligation to provide one's wife with household goods and a dwelling stems from the Torah itself and is not merely a Rabbinic ordinance.

4. Similarly, he is obligated to provide her with ornaments - e.g., colored cloths to wrap her head and forehead, eye-makeup, rouge and the like - so that she will not appear unattractive to him.

5. When does the above apply? With regard to a poor Jewish man. Concerning a rich man, by contrast, all [of his obligations are judged] according to the extent of his wealth.[4] If it would be appropriate for him to buy her silk and embroidered clothing and golden articles, he is compelled to provide her with these.

Similarly, the dwelling [he is required to give her] is judged according to his wealth, as are the ornaments and the household goods. If he does not have the means to provide her with the minimum required of a poor Jewish man, he is compelled to divorce her.[5] The money due her by virtue of her *ketubah* is considered to be a debt that he is required to pay when he gains the means.

6. [A man] is obligated to provide the necessary clothing, dwelling and household goods, not only for his wife, but also for his sons and daughters who are six years old or less.[6] He is not, however, required to provide for them according to his wealth; all that is necessary is that he provide for their needs.

This is the governing principle: whenever a husband [or his estate] is required to provide for a person's subsistence - whether the husband is alive or deceased - the husband [or his estate] is also obligated to provide for the person's clothing, household goods and dwelling. Whenever a court must sell [a person's property] to provide for [a dependent's] subsistence,[7] they also sell [his property] to provide [the dependent] with clothing, household goods and a dwelling.

7. When a woman's husband has departed on a journey, and the court allots [money from his property] for her subsistence, her clothes, her household goods and the renting of a dwelling, they do not allot her money for ornaments. For she does not have a husband [present] for whom to make herself attractive. If, by contrast, a woman's husband loses his mental faculties or becomes a deaf mute, she is granted an allotment for ornaments.[8]

The laws that apply to the claims and counterclaims between a woman and her husband with regard to garments, clothing and the rental of a dwelling [in the event of the husband's departure on an extended journey] are the same as those that apply with regard to her subsistence. If he claims to have provided for her and she denies [his claim], the same rulings apply to all claims.

8. [The following rules apply if a husband] takes a vow that prevents[9] his wife from wearing any type of ornament. If the couple are poor, they may

ד וְכֵן מְחַיְּבִין אוֹתוֹ לִתֵּן לָהּ תֵּן תַּכְשִׁיטִים, כְּגוֹן בִּגְדֵי צִבְעוֹנִין לְהַקִּיף עַל רֹאשָׁהּ וּפַדַּחְתָּהּ, וּפוּךְ וְשָׂרָק וְכַיּוֹצֵא בָהֶן, כְּדֵי שֶׁלֹּא תִתְגַּנֶּה עָלָיו.

ה בַּמֶּה דְבָרִים אֲמוּרִים? בְּעָנִי שֶׁבְּיִשְׂרָאֵל; אֲבָל בְּעָשִׁיר — הַכֹּל לְפִי עָשְׁרוֹ. וַאֲפִלּוּ הָיָה רָאוּי לִקְנוֹת לָהּ כְּלֵי מֶשִׁי וְרִקְמָה וּכְלֵי זָהָב — כּוֹפִין אוֹתוֹ וְנוֹתֵן. וְכֵן הַמָּדוֹר — לְפִי עָשְׁרוֹ, וְהַתַּכְשִׁיט וּכְלֵי הַבַּיִת — הַכֹּל לְפִי עָשְׁרוֹ. וְאִם קָצְרָה יָדוֹ לִתֵּן לָהּ אֲפִלּוּ בְּעָנִי שֶׁבְּיִשְׂרָאֵל — כּוֹפִין אוֹתוֹ לְהוֹצִיא, וְתִהְיֶה הַכְּתֻבָּה עָלָיו חוֹב עַד שֶׁיַּעֲשִׁיר.

ו וְלֹא הָאִשָּׁה בִּלְבַד, אֶלָּא בָּנָיו וּבְנוֹתָיו הַקְּטַנִּים, בְּנֵי שֵׁשׁ אוֹ פָחוֹת — חַיָּב לִתֵּן לָהֶם כְּסוּת הַמַּסְפֶּקֶת לָהֶם, וּכְלֵי תַּשְׁמִישׁ, וּמָדוֹר לִשְׁכֹּן בּוֹ. וְאֵינוֹ נוֹתֵן לָהֶם לְפִי עָשְׁרוֹ, אֶלָּא כְּפִי צָרְכָּן בִּלְבַד. זֶה הַכְּלָל: כָּל מִי שֶׁיֵּשׁ לוֹ עָלָיו מְזוֹנוֹת בֵּין בְּחַיָּיו בֵּין אַחַר מוֹתוֹ — יֵשׁ לוֹ כְּסוּת וּכְלֵי בַּיִת וּמָדוֹר; וְכָל שֶׁבֵּית דִּין מוֹכְרִין לִמְזוֹנוֹתָיו, כָּךְ מוֹכְרִין לִכְסוּתוֹ וּכְלֵי בֵּיתוֹ וּמָדוֹרוֹ.

ז הָאִשָּׁה שֶׁהָלַךְ בַּעְלָהּ, וּפָסְקוּ לָהּ בֵּית דִּין מְזוֹנוֹת וּכְסוּת וּכְלֵי בַיִת וּשְׂכַר מָדוֹר — אֵין פּוֹסְקִין לָהּ תַּכְשִׁיט, שֶׁהֲרֵי אֵין לָהּ בַּעַל שֶׁתִּתְקַשֵּׁט לוֹ; אֲבָל מִי שֶׁנִּשְׁתַּטָּה בַעְלָהּ אוֹ שֶׁנִּתְחָרֵשׁ — פּוֹסְקִין לָהּ תַּכְשִׁיט. וְדִין הַבַּעַל עִם אִשְׁתּוֹ בְּטַעֲנַת הַכְּסוּת וְהַכֵּלִים וּשְׂכַר הַמָּדוֹר — כְּדִינָם בְּטַעֲנַת הַמְּזוֹנוֹת. אִם אָמַר הוּא: נָתַתִּי, וְהִיא אוֹמֶרֶת: לֹא נָתַתָּ — דִּין אֶחָד לַכֹּל.

ח הַמַּדִּיר אֶת אִשְׁתּוֹ שֶׁלֹּא תִתְקַשֵּׁט בְּאֶחָד מִכָּל הַמִּינִין —

4. I.e., a man is obligated to provide his wife with the clothes appropriate for a woman of her social standing (or his social standing, if he is of higher social standing than she) in the country in which they dwell.

5. For she should be given the opportunity to marry a man who can provide her with her basic necessities. (See Chapter 12, Halachah 11 and notes.)

6. Similarly, if he is capable of giving charity, he should provide for his sons and daughters above the age of six, as explained in Chapter 12, Halachah 15 (*Chelkat Mechokek* 73:5).

7. See Chapter 12, Halachah 16.

8. *Rashi, Ketubot* 48a, explains the difference between the two instances. When the husband left on the journey, he decided to leave his wife without adornments. Hence, we may not expropriate the money for them from his property. When, by contrast, a man loses his mental faculties, the court attempts to support the man's wife as her husband would have liked to. And we assume that he would have preferred that his wife have ornaments to adorn herself.

9. See the notes on Chapter 12, Halachah 24.

remain married for a year while the vow is in effect.[10] If [it remains in effect] for a longer period, he must either absolve himself of the vow, or divorce [his wife] and pay her [the money due her by virtue of her] *ketubah.*

If the couple are wealthy, they may remain married for a month while the vow is in effect. If [it remains in effect] for a longer period, he must either absolve himself of the vow or divorce [his wife] and pay her [the money due her by virtue of her] *ketubah.*

9. [The following rules apply if a husband] takes a vow that prevents his wife from going to the bathhouse. [The couple may remain married for only] one week in a large city and two weeks in a village [if the vow remains in effect]. If he takes a vow that prevents his wife from wearing shoes [the couple may remain married for only] three days[11] in a village and one day in a large city.[12] If [the vow remains in effect] for a longer period, he must either absolve himself of the vow or divorce [his wife] and pay her [the money due her by virtue of her] *ketubah.*

10. If [a husband] takes a vow that prevents his wife from borrowing or lending household goods that are frequently lent and borrowed between neighbors - e.g., a sifter, a sieve, a mill, an oven or the like - he must either absolve himself of the vow, or divorce [his wife] and pay her [the money due her by virtue of her] *ketubah.*[13] [The rationale is that his vow] causes her to have a bad reputation among her neighbors.

Similarly, if she takes an oath[14] not to borrow or lend [neighbors] a sifter, a sieve, a mill, an oven or the like, or not to weave attractive garments for her sons in places where it is customary to do so, he may divorce her without paying her [the money due her by virtue of her] *ketubah.* [The rationale is that her vow] causes him to have a reputation as a miser among his neighbors.

11. In a place where it is customary for a woman not to go out to the market place wearing merely a cap on her head, but also a veil that covers her entire body like a cloak, her husband must provide at least the least expensive type of veil for her. If he is wealthy, [he must provide her with a veil whose quality] is commensurate with his wealth.

[He must give her this veil] so that she can visit her father's home, a house of mourning or a wedding celebration. For every woman should be given the opportunity to visit her father and to go to a house of mourning or a wedding celebration as an expression of kindness to her friends and relatives, for [this will have a reciprocal effect], and they will return the visits. For a woman [at home] is not confined in a jail, from which she cannot come and go.

Nevertheless, it is uncouth for a woman always to leave home - this time to go out and another time to go on the street. Indeed, a husband should

בָּעֲנִיּוֹת: שָׁנָה אַחַת — יְקַיֵּם, יָתֵר עַל כֵּן — אוֹ יַתִּיר אֶת נִדְרוֹ אוֹ יוֹצִיא וְיִתֵּן כְּתֻבָּה;
וּבָעֲשִׁירוֹת: שְׁלֹשִׁים יוֹם — יְקַיֵּם, יָתֵר עַל כֵּן — יַתִּיר אֶת נִדְרוֹ אוֹ יוֹצִיא וְיִתֵּן כְּתֻבָּה.

ט הִדִּירָהּ שֶׁלֹּא תֵּלֵךְ לְמֶרְחָץ: בִּכְרַכִּים — שַׁבָּת אַחַת, בִּכְפָרִים שְׁתֵּי שַׁבָּתוֹת.
שֶׁלֹּא תִּנְעַל מִנְעָל: בִּכְפָרִים — שְׁלֹשָׁה יָמִים, וּבִכְרַכִּים — מֵעֵת לְעֵת.
יָתֵר עַל זֶה — יַתִּיר אֶת נִדְרוֹ אוֹ יוֹצִיא וְיִתֵּן כְּתֻבָּה.

י הִדִּירָהּ שֶׁלֹּא תִּשְׁאַל וְלֹא תַשְׁאִיל מִכְּלֵי הַבַּיִת שֶׁדֶּרֶךְ כָּל הַשְּׁכֵנוֹת לִשְׁאֹל אוֹתָן וּלְהַשְׁאִילָן,
כְּגוֹן נָפָה וּכְבָרָה, רֵחַיִם וְתַנּוּר וְכַיּוֹצֵא בָּהֶם — יַתִּיר אֶת נִדְרוֹ אוֹ יוֹצִיא וְיִתֵּן כְּתֻבָּה,
מִפְּנֵי שֶׁמַּשִּׂיאָהּ שֵׁם רַע בִּשְׁכוּנָתָהּ.
וְכֵן הִיא שֶׁנָּדְרָה שֶׁלֹּא תִּשְׁאַל וְלֹא תַשְׁאִיל נָפָה וּכְבָרָה וְרֵחַיִם וְתַנּוּר וְכַיּוֹצֵא בָּהֶם, וְשֶׁלֹּא
תֶאֱרֹג בְּגָדִים נָאִים לַבָּנִים, בְּמָקוֹם שֶׁדַּרְכָּן לֶאֱרֹג אוֹתָם לַבָּנִים — תֵּצֵא בְּלֹא כְּתֻבָּה,
מִפְּנֵי שֶׁמַּשִּׂיאַתּוּ שֵׁם רַע בִּשְׁכוּנָתוֹ שֶׁהוּא כִּילַי.

יא מָקוֹם שֶׁדַּרְכָּן שֶׁלֹּא תֵצֵא אִשָּׁה לַשּׁוּק בְּכִפָּה שֶׁעַל רֹאשָׁהּ בִּלְבַד, עַד שֶׁיִּהְיֶה עָלֶיהָ רְדִיד
הַחוֹפֶה אֶת כָּל גּוּפָהּ כְּמוֹ טַלִּית — נוֹתֵן לָהּ בִּכְלַל הַכְּסוּת רְדִיד הַפָּחוּת מִכָּל הָרְדִידִין.
וְאִם הָיָה עָשִׁיר — נוֹתֵן לָהּ לְפִי עָשְׁרוֹ.
כְּדֵי שֶׁתֵּצֵא בּוֹ לְבֵית אָבִיהָ אוֹ לְבֵית הָאֵבֶל אוֹ לְבֵית הַמִּשְׁתֶּה.
לְפִי שֶׁכָּל אִשָּׁה יֵשׁ לָהּ לָצֵאת וְלֵילֵךְ לְבֵית אָבִיהָ לְבַקְּרוֹ, וּלְבֵית הָאֵבֶל וּלְבֵית הַמִּשְׁתֶּה לִגְמֹל
חֶסֶד לְרֵעוֹתֶיהָ, כְּדֵי שֶׁיָּבוֹאוּ הֵם לָהּ,
שֶׁאֵינָהּ בְּבֵית הַסֹּהַר עַד שֶׁלֹּא תֵּצֵא וְלֹא תָבוֹא.
אֲבָל גְּנַאי הוּא לְאִשָּׁה שֶׁתִּהְיֶה יוֹצְאָה תָּמִיד, פַּעַם בַּחוּץ פַּעַם בָּרְחוֹבוֹת.

---

10. A poor woman does not wear ornaments very frequently and will not feel deprived if she does not adorn herself for a year. A rich woman, by contrast, cannot bear not to wear ornaments for such an extended period.

11. This law is based on the Jerusalem Talmud (*Ketubot* 7:4). The standard printed text of that source, however, has a slightly different version, stating "three months" instead of three days.

12. These rulings were dependent on the socio-economic conditions prevalent in the Talmudic period. If the norms are different in other societies, the rulings also change.

13. The *Maggid Mishneh* states that the husband is given thirty days to consider absolving his vow. The *Shulchan Aruch* (*Even HaEzer* 74:3) states he must divorce her immediately. If the husband makes the vow dependent on marital relations, he is given a week to consider the matter (*Shulchan Aruch, loc. cit.* 74:3).

14. Note the slight deviation between the wording chosen by the Rambam and that employed by the *Tur* and the *Shulchan Aruch* (*loc. cit.*).

prevent a wife from doing this and not allow her to go out more than once or twice a month, as is necessary.[15] For there is nothing more attractive for a woman than to sit in the corner of her home, as [implied by Psalms 45:14]: "All the glory of the king's daughter is within."

12. [The following rules apply when a husband] takes a vow that prevents his wife from going to her father's home. If he lives in the same city, [the husband] is granted a respite of one month. [If he desires to maintain his vow at the beginning of] the second month, he must divorce [his wife] and pay her [the money due her by virtue of her] *ketubah*. If [the wife's father lives] in another city, [the husband] is granted respite until the first festival.[16] [If he desires to maintain his vow until] the second [festival], he must divorce [his wife] and pay her [the money due her by virtue of her] *ketubah*.

13. [The following rules apply when a husband] takes a vow that prevents his wife from going to a house of mourning or to wedding celebrations. He must either absolve himself of the vow or divorce [his wife] and pay her [the money due her by virtue of her] *ketubah*. For this is like placing her in jail and locking her in.

If [the husband] claims: "[I forbade her from going] because of indecent people who were present at that house of mourning or wedding," and it was discovered that indeed, indecent people were present, he is given the prerogative [of making that vow].

14. When a person tells his wife, "I do not desire that your father, your mother, your brothers and your sisters come into my domain," he is given that prerogative. Instead, she should visit them when an [unusual] event occurs to them. And she should visit her father's house once a month and on each festival. They, by contrast, should visit her only when an unusual event of great import occurs - e.g., sickness or birth. For a person should not be forced to have others enter his domain.

Similarly, if [the wife] says: "I do not want your mother and your sisters to visit, nor will I live together with them in one courtyard, because they cause me difficulties and distress," she is given that prerogative.[17] For a person should not be forced to have others dwell with him in his domain.

15. When a husband says: "I will not dwell in this home, because there are wicked or indecent people or gentiles in this neighborhood, and I fear them," he is given that prerogative. This applies even if it has not been established that there are indecent people living there. For our Sages ordained:[18] "Keep away from a bad neighbor." Even if the dwelling belongs to the woman, she is forced to leave it, and they should establish their dwelling among worthy people.[19]

וְיֵשׁ לַבַּעַל לִמְנֹעַ אִשְׁתּוֹ מִזֶּה, וְלֹא יַנִּיחֶנָּה לָצֵאת אֶלָּא כְּמוֹ פַּעַם אַחַת בְּחֹדֶשׁ אוֹ כְּמוֹ פַּעֲמַיִם בְּחֹדֶשׁ, לְפִי הַצֹּרֶךְ.

שֶׁאֵין יֹפִי לְאִשָּׁה אֶלָּא לֵישֵׁב בְּזָוִית בֵּיתָהּ, שֶׁכָּךְ כָּתוּב: כָּל כְּבוּדָּה בַת מֶלֶךְ פְּנִימָה.

יב הַמַּדִּיר אֶת אִשְׁתּוֹ שֶׁלֹּא תֵלֵךְ לְבֵית אָבִיהָ —

בִּזְמַן שֶׁהוּא עִמָּהּ בָּעִיר: חֹדֶשׁ אֶחָד — מַמְתִּינִין לוֹ, שְׁנַיִם — יוֹצִיא וְיִתֵּן כְּתֻבָּה;

וּבִזְמַן שֶׁהוּא בְּעִיר אַחֶרֶת: רֶגֶל אֶחָד — מַמְתִּינִין לוֹ, שְׁנַיִם — יוֹצִיא וְיִתֵּן כְּתֻבָּה.

יג הַמַּדִּיר אֶת אִשְׁתּוֹ שֶׁלֹּא תֵלֵךְ לְבֵית הָאֵבֶל אוֹ לְבֵית הַמִּשְׁתֶּה — אוֹ יַתִּיר אֶת נִדְרוֹ אוֹ יוֹצִיא וְיִתֵּן כְּתֻבָּה;

שֶׁזֶּה כְּמִי שֶׁאֲסָרָהּ בְּבֵית הַסֹּהַר וְנָעַל בְּפָנֶיהָ.

וְאִם הָיָה טוֹעֵן מִפְּנֵי בְּנֵי אָדָם פְּרוּצִים שֶׁיֵּשׁ בְּאוֹתוֹ בֵּית הָאֵבֶל אוֹ בְּבֵית הַמִּשְׁתֶּה, וְהֶחֱזִיקוּ שָׁם פְּרוּצִים — שׁוֹמְעִין לוֹ.

יד הָאוֹמֵר לְאִשְׁתּוֹ: אֵין רְצוֹנִי שֶׁיָּבוֹאוּ לְבֵיתִי אָבִיךְ וְאִמֵּךְ, אַחַיִךְ וְאַחְיוֹתַיִךְ — שׁוֹמְעִין לוֹ.

וְתִהְיֶה הִיא הוֹלֶכֶת לָהֶם כְּשֶׁיֶּאֱרַע לָהֶם דָּבָר, וְתֵלֵךְ לְבֵית אָבִיהָ פַּעַם בְּחֹדֶשׁ וּבְכָל רֶגֶל וָרֶגֶל;

וְלֹא יִכָּנְסוּ הֵם לָהּ אֶלָּא אִם אֵרַע לָהּ דָּבָר, כְּגוֹן חֳלִי אוֹ לֵדָה.

שֶׁאֵין כּוֹפִין אֶת הָאָדָם שֶׁיִּכָּנְסוּ אֲחֵרִים בִּרְשׁוּתוֹ.

וְכֵן הִיא שֶׁאָמְרָה: אֵין רְצוֹנִי שֶׁיִּכָּנְסוּ אֶצְלִי אִמֵּךְ וְאַחְיוֹתֶיךָ, וְאֵינִי שׁוֹכֶנֶת עִמָּהֶם בְּחָצֵר אַחַת, מִפְּנֵי שֶׁמְּרַעִין לִי וּמְצֵרִין לִי — שׁוֹמְעִין לָהּ;

שֶׁאֵין כּוֹפִין אֶת הָאָדָם שֶׁיֵּשְׁבוּ אֲחֵרִים עִמּוֹ בִּרְשׁוּתוֹ.

טו הָאִישׁ שֶׁאָמַר: אֵינִי דָר בְּמָדוֹר זֶה, מִפְּנֵי שֶׁבְּנֵי אָדָם רָעִים אוֹ פְּרוּצִים אוֹ עַכּוּ״ם בִּשְׁכוּנָתִי וַאֲנִי מִתְיָרֵא מֵהֶם — שׁוֹמְעִים לוֹ,

וְאַף־עַל־פִּי שֶׁלֹּא הֶחֱזִיקוּ בִּפְרִיצוּת, שֶׁכָּךְ צִוּוּ חֲכָמִים: הַרְחֵק מִשָּׁכֵן רָע.

וַאֲפִלּוּ הָיָה הַמָּדוֹר שֶׁלָּהּ — מוֹצִיאִין אוֹתָהּ מִמֶּנּוּ, וְשׁוֹכֵן בֵּין בְּנֵי אָדָם כְּשֵׁרִים.

---

15. While the spirit of the Rambam's words is appreciated, in most communities the norm is for women to leave their homes far more frequently.

16. For it is customary for a daughter to visit her parents during the festivals.

17. Based on the views of the Ra'avad and others, the Ramah (*Even HaEzer* 74:10) explains that the woman's rights are different from her husband's. Since the dwelling belongs to him, he may invite his mother and sisters. Nevertheless, efforts should be made to mediate between them and his wife. If necessary, a man or a woman should be placed in the home to see who is the cause of the difficulty.

18. *Avot* 1:7.

19. See *Hilchot De'ot* 6:1, where the Rambam emphasizes the importance of eschewing an undesirable environment and dwelling in a favorable one.

The same law applies if the woman makes such a demand. Although [the husband] says, "I do not object to them," her will is followed. [The rationale is that] she can say, "I do not want to get a bad reputation in these neighborhoods."

16. All of the earth is divided into different lands - e.g., the Land of Canaan, the Land of Egypt, the Land of Yemen, the Land of Ethiopia, the Land of Babylonia and the like.[20] Every land is subdivided into large cities[21] and villages. With regard to the subject of marriage, the cities of *Eretz Yisrael* are considered to be divided into three different lands: Judea, Transjordan and the Galilee.

17. When a man from one of these lands marries a woman in another land, she is compelled to follow him to his land, or to accept a divorce without receiving [the money due her by virtue of her] *ketubah*. [The rationale is that,] although it was not specifically stated, [it can be assumed] that he married her on this condition.[22]

When, however, a person marries a woman in a particular land and he[23] is from that land, he does not have the right to [compel] her to move to another land. He may, nevertheless, [compel] her to move from city to city and from village to village within that land.

He may not, however, [compel] her to move from a city to a village, or from a village to a city. For there are certain advantages to living in a city, and other advantages to living in a village.

18. When he [compels] her to move from one city to another, or from one village to another within a particular land, he may not compel her to move from pleasant surroundings[24] to unpleasant surroundings, nor from unpleasant [surroundings] to pleasant ones. [Although seemingly, the latter move would be beneficial for her, her consent is, nevertheless, required] because she must care for and check herself in the pleasant surroundings, so that she will not be considered inferior and unattractive.[25]

Similarly, [her husband] may not [compel] her to move from an area inhabited primarily by Jews to an area inhabited primarily by gentiles.

20. The Ramah (*Even HaEzer* 75:1) states that it is a difference in language that divides one land from another. The Rivash (Responsum 177) states that the determining factor is the government of the land. This matter is discussed by the later authorities, particularly in light of the emergence of large countries comprising many times the area of *Eretz Yisrael* in the Talmudic period. Many commentaries define a land as a place inhabited by people who speak the same language and are governed by the same authority. Even that is common today.

וְכֵן הִיא שֶׁאָמְרָה כֵּן, אַף־עַל־פִּי שֶׁהוּא אוֹמֵר: אֲנִי אֵינִי מַקְפִּיד עֲלֵיהֶם — שׁוֹמְעִין לָהּ, מִפְּנֵי שֶׁהִיא אוֹמֶרֶת: אֵין רְצוֹנִי שֶׁיֵּצֵא עָלַי שֵׁם רַע בִּשְׁכֵנוֹת אֵלּוּ.

טז כָּל הַיִּשּׁוּב אֲרָצוֹת אֲרָצוֹת הוּא, כְּגוֹן אֶרֶץ כְּנַעַן וְאֶרֶץ מִצְרַיִם וְאֶרֶץ תֵּימָן וְאֶרֶץ כּוּשׁ וְאֶרֶץ שִׁנְעָר וְכַיּוֹצֵא בָּהֶן.

וְכָל אֶרֶץ וָאֶרֶץ — מְדִינוֹת וּכְפָרִים.

וְעָרֵי יִשְׂרָאֵל לְעִנְיַן נִשּׂוּאִין שָׁלֹשׁ אֲרָצוֹת הָיוּ: יְהוּדָה, וְעֵבֶר הַיַּרְדֵּן, וְהַגָּלִיל.

יז אִישׁ שֶׁהָיָה מֵאֶרֶץ מִן הָאֲרָצוֹת, וְנָשָׂא אִשָּׁה בְּאֶרֶץ אַחֶרֶת — כּוֹפִין אוֹתָהּ וְיוֹצְאָה עִמּוֹ לְאַרְצוֹ, אוֹ תֵּצֵא בְּלֹא כְתֻבָּה;

שֶׁעַל מְנָת כֵּן נְשָׂאָהּ, אַף־עַל־פִּי שֶׁלֹּא פֵּרֵשׁ.

אֲבָל הַנּוֹשֵׂא אִשָּׁה בְּאַחַת מִן הָאֲרָצוֹת, וְהִיא מֵאַנְשֵׁי אוֹתָהּ הָאָרֶץ — אֵינוֹ יָכוֹל לְהוֹצִיאָהּ לְאֶרֶץ אַחֶרֶת;

אֲבָל מוֹצִיאָהּ מִמְּדִינָה לִמְדִינָה וּמִכְּפָר לִכְפָר בְּאוֹתָהּ הָאָרֶץ.

וְאֵינוֹ יָכוֹל לְהוֹצִיאָהּ מִמְּדִינָה לִכְפָר, וְלֹא מִכְּפָר לִמְדִינָה;

שֶׁיֵּשׁ דְּבָרִים שֶׁיְּשִׁיבַת הַמְּדִינָה טוֹבָה לָהֶם, וְיֵשׁ דְּבָרִים שֶׁיְּשִׁיבַת הַכְּפָרִים טוֹבָה לָהֶם.

יח וּכְשֶׁמּוֹצִיאָהּ מִמְּדִינָה לִמְדִינָה וּמִכְּפָר לִכְפָר בְּאוֹתָהּ הָאָרֶץ — אֵינוֹ יָכוֹל לְהוֹצִיאָהּ מִנָּוֶה הַיָּפֶה לְנָוֶה הָרַע, וְלֹא מֵרַע לְיָפֶה;

מִפְּנֵי שֶׁהִיא צְרִיכָה לְהִטַּפֵּל וְלִבְדֹּק עַצְמָהּ בַּנָּוֶה הַיָּפֶה, כְּדֵי שֶׁלֹּא תִהְיֶה בּוֹ קָלָה וּכְעוּרָה.

וְכֵן לֹא יוֹצִיאָהּ מִמָּקוֹם שֶׁרֻבּוֹ יִשְׂרָאֵל לְמָקוֹם שֶׁרֻבּוֹ עַכּוּ"ם.

---

21. Our translation is based on the Rambam's Commentary on the Mishnah (*Ketubot* 13:10). The contemporary translation of מדינה as "state" or "country" is not appropriate in this context.

22. The Ramah (*Even HaEzer* 75:1) quotes the opinion of Rabbenu Tam (*Ketubot* 110b), which states that when the two come from different lands and the marriage is held in one of these lands, the place where the couple marries determines their future dwelling. If, however, they each come from a different land from that in which the marriage is held, the woman may compel her husband to live in her native land. See also the opinion of *Terumat HaDeshen* (Responsum 416, quoted by the Ramah, *loc. cit.*), which states that if the man cannot earn a livelihood in the locale in which he is living, he may compel his wife to follow him to any place where he can.

23. Our text follows the version found in many manuscripts and early printings of the *Mishneh Torah* and that which is quoted by the *Shulchan Aruch* (*Even HaEzer* 75:1). The standard published version states "she" instead of "he."

24. I.e., the neighborhood and its scenery. Our translation is based on the *Ma'aseh Rokeach*. Others translate נוה as "dwelling" - i.e., the home in which the couple reside.

25. The Rambam appears to be saying that the woman must dress and present herself in an appropriate way in an attractive setting, and she might not desire to make such an effort. Rashi (*Ketubot* 110b) explains that the change in lifestyle may cause illness.

Wherever [the couple lives], they should move[26] from an area inhabited primarily by gentiles to an area inhabited primarily by Jews.

19. When does the above apply? When moving from one place in the diaspora to another, or from one place in *Eretz Yisrael* to another. But if [the husband desires to move] from the diaspora to *Eretz Yisrael*, the woman should be compelled to move.[27] [This applies even when moving involves leaving] pleasant surroundings for unpleasant ones. Even [when it is necessary to leave] an area inhabited primarily by Jews for an area inhabited primarily by gentiles, one should [move to *Eretz Yisrael*].

One should not leave *Eretz Yisrael* for the diaspora,[28] even if the move enables one to relocate from unpleasant [surroundings] to pleasant ones, and even when it enables one to move from an area inhabited primarily by gentiles to an area inhabited primarily by Jews.

20. When a husband desires to move to *Eretz Yisrael* and [his wife] does not desire to do so, he may divorce her without paying her [the money due her by virtue of her] *ketubah*. If she desires to move [to *Eretz Yisrael*] and he does not desire to do so, he must divorce her and pay her [the money due her by virtue of her] *ketubah*.[29]

The same laws apply with regard to moving from other places in *Eretz Yisrael* to Jerusalem. [Just as] everyone should move to *Eretz Yisrael*, and no one should leave there, [so too,] everyone should move to Jerusalem, and no one should leave there.[30]

26. Our translation is based on the *Bayit Chadash* (*Even HaEzer* 75), which states that the woman may compel her husband to make such a move. Note, however, the *Chelkat Mechokek* 75:12, which states that this interpretation need not be accepted.
27. As reflected in *Hilchot Melachim*, Chapter 5, the Rambam does not consider living in *Eretz Yisrael* a mitzvah [in contrast to the view of the Ramban (*Hosafot l'Sefer HaMitzvot*, Positive Mitzvah 4) and others, who do]. Nevertheless, he states (*Hilchot Melachim* 5:12): "At all times... a person should dwell in *Eretz Yisrael*... rather than in the diaspora."

The commentaries interpret the expression "At all times" to include even the present age. *Tosafot, Ketubot* 110b, explains that because we are unsure how to fulfill the agricultural laws of *Eretz Yisrael*, there is no obligation to live there in the present age. Others explain that because of the dangers that exist in *Eretz Yisrael*, there is no obligation. (See *Shulchan Aruch, Even HaEzer* 75:5.) As reflected in this ruling and in one of his responsa, the Rambam negates those views and advocates living in *Eretz Yisrael*, even in the present age.

וּבְכָל מָקוֹם מוֹצִיאִין מִמְּקוֹם שֶׁרֻבּוֹ עַכּוּ"ם לְמָקוֹם שֶׁרֻבּוֹ יִשְׂרָאֵל.

יט בַּמֶּה דְּבָרִים אֲמוּרִים? מֵחוּצָה לָאָרֶץ לְחוּצָה לָאָרֶץ, אוֹ מֵאֶרֶץ יִשְׂרָאֵל לְאֶרֶץ יִשְׂרָאֵל; אֲבָל מֵחוּצָה לָאָרֶץ לְאֶרֶץ יִשְׂרָאֵל — כּוֹפִין אוֹתָהּ לַעֲלוֹת.
אֲפִלּוּ מִנָּוֶה הַיָּפֶה לְנָוֶה הָרַע, וַאֲפִלּוּ מִמָּקוֹם שֶׁרֻבּוֹ יִשְׂרָאֵל לְמָקוֹם שֶׁרֻבּוֹ עַכּוּ"ם — מַעֲלִין.
וְאֵין מוֹצִיאִין מֵאֶרֶץ יִשְׂרָאֵל לְחוּצָה לָאָרֶץ,
וַאֲפִלּוּ מִנָּוֶה הָרַע לְנָוֶה הַיָּפֶה, [וַאֲפִלּוּ מִמָּקוֹם] שֶׁרֻבּוֹ עַכּוּ"ם לְמָקוֹם שֶׁרֻבּוֹ יִשְׂרָאֵל.

כ אָמַר הָאִישׁ לַעֲלוֹת לְאֶרֶץ יִשְׂרָאֵל, וְהִיא אֵינָהּ רוֹצָה — תֵּצֵא בְּלֹא כְּתֻבָּה.
אָמְרָה הִיא לַעֲלוֹת, וְהוּא אֵינוֹ רוֹצֶה — יוֹצִיא וְיִתֵּן כְּתֻבָּה.
וְהוּא הַדִּין לְכָל מָקוֹם מֵאֶרֶץ יִשְׂרָאֵל עִם יְרוּשָׁלַיִם.
שֶׁהַכֹּל מַעֲלִין לְאֶרֶץ יִשְׂרָאֵל, וְאֵין הַכֹּל מוֹצִיאִין מִשָּׁם;
הַכֹּל מַעֲלִין לִירוּשָׁלַיִם, וְאֵין הַכֹּל מוֹצִיאִין מִשָּׁם.

28. See *Hilchot Melachim* 5:9, which states that it is forbidden to leave *Eretz Yisrael* for the purpose of settling in the diaspora, unless there is a famine of extreme severity. Even then, abandoning the land is not considered desirable. In *Hilchot Melachim* 5:12, the Rambam states: "Whoever leaves [*Eretz Yisrael*] for the diaspora is considered as though he worships idols."

29. As mentioned above, there are opinions that maintain that in the present age, there is no obligation to dwell in *Eretz Yisrael*. According to these views, this ruling does not apply. Although the *Shulchan Aruch* (*Even HaEzer* 75:4-5) also mentions the opposing view, it appears to follow the opinion stated by the Rambam. Nevertheless, many Ashkenazic authorities maintain (see *Ba'er Heteiv* 75:19) that at present one may not divorce a woman without paying her the money due her for her *ketubah* because she does not desire to move to *Eretz Yisrael*. Although the *Pitchei Teshuvah* 75:7 speaks extensively about the positive value of living in *Eretz Yisrael* in the present age, it mentions another factor - the difficulty of earning a living in *Eretz Yisrael* - and states that unless one is assured of being able to sustain himself through work - as opposed to receiving charity - one may not compel one's family to relocate.

30. There are opinions (Mordechai, at the conclusion of *Ketubot*) that maintain that in the present age, when there is no Temple, there is no difference between Jerusalem and other cities in *Eretz Yisrael*. Nevertheless, the fact that this law is quoted by the *Shulchan Aruch* (*Even HaEzer* 75:4), a text that deals only with laws applicable at present, appears to imply that the Rambam's ruling should be applied in the present age as well.

CHAPTER FOURTEEN

1. The [obligation of] conjugal rights[1] as prescribed by the Torah [is individual in nature], depending on the strength of each particular man and the [type of] work that he performs.

What is implied? Healthy men who are pampered and indulged, and who are not employed in labor that weakens their strength - but rather eat, drink and spend [the majority of their day] at home - should fulfill their conjugal duties every night.

[The following rules apply to] workers - e.g., tailors, weavers, construction workers and the like. If they work in the city [in which they live], they should fulfill their conjugal duties twice a week. If they work in another city, they should fulfill their conjugal duties once a week.

Donkey-drivers should fulfill their conjugal duties once a week. Camel-drivers should fulfill their conjugal duties once every thirty days. Seamen should fulfill their conjugal duties once every six months.

Students of the Torah should fulfill their conjugal duties once a week. [Their obligation is limited,] because the Torah weakens their strength. It is the practice of Torah scholars to engage in marital relations on Friday night.[2]

2. A wife has the right to prevent her husband from making business trips except to close places, so that he will not be prevented from fulfilling his conjugal duties. He may make such journeys only with her permission.

Similarly, she has the prerogative of preventing him from changing from a profession that grants her more frequent conjugal rights to one that grants her less frequent rights - e.g., a donkey-driver who wishes to become a camel-driver, or a camel-driver who wishes to become a seaman.[3]

Students of the Torah may, however, depart for Torah study for two or three years without their wives' permission. Similarly, a wife cannot prevent a husband who is pampered and indulged from becoming a student of the Torah.

3. A man [has the prerogative of] marrying several wives[4] - even 100, whether at one time or one after the other. His wife may not object to this, provided he has the means to provide each [wife] with her subsistence, clothing and conjugal rights as befits her. He may not, however, compel his wives to live in the same courtyard. Instead, each one is entitled to her own household.[5]

---

1. The very word *onah* - and its translation as "conjugal rights" - conveys a fundamental conception with regard to the Torah's conception of marital intimacy. Marital intimacy

פֶּרֶק אַרְבָּעָה עָשָׂר

א עוֹנָה הָאֲמוּרָה בַּתּוֹרָה — לְכָל אִישׁ וָאִישׁ כְּפִי כֹחוֹ וּכְפִי מְלַאכְתּוֹ.

כֵּיצַד? בְּנֵי אָדָם הַבְּרִיאִים וְהָרַכִּים וְהָעֲנֻגִּים, שֶׁאֵין לָהֶם מְלָאכָה שֶׁמַּכְשֶׁלֶת כֹּחָן, אֶלָּא אוֹכְלִין וְשׁוֹתִין וְיוֹשְׁבִין בְּבָתֵּיהֶן — עוֹנָתָן בְּכָל לַיְלָה.

הַפּוֹעֲלִין, כְּגוֹן הַחַיָּטִין וְהָאוֹרְגִין וְהַבּוֹנִים וְכַיּוֹצֵא בָהֶן:

אִם הָיְתָה מְלַאכְתָּן בָּעִיר — עוֹנָתָן פַּעֲמַיִם בְּשַׁבָּת,

וְאִם הָיְתָה מְלַאכְתָּן בְּעִיר אַחֶרֶת — עוֹנָתָן פַּעַם אַחַת בְּשַׁבָּת.

הַחַמָּרִים — פַּעַם אַחַת בְּשַׁבָּת.

וְהַגַּמָּלִים — אַחַת לִשְׁלֹשִׁים יוֹם.

וְהַמַּלָּחִין — אַחַת לְשִׁשָּׁה חֳדָשִׁים.

תַּלְמִידֵי חֲכָמִים — עוֹנָתָן פַּעַם אַחַת בְּשַׁבָּת, מִפְּנֵי שֶׁתַּלְמוּד תּוֹרָה מַתִּישׁ כֹּחָן. וְדֶרֶךְ תַּלְמִידֵי חֲכָמִים לְשַׁמֵּשׁ מִטָּתָן מִלֵּילֵי שַׁבָּת לְלֵילֵי שַׁבָּת.

ב יֵשׁ לְאִשָּׁה לְעַכֵּב עַל בַּעְלָהּ שֶׁלֹּא יֵצֵא לִסְחוֹרָה אֶלָּא לְמָקוֹם קָרוֹב, שֶׁלֹּא יִמְנַע מֵעוֹנָתָהּ וְלֹא יֵצֵא אֶלָּא בִּרְשׁוּתָהּ.

וְכֵן יֵשׁ לָהּ לְמָנְעוֹ לָצֵאת מִמְּלָאכָה שֶׁעוֹנָתָהּ קְרוֹבָה לִמְלָאכָה שֶׁעוֹנָתָהּ רְחוֹקָה, כְּגוֹן חַמָּר שֶׁבִּקֵּשׁ לְהֵעָשׂוֹת גַּמָּל, אוֹ גַמָּל לְהֵעָשׂוֹת מַלָּח.

וְתַלְמִידֵי חֲכָמִים יוֹצְאִין לְתַלְמוּד תּוֹרָה שֶׁלֹּא בִּרְשׁוּת נְשׁוֹתֵיהֶן שְׁתַּיִם וְשָׁלֹשׁ שָׁנִים. וְכֵן רַךְ וְעָנֹג שֶׁנַּעֲשָׂה תַּלְמִיד חָכָם — אֵין אִשְׁתּוֹ יְכוֹלָה לְעַכֵּב.

ג נוֹשֵׂא אָדָם כַּמָּה נָשִׁים, אֲפִלּוּ מֵאָה, בֵּין בְּבַת אַחַת בֵּין בְּזוֹ אַחַר זוֹ, וְאֵין אִשְׁתּוֹ יְכוֹלָה לְעַכֵּב.

וְהוּא, שֶׁיִּהְיֶה יָכוֹל לִתֵּן שְׁאָר כְּסוּת וְעוֹנָה כָּרָאוּי לְכָל אַחַת וְאֶחָת.

וְאֵינוֹ יָכוֹל לָכֹף אוֹתָן לִשְׁכֹּן בְּחָצֵר אַחַת, אֶלָּא כָּל אַחַת וְאַחַת לְעַצְמָהּ.

---

is not for the husband's sake, but rather for his wife's. *Onah* also means "respond." A man should be responding to his wife's desires and satisfying her wishes for closeness.

2. See *Hilchot Shabbat* 30:14, where the Rambam states that marital relations are one of the expressions of *oneg Shabbat*, "Sabbath delight." (See also *Hilchot De'ot* 4:19, 5:4.)

3. *Ketubot* 62b states that even if the other profession is more profitable, the prerogative is granted to the woman, for a woman values intimacy with her husband more than financial advancement.

4. *Yevamot* 65a states that if it is the local custom for a man to have only one wife, a man may not deviate from that custom. In the Ashkenazic community, as ordained by the ban of Rabbenu Gershom, it is forbidden for a man to marry more than one wife. (See *Shulchan Aruch* (*Even HaEzer* 1:9-10).)

5. The commentaries draw support for this law from the Biblical narrative (Genesis 31:33), which mentions that Jacob had separate tents for Leah, Rachel, Bilhah and Zilpah. (See also Chapter 13, Halachah 14.)

4. What are [his obligations with regard to his wives'] conjugal rights? [They are determined according to] the number [of wives he has.]

What is implied? If a worker has two wives, he is obligated to fulfill his duties towards each one once a week. If he has four wives, he is obligated to fulfill his duties towards each one once every two weeks. Similarly, a seaman who has four wives is obligated to fulfill his duties towards each one once every two years.

Therefore, our Sages[6] commanded that a person should not marry more than four wives, although he has ample financial resources, so that he will be able to fulfill his conjugal obligations towards each one once a month.[7]

5. When a man makes a vow requiring his wife to tell other people what he told her - or what she told him - of the jests and frivolities that a man and his wife will [occasionally] speak [in preparation for] marital relations, he must divorce [his wife] and pay her [the money due her by virtue of her] *ketubah*. For a woman may not [be compelled] to speak brazenly and tell others lascivious things.

Similarly, if a man makes a vow requiring his wife to take actions during marital relations to prevent conception, or if he makes a vow requiring her to act foolishly, [performing] acts that have no meaning and are merely foolishness,[8] he must divorce [his wife] and pay her [the money due her by virtue of her] *ketubah.*

6. When a man makes a vow causing marital relations with his wife to be forbidden, he is given a respite of one week.[9] After that time, he must divorce [his wife] and pay her [the money due her by virtue of her] *ketubah*, or absolve his vow. [This ruling applies even if the man] is a seaman whose obligation towards conjugal duties is once every six months. [The rationale is that] since he took a vow, he has caused his wife distress, and she despairs [of ever resuming intimacy].

How can such a vow be effective? If he tells her: "Marital relations with me are forbidden for you," or he takes an oath not to engage in marital relations, his vow is of no consequence, and by taking an oath he violates the prohibition against taking a false oath, for he is obligated [by the Torah to engage in relations with her].[10] If, however, he tells her, "The satisfaction of engaging in relations with you is forbidden to me," it is a [binding] vow, and he is forbidden to engage in relations with her.[11] For a person should not be fed food that is forbidden to him.

7. It is forbidden for a man to deprive his wife of her conjugal rights. If he transgresses and deprives her of these rights in order to cause her distress, he violates one of the Torah's negative commandments, as [Exodus 21:10] states: "Do not deprive [her] of her sustenance, garments or conjugal rights."[12]

ד וְכַמָּה הִיא עוֹנָתָן? לְפִי מִנְיָן.

כֵּיצַד? פּוֹעֵל שֶׁהָיוּ לוֹ שְׁתֵּי נָשִׁים — יֵשׁ לָזוֹ עוֹנָה אַחַת בְּשַׁבָּת, וְיֵשׁ לָזוֹ עוֹנָה אַחַת בְּשַׁבָּת. הָיוּ לוֹ אַרְבַּע נָשִׁים — נִמְצָא עוֹנַת כָּל אַחַת מֵהֶן פַּעַם אַחַת בִּשְׁתֵּי שַׁבָּתוֹת.

וְכֵן אִם הָיָה מֶלֶךְ וְיֵשׁ לוֹ אַרְבַּע נָשִׁים — תִּהְיֶה עוֹנַת כָּל אַחַת מֵהֶן פַּעַם אַחַת בִּשְׁתֵּי שָׁנִים. לְפִיכָךְ צִוּוּ חֲכָמִים, שֶׁלֹּא יִשָּׂא אָדָם יוֹתֵר עַל אַרְבַּע נָשִׁים, אַף־עַל־פִּי שֶׁיֵּשׁ לוֹ מָמוֹן הַרְבֵּה, כְּדֵי שֶׁתַּגִּיעַ לָהֶן עוֹנָה פַּעַם אַחַת בְּחֹדֶשׁ.

ה הַמַּדִּיר אֶת אִשְׁתּוֹ שֶׁתֹּאמַר שֶׁתֹּאמַר לַאֲחֵרִים מַה שֶּׁאָמַר לָהּ אוֹ מַה שֶּׁאָמְרָה לוֹ מִדִּבְרֵי שְׂחוֹק וְקַלּוּת רֹאשׁ שֶׁמְּדַבֵּר אָדָם עִם אִשְׁתּוֹ עַל עִסְקֵי תַּשְׁמִישׁ — הֲרֵי זֶה יוֹצִיא וְיִתֵּן כְּתֻבָּה;

שֶׁאֵין זוֹ יְכוֹלָה לְהָעֵז לְהָעֵז פָּנֶיהָ וְלוֹמַר לַאֲחֵרִים דִּבְרֵי קָלוֹן.

וְכֵן אִם הַדִּירָהּ שֶׁתִּהְיֶה פּוֹעֶלֶת בְּעֵת תַּשְׁמִישׁ שֶׁלֹּא תִתְעַבֵּר,

אוֹ שֶׁהַדִּירָהּ שֶׁתַּעֲשֶׂה מַעֲשֶׂה שׁוֹטִים וּדְבָרִים שֶׁאֵין בָּהֶן מַמָּשׁ אֶלָּא כְּשְׁטוּת — הֲרֵי זֶה יוֹצִיא וְיִתֵּן כְּתֻבָּה.

ו הַמַּדִּיר אֶת אִשְׁתּוֹ מִתַּשְׁמִישׁ הַמִּטָּה:

שַׁבָּת אַחַת — מַמְתִּינִין לוֹ, יָתֵר עַל כֵּן — יוֹצִיא וְיִתֵּן כְּתֻבָּה אוֹ יָפֵר נִדְרוֹ.

אֲפִלּוּ הָיָה מַלָּח, שֶׁעוֹנָתוֹ לְשִׁשָּׁה חֳדָשִׁים; שֶׁכֵּיוָן שֶׁנָּדַר — הֲרֵי צְעָרָהּ וְנִתְיָאֲשָׁה.

וְכֵיצַד מַדִּירָהּ? אִם אָמַר לָהּ: תַּשְׁמִישִׁי אָסוּר עָלַיִךְ, אוֹ שֶׁנִּשְׁבַּע שֶׁלֹּא יְשַׁמֵּשׁ מִטָּתוֹ — לֹא נָדַר כְּלוּם, וְאִם נִשְׁבַּע — נִשְׁבַּע לַשָּׁוְא, מִפְּנֵי שֶׁהוּא מְשֻׁעְבָּד לָהּ.

אָמַר לָהּ: הֲנָאַת תַּשְׁמִישֵׁךְ אֲסוּרָה עָלַי — הֲרֵי זֶה נֶדֶר, וְאָסוּר לְשַׁמֵּשׁ; שֶׁאֵין מַאֲכִילִין לְאָדָם דָּבָר הָאָסוּר לוֹ.

ז אָסוּר לְאָדָם לִמְנֹעַ אִשְׁתּוֹ מֵעוֹנָתָהּ.

וְאִם עָבַר וּמָנַע כְּדֵי לְצַעֲרָהּ — עָבַר בְּלֹא תַעֲשֶׂה שֶׁבַּתּוֹרָה, שֶׁנֶּאֱמַר: שְׁאֵרָהּ כְּסוּתָהּ וְעֹנָתָהּ לֹא יִגְרָע.

6. *Yevamot* 65a.

7. From this, it appears that the custom of engaging in sexual relations once a week was not the practice of Torah scholars alone.

8. E.g., to fill up pitchers of water and dump them down the drain (*Ketubot* 7:3; *Even HaEzer* 76:12).

9. In this time, it is hoped that he will change his mind and retract his vow.

10. As mentioned in Chapter 12, Halachah 2, a husband is obligated by the Torah to give his wife conjugal rights. Once an obligation is imposed on a person by the Torah, he may not free himself of it by taking a vow or an oath.

11. Since this vow does not forbid anything to the woman, but states instead, that her husband is prohibited from appreciating pleasure that results from relations with her, it can be effective.

12. Rav Kapach notes that although this prohibition involves three rights, the Rambam

If he becomes sick or his virility is weakened, and he is unable to engage in sexual relations, he is given a period of six months[13] - for [a woman is never required to wait] longer for her conjugal rights than this - in the hope that he recovers. Afterwards, the prerogative is hers [whether to remain married] or whether he must divorce her and pay her [the money due her by virtue of her] *ketubah*.

8. A woman who withholds marital intimacy from her husband is called a *moredet* ("a rebel"). She is asked why she has rebelled. If she answers: "Because I am repulsed by him and I cannot voluntarily engage in relations with him," her husband should be compelled to divorce her immediately. For she is not like a captive, [to be forced] to engage in relations with one she loathes.[14]

[In such an instance, as part of] the divorce [settlement], she does not receive any of the money promised her in her *ketubah*.[15] She is entitled to whatever remains of the possessions she brought into the marriage arrangement, both those for which her husband assumed responsibility and those for which he did not assume responsibility - i.e., *nichsei m'log*.[16]

She is not entitled to anything that belongs to her husband. She should remove even the shoe on her foot and her head-covering that he gave her and return them to him. [Similarly,] she should return to him any presents that he gave her. For he did not give them to her with the intent that she take them and [leave his home].

9. [Different rules apply, however,] if she rebelled against her husband with the intent of causing him distress,[17] saying: "I intend to cause him distress this way, because he did this or this to me," "...because he cursed me," "...because he has caused me strife," or the like, she is sent a messenger from the court, [who] tells her: "Take note. If you continue your rebellious conduct, you will forfeit your *ketubah*, even if it is worth one hundred *maneh*."[18]

Afterwards, announcements are made concerning her in the synagogues and the houses of study each day for four consecutive weeks,[19] saying: "So and so has rebelled against her husband."[20]

mentions its violation only with regard to the denial of conjugal rights. He explains that with regard to her sustenance and garments, a woman can take legal recourse and sue for the money due. This, however, is not possible with regard to conjugal rights.

13. The later authorities (*Chelkat Mechokek* 76:18; *Beit Shmuel* 76:17) quote the opinion in the *Shiltei HaGiborim* that states that if a man is afflicted with an ailment that will heal, his wife is required to remain married to him, despite the fact that the treatment will last longer than six months.

14. The *Maggid Mishneh* and many other authorities differ with the Rambam on this point and maintain that a man should not be forced to divorce his wife even in such a situation. This view is followed by the *Shulchan Aruch* (*Even HaEzer* 77:2). Even those

וְאִם חָלָה אוֹ תָּשַׁשׁ כֹּחוֹ וְאֵינוֹ יָכוֹל לִבְעוֹל — יַמְתִּין שִׁשָּׁה חֲדָשִׁים שֶׁמָּא יַבְרִיא, שֶׁאֵין לָךְ עוֹנָה גְדוֹלָה מִזּוֹ,

וְאַחַר כָּךְ אוֹ יִטֹּל מִמֶּנָּה רְשׁוּת אוֹ יוֹצִיא וְיִתֵּן כְּתֻבָּה.

ח הָאִשָּׁה שֶׁמָּנְעָה בַּעְלָהּ מִתַּשְׁמִישׁ הַמִּטָּה, הִיא הַנִּקְרֵאת מוֹרֶדֶת.

וְשׁוֹאֲלִין אוֹתָהּ מִפְּנֵי מָה מָרָדָה.

אִם אָמְרָה: מְאַסְתִּיהוּ וְאֵינִי יְכוֹלָה לְהִבָּעֵל לוֹ מִדַּעְתִּי — כּוֹפִין אוֹתוֹ לְשָׁעָתוֹ לְגָרְשָׁהּ, לְפִי שֶׁאֵינָהּ כִּשְׁבוּיָה שֶׁתִּבָּעֵל לְשָׂנוּא לָהּ.

וְתֵצֵא בְּלֹא כְתֻבָּה כְּלָל.

וְתִטֹּל בְּלָאוֹתֶיהָ הַקַּיָּמִין — בֵּין מִנְּכָסִים שֶׁהִכְנִיסָה לְבַעְלָהּ וְנִתְחַיֵּב בְּאַחֲרָיוּתָן, בֵּין מִנִּכְסֵי מְלוֹג שֶׁלֹּא נִתְחַיֵּב בְּאַחֲרָיוּתָן.

וְאֵינָה נוֹטֶלֶת בְּשֶׁל בַּעַל כְּלוּם. וַאֲפִלּוּ מִנְעָל שֶׁבְּרַגְלֶיהָ וּמִטְפַּחַת שֶׁבְּרֹאשָׁהּ שֶׁלְּקָחָן לָהּ, פּוֹשֶׁטֶת וְנוֹתֶנֶת לוֹ.

וְכָל מַה שֶּׁנָּתַן לָהּ מַתָּנָה מַחֲזֶרֶת אוֹתוֹ, שֶׁלֹּא נָתַן לָהּ עַל מְנָת שֶׁתִּטֹּל וְתֵצֵא.

ט וְאִם מָרְדָה מִתַּחַת בַּעְלָהּ כְּדֵי לְצַעֲרוֹ, וְאָמְרָה: הֲרֵינִי מְצַעֶרֶת אוֹתוֹ בְּכָךְ מִפְּנֵי שֶׁעָשָׂה לִי כָּךְ וְכָךְ, אוֹ מִפְּנֵי שֶׁקִּלְלַנִי, אוֹ מִפְּנֵי שֶׁעָשָׂה עִמִּי מְרִיבָה, וְכַיּוֹצֵא בִּדְבָרִים אֵלּוּ —

שׁוֹלְחִים לָהּ מִבֵּית דִּין וְאוֹמְרִין לָהּ: הֱוֵי יוֹדַעַת, שֶׁאִם אַתְּ עוֹמֶדֶת בְּמִרְדֵּךְ — אֲפִלּוּ כְּתֻבָּתֵךְ מֵאָה מָנֶה, הִפְסַדְתְּ אוֹתָהּ.

וְאַחַר כָּךְ מַכְרִיזִין עָלֶיהָ בְּבָתֵּי כְנֵסִיּוֹת וּבְבָתֵּי מִדְרָשׁוֹת בְּכָל יוֹם, אַרְבַּע שַׁבָּתוֹת זוֹ אַחַר זוֹ, וְאוֹמְרִים: פְּלוֹנִית מָרְדָה עַל בַּעְלָהּ.

opinions that favor the Rambam's ruling emphasize that the court should seek to clarify that the woman is not making her statements because she fell in love with another man and seeks to end her previous marriage because of him.

15. For, as implied by the Rambam's statements below, this money was promised to her only on the condition that she maintain the marriage relationship.

16. Those authorities who differ with the Rambam regarding whether the husband is compelled to divorce his wife also differ with regard to this point. They maintain that even with regard to the possessions for which her husband accepted responsibility, the woman is granted only what she takes possession of. (See *Maggid Mishneh*; Ramah (*Even HaEzer, loc. cit.*).

17. I.e., she is not necessarily interested in terminating the marriage, but rather in withholding marital relations as a means to communicate her position to her husband.

18. A *maneh* is equivalent to 100 *dinarim*.

19. The *Shulchan Aruch* (*Even HaEzer* 77:2) quotes the Rambam's wording. The Ramah, however, differs, stating that the announcement need be made only on four consecutive Sabbaths.

20. The purpose of these announcements is obviously to shame her and to cause her to reconsider her course of behavior.

10. After the announcement has been made, the court sends her a messenger a second time. He tells her: "If you continue your rebellious conduct, you have forfeited your *ketubah*." If, nevertheless, she continues this conduct and does not retract, she is consulted by the court. [If she does not change her mind,] she then forfeits her *ketubah* and has no rights to a *ketubah* at all.21

She is not given a divorce until twelve months pass.22 During these twelve months, [her husband is] not [required] to provide for her subsistence. If she dies before being divorced, her husband inherits her [property].

11. This is the sequence followed with regard to a woman who rebels [against her husband] in order to cause him distress. These laws apply even when the woman is in the *niddah* state or when she is ill and is not fit to engage in sexual relations. Similarly, they apply even when her husband is a seaman whose conjugal duties are only once in six months, and even when [her husband] has another wife.23

12. Similarly, when the time comes for an *arusah* to enter *nisu'in*,24 and she refuses to do so, rebelling in order to cause [her husband] distress, she is considered to be one who rebels [and refuses to engage] in marital relations. Similarly, the above sequence is followed when a *yevamah* refuses to undergo *yibbum* in order to cause [her *yavam*] distress.25

13. When this woman who rebels is divorced after twelve months without receiving [any of the money due her because of] her *ketubah*, she must also return everything that belongs to her husband.

With regard to the property that she brought to [the marriage arrangement] and what remains [of her trousseau, different rules apply].26 If she takes physical possession of these articles, they are not taken from her, but if her husband takes physical possession of them,27 they are not taken from

---

21. I.e., she does not receive the fundamental requirement of the *ketubah*, nor any additional amount that her husband promised her (*tos'fot ketubah*).

22. The *Maggid Mishneh* explains that, as a favor, the court requests the husband not to divorce his wife until this time has passed, for it is disgraceful for a Jewish couple to part because of strife. It is hoped that during the twelve months they are required to wait, they will resolve their differences.

There are opinions that state that in the present age, the husband is not required to wait an entire year and may instead divorce his wife immediately. Nevertheless, the majority of authorities do not accept this view (Ramah, *loc. cit.*).

According to the Rambam, during these twelve months, the husband has no financial responsibilities to his wife whatsoever. If she is held captive, he is not required to redeem her, and if he dies, she does not inherit her *ketubah* from his estate. Rabbenu Asher

י וְאַחַר הַהַכְרָזָה שׁוֹלְחִין לָהּ בֵּית דִּין פַּעַם שְׁנִיָּה וְאוֹמְרִים לָהּ: אִם אַתְּ עוֹמֶדֶת בְּמִרְדֵּךְ, הִפְסַדְתְּ כְּתֻבָּתִיךְ.

אִם עָמְדָה בְּמִרְדָּהּ וְלֹא חָזְרָה — נִמְלָכִין בָּהּ, וּתְאַבֵּד כְּתֻבָּתָהּ, וְלֹא יִהְיֶה לָהּ כְּתֻבָּה כְּלָל. וְאֵין נוֹתְנִין לָהּ גֵּט עַד שְׁנֵים עָשָׂר חֹדֶשׁ, וְאֵין לָהּ מְזוֹנוֹת כָּל שְׁנֵים עָשָׂר חֹדֶשׁ. וְאִם מֵתָה קֹדֶם הַגֵּט — בַּעְלָהּ יוֹרְשָׁהּ.

יא כַּסֵּדֶר הַזֶּה עוֹשִׂין לָהּ אִם אִם מָרְדָה כְּדֵי לְצַעֲרוֹ. וַאֲפִלּוּ הָיְתָה נִדָּה אוֹ חוֹלָה, שֶׁאֵינָהּ רְאוּיָה לְתַשְׁמִישׁ. וַאֲפִלּוּ הָיָה בַּעְלָהּ מַלָּח, שֶׁעוֹנָתוֹ לְשִׁשָּׁה חֳדָשִׁים. וַאֲפִלּוּ יֵשׁ לוֹ אִשָּׁה אַחֶרֶת.

יב וְכֵן אֲרוּסָה שֶׁהִגִּיעַ זְמַנָּהּ לְהִנָּשֵׂא, וּמָרְדָה כְּדֵי לְצַעֲרוֹ וְלֹא נִשֵּׂאת — הֲרֵי זוֹ מוֹרֶדֶת מִתַּשְׁמִישׁ.

וְכֵן יְבָמָה שֶׁלֹּא רָצְתָה לְהִתְיַבֵּם כְּדֵי לְצַעֲרוֹ, כַּסֵּדֶר הַזֶּה עוֹשִׂין לָהּ.

יג הַמּוֹרֶדֶת הַזֹּאת, כְּשֶׁהִיא יוֹצֵאת אַחַר שְׁנֵים עָשָׂר חֹדֶשׁ בְּלֹא כְּתֻבָּה, תַּחֲזִיר כָּל דָּבָר שֶׁהוּא שֶׁל בַּעַל.

אֲבָל נְכָסִים שֶׁהִכְנִיסָה לוֹ וּבְלָאוֹתֵיהֶן קַיָּמִים: אִם תָּפְסָה — אֵין מוֹצִיאִים מִיָּדָהּ, וְאִם תְּפָסָן הַבַּעַל — אֵין מוֹצִיאִין מִיָּדוֹ.

(as interpreted by the *Tur, Even HaEzer* 77) differs and maintains that during these twelve months, the woman's *ketubah* is still in effect. The *Shulchan Aruch* (*Even HaEzer* 77:2) cites the Rambam's view, while the Ramah follows that of Rabbenu Asher.

23. In all the instances mentioned in this halachah, the governing principle is that the fact that a woman makes a categorical statement refusing to engage in marital relations in the future is sufficient to warrant her being placed in this category, despite the fact that her conduct is of no immediate consequence.

24. One year, for a *na'arah*, one month for a *bogeret*, as stated in Chapter 10, Halachah 17.

25. *Yibbum* refers to the marriage of the widow (the *yevamah*) of a childless man by his brother (the *yavam*). The Rambam's ruling is dependent on his decision that even in the present age, the mitzvah of *yibbum* takes precedence over the mitzvah of *chalitzah* (*Hilchot Yibbum* 1:2). The latter decision is not accepted in the Ashkenazic community, and therefore, the ruling in our halachah is also a matter of dispute. (See Ramah, *Even HaEzer* 165:1.)

26. I.e., the laws governing a woman who rebels against her husband differ from those governing a woman who claims that she is repulsed by her husband, as described in Halachah 8.

27. In both the *Kessef Mishneh* and the *Shulchan Aruch* (*Even HaEzer* 77:3), Rav Yosef Karo states that the husband does not have to take physical possession of this property. As long as the wife does not take possession of it, it is considered to be his.

him. Similarly, her husband is not held liable for anything that has been lost from her possessions for which he accepted responsibility.[28] This is the law prescribed by the Talmud with regard to a woman who rebels [against her husband].

14. There are *geonim* who say that in Babylonia different customs were followed with regard to a woman who rebels [against her husband].[29] These customs have not, however, spread throughout the majority of the Jewish community, and in most places within the Jewish community, there are many sages of stature who differ with them. [Therefore,] it is proper to follow the laws prescribed by the Talmud.

15. [The following ruling applies when] a man rebels against his wife and says, "I will support her and provide her with her subsistence, but I will not be intimate with her, because she has become loathsome to me." He must increase her *ketubah* by the equivalent of 36 barleycorns worth of [pure] silver[30] each week. They may remain married without engaging in relations for as long as she desires.[31]

Although her *ketubah* continues to increase, [her husband] also transgresses a negative commandment, for [Exodus 21:10] states: "Do not deprive [her of her... conjugal rights]." If the husband hates her, let him divorce her; causing her anguish, however, is forbidden.

Why is he not punished by lashes for [violating] this negative commandment? Because its [violation] does not involve a deed.[32]

16. [The following rules apply when] a man and his wife come to court and he claims that his wife refuses to engage in marital relations, and she replies: "I follow the way of the world with him," or if she claims that he deprives her of her conjugal rights, and he replies that he "follows the way of the world with her." At first, a ban of ostracism is issued against anyone who denies his or her spouse marital intimacy and refuses to acknowledge the matter before the court.[33]

Afterwards, if acknowledgement is [still] not made, the couple are asked to enter into privacy in the presence of witnesses. If they do this, and yet the claims continue as before, a request is made of the defendant, and a compromise is made [as just] as the judge can make. It is, however, forbidden to engage in relations in the presence of others. For it is forbidden to engage in relations in the presence of any living being.

---

28. This refers to *nichsei tzon barzel*, property whose full value must ordinarily be returned to the woman. In contrast, *nichsei m'log* - property for which the husband did not accept responsibility and is returned to the woman in whatever condition it is, regardless

וְכֵן כָּל מַה שֶׁאָבַד מִנְּכָסֶיהָ שֶׁקִּבֵּל הַבַּעַל אַחֲרָיוּתָן עָלָיו, אֵינוֹ מְשַׁלֵּם לָהּ כְּלוּם. זֶה הוּא דִּין הַגְּמָרָא בְּמוֹרֶדֶת.

יד וְאָמְרוּ הַגְּאוֹנִים, שֶׁיֵּשׁ לָהֶם בְּבָבֶל מִנְהָגוֹת אֲחֵרוֹת בְּמוֹרֶדֶת. וְלֹא פָּשְׁטוּ אוֹתָן הַמִּנְהָגוֹת בְּרֹב יִשְׂרָאֵל, וְרַבִּים וּגְדוֹלִים חוֹלְקִין עֲלֵיהֶם בְּרֹב הַמְּקוֹמוֹת. וּכְדִין הַגְּמָרָא רָאוּי לִתְפֹּס וְלָדוּן.

טו הַמּוֹרֵד עַל אִשְׁתּוֹ וְאָמַר: הֲרֵינִי זָן וּמְפַרְנֵס אוֹתָהּ, אֲבָל אֵינִי בָּא עָלֶיהָ מִפְּנֵי שֶׁשְּׂנֵאתִיהָ — מוֹסִיפִין לָהּ עַל כְּתֻבָּתָהּ מִשְׁקַל שֵׁשׁ וּשְׁלֹשִׁים שְׂעוֹרוֹת שֶׁל כֶּסֶף בְּכָל שַׁבָּת וְשַׁבָּת. וְיֵשֵׁב וְלֹא יְשַׁמֵּשׁ כָּל זְמַן שֶׁתִּרְצֶה הִיא לֵישֵׁב. וְאַף־עַל־פִּי שֶׁכְּתֻבָּתָהּ הוֹלֶכֶת וְנוֹסֶפֶת, הֲרֵי הוּא עוֹבֵר בְּלֹא תַעֲשֶׂה, שֶׁנֶּאֱמַר: לֹא יִגְרַע. שֶׁאִם שְׂנֵאָהּ — יְשַׁלְּחָהּ, אֲבָל לַעֲנוֹת — אָסוּר. וְלָמָּה לֹא יִלְקֶה עַל לָאו זֶה? מִפְּנֵי שֶׁאֵין בּוֹ מַעֲשֶׂה.

טז אִישׁ וְאִשְׁתּוֹ שֶׁבָּאוּ לְבֵית דִּין, הוּא אוֹמֵר: זוֹ מוֹרֶדֶת מִתַּשְׁמִישׁ, וְהִיא אוֹמֶרֶת: לֹא כִי, אֶלָּא כְּדֶרֶךְ כָּל הָאָרֶץ אֲנִי עִמּוֹ; וְכֵן אִם טָעֲנָה הִיא וְאָמְרָה שֶׁהוּא מוֹרֵד מִתַּשְׁמִישׁ, וְהוּא אוֹמֵר: לֹא כִי, אֶלָּא כְּדֶרֶךְ כָּל הָאָרֶץ אֲנִי עִמָּהּ — מַחֲרִימִין בַּתְּחִלָּה עַל מִי שֶׁהוּא מוֹרֵד וְלֹא יוֹדֶה בְּבֵית דִּין, וְאַחַר כָּךְ, אִם לֹא הוֹדוּ, אוֹמְרִין לָהֶם: הִתְיַחֲדוּ בִּפְנֵי עֵדִים. נִתְיַחֲדוּ, וַעֲדַיִן הֵם טוֹעֲנִין — מְבַקְּשִׁין מִן הַנִּטְעָן וְעוֹשִׂין פְּשָׁרָה כְּפִי כֹּחַ הַדַּיָּן. אֲבָל לִבְעֹל בִּפְנֵי בְּנֵי אָדָם אִי אֶפְשָׁר, לְפִי שֶׁאָסוּר לִבְעֹל בִּפְנֵי כָּל בְּרִיָּה.

of its worth - must be returned to her, even if she rebels against him. (See Ramah, *Even HaEzer* 77:2.)

The rationale for this distinction is that since he takes responsibility for the *nichsei tzon barzel*, these articles are considered to be possessed by him unless she takes physical possession of them. With regard to the *nichsei m'log*, by contrast, since the husband does not take responsibility, they are not considered to be in his possession.

29. The customs of these *geonim* are quoted in the *Halachot* of Rav Yitzchak Alfasi. They are far more considerate of the woman's position and interests. The Ramah (*Even HaEzer* 77:3) states that if the woman gives a reasonable explanation for her conduct, these customs should be followed.

30. I.e., three *dinarim* of the currency employed during the Talmudic period.

31. If she does not desire to remain married, she may ask the court to compel him to grant her a divorce, as stated in Halachah 7.

32. And lashes are given only for a transgression that involves a deed (*Hilchot Sanhedrin* 18:2).

33. Although the Ra'avad differs with the Rambam's ruling, it is quoted by the *Shulchan Aruch* (*Even HaEzer* 77:4).

17. When a woman becomes ill, [her husband] is obligated [to provide] medical treatment for her until she recovers. If the husband sees that her illness is prolonged, and he will be forced to spend much money treating her, he may tell her: "Here is the money due you by virtue of your *ketubah*. Either pay for your treatment from this money, or I will divorce you and pay you what is due you and abandon you." [Although] he is given this prerogative, it is not ethical to act in this manner.[34]

18. [When a man's wife] is taken captive, he is obligated to redeem her. If he is a priest, [although] she has become forbidden to him,[35] he must redeem her and have her returned to her father's home. If he was in another city, he must still provide for her until she is returned to her native locale. [Then] he must divorce her and pay her [the money due her by virtue of her] *ketubah*.

If her husband was an Israelite - who is permitted to remain married to a woman who was held captive[36] - he must return her to her station as his wife, as she was previously.[37] Afterwards, if he desires,[38] he may divorce her, [provided] he pays her [the money due her by virtue of her] *ketubah*.

19. A husband is not obligated to redeem his wife for more than her worth. Instead, [the laws applying] to her [redemption] are the same as with regard to others held captive.[39]

When her ransom exceeds [the money due her by virtue of] her *ketubah*, her husband is not given the prerogative of saying: "I will divorce her. Here is [the money due her by virtue of] her *ketubah*. Let her redeem herself." Instead, [if necessary,] he should be compelled to redeem her, even if her ransom is ten times [the value of] her *ketubah* - even if it is equivalent to all of his assets.

When does the above apply? On the first occasion [that she is held captive].

34. As mentioned by the *Maggid Mishneh* and the *Kessef Mishneh*, there are authorities who maintain that there is an explicit prohibition preventing a husband from divorcing a wife who is too ill to care for herself. The later authorities, however, follow the Rambam's view.

In the Ashkenazic community, there is a question if the Rambam's ruling applies in the present age, after the ban of Rabbenu Gershom, which prevents divorcing a woman against her will. (See the *Chelkat Mechokek* 79:3, which quotes an opinion that states that as long as the husband is prepared to meet all the financial obligations of the divorce, he has the prerogative to divorce a woman against her will, even when she is ill.)

35. As mentioned in Chapter 24, Halachah 21, a priest is forbidden to have relations with a woman who engaged in sexual relations with a gentile, even when she was raped. Our Sages assumed that women taken captive by gentiles were raped by them, and

יז הָאִשָּׁה שֶׁחָלְתָה — חַיָּב לְרַפְּאוֹת אוֹתָהּ עַד שֶׁתַּבְרִיא.

רָאָה שֶׁהֶחֱלִי אָרֹךְ וְיַפְסִיד מָמוֹן הַרְבֵּה לִרְפוּאָה, וְאָמַר לָהּ: הֲרֵי כְּתֻבָּתִיךְ מֻנַּחַת, אוֹ רַפְּאִי עַצְמֵךְ מִכְּתֻבָּתִיךְ אוֹ הֲרֵינִי מְגָרְשֵׁךְ וְנוֹתֵן כְּתֻבָּה וְהוֹלֵךְ — שׁוֹמְעִין לוֹ. וְאֵין רָאוּי לַעֲשׂוֹת כֵּן, מִפְּנֵי דֶּרֶךְ אֶרֶץ.

יח נִשְׁבֵּת — חַיָּב לִפְדּוֹתָהּ.

וְאִם הָיָה כֹּהֵן, שֶׁכְּבָר נֶאֶסְרָה עָלָיו — פּוֹדֶה אוֹתָהּ וּמַחֲזִירָהּ לְבֵית אָבִיהָ. אֲפִלּוּ הָיָה בְּעִיר אַחֶרֶת — מְטַפֵּל לָהּ עַד שֶׁמַּחֲזִירָהּ לִמְדִינָתָהּ. וּמְגָרְשָׁהּ וְנוֹתֵן לָהּ כָּל כְּתֻבָּתָהּ.

הָיָה בַּעְלָהּ יִשְׂרָאֵל, שֶׁהַשְּׁבוּיָה מֻתֶּרֶת לוֹ, מַחֲזִירָהּ לוֹ לְאִשָּׁה כְּמוֹ שֶׁהָיְתָה. וְאִם רָצָה אַחַר כָּךְ, מְגָרְשָׁהּ וְנוֹתֵן לָהּ כְּתֻבָּתָהּ.

יט אֵין מְחַיְּבִין אֶת הַבַּעַל לִפְדּוֹת אֶת אִשְׁתּוֹ יוֹתֵר עַל דָּמֶיהָ, אֶלָּא כַּמָּה שֶׁהִיא שָׁוָה כִּשְׁאָר הַשְּׁבוּיוֹת.

הָיוּ דָמֶיהָ יוֹתֵר עַל כְּדֵי כְתֻבָּתָהּ, וְאָמַר: הֲרֵינִי מְגָרְשָׁהּ, וְזוֹ כְּתֻבָּתָהּ, וְתֵלֵךְ וְתִפְדֶּה אֶת עַצְמָהּ — אֵין שׁוֹמְעִין לוֹ, אֶלָּא כּוֹפִין אוֹתוֹ וּפוֹדֶה אוֹתָהּ. אֲפִלּוּ הָיוּ דָמֶיהָ עַד עֲשָׂרָה בִּכְתֻבָּתָהּ, וַאֲפִלּוּ אֵין לוֹ אֶלָּא כְּדֵי פִדְיוֹנָהּ.

בַּמֶּה דְּבָרִים אֲמוּרִים? בְּפַעַם רִאשׁוֹנָה;

therefore prohibited a priest from remaining married to such a woman. (See *Hilchot Issurei Bi'ah* 18:17-30.)

36. The Ramah (*Even HaEzer* 78:6) notes that even an Israelite is forbidden to remain married to a woman who is held captive by gentiles if she willingly engaged in relations with one of them. In such instances, he is not obligated to redeem her.

37. I.e., he may not merely redeem her and send her a divorce.

38. I.e., out of suspicion that she willingly engaged in relations with her captors, or because he does not want to live with a woman who had relations with others (*Ma'aseh Rokeach*).

39. As explained in *Hilchot Matnot Ani'yim* 8:12, our Sages decreed that captives should not be redeemed for more than their worth, so that the gentiles will not be overwhelmingly encouraged to seize Jews as captives.

The Rambam's wording has aroused the attention of the later authorities (*Chelkat Mechokek* 78:2; *Beit Shmuel* 78:2), for it implies that if the husband desires to redeem her for more than her worth, he may, while with regard to other captives it is forbidden to do so. They interpret the Rambam's words as applying this prohibition to the husband as well. The *Beit Shmuel* interprets the ruling of the Ramah (*Even HaEzer* 78:2) as meaning that a husband is required to redeem his wife even though her captors demand more than her worth.

If, however, he redeems her and she is taken captive again, if he desires to divorce her he may divorce her, pay [her the money due her by virtue of] her *ketubah*, and [then] she must redeem herself.[40]

20. When a man's wife is taken captive and he is abroad, the court expropriates his assets and sells them after announcements have been made,[41] and redeems his wife as he would be required to.

21. When a person causes his wife to be bound by a vow that requires him to divorce her[42] and pay her [the money due her by virtue of] her *ketubah*, and she is taken captive after he causes her to be bound by this vow, he is not required to redeem her. For from the time he caused her to be bound by the vow, he was obligated to divorce her and pay her [the money due her by virtue of her] *ketubah*.[43]

22. When a woman who is forbidden to [engage in relations] with her husband because of one of the Torah's prohibitions is taken captive, he is not obligated to redeem her.[44] Instead, he must provide her with [the money due her by virtue of] her *ketubah*, and she must redeem herself.

[One might ask: Why is this instance different from the wife of a priest who is taken captive?] A woman who has been taken captive is forbidden to a priest, and yet he is obligated to redeem [his wife in such an instance]. [There is, however, a difference between the two instances. The priest's wife] was not forbidden to him beforehand. It is the prohibition stemming from her being taken captive that causes [their relationship to be forbidden].[45]

23. When a man's wife dies, he is obligated to bury her and to have eulogies and lamentations performed as is the local custom. Even a poor Jewish man should provide at least two flutes[46] and one woman to lament. If [her husband] is rich, [the funeral should be carried out] in a manner appropriate to his wealth.

If the social standing of [a man's wife] exceeded his own, he must have her buried in a manner appropriate to her social standing. For [when she marries,] a woman ascends to her husband's social standing [if his is higher than hers], but does not descend [to his, if her social standing surpasses his].[47] [This principle applies] even after death.

---

40. In both the *Kessef Mishneh* and in the *Beit Yosef* (*Even HaEzer* 78), Rav Yosef Karo states that the husband is not obligated to redeem his wife a second time. If he desires, he may remain married to her without redeeming her. Many, however, differ with this as the interpretation of the Rambam's words. (See *Chelkat Mechokek* 78:4; *Beit Shmuel* 78:4.)
41. See *Hilchot Malveh V'Loveh* 12:8-11, which states that an announcement is made regarding the sale of the person's property so that he will receive the best price.

אֲבָל אִם פְּדָאָהּ וְנִשְׁבֵּת פַּעַם שְׁנִיָּה, וְרָצָה לְגָרְשָׁהּ — הֲרֵי זֶה מְגָרְשָׁהּ וְנוֹתֵן כְּתֻבָּה, וְהִיא תִּפְדֶּה אֶת עַצְמָהּ.

כ מִי שֶׁנִּשְׁבֵּת אִשְׁתּוֹ וְהוּא בִּמְדִינַת הַיָּם — בֵּית דִּין יוֹרְדִין לִנְכָסָיו וּמוֹכְרִין בְּהַכְרָזָה, וּפוֹדִין אוֹתָהּ כְּדֶרֶךְ שֶׁהַבַּעַל פּוֹדֶה.

כא הַמַּדִּיר אֶת אִשְׁתּוֹ נֶדֶר שֶׁהוּא חַיָּב בִּגְלָלוֹ לְגָרְשָׁהּ וְלִתֵּן כְּתֻבָּה, וְנִשְׁבֵּת אַחַר שֶׁהִדִּירָהּ — אֵינוֹ חַיָּב לִפְדּוֹתָהּ;

שֶׁמִּשָּׁעָה שֶׁהִדִּירָהּ נִתְחַיֵּב לְגָרְשָׁהּ וְלִתֵּן לָהּ כְּתֻבָּהּ.

כב הָאִשָּׁה שֶׁהָיְתָה אֲסוּרָה עַל בַּעְלָהּ מֵאִסּוּרֵי לָאוִין, וְנִשְׁבֵּת — אֵינוֹ חַיָּב לִפְדּוֹתָהּ, אֶלָּא נוֹתֵן לָהּ כְּתֻבָּתָהּ וְהִיא תִּפְדֶּה אֶת עַצְמָהּ. וַהֲלֹא הַשְּׁבוּיָה אֲסוּרָה לַכֹּהֵן וַהֲרֵי הוּא פּוֹדֶה אוֹתָהּ? מִפְּנֵי שֶׁלֹּא הָיְתָה אֲסוּרָה מִקֹּדֶם, וְאִסּוּר הַשְּׁבִיָּה הוּא שֶׁגָּרַם לָהּ.

כג מֵתָה אִשְׁתּוֹ — חַיָּב בִּקְבוּרָתָהּ, וְלַעֲשׂוֹת לָהּ מִסְפֵּד וְקִינִים כְּדֶרֶךְ כָּל הַמְּדִינָה. וַאֲפִלּוּ עָנִי שֶׁבְּיִשְׂרָאֵל לֹא יִפְחֲתוּ לוֹ מִשְּׁנֵי חֲלִילִין וּמְקוֹנֶנֶת. אִם הָיָה עָשִׁיר — הַכֹּל לְפִי כְּבוֹדוֹ. וְאִם הָיָה כְּבוֹדָהּ יוֹתֵר מִכְּבוֹדוֹ — קוֹבְרִין אוֹתָהּ לְפִי כְּבוֹדָהּ; שֶׁהָאִשָּׁה עוֹלָה עִם בַּעְלָהּ, וְאֵינָהּ יוֹרֶדֶת אֲפִלּוּ לְאַחַר מִיתָה.

---

42. E.g., the vows mentioned in Chapter 13, Halachah 8ff.

43. The obligation for a husband to redeem his wife stems from her *ketubah*, which states: "If you are taken captive, I will redeem you and take you back as my wife." Since he is already obligated to divorce her, he is not bound by this clause.

44. The rationale for this ruling is that the obligation to redeem one's wife involves returning her to her status as a wife, and this is forbidden in this instance. Nevertheless, although this is the rationale, the same ruling applies with regard to a High Priest who married a widow, or an ordinary priest who married a divorcee.

In these instances, the obligation of the woman's *ketubah* - that she be redeemed and returned to her native land - could be fulfilled without transgressing a prohibition of the Torah. Nevertheless, since relations with her were forbidden previously, her husband is not obligated to redeem her (*Ketubot* 52a).

45. With regard to a woman forbidden to her husband by virtue of a Torah prohibition, by contrast, the prohibition existed before she was taken captive.

46. Flutes have a mournful tone that arouses tears (Rambam's Commentary on the Mishnah, *Shabbat* 23:4).

47. This principle applies to many aspects of the financial relationship of the marriage bond - e.g., the woman's subsistence, her garments and her lodging. It is curious that this instance is the first time the Rambam mentions it explicitly.

24. If a husband does not desire [to pay for] the burial of his wife, and another person voluntarily takes the initiative and has her buried, [the costs of the burial] should be expropriated from her husband against his will and given to the person [who arranged the burial].[48] [The rationale is to prevent the body of a Jew] from being thrown to the dogs.

If a man is in another city when his wife dies, the court should expropriate his property and sell it without an announcement.[49] The woman should be buried as appropriate to her husband's financial resources and his social standing or her social standing.

CHAPTER FIFTEEN

1. It is permissible for a woman to authorize her husband to ignore her conjugal rights. When does this apply? When he has children already and has fulfilled the mitzvah to be fruitful and multiply. If, however, he has not fulfilled the mitzvah of being fruitful and multiplying, he is obligated to engage in sexual relations whenever his conjugal duties require, until he fathers children.[1] For this is a positive commandment of the Torah, as [Genesis 1:28] states: "Be fruitful and multiply."[2]

2. The mitzvah of being fruitful and multiplying is incumbent on the husband and not on his wife.[3]

When does a man become obligated to fulfill this mitzvah? From the time he reaches seventeen.[4] If he reaches twenty and has not married, he is considered to have transgressed and negated [the observance of] this positive commandment.[5]

If, however, he is occupied with the study of Torah and absorbed in [this endeavor] and is hesitant of marrying, lest he be forced to work to support

---

48. Although the Rambam makes a distinction between this instance and a similar situation mentioned in Chapter 12, Halachah 19, the Rashba and others do not. The *Shulchan Aruch* (*Even HaEzer* 89:2) quotes the Rambam's view, but the *Beit Shmuel* 89:2 states that because of the other views, the husband's property may not be expropriated against his will.

49. Although usually announcements are made for 30 days prior to the sale of property by the court, an exception is made in this instance, so that the woman's burial will not be delayed (*Ketubot* 100b).

1. Conjugal rights are a privilege granted to a wife, and she has the right to forego them if she and her husband consent. Fathering children, by contrast, is one of the Torah's commandments, and a woman may not prevent her husband from fulfilling his obligation. See *Yevamot* 65b.

כד לֹא רָצָה לְקַבֹּר אֶת אִשְׁתּוֹ, וְעָמַד אֶחָד מִדַּעַת עַצְמוֹ וּקְבָרָהּ — מוֹצִיאִין מִבַּעֲלָהּ עַל
כָּרְחוֹ וְנוֹתְנִין לָזֶה,
כְּדֵי שֶׁלֹּא תִּהְיֶה זוֹ מֻשְׁלֶכֶת לַכְּלָבִים.
הָיָה בִּמְדִינָה אַחֶרֶת כְּשֶׁמֵּתָה אִשְׁתּוֹ — בֵּית דִּין יוֹרְדִין לִנְכָסָיו וּמוֹכְרִין בְּלֹא הַכְרָזָה, וְקוֹבְרִין
אוֹתָהּ לְפִי מָמוֹן הַבַּעַל וּלְפִי כְּבוֹדוֹ אוֹ לְפִי כְּבוֹדָהּ.

פֶּרֶק חֲמִשָּׁה עָשָׂר

א הָאִשָּׁה שֶׁהִרְשָׁת אֶת בַּעֲלָהּ אַחַר הַנִּשּׂוּאִין שֶׁיִּמְנַע עוֹנָתָהּ — הֲרֵי זֶה מֻתָּר.
בַּמֶּה דְּבָרִים אֲמוּרִים? בְּשֶׁהָיוּ לוֹ בָּנִים, שֶׁכְּבָר קִיֵּם מִצְוַת פְּרִיָּה וּרְבִיָּה;
אֲבָל לֹא קִיֵּם — חַיָּב לִבְעֹל בְּכָל עוֹנָה עַד שֶׁיִּהְיוּ לוֹ בָּנִים,
מִפְּנֵי שֶׁהִיא מִצְוַת עֲשֵׂה שֶׁל תּוֹרָה, שֶׁנֶּאֱמַר: פְּרוּ וּרְבוּ.

ב הָאִישׁ מְצֻוֶּה עַל פְּרִיָּה וּרְבִיָּה, אֲבָל לֹא הָאִשָּׁה.
וְאֵימָתַי הָאִישׁ נִתְחַיֵּב בְּמִצְוָה זוֹ? מִבֶּן שְׁבַע עֶשְׂרֵה.
וְכֵיוָן שֶׁעָבְרוּ עֶשְׂרִים שָׁנָה וְלֹא נָשָׂא אִשָּׁה — הֲרֵי זֶה עוֹבֵר וּמְבַטֵּל מִצְוַת עֲשֵׂה.
וְאִם הָיָה עוֹסֵק בַּתּוֹרָה וְטָרוּד בָּהּ, וְהָיָה מִתְיָרֵא מִלִּשָּׂא אִשָּׁה, כְּדֵי שֶׁלֹּא יִטְרַח בִּמְזוֹנוֹת

The *Turei Zahav* (*Even HaEzer* 1:1) and the *Beit Shmuel* 1:1 question the Rambam's decision. For, as stated in Halachah 16, even after the person has fulfilled the mitzvah of being fruitful and multiplying, he is obligated by rabbinic law to continue to father children. Seemingly, just as a man's wife may not prevent him from fulfilling the obligations imposed on him by the Torah, so too, she may not prevent him from fulfilling the obligations imposed on him by our Sages.

The *Pitchei Teshuvah* 1:1 resolves this difficulty by quoting the *Chidah*, who explains that our Sages did not equate the obligation to continue to father children with the Torah's obligation to be fruitful and multiply. As long as a man endeavors to continue to father children from time to time, it is acceptable. There is no need to persist with the same perseverance as one who has not yet fulfilled this mitzvah. (See also the notes on Halachah 7.)

2. *Sefer HaMitzvot* (Positive Commandment 212) and *Sefer HaChinuch* (Mitzvah 1) include this as one of the Torah's 613 mitzvot.

3. Rabbenu Nissim explains that although the mitzvah is incumbent on the man, since the woman takes an active part in its fulfillment, she receives a portion of the reward.

4. The *Mishnah* (*Avot* 5:22; according to the Rambam, this is a *baraita*) states: "At eighteen, to the wedding chamber." The Rambam interprets this to mean: in one's eighteenth year of life.

Note the *Shulchan Aruch* (*Even HaEzer* 1:3), which states that the optimum way of performing the mitzvah is to marry earlier.

5. The *Shulchan Aruch* (*ibid.*) states that the Jewish court should compel a Jewish male

his wife and thus be prevented from [studying] Torah, he is permitted to delay [marriage]. For a person who is occupied in the performance of one mitzvah is freed from the obligation to perform another. Surely [this applies with regard to] the study of Torah.

2. When a person's soul desires [to study] Torah at all times and is obsessed with its [study] as was ben Azzai,[6] and clings to it throughout his life, without marrying, he is not considered to have transgressed.[7]

[This applies] provided a man's natural inclination does not overcome him.[8] If, however, his natural inclination overcomes him, he is obligated to marry, even if he has already fathered children, lest he be prompted to [sexual] thoughts.[9]

4. How many children is it necessary for a man to have fathered to be considered to have fulfilled this mitzvah? One boy and one girl,[10] as [implied by Genesis 5:2]: "He created them, a male and a female." If the son was a *saris* or the daughter an *aylonit*, he is not considered to have fulfilled this mitzvah.[11]

5. A man is considered to have fulfilled the mitzvah of being fruitful and multiplying [even when] he fathers [children] and they die, so long as [his children] have left behind children [of their own]. For grandchildren are considered to be children.

When does the above apply? When the person's grandchildren are both male and female, and they are descended from a male and a female, even though the male grandchild is the son of the man's daughter, and the female grandchild is the daughter of the man's son.[12] Since they come from two of his children, he is considered to have fulfilled the mitzvah of being fruitful and multiplying. If, however, he had a son and a daughter who both died, and [one did not leave any children, while] one left a son and a daughter, the grandfather is not considered to have fulfilled this mitzvah.

6. When [a convert] had fathered children as a gentile, and both he and they convert,[13] he is considered to have fulfilled this mitzvah. By contrast, a freed slave who had fathered children as a slave is not considered to have fulfilled this mitzvah, although his children were also freed. Instead, he must father children after he has been freed. [The rationale is that] a slave is not considered to have any paternal lineage.

to marry at twenty if he is not devoting his time to the study of Torah. The Ramah, however, states that this is not the custom in the present age.
6. See *Yevamot* 63b.

בַּעֲבוּר אִשְׁתּוֹ וִיבַטֵּל מִן הַתּוֹרָה — הֲרֵי זֶה מֻתָּר לְהִתְאַחֵר;
שֶׁהָעוֹסֵק בְּמִצְוָה פָּטוּר מִן הַמִּצְוָה, וְכָל שֶׁכֵּן בְּתַלְמוּד תּוֹרָה.

ג מִי שֶׁחָשְׁקָה נַפְשׁוֹ בַּתּוֹרָה תָּמִיד וְשׁוֹגֶה בָּהּ כְּבֶן עַזַּאי, וְדָבַק בָּהּ כָּל יָמָיו וְלֹא נָשָׂא אִשָּׁה
— אֵין בְּיָדוֹ עָוֹן.
וְהוּא, שֶׁלֹּא יִהְיֶה יִצְרוֹ מִתְגַּבֵּר עָלָיו;
אֲבָל אִם הָיָה יִצְרוֹ מִתְגַּבֵּר עָלָיו — חַיָּב לִשָּׂא אִשָּׁה, וַאֲפִלּוּ הָיוּ לוֹ בָּנִים, שֶׁמָּא יָבוֹא לִידֵי
הַרְהוּר.

ד כַּמָּה בָנִים יִהְיוּ לְאִישׁ וְתִתְקַיֵּם מִצְוָה זוֹ בְּיָדוֹ? זָכָר וּנְקֵבָה. שֶׁנֶּאֱמַר: זָכָר וּנְקֵבָה בְּרָאָם.
הָיָה הַבֵּן סָרִיס, אוֹ שֶׁהָיְתָה הַבַּת אַיְלוֹנִית — לֹא קִיֵּם מִצְוָה זוֹ.

ה נוֹלְדוּ לוֹ וָמֵתוּ וְהִנִּיחוּ בָנִים — הֲרֵי זֶה קִיֵּם מִצְוַת פְּרִיָּה וּרְבִיָּה.
בְּנֵי בָנִים הֲרֵי הֵם כְּבָנִים.
בַּמֶּה דְּבָרִים אֲמוּרִים? בְּשֶׁהָיוּ בְּנֵי הַבָּנִים זָכָר וּנְקֵבָה, וְהָיוּ בָּאִים מִזָּכָר וּנְקֵבָה.
אַף־עַל־פִּי שֶׁהַזָּכָר בֶּן בִּתּוֹ וְהַנְּקֵבָה בַּת בְּנוֹ — הוֹאִיל וְהֵם מִשְּׁנֵי בָּנָיו הֵן בָּאִים, הֲרֵי קִיֵּם
מִצְוַת פְּרִיָּה וּרְבִיָּה.
אֲבָל אִם הָיוּ לוֹ בֵּן וּבַת וָמֵתוּ, וְהִנִּיחַ אֶחָד מֵהֶן זָכָר וּנְקֵבָה — עֲדַיִן לֹא קִיֵּם הַמִּצְוָה.

ו הָיוּ לוֹ בָּנִים בְּגֵיּוּתוֹ, וְנִתְגַּיֵּר הוּא וָהֵם — הֲרֵי זֶה קִיֵּם מִצְוָה זוֹ.
הָיוּ לוֹ בָּנִים וְהוּא עֶבֶד, וְנִשְׁתַּחְרֵר הוּא וָהֵם — לֹא קִיֵּם מִצְוַת פְּרִיָּה וּרְבִיָּה עַד שֶׁיּוֹלִיד
אַחַר שֶׁנִּשְׁתַּחְרֵר;
שֶׁהָעֶבֶד אֵין לוֹ יִחוּס.

7. The *Turei Zahav* 1:6 interprets this expression as meaning that, at the outset, this is not a desirable course of action to follow.
8. This condition applies also to the license to delay marriage mentioned in the previous halachah.
9. In connection with this law, the commentaries cite *Yoma* 29a, which states: "Thoughts of sin are more damaging than sin itself." Instead of pointing his life to spiritual refinement, the individual is directing himself to sinful thoughts.
10. But if a man has only several sons or only several daughters, he is not considered to have fulfilled the mitzvah.
11. See Chapter 2 for a definition of these terms. Since this child is incapable of conceiving children, the child's father is not considered to have fulfilled the mitzvah.
12. *Tosafot* (*Yevamot* 62b) states that even if the grandchildren are two males or two females, one is considered to have fulfilled this mitzvah. The *Shulchan Aruch* (*Even HaEzer* 1:6), however, quotes the Rambam's view.
13. *Tosafot* states that even if the convert's children did not themselves convert, the convert is considered to have fulfilled this mitzvah. (See *Beit Shmuel* 1:12.)

7. A man should not marry a barren women, an elderly woman, an *aylonit* or a minor who is not fit to bear a child[14] unless he has already fulfilled the mitzvah of being fruitful and multiplying,[15] or he has another wife with whom he can father children.[16]

When a man has married a woman and remained married to her for ten years[17] without her bearing children,[18] he must divorce her and pay her [the money due her by virtue of her] *ketubah*, or marry a woman who is fit to bear children.

If he does not desire to divorce her, he should be compelled to do so; he should be beaten with a rod until he divorces her.[19] Even when he says, "I will not engage in marital relations with her. Instead, we will dwell together with witnesses so that we will not ever be in private," regardless of whether it is he or she who offers this proposition,[20] it is not accepted. Rather, he is required to divorce [his wife] or marry another woman who is fit to bear children.

8. When a man has lived [together with his wife] for ten years without her bearing children, and he releases semen as one shoots an arrow,[21] it can be assumed that the affliction comes from her.[22] Therefore, he should divorce her without paying her [the essential requirement of] the *ketubah*. She is, however, entitled to the additional sum [by which the *ketubah* was increased]. [The rationale is that] such a woman should not be judged more severely than an *aylonit* whose husband did not recognize her condition, who is granted the additional amount, as will be explained.[23]

If [the husband] does not [release semen] as one shoots an arrow, it can be assumed that the affliction comes from him alone. When he divorces her, he must pay her [the entire sum due her by virtue of her] *ketubah*: the essential requirement and the additional sum.

14. From the *Shulchan Aruch* (*Even HaEzer* 23:1), one can infer that sexual relations with a minor are considered as emitting wasted seed, one of the more severe prohibitions of the Torah. The Ramah (*loc. cit.*:5) and other authorities, however, differ and explain that as long as relations are carried out in an ordinary manner, having relations with a minor or an *aylonit* does not violate this prohibition.
15. Rav Moshe Cohen states that since, as mentioned in Halachah 16, a person is obligated to continue fathering children, a man is obligated to marry a woman who can bear children even after fulfilling the mitzvah. The *Maggid Mishneh* states that in principle the Rambam also accepts this ruling, as indicated by his wording in *Hilchot Issurei Bi'ah* 21:26. In this instance, he was merely stating the law required by the Torah.

The Ramah (*Even HaEzer* 1:3) states although it would be proper to rebuke a person for marrying such a woman, this is not done in the present age.
16. As mentioned previously, in the Ashkenazic community it is customary not to marry more than one wife. All the laws mentioned in this halachah must be viewed with that principle in mind.
17. In his Commentary on the Mishnah (*Yevamot* 6:7), the Rambam writes that the

ז לֹא יִשָּׂא אָדָם עֲקָרָה וּזְקֵנָה וְאַיְלוֹנִית וּקְטַנָּה שֶׁאֵינָהּ רְאוּיָה לֵילֵד, אֶלָּא אִם כֵּן קִיֵּם מִצְוַת פְּרִיָּה וּרְבִיָּה, אוֹ שֶׁהָיְתָה לוֹ אִשָּׁה אַחֶרֶת לִפְרוֹת וְלִרְבּוֹת מִמֶּנָּה.

נָשָׂא אִשָּׁה וְשָׁהֲתָה עִמּוֹ עֶשֶׂר שָׁנִים וְלֹא יָלְדָה — הֲרֵי זֶה יוֹצִיא וְיִתֵּן כְּתֻבָּה, אוֹ יִשָּׂא אִשָּׁה הָרְאוּיָה לֵילֵד.

וְאִם לֹא רָצָה לְהוֹצִיא — כּוֹפִין אוֹתוֹ וּמַכִּין אוֹתוֹ בְּשׁוֹט עַד שֶׁיּוֹצִיא.

וְאִם אָמַר: אֵינִי בּוֹעֲלָהּ, וַהֲרֵינִי שׁוֹכֵן עִמָּהּ בִּפְנֵי עֵדִים כְּדֵי שֶׁלֹּא אִתְיַחֵד עִמָּהּ — בֵּין שֶׁאָמְרָה הִיא, בֵּין שֶׁאָמַר הוּא — אֵין שׁוֹמְעִין, אֶלָּא יוֹצִיא אוֹ יִשָּׂא אִשָּׁה הָרְאוּיָה לֵילֵד.

ח שָׁהֲתָה עֶשֶׂר שָׁנִים וְלֹא יָלְדָה, וַהֲרֵי הוּא יוֹרֶה כְּחֵץ שִׁכְבַת זֶרַע — חֶזְקַת הַחֳלִי מִמֶּנָּה, וְתֵצֵא שֶׁלֹּא בִּכְתֻבָּה.

וְיֵשׁ לָהּ תּוֹסֶפֶת. לֹא תִהְיֶה זוֹ פְּחוּתָה מֵאַיְלוֹנִית שֶׁלֹּא הִכִּיר בָּהּ, שֶׁיֵּשׁ לָהּ תּוֹסֶפֶת, כְּמוֹ שֶׁיִּתְבָּאֵר.

וְאִם אֵינוֹ יוֹרֶה כְּחֵץ — חֶזְקַת הַחֳלִי מִמֶּנּוּ בִּלְבַד, וְיוֹצִיא וְיִתֵּן הַכְּתֻבָּה כֻּלָּהּ, עִקָּר וְתוֹסֶפֶת.

---

source for this practice is Sarah's giving Hagar to Abraham: "After ten years in which Abram had lived in the Land of Canaan" (Genesis 16:3). Since this period passed without her bearing children, she provided him with another wife who could.

18. The Rivash (Responsum 15, quoted by the Ramah 154:10) explains that if after having one child together, a couple do not have children for ten years, they are not forced to divorce.

19. The Ramah (*Even HaEzer* 1:3) states that in his time, it was no longer customary to compel a man to divorce a woman who has not borne children to her husband. (See also the *Hagahot Maimoniot*, which quote opinions that state that in this age, and particularly in the diaspora, there is no obligation to divorce a woman even though she has not borne children in this amount of time. At present, there are many Rabbis who have divorced their wives in such a situation, but at least an equal number who have not. Every person has the prerogative of making his own decision regarding this matter.)

20. I.e., rather than bear the expense of paying her *ketubah* immediately, the man desires to remain married; or from the woman's perspective, rather than have to earn her own subsistence, she desires to remain married.

21. *Chaggigah* 15a states that unless a man releases semen as one shoots an arrow, he will not be able to father children.

22. As reflected in the following halachah, the Rambam maintains that unless the man's wife explicitly claims that he does not release semen as one shoots an arrow, it is assumed that the affliction is the woman's. Therefore, she is not entitled to the essential requirement of the *ketubah*.

The Ra'avad differs and maintains that for the responsibility to be placed on the woman, she must have been married to two other men previously, and in both instances, divorced after ten years for not bearing children. The Ramah (*Even HaEzer* 154:6) accepts this opinion.

23. See Chapter 23, Halachot 2 and 3.

9. [The following rules apply when there is a dispute with regard to which of the couple it is whose affliction prevents the couple from having children. The husband] claims: "It is she who cannot bear children," and she claims "He cannot conceive children, for he does not [release semen] as one shoots an arrow." Her word is accepted. He may, however, have a ban of ostracism issued conditionally against anyone who makes a claim that she does not definitely know to be true. Afterwards, he must pay her [the money due her by virtue of her] *ketubah*.

If she says, "I do not know if the difficulty stems from me or from him," she is not entitled to the essential requirement of the *ketubah*, as explained. [The rationale is that] the money should stay in the possession of its owner until she makes a definite claim[24] that he does not [release semen] as one shoots an arrow.

Why is the woman's word accepted when she makes such a claim? Because she can feel whether or not he [releases semen] as one shoots an arrow, and he cannot make such a distinction.

10. When a woman demands of her husband to divorce her after ten years [of marriage], because she has not given birth,[25] and she claims that he does not [release semen] as one shoots an arrow, her request is accepted.[26] Although she is not commanded to fulfill the mitzvah of being fruitful and multiplying, she needs sons [to assist] her in her old age.[27] [Therefore,] he should be compelled to divorce her.

He is required to give her only the essential requirement of the *ketubah*. [He is not required to give her the additional amount,] because he did not promise her this additional amount with the intent that she leave him at her will and take this money.

11. If [a husband] travels on an [extended] business trip during these ten years, or either the husband or the wife were ill or confined in prison, [the time that the couple did not share together] is not included in the calculation [of the ten years].[28]

12. If a woman miscarries, [the ten years are] recalculated from the day of the miscarriage.

---

24. The husband keeps possession of the money he is required to pay his wife by virtue of her *ketubah*. Although our Sages accepted her word when she issues a claim against her husband, they did so only when that claim was definite. If she is in doubt, the money should remain in the possession of its immediate owner.
25. The *Beit Yosef* (*Even HaEzer* 154) states that as long as a woman has given birth

ט הוּא אוֹמֵר: מִמֶּנָּה נִמְנַע הַוָּלָדָה, וְהִיא אוֹמֶרֶת: מִמֶּנּוּ נִמְנַע, מִפְּנֵי שֶׁאֵינוֹ יוֹרֶה כְּחֵץ — נֶאֱמֶנֶת.

וְיֵשׁ לוֹ לְהַחֲרִים סְתָם עַל מִי שֶׁטּוֹעֶנֶת דָּבָר שֶׁאֵינָהּ יוֹדַעַת בּוֹ בְּוַדַּאי, וְאַחַר כָּךְ יִתֵּן כְּתֻבָּה.

וְאִם אָמְרָה: אֵינִי יוֹדַעַת אִם מִמֶּנִּי אִם מִמֶּנּוּ — אֵין לָהּ עִקַּר כְּתֻבָּה, כְּמוֹ שֶׁאָמַרְנוּ.

הֶעֱמֵד מָמוֹן בְּחֶזְקַת בְּעָלָיו, עַד שֶׁתִּטְעַן בְּוַדַּאי שֶׁאֵינוֹ יוֹרֶה כְּחֵץ.

וְלָמָּה נֶאֱמֶנֶת הִיא בְּטַעֲנָה זוֹ?

מִפְּנֵי שֶׁהִיא מַרְגֶּשֶׁת אִם יוֹרֶה כְּחֵץ אִם לֹא יוֹרֶה כְּחֵץ, וְהוּא אֵינוֹ מַרְגִּישׁ.

י הָאִשָּׁה שֶׁבָּאָה לִתְבֹּעַ מִבַּעְלָהּ לְגָרְשָׁהּ אַחַר עֶשֶׂר שָׁנִים מִפְּנֵי שֶׁלֹּא יָלְדָה, וְהִיא אוֹמֶרֶת שֶׁאֵינוֹ יוֹרֶה כְּחֵץ — שׁוֹמְעִין לָהּ.

אַף־עַל־פִּי שֶׁאֵינָהּ מְצֻוָּה עַל פְּרִיָּה וּרְבִיָּה, צְרִיכָה הִיא לְבָנִים לְזִקְנוּתָהּ.

וְכוֹפִין אוֹתוֹ לְהוֹצִיא, וְיִתֵּן עִקַּר כְּתֻבָּה בִּלְבַד; שֶׁלֹּא כָּתַב לָהּ הַתּוֹסֶפֶת עַל מְנָת שֶׁתֵּצֵא לִרְצוֹנָהּ וְתִטֹּל.

יא הָלַךְ בִּסְחוֹרָה בְּתוֹךְ עֶשֶׂר שָׁנִים,

אוֹ שֶׁהָיָה הַבַּעַל חוֹלֶה, אוֹ שֶׁהָיְתָה הִיא חוֹלָה,

אוֹ שֶׁהָיוּ חֲבוּשִׁין בְּבֵית הָאֲסוּרִין — אֵין עוֹלֶה לָהֶן אוֹתוֹ זְמַן מִן הַמִּנְיָן.

יב הִפִּילָה — מוֹנָה מִיּוֹם שֶׁהִפִּילָה.

to one child, whether a son or a daughter, she is not given the prerogative of making such a claim.

The *Ma'aseh Rokeach* explains that this refers to an instance in which the man fathered children before marrying this woman, but then his physical condition deteriorated, and, according to the woman's claim, he is no longer able to release semen in an ordinary way. Were this not the case, he would be compelled to divorce her in order to fulfill the mitzvah of having children. Since he has, however, fulfilled that mitzvah, he is not compelled to divorce his wife. Therefore, it is the woman who must take the initiative.

26. As reflected in the ruling of the *Shulchan Aruch* (*Even HaEzer* 154:6), other authorities emphasize that the woman's request must be made solely for this reason. If the court feels that she desires the money due her by virtue of her *ketubah* or to marry another man, her request is not accepted (*Be'urei HaGra* 154:25).

27. *Yevamot* 65b states "she needs a staff for support and a spade for burial" - i.e., sons to support her in her old age and to take care of her funeral arrangements.

28. The *Shulchan Aruch* (*Even HaEzer* 154:11) follows the understanding of Rabbenu Asher, who interprets this ruling as applying even when it was possible for the couple to engage in marital relations during the situations mentioned. It is possible that just as their conduct aroused negative spiritual influences resulting in illness or imprisonment, those negative influences - and not the physical condition of the man or woman - prevented them from having children. From the Rambam's Commentary on the Mishnah (*Yevamot* 6:7), it does not appear that he shares this understanding.

If a woman has three successive miscarriages,[29] we can presume that she will continue to miscarry, and there is the possibility that [her husband] will not merit to have children from her. Therefore, he should divorce her,[30] and pay her [the money due her by virtue of her] *ketubah.*

13. [The following rules apply when there is a difference between the information stemming from the claims of a husband and his wife.] He claims that she has miscarried within the ten years so that they can continue [their marriage], and she denies the miscarriage. [Her claim] is believed; [if it were not true,] she would not cause herself to be considered barren.[31]

If he claims that she has miscarried twice, and she claims to have miscarried three times, [her claim] is believed. [If it were not true,] she would not cause herself to be considered a woman who [continually] miscarries.

[Therefore, in both instances,] he should divorce her and pay her [the money due her by virtue of her] *ketubah.* With regard to the above situations, he may require her to take a Rabbinic oath that she did not miscarry or that she miscarried three times. For this claim obligates him to pay her [the money due her by virtue of her] *ketubah.*[32]

14. [When a woman] marries one man, remains married to him for ten years without bearing a child and is divorced [for that reason], she is permitted to marry a second husband.[33] If she remained married to the second husband for ten years without bearing a child, she should not marry a third husband.[34]

If she marries a third husband, she should be divorced; [he is] not [required to pay her the money due her by virtue of] her *ketubah.*[35] [This applies] unless he has another wife, or he has already fulfilled the mitzvah of being fruitful and multiplying.

15. [The following laws apply when] a woman comes to court and claims that her husband cannot perform sexually in an ordinary way that will lead to the conception of children, or that he does not [release semen] as one shoots an arrow.[36] The judges should try to arrange a compromise,[37] telling the woman: "It is proper for you to conduct yourself with your husband [as follows]: Remain [married] for ten years. [If] you do not give birth, come to him with a claim at that time."

29. Even within a period shorter than ten years (Rabbenu Asher).
30. She is, however, permitted to marry another man (*Shulchan Aruch, Even HaEzer* 154:12).
31. The *Beit Shmuel* 154:29 emphasizes that this law and the following law apply only when the court does not suspect that the woman desires to marry another man. This is also reflected in the Rambam's wording, which indicates that her claim comes as a response to the court's initiative.
32. Although the Ra'avad differs and does not require an oath in this situation, the *Maggid*

אִם הִפִּילָה וְחָזְרָה וְהִפִּילָה שָׁלֹשׁ פְּעָמִים — הֻחְזְקָה לִנְפָלִים,
וְשֶׁמָּא לֹא זָכָה לְהִבָּנוֹת מִמֶּנָּה, וְיוֹצִיא וְיִתֵּן כְּתֻבָּה.

יג הוּא אוֹמֵר: הִפִּילָה בְּתוֹךְ עֶשֶׂר, כְּדֵי שֶׁיִּשְׁהֶה עִמָּהּ, וְהִיא אוֹמֶרֶת: לֹא הִפַּלְתִּי — נֶאֱמֶנֶת,
שֶׁאֵינָהּ מַחְזֶקֶת עַצְמָהּ בַּעֲקָרוּת.
הוּא אוֹמֵר: הִפִּילָה שְׁנַיִם, וְהִיא אוֹמֶרֶת: הִפַּלְתִּי שְׁלֹשָׁה — נֶאֱמֶנֶת, שֶׁאֵינָהּ מַחְזֶקֶת עַצְמָהּ
בְּמַפֶּלֶת, וְיוֹצִיא וְיִתֵּן כְּתֻבָּה.
וּבְכָל זֶה מַשְׁבִּיעָהּ שְׁבוּעַת הֶסֵּת שֶׁלֹּא הִפִּילָה אוֹ שֶׁהִפִּילָה שְׁלֹשָׁה, שֶׁבִּטַעֲנָה זוֹ יִתְחַיֵּב לָתֵן
כְּתֻבָּה.

יד נִשֵּׂאת לָרִאשׁוֹן וְשָׁהֲתָה עִמּוֹ עֶשֶׂר שָׁנִים וְלֹא יָלְדָה וְהוֹצִיאָהּ — מֻתֶּרֶת לְהִנָּשֵׂא לְשֵׁנִי.
שָׁהֲתָה עִם הַשֵּׁנִי עֶשֶׂר שָׁנִים וְלֹא יָלְדָה — לֹא תִנָּשֵׂא לִשְׁלִישִׁי.
וְאִם נִשֵּׂאת לִשְׁלִישִׁי — תֵּצֵא שֶׁלֹּא בִכְתֻבָּה, אֶלָּא אִם כֵּן יֵשׁ לוֹ אִשָּׁה אַחֶרֶת אוֹ שֶׁקִּיֵּם מִצְוַת
פְּרִיָּה וּרְבִיָּה.

טו הָאִשָּׁה שֶׁבָּאָה לְבֵית דִּין וְאָמְרָה: בַּעְלִי אֵינוֹ יָכוֹל לְשַׁמֵּשׁ כְּדֶרֶךְ כָּל הָאָרֶץ שִׁמּוּשׁ
שֶׁמּוֹלִיד, אוֹ שֶׁאֵינוֹ יוֹרֶה כְּחֵץ — יַעֲשׂוּ הַדַּיָּנִין פְּשָׁרָה.
וְאוֹמְרִים לָהּ: רְאוּי לִיךְ שֶׁתִּתְנַהֲגִי עִם בַּעְלִיךְ עַד שֶׁתִּשְׁהִי עֶשֶׂר שָׁנִים וְלֹא תוֹלִידִי, וְאַחַר כָּךְ
תִּתְבְּעִי.

Mishneh and the *Kessef Mishneh* support the Rambam's position. It is the Rambam's position that is accepted by the *Shulchan Aruch (Even HaEzer* 154:15).
33. It is possible that the woman is not barren. It was merely that the two did not merit to conceive children together (*Yevamot* 64a).
34. Although a factor must normally repeat itself three times for a *chazakah* (a presumption that can be relied on) to be established, an exception is made with regard to the laws of marriage. In this context, the opinion that considers a twofold occurrence to be a *chazakah* is followed.
35. This ruling applies only if the husband had been unaware of the woman's condition previously. If he knew of that she was incapable of bearing children, he is obligated to pay her the money due her by virtue of her *ketubah*, as is the law with regard to an *aylonit* (Chapter 24:1-2).
36. As reflected in the Rambam's Commentary on the Mishnah (the conclusion of *Nedarim*), the Rambam does not interpret this as referring to an instance where the husband is sexually impotent entirely. Instead, it refers to a situation in which he can function, but it is the woman's belief that he will never conceive children. See the *Lechem Mishneh* and the interpretation of the Ralbach (Responsum 32). If, however, the woman were to claim that her husband is impotent, her word would be accepted.
Note, however, the Rashba (Vol. I, Responsum 628) and *K'nesset HaGedolah (Even HaEzer* 154:60), which interpret this halachah as speaking about an instance where the husband is sexually impotent.
37. In his Commentary on the Mishnah (*loc. cit.*), the Rambam states that, in theory, it

We protract the negotiations of this matter with her; we do not require her to continue living with him, nor do we judge her as a woman who rebels against her husband. Instead, the dealings are prolonged until the two parties reach a compromise.

16. Although a man has fulfilled the mitzvah of being fruitful and multiplying, he is bound by a Rabbinic commandment not to refrain from being fruitful and multiplying as long as he is physically potent.[38] For anyone who adds a soul to the Jewish people is considered as if he built an entire world.[39]

Similarly, it is a mitzvah of our Sages that a man should not live without a wife,[40] so that he will not be prompted to [sexual] thoughts.[41] Similarly, a woman should not live without a man,[42] so that she will not be suspected [of immoral conduct].

17. It is an obligation for a man to admonish[43] his wife. Our Sages declared:[44] "A man will not admonish his wife unless a spirit of purity enters his being." [Nevertheless,] he should not admonish her more than necessary.[45]

[A man] should never compel [his wife] to engage in sexual relations against her will. Instead, [relations] should be with her agreement, [preceded by] conversation and a spirit of joy.[46]

18. Similarly, our Sages commanded a woman to conduct herself modestly at home, not to proliferate levity or frivolity before her husband, not to request intimacy verbally,[47] nor to speak about this matter.

She should not deny her husband [intimacy] to cause him anguish, so that he should increase his love for her. Instead, she should oblige him whenever he desires. She should keep her distance from his relatives and the members

would be proper to compel the husband to grant his wife a divorce immediately. This is not done, however, out of fear that her claim is untrue and she merely desires to marry another man.

He continues, stating that the court should try to develop communication between the couple. If those efforts fail, a compromise should be negotiated - e.g., in return for not compelling the woman to wait ten years for the divorce, the amount of money the husband is required to pay because of the *ketubah* should be reduced.

38. *Yevamot* 62a states: "[Although a man] fathers children in his youth, he should continue to do so at an advanced age, as implied by [Ecclesiastes 11:6]: 'In the morning, sow your seed; and in the evening, do not withhold your hand.'"

As mentioned above, the *Chidah* explains that as long as a man endeavors to continue fathering children from time to time, it is acceptable. One need not attempt to conceive children at every opportunity. Based on this decision, there are authorities who permit the limited use of certain birth control devices. The matter is not, however, entirely clear

וּמְגַלְגְּלִין עִמָּה בְּדָבָר זֶה. וְאֵין כּוֹפִין אוֹתָהּ לֵישֵׁב, וְלֹא דָנִין אוֹתָהּ כְּדִין הַמּוֹרֶדֶת, אֶלָּא מַאֲרִיכִין בְּדָבָר זֶה עַד שֶׁיַּעֲשׂוּ פְּשָׁרָה.

טז אַף־עַל־פִּי שֶׁקִּיֵּם אָדָם מִצְוַת פְּרִיָּה וּרְבִיָּה, הֲרֵי הוּא מְצֻוֶּה מִדִּבְרֵי סוֹפְרִים שֶׁלֹּא יְבַטֵּל מִלִּפְרוֹת וְלִרְבּוֹת כָּל זְמַן שֶׁיֵּשׁ בּוֹ כֹּחַ; שֶׁכָּל הַמּוֹסִיף נֶפֶשׁ אַחַת בְּיִשְׂרָאֵל — כְּאִלּוּ בָּנָה עוֹלָם.

וְכֵן מִצְוַת חֲכָמִים הִיא, שֶׁלֹּא יֵשֵׁב אָדָם בְּלֹא אִשָּׁה, שֶׁלֹּא יָבוֹא לִידֵי הִרְהוּר; וְלֹא תֵשֵׁב אִשָּׁה בְּלֹא אִישׁ, שֶׁלֹּא תֵחָשֵׁד.

יז וְחוֹבָה עַל כָּל אִישׁ לְקַנֹּאת לְאִשְׁתּוֹ.
אָמְרוּ חֲכָמִים: אֵין אָדָם מְקַנֵּא לְאִשְׁתּוֹ אֶלָּא אִם כֵּן נִכְנְסָה בּוֹ רוּחַ טָהֳרָה.
וְלֹא יְקַנֵּא לָהּ בְּיוֹתֵר מִדַּי.
וְלֹא יֶאֱנֹס אוֹתָהּ וְיִבְעַל בְּעַל כָּרְחָהּ, אֶלָּא בְּדַעְתָּהּ וּמִתּוֹךְ שִׂיחָה וְשִׂמְחָה.

יח וְכֵן צִוּוּ חֲכָמִים עַל הָאִשָּׁה, שֶׁתִּהְיֶה צְנוּעָה בְּתוֹךְ בֵּיתָהּ,
וְלֹא תַרְבֶּה שְׂחוֹק וְקַלּוּת רֹאשׁ בִּפְנֵי בַעְלָהּ.
וְלֹא תִתְבַּע תַּשְׁמִישׁ הַמִּטָּה בְּפִיהָ,
וְלֹא תִהְיֶה מְדַבֶּרֶת בְּעֵסֶק זֶה.
וְלֹא תִמְנַע מִבַּעְלָהּ כְּדֵי לְצַעֲרוֹ עַד שֶׁיּוֹסִיף בְּאַהֲבָתָהּ, אֶלָּא נִשְׁמַעַת לוֹ בְּכָל עֵת שֶׁיִּרְצֶה.

---

cut and should be discussed with a competent Rabbinic authority with regard to one's actual conduct.

39. Similarly, having children leads to the coming of the Redemption. *Yevamot* 63b states that the *Mashiach* will not come until all the souls destined to be conceived are born.

40. The *Shulchan Aruch* (*Even HaEzer* 1:8) explains that this commandment applies when the husband cannot support a wife who can bear children and increase the size of his family.

41. See *Yevamot* 62b, which states: "Any man who is unmarried is left without happiness, without good and without blessing."
Rav David Cohen quotes Rav Yitzchak Alfasi as maintaining that the requirement to marry stems from the Torah and not from our Sages, as the Rambam maintains.

42. See *Hilchot Issurei Bi'ah* 21:26, which states that it is permissible for a woman never to marry.

43. Here the term לקנאת, translated as "admonish," has a specific meaning: to warn one's wife not to enter into privacy with another man. If this warning is disobeyed, the woman must undergo the rites of a *sotah* to continue her marriage.

44. *Sotah* 3a. Although this is the subject of a difference of opinion among our Sages, the Rambam follows the opinion of Rabbi Akiva.

45. See the conclusion of *Hilchot Sotah* for a more detailed treatment of this subject.

46. See *Hilchot De'ot* 5:4-5.

47. *Eruvin* 100b states that a woman requests intimacy with her heart.

of his household so that he will not be provoked by jealousy and should avoid scandalous situations - indeed, any trace of scandal.[48]

19. Similarly, our Sages commanded that a man honor his wife more than his own person, and love her as he loves his own person. If he has financial resources, he should offer her benefits in accordance with his resources. He should not cast a superfluous measure of fear over her. He should talk with her gently, being neither sad nor angry.

20. And similarly, they commanded a woman to honor her husband exceedingly and to be in awe of him. She should carry out all her deeds according to his directives, considering him to be an officer or a king. She should follow the desires of his heart and shun everything that he disdains.

This is the custom of holy and pure Jewish women and men in their marriages. And these ways will make their marriage pleasant and praiseworthy.

CHAPTER SIXTEEN

1. The property that a woman brings to her husband's [resources] - be it landed property, movable property or servants - is not referred to with the term *ketubah*, but rather with the term *nedunyah*.

[More particularly, there are two subdivisions within this category.] When the husband accepts responsibility for the *nedunyah* and it is considered to be his property[1] - i.e., if it decreases in value he suffers the loss, and if it increases in value the gain is his - the property is referred to as *nichsei tzon barzel*.[2]

If the husband did not accept responsibility for the *nedunyah*,[3] and it instead remained the property of the woman[4] - if it decreases in value she suffers the loss, and if it increases in value the gain is hers - the property is referred to as *nichsei m'log*.[5]

2. Similarly, all the property that a woman owns that she did not bring to her husband's household, nor had written in her *ketubah*, but rather left as her

---

48. See Chapter 24, Halachah 15ff.

1. I.e., the article or land that the woman brings to the household is evaluated, and the husband takes responsibility for the value of the article. From this time onward, it is as if the article were his, and he is obligated to pay his wife a fixed amount if he divorces her or she is widowed.
2. This term literally means "property [that is like] iron sheep." The term iron is used to indicate that the husband's obligation is unchanging, like iron. The reference to sheep stems from the fact that during the Talmudic period in *Eretz Yisrael*, a similar agreement

וְתִזָּהֵר מִקְּרוֹבָיו וּבְנֵי בֵיתוֹ, כְּדֵי שֶׁלֹּא יַעֲבֹר עָלָיו רוּחַ קִנְאָה.
וְתִתְרַחֵק מִן הַכִּעוּר וּמִן הַדּוֹמֶה לַכִּעוּר.

יט וְכֵן צִוּוּ חֲכָמִים, שֶׁיְּהֵא אָדָם מְכַבֵּד אֶת אִשְׁתּוֹ יוֹתֵר מִגּוּפוֹ, וְאוֹהֲבָהּ כְּגוּפוֹ.
וְאִם יֵשׁ לוֹ מָמוֹן, מַרְבֶּה בְּטוֹבָתָהּ כְּפִי מָמוֹנוֹ.
וְלֹא יָטִיל עָלֶיהָ אֵימָה יְתֵרָה.
וְיִהְיֶה דִּבּוּרוֹ עִמָּהּ בְּנַחַת.
וְלֹא יִהְיֶה עָצֵב וְלֹא רַגְזָן.

כ וְכֵן צִוּוּ עַל הָאִשָּׁה, שֶׁתִּהְיֶה מְכַבֶּדֶת אֶת בַּעְלָהּ בְּיוֹתֵר מִדַּי,
וְיִהְיֶה עָלֶיהָ מוֹרָא מִמֶּנּוּ, וְתַעֲשֶׂה כָּל מַעֲשֶׂיהָ עַל פִּיו.
וְיִהְיֶה בְּעֵינֶיהָ כְּמוֹ שַׂר אוֹ מֶלֶךְ, מְהַלֶּכֶת בְּתַאֲוַת לִבּוֹ וּמְרַחֶקֶת כָּל מַה שֶׁיִּשְׂנָא.
וְזֶה דֶּרֶךְ בְּנוֹת יִשְׂרָאֵל וּבְנֵי יִשְׂרָאֵל הַקְּדוֹשִׁים וְהַטְּהוֹרִים בְּזִוּוּגָן. וּבִדְרָכִים אֵלּוּ יִהְיֶה יִשׁוּבָן נָאֶה וּמְשֻׁבָּח.

פֶּרֶק שִׁשָּׁה עָשָׂר

א הַנְּכָסִים שֶׁמַּכְנֶסֶת הָאִשָּׁה לְבַעְלָהּ — בֵּין קַרְקַע, בֵּין מִטַּלְטְלִין, בֵּין עֲבָדִים — אַף־עַל־פִּי שֶׁהֵן נִכְתָּבִין בִּשְׁטַר הַכְּתֻבָּה, אֵין נִקְרָאִין כְּתֻבָּה, אֶלָּא נְדוּנְיָא שְׁמָם.
וְאִם קִבֵּל הַבַּעַל אַחֲרָיוּת הַנְּדוּנְיָא עָלָיו וְנַעֲשֵׂת בִּרְשׁוּתוֹ — אִם פָּחֲתָה פָּחֲתָה לוֹ, וְאִם הוֹתִירָה הוֹתִירָה לוֹ — הֲרֵי זוֹ נִקְרֵאת נִכְסֵי צֹאן בַּרְזֶל.
וְאִם לֹא קִבֵּל אַחֲרָיוּת הַנְּדוּנְיָא עָלָיו, אֶלָּא הֲרֵי הִיא בִּרְשׁוּת הָאִשָּׁה — אִם פָּחֲתָה פָּחֲתָה לָהּ, וְאִם הוֹתִירָה הוֹתִירָה לָהּ — הֲרֵי זוֹ נִקְרֵאת נִכְסֵי מְלוֹג.

ב וְכֵן כָּל נְכָסִים שֶׁיֵּשׁ לָאִשָּׁה, שֶׁלֹּא הִכְנִיסָה אוֹתָן לְבַעְלָהּ וְלֹא כָּתְבוּ אוֹתָן בַּכְּתֻבָּה,

was frequently made with a shepherd with regard to the sheep entrusted to him. He was given a herd that was evaluated at a given price, and he was obligated to return either sheep of that value, or payment for them to their owner. (See the commentary of Rav Ovadiah of Bertinoro, *Yevamot* 7:1.)

3. With this statement, the Rambam indicates that - in contrast to the opinion of certain authorities - the property belonging to a woman does not automatically become *nichsei tzon barzel*. For it to be placed in that category, the husband must explicitly accept responsibility for it (*Maggid Mishneh*). (See *Shulchan Aruch, Even HaEzer* 85:3.)

4. With regard to this type of property as well, the husband has the privilege to manage the use of the property and reap its benefits during the time he remains married to the woman, but the property itself belongs to her.

5. The term *m'log* means "to pull out hairs" (Jerusalem Talmud, *Yevamot* 7:1). Just

own, or property that came to her as an inheritance, or that was given to her as a present - all of this is referred to as *nichsei m'log*, for it is all in her possession.

The term *ketubah*, by contrast, refers only to the fundamental requirement of the marriage contract - i.e., 100 [*zuz* for a non-virgin] or 200 [*zuz* for a virgin] and the additional amount that [the husband promised].[6]

3. We have already explained that our Sages established the fundamental requirement of the marriage contract, and that the laws governing the additional amount [promised by the husband] are the same as those governing the fundamental requirement.[7]

[Our Sages] did not grant a woman the option of collecting [the money due her by virtue of] her *ketubah* whenever she desired. Instead, it is like a debt, which is not payable until a given date. For a *ketubah*, the time when payment is due is not until after the woman's husband dies or divorces her.

Similarly, our Sages ordained that if a husband has fields [of varying quality] - good, bad and intermediate - when the woman comes to collect [the money due her by virtue of] her *ketubah* from this property, she is entitled to collect only from the inferior fields.[8] They are referred to as *ziboorit*.[9]

4. Similarly, our Sages ordained that when a woman comes to collect [the money due her by virtue of] her *ketubah* after her husband's death, she may not collect [this sum] until she takes an oath while holding a sacred article,[10] that her husband did not leave any property in her possession,[11] that she had not sold her *ketubah* to him, nor waived payment of it.[12] [Her wardrobe, even] the garments she is wearing should be evaluated and the sum deducted from [the money due her by virtue of] her *ketubah*.[13]

If, however, he voluntarily divorces her, she may collect [the money due her] without taking an oath,[14] nor should [her wardrobe] be evaluated.[15] [The rationale is that] he bought them for her, she acquired them, and it is he who desires to divorce her, and not the reverse.[16]

as a person pulls out the hairs from a head, leaving it uncovered, so too, the husband continues to use his wife's property even though its value depreciates.

6. By making a distinction between the money due a woman by virtue of her *ketubah* and her *nedunyah*, the Rambam is emphasizing that they are governed by different laws. With regard to the money of the *ketubah*, the husband or his estate is granted certain leniencies. But with regard to the *nedunyah*, by contrast, the woman is considered the same as any other of her husband's creditors (*Maggid Mishneh*). The *Beit Yosef* and the Ramah (*Even HaEzer* 100:2) quote this explanation.

7. See Chapter 10, Halachah 7.

8. Although a creditor has the right to collect his due from the properties of intermediate

אֶלָּא נִשְׁאֲרוּ לְעַצְמָהּ, אוֹ נָפְלוּ לָהּ בִּירֻשָּׁה אַחַר שֶׁנִּתְאָרְסָה, אוֹ נָתְנוּ לָהּ בְּמַתָּנָה — הַכֹּל נִקְרָאִין נִכְסֵי מְלוֹג, שֶׁכֻּלָּן בִּרְשׁוּתָהּ הֵן.

וְאֵין נִקְרָאִין כְּתֻבָּה אֶלָּא עִקַּר כְּתֻבָּה, שֶׁהוּא מֵאָה אוֹ מָאתַיִם, עִם הַתּוֹסֶפֶת בִּלְבַד.

ג כְּבָר הוֹדַעְנוּ, שֶׁחֲכָמִים תִּקְּנוּ כְּתֻבָּה לָאִשָּׁה, וְדִין הַתּוֹסֶפֶת כְּדִין הָעִקָּר. וְלֹא תִּקְּנוּ לִגְבוֹתָהּ כָּל זְמַן שֶׁתִּרְצֶה, אֶלָּא הֲרֵי הִיא כְּחוֹב שֶׁיֵּשׁ לוֹ זְמַן, וְאֵין הַכְּתֻבָּה נִגְבֵּית אֶלָּא לְאַחַר מִיתַת הַבַּעַל אוֹ אִם גֵּרְשָׁהּ.

וְכֵן הִתְקִינוּ, שֶׁאִם הָיוּ לַבַּעַל שָׂדוֹת טוֹבוֹת וְרָעוֹת וּבֵינוֹנִיּוֹת, וּבָאָה הָאִשָּׁה לִגְבּוֹת כְּתֻבָּתָהּ מִמֶּנּוּ, שֶׁלֹּא תִּגְבֶּה אֶלָּא מִן הָרָעָה שֶׁבִּנְכָסָיו, וְהִיא הַנִּקְרֵאת זִבּוּרִית.

ד וְכֵן הִתְקִינוּ, שֶׁכְּשֶׁתָּבוֹא לִגְבּוֹת כְּתֻבָּתָהּ אַחַר מוֹתוֹ — לֹא תִּגְבֶּה עַד שֶׁתִּשָּׁבַע בִּנְקִיטַת חֵפֶץ שֶׁלֹּא הִנִּיחַ אֶצְלָהּ כְּלוּם, וְלֹא מָכְרָה לוֹ כְּתֻבָּתָהּ, וְלֹא מָחֲלָה אוֹתָהּ. וְשָׁמִין לָהּ כָּל מַה שֶּׁעָלֶיהָ, וּפוֹחֲתִין אוֹתוֹ מִכְּתֻבָּתָהּ.

אֲבָל אִם גֵּרְשָׁהּ לִרְצוֹנוֹ — גּוֹבָה בְּלֹא שְׁבוּעָה, וְאֵין שָׁמִין כְּסוּת שֶׁעָלֶיהָ; שֶׁהֲרֵי לְקָחָן לָהּ וְזָכְתָה בָּהֶן, וְהוּא רוֹצֶה לְהוֹצִיאָהּ, לֹא הִיא.

value, the woman is given this disadvantage. The rationale is that a woman desires to marry and therefore is willing to accept this stipulation (*Gittin* 50a).

9. The *Aruch HaShalem* interprets this term as being derived from an Arab word meaning "a rocky field." The Ramah (*Choshen Mishpat* 101:5) states that it refers to a bee that stings and is therefore considered one of the lower forms of life.

10. I.e., a Torah scroll, as mentioned in *Hilchot Sh'vuot* 11:8. An oath is required because the woman is seeking to collect money from an estate bequeathed to heirs, and whenever payment is to be collected from an estate, an oath is necessary (*Ketubot* 87a; *Hilchot Malveh V'Loveh* 14:1).

11. The *Tur* (*Even HaEzer* 96) states that the woman must also take an oath that she did not seize any of her husband's property. The *Shulchan Aruch* (*Even HaEzer* 96:2) quotes this view.

12. In contrast to the opinion of the *Tur* (*loc. cit.*) and the *Hagahot Maimoniot*, the Rambam maintains that even if a woman is in possession of her *ketubah*, she is required to take these oaths. (See Halachah 21.) The *Shulchan Aruch* (*loc. cit.*) mentions the Rambam's view, but appears to favor that of the *Tur*.

13. This refers to a trousseau given to the woman by her husband. Although the husband gave his wife these clothes as a gift, he did not give them to her with the intent that she take them and leave his household (*Ketubot* 54a).

14. In the first half of this halachah, the oath is instituted by the court to protect the interests of the heirs. In this instance, however, unless the husband himself issues a claim requiring an oath (see Halachah 19), no oath is required.

15. From *Hilchot Malveh V'Loveh* 1:5, it appears that this does not apply to a woman's Sabbath and festival clothing, or to her jewelry. Similarly, the *Shulchan Aruch* (*Even HaEzer* 99:1) states that those articles should be evaluated and deducted from the sum due her by virtue of her *ketubah*.

16. If, however, the husband is compelled to divorce his wife, her wardrobe should

5. Similarly, [our Sages] ordained that a widow[17] should collect [the money due her by virtue of] her *ketubah* from landed property only.[18] [Moreover,] she may not collect [her due] from the increment in the value of that property after the husband died.[19] Similarly, after their father's death, [the woman's] daughters do not receive their subsistence[20] from the increment in the value of that property after his death.

Similarly, a woman may not collect [the money due her by virtue of] her *ketubah* from the increment in the value of [landed] property accomplished through the efforts of a purchaser, although other creditors are entitled to collect their due from that increment.[21] These rulings are among the leniencies [granted with regard to the the payment of the money due a woman by virtue] of her *ketubah*.

6. Similarly, among the leniencies [granted with regard to the payment of the money due a woman by virtue] of her *ketubah* is that a woman will collect the money due her from the coinage that is of least value.

What is implied? A man married a woman in one country and divorced her in another. If the coinage of the country in which the couple married is more valuable than the coinage of the country in which they divorced, he may pay her with the coinage of the country in which they divorced. If, by contrast, the coinage of the country in which the couple divorced is more valuable than the coinage of the country in which they married, he may pay her with the coinage of the country in which they married.[22]

When does the above apply? When her *ketubah* states a sum of coins without specification. If, however, a specific type of coin is explicitly mentioned, whether with regard to the fundamental requirement of the *ketubah*, or with regard to the extra amount added by the husband, the law is the same as when a person lends a colleague a specific type of coin - he must return the loan in the coinage that he took, as will be explained in *Hilchot Halva'ah*.[23]

7. The *geonim* of all the *yeshivot* ordained that after the death of a man, a woman should be able to collect her [money due her by virtue of her] *ketubah* from movable property,[24] just as they ordained that a creditor can

be evaluated and deducted from the money due her by virtue of her *ketubah* (*Maggid Mishneh*; see *Ketubot* 77a).

1/. This restriction applies to a widow, but not to a divorcee. The Rashba and other authorities differ and maintain that the same ruling applies to a divorcee. It appears that it is their opinion that is accepted by the *Shulchan Aruch* (*Even HaEzer* 100:1).

18. I.e., and not from movable property. This ruling also applies to other creditors, as stated in *Hilchot Nizkei Mammon* 8:11. (See, however, Halachah 7 below.)

19. E.g., a woman was owed 200 *zuz* by virtue of her *ketubah*. Her husband's property was worth 150 *zuz* at the time of his death. Although its value rose afterwards to 200, the

ה וְכֵן הִתְקִינוּ, שֶׁלֹּא תִּגְבֶּה הָאַלְמָנָה כְּתֻבָּתָהּ אֶלָּא מִן הַקַּרְקַע.
וְאֵינָהּ גּוֹבָה מִשֶּׁבַח שֶׁשָּׁבְחוּ נְכָסִים לְאַחַר מִיתַת הַבַּעַל.
וְאֵין הַבָּנוֹת נִזּוֹנוֹת לְאַחַר מִיתַת אֲבִיהֶן מִשֶּׁבַח שֶׁשָּׁבְחוּ נְכָסִים לְאַחַר מִיתָתוֹ.
וְאֵינָהּ טוֹרֶפֶת בִּכְתֻבָּתָהּ בְּשֶׁבַח שֶׁהִשְׁבִּיחַ הַלּוֹקֵחַ, אַף-עַל-פִּי שֶׁבַּעַל חוֹב גּוֹבֶה אֶת הַשֶּׁבַח.
וּדְבָרִים אֵלּוּ מִקֻּלֵּי כְּתֻבָּה הֵם.

ו וְכֵן מִקֻּלֵּי כְתֻבָּה, שֶׁתִּטֹּל הָאִשָּׁה בִּכְתֻבָּתָהּ מִן הַפָּחוּת שֶׁבַּמַּטְבְּעוֹת.
כֵּיצַד? נָשָׂא אִשָּׁה בְּמָקוֹם אֶחָד, וְגֵרְשָׁהּ בְּמָקוֹם אַחֵר:
אִם הָיוּ מְעוֹת מְקוֹם הַנִּשּׂוּאִין טוֹבִים מִמְּעוֹת מְקוֹם הַגֵּרוּשִׁין — נוֹתֵן לָהּ מִמְּעוֹת מְקוֹם הַגֵּרוּשִׁין;
וְאִם הָיוּ מְעוֹת מְקוֹם הַגֵּרוּשִׁין טוֹבִים מִמְּעוֹת מְקוֹם הַנִּשּׂוּאִין — נוֹתֵן לָהּ מִמְּעוֹת מְקוֹם הַנִּשּׂוּאִין.
בַּמֶּה דְּבָרִים אֲמוּרִים? בְּשֶׁהָיָה בִּכְתֻבָּתָהּ מָעוֹת סְתָם;
אֲבָל אִם פֵּרֵשׁ בָּהּ מַטְבֵּעַ יָדוּעַ, בֵּין בְּעָקָר בֵּין בַּתּוֹסֶפֶת — הֲרֵי הִיא כְּדִין הַמַּלְוֶה אֶת חֲבֵרוֹ מַטְבֵּעַ יָדוּעַ, שֶׁנּוֹתֵן לוֹ כַּמָּה שֶׁהִלְוָהוּ, כְּמוֹ שֶׁיִּתְבָּאֵר בְּהִלְכוֹת הַלְוָאָה.

ז תִּקְּנוּ הַגְּאוֹנִים בְּכָל הַיְשִׁיבוֹת, שֶׁתִּהְיֶה הָאִשָּׁה גּוֹבָה כְּתֻבָּתָהּ אַחֲרֵי מוֹת בַּעְלָהּ אַף מִן הַמִּטַּלְטְלִין, כְּדֶרֶךְ שֶׁהִתְקִינוּ לְבַעַל חוֹב לִגְבּוֹת מִן הַמִּטַּלְטְלִין.

woman is entitled to only 150, because that was its value at the time of her husband's death.
20. This is one of the conditions of a woman's *ketubah*.
21. Landed property that was owned by a man at the time of his marriage or acceptance of a financial obligation is considered to be on lien to his wife or to his creditor. Even if it is sold to another person, the debt can be collected from it, if the person or his estate has no other property, as stated in Halachah 10. (See also *Hilchot Malveh V'Loveh*, Chapter 19.)
As mentioned in *Hilchot Malveh V'Loveh* 21:1, a creditor is entitled to collect not only the property itself, but also any increment in its value, whether an increment that comes naturally, or even one that results because of effort on the part of the purchaser. A woman is not, however, given this privilege with regard to the money due her by virtue of her *ketubah*.
22. I.e., the woman's *ketubah* mentioned 200 silver coins without specifying the type of coin, and there was a difference between the value of the silver coins used in the country where the *ketubah* was written and those used in the country where the divorce takes place. If this were a loan contract, we would say that the intent is the coins of the country in which the loan was given. As a leniency to the husband, however, the law is different with regard to a *ketubah*, and he is obligated to pay only the lesser of the two values.
The *Maggid Mishneh* and the *Shulchan Aruch* (*Even HaEzer* 100:5) state that this law applies only when the value of the money the woman receives is not less than 100 *zuz* of the Talmudic period for a non-virgin, and 200 *zuz* for a virgin.
23. *Hilchot Malveh V'Loveh* 4:11.
24. The *Maggid Mishneh* explains that this ruling reflects a difference in the socio-economic

collect the debt owed him from movable property.[25] This mandate spread throughout the majority of the Jewish people.[26]

Similarly, the other conditions of a woman's *ketubah* are governed by the same rules as [the fundamental requirement of] the *ketubah*, and they are binding on the movable property of the deceased's estate, as well as on the landed property. There is, however, one exception - the right of the sons to inherit their mother's *ketubah*. Since the custom of granting them this inheritance was not universally accepted by all the *yeshivot*,[27] I maintain that the law of the Talmud should be applied in this instance, and they should inherit the money due their mother by virtue of her *ketubah* only from the landed property [within the estate].[28]

8. In all the [Jewish] communities of which I know and have heard reports from, it has already become the custom to write the *ketubah* so that [its obligations are binding] on both the landed property and the movable property [in the estate].[29]

[Making] this addition is a great asset; it was ordained by learned men of great stature. For it is a monetary stipulation, and thus a widow is entitled to collect [the money due her] from the movable property [in her husband's] estate by virtue of this stipulation, and not by virtue of the mandate of the later sages.[30]

9. [The following rules apply when] this stipulation was not included in the text of the *ketubah*, but instead [the couple] married without making an explicit statement [in this regard]. If the husband knew of this ordinance established by the *geonim*, the woman may collect [the money due her from the movable property in his estate].

If, however, he was not [aware of this ordinance], or we are unsure whether he knew of it, we deliberate at length concerning this matter. For an ordinance of the *geonim* does not have the power to be applied and to have money expropriated from the heirs because of it, when it was not explicitly stated, as is the law regarding the conditions of the *ketubah*.[31] [The distinction between the two is that the conditions of the *ketubah*] are ordinances instituted by the Great *Sanhedrin*.

10. Our Sages also ordained that all of a husband's property should be on lien for the woman's *ketubah*. Even if the woman's *ketubah* is [only 100 *zuz*] and [her husband] owns property worth several thousand gold pieces, it is all under lien to her *ketubah*.

---

status of the Jewish people. Land was commonly owned in the Talmudic period, and hence a woman would not feel secure unless the obligation of her *ketubah* were supported by land. In contrast, the ownership of land was less common in the era of the *geonim*.

וּפָשְׁטָה תַּקָּנָה זוֹ בְּרֹב יִשְׂרָאֵל.

וְכֵן שְׁאָר תְּנָאֵי כְתֻבָּה — כֻּלָּן כַּכְּתֻבָּה הֵן, וְיֵשְׁנָן בְּמִטַּלְטְלִין כְּבַקַּרְקַע.

חוּץ מִכְּתֻבַּת 'בְּנִין דִּכְרִין', שֶׁלֹּא מָצָאנוּ מִנְהַג יְרֵשָׁתָן פָּשׁוּט בְּכָל הַיְשִׁיבוֹת.

לְפִיכָךְ אֲנִי אוֹמֵר: מַעֲמִידִין אוֹתָהּ עַל דִּין הַגְּמָרָא, שֶׁאֵין יוֹרְשִׁין כְּתֻבַּת אִמָּן אֶלָּא מִן הַקַּרְקַע.

ח כְּבָר נָהֲגוּ בְּכָל הַמְּקוֹמוֹת שֶׁיָּדַעְנוּ וְשֶׁשָּׁמַעְנוּ שִׁמְעָן, שֶׁיִּכְתְּבוּ בַּכְּתֻבָּה: בֵּין מִמְּקַרְקְעֵי בֵּין מִמְּטַלְטְלֵי.

וְדָבָר זֶה תִּקּוּן גָּדוֹל הוּא, וַאֲנָשִׁים גְּדוֹלִים וּנְבוֹנִים הִנְהִיגוּ דָבָר זֶה; שֶׁהֲרֵי זֶה תְּנַאי שֶׁבְּמָמוֹן, וְנִמְצָא הָאַלְמָנָה גּוֹבָה מִן הַמִּטַּלְטְלִין בִּתְנַאי זֶה, לֹא בְּתַקָּנַת אֲחֵרוֹנִים.

ט הֲרֵי שֶׁלֹּא כָתַב כָּךְ בִּשְׁטַר הַכְּתֻבָּה, אֶלָּא נָשָׂא סְתָם:

אִם הָיָה יוֹדֵעַ בְּתַקָּנָה זוֹ שֶׁל גְּאוֹנִים — גּוֹבָה,

וְאִם לָאו, אוֹ שֶׁנִּסְתַּפֵּק לָנוּ הַדָּבָר — מְתִיָּשְׁבִין בַּדָּבָר הַרְבֵּה;

שֶׁאֵין כֹּחַ בְּתַקָּנַת הַגְּאוֹנִים לָדוּן בָּהּ אַף־עַל־פִּי שֶׁלֹּא נִתְפָּרְשָׁה, כְּדִין תְּנָאֵי כְתֻבָּה שֶׁהֵם תַּקָּנַת הַסַּנְהֶדְרִין הַגְּדוֹלָה, עַד שֶׁנּוֹצִיא בָּהּ מָמוֹן מִן הַיּוֹרְשִׁים.

י וְעוֹד תִּקְּנוּ חֲכָמִים, שֶׁיִּהְיוּ כָּל נִכְסֵי הַבַּעַל אַחֲרָאִין וְעַרְבָאִין לַכְּתֻבָּה. אֲפִלּוּ כְּתֻבָתָהּ מָנֶה, וְיֵשׁ לוֹ קַרְקַע בַּאֲלָפִים זְהוּבִים — הַכֹּל תַּחַת שִׁעְבּוּד הַכְּתֻבָּה.

Movable property, thus, rose in importance, and a woman would feel secure even when an obligation was supported only by movable property.

25. See *Hilchot Nizkei Mammon* 8:12.

26. Since it was accepted by the majority of the Jewish people, it should be adhered to. See, however, the following halachot.

27. I.e., in certain places this practice was not followed. Although the Rambam maintains that the sons should be granted that privilege, their rights should not be extended beyond their original scope.

28. The Rambam's opinion is accepted by many authorities. Nevertheless, there are dissenting views. The *Shulchan Aruch* (*Even HaEzer* 111:14) mentions both views without appearing to favor either one.

29. See the Rambam's text of the *ketubah, Hilchot Yibbum* 4:33.

30. A person has the license to bind his estate to a particular obligation, although he would not be required to pay it by law. Once he makes such a commitment, his estate is bound by it.

31. The *Kessef Mishneh* explains that in the Rambam's era, the observance of this ordinance had not spread throughout the entire Jewish world. Note the introduction to the *Mishneh Torah* which states that, in contrast to the ordinances of the Sages of the Talmud, an ordinance instituted by the *geonim* is not binding unless its observance has spread throughout the entire Jewish people.

The *Chelkat Mechokek* 100:2 and the *Beit Shmuel* 100:2 emphasize that the observance of this ordinance spread in the subsequent generations, and it is now universal Jewish

[Her husband] is entitled to sell all his property if he desires, and his sale is binding. Nevertheless, all the property that he sells after his marriage can be expropriated [from the purchaser] by his widow [in lieu of payment for] her *ketubah* when he divorces her or when he dies, if he does not possess property that has not been sold.[32]

When a woman expropriates property [from a purchaser], she must take an oath holding a sacred article, as is taken by any of [a person's] creditors [who seek to expropriate property from its purchasers]. This provision was instituted so that he should not view [the obligation of] the *ketubah* lightly.

11. When the court or the heirs require a widow to take an oath when she comes to collect [the money due her by virtue of] her *ketubah*, the oath should be taken only outside the court.[33] For the court would refrain from administering the oath, lest she not be precise with herself when making it.[34]

If the heirs desired that she make a vow [instead of an oath], she may make a vow linked to any object they desire.[35] This vow may be administered in a court. Afterwards, she should collect [the money due her by virtue of] her *ketubah*.

12. If a widow dies before taking this oath, her heirs should not inherit her *ketubah* at all, for she does not have any rights to her *ketubah* until she takes an oath.[36]

If the woman marries [a second time] before taking an oath [with regard to [the money due her by virtue of] her *ketubah* from her previous husband's estate], she may take an oath after her remarriage and collect her due whenever she desires. She does not, however, have the option of making a vow, lest her [second] husband annul it.[37]

13. If [a woman's husband] designated a plot of land for her in her *ketubah*, whether he specified [only] one of its borders or all four of its borders, she may collect her *ketubah* from this plot of land without taking an oath.

Similarly, if he specified movable property [in the *ketubah*] and this movable property exists, she may take it without taking an oath. [Moreover,] if the [movable property that was specified] was sold and other movable property purchased with the proceeds, it being known that these goods were purchased with the proceeds of [the movable property specified in the *ketubah*], she may take them without taking an oath.

practice. Therefore, it is binding even when it was not explicitly stated in the *ketubah*, and the husband's heirs claim that he was unaware of it.

32. If, however, the husband or his estate possesses property that has not been sold, neither the woman nor another creditor may expropriate property that has already been sold (*Gittin* 5:2).

33. Rashi, the Ramban and the Rashba state that when an oath is made outside the court,

וְכָל שֶׁיִּמְכֹּר אַחַר הַנִּשּׂוּאִין מִנְּכָסָיו, אַף־עַל־פִּי שֶׁמִּמְכָּרוֹ קַיָּם וְיֵשׁ לוֹ לִמְכֹּר כָּל נְכָסָיו אִם יִרְצֶה — יֵשׁ לָהּ לִטְרֹף אוֹתָן בִּכְתֻבָּתָהּ כְּשֶׁיְּגָרְשֶׁנָּה אוֹ כְּשֶׁיָּמוּת, אִם לֹא תִּמְצָא נְכָסִים בְּנֵי חֹרִין.

וּכְשֶׁתִּטְרֹף — לֹא תִּטְרֹף אֶלָּא בִּשְׁבוּעָה בִּנְקִיטַת חֵפֶץ, כְּדִין כָּל בַּעֲלֵי חוֹבוֹת.

וְתַקָּנָה זוֹ, כְּדֵי שֶׁלֹּא תִּהְיֶה כְּתֻבָּה קַלָּה בְּעֵינָיו.

יא כְּשֶׁמַּשְׁבִּיעִין בֵּית דִּין אוֹ הַיּוֹרְשִׁין אֶת הָאַלְמָנָה כְּשֶׁתָּבוֹא לִגְבּוֹת כְּתֻבָּתָהּ — אֵין מַשְׁבִּיעִין אוֹתָהּ אֶלָּא חוּץ לְבֵית דִּין;

מִפְּנֵי שֶׁבָּתֵּי דִינִין הָיוּ נִמְנָעִין מִלְהַשְׁבִּיעָהּ, שֶׁחוֹשְׁשִׁין לָהּ שֶׁמָּא לֹא תְּדַקְדֵּק עַל עַצְמָהּ בַּשְּׁבוּעָה.

וְאִם רָצוּ הַיְתוֹמִים לְהַדִּירָהּ — נוֹדֶרֶת לָהֶן כָּל מַה שֶּׁיִּרְצוּ, וּמַדִּירִין אוֹתָהּ בְּבֵית דִּין, וְאַחַר כָּךְ נוֹטֶלֶת כְּתֻבָּתָהּ.

יב מֵתָה הָאַלְמָנָה קֹדֶם שֶׁתִּשָּׁבַע — אֵין יוֹרְשֶׁיהָ יוֹרְשִׁין מִכְּתֻבָּתָהּ כְּלוּם; שֶׁאֵין לָהּ כְּתֻבָּה עַד שֶׁתִּשָּׁבַע.

וְאִם נִשֵּׂאת קֹדֶם שֶׁתִּשָּׁבַע — הֲרֵי זוֹ נִשְׁבַּעַת אַחַר הַנִּשּׂוּאִין, וְנוֹטֶלֶת כָּל זְמַן שֶׁתִּרְצֶה; אֲבָל אֵינָהּ נוֹדֶרֶת וְנוֹטֶלֶת, שֶׁמָּא יָפֵר לָהּ הַבַּעַל.

יג יִחֵד לָהּ קַרְקַע בִּכְתֻבָּתָהּ — בֵּין שֶׁיִּחֵד לָהּ בְּאַרְבַּעַת הַמְּצָרִים, בֵּין בְּמֵצֶר אֶחָד — גּוֹבָה אֶת כְּתֻבָּתָהּ מִמֶּנּוּ בְּלֹא שְׁבוּעָה.

וְכֵן אִם כָּתַב לָהּ מִטַּלְטְלִין, וְהֵן עַצְמָן קַיָּמִין — נוֹטֶלֶת אוֹתָן בְּלֹא שְׁבוּעָה.

וְכֵן אִם נִמְכְּרוּ וְנִלְקַח בָּהֶן מִטַּלְטְלִין אֲחֵרִים, וְנוֹדַע שֶׁאֵלּוּ הַשְּׁנִיִּים מִדְּמֵי הַמִּטַּלְטְלִין הָרִאשׁוֹנִים — נוֹטַלְתָּן בְּלֹא שְׁבוּעָה.

God's name is not mentioned, and a Torah scroll is not held. The *Shulchan Aruch* (*Even HaEzer* 96:19) quotes this view. The *Maggid Mishneh* states, however, that the fact that the Rambam does not mention such a distinction indicates that he does not accept this concept.

34. *Gittin* 35a explains that since a widow carries out certain activities on behalf of the heirs of her deceased husband's estate (who are, in most instances, her children), she feels free to take certain articles belonging to the estate, without taking this into consideration. Hence, she might be ready to take an oath that she did not benefit from the estate, when in fact she did.

Since the sin of - and the punishment for - taking a false oath is very harsh, our Sages wished to reduce this severity by having the oath administered outside the court.

35. I.e., the woman will vow never to eat bread on the condition that she benefited from property belonging to the estate. Breaking a vow is considered a less severe transgression than taking a false oath.

36. This principle applies universally: Whenever a person is entitled to property only after taking an oath, that property is not transferred to the person's heirs if the oath had not been taken (*Shulchan Aruch, Even HaEzer* 96:1).

37. Since the woman's second husband has the option of annulling any vows made by

14. A woman who diminishes [the amount of money due her by virtue of] her *ketubah* may collect her due only after taking an oath.[38]

What is implied? A woman produces a *ketubah* that states [that she is due] 1000 *zuz*. Her husband claims that she received the entire amount, while she claims to have received only a portion of the amount. Even if there are witnesses who testify that she received the amount that she admits to having received,[39] and even if she is extremely precise in accounting what she took, mentioning even [the last] half-*p'rutah*, she may collect the remainder only after taking an oath.[40]

15. [An oath is also required in the following instance.] The husband claims that [his wife] received all [the money due her by virtue of] her *ketubah*], while the woman claims not to have received the money, and one witness testifies that she received either the entire sum or a portion of it. [The woman] may collect the entire [sum mentioned in] the *ketubah*, but only after taking an oath.[41]

16. [When a divorcee collects the money due her by virtue of her *ketubah*] outside the presence of her husband, she must take an oath before doing so.

What is implied? A man divorced his wife and departed. After his wife takes an oath, the court should expropriate his property and give [the woman the money due her by virtue of] her *ketubah*.

The above applies when the husband is in a distant place, where there is difficulty in notifying him. If, however, he is in a nearby place [where it is possible] to notify him, a message should be sent to notify him [of the court's impending action]. If he does not come, the woman should take the oath and collect [her due].

17. A woman who reduces the value of her *ketubah* is not required to take an oath before collecting [her due].[42]

What is implied? A woman produces a *ketubah* that states [that she is due] 1000 *zuz*. Her husband claims that she received the entire amount, while she claims not to have received anything at all, but she admits: "I am owed only 500 *zuz*. Although he wrote 1000 for me [in the *ketubah*], there was an understanding between me and him [concerning this]." In this instance, she is not required to take an oath before collecting [her due].

If, however, [in the above situation,] the woman says: "My *ketubah* states only 500 *zuz*," she may not collect with this document that says [she is due] 1000 *zuz*, for she has negated it. It is as if she has admitted that it is false. Therefore, [the husband] may take a rabbinic oath [to support his claim]; he is then freed [of all obligations].

his wife, it is possible that she will take a false vow, relying on her husband to nullify it (*Gittin* 35b).

יד הַפּוֹגֶמֶת כְּתֻבָּתָהּ — לֹא תִּפָּרַע אֶלָּא בִּשְׁבוּעָה.

כֵּיצַד? הוֹצִיאָה שְׁטַר כְּתֻבָּה שֶׁיֵּשׁ בּוֹ אֶלֶף זוּז, הַבַּעַל אוֹמֵר: נִתְקַבַּלְתְּ הַכֹּל, וְהִיא אוֹמֶרֶת: לֹא נִתְקַבַּלְתִּי אֶלָּא כָּךְ וְכָךְ.

וַאֲפִלּוּ יֵשׁ עָלֶיהָ עֵדִים בְּמִקְצָת שֶׁנָּטְלָה, וַאֲפִלּוּ דְּקִדְּקָה עַצְמָהּ בְּחֶשְׁבּוֹן מַה שֶּׁנָּטְלָה בַּחֲצִי פְרוּטָה — לֹא תִּטֹּל הַשְּׁאָר אֶלָּא בִּשְׁבוּעָה.

טו אָמַר הַבַּעַל: נִתְקַבַּלְתְּ הַכֹּל, וְהִיא אוֹמֶרֶת: לֹא נִתְקַבַּלְתִּי כְּלוּם, וְעֵד אֶחָד מֵעִיד עָלֶיהָ שֶׁנִּתְקַבְּלָה הַכֹּל אוֹ מִקְצָת — לֹא תִּפָּרַע כָּל הַכְּתֻבָּה אֶלָּא בִּשְׁבוּעָה.

טז הַנִּפְרַעַת שֶׁלֹּא בְּפָנָיו — לֹא תִּפָּרַע אֶלָּא בִּשְׁבוּעָה.

כֵּיצַד? הֲרֵי שֶׁגֵּרַשׁ אֶת אִשְׁתּוֹ וְהָלַךְ לוֹ — בֵּית דִּין יוֹרְדִין לִנְכָסָיו וּמַגְבִּין אוֹתָהּ כְּתֻבָּתָהּ.

וְהוּא, שֶׁיִּהְיֶה בְּמָקוֹם רָחוֹק, שֶׁיֵּשׁ לָהֶן טֹרַח לְהוֹדִיעוֹ;

אֲבָל אִם הָיָה בְּמָקוֹם קָרוֹב לְהוֹדִיעוֹ — שׁוֹלְחִין לוֹ וּמוֹדִיעִין אוֹתוֹ, וְאִם לֹא יָבוֹא — תִּשָּׁבַע וְתִטֹּל.

יז הַפּוֹחֶתֶת כְּתֻבָּתָהּ — נִפְרַעַת שֶׁלֹּא בִּשְׁבוּעָה.

כֵּיצַד? הוֹצִיאָה שְׁטַר כְּתֻבָּה בְּאֶלֶף זוּז, הוּא אוֹמֵר: נִתְקַבַּלְתְּ הַכֹּל, וְהִיא אוֹמֶרֶת: לֹא נִתְקַבַּלְתִּי כְּלוּם, וְאֵין לִי אֶלָּא חֲמֵשׁ מֵאוֹת זוּז; וְזֶה שֶׁכָּתַב לִי אֶלֶף, אֲמָנָה הָיְתָה בֵּינִי לְבֵינוֹ — הֲרֵי זוֹ נִפְרַעַת שֶׁלֹּא בִּשְׁבוּעָה.

אֲבָל אִם אָמְרָה: אֵין בִּשְׁטַר כְּתֻבָּתִי אֶלָּא חֲמֵשׁ מֵאוֹת — אֵינָהּ נִפְרַעַת בִּשְׁטָר זֶה שֶׁיֵּשׁ בּוֹ אֶלֶף זוּז כְּלוּם, שֶׁהֲרֵי בִּטְלָה אוֹתוֹ וּכְאִלּוּ הוֹדַת שֶׁהוּא שֶׁקֶר. לְפִיכָךְ נִשְׁבַּע שְׁבוּעַת הֶסֵּת וְנִפְטָר.

---

38. Our Sages required the woman to take an oath because they were not sure that she made a complete account of the money she received. Requiring her to take an oath insures that she will, in fact, be careful regarding this account (*Ketubot* 87b).

39. The fact that witnesses were made to observe payment of one portion of the *ketubah* is no proof that a second payment was not made without being observed by witnesses.

40. The fact that she appears precise in reporting what she admits to having received is not proof that she has made a totally precise accounting (*Ketubot*, loc. cit.).

Similar laws apply to a creditor who states that he is actually owed a lesser amount than is stated in the contract of loan (*Hilchot Malveh V'Loveh* 14:1).

41. Since the husband has only one witness to support his claim, and the woman's claim is supported by her *ketubah*, she is entitled to collect her full claim. Nevertheless, because of the witness, an oath is required.

42. In contrast to a woman who diminishes the amount of money due her by virtue of her *ketubah* (Halachah 14), this woman does not admit receiving any funds. Hence, there is no need to require an oath so that she will make a careful account (*Bayit Chadash, Even HaEzer* 96).

18. Whenever we have stated that a woman may not collect [her due] unless she takes an oath, the court tells her: "Take the oath and collect [your due]." Whenever we said that she may collect her due without an oath, [the court] tells the husband: "Give her [what is due her]. Your claim is not acceptable until you bring proof to support it."

19. [If in the latter instances], on his own initiative, the husband asks that [the woman] take an oath [denying] his claim, [the court] tells her: "Take the oath and collect [your due]." She must take this oath holding a sacred article.

If, [originally,] she made a stipulation with [her husband] enabling her to collect [the money due her by virtue of] her *ketubah* without taking an oath, or that her word would be accepted regardless of what she claims, she may collect [her due] from him [in the event of a divorce] without taking any oath at all. [In the event of his death,] however, she must take an oath before collecting [her due] from his heirs.[43]

20. If, [originally,] she made a stipulation with [her husband] enabling her to collect [the money due her by virtue of] her *ketubah* from his heirs without taking an oath, or that her word would be accepted by his heirs regardless of what she claims, she may collect [her due] from the heirs without taking any oath at all.[44]

If, however, she comes to collect [her due] from property that has been sold, she must take an oath before collecting. Although her husband was willing to accept her word, the stipulation he made is binding only on himself and [the estate he left to] his heirs. It does not have the power to cause others to incur a financial loss.[45]

21. A widow who is in possession of her [the document recording her] *ketubah* may collect her due, after taking an oath, even though 100 years have passed since her husband's death.[46] This applies regardless of whether she resides in her [deceased] husband's home or in her father's home.[47]

If, however, she does not have possession of her *ketubah*, she is not entitled to anything, even if she makes her claim on the day her husband dies.[48] Similarly, a divorcee is not entitled even to the fundamental requirement of the *ketubah* until she produces her *ketubah*.

22. When does the above apply? In a place where it is customary to compose a

43. Unless a specific statement was made to that effect, the stipulation that her husband accepted at the time of the composition of the *ketubah* applies only to himself and not to his heirs.
44. The Rambam's opinion is accepted by the *Shulchan Aruch* (*Even HaEzer* 98:6). The

יח כָּל מָקוֹם שֶׁאָמַרְנוּ: לֹא תִּפָּרַע אֶלָּא בִּשְׁבוּעָה — אוֹמְרִים לָהּ בֵּית דִּין: הִשָּׁבְעִי וּטְלִי;
וּמָקוֹם שֶׁאָמַרְנוּ: תִּפָּרַע שֶׁלֹּא בִּשְׁבוּעָה — אוֹמְרִים לַבַּעַל: עֲמֹד וְתֵן לָהּ, וְאֵין אַתָּה נֶאֱמָן
בְּטַעֲנָה זוֹ עַד שֶׁתָּבִיא רְאָיָה לִדְבָרֶיךָ.

יט אָמַר הַבַּעַל מֵעַצְמוֹ: תִּשָּׁבַע לִי עַל טַעֲנָתִי — אוֹמְרִין לָהּ: הִשָּׁבְעִי וּטְלִי, וְתִשָּׁבַע בִּנְקִיטַת
חֵפֶץ.
הִתְנָה עִמּוֹ שֶׁתִּגְבֶּה כְּתֻבָּתָהּ שֶׁלֹּא בִּשְׁבוּעָה, אוֹ שֶׁתְּהֵא נֶאֱמֶנֶת בְּכָל מַה שֶׁתִּטְעַן — גּוֹבָה
מִמֶּנּוּ בְּלֹא שְׁבוּעָה כְּלָל.
אֲבָל אִם בָּאָה לִגְבּוֹת מִיּוֹרְשָׁיו — תִּשָּׁבַע וְאַחַר כָּךְ תִּטֹּל.

כ הִתְנָה עִמּוֹ שֶׁתִּגְבֶּה כְּתֻבָּתָהּ מִיּוֹרְשָׁיו בְּלֹא שְׁבוּעָה, אוֹ שֶׁתִּהְיֶה נֶאֱמֶנֶת בְּכָל מַה שֶׁתִּטְעַן
עַל יוֹרְשָׁיו — הֲרֵי זוֹ נוֹטֶלֶת מֵהֶן בְּלֹא שְׁבוּעָה.
אֲבָל אִם בָּאָה לִטְרֹף מִנְּכָסִים מְשֻׁעְבָּדִים — לֹא תִּטְרֹף אֶלָּא בִּשְׁבוּעָה, וְאַף-עַל-פִּי שֶׁהֶאֱמִינָהּ
הַבַּעַל;
שֶׁאֵין תְּנַאי הַבַּעַל מוֹעִיל אֶלָּא עָלָיו וְעַל יוֹרְשָׁיו, אֲבָל לְהַפְסִיד מָמוֹן אֲחֵרִים אֵינוֹ מוֹעִיל.

כא אַלְמָנָה שֶׁהָיָה שְׁטַר כְּתֻבָּה יוֹצֵא מִתַּחַת יָדָהּ — נִשְׁבַּעַת וְגוֹבָה כְּתֻבָּתָהּ לְעוֹלָם, אֲפִלּוּ
אַחַר מֵאָה שָׁנָה.
בֵּין שֶׁהָיְתָה בְּבֵית בַּעְלָהּ, בֵּין שֶׁהָיְתָה בְּבֵית אָבִיהָ.
וְאִם אֵין שְׁטַר כְּתֻבָּה יוֹצֵא מִתַּחַת יָדָהּ — אֵין לָהּ כְּלוּם, וַאֲפִלּוּ עִקַּר כְּתֻבָּה, וַאֲפִלּוּ תְּבָעָה
בְּיוֹם מִיתַת בַּעְלָהּ.
וְכֵן הַגְּרוּשָׁה, אֲפִלּוּ עִקַּר כְּתֻבָּה אֵין לָהּ עַד שֶׁתּוֹצִיא שְׁטַר כְּתֻבָּה.

כב בַּמֶּה דְּבָרִים אֲמוּרִים? בְּמָקוֹם שֶׁדַּרְכָּן לִכְתֹּב כְּתֻבָּה;

Ramah, however, cites the opinion of Rabbenu Asher and other Ashkenazic authorities, who maintain that the husband's stipulation is not binding upon his heirs.

45. The Ra'avad maintains that the woman's claim should be accepted without an oath. Since the husband made such a stipulation, it would have become public knowledge. Any person who purchased the property knew about the matter and accepted the risk. It is, however, the Rambam's ruling that is accepted by the *Shulchan Aruch* (*loc. cit.*).

46. The fact that she maintained possession of her *ketubah* indicates that her delay in presenting her claim does not indicate a willingness to forego it.

47. This distinction is, however, relevant in Halachah 23.

48. For perhaps she has already received the money due her by virtue of her *ketubah*, or she has waived payment of this debt.

The *Shulchan Aruch* (*Even HaEzer* 100:6) quotes the Rambam's rulings. The Ramah quotes rulings that allow the woman to collect the money due her even in such an instance. Nevertheless, he states that the prevailing custom is not to allow a woman to collect her claim unless she is in possession of her *ketubah*.

document [recording] the *ketubah*. [Different rules apply,] however, in a place where it is not customary to compose a document [recording] the *ketubah*. [In such places, [the couple] rely on the conditions established by the Jewish court.[49]

[In such a situation, the woman is entitled to] collect the essential requirement of the *ketubah*[50] even when she is not in possession of a document recording the *ketubah*, regardless of whether she was widowed or divorced, or whether she [continues to] reside in her husband's home or [has returned to] her father's home. She is not, however, given [anything she claims her husband promised her] in addition unless she has definite proof [of such an obligation].[51]

23. Until when is a widow entitled to collect the essential requirement of the *ketubah*[52] in a place where it is not customary to compose a *ketubah*? If she [continues to reside] in her husband's home, there is no limit on the time she is granted.[53] If she [resides] in her father's home,[54] [she has this prerogative] for twenty-five years.

If, [however,] she comes to collect [the money due her because of her *ketubah*] after twenty-five years, she is not entitled to anything. [The rationale is that] had she not foregone [the money due her], she would not have remained silent for this long. Nor is she living together with the heirs, so that she could [excuse her silence,] explaining that she was embarrassed to sue them while she was living together with them in [one] home.

24. For this reason, if [one of] the heirs was in the habit of bringing her subsistence while she was residing in her father's home and caring for her needs, she has the prerogative of demanding [her due] even after twenty-five years have passed. The reason why she remained silent and did not present her claim is that she was ashamed [to sue] the heir.

25. [The following rules apply when there is a difference between the claims of a husband - or his heirs - and his wife regarding the size of the essential requirement of her *ketubah*.] She says, "I was a virgin when I married, and the essential requirement of my *ketubah* is 200 [*zuz*]." Her husband or his heirs claim, "She was not a virgin, and she is due only 100."

If there are witnesses who saw that the customs that people in that locale carry out when virgins are wed were carried out on her behalf - e.g., there were different types of celebrations, [she wore a] crown or a particular garment [designated for this purpose], or other rites that are performed only for the

49. In the Talmudic period, there were places where it was not customary to compose a written document spelling out the marriage contract. Nevertheless, it was understood by

אֲבָל בְּמָקוֹם שֶׁאֵין דַּרְכָּן לִכְתֹּב כְּתֻבָּה, אֶלָּא סוֹמְכִין עַל תְּנָאֵי בֵּית דִּין — הֲרֵי זוֹ גּוֹבָה עִקַּר כְּתֻבָּה אַף-עַל-פִּי שֶׁאֵין בְּיָדָהּ שְׁטַר כְּתֻבָּה — בֵּין נִתְגָּרְשָׁה בֵּין נִתְאַלְמְנָה, בֵּין שֶׁהָיְתָה בְּבֵית בַּעְלָהּ בֵּין שֶׁהָיְתָה בְּבֵית אָבִיהָ,
אֲבָל תּוֹסֶפֶת אֵין לָהּ בְּכָל מָקוֹם אֶלָּא בִּרְאָיָה בְּרוּרָה.

כג וְעַד כַּמָּה תִּגְבֶּה הָאַלְמָנָה הָעִקָּר בְּמָקוֹם שֶׁאֵין כּוֹתְבִין כְּתֻבָּה?
אִם הָיְתָה בְּבֵית בַּעְלָהּ — גּוֹבָה לְעוֹלָם,
וְאִם הָיְתָה בְּבֵית אָבִיהָ — עַד עֶשְׂרִים וְחָמֵשׁ שָׁנָה.
וְאִם בָּאָה לִתְבֹּעַ אַחַר עֶשְׂרִים וְחָמֵשׁ שָׁנָה — אֵין לָהּ כְּלוּם; שֶׁאִלּוּ לֹא מָחֲלָה — לֹא שָׁתְקָה כָּל זְמַן זֶה,
וַהֲרֵי אֵינָהּ עִם הַיּוֹרְשִׁים כְּדֵי שֶׁתֹּאמַר: נִכְלַמְתִּי מִלְּתָבְעָן וְהֵן עִמִּי בַּבַּיִת.

כד לְפִיכָךְ, אִם הָיָה הַיּוֹרֵשׁ עַצְמוֹ מוֹלִיךְ מְזוֹנוֹתֶיהָ לְבֵית אָבִיהָ וּמִטַּפֵּל בָּהּ — יֵשׁ לָהּ לִתְבֹּעַ כְּתֻבָּתָהּ וַאֲפִלּוּ אַחַר עֶשְׂרִים וְחָמֵשׁ שָׁנָה;
מִפְּנֵי שֶׁזּוֹ שֶׁשָּׁתְקָה וְלֹא תָבְעָה, מִפְּנֵי שֶׁהִיא בּוֹשָׁה מִן הַיּוֹרֵשׁ.

כה הִיא אוֹמֶרֶת: בְּתוּלָה נִשֵּׂאתִי וְעִקַּר כְּתֻבָּתִי מָאתַיִם, וְהַבַּעַל אוֹ יוֹרְשָׁיו אוֹמְרִים: בְּעוּלָה נִשֵּׂאת וְאֵין לָהּ אֶלָּא מֵאָה —
אִם יֵשׁ עֵדִים שֶׁרָאוּ שֶׁעָשׂוּ לָהּ הַמִּנְהָגוֹת שֶׁנָּהֲגוּ אַנְשֵׁי הָעִיר אוֹתָהּ לַעֲשׂוֹתָן לִבְתוּלָה, כְּגוֹן מִינֵי שִׂמְחָה אוֹ כְּתָרִים אוֹ מַלְבּוּשׁ יָדוּעַ, אוֹ שְׁאָר דְּבָרִים שֶׁאֵין עוֹשִׂין כָּךְ אֶלָּא לִבְתוּלָה — הֲרֵי

---

both the husband and the wife that the financial dimensions of their marriage would be governed by the rules expressed in our Sages' requirements for the *ketubah*.

50. When the husband claims to have paid the woman her due, he must prove his assertion. Otherwise, the woman's claim is accepted (*Maggid Mishneh*).

51. This amount is granted the woman voluntarily by her husband and is not required by Jewish law. Therefore, unless the woman has proof that the commitment was made, she is not entitled to collect anything from her husband (*Maggid Mishneh*).

The *Tur* (*Even HaEzer* 100) states that even if a woman can prove that her husband made a commitment for an additional amount to her at the time of the marriage, she must also prove that this commitment was not met.

52. The *Tur* (*Even HaEzer* 101) maintains that the Rambam's wording indicates that even if she remains silent, she foregoes only the essential requirement of the *ketubah*, but not the additional commitment that her husband made. However, Rav Yosef Karo dismisses this interpretation in the *Kessef Mishneh* and does not mention it in the *Shulchan Aruch* (*Even HaEzer* 101).

53. As reflected in the conclusion of this halachah, although a widow has the right to continue dwelling in her deceased husband's home, the heirs also have the right to dwell there. Since she is deriving her subsistence from them, she is ashamed to demand payment of her due from them.

54. Or she remarries (*Ramah, Even HaEzer* 101:1).

sake of virgins were performed [for her] - she is entitled to 200 [*zuz*]. If there are no witnesses to this, she is entitled to only 100 [*zuz*].

[In the latter instance,] if her husband is alive, she can require him to take an oath required by the Torah,[55] for he has acknowledged a portion of a claim.

[In cases of this nature,] testimony is accepted [from a person][56] once he became an adult, who says: "I remember that when I was a child, the rites performed for virgin brides were performed on behalf of such and such."[57]

As mentioned, all the above applies [only] in places where it is customary not to compose a document recording the *ketubah*.[58]

26. When a woman tells her husband, "You divorced me," her word is accepted. [The rationale is that if this were not the truth,] she would not speak so boldly to her husband.[59]

Accordingly, when a woman produces her *ketubah*, [even] without having a bill of divorce, and tells her husband: "You divorced me. I lost my bill of divorce. Give me [the money due me by virtue of] my *ketubah*," [her claim is accepted, and her husband] is obligated to pay her the essential requirement of the marriage contract, even though he claims that he never divorced her.[60] He is not, however, [obligated to] give her the additional amount he promised,[61] unless she brings proof that she has been divorced, or she manifests possession of both the bill of divorce and her *ketubah*.

27. [In the above situation,] if [the woman's] husband said: "This is what happened. I divorced her and paid her all [the money due her by virtue of] her *ketubah*, both the essential requirement and the additional amount. She

---

55. Objections to this statement are raised by the Ra'avad, Rav Moshe HaCohen and others. The claim for which the husband is required to take an oath involves a liability for which landed property is under lien. In such instances, a Torah oath is never administered. The *Tur* (*Even HaEzer* 96) and others, therefore, maintain that a rabbinic oath (*sh'vuat hesset*) is administered.

The *Maggid Mishneh* explains that the Rambam is referring to an instance in his time, when, as stated in Halachot 8-9, the lien of the *ketubah* applies to movable as well as landed property. Nevertheless, the *Maggid Mishneh's* explanation is challenged by other authorities, and even the *Maggid Mishneh* himself raises questions. The *Shulchan Aruch* (*Even HaEzer* 96:16) mentions both opinions.

56. As in all cases of Torah law, the testimony of two witnesses is required in this instance. The *Maggid Mishneh* states that according to the Rambam, both of these witnesses may have witnessed the events under consideration when they were minors. In both the *Kessef Mishneh* and in the *Shulchan Aruch* (*loc. cit.*), Rav Yosef Karo differs and states that it is acceptable if one of these witnesses observed the events as a minor, but the other must have been past majority at that time.

57. Generally, a witness's testimony is not accepted unless he is past majority - not only

זוֹ נוֹטֶלֶת מָאתַיִם;

וְאִם אֵין לָהּ עֵדִים בָּזֶה — הֲרֵי זוֹ נוֹטֶלֶת מָנֶה.

וְאִם הָיָה הַבַּעַל קַיָּם — יֵשׁ לָהּ לְהַשְׁבִּיעוֹ שְׁבוּעַת הַתּוֹרָה, שֶׁהֲרֵי הוֹדָה בְּמִקְצָת הַטַּעֲנָה.

וְנֶאֱמָן הַקָּטָן לְהָעִיד בִּגְדֻלוֹ וְלוֹמַר: זָכוּר אֲנִי כְּשֶׁהָיִיתִי קָטָן שֶׁנָּשֵׂאָה לִפְלוֹנִית מִנְהַג הַבְּתוּלוֹת.

וְכָל הַדְּבָרִים הָאֵלּוּ — בְּמָקוֹם שֶׁאֵין כּוֹתְבִין כְּתֻבָּה, כְּמוֹ שֶׁאָמַרְנוּ.

כו הָאִשָּׁה שֶׁאָמְרָה לְבַעְלָהּ: גֵּרַשְׁתַּנִי — נֶאֱמֶנֶת, שֶׁאֵינָהּ מְעִזָּה פָּנֶיהָ בִּפְנֵי בַּעְלָהּ.

לְפִיכָךְ, הָאִשָּׁה שֶׁהוֹצִיאָה שְׁטַר כְּתֻבָּה וְאֵין עִמָּהּ גֵּט, וְאָמְרָה לְבַעְלָהּ: גֵּרַשְׁתַּנִי וְאָבַד גִּטִּי, תֵּן לִי כְּתֻבָּתִי, וְהוּא אוֹמֵר: לֹא גֵרַשְׁתִּיךְ — חַיָּב לִתֵּן לָהּ עִקַּר כְּתֻבָּה;

אֲבָל אֵינוֹ נוֹתֵן לָהּ הַתּוֹסֶפֶת, עַד שֶׁתָּבִיא רְאָיָה שֶׁגֵּרְשָׁהּ, אוֹ שֶׁיֵּצֵא גֵט עִם הַכְּתֻבָּה מִתַּחַת יָדָהּ.

כז אָמַר לָהּ הַבַּעַל: כָּךְ הָיָה, גֵּרַשְׁתִּי וְנָתַתִּי לָהּ כָּל הַכְּתֻבָּה, עִקָּר וְתוֹסֶפֶת, וְכָתְבָה לִי שׁוֹבֵר,

at the time he testifies in court, but also at the time he sees the event under discussion. In this instance, however, leniency is granted, because we rely on the fact that, by and large, most women are virgins when they marry. Moreover, the obligation of the *ketubah* is a point of Rabbinic law (*Ketubot* 28a; *Hilchot Edut* 14:3).

58. For if a *ketubah* was composed, the text of the *ketubah* will clarify the matter. There is, however, an instance where this ruling would be applicable in a place where it is customary to compose a *ketubah*: an instance where the woman brings witnesses who testify that her *ketubah* was lost (*Maggid Mishneh*).

59. The simple meaning of the Rambam's words is that if a woman makes such a statement, she is free to marry another person. As in Chapter 4, Halachah 13, the Ra'avad differs, explaining that the woman's statements are accepted only after the fact - i.e., after she has already married another person - and only insomuch as to require that other person to divorce her.

The *Shulchan Aruch* (*Even HaEzer* 17:2) quotes the Rambam's view, while the Ra'avad's position is quoted by the Ramah. The Ramah also mentions that in the present age, since brash conduct has become more widespread, this claim is no longer accepted when presented by a woman. The *Beit Shmuel* 17:4 mentions that, at present, since it is customary for a record of divorces to be kept by the rabbinical court that issues them, this claim is no longer accepted. This is particularly true in the present age, when record-keeping and communication have advanced.

60. The Ra'avad and the Ramah differ, as above.

61. The essential requirement of the *ketubah* is an obligation imposed by our Sages, granted so that she would have the means to marry another person in the case of divorce or widowhood. Hence, since she is granted the opportunity of remarrying in this instance, she is also entitled to the money due her by virtue of the *ketubah*. The additional amount, by contrast, is not an obligation, but rather a present promised by her husband. It is self-understood that he did not make this promise to enable her to marry another man, when he does not admit that a divorce took place (*Maggid Mishneh*).

wrote me a receipt, but I lost it," [the following rules apply]. He requires her to take an oath while holding a sacred article [that he is liable to pay her] the essential requirement [of the *ketubah*], and then he must give her [that sum].[62]

With regard to the additional amount, his word is accepted. [The rationale is that] he could have claimed that he never divorced her, and in such an instance he would not be held liable for the additional amount. [We assume that had he desired to lie, he would have used that alternative.] He is, however, required to take a rabbinic oath with regard to the additional amount.

28. [The following rules apply when] a woman produces a bill of divorce, but does not have her *ketubah* in her possession. If the local custom is not to compose a *ketubah*, she is entitled to collect the essential requirement of her *ketubah* by [virtue of] the bill of divorce she is holding. If, however, it is the local custom to compose a *ketubah*, she is not entitled even to the fundamental requirement of the *ketubah* until she produces her *ketubah*, as was explained.[63] Her husband must take a rabbinic oath denying her claim, and he is freed of liability.

29. [When] a woman produces two bills of divorce and two *ketubot*, she is entitled to collect the amount due her by virtue of both *ketubot*.[64] If she produces two *ketubot* and one bill of divorce, she is entitled to collect only [the money due her for] one *ketubah*.[65]

Which *ketubah* should she collect? If they are both for the same amount, the later *ketubah* negates the earlier one, and she is entitled to collect [property that was sold to others] from the date of the later [*ketubah*].[66] If one of them is for a greater sum than the other, she may collect whichever she desires, and the other one is voided.[67]

30. [When] a woman produces two bills of divorce and one *ketubah*, she has [the right to collect] only [the amount due her by virtue of] one *ketubah*.[68] For when a man divorces his wife and remarries her without specifying any conditions, [it can be assumed] that he remarried her with the intent that her original *ketubah* [become binding again].

[The following rules apply when] a woman produces a bill of divorce and a *ketubah* after the death of her husband: If the bill of divorce is dated prior to the *ketubah*,[69] [in a place where] it is not customary to compose

62. The authorities who free the husband of obligation in the previous halachah also free him of all liability in this instance (*Chelkat Mechokek* 100:40; *Beit Shmuel* 100:40).
63. Halachot 21-22.
64. We assume that the man divorced his wife and did not pay her the money due her by

וְאָבַד שׁוֹבְרִי —

מִתּוֹךְ שֶׁיָּכוֹל לוֹמַר 'לֹא גֵּרַשְׁתִּי' וְלֹא יִתְחַיֵּב בַּתּוֹסֶפֶת, נֶאֱמָן.

וּמַשְׁבִּיעָהּ בִּנְקִיטַת חֵפֶץ, וְנוֹתֵן לָהּ אֶת הָעִקָּר, וְנִשְׁבָּע הוּא שְׁבוּעַת הֶסֵּת עַל הַתּוֹסֶפֶת.

כח הוֹצִיאָה גֵט וְאֵין בְּיָדָהּ שְׁטַר כְּתֻבָּה:

אִם דֶּרֶךְ אוֹתוֹ מָקוֹם שֶׁלֹּא יִכְתְּבוּ כְּתֻבָּה — גּוֹבָה עִקַּר כְּתֻבָּתָהּ בַּגֵּט שֶׁבְּיָדָהּ;

וְאִם דַּרְכָּן לִכְתֹּב כְּתֻבָּה — אֲפִלּוּ עִקָּר אֵין לָהּ עַד שֶׁתּוֹצִיא שְׁטַר כְּתֻבָּה, כְּמוֹ שֶׁבֵּאַרְנוּ.

וְנִשְׁבָּע הַבַּעַל שְׁבוּעַת הֶסֵּת עַל טַעֲנָתָהּ, וְנִפְטָר.

כט הוֹצִיאָה שְׁתֵּי גִטִּין וּשְׁתֵּי כְּתֻבּוֹת — גּוֹבָה שְׁתֵּי כְּתֻבּוֹת.

הוֹצִיאָה שְׁתֵּי כְּתֻבּוֹת וְגֵט אֶחָד — אֵינָהּ גּוֹבָה אֶלָּא כְּתֻבָּה אַחַת.

וְאֵי זוֹ מֵהֶן גּוֹבָה?

אִם שְׁתֵּיהֶן שָׁוֶה — בִּטְּלָה הָאַחֲרוֹנָה אֶת הָרִאשׁוֹנָה, וְאֵינָהּ טוֹרֶפֶת אֶלָּא מִזְּמַן הָאַחֲרוֹנָה;

וְאִם הָיָה בְּאַחַת מִשְּׁתֵּיהֶן תּוֹסֶפֶת עַל חֲבֶרְתָּהּ — גּוֹבָה בְּאֵיזֶה מֵהֶן שֶׁתִּרְצֶה, וּתְבַטֵּל הַשְּׁנִיָּה.

ל הוֹצִיאָה שְׁתֵּי גִטִּין וּכְתֻבָּה אַחַת — אֵין לָהּ אֶלָּא כְּתֻבָּה אַחַת;

שֶׁהַמְגָרֵשׁ אֶת אִשְׁתּוֹ וְהֶחֱזִירָהּ סְתָם — עַל כְּתֻבָּתָהּ הָרִאשׁוֹנָה הֶחֱזִירָהּ.

הוֹצִיאָה גֵט וּכְתֻבָּה אַחַר מִיתַת הַבַּעַל:

אִם גֵּט קוֹדֵם לַכְּתֻבָּה — גּוֹבָה בְּגֵט זֶה עִקָּר כְּתֻבָּה, אִם אֵין דַּרְכָּן לִכְתֹּב כְּתֻבָּה,

virtue of her *ketubah*. Afterwards, the couple remarried, and the husband subsequently divorced her a second time, without paying her the money due her by virtue of her *ketubah*.

65. The laws that follow apply when the dates of both the *ketubot* precede the date of the bill of divorce, and thus it is apparent that the woman was divorced only once.

66. As mentioned previously, all of a husband's property is under lien to the *ketubah*. Therefore, if he sells his landed property to others and he does not possess sufficient property after the divorce to give his wife her due, she may collect that money by expropriating property that was sold. In this instance, we say that the woman waived payment of her *ketubah* originally to free from the lien property that was sold. Afterwards, her husband wrote her a second *ketubah* for the same amount.

67. In this instance, we assume that the husband wrote the woman a second *ketubah* that would preempt the first one. In this instance, the woman has the choice of selecting which *ketubah* she desires - the one with the greater sum, or the one that is dated first and thus gives her greater power with regard to the expropriation of property that has been sold.

68. As reflected in the continuation of the Rambam's statements, this refers to a situation in which the man divorced his wife and did not pay her the money due her by virtue of her *ketubah*. Afterwards, he remarried her without composing a second *ketubah*.

69. We assume that her husband divorced her and did not pay her the money due her by virtue of her *ketubah*. Afterwards, he remarried her and composed a *ketubah*.

a *ketubah*, she is entitled to collect the essential requirement of her *ketubah* by [virtue of this] bill of divorce,[70] and she is entitled to collect the entire sum [mentioned] in the second *ketubah*, for she acquires this sum by virtue of [her husband's] death.

If her *ketubah* is dated prior to the bill of divorce, she is entitled to collect [the money due her by virtue of] the *ketubah* only once. [We assume] that when he remarried her, his intent was that her original *ketubah* [become binding again].

31. A woman's word is accepted if she says: "My husband died," so that she [be granted permission to] remarry, as will be explained in *Hilchot Gerushin.*[71] One of the conditions of the *ketubah* is that if a woman remarries after the death of her husband, she is entitled to collect the entire sum written in her *ketubah*.

Therefore, if she came to the court and said: "My husband died. Grant me permission to remarry," without mentioning [the collection of the money due her by virtue of] her *ketubah* at all, she is granted permission to remarry. [Afterwards,] she is required to take an oath,[72] and then she is given [the money due her by virtue of] her *ketubah*.

If she says, "My husband died. Give me the money due me by virtue of my *ketubah*," [not only is she not granted this money,] she is not even permitted to remarry. [We assume that] she came [only] because of the matter of the *ketubah*. Our presumption is that her husband has not died. Her intent is not to remarry, but merely to collect [the money due her by virtue of] the *ketubah* during [her husband's] lifetime.

If she came and said: "My husband died. Grant me permission to remarry and give me [the money due me by virtue of] my *ketubah*," she is permitted to remarry and is granted [the money due her by virtue of] her *ketubah*. The rationale is that her primary intent is remarriage. If, however, she comes and says: "My husband died. Give me [the money due me by virtue of] my *ketubah*, and grant me permission to remarry," she is permitted to remarry, but she is not granted [the money due her by virtue of] her *ketubah*.[73] If, however, she seizes possession [of this sum], the court should not expropriate it from her possession.

CHAPTER SEVENTEEN

1. [The following laws apply when] a person dies after having been married to several wives. Whichever of his wives was married first has the right to collect [the money due her by virtue of] her *ketubah* [before the others]. None may collect [her due] without taking an oath.[1]

---

70. As explained in Halachah 28.

וְגוֹבָה כָּל מַה שֶּׁיֵּשׁ בִּכְתֻבָּתָהּ זוֹ, שֶׁהֲרֵי זָכְתָה בָּהּ בְּמִיתָתוֹ;

וְאִם כְּתֻבָּה קָדְמָה אֶת הַגֵּט — אֵין לָהּ אֶלָּא כְּתֻבָּה אַחַת, שֶׁעַל כְּתֻבָּתָהּ הָרִאשׁוֹנָה הֶחֱזִירָהּ.

לֹא הָאִשָּׁה נֶאֱמֶנֶת לוֹמַר 'מֵת בַּעְלִי' כְּדֵי שֶׁתִּנָּשֵׂא, כְּמוֹ שֶׁיִּתְבָּאֵר בְּהִלְכוֹת גֵּרוּשִׁין.

וּמִתְּנָאֵי הַכְּתֻבָּה — שֶׁאִם תִּנָּשֵׂא לְאַחֵר אַחַר מוֹתוֹ, תִּטֹּל כָּל מַה שֶּׁכָּתַב לָהּ בִּכְתֻבָּתָהּ.

לְפִיכָךְ, אִם בָּאָה לְבֵית דִּין וְאָמְרָה: מֵת בַּעְלִי, הַתִּירוּנִי לְהִנָּשֵׂא, וְלֹא הִזְכִּירָה שָׁם כְּתֻבָּה בָּעוֹלָם — מַתִּירִין אוֹתָהּ לְהִנָּשֵׂא, וּמַשְׁבִּיעִין אוֹתָהּ וְנוֹתְנִין לָהּ כְּתֻבָּתָהּ.

בָּאָה וְאָמְרָה: מֵת בַּעְלִי, תְּנוּ לִי אֶת כְּתֻבָּתִי — אַף לְהִנָּשֵׂא אֵין מַתִּירִין אוֹתָהּ;

שֶׁעַל עִסְקֵי הַכְּתֻבָּה בָּאָה, וַהֲרֵי זֶה בְּחֶזְקַת שֶׁלֹּא מֵת, וְאֵין דַּעְתָּהּ לְהִנָּשֵׂא, אֶלָּא לִטֹּל כְּתֻבָּה מֵחַיִּים בִּלְבָד.

בָּאָה וְאָמְרָה: מֵת בַּעְלִי, הַתִּירוּנִי לְהִנָּשֵׂא וּתְנוּ לִי אֶת כְּתֻבָּתִי — מַתִּירִין אוֹתָהּ לְהִנָּשֵׂא וְנוֹתְנִין לָהּ כְּתֻבָּתָהּ, מִפְּנֵי שֶׁעִקַּר דְּבָרֶיהָ עַל עִסְקֵי הַנִּשּׂוּאִין בָּאָה;

אֲבָל אִם בָּאָה וְאָמְרָה: תְּנוּ לִי אֶת כְּתֻבָּתִי וְהַתִּירוּנִי לְהִנָּשֵׂא — מַתִּירִין אוֹתָהּ, וְאֵין נוֹתְנִין לָהּ כְּתֻבָּה.

וְאִם תָּפְשָׂה — אֵין מוֹצִיאִין מִיָּדָהּ.

פֶּרֶק שִׁבְעָה עָשָׂר

א מִי שֶׁהָיָה נָשׂוּי נָשִׁים רַבּוֹת וָמֵת — כָּל שֶׁנִּשֵּׂאת בַּתְּחִלָּה קוֹדֶמֶת לִטֹּל כְּתֻבָּתָהּ. וְאֵין אַחַת מֵהֶן נוֹטֶלֶת אֶלָּא בִּשְׁבוּעָה.

71. Chapter 12, Halachah 15. (See also *Hilchot Nachalot* 7:2.)

72. I.e., the oath made by all widows before collecting the money due them by virtue of their *ketubah* (*Maggid Mishneh; Kessef Mishneh*), in contrast to the opinion of the *Tur* (*Even HaEzer* 100), who requires the woman to take an oath that her husband died. (See *Chelkat Mechokek* 17:83.)

73. This is a question that is left unresolved by the Talmud (*Yevamot* 117a). The Rambam rules that since the matter is very severe - if the woman remarries, and it is discovered that she lied, she will be prohibited to remain married to both her first or second husbands, and her children from her second husband will be considered illegitimate - and if her first husband is alive, it is likely that the fact will be discovered - in theory, the woman should be allowed to remarry. Because she mentions her *ketubah*, however, there is a doubt, and because of the doubt, the money in question is allowed to remain in the hands of the party in whose possession it is at the time the question is raised - i.e., the heirs. That doubt, however, applies only to the financial dimension of the relationship, and not to the permission to remarry (*Kessef Mishneh*).

Rabbenu Asher differs and maintains that the doubt raised by the Talmud also applies with regard to the woman's permission to remarry. Both opinions are mentioned by the *Shulchan Aruch* (*Even HaEzer* 17:44), although it appears that the Rambam's approach is favored.

1. In his Commentary on the Mishnah (*Ketubot* 10:4), the Rambam explains that this oath

The [wives who married] last are entitled to [collect their due] only from what remains after [those who married previously collect theirs].[2] Even the last wife [to collect] must take an oath [before] she collects what remains.[3]

Similarly, when there is [also] a promissory note [owed by the husband's estate], if the promissory note was dated before [the *ketubot*], the promissory note should be collected first. If the *ketubot* were each dated before [the promissory note], the woman should collect [her due] first, and the person owed the promissory note [should collect from] the remainder.

2. When does the above apply? When the land from which [the wives and the creditor] desire to collect was owned by [the deceased] at the time he married the women and took the loan. For [in such a situation], the law is that whoever's document is dated first takes precedence.

If, however, a man married several women in succession, and borrowed money - whether before marrying the women or afterwards - and [then - i.e.,] after marrying and borrowing he purchased land - it should be divided among all of them equally, for all their liens took effect at the same time. At the time he purchased the land, each one established a lien on it. None has precedence over the others.[4]

3. Similarly, if all the *ketubot* and promissory notes were dated on one day - or at a specific time, in a place where it is customary to [include] the time [of a legal document] - it should be divided among all of them equally; none has precedence over the others.

Under all circumstances, [if one of the creditors or one of the wives] took possession of movable property [belonging to the estate as payment for] the loan or *ketubah*, the property that they took should not be expropriated from him or her. For no creditor has precedence over another with regard to movable property.[5]

4. [The following rules apply when] a person divorces his wife at the time he has an outstanding promissory note, and his creditor and his divorcee come to collect [their due]. If the husband owns [enough] money and land to settle the debt and the obligations stemming from the *ketubah*, the creditor should be awarded the money,[6] and his divorcee should collect [the money due her by virtue of] her *ketubah* from the landed property.[7]

---

differs from the oath that all widows take before collecting from an estate, as mentioned in Chapter 16, Halachah 4, and must be taken even when the wives are not obligated to take that oath. The woman must take this oath for the other widows, stating that she did not collect any money from their husband's estate previously. The *Shulchan Aruch* (*Even HaEzer* 96:16), however, states that the first widow takes an oath to the second, the second to the third, the third to the fourth, and the fourth to the heirs.

2. This procedure is followed even if doing so prevents one of the wives from collecting

וְאֵין לָאַחֲרוֹנָה אֶלָּא מַה שֶּׁשִּׁיְּרָה שֶׁלְּפָנֶיהָ, וְגַם הִיא נִשְׁבַּעַת וְנוֹטֶלֶת הַשְּׁאָר.

וְכֵן אִם הָיָה עָלָיו שְׁטַר חוֹב:

אִם הָיָה הַחוֹב קוֹדֵם — גּוֹבֶה בַּעַל חוֹב תְּחִלָּה;

וְאִם הַכְּתֻבָּה קָדְמָה — גּוֹבָה הָאִשָּׁה בַּתְּחִלָּה, וְהַנִּשְׁאָר לְבַעַל חוֹב.

ב בַּמֶּה דְּבָרִים אֲמוּרִים? כְּשֶׁהָיְתָה הַקַּרְקַע שֶׁבָּאוּ לִגְבּוֹת מִמֶּנָּה קְנוּיָה לוֹ בִּשְׁעַת נִשּׂוּאִים וּבִשְׁעָה שֶׁלָּוָה הוּא;

שֶׁהַדִּין נוֹתֵן, שֶׁכָּל הַקּוֹדֵם בִּשְׁטָר תְּחִלָּה זָכָה תְּחִלָּה.

אֲבָל אִם נָשָׂא נָשִׁים זוֹ אַחַר זוֹ וְלָוָה, בֵּין קֹדֶם נִשּׂוּאִין בֵּין אַחַר נִשּׂוּאִין, וְאַחַר שֶׁנָּשָׂא וְלָוָה קָנָה קַרְקַע — כֻּלָּן חוֹלְקִין כְּאֶחָד;

שֶׁשִּׁעְבּוּד כֻּלָּן כְּאֶחָד בָּא, שֶׁבְּשָׁעָה שֶׁקָּנָה הָיָה מְשֻׁעְבָּד לַכֹּל, וְאֵין כָּאן דִּין קְדִימָה.

ג וְכֵן אִם הָיָה זְמַן הַכְּתֻבּוֹת וְהַשְּׁטָרוֹת כֻּלָּן יוֹם אֶחָד אוֹ שָׁעָה אַחַת, בְּמָקוֹם שֶׁכּוֹתְבִין שָׁעוֹת — חוֹלְקִין כְּאֶחָד, שֶׁאֵין שָׁם קוֹדֵם.

וּלְעוֹלָם, כָּל שֶׁקָּדַם וְזָכָה בִּמְטַלְטְלִין כְּדֵי חוֹבוֹ אוֹ כְּדֵי כְתֻבָּתָה — אֵין מוֹצִיאִין מִיָּדוֹ, שֶׁאֵין דִּין קְדִימָה בִּמְטַלְטְלִין.

ד מִי שֶׁגֵּרֵשׁ אֶת אִשְׁתּוֹ וְעָלָיו שְׁטַר חוֹב, וּבָא בַּעַל חוֹב וְהָאִשָּׁה לִגְבּוֹת, וְהָיוּ לוֹ מָעוֹת וְקַרְקַע כְּדֵי הַחוֹב וְהַכְּתֻבָּה — בַּעַל חוֹב נוֹטֵל מָעוֹת, וְהָאִשָּׁה נוֹטֶלֶת כְּתֻבָּתָהּ מִן הַקַּרְקַע.

all that is due her. Indeed, even if there is nothing left for her at all, this order should be followed.

3. This ruling follows the opinion of ben Nanas in the above-mentioned *mishnah*. It involves a reversal of opinion for the Rambam, who, in his Commentary on the Mishnah favored the view of the other Sages.

4. This refers to a situation where the property owned by the estate is sufficient to cover all the obligations. Otherwise, the creditor takes precedence over the widows, as explained in Halachot 4-5 (*Maggid Mishneh*).

5. If one of the wives or creditors did not wait for the formal deposition of the estate's property, but took possession of some of the movable property on his or her own initiative, they are allowed to retain possession. For in contrast to landed property, the ownership of movable property is not a matter of public knowledge. Hence a creditor does not know whether another creditor preceded him, and therefore no creditor is given the right to collect his due from such property.

As reflected in the rulings of the *Tur* and the *Shulchan Aruch* (*Even HaEzer* 102:2), this ruling applies only when the movable property was not acquired together with and via the acquisition of landed property (*kinyan agav*). In the latter situation, the ownership of the movable property also becomes public knowledge, and therefore the order in which the liens were established is significant.

The Ramah quotes the opinion of the Mordechai, who states that, in the latter instance, if one of the widows seizes possession of the property, it should be expropriated from her.

6. For it was money that he gave him.

7. For a woman's *ketubah* did not require an outlay of money on her part. A woman

If all [the husband] possesses is land that is not of sufficient value to settle both debts, and neither [his divorcee nor his creditor] has a prior claim to this land, it should be given [toward the payment of the debt owed to] the creditor. If any [land] remains [after the settlement of the debt], it should be given to the divorcee. If nothing remains, the divorcee must yield to the creditor. [The rationale is that] the creditor suffered a loss; he [lent] money [to the husband]. The woman, by contrast, did not lose anything. For more than a man desires to marry, a woman desires to be married.

5. Similarly, if a man dies leaving a widow and a creditor, and land to which neither of them has a prior claim, the widow must yield to the creditor, and he collects the debt owed him first.

6. Since the *geonim* ordained[8] that a woman and a creditor may collect their due from movable property, and as is well known, no creditors are given precedence with regard to movable property[9] [the following rules apply]. If the husband did not leave enough movable property to settle both accounts, the creditor is allowed to collect the entire debt [owed him] first. If anything remains [after the settlement of the debt] for the wife to receive [by virtue of] her *ketubah*, it should be given to her. If nothing remains, the wife must yield.

7. [The following rule applies when] *nichsei tzon barzel* were recorded in a woman's *ketubah* and she claims that they were lost or taken by her husband. With regard to *nichsei tzon barzel*, a woman is regarded like any other creditor.[10]

Therefore, she is required to take an oath that she did not take possession of them, give them away or forego the obligation [to her husband]. Afterwards, she receives a share in the estate together with the other creditors.

8. When a person who has many wives and who dies or divorces them when none of them has a claim of higher priority to his property than the others, and his holdings are not of sufficient value to pay them each the money due them by virtue of their *ketubot*, how are his holdings divided? If his holdings are sufficiently valuable to provide only the wife with the *ketubah* of the least value, or if they are less valuable than that, all of his wives divide [his holdings] equally.

If his holdings are more valuable than that, they should be divided equally to provide the wife with [the money due her by virtue of] the *ketubah* of the least value. Afterwards, the remainder is divided among the remaining wives according to the same pattern.

What is implied? [To explain by example:] A man was married to four wives. The *ketubah* of the first was for 400 [*zuz*], that of the second for

וְאִם אֵין לוֹ אֶלָּא קַרְקַע שֶׁאֵין בָּהּ כְּדֵי לִגְבוֹת לִשְׁנֵיהֶם, וְלֹא הָיָה בָּהּ דִּין קְדִימָה — נוֹתְנִין אוֹתוֹ לְבַעַל חוֹב.

וְאִם נִשְׁאַר לָאִשָּׁה כְּלוּם — תִּטֹּל, וְאִם לָאו — תִּדָּחֶה מִפְּנֵי בַעַל חוֹב.

שֶׁהֲרֵי בַּעַל חוֹב הִפְסִיד וְהוֹצִיא מָעוֹתָיו, וְהָאִשָּׁה לֹא חָסְרָה דָבָר; שֶׁיּוֹתֵר מִשֶּׁהָאִישׁ רוֹצֶה לִשָּׂא, אִשָּׁה רוֹצָה לְהִנָּשֵׂא.

ה וְכֵן מִי שֶׁמֵּת וְהִנִּיחַ אִשָּׁה וּבַעַל חוֹב וְקַרְקַע שֶׁאֵין בָּהּ דִּין קְדִימָה — הָאִשָּׁה נִדְחֵית מִפְּנֵי בַּעַל חוֹב, וְהוּא גוֹבֶה חוֹבוֹ תְּחִלָּה.

ו וְכֵיוָן שֶׁתִּקְּנוּ הַגְּאוֹנִים, שֶׁתִּגָּבֶה הָאִשָּׁה וּבַעַל חוֹב מִן הַמִּטַּלְטְלִין, וְהַדָּבָר יָדוּעַ שֶׁאֵין דִּין קְדִימָה בְּמִטַּלְטְלִין, אִם לֹא הִנִּיחַ מִטַּלְטְלִין כְּדֵי לִתֵּן לִשְׁנֵיהֶם — נוֹתְנִין לְבַעַל חוֹב כָּל חוֹבוֹ תְּחִלָּה;

וְאִם נִשְׁאַר לָאִשָּׁה מַה שֶּׁתִּטֹּל בִּכְתֻבָּתָהּ — תִּטֹּל, וְאִם לָאו — תִּדָּחֶה.

ז הָיוּ כְּתוּבִין בִּכְתֻבָּתָהּ נִכְסֵי צֹאן בַּרְזֶל, וְטָעֲנָה שֶׁאָבְדוּ אוֹ שֶׁלְּקָחָם הַבַּעַל — הֲרֵי הִיא בְּנִכְסֵי צֹאן בַּרְזֶל שֶׁלָּהּ כִּשְׁאָר בַּעֲלֵי חוֹבוֹת,

וְנִשְׁבַּעַת שֶׁלֹּא לָקְחָה אוֹתָן וְלֹא נָתְנָה וְלֹא מָחֲלָה, וְחוֹלֶקֶת עִם בַּעֲלֵי חוֹבוֹת.

ח מִי שֶׁמֵּת אוֹ גֵרֵשׁ, וְיֵשׁ לוֹ נָשִׁים רַבּוֹת, וְאֵין שָׁם דִּין קְדִימָה, וְאֵין לוֹ כְּדֵי כָּל הַכְּתֻבּוֹת — כֵּיצַד הֵן חוֹלְקוֹת?

רוֹאִים: אִם כְּשֶׁיֵּחָלֵק הַמָּמוֹן עַל מִנְיַן הַנָּשִׁים, יַגִּיעַ לַפְּחוּתָה שֶׁבָּהֶן כְּדֵי כְּתֻבָּתָהּ אוֹ פָחוֹת — חוֹלְקוֹת בְּשָׁוֶה;

וְאִם הָיָה הַמָּמוֹן יוֹתֵר עַל זֶה — חוֹלְקִים מִמֶּנּוּ כְּדֵי שֶׁיַּגִּיעַ לַפְּחוּתָה שֶׁבָּהֶן כְּשִׁעוּר כְּתֻבָּתָהּ, וְחוֹזְרוֹת וְחוֹלְקוֹת אֶת הַמּוֹתָר בֵּין הַנּוֹתָרוֹת עַל דֶּרֶךְ הָרִאשׁוֹן.

כֵּיצַד? מִי שֶׁהָיָה נָשׂוּי אַרְבַּע נָשִׁים, כְּתֻבָּתָהּ שֶׁל רִאשׁוֹנָה אַרְבַּע מֵאוֹת, וְשֶׁל שְׁנִיָּה

always relies on the fact that she will ultimately be able to collect the money due her by virtue of her *ketubah* from the landed property in her husband's estate (*Ketubot* 86a). Different laws apply with regard to her dowry, however, for there she did make an outlay of money and
or goods.

8. See Chapter 16, Halachah 7, and notes which explain that this ordinance of the *geonim* was accepted in many communities and therefore, it must be respected. Nevertheless, it does not have the same legal power as an ordinance instituted by the Sages of the Talmud.

9. See the notes on Halachah 3 with regard to a *kinyan agav*.

10. The term *nichsei tzon barzel* refers to property that the woman brought to the household, for which the husband obligated himself to pay a fixed value. In this instance, since the woman, like a creditor, gave up something of value, she is considered on a higher level of precedence than usual.

300, that of the third for 200, and that of the first for 100. The total sum is thus 1000 [*zuz*]. [The following rules apply] if he divorces all of them or dies. If his holdings are worth 400 [*zuz*] or less, they divide his holdings equally, and each receives 100 or less. If his holdings are worth 800 [it would be improper to divide them equally]. For if they were divided equally, the fourth wife would receive 200 [*zuz*], and [the money due her by virtue of] her *ketubah* is only 100.

What is done instead? 400 [*zuz*] are set aside and divided equally, each receiving 100. Thus, the fourth wife has received [the full amount due her by virtue of] her *ketubah* and she withdraws [from the suit]. Thus, 400 [*zuz*] are left for three wives, each of whom has already received 100 *zuz*]. If the 400 were divided equally among the three of them [it would be unfair]. For the third wife would receive 233 and [the amount due her by virtue of] her *ketubah* was only 200. Therefore, 300 [*zuz*] are separated from the 400, and these are divided equally among the three. Thus, the third wife receives her 200 and withdraws [from the suit]. There remain two wives and 100 *[zuz]*. This sum is divided equally between the first and second wife. Thus, the first and second wife each received 250 *zuz*; the third wife received 200; and the fourth wife, 100. This pattern of allocation is followed even when there are 100 [wives].[11]

9. A person who guarantees the value of a woman's *ketubah* is not obligated to pay [her the money due her in the event that her husband's holdings are not sufficient if he dies or divorces her]. [This applies] even when he affirmed his commitment with a contractual act.[12] [The rationale is that] his [intent is to] perform a mitzvah,[13] and he did not cause the woman to lose anything.[14]

If, however, a person guarantees the *ketubah* of his son and affirms his commitment with a contractual act,[15] he is obligated to pay. For a father will make a binding commitment on behalf of his son and decide to obligate himself.

A person who underwrites a *ketubah*, by contrast, is obligated to pay, even though he did not affirm his commitment with a contractual act. What is meant by a person who underwrites a *ketubah*? One who tells a woman: "Marry this man. I will give [the money for] this *ketubah*." If, however, he says: "I will guarantee this *ketubah*," "I will pay this *ketubah*," "I am obligated for it" or the like, he is not liable unless he is the father [of the groom].

---

11. This pattern is also followed in the allocation of a person's holdings when they are not sufficient to pay the debts he owes, as explained in *Hilchot Malveh V'Loveh*, Chapter 20. The Ra'avad differs with the Rambam's approach and follows the minority view that the Rambam cites in that source, which maintains that the money should be divided proportionately. The Rambam's view is followed by most other *Rishonim* (Rashi,

שָׁלֹשׁ מֵאוֹת, וְשֶׁל שְׁלִישִׁית מָאתַיִם, וְשֶׁל רְבִיעִית מֵאָה, נִמְצָא הַכֹּל אֶלֶף, וְגֵרֵשׁ כֻּלָּן אוֹ מֵת:

אִם הִנִּיחַ אַרְבַּע מֵאוֹת אוֹ פָחוֹת — חוֹלְקוֹת בְּשָׁוֶה, וְכָל אַחַת נוֹטֶלֶת מֵאָה אוֹ פָחוֹת. הִנִּיחַ שְׁמוֹנֶה מֵאוֹת — אִם תֵּחָלֵק בֵּין כֻּלָּן בְּשָׁוֶה, נִמְצֵאת הָרְבִיעִית נוֹטֶלֶת מָאתַיִם, וַהֲרֵי אֵין בִּכְתֻבָּתָהּ אֶלָּא מֵאָה.

אֶלָּא כֵּיצַד עוֹשִׂין? לוֹקְחִין אַרְבַּע מֵאוֹת זוּז וְחוֹלְקִין אוֹתָן בֵּינֵיהֶן בְּשָׁוֶה מֵאָה מֵאָה, נִמְצֵאת הָרְבִיעִית נָטְלָה כְּדֵי כְּתֻבָּתָהּ וְהָלְכָה לָהּ.

נִשְׁאַר כָּאן אַרְבַּע מֵאוֹת זוּז וְשָׁלֹשׁ נָשִׁים, שֶׁבְּיַד כָּל אַחַת מִשָּׁלָשְׁתָּן מֵאָה זוּז. אִם תֵּחָלֵק הָאַרְבַּע מֵאוֹת בֵּין שְׁלָשְׁתָּן בְּשָׁוֶה, נִמְצָא הַשְּׁלִישִׁית נוֹטֶלֶת מָאתַיִם וּשְׁלֹשִׁים וְשָׁלֹשׁ וּשְׁלִישׁ, וַהֲרֵי אֵין בִּכְתֻבָּתָהּ אֶלָּא מָאתַיִם.

לְפִיכָךְ לוֹקְחִין מֵאַרְבַּע הַמֵּאוֹת שָׁלֹשׁ מֵאוֹת, וְחוֹלְקִין בֵּין שְׁלָשְׁתָּן בְּשָׁוֶה, שֶׁנִּמְצֵאת הַשְּׁלִישִׁית שֶׁנָּטְלָה מָאתַיִם שֶׁלָּהּ וְהָלְכָה לָהּ.

נִשְׁאַר כָּאן מֵאָה וּשְׁתֵּי נָשִׁים. חוֹלְקִין אֶת הַמֵּאָה בְּשָׁוֶה בֵּין רִאשׁוֹנָה וּשְׁנִיָּה. נִמְצָא בְּיַד הָרִאשׁוֹנָה מָאתַיִם וַחֲמִשִּׁים, וְכֵן בְּיַד הַשְּׁנִיָּה, וְנִמְצָא בְּיַד הַשְּׁלִישִׁית מָאתַיִם, וּבְיַד הָרְבִיעִית מֵאָה.

וְעַל דֶּרֶךְ זוֹ חוֹלְקוֹת לְעוֹלָם, אֲפִלּוּ הֵן מֵאָה.

ט הֶעָרֵב לְאִשָּׁה בִּכְתֻבָּתָהּ — אַף־עַל־פִּי שֶׁקָּנוּ מִיָּדוֹ, אֵינוֹ חַיָּב לְשַׁלֵּם; שֶׁמִּצְוָה עָשָׂה, וַהֲרֵי לֹא חָסְרָה כְּלוּם.

וְאִם עָרֵב שֶׁל כְּתֻבַּת בְּנוֹ הוּא, וְקָנוּ מִיָּדוֹ — חַיָּב לְשַׁלֵּם; שֶׁהָאָב בִּגְלַל בְּנוֹ מְשַׁעְבֵּד עַצְמוֹ וְגוֹמֵר וּמַקְנֶה.

וְקַבְּלָן שֶׁל כְּתֻבָּה — חַיָּב לְשַׁלֵּם, אַף־עַל־פִּי שֶׁלֹּא קָנוּ מִיָּדוֹ. וְאֵי זֶה הוּא קַבְּלָן? זֶה שֶׁאָמַר לְאִשָּׁה: הִנָּשְׂאִי לָזֶה, וַאֲנִי נוֹתֵן כְּתֻבָּה זוֹ. אֲבָל אִם אָמַר לָהּ: הֲרֵינִי עָרֵב כְּתֻבָּה זוֹ, אֲנִי פּוֹרֵעַ כְּתֻבָּה זוֹ, אֲנִי חַיָּב בָּהּ, וְכַיּוֹצֵא בָּזֶה — פָּטוּר, אֶלָּא אִם כֵּן הָיָה אָבִיו.

Rabbenu Yitzchak Alfasi, the Rashba and Rabbenu Asher) and is accepted by the *Shulchan Aruch* (*Even HaEzer* 96:18).

12. *Bava Batra* 174b explains that the guarantor is not serious about his commitment. He feels that the couple needs only a small push to get married, and that is his intent, rather than making a serious financial commitment. Even a contractual act, which in other contexts serves as an indication of seriousness of purpose, is not sufficient in this instance.

The Ra'avad and the *Tur* (*Even HaEzer* 102) differ, and maintain that if a guarantor affirms his commitment with a contractual act, he is liable. The *Shulchan Aruch* (*Even HaEzer* 102:6) quotes the Rambam's view, while the Ramah cites that of the Ra'avad.

13. I.e., he brought about the marriage between the couple.

14. As can be deduced from the Rambam's wording, the *Maggid Mishneh* states that if a person guarantees a woman's *nedunyah* (the goods she brought to the household), his commitment is binding. For in this instance, the woman did give up something of value.

15. In this instance as well, the Ra'avad and the *Tur* differ and hold the father liable, even

When a person divorces a wife [whose *ketubah* has been underwritten in the above fashion], he must first take a vow[16] that she is forbidden to derive benefit from him. Only then may she collect her *ketubah* from the underwriter or the [husband's] father, if he guaranteed it. [This precaution was instituted,] lest the husband remarry her,[17] and thus the two will [have acquired] the property of [the underwriter] through subterfuge.

10. Similarly, a person who consecrates his property and then divorces his wife must take a vow that she is forbidden to derive benefit from him. Only then may she collect [the money due her by virtue of her *ketubah*] from the person who redeems the property from the Temple treasury.[18] [This precaution was instituted,] lest the two attempt to deceive the Temple treasury.[19]

When, however, a person divorces his wife, and she comes to collect [the money due her by virtue of her *ketubah*] from the [property that was sold to] purchasers, he is not required to take a vow that she is forbidden to derive benefit from him. Instead, she must take the oath required of her, and then she [is entitled to] collect [her due]. If afterwards she desires, she may return to her husband. For the purchasers know that the property was under lien to the *ketubah* of a woman, and they caused themselves the loss by taking property that was under such a lien.

11. When a husband sold his property, and afterwards the woman agreed to [her husband's] act and wrote the purchaser: "I have no claim against you," she may, nevertheless, collect [the money due her by virtue of her *ketubah* by expropriating this property].[20] [This applies] even when she affirmed [her commitment] with a contractual act.[21] [The rationale is] that she wrote this [statement to the purchaser] only so that there will not be strife between her and her husband. She can [therefore excuse herself], saying: "I was [merely intending] to please my husband."[22]

[A different rule applies, however, when the purchaser] enters into an agreement with the woman that she foregoes her lien on this property [before purchasing it from her husband]. If this agreement is affirmed with a contractual act, and afterwards the husband sells the property [to him], [the woman is not entitled to] expropriate this property.[23]

Similarly, [a woman is not entitled to expropriate property sold by her husband in the following circumstance]. Her husband sold a property [on a previous occasion, and at that time] asked his wife to write the purchaser, "I have no claim to this property," and the woman refused, causing the

הַמְגָרֵשׁ אֶת אִשְׁתּוֹ — יַדִּירֶנָּה הֲנָאָה וְאַחַר כָּךְ תִּפָּרַע כְּתֻבָּתָהּ מִן הַקַּבְּלָן אוֹ מֵאָבִיו, אִם הָיָה עָרֵב;

שֶׁמָּא יַחֲזִירֶנָּה, וְנִמְצְאוּ עוֹשִׂין קְנוּנְיָא עַל נְכָסָיו שֶׁל זֶה.

י וְכֵן הַמַּקְדִּישׁ נְכָסָיו וְגֵרֵשׁ אֶת אִשְׁתּוֹ — יַדִּירֶנָּה הֲנָאָה וְאַחַר כָּךְ תִּפָּרַע מִן הַפּוֹדֶה מִיַּד הַהֶקְדֵּשׁ; שֶׁמָּא יַעֲשׂוּ קְנוּנְיָא עַל הַהֶקְדֵּשׁ.

אֲבָל הַמְגָרֵשׁ אֶת אִשְׁתּוֹ וּבָאָה לִטְרֹף מִן הַלָּקוֹחוֹת — אֵין מְחַיְּבִין אוֹתוֹ לְהַדִּירָהּ, אֶלָּא נִשְׁבַּעַת וְטוֹרֶפֶת.

וְאִם רָצְתָה, תַּחֲזֹר לְבַעְלָהּ.

שֶׁכְּבָר יָדְעוּ הַלָּקוֹחוֹת שֶׁיֵּשׁ עָלָיו כְּתֻבַּת אִשָּׁה, וְהֵם הִפְסִידוּ עַל עַצְמָם שֶׁלָּקְחוּ נְכָסִים שֶׁתַּחַת שִׁעְבּוּדָהּ.

יא הַבַּעַל שֶׁמָּכַר נְכָסָיו, וְאַחַר כָּךְ כָּתְבָה אִשְׁתּוֹ לַלּוֹקֵחַ: דִּין וּדְבָרִים אֵין לִי עִמְּךָ, וְהִסְכִּימָה לְמַעֲשָׂיו — אַף־עַל־פִּי שֶׁקָּנוּ מִמֶּנָּה, הֲרֵי זוֹ טוֹרֶפֶת;

שֶׁלֹּא כָתְבָה לוֹ אֶלָּא שֶׁלֹּא תִהְיֶה בֵּינָה לְבֵין בַּעְלָהּ קְטָטָה, וְיֵשׁ לָהּ לוֹמַר: נַחַת רוּחַ עָשִׂיתִי לְבַעְלִי.

אֲבָל אִם קָנוּ מִיַּד הָאִשָּׁה תְּחִלָּה שֶׁאֵין לָהּ שִׁעְבּוּד עַל מָקוֹם זֶה, וְאַחַר כָּךְ מָכַר אוֹתוֹ הַבַּעַל — אֵינָהּ טוֹרֶפֶת אוֹתוֹ.

וְכֵן אִם מָכַר הַבַּעַל, וְאָמַר לְאִשְׁתּוֹ לִכְתֹּב לַלּוֹקֵחַ: דִּין וּדְבָרִים אֵין לִי עִמְּךָ, וְלֹא כָתְבָה וְלֹא

---

16. Moreover, this vow must be taken *al da'at rabbim*, based on the judgement of the public, and it thus cannot be nullified (*Shulchan Aruch, Even HaEzer* 102:7).

17. I.e., after the woman collected the money due her by virtue of her *ketubah* from him.

18. The woman may not collect the money due her by virtue of her *ketubah* from the property while it is the possession of the Temple treasury. After it is redeemed, however, she may collect her due from the property. The person who redeems the property must, however, be advised that the property is on lien to a woman's *ketubah*. (See *Hilchot Malveh V'Loveh* 18:7; *Hilchot Arachin VaCharamin* 7:14-15.)

19. I.e., the woman will collect her husband's property because it is on lien on her *ketubah*. Afterwards, she will remarry her husband, and he will be able to use his property, because of his rights as the woman's husband.

20. The sale is valid, however, until the woman seeks to claim the property. If, by contrast, the husband sells property that belonged to the woman, or property from which she was designated to collect the money due her by virtue of her *ketubah*, the sale is nullified immediately (*Maggid Mishneh*). (See *Hilchot Mechirah* 30:3.)

21. Note the Ramah (*Even HaEzer* 90:17), who states that if the woman received money from the purchaser, her commitment is binding.

22. I.e., the woman is saying that her commitment was not sincere and was made only to satisfy her husband.

23. Since she entered into the agreement with the purchaser before her husband made the sale, she cannot excuse herself by saying that she made her statements only to please her husband.

sale to be nullified.[24] [If,] afterwards, the husband sells [property] - whether the same field he had sold previously or another field - to another person, and after the husband's sale the woman agreed, [made a commitment] that she has no claim to this field and affirmed it with a contractual act, she may not expropriate it. For she cannot say, "I did this [merely] to please my husband," since on the previous occasion, when she did not want [to waive her rights], she did not follow her husband's desires.

12. [The above ruling is also relevant in the following situation.] A man had two wives. He sold a field, and the purchaser had entered into a contractual act with one of [the husband's] wives, waiving her lien to this field in a manner in which the agreement was effective and the woman no longer had the privilege of claiming, "I did this [merely] to please my husband." Afterwards, the husband died or divorced both his wives.

The second wife may expropriate the property from the purchaser, for she did not enter into any agreement with him. The first wife may then expropriate [the property] from the second wife, for she had a prior claim to it, and she waived her lien only with regard to the purchaser [and not with regard to anyone else]. When the property comes into the possession of the first [wife], the purchaser may expropriate it from her, since she made an agreement with him. [The second wife can then expropriate it from the purchaser,] and the cycle continues until they reach a compromise among themselves.[25]

13. [In the event of her husband's death,] a widow - regardless of whether she was widowed from *erusin* or *nisu'in* - may take the oath [required of her], sell land belonging to her husband and collect [the money due her by virtue of] her *ketubah*. [The sale may be carried out] in a court of expert judges, or in a court whose judges are not expert,[26] provided it consists of three trustworthy men who are knowledgeable with regard to the evaluation of land. The responsibility for the sale falls on the estate belonging to the heirs.[27] A divorcee, by contrast, may sell [her ex-husband's property] only in a court of expert judges.[28]

Whenever a woman has property sold in court, she must have it sold after a public announcement has been made. In the laws of loans,[29] the guidelines for the sale [of property] will be explained. When, by contrast, a woman sells

---

24. The *Maggid Mishneh* questions the reason for this phrase. When this law is cited in the *Tur* and the *Shulchan Aruch* (*Even HaEzer* 90:17), this phrase is omitted. Nevertheless, based on the Rambam's Commentary on the Mishnah (*Ketubot* 10:5), the *Ma'aseh Rokeach* maintains that, according to the Rambam, a sale must have been nullified in order for the woman's commitment to be binding later on.

25. A three-way compromise would obviously be most desirable. Nevertheless, any compromise between two of the three parties that causes one to renounce his right to expropriate the property is sufficient to stop the cycle (*Chelkat Mechokek* 100:26).

הִסְכִּימָה לְמַעֲשָׂיו, וְנִפְסַד הַמֶּכֶר, וְחָזַר הַבַּעַל וּמָכַר לְאִישׁ אַחֵר, בֵּין אוֹתָהּ שָׂדֶה בֵּין שָׂדֶה אַחֶרֶת, וְאַחַר שֶׁמָּכַר הַבַּעַל הִסְכִּימָה לְמַעֲשָׂיו, וְקָנוּ מִיָּדָהּ שֶׁאֵין לָהּ שִׁעְבּוּד עַל שָׂדֶה זוֹ — אֵינָהּ יְכוֹלָה לִטְרוֹף;
שֶׁאֵינָהּ יְכוֹלָה לוֹמַר 'נַחַת רוּחַ עָשִׂיתִי לְבַעֲלִי', שֶׁהֲרֵי בָּרִאשׁוֹנָה, כְּשֶׁלֹּא רָצְתָה, לֹא הָלְכָה בִּרְצוֹן בַּעְלָהּ.

יב מִי שֶׁהָיוּ לוֹ שְׁתֵּי נָשִׁים, וּמָכַר אֶת שָׂדֵהוּ, וְקָנוּ מִיַּד הָרִאשׁוֹנָה שֶׁאֵין לָהּ שִׁעְבּוּד עַל שָׂדֶה זוֹ וְאֵינָהּ טוֹרֶפֶת אוֹתוֹ מִן הַלּוֹקֵחַ, וְהָיָה הַקִּנְיָן מוֹעִיל שֶׁאֵינָהּ יְכוֹלָה לִטְעֹן בּוֹ 'נַחַת רוּחַ עָשִׂיתִי לְבַעֲלִי', וְאַחַר כָּךְ מֵת הַבַּעַל אוֹ גֵּרֵשׁ שְׁתֵּיהֶן —
הַשְּׁנִיָּה מוֹצִיאָה מִיַּד הַלּוֹקֵחַ, שֶׁהֲרֵי לֹא קָנוּ מִיָּדָהּ לַלּוֹקֵחַ,
וְהָרִאשׁוֹנָה מוֹצִיאָה מִיַּד הַשְּׁנִיָּה, מִפְּנֵי שֶׁהִיא קָדְמָה, וְלֹא הֵסִירָה שֶׁעְבּוּדָהּ אֶלָּא מֵעַל הַלּוֹקֵחַ.
וּכְשֶׁתַּחֲזֹר הַשָּׂדֶה לָרִאשׁוֹנָה, חוֹזֵר הַלּוֹקֵחַ וּמוֹצִיאָהּ מִיָּדָהּ, שֶׁהֲרֵי קָנוּ לוֹ. וְחוֹזְרוֹת חֲלִילָה, עַד שֶׁיַּעֲשׂוּ פְּשָׁרָה בֵּינֵיהֶן.

יג אַלְמָנָה, בֵּין מִן הַנִּשּׂוּאִין בֵּין מִן הָאֵרוּסִין, נִשְׁבַּעַת וּמוֹכֶרֶת מִקַּרְקַע בַּעְלָהּ וְנִפְרַעַת כְּתֻבָּתָהּ בֵּין בְּבֵית דִּין מֻמְחִין בֵּין בְּבֵית דִּין שֶׁאֵינָן מֻמְחִין.
וְהוּא, שֶׁיִּהְיוּ הַשְּׁלֹשָׁה הָאֲנָשִׁים נֶאֱמָנִין וְיוֹדְעִין בְּשׁוּמַת הַקַּרְקַע.
וְאַחֲרָיוּת הַמֶּכֶר עַל נִכְסֵי יְתוֹמִים.
אֲבָל הַגְּרוּשָׁה לֹא תִמְכּוֹר אֶלָּא בְּבֵית דִּין מֻמְחִין.
וְכָל הַמּוֹכֶרֶת בְּבֵית דִּין — לֹא תִמְכּוֹר אֶלָּא בְּהַכְרָזָה.
וּבְהִלְכוֹת הַלְוָאָה יִתְבָּאֵר מִשְׁפַּט מְכִירַת בֵּית דִּין הֵיאַךְ הִיא.

26. Our Sages understood that the necessity to pursue judicial proceedings is a cause of hardship and embarrassment for women. They felt that rather than subject his wife to such distress, any husband would willingly grant her the right to collect the money due her by virtue of her *ketubah* by selling his property without appearing in court (*Ketubot* 97b).

Therefore, rather than require her to take the matter to a formal court, they enabled her to resolve the issue by having the property evaluated by three acquaintances who possess the qualities mentioned above. Although these men would not be considered capable of participating in an ordinary court, an exception was made in this case. If, however, the widow has already remarried, she is required to undergo the ordinary judicial procedure.

27. I.e., should the property be expropriated by a creditor of the deceased, his heirs must reimburse the purchaser.

28. With regard to a divorcee, by contrast, our Sages (*op. cit.*) felt that her ex-husband would not be disturbed by her being subjected to hardship when this is necessary to protect his own interests.

Although there are *Rishonim* who maintain that the provision made for a widow also applies to a divorcee, the Rambam's ruling is accepted by the *Shulchan Aruch* (*Even HaEzer* 103:3).

29. See *Hilchot Malveh V'Loveh* 12:8,10, which explains that public announcements that a property will be sold are made daily for thirty days (or on Mondays and Thursdays, for a period of sixty days).

property without the participation of the court,[30] a public announcement [of the sale] need not be made. It is, nevertheless, necessary [to consult] with three trustworthy men who are knowledgeable with regard to the evaluation [of property].

14. [The following rules apply when] a widow sells [her husband's] landed property privately in order to collect the money due her by virtue of her *ketubah*:[31] If she sold the property at its proper value, the sale is binding.[32] [All that is necessary is for] her to take the oath required of widows after the sale.[33]

The above applies when she sells the property to another individual. If she takes it as her own after evaluating it, her act is of no significance.[34] [This applies even when] she had announced the sale of the property [and received no better offer].

15. [In the above situation,] if the woman's *ketubah* was for 200 [*zuz*], and she sold [property] that was worth 100 [*zuz*] for 200,[35] or property that was worth 200 for 100,[36] she has received the value of her *ketubah* and is no longer owed anything. She must, however, take the oath required of a widow.

If her *ketubah* was for 100 [*zuz*] and she sold [property] worth 101 [*zuz*] for 100, the sale is nullified.[37] [This applies] even if she says, "I will [accept the loss and] return the [outstanding] *dinar* to the heirs."

16. If her *ketubah* was for 400 *zuz* and she sold [four pieces of property], three that were each worth 100 [*zuz*] for 100 [*zuz*] each, and one that was worth 101 *zuz* for 100 [*zuz*] - the final sale is nullified, but the [first three] are all binding.

17. A woman has the privilege of selling [the rights to] her *ketubah* or giving [them] as a present.[38] If her husband dies or divorces her, [the purchaser or the recipient] is entitled to come and collect [the money due her by virtue of her *ketubah*].[39] If she dies in the lifetime of her husband or [after his death, but] before she takes the oath [required of widows], he is not entitled to anything.

18. Although a woman sold [the rights to] a portion of her *ketubah*, used them as security [for a loan] or gave them as a present, she may sell landed property belonging to her husband and collect the remainder of [the money due her by virtue of] her *ketubah*. [This sale may be carried out] in a court of three expert judges or through three trustworthy men.

30. I.e., without the participation of a formal court.
31. I.e., without even the participation of the three acquaintances mentioned in the previous halachah.

אֲבָל הַמּוֹכֶרֶת שֶׁלֹּא בְּבֵית דִּין — אֵינָהּ צְרִיכָה הַכְרָזָה. וְאַף־עַל־פִּי־כֵן צָרִיךְ שְׁלֹשָׁה שֶׁהֵם נֶאֱמָנִים וְיוֹדְעִים בְּשׁוּמָא.

יד אַלְמָנָה שֶׁמָּכְרָה קַרְקַע בִּכְתֻבָּתָהּ בֵּינָהּ לְבֵין עַצְמָהּ, אִם מָכְרָה שָׁוֶה בְּשָׁוֶה — מִכְרָהּ קַיָּם, וְנִשְׁבַּעַת שְׁבוּעַת אַלְמָנָה אַחַר שֶׁמָּכְרָה.
וְהוּא, שֶׁמָּכְרָה לְאַחֵר; אֲבָל אִם שָׁמָה לְעַצְמָהּ — לֹא עָשְׂתָה כְּלוּם, וַאֲפִלּוּ הִכְרִיזָה.

טו הָיְתָה כְּתֻבָּתָהּ מָאתַיִם, וּמָכְרָה שָׁוֶה מֵאָה בְּמָאתַיִם, אוֹ שָׁוֶה מָאתַיִם בְּמֵאָה — נִתְקַבְּלָה כְּתֻבָּתָהּ וְאֵין לָהּ כְּלוּם, וּבִלְבַד שֶׁתִּשָּׁבַע שְׁבוּעַת אַלְמָנָה.
הָיְתָה כְּתֻבָּתָהּ מֵאָה, וּמָכְרָה שָׁוֶה מֵאָה וְדִינָר בְּמֵאָה — מִכְרָהּ בָּטֵל, וַאֲפִלּוּ אָמְרָה: אֲנִי אַחֲזִיר אֶת הַדִּינָר לַיּוֹרְשִׁים.

טז הָיְתָה כְּתֻבָּתָהּ אַרְבַּע מֵאוֹת זוּז, וּמָכְרָה לָזֶה בְּמָנֶה וְלָזֶה בְּמָנֶה שָׁוֶה בְּשָׁוֶה, וְלָאַחֲרוֹן שָׁוֶה מֵאָה וְדִינָר בְּמֵאָה — שֶׁל אַחֲרוֹן בָּטֵל, וְשֶׁל כֻּלָּם קַיָּם.

יז יֵשׁ לְאִשָּׁה לִמְכֹּר כְּתֻבָּתָהּ אוֹ לִתְּנָהּ בְּמַתָּנָה.
אִם מֵת הַבַּעַל אוֹ גֵרְשָׁהּ — יָבוֹא הַלָּהּ וְיִטֹּל; וְאִם מֵתָה הִיא בְּחַיֵּי בַּעְלָהּ אוֹ קֹדֶם שֶׁנִּשְׁבְּעָה — אֵין לוֹ כְּלוּם.

יח הֲרֵי שֶׁמָּכְרָה מִקְצָת כְּתֻבָּתָהּ, אוֹ מִשְׁכְּנָה מִקְצָת כְּתֻבָּתָהּ, אוֹ נָתְנָה לְאַחֵר מִקְצָת כְּתֻבָּתָהּ — מוֹכֶרֶת מִקַּרְקַע בַּעְלָהּ וְתִגְבֶּה הַשְּׁאָר בֵּין בְּבֵית דִּין מֻמְחִין בֵּין בִּשְׁלֹשָׁה נֶאֱמָנִים.

32. Although the *Shulchan Aruch* (*Even HaEzer* 103:1) appears to favor the Rambam's view, it does mention other opinions that differ.
33. It would appear that the Rambam requires her merely to take the oath required of all widows before collecting the money due her by virtue of her *ketubah*. In this instance, the *Shulchan Aruch* (*Even HaEzer* 103:4) requires the woman to take an additional oath, stating that she did not sell the property for less than its worth.
34. The *Maggid Mishneh* and *Chelkat Mechokek* 103:11 state that, according to the Rambam, if the woman has the property evaluated by three trustworthy men who are knowledgeable with regard to the value of property, she is allowed to take the property as her own. Other opinions differ and maintain that this is possible only when the property is evaluated by a proper Rabbinical court.
35. When selling the property, the woman is considered to be the agent of the heirs, and the profit belongs to them and not to her (*Ketubot* 98b).
36. In this instance, the woman must accept the loss herself, because she took property that was worth the full value of her *ketubah*.
37. For she has no right to sell any property that is worth more than her *ketubah*.
38. The requirement of a *ketubah* was instituted so that the husband will not consider divorce a light matter, because of the severity of the financial obligation that will result. This remains true even if the woman does not receive the money herself.
39. As reflected in the continuation of the Rambam's words, the woman must first take

[A woman] may sell [portions of her husband's property] many times. [These sales may be carried out] in a court of three expert judges or through three trustworthy men who are knowledgeable with regard to the evaluation of property.

19. When a woman sells [the rights to] her *ketubah* - whether to another person or to her husband - she does not forfeit the other privileges of her *ketubah*.[40] [As such,] if she has a son, [and she dies before her husband does,] he inherits the worth of her *ketubah* - [although it] was sold from his father's estate - in addition to his share [in the estate, as will be explained].[41]

If, by contrast, a woman waives her *ketubah* in favor of her husband, she forfeits all the privileges associated with her *ketubah*. [Her husband] is not required to provide her even with her subsistence.[42]

The waiver of a *ketubah* [in favor of the woman's husband] need not [be affirmed by] a contractual act nor [be observed by] witnesses,[43] just as the forfeiture [of any obligations] does not require [affirmation by] a contractual act nor [the observation of] witnesses. Through one's words alone [the forfeiture is binding], provided the statement is made seriously, [in a manner that] can be relied upon, rather than facetiously, as a joke, or rhetorically.[44]

CHAPTER EIGHTEEN

1. A widow is entitled to receive support from the estate [inherited by her husband's] heirs as long as she remains a widow, unless she collects [the money due her by virtue of] her *ketubah*.[1] From the time she demands payment for her *ketubah* in court, however, she is no longer entitled to receive her subsistence.[2]

Similarly, if she sold [the rights to] her entire *ketubah*, gave them as security [for a loan] or made her *ketubah* an *ipotiki* for another person - i.e., she told him "Collect your debt from here" - she is not entitled to receive her

the oaths required of her as if she herself were to collect the money due her by virtue of her *ketubah*.
40. I.e., her rights to support, medical attention and the like.
41. Chapter 19, Halachah 2.
42. From the Rambam's wording, it appears that the woman is not entitled to her subsistence even during her husband's lifetime, while they remain married. (Note Chapter 10, Halachah 10, which states that if a woman waives her *ketubah* in favor of her husband, he must write her a new *ketubah*.) The *Shulchan Aruch* (*Even HaEzer* 93:9) quotes the opinion that even during the husband's lifetime, he is not required to support his wife, but appears to favor the view of other *Rishonim* (Rashi, the Ramban and

וּמוֹכֶרֶת לִכְתֻבָּתָהּ אֲפִלּוּ פְעָמִים רַבּוֹת בֵּין בְּבֵית דִּין בֵּין בִּשְׁלֹשָׁה נֶאֱמָנִים וְיוֹדְעִים שׁוּמַת הַקַּרְקַע.

יט הַמּוֹכֶרֶת כְּתֻבָּתָהּ, בֵּין לַאֲחֵרִים בֵּין לְבַעְלָהּ, לֹא אִבְּדָה שְׁאָר תְּנָאֵי כְּתֻבָּה.

וְאִם הָיָה לָהּ בֵּן זָכָר — יוֹרֵשׁ כְּנֶגֶד הַכְּתֻבָּה הַזֹּאת שֶׁנִּמְכְּרָה מִנִּכְסֵי אָבִיו יוֹתֵר עַל חֶלְקוֹ, כְּדִין תְּנַאי זֶה.

אֲבָל הַמּוֹחֶלֶת כְּתֻבָּתָהּ לְבַעְלָהּ — אִבְּדָה כָּל תְּנָאֵי כְּתֻבָּתָהּ, וַאֲפִלּוּ מְזוֹנוֹת אֵין לָהּ עָלָיו.

וּמוֹחֶלֶת כְּתֻבָּתָהּ אֵינָהּ צְרִיכָה קִנְיָן וְלֹא עֵדִים; כִּשְׁאָר כָּל הַמּוֹחֲלִים, שֶׁאֵינָן צְרִיכִין לֹא עֵדִים וְלֹא קִנְיָן, אֶלָּא בִּדְבָרִים בִּלְבַד.

וְהוּא, שֶׁיִּהְיוּ דְבָרִים שֶׁהַדַּעַת סוֹמֶכֶת עֲלֵיהֶן, וְלֹא יִהְיוּ דִבְרֵי שְׂחוֹק וְהִתּוּל אוֹ דִבְרֵי תֵמַהּ, אֶלָּא בְּדַעַת נְכוֹנָה.

פֶּרֶק שְׁמוֹנָה עָשָׂר

א אַלְמָנָה נִזּוֹנֶת מִנִּכְסֵי יוֹרְשִׁין כָּל זְמַן אַלְמְנוּתָהּ עַד שֶׁתִּטֹּל כְּתֻבָּתָהּ.

וּמִשֶּׁתִּתְבַּע כְּתֻבָּתָהּ בְּבֵית דִּין, אֵין לָהּ מְזוֹנוֹת.

וְכֵן אִם מָכְרָה כְּתֻבָּתָהּ כֻּלָּהּ, אוֹ מִשְׁכְּנָה כְתֻבָּתָהּ, אוֹ עָשְׂתָה כְּתֻבָּתָהּ אַפּוֹתֵיקֵי לְאַחֵר, וְהוּא שֶׁתֹּאמַר לוֹ: פֹּה תִּגְבֶּה חוֹבְךָ —

---

the Rashba), who grant a woman the right to support during her husband's lifetime in such a situation.

See also Chapter 19, Halachah 12, which discusses another consequence of a woman's waiver of her *ketubah* in favor of her husband.

43. In contrast to their role with regard to marriage and divorce, in financial matters witnesses are necessary only to confirm what happened. Their presence does not make a transaction or a commitment binding, nor hinder it from becoming so. (See *Hilchot Mechirah* 5:9.)

44. See *Hilchot Mechirah* 5:11-13.

1. Rashi (*Gittin* 35a) states that as long as the widow does not contemplate remarriage, she is showing honor to her deceased husband, and therefore our Sages ordained that she should receive her subsistence from his estate. However, by demanding payment of the money due her by virtue of her *ketubah*, she indicates that she is seeking to remarry. From that time onward, her deceased husband's estate is no longer obligated to support her.

The option whether to continue receiving her subsistence or to demand payment of the money due her by virtue of her *ketubah* is hers. The heirs cannot compel her to receive the money due her by virtue of her *ketubah* and cease giving her support (*Ketubot* 95b; *Maggid Mishneh*).

2. The *Beit Shmuel* 93:13 explains that if the woman asks for payment of the money due her by virtue of her *ketubah*, and the heirs refuse to pay her or are unable to do so, she is still entitled to support.

subsistence from the heirs.[3] [The above applies] whether these exchanges were made in a court of expert judges or outside a court, or whether they were made in her husband's lifetime or after his death.

If, however, she sold [the rights to] only a portion of her *ketubah*, she is entitled to receive her subsistence.[4] When a widow becomes consecrated[5] [to a new husband], she forfeits [her rights to receive] subsistence [from her deceased husband's estate].[6]

2. Just as the woman receives her subsistence from her husband's estate after his death, so, too, is she granted a wardrobe, household utensils and [the right to continue] living in the dwelling she lived in during her husband's lifetime.[7] She may continue to make use of the pillows, spreads, servants and maidservants that she made use of during her husband's lifetime.

If the dwelling falls, the heirs are not required to rebuild it.[8] [Even] if the widow asked, "Allow me to rebuild it at my own expense," she is not granted this option. Similarly, she may not repair it, nor have the walls sealed [and painted].

She must [continue to] dwell in it in the condition it [was in her husband's passing], or she must leave [and find other accommodations]. Should the heirs sell the dwelling in which a widow is living, their deed is of no consequence.

3. If the dwelling [in which she was living fell] or her husband had been renting a dwelling, [the estate must] provide her with a dwelling appropriate to her social standing. Similarly, her subsistence and the wardrobe given her are granted according to her social standing.

If her husband's social standing exceeded her own, she is granted the above according to his social standing. For a woman's [social standing] ascends according to [her husband's] social standing, but does not descend [according to his]. [This applies] even after his death.

4. [The widow is given her subsistence as a member of] the household at large. What is the intent of [the latter term]? When five people who would each require a *kav* of food when they eat alone [live] in the same house and eat together [their needs are reduced]. Four *kabbim* will be sufficient for them. The same applies with regard to other necessary household [supplies].

Therefore, if a widow says: "I will not leave my father's house. Ascertain the amount of support I deserve for my subsistence and give it to me there," the heirs have the right to tell her: "If you desire to dwell with us, you will receive [a full measure of] support. If not, we will give you only your share as a member of the household at large."

3. In all these instances, it is considered as if she has already collected the money due her by virtue of her *ketubah*.

בֵּין שֶׁעֲשָׂתָה אֵלּוּ בְּבֵית דִּין מַמְחִין בֵּין שֶׁלֹּא בְּבֵית דִּין, בֵּין שֶׁעֲשָׂתָה בְּחַיֵּי בַּעְלָהּ בֵּין שֶׁעֲשָׂתָה לְאַחַר מִיתַת בַּעְלָהּ — אֵין לָהּ מְזוֹנוֹת מִן הַיּוֹרְשִׁים. אֲבָל אִם מָכְרָה מִקְצָתָהּ — יֵשׁ לָהּ מְזוֹנוֹת. וּמִשֶּׁתִּתְאָרֵס הָאַלְמָנָה אָבְדָה מְזוֹנוֹתֶיהָ.

ב כְּשֵׁם שֶׁנִּזּוֹנֶת אַחַר מוֹתוֹ מִנְּכָסָיו, כָּךְ נוֹתְנִין לָהּ כְּסוּת וּכְלֵי תַשְׁמִישׁ, וְיוֹשֶׁבֶת בַּמָּדוֹר שֶׁהָיְתָה בּוֹ בְּחַיֵּי בַּעְלָהּ, וּמִשְׁתַּמֶּשֶׁת בַּכָּרִים וּכְסָתוֹת בָּעֲבָדִים וּבַשְּׁפָחוֹת שֶׁנִּשְׁתַּמְּשָׁה בָּהֶן בְּחַיֵּי בַּעְלָהּ.
נָפַל הַמָּדוֹר — אֵין הַיּוֹרְשִׁין חַיָּבִין לִבְנוֹתוֹ.
וְאִם אָמְרָה: הַנִּיחוּ לִי וַאֲנִי אֶבְנֶנּוּ מִשֶּׁלִּי — אֵין שׁוֹמְעִין לָהּ.
וְכֵן לֹא תְחַזֵּק בִּדְקוֹ וְלֹא תִּטְחֶה אוֹתוֹ, אֶלָּא תֵּשֵׁב בּוֹ כְּמָה שֶׁהוּא אוֹ תֵּצֵא.
וְיוֹרְשִׁין שֶׁמָּכְרוּ מָדוֹר אַלְמָנָה — לֹא עָשׂוּ וְלֹא כְלוּם.

ג נָפַל הַבַּיִת אוֹ שֶׁלֹּא הָיָה לְבַעְלָהּ בַּיִת אֶלָּא בְּשָׂכָר — נוֹתְנִין לָהּ מָדוֹר לְפִי כְּבוֹדָהּ.
וְכֵן מְזוֹנוֹתֶיהָ וּכְסוּתָהּ — לְפִי כְּבוֹדָהּ.
וְאִם הָיָה כְבוֹד הַבַּעַל גָּדוֹל מִכְּבוֹדָהּ — נוֹתְנִין לָהּ לְפִי כְּבוֹדוֹ; מִפְּנֵי שֶׁעוֹלָה עִמּוֹ, וְאֵינָהּ יוֹרֶדֶת אֲפִלּוּ לְאַחַר מִיתָה.

ד בִּרְכַּת הַבַּיִת מְרֻבָּה. כֵּיצַד?
חֲמִשָּׁה שֶׁהָיָה מְזוֹנוֹת כָּל אֶחָד מֵהֶן קַב בְּשֶׁיֹּאכַל לְבַדּוֹ, אִם הָיוּ חֲמִשְׁתָּן בְּבַיִת אֶחָד וְאוֹכְלִין בְּעֵרוּב — מַסְפִּיק לָהֶן אַרְבַּע קַבִּין. וְהוּא הַדִּין לִשְׁאָר צָרְכֵי הַבַּיִת.
לְפִיכָךְ, אַלְמָנָה שֶׁאָמְרָה: אֵינֶנִּי זָזָה מִבֵּית אָבִי, פִּסְקוּ לִי מְזוֹנוֹת וּתְנוּ לִי שָׁם — יְכוֹלִין הַיּוֹרְשִׁין לוֹמַר לָהּ: אִם אַתְּ אֶצְלֵנוּ — יֵשׁ לָךְ מְזוֹנוֹת, וְאִם לָאו — אֵין אָנוּ נוֹתְנִים לָךְ אֶלָּא כְּפִי בִּרְכַּת הַבַּיִת.

---

4. In this instance, however, the heirs have the right to pay her the remainder of the money due her by virtue of her *ketubah*, and thus prevent her from continuing to collect her subsistence from the estate. If this provision were not granted, every widow would collect all the money due her by virtue of her *ketubah* except for the final *p'rutah*, and continue to receive support (Rabbenu Asher, quoted by the *Shulchan Aruch, Even HaEzer* 93:10.).

5. In the present age, this law applies even when the woman has merely become engaged to a new husband (*Beit Yosef, Even HaEzer* 93, as quoted by the Ramah, *Even HaEzer* 93:7).

6. Even if she has not collected the money due her by virtue of her *ketubah*.

7. Nevertheless, the dwelling becomes the property of the heirs, and they are also entitled to live there. The widow is, however, granted a place of dignity in the household (*Maggid Mishneh*; Ramah, *Even HaEzer* 94:1).

8. Nor are they required to give her a room in it if they rebuild it themselves. Instead, they may rent her a different dwelling, as stated in the following halachah.

If she explains [that she desires not to live with them] because she is young, and they are young [and the situation would be immodest, her claim is accepted]. [The heirs are required] to provide her with support sufficient for her as she lives alone, while she lives in her father's home.

[Any money] remaining from [the funds granted for] the support of a widow or from her wardrobe belongs to the heirs.[9]

5. [The following laws apply when] a widow becomes sick. If she requires medical treatment that is of an undefined nature, it is considered as support for her subsistence, and the heirs must provide her with it.[10] If, however, she requires medical treatment of a limited nature, the treatment [should be paid for by deducting it] from [the money due her by virtue of] her *ketubah*.

If she is taken captive, the heirs are not required to redeem her. [This applies] even if she is a *yevamah* [and it is a mitzvah for her late husband's brother to marry her]. [Indeed,] even when she was taken captive during her husband's lifetime [and he was thus obligated to redeem her], if he dies while she is in captivity, there is no obligation to redeem her from his estate. Instead, she must be redeemed from her private funds, or she must collect [the money due her by virtue of] her *ketubah* and redeem herself.

6. When a widow dies, her late husband's heirs are responsible for her burial. If, however, she had already taken the oath required of a widow [before collecting the money due her by virtue of her *ketubah*], her heirs inherit her *ketubah*, and they are required to bury her, and not her late husband's heirs.[11]

[Her late husband's] heirs are entitled to the income [from the work] of the widow. If the heirs tell the widow, "Take the income you generate in exchange for [receiving] your subsistence," their words are of no substance. If, however, she desires such an arrangement, she is given this prerogative.[12]

7. All the household tasks that a wife performs on behalf of her husband, a widow must perform on behalf of his heirs, with the exception of pouring them drinks, making their beds and washing their face, hands and feet.[13]

8. An ownerless article discovered by a widow and the benefit that accrues from the property that the woman brought to her husband's household belong to the woman herself; the heirs [to her husband's estate] have no right to them at all.[14]

9. The Ra'avad differs with the Rambam and maintains that these funds are granted to the widow, but the *Shulchan Aruch* (*Even HaEzer* 95:5) follows the Rambam's ruling.
10. The heirs may, however, fix a price with the physician for the widow's treatment, and then she becomes responsible for the financial burden (*Ketubot* 52b; *Shulchan Aruch, Even HaEzer* 79:2).

וְאִם הָיְתָה טוֹעֶנֶת: מִפְּנֵי שֶׁהִיא יַלְדָּה וְהֵם יְלָדִים — נוֹתְנִין לָהּ מְזוֹנוֹת הַמַּסְפִּיקִין לָהּ לְבַדָּהּ וְהִיא בְּבֵית אָבִיהָ.

וּמוֹתַר מְזוֹנוֹת הָאַלְמָנָה וּמוֹתַר הַכְּסוּת — לַיּוֹרְשִׁין.

ה אַלְמָנָה שֶׁחָלְתָה: אִם צְרִיכָה לִרְפוּאָה שֶׁאֵין לָהּ קִצְבָּה — הֲרֵי זוֹ כִּמְזוֹנוֹת וְיוֹרְשִׁין חַיָּבִין בָּהּ;

וְאִם הִיא צְרִיכָה רְפוּאָה שֶׁיֵּשׁ לָהּ קִצְבָּה — הֲרֵי זוֹ מִתְרַפְּאָה מִכְּתֻבָּתָהּ. נִשְׁבֵּת — אֵין הַיּוֹרְשִׁין חַיָּבִין לִפְדּוֹתָהּ.

אֲפִלּוּ הָיְתָה יְבָמָה, וַאֲפִלּוּ נִשְׁבֵּת בְּחַיֵּי בַּעֲלָהּ וּמֵת וְהִיא בַּשִּׁבְיָה — אֵין חַיָּבִין לִפְדּוֹתָהּ מִנְּכָסָיו;

אֶלָּא נִפְדֵּית מִשֶּׁל עַצְמָהּ, אוֹ תִּטֹּל כְּתֻבָּתָהּ וְתִפְדֶּה עַצְמָהּ.

ו מֵתָה הָאַלְמָנָה — יוֹרְשֵׁי הַבַּעַל חַיָּבִין בִּקְבוּרָתָהּ.

וְאִם נִשְׁבְּעָה שְׁבוּעַת אַלְמָנָה וְאַחַר כָּךְ מֵתָה — יוֹרְשֶׁיהָ יוֹרְשִׁין כְּתֻבָּתָהּ וְהֵן חַיָּבִין בִּקְבוּרָתָהּ, אֲבָל לֹא יוֹרְשֵׁי הַבַּעַל.

מַעֲשֵׂה יְדֵי הָאַלְמָנָה — לַיּוֹרְשִׁין.

וְיוֹרֵשׁ שֶׁאָמַר לָאַלְמָנָה: טְלִי מַעֲשֵׂה יָדַיִךְ בִּמְזוֹנוֹתַיִךְ — אֵין שׁוֹמְעִין לוֹ; אֲבָל הִיא שֶׁרָצְתָה בָּזֶה — שׁוֹמְעִין לָהּ.

ז וְכָל מְלָאכוֹת שֶׁהָאִשָּׁה עוֹשָׂה לְבַעְלָהּ, אַלְמָנָה עוֹשָׂה לַיְתוֹמִים, חוּץ מִמְּזִיגַת הַכּוֹס וְהַצָּעַת הַמִּטָּה וְהַרְחָצַת פָּנָיו יָדָיו וְרַגְלָיו.

ח מְצִיאַת הָאַלְמָנָה וּפֵרוֹת נְכָסִים שֶׁהִכְנִיסָה לַבַּעַל — לְעַצְמָהּ, וְאֵין לַיּוֹרֵשׁ בָּהֶם כְּלוּם.

11. The rationale is, as stated in Chapter 12, Halachah 4, that the burial of the woman was granted her in return for the husband's right to inherit her *ketubah*. If her heirs can collect the money due her by virtue of her *ketubah*, they are required to bury her. If not, since the money for her *ketubah* remains within the husband's estate, his heirs are responsible for her burial.

Although this is the Rambam's view, the Ra'avad and Rabbenu Nissim do not accept it. The *Shulchan Aruch* (*Even HaEzer* 89:4) mentions the Rambam's view and states that it was not accepted by the other authorities.

12. The same laws apply with regard to her husband during his lifetime, as stated in Chapter 12, Halachah 4.

13. These tasks are acts of endearment, appropriate only for a wife to her husband.

14. Although a husband is granted these rights (Chapter 12, Halachah 3), his heirs are not. The husband is granted the rights to the objects his wife finds so that strife will not arise between them. That rationale is not considered with regard to his heirs (*Ketubot* 96a).

With regard to the rights to her property: as mentioned in Chapter 12, Halachah 4, our Sages associated the rights to a woman's property with her redemption from captivity. Since the heirs are not obligated to redeem her, they are not entitled to this privilege.

9. The property that [a woman brought to the household as] her *nedunyah* may be taken by the woman without her having to take an oath.[15] The heirs to her husband's estate have no claim with regard to it, except if the *nichsei tzon barzel* have increased in value during her husband's lifetime. [In this instance,] the increase belongs to the husband[16] [and is given to his heirs].

[Even] if a widow dies without taking the oath [required of her], her heirs inherit her *nedunyah*, even if it is *nichsei tzon barzel*. If, however, it has increased in value, the increase must go to her husband's heirs.

10. When a woman seizes movable property [belonging to her husband's estate, so that she can sell it and use the money] for her subsistence, the property should not be removed from her possession.[17] [This applies regardless of] whether she took possession of the movable property during her husband's lifetime or afterwards. Even if she takes possession of a talent of gold[18] [it is not removed from her possession].

Instead, the court documents what she has taken into her possession and defines the amount she should be given for her subsistence. Calculations are made, and she is allowed to derive her subsistence from [the property] in her possession until she dies or until she is no longer entitled to support for her subsistence. [At that time,] the heirs are granted the remainder.

11. Similarly, if she took possession of movable property during her husband's lifetime [to provide] for [the money due her by virtue of] her *ketubah*, she may collect [the money due her] from this [property after he dies]. If, however, she took possession of it after her husband's death [to provide] for [the money due her by virtue of] her *ketubah*, she may not collect [her due] from it.[19]

12. [20]The *geonim* ordained that a woman may collect [the money due her by virtue of] her *ketubah* and every obligation due her as a stipulation of her *ketubah* from the movable property [in her husband's estate]. Based on this

---

15. The property that a woman brings to her household belongs to her. Her husband has merely the right to derive benefit from it; he is not the owner. With regard to this property, she is treated like any of the other creditors of the estate, and no oath is required of her.
16. *Nichsei tzon barzel* is property that the husband has had evaluated, and it is the value of the article for which he obligates himself or his estate. Nevertheless, if the property itself exists, it is given to the woman. If the property has increased in value, however, the husband - and therefore his heirs - are entitled to the increase.

The *Maggid Mishneh* and the *Shulchan Aruch* (*Even HaEzer* 96:1) state that this law refers only in an instance where the property that the woman brought to the household - or an article exchanged for it - is still intact. Otherwise, she is required to take an oath before collecting the money paid in lieu of the property.
17. Although the movable property in her husband's estate is not under lien for her subsistence, it is not taken away from her if she takes possession of it. As the *Kessef*

ט וְהַנְּכָסִים עַצְמָם שֶׁהֵם נְדוּנְיָתָהּ — נוֹטֶלֶת אוֹתָן בְּלֹא שְׁבוּעָה,
וְאֵין לַיּוֹרְשִׁים בָּהֶם דִּין לְעוֹלָם, אֶלָּא אִם כֵּן הוֹתִירוּ בְּחַיֵּי הַבַּעַל וְהָיוּ נִכְסֵי צֹאן בַּרְזֶל
שֶׁהַמּוֹתָר לַבַּעַל.
וְאִם מֵתָה הָאַלְמָנָה בְּלֹא שְׁבוּעָה — יוֹרְשֶׁיהָ יוֹרְשִׁים נְדוּנְיָתָהּ, אַף־עַל־פִּי שֶׁהוּא נִכְסֵי צֹאן
בַּרְזֶל.
וְאִם הָיָה בָּהֶן מוֹתָר — הַמּוֹתָר לְיוֹרְשֵׁי הַבַּעַל.

י אַלְמָנָה שֶׁתָּפְסָה מִטַּלְטְלִין כְּדֵי שֶׁתִּזּוֹן מֵהֶן — בֵּין שֶׁתָּפְסָה מֵחַיִּים בֵּין שֶׁתָּפְסָה אַחַר
מוֹתוֹ, אֲפִלּוּ תָּפְסָה כִּכַּר זָהָב — אֵין מוֹצִיאִין מִיָּדָהּ;
אֶלָּא כּוֹתְבִין עָלֶיהָ בֵּית דִּין מַה שֶּׁתָּפְסָה, וּפוֹסְקִין לָהּ מְזוֹנוֹת, וּמְחַשְּׁבִין עִמָּהּ, וְהִיא
נִזּוֹנֶת מִמַּה שֶּׁבְּיָדָהּ עַד שֶׁתָּמוּת אוֹ עַד שֶׁלֹּא יִהְיוּ לָהּ מְזוֹנוֹת, וְיִקְחוּ הַיּוֹרְשִׁין אֶת
הַשְּׁאָר.

יא וְכֵן אִם תָּפְסָה מִטַּלְטְלִין בִּכְתֻבָּתָהּ בְּחַיֵּי בַּעְלָהּ, וָמֵת — גּוֹבָה מֵהֶן;
אֲבָל אִם תָּפְסָה אַחַר מוֹתוֹ לִכְתֻבָּתָהּ — אֵינָהּ גּוֹבָה מֵהֶן.

יב תִּקְּנוּ הַגְּאוֹנִים שֶׁתִּגְבֶּה הַכְּתֻבָּה וּתְנָאֵי הַכְּתֻבָּה מִן הַמִּטַּלְטְלִין.

Mishneh emphasizes, the above applies with regard to the Talmudic era. As stated in the
following halachah, it is customary at present to consider movable property as under lien
to all a husband's obligations.

    There are some *Rishonim* who differ with the Rambam and equate the provisions
for the widow's subsistence with the collection of the money due her by virtue of her
ketubah. (See the following halachah.) The *Shulchan Aruch* (*Even HaEzer* 93:20) follows
the Rambam's view.

18. I.e., a sum that will last far longer than thirty days - the length of time for which
the court sells property to provide her with her subsistence - or perhaps more than the
worth of the woman's entire *ketubah*.

19. Instead, it must be returned to the heirs.

    Tosafot (*Ketubot* 96a) explains the distinction between a woman's taking possession
of movable property to collect for her subsistence and the collection of the money due
her by virtue of her *ketubah* as follows. Our Sages ordained that a woman may collect
the money due her by virtue of her *ketubah* from property that had belonged to her
husband and was sold. Therefore, it is likely that the woman will ultimately receive
her due. As such, she is required to return the movable property. With regard to her
subsistence, however, no such provision was made. Hence, she is given an alternative, to
take possession of movable property.

    As explained in the following note, according to the *Kessef Mishneh* and others this
law describes the practices of the Talmudic age and not those of the present era.

20. *K'nesset HaGedolah* explains that, contrary to the standard published texts of the
Mishneh Torah, Halachah 12 begins here. This is not a continuation of the previous
halachah, because there is a difference with regard to the laws governing movable property
between the practices of the Talmudic age and those of the present era.

[provision], a woman may receive her subsistence from [the sale of] movable property [from her husband's estate].

Nevertheless, if her husband left movable property and she did not take possession of it, the heirs take possession of it, and they must provide her with her subsistence. She has no right to prevent them from taking possession, by saying: "Have the movable property held in the court [so that] I can derive my subsistence from it, lest it become depleted,[21] and I will have no means of support." Even if an explicit stipulation was made [by her husband at the time her *ketubah* was composed] that she could derive her subsistence from this movable property, she cannot prevent [the heirs] from taking possession of it.[22] This is the ruling that is universally followed in all courts.

13. If, however, her husband left landed property, she has the right to prevent the heirs from selling it. If they do sell it, however, she does not have the right to expropriate [the property] from the purchasers. A widow and a man's daughters may derive their subsistence only from the property that remains in his estate. [In this regard, they have no claim to property that was sold.][23]

14. If the deceased left many wives, they all have equal rights to receive their subsistence. [This applies] even when he married them one after the other. For the concept of a prior claim does not exist with regard to a claim for support.[24]

15. [The following rules apply with regard to] a widow who has an obligation to marry a *yavam*.[25] During the first three months,[26] she derives her subsistence from her deceased husband's estate.[27] If it can be determined that she is pregnant, or if it was known that she was pregnant when her husband died, she continues to derive her support [from his estate] until she gives birth. If she bears a viable child, she may continue to derive her subsistence throughout her widowhood as other women do.

If after three months have passed, it is [either] not evident that she is pregnant or she miscarries, she is not entitled to support from either her husband's estate or from her *yavam*. Instead, she must file a suit against her *yavam* either to marry her or [to free her of her obligation through] *chalitzah*.

---

21. For if the heirs sell it, the woman has no claim to the proceeds of the sale, nor may she expropriate the property from the purchasers. Similarly, if the heirs destroy the movable property, she has no claim against them. From an ethical perspective, however, the heirs are enjoined not to sell this movable property.

22. The *Chelkat Mechokek* 93:36 states that if a specific clause was included in the

לְפִיכָךְ תִּזּוֹן הָאַלְמָנָה מִן הַמִּטַּלְטְלִין אַף־עַל־פִּי שֶׁלֹּא תָפְסָה. וְאִם הִנִּיחַ בַּעְלָהּ מִטַּלְטְלִין וְלֹא תָפְסָה אוֹתָן — הַיּוֹרְשִׁין נוֹטְלִין אוֹתָן וְהֵן מַעֲלִין לָהּ מְזוֹנוֹת, וְאֵינָהּ יְכוֹלָה לְעַכֵּב עֲלֵיהֶן וְלוֹמַר: יִהְיוּ הַמִּטַּלְטְלִין מֻנָּחִין בְּבֵית דִּין עַד שֶׁאֵזּוֹן מֵהֶן, שֶׁמָּא יֹאבְדוּ וְלֹא יִהְיוּ לִי מְזוֹנוֹת.

וַאֲפִלּוּ הִתְנְתָה עָלָיו בְּפֵרוּשׁ שֶׁתִּזּוֹן מִן הַמִּטַּלְטְלִין — אֵינָהּ מְעַכֶּבֶת. וְכָזֶה דָנִין תָּמִיד בְּכָל בָּתֵּי דִינִין.

יג אֲבָל אִם הִנִּיחַ קַרְקַע — יְכוֹלָה הִיא לְעַכֵּב עֲלֵיהֶן שֶׁלֹּא יִמְכְּרוּ. וְאִם מָכְרוּ — אֵינָהּ מוֹצִיאָה מִיַּד הַלָּקוֹחוֹת; שֶׁאֵין הָאִשָּׁה וְהַבָּנוֹת נִזּוֹנוֹת אֶלָּא מִנְּכָסִים בְּנֵי חֹרִין.

יד הִנִּיחַ נָשִׁים רַבּוֹת, אַף־עַל־פִּי שֶׁנְּשָׂאָן זוֹ אַחַר זוֹ — נִזּוֹנוֹת בְּשָׁוֶה, שֶׁאֵין דִּין קְדִימָה בְּמִטַּלְטְלִין.

טו אַלְמָנָה שֶׁנָּפְלָה לִפְנֵי יָבָם:
בִּשְׁלֹשָׁה חֳדָשִׁים הָרִאשׁוֹנִים — נִזּוֹנֶת מִשֶּׁל בַּעַל.
וְאִם הֻכַּר הָעֻבָּר, וְכֵן אִם הִנִּיחָהּ מְעֻבֶּרֶת — נִזּוֹנֶת וְהוֹלֶכֶת עַד שֶׁתֵּלֵד.
יָלְדָה בֵּן שֶׁל קַיָּמָא — נִזּוֹנֶת וְהוֹלֶכֶת כָּל יְמֵי אַלְמְנוּתָהּ, כִּשְׁאָר כָּל הַנָּשִׁים.
לֹא נִמְצֵאת מְעֻבֶּרֶת אַחַר שְׁלֹשָׁה חֳדָשִׁים, אוֹ שֶׁהִפִּילָה — אֵינָהּ נִזּוֹנֶת לֹא מִשֶּׁל בַּעַל וְלֹא מִשֶּׁל יָבָם, אֶלָּא תּוֹבַעַת יְבָמָהּ לִכְנֹס אוֹ לַחֲלֹץ.

ketubah regarding this matter, although the widow cannot nullify the sale she has a right to receive her subsistence from its proceeds.

23. The Rashba states that if a clause was added to the *ketubah* specifically stating that the woman has the right to collect her subsistence from movable property after her husband's death, then she is allowed to expropriate the landed property from the purchasers (*Maggid Mishneh; Ramah, Even HaEzer* 93:21).

24. Our translation is based on manuscripts and early printings of the *Mishneh Torah*. The standard printed texts substitute "movable property" for "claim for support." Apparently, this version reached the Ra'avad who objects, and states - as is the halachah - that the principle applies with regard to landed property as well.

25. I.e., her husband died childless, and he had a brother who is commanded to marry his widow.

26. This time period is granted in order to determine whether the woman was made pregnant by her husband before he died. If three months pass without pregnancy becoming noticeable, we can assume that a child was not conceived.

27. Until she gives birth or miscarries, she is not entitled to remarry, lest she become bound by the obligation of *yibbum*. Since it is because of her husband that she may not remarry, his estate is required to provide for her (Rashi, *Yevamot* 41b).

16. If she filed a suit against her *yavam* either to marry her or [to free her of her obligation through] *chalitzah*, he appeared in court and then fled or became ill, or if the *yavam* lives overseas,[28] the woman is entitled to derive her support from the property of the *yavam* without taking any oath at all.[29]

17. If the *yavam* she was obligated to marry is a minor,[30] she is not entitled to receive her support from him until he comes of age and resembles other *yevamim*.[31]

18. Should a person designate a portion of land to be used for support of his wife after his death, by saying: "This particular place will be for [my wife's] support,"[32] he has granted her additional rights with regard to her support.

If the income [from this land] is less than the support due her, she is entitled [to collect] the remainder from the other portions of his estate. If the income [from those portions of land] is less than the support due her, she is entitled to the entire amount.

If, however, he told her, "Your support will come from this particular place," and she remained silent,[33] her sole source of support is the income from that particular place. [Her husband] has specificied [the source for] her support.

19. There are those who have ruled that when a widow comes to the court to ask for support she should be allotted support without requiring her to take an oath.[34] This ruling should not be followed; they have misunderstood [the situation, erroneously associating it with that of] a woman whose husband left on an overseas journey.[35]

My teachers[36] ruled that she should not be allotted support until she takes an oath in court.[37] For she is coming to collect from property in the possession of heirs, and anyone who collects property in the possession of heirs may do so only after an oath has been taken. My own conception [also] follows [this approach], and it is proper to rule accordingly.

---

28. The *Maggid Mishneh* states that the latter two clauses - that the *yavam* became sick or that he lived overseas - apply also only if the *yavam* had previously appeared in court. If, however, he has never appeared in court, he is not under any obligation.

The *Shulchan Aruch* (*Even HaEzer* 160:1) follows the opinion of Rabbenu Asher, who states that the *yavam* is obligated to support her in the latter instances only when he consented to marry her. If he desired to perform *chalitzah*, he is under no obligation to her.

29. There is no need for her to take an oath that the *yavam* had not given her property. For since they have not established a relationship, such suspicions are unfounded (*Ketubot* 107b).

30. Who should not perform the mitzvah of *yibbum* until he attains majority.

31. Since he is forbidden to marry her, he is not required to support her. Nor is she entitled

טז תָּבְעָה יְבָמָהּ לִכְנֹס אוֹ לַחֲלֹץ, וְעָמַד בְּבֵית דִּין, וּבָרַח אוֹ שֶׁחָלָה, אוֹ שֶׁהָיָה הַיָּבָם בִּמְדִינַת הַיָּם — הֲרֵי זוֹ נִזּוֹנֶת מִשֶּׁל יָבָם בְּלֹא שְׁבוּעָה כְּלָל.

יז נָפְלָה לִפְנֵי יָבָם קָטָן — אֵין לָהּ מְזוֹנוֹת עַד שֶׁיִּגְדַּל וְיִהְיֶה כִּשְׁאָר הַיְבָמִין.

יח מִי שֶׁיִּחֵד קַרְקַע לְאִשְׁתּוֹ בִּמְזוֹנוֹתֶיהָ בִּשְׁעַת מִיתָה, וְאָמַר: יִהְיֶה מָקוֹם פְּלוֹנִי לִמְזוֹנוֹת — הֲרֵי רִבָּה לָהּ מְזוֹנוֹת.
וְאִם הָיָה שְׂכָרוֹ פָּחוֹת מִמְּזוֹנוֹת הָרְאוּיוֹת לָהּ — נוֹטֶלֶת הַשְּׁאָר מִשְּׁאָר נְכָסִים;
וְאִם הָיָה שְׂכָרוֹ יוֹתֵר מִן הָרָאוּי לָהּ — נוֹטֶלֶת הַכֹּל.
אֲבָל אִם אָמַר לָהּ: יִהְיֶה בְּמָקוֹם פְּלוֹנִי בִּמְזוֹנוֹתֶיהָ, וְשָׁתְקָה — אֵין לָהּ אֶלָּא פֵּרוֹת אוֹתוֹ מָקוֹם בִּלְבַד, שֶׁהֲרֵי קָצַץ לָהּ מְזוֹנוֹת.

יט אַלְמָנָה שֶׁבָּאָה לְבֵית דִּין לִתְבֹּעַ מְזוֹנוֹת — יֵשׁ מִי שֶׁהוֹרָה, שֶׁפּוֹסְקִין לָהּ מְזוֹנוֹת וְאֵין מַשְׁבִּיעִים אוֹתָהּ.
וְאֵין רָאוּי לִסְמֹךְ עַל הוֹרָאָה זוֹ, מִפְּנֵי שֶׁנִּתְחַלֵּף לוֹ הַדָּבָר בְּאִשָּׁה שֶׁהָלַךְ בַּעְלָהּ לִמְדִינַת הַיָּם.
וְרַבּוֹתַי הוֹרוּ, שֶׁאֵין לָהּ מְזוֹנוֹת מִבֵּית דִּין עַד שֶׁתִּשָּׁבַע;
שֶׁהֲרֵי זוֹ בָּאָה לְהִפָּרַע מִנִּכְסֵי יְתוֹמִים, וְכָל הַנִּפְרָע מִנִּכְסֵי יְתוֹמִים — לֹא תִּפָּרַע אֶלָּא בִּשְׁבוּעָה.
וְלָזֶה דַּעְתִּי נוֹטָה, וְכֵן רָאוּי לָדוּן.

to support from her husband's estate. *Yevamot* 41b says that it is as if she is penalized from heaven.
32. The Rambam is referring to statements made by a dying man with regard to the allocation of his property. If these statements are observed by witnesses, they are binding. This practice, referred to as a *matnat sh'chiv me'ra* (the oral will of a dying man) is described in *Hilchot Zechiyah UMatanah* 8:2).
33. I.e., since it is possible that the woman will suffer a loss, she has the right to protest. If, however, she remained silent, we assume that she accepted her husband's decision.
34. The reference is to Rabbenu Yitzchak Alfasi, who ruled this way in a responsum. His opinion is favored also by the Ra'avad, the Ramban, the Rashba and Rabbenu Asher. *Ketubot* 105a states that the woman should take an oath "at the end and not at the beginning." They explain that this refers to a woman whose husband has died. The woman should take the oath when she comes to collect the money due her by virtue of her *ketubah*, and not when she comes asking for support. The *Shulchan Aruch* (*Even HaEzer* 93:19) appears to favor this view, and the Ramah states that it should be followed.
35. See Chapter 12, Halachah 16.
36. Rav Yosef Migash.
37. They interpret *Ketubot* (*loc. cit.*) to be referring to a woman whose husband traveled overseas. She should not take an oath at the outset - i.e., when she comes to collect her subsistence - but rather at the end, if her husband comes and requires this of her. See Chapter 12, Halachah 21.

20. When a woman comes to the court to collect support for her subsistence, an oath is administered to her at the outset. The property is then sold without being publicized, and an allotment is made for her subsistence.[38]

Similarly, she is entitled to sell property for her subsistence without involving a court of expert judges; three trustworthy individuals are sufficient, and the sale need not be publicized. Similarly, if she sells property by herself for its appropriate value to provide for her subsistence, the sale is binding.[39] When the heirs come and require her to take an oath, she must take the oath.

21. How much property is sold to provide for her subsistence? Enough to provide for her support for six months,[40] but not for longer than that. The sale is made on the condition that the purchaser give the widow an allotment for food every thirty days.[41] Afterwards, another parcel of property is sold for another six months.

The property should continue to be sold in this manner until all that remains from the estate is [the money due her by virtue of] her *ketubah*. She should collect this sum and complete her dealings with the court.[42]

22. When the court allots a widow support for her subsistence, they do not reckon the money she earns until the heirs come and demand it. [If such a demand is made,] and the woman has earned money, they are entitled to it. If not, they have no further claim against her.

I maintain [however] that if the heirs are below majority, the court should make a reckoning with the widow with regard to [her income].[43] Just as she is allotted a subsistence, the court declares that her income [should be given to the orphans].

23. When a widow does not manifest possession of her *ketubah*, she is not granted money for her subsistence. [The rationale is that] perhaps she waived her *ketubah* [in favor of her husband] or sold it or gave it as security [for a loan].[44]

Even when the heir[s] do not issue such a claim against her, the court makes this claim on their behalf and tells her: "Bring your *ketubah*, take the required oath and collect [the money for] your subsistence." [This law applies] unless

The dissenting authorities refute this interpretation, explaining that it is far more reasonable to require an oath of a woman when her husband is alive than after his death, for after his death it is very likely that the woman will soon take an oath to collect her *ketubah*.

38. In contrast to the sale of property so that the woman can collect the money due her by virtue of her *ketubah* (Chapter 17, Halachah 13), in this instance the sale need not be publicized. The rationale is that the woman needs the money for her subsistence immediately and should not be required to wait.

39. Rabbenu Chanan'el and the Ramban differ with the Rambam on this point. Although

כ אַלְמָנָה שֶׁבָּאָה לְבֵית דִּין לִתְבֹּעַ דִּין לְתְבֹּעַ דִּין מְזוֹנוֹת — מַשְׁבִּיעִין אוֹתָהּ בַּתְּחִלָּה, וּמוֹכְרִין בְּלֹא הַכְרָזָה, וְנוֹתְנִין לָהּ מְזוֹנוֹת.

וְכֵן יֵשׁ לָהּ לִמְכֹּר לִמְזוֹנוֹת שֶׁלֹּא בְּבֵית דִּין מֻמְחִין, אֶלָּא בִּשְׁלֹשָׁה אֲנָשִׁים נֶאֱמָנִים, בְּלֹא הַכְרָזָה.

וְכֵן אִם מָכְרָה לִמְזוֹנוֹת בֵּינָהּ לְבֵין עַצְמָהּ שָׁוֶה בְּשָׁוֶה — מִכְרָהּ קַיָּם.

וּכְשֶׁיָּבוֹאוּ הַיּוֹרְשִׁין לְהַשְׁבִּיעַ אוֹתָהּ — נִשְׁבַּעַת.

כא וְכַמָּה מוֹכְרִין לִמְזוֹנוֹת? כְּדֵי לָזוּן מֵהֶם שִׁשָּׁה חֳדָשִׁים, לֹא יוֹתֵר עַל זֶה. וּמוֹכְרִין עַל מְנָת שֶׁיִּהְיֶה הַלּוֹקֵחַ נוֹתֵן לָהּ מְזוֹן שְׁלֹשִׁים יוֹם. וְחוֹזֶרֶת וּמוֹכֶרֶת פַּעַם שְׁנִיָּה לְשִׁשָּׁה חֳדָשִׁים.

וְכֵן מוֹכֶרֶת וְהוֹלֶכֶת לְעוֹלָם, עַד שֶׁיִּשָּׁאֵר מִן הַנְּכָסִים כְּדֵי כְתֻבָּתָהּ, גּוֹבָה כְּתֻבָּתָהּ מִן הַשְּׁאָר וְהוֹלֶכֶת לָהּ.

כב אַלְמָנָה שֶׁפָּסְקוּ לָהּ בֵּית דִּין מְזוֹנוֹת — אֵין מְחַשְּׁבִין עִמָּהּ עַל מַעֲשֵׂה יָדֶיהָ, עַד שֶׁיָּבוֹאוּ הַיּוֹרְשִׁים וְיִתְבְּעוּהָ.

אִם מָצְאוּ לָהּ מַעֲשֵׂה יָדֶיהָ — נוֹטְלִין אוֹתוֹ, וְאִם לָאו — הוֹלְכִין לְדַרְכָּם.

וַאֲנִי אוֹמֵר, שֶׁאִם הָיוּ הַיּוֹרְשִׁים קְטַנִּים — בֵּית דִּין מְחַשְּׁבִין עִמָּהּ, וּפוֹסְקִין מַעֲשֵׂה יָדֶיהָ, כְּדֶרֶךְ שֶׁפּוֹסְקִין לָהּ מְזוֹנוֹת.

כג אַלְמָנָה שֶׁאֵין שְׁטַר כְּתֻבָּה יוֹצֵא מִתַּחַת יָדָהּ — אֵין לָהּ מְזוֹנוֹת; שֶׁמָּא מָחֲלָה כְּתֻבָּתָהּ, אוֹ מָכְרָה אוֹ מִשְׁכְּנָה אוֹתָהּ.

אַף־עַל־פִּי שֶׁלֹּא טָעַן יוֹרֵשׁ — טוֹעֲנִין אָנוּ לוֹ וְאוֹמְרִים לָהּ: הָבִיאִי כְּתֻבָּתֵיךְ וְהִשָּׁבְעִי וּטְלִי מְזוֹנוֹתַיִךְ.

---

their opinion is also mentioned by the *Shulchan Aruch* (*Even HaEzer* 93:25), it appears that the Rambam's opinion is favored.

40. In this manner, a large amount of property is sold. If a smaller amount were sold, the parcel of land would be too small to fetch a proper price.

41. I.e., the purchaser gives the widow only enough money to support herself for thirty days at a time. The rationale is that if she remarries or seeks to collect her *ketubah*, she is no longer entitled to receive support for her subsistence. Since there is the possibility that this will happen at any given time, she is given support for only a limited period of time. In the event that she remarries, the remainder of the money left from the sale is given to the heirs (Rashi, *Ketubot* 97a).

42. The *Maggid Mishneh* explains that this is simply proper advice for the woman. For she can sell all the land necessary to provide her with the money due her by virtue of her *ketubah* at one time, while to collect her subsistence she must sell the land in small parcels. If she chooses, however, she may take the latter alternative.

43. Since the heirs are orphans, the court is obligated to look after their interests. Therefore, it is obligated to ensure that the woman's earnings are given to them.

44. In all these cases, the widow is no longer entitled to receive support from her deceased's husband's estate, as stated in Chapter 12, Halachah 18.

it is not customary [in a particular locale] to compose a document recording the *ketubah*.[45]

24. [The following laws apply when] a woman and her husband traveled overseas, and she returned, claiming [her husband] died. If she desires, she is entitled to receive her subsistence from her husband's estate, as are other widows. If she desires, she may collect [the money due her by virtue of] her *ketubah*.[46]

If she claims, "My husband divorced me," her word is not accepted.[47] She is, however, entitled to derive her subsistence from his estate until she receives a sum equal to [the money due her by virtue of] her *ketubah*. [The rationale is] that if she is still his wife, she is entitled to receive her subsistence [from his holdings]. If he divorced her, she is entitled to receive [the money due her by virtue of] her *ketubah*, [provided] she manifests possession of her *ketubah*. Therefore, she may collect the support for her subsistence until she receives [the money due her by virtue of] her *ketubah*. [From this point on,] she has completed her dealings with the court.

25. [The following laws apply when] there is doubt whether a woman was divorced, and her husband died [afterwards]. She is not entitled to receive her subsistence from his estate, for property cannot be expropriated from an heir on the basis of a doubtful claim.[48] During her husband's lifetime, by contrast, she is entitled to her subsistence until she is divorced in a complete and binding manner.[49]

26. If a poor[50] widow waits two years before she sues for support - or if a rich widow waits three years - it can be assumed that she has waived her claim to support for the previous years.[51] Therefore, she is not granted support for that period. From the time she issues a claim onward, however, she is entitled to support.

If, however, she waited even one day less [before presenting her claim], she is not considered to have waived her claim, and she may collect her support for the previous years.

27. [The following rules apply when] a widow demands support for her subsistence from the heirs, and they claim to have paid her, while she claims that she did not receive payment. Until she remarries, the burden of proof is

---

45. In this instance, since the probability is that the woman would not have been given a document recording her *ketubah*, the fact that she does not have such a document in her possession is not considered detrimental to her position.
46. See Chapter 16, Halachah 31.

אֶלָּא אִם אֵין דַּרְכָּם לִכְתֹּב כְּתֻבָּה.

כד הָאִשָּׁה שֶׁהָלְכָה הִיא וּבַעְלָהּ לִמְדִינַת הַיָּם, וּבָאָה וְאָמְרָה: מֵת בַּעְלִי —
רָצְתָה — נִזּוֹנֶת כְּדִין כָּל הָאַלְמָנוֹת, רָצְתָה — נוֹטֶלֶת כְּתֻבָּה.
אָמְרָה: גֵּרְשַׁנִי בַּעְלִי — אֵינָהּ נֶאֱמֶנֶת, וְנִזּוֹנֶת מִנְּכָסָיו עַד כְּדֵי כְּתֻבָּתָהּ מִכָּל פָּנִים:
שֶׁאִם עֲדַיִן הִיא אִשְׁתּוֹ — יֵשׁ לָהּ מְזוֹנוֹת,
וְאִם גֵּרְשָׁהּ כְּמוֹ שֶׁאָמְרָה — יֵשׁ לָהּ כְּתֻבָּה, שֶׁהֲרֵי כְּתֻבָּתָהּ בְּיָדָהּ.
לְפִיכָךְ נוֹטֶלֶת מְזוֹנוֹת עַד כְּדֵי כְּתֻבָּתָהּ וְהוֹלֶכֶת לָהּ.

כה הָאִשָּׁה שֶׁהָיָה לָהּ סְפֵק גֵּרוּשִׁין וּמֵת בַּעְלָהּ — אֵינָהּ נִזּוֹנֶת מִנְּכָסָיו, שֶׁאֵין מוֹצִיאִין מִיַּד
הַיּוֹרֵשׁ מִסָּפֵק.
אֲבָל בְּחַיֵּי בַּעְלָהּ — יֵשׁ לָהּ מְזוֹנוֹת עַד שֶׁתִּתְגָּרֵשׁ גֵּרוּשִׁין גְּמוּרִין.

כו אַלְמָנָה עֲנִיָּה שֶׁשָּׁהֲתָה שְׁתֵּי שָׁנִים וְלֹא תָבְעָה מְזוֹנוֹת, אוֹ עֲשִׁירָה שֶׁשָּׁהֲתָה שָׁלֹשׁ שָׁנִים
וְלֹא תָבְעָה — וִתְּרָה,
וְאֵין לָהּ מְזוֹנוֹת בַּשָּׁנִים שֶׁעָבְרוּ, אֶלָּא מִשָּׁעָה שֶׁתְּבָעָה.
וְאִם שָׁהֲתָה פָּחוֹת מִזֶּה אֲפִלּוּ בְּיוֹם אֶחָד — לֹא וִתְּרָה, אֶלָּא תּוֹבַעַת וְנוֹטֶלֶת מְזוֹן הַשָּׁנִים
שֶׁעָבְרוּ.

כז אַלְמָנָה שֶׁתָּבְעָה מְזוֹנוֹת מִן הַיּוֹרְשִׁים, הֵם אוֹמְרִים: נָתַנּוּ, וְהִיא אוֹמֶרֶת: לֹא נָטַלְתִּי —

---

47. See *Hilchot Gerushin* 12:1.
48. Since her status is questionable, she is not entitled to support. For this is granted only to a man's wife and not to his divorcee.
49. Since divorce is dependent on the husband's initiative, as long as a woman's status is in question - and for that reason she may not marry another person - he is required to continue to support her (Rashi, *Ketubot* 97b).
50. *Ketubot* 96a mentions two years and three years, stating that the difference is between a rich widow (who can afford to wait) and a poor one; alternatively, between a brash widow (who is not embarrassed to appear in court) and a modest one (who will hesitate before coming). The Rambam does not mention the second opinion at all (although generally, when the Talmud mentions two opinions, he rules according to the second opinion), nor does the *Shulchan Aruch* (*Even HaEzer* 93:14). Rabbenu Asher and the *Chelkat Mechokek* 93:26, however, do mention the latter opinion.
51. The Rashba maintains that if, however, the woman took property as security, or if she borrowed money to be repaid with the money she will receive for her support, she is still entitled to receive the money retroactively. This opinion is cited by the *Maggid Mishneh* and the *Shulchan Aruch* (*op. cit.*).

on the orphans. [If they do not support their claim,] the widow is entitled to take a rabbinical oath and collect the money due her.[52] If she has already remarried, the burden of proof is upon her. [If she does not support her claim,] the heirs are entitled to take a rabbinic oath that they paid her [and are freed of obligation].[53]

28. The laws governing the extra sum added by the husband to the *ketubah* are the same as those governing the fundamental requirement of the *ketubah*. Therefore, if a widow demands payment of this additional amount - or sells it, waives payment of it [in favor of her husband] or gives it as security - together with the fundamental requirement of the *ketubah*, she is not entitled to support for her subsistence.

If she demanded payment for a portion and left a portion uncollected,[54] it is as if she demanded payment for a portion of the fundamental requirement of the *ketubah* and left a portion uncollected.[55]

Whenever a woman sells or waives payment of her *ketubah* without making any further specification, she is considered to have sold or waived this additional amount together with the fundamental requirement of the *ketubah*. For the term *ketubah* is universally used to refer to both these items.

CHAPTER NINETEEN

1. One of the provisions of [a woman's] *ketubah* is that her male offspring will inherit the money due their mother by virtue of her *ketubah* and the *nedunyah* she brought to the household as *nichsei tzon barzel*.[1] Afterwards, these children divide the remainder of the estate with their brothers equally.[2]

2. What is implied? A man married a woman whose *ketubah* and *nedunyah* were together valued at 1000 [*zuz*]. She bore a son, and then she died within [her husband's] lifetime. Afterwards, the man married another woman whose *ketubah* and *nedunyah* were together valued at 200 [*zuz*]. She bore a son, and then she died within [her husband's] lifetime. Afterwards, the man died, leaving an estate worth 2000 [*zuz*].

His first wife's son should inherit 1000 [*zuz*] by virtue of his mother's *ketubah*, and his second wife's son should inherit 200 [*zuz*] by virtue of his mother's *ketubah*, and the remainder they should [both] inherit and [divide] equally. Thus, the first wife's son will receive 1400 [*zuz*], and the second wife's son will receive 600 [*zuz*].

52. As long as she has not remarried, the property of her husband's estate is considered under lien to her and in her possession. Hence, she is given this privilege.

כָּל זְמַן שֶׁלֹּא נִשֵּׂאת — עַל הַיְתוֹמִים לְהָבִיא רְאָיָה, אוֹ תִּשָּׁבַע שְׁבוּעַת הֶסֵּת וְתִטֹּל;

מִשֶּׁנִּשֵּׂאת — עָלֶיהָ לְהָבִיא רְאָיָה, אוֹ יִשָּׁבְעוּ הַיּוֹרְשִׁים שְׁבוּעַת הֶסֵּת שֶׁנְּתָנוּ לָהּ.

כח דִּין תּוֹסֶפֶת כְּתֻבָּה כְּדִין הָעִקָּר.

לְפִיכָךְ, אַלְמָנָה שֶׁתָּבְעָה אוֹ מָכְרָה אוֹ מָחֲלָה אוֹ מִשְׁכְּנָה תּוֹסֶפֶת כְּתֻבָּתָהּ עִם הָעִקָּר — אֵין לָהּ מְזוֹנוֹת.

וְאִם תָּבְעָה מִקְצָת וְהִנִּיחָה מִקְצָת — הֲרֵי זוֹ כְּמִי שֶׁתָּבְעָה מִקְצָת הָעִקָּר וְהִנִּיחָה מִקְצָתוֹ.

וְכָל הַמּוֹכֶרֶת אוֹ הַמּוֹחֶלֶת סְתָם — מָכְרָה וּמָחֲלָה הַתּוֹסֶפֶת עִם הָעִקָּר; שֶׁשְּׁנֵיהֶם כְּתֻבָּה שְׁמָם בְּכָל מָקוֹם.

פֶּרֶק תִּשְׁעָה עָשָׂר

א מִתְּנָאֵי הַכְּתֻבָּה, שֶׁיִּהְיוּ בָּנִים הַזְּכָרִים יוֹרְשִׁים כְּתֻבַּת אִמָּן וּנְדוּנְיָתָהּ שֶׁהִכְנִיסָה בְּתוֹרַת נִכְסֵי צֹאן בַּרְזֶל, וְאַחַר כָּךְ חוֹלְקִין שְׁאָר הַיְרֻשָּׁה עִם אֲחֵיהֶם בְּשָׁוֶה.

ב כֵּיצַד? נָשָׂא אִשָּׁה, כְּתֻבָּתָהּ וּנְדוּנְיָתָהּ אֶלֶף, וְיָלְדָה בֵּן, וּמֵתָה בְּחַיָּיו.

וְאַחַר כָּךְ נָשָׂא אִשָּׁה אַחֶרֶת, כְּתֻבָּתָהּ וּנְדוּנְיָתָהּ מָאתַיִם, וְיָלְדָה בֵּן, וּמֵתָה בְּחַיָּיו. וְאַחַר כָּךְ מֵת הוּא, וְהִנִּיחַ אַלְפַּיִם.

בְּנוֹ מִן הָרִאשׁוֹנָה יוֹרֵשׁ אֶלֶף שֶׁבִּכְתֻבַּת אִמּוֹ, וּבְנוֹ מִן הַשְּׁנִיָּה יוֹרֵשׁ מָאתַיִם שֶׁבִּכְתֻבַּת אִמּוֹ, וְהַשְּׁאָר יוֹרְשִׁים אוֹתוֹ בְּשָׁוֶה.

נִמְצָא בְּיַד בֶּן הָרִאשׁוֹנָה אֶלֶף וְאַרְבַּע מֵאוֹת, וּבְיַד בֶּן הַשְּׁנִיָּה שֵׁשׁ מֵאוֹת.

---

53. For once she remarries, the property is considered to be in the possession of the heirs. Hence, they are given this privilege.

54. The same law applies if the widow demanded payment of the fundamental requirement of the *ketubah*, but did not demand payment for the additional amount.

55. See Halachah 1.

1. This and the laws that follow are relevant only in situations where a man has children from two different wives and he did not divorce the wives before their death. When a man's wives die before he does, he inherits their *nedunyah* and is not required to pay them the money due them by virtue of their *ketubot*. Nevertheless, our Sages ordained that a woman's children should benefit from her investment in the household and the commitment made to her. Hence, before the father's estate is divided among all the heirs, the children of each of his wives are entitled to receive the monies mentioned above.

2. Note the statements of the Ramah (*Even HaEzer* 111:16), who states that this practice

3. When does the above apply? When [the estate] is worth at least one *dinar* more than the amount [due the children by virtue of their mothers'] *ketubot*. If, however, there is not a *dinar* or more remaining [in the estate],[3] the entire estate should be divided equally [without applying the provision mentioned above].

[The rationale is that] if [the children of one of the mothers] will inherit [what is due them by virtue of] their mother's *ketubah*, [the other mother's children] will inherit [what is due them by virtue of] their mother's *ketubah*, and at least one *dinar* will not remain to be divided among the heirs, then this provision [which is of Rabbinic origin] will supersede [entirely] the equal division of the estate among the children that is required by Scriptural law.

4. The same law applies to a man who married many wives, whether one after the other or several at one time. If they have all died in his lifetime, and they have all borne male children from this man, if his estate contains at least a *dinar* more than the *ketubot* of all his wives, each of the [sets of] sons inherits the money due their mother by virtue of her *ketubah*. The remainder [of the estate] is divided equally.

5. [Should the estate not be large enough to satisfy the obligations of both *ketubot* and the additional *dinar*,] and the heirs say: "We will increase the value of our father's estate so that there will be more than a *dinar* [in addition to the value of the *ketubot*]," so that they can collect [the money due their mother by virtue of] her *ketubah*, their request is not accepted. Instead, the estate should be evaluated in court according to its value at the time of their father's death [and the decision rendered on the basis of this figure].

Even if the value of the estate increases or decreases [in the time between] the death of their father and the actual division of the property, [the decision whether to grant the heirs their mothers' *ketubot*] depends only on the value of the estate at the time of their father's death.

6. If the value of the estate was a *dinar* or more than the sum of the two *ketubot*, each of the sons inherits the money due his mother by virtue of her *ketubah*. Even if there is a promissory note due against the estate for the amount that exceeds the value of the *ketubot*, it is not considered to have reduced [the value of the estate].

7. [The following rules apply when a man] was married to two wives. One died within his lifetime and one died afterwards, and he has sons from both wives. Although the value of the estate he left does not exceed the value of the two *ketubot*, the sons of the [wife who died after her husband's death] have the right to inherit the money due their mother by virtue of her *ketubah* first, [provided] she took the oath required of a widow before she died.

ג בַּמֶּה דְּבָרִים אֲמוּרִים? בְּשֶׁהִנִּיחַ יוֹתֵר עַל כְּדֵי שְׁתֵּי כְתֻבּוֹת דִּינָר אֶחָד אוֹ יוֹתֵר כְּדֵי שֶׁיַּחְלְקוּ הַשְּׁאָר בְּשָׁוֶה;

אֲבָל אִם לֹא הִנִּיחַ יוֹתֵר דִּינָר — חוֹלְקִים הַכֹּל בְּשָׁוֶה.

שֶׁאִם יִרְשׁוּ אֵלּוּ כְתֻבַּן אִמָּן וְאֵלּוּ כְתֻבַּת אִמָּן, וְלֹא יִשָּׁאֵר דִּינָר אֶחָד לַחֲלֹק אוֹתוֹ בֵּין הַיּוֹרְשִׁים, נִמְצָא תְנַאי זֶה מְבַטֵּל חִלּוּק יְרֻשָּׁה בֵּין הַבָּנִים בְּשָׁוֶה שֶׁהוּא מִן הַתּוֹרָה.

ד וְהוּא הַדִּין לְמִי שֶׁנָּשָׂא נָשִׁים רַבּוֹת, בֵּין בָּזוֹ אַחַר זוֹ בֵּין בְּבַת אַחַת, וּמֵתוּ כֻּלָּן בְּחַיָּיו, וְלֹא מֵהֶן בָּנִים זְכָרִים,

אִם הָיָה שָׁם יוֹתֵר עַל כְּדֵי כָּל הַכְּתֻבּוֹת דִּינָר — כָּל אֶחָד וְאֶחָד יוֹרֵשׁ כְּתֻבַּת אִמּוֹ, וְהַשְּׁאָר חוֹלְקִין בְּשָׁוֶה.

ה אָמְרוּ הַיְתוֹמִים: הֲרֵי אָנוּ מַעֲלִין עַל נִכְסֵי אָבִינוּ יוֹתֵר דִּינָר, כְּדֵי שֶׁיִּטְּלוּ כְּתֻבַּת אִמָּן — אֵין שׁוֹמְעִין לָהֶם,

אֶלָּא שָׁמִין אֶת הַנְּכָסִים בְּבֵית דִּין כַּמָּה שֶׁהָיוּ שָׁוִין בִּשְׁעַת מִיתַת אֲבִיהֶן.

וְאַף־עַל־פִּי שֶׁנִּתְרַבּוּ אוֹ נִתְמַעֲטוּ אַחֲרֵי מִיתַת אֲבִיהֶן קֹדֶם שֶׁיָּבוֹאוּ לַחֲלֹק — אֵין שָׁמִין אוֹתָן אֶלָּא כִּשְׁעַת מִיתַת אֲבִיהֶן.

ו הָיָה שָׁם יוֹתֵר עַל כְּדֵי כָּל הַכְּתֻבּוֹת דִּינָר אוֹ יוֹתֵר, אַף־עַל־פִּי שֶׁיֵּשׁ עָלָיו שְׁטַר חוֹב כְּנֶגֶד הַיּוֹתֵר — אֵינוּ מְמַעֵט, אֶלָּא כָּל אֶחָד מֵהֶן יוֹרֵשׁ כְּתֻבַּת אִמּוֹ.

ז מִי שֶׁהָיָה נָשׂוּי שְׁתֵּי נָשִׁים, וּמֵתָה אַחַת מֵהֶן בְּחַיָּיו וְאַחַת אַחַר מוֹתוֹ, וְלוֹ בָּנִים מִשְׁתֵּיהֶן, אַף־עַל־פִּי שֶׁלֹּא הִנִּיחַ יָתֵר עַל שְׁתֵּי הַכְּתֻבּוֹת:

אִם נִשְׁבְּעָה הַשְּׁנִיָּה שְׁבוּעַת אַלְמָנָה קֹדֶם שֶׁתָּמוּת — בָּנֶיהָ קוֹדְמִים לִירֻשַּׁת כְּתֻבָּתָהּ,

is not followed in the present age. The rationale is that the practice was instituted in the Talmudic era to encourage a father to give his daughter a generous *nedunyah*. (For because of this practice, he can be assured that the money he gives will remain within his family.) In the present age, however, this encouragement is not necessary, for it has become customary for parents to endow their daughters generously before marriage.

3. As the Rambam stated in Chapter 16, Halachah 7, the children's inheritance of the money due their mother by virtue of her *ketubah* applies only when there is enough landed property remaining in the estate to pay for both *ketubot*.

From the wording of the Rambam, it would, nevertheless, appear that it is sufficient that the additional *dinar* be movable property; it need not be landed property. This indeed is the ruling of the *Shulchan Aruch* (*Even HaEzer* 111:14). If this is the intent, it would reflect a change in the Rambam's decision from his ruling in his Commentary on the Mishnah (*Ketubot* 10:3).

[The rationale is] that they do not inherit their mother's *ketubah* by virtue of this provision, but rather through the Torah's laws of inheritance.[4] Afterwards, the sons of the wife [who died during her husband's lifetime] inherit [the money due their mother by virtue of her] *ketubah* on the basis of this provision. If anything remains in the estate afterwards, it should be divided equally.[5]

If [the woman who died after her husband] died before she was able to take the oath [required of her], only the sons of [the woman who died in her husband's lifetime] are entitled to inherit [the money due their mother by virtue of] her *ketubah*.[6] The remainder is divided equally.

8. [The following rules apply when a man] was married to two wives, fathered sons with both of them and then died. If the wives died after the father did, but after taking the oath [required of widows], each of their sons is entitled to inherit [the money due his mother by virtue of] her *ketubah* according to the Torah's laws of inheritance, and not by virtue of this provision. Therefore, in this instance it is not significant whether the estate is more valuable than the sum of the two *ketubot* or not. [The claim of] the heirs of the wife married first takes precedence over the claim of the wife married afterwards.

If neither of the wives took [the required] oath, the sons [of both women] divide the entire estate equally. Neither has the right to inherit [his mother's] *ketubah*, for a widow is not entitled to her *ketubah* until she takes the [required] oath.[7]

9. [In the above instance,] if one of the widows took the [required] oath and one did not, the sons of the one who took the oath inherit [the money due their mother by virtue of] her *ketubah* first, and then the remainder of the estate is divided equally [among all the heirs].[8]

Whenever [a son] inherits [the money due his mother by virtue of] her *ketubah* after she died in his father's lifetime, he does not have the right to expropriate property that was sold to others; [he inherits] only property in the possession of the estate.

10. Among the provisions of the *ketubah* is that after the death of their father, [his wife's] daughters have the right to receive support for their sustenance from their father's estate[9] until they become consecrated[10] or until they reach the age of *bagrut*.[11]

If a daughter reaches the age of *bagrut* but has not been consecrated, or if she is consecrated before she reaches the age of *bagrut*,[12] she is not entitled to receive her sustenance.

4. I.e., once the woman took the oath required of her, the money due her by virtue of her *ketubah* is considered to be justly hers. Her children then inherit her property.
5. In this instance, they are entitled to inherit the money due their mother by virtue of her

מִפְּנֵי שֶׁאֵינָן יוֹרְשִׁין כְּתֻבַּת אִמָּן בִּתְנַאי זֶה, אֶלָּא יְרֻשָּׁה שֶׁל תּוֹרָה,
וְאַחַר כָּךְ יוֹרְשִׁין בְּנֵי הָרִאשׁוֹנָה כְּתֻבַּת אִמָּן בִּתְנַאי זֶה.
וְאִם נִשְׁאַר שָׁם כְּלוּם — חוֹלְקִין אוֹתוֹ בְּשָׁוֶה.
וְאִם מֵתָה קֹדֶם שֶׁתִּשָּׁבַע — בְּנֵי הָרִאשׁוֹנָה יוֹרְשִׁים כְּתֻבַּת אִמָּן בִּלְבַד, וְהַשְּׁאָר חוֹלְקִין בְּשָׁוֶה.

ח הָיָה נָשׂוּי שְׁתֵּי נָשִׁים, וְהָיוּ לוֹ בָנִים מֵהֶן, וָמֵת, וְאַחַר כָּךְ מֵתוּ הַנָּשִׁים:
אִם נִשְׁבְּעוּ וְאַחַר כָּךְ מֵתוּ — כָּל אֶחָד וְאֶחָד יוֹרֵשׁ כְּתֻבַּת אִמּוֹ בִּירֻשָּׁה שֶׁל תּוֹרָה, וְלֹא בִּתְנַאי זֶה.
לְפִיכָךְ אֵין מַשְׁגִּיחִין אִם יֵשׁ שָׁם מוֹתָר אוֹ אֵין שָׁם.
וְיוֹרְשֵׁי הָרִאשׁוֹנָה קוֹדְמִין לְיוֹרְשֵׁי הַשְּׁנִיָּה.
וְאִם לֹא נִשְׁבְּעוּ — חוֹלְקִין הַבָּנִים הַכֹּל בְּשָׁוֶה; וְאֵין שָׁם יְרֻשַּׁת כְּתֻבָּה, לְפִי שֶׁאֵין לְאַלְמָנָה כְּתֻבָּה עַד שֶׁתִּשָּׁבַע.

ט אַחַת נִשְׁבְּעָה וְאַחַת לֹא נִשְׁבְּעָה — זוֹ שֶׁנִּשְׁבְּעָה בָּנֶיהָ יוֹרְשִׁין כְּתֻבָּתָהּ תְּחִלָּה, וְהַשְּׁאָר חוֹלְקִין אוֹתוֹ בְּשָׁוֶה.
וְכָל הַיּוֹרֵשׁ כְּתֻבַּת אִמּוֹ שֶׁמֵּתָה בְּחַיֵּי אָבִיו — אֵינוֹ טוֹרֵף מִנְּכָסִים מְשֻׁעְבָּדִים, אֶלָּא מִבְּנֵי חֹרִין, כְּכָל הַיּוֹרְשִׁין.

י וּמִתְּנָאֵי כְתֻבָּה, שֶׁתִּהְיֶינָה הַבָּנוֹת נִזּוֹנוֹת מִנִּכְסֵי אֲבִיהֶן אַחַר מוֹתוֹ עַד שֶׁיִּתְאָרְסוּ אוֹ עַד שֶׁיִּבְגְּרוּ.
בָּגְרָה הַבַּת אַף־עַל־פִּי שֶׁלֹּא נִתְאָרְסָה, אוֹ נִתְאָרְסָה אַף־עַל־פִּי שֶׁלֹּא בָגְרָה — אֵין לָהּ מְזוֹנוֹת.

---

ketubah even if the estate is not large enough to allow for the division of the inheritance according to Scriptural law afterwards (*Ketubot* 91a; *Shulchan Aruch, Even HaEzer* 111:8).

6. Since the woman did not take the oath required of a widow, there is room to suspect that her husband already gave her the money due her by virtue of her *ketubah*, or that she took possession of it herself. Therefore, her sons are not entitled to collect her *ketubah*.

7. Nor are the sons entitled to inherit the money due their mothers by virtue of their *ketubot* based on the provision mentioned above, because this is applicable only when the woman dies in her husband's lifetime.

8. The sons of the widow who did not take the oath are not entitled to inherit the money due their mother by virtue of her *ketubah*.

9. See Chapter 21, Halachah 18, which states that the daughters are granted this right even when their father divorced their mother before his death, and they took up residence with their mother.

10. Once the daughter is consecrated by a husband, her support is no longer the responsibility of her father's estate. (See also Halachah 15.)

11. During a man's lifetime, he is required only to provide his daughters with their sustenance until the age of six (Chapter 12, Halachah 14). After his death, however, they are entitled to support until the age of twelve and a half.

12. From the Rambam's wording, it would appear that he maintains that a girl forfeits

When a daughter receives her sustenance from her father's estate after his death, her earnings and the ownerless objects she discovers belong to her, not to her brothers.[13]

11. An allotment of support, garments and living quarters should be made for a man's daughters from his estate, just as it is made for his widow. His [landed property] may be sold to provide his daughters with their sustenance and garments without a public announcement, just as it is sold to provide for his widow's sustenance and garments.

[There is, however, one difference between the two.] The allotment to the widow is made according to her social standing and that of her husband, while his daughters are given only their necessities. The daughters are not, however, required to take an oath.[14]

12. A man's sons are not entitled to inherit [the money due their mother by virtue of] her *ketubah*, nor are his daughters entitled to receive their sustenance according to the provisions mentioned above unless they manifest possession of the document [recording their mother's] *ketubah*.[15] If, however, they do not manifest possession of the document, they are not entitled to anything, for it is possible that their mother waived her *ketubah* [in favor of her husband]. In a locale where it is not customary to record the *ketubah* in a document, however, the children are entitled to [the benefits stemming from] these provisions.

13. When, shortly before his passing, a man orders that one of the provisions of [his wife's] *ketubah* be ignored - e.g., he said: "My daughters should not derive their sustenance from my estate," "My widow should not derive her sustenance from my estate," or "My sons should not inherit the money due their mother by virtue of her *ketubah*" - his words are of no consequence.[16]

[Although] person gives his entire estate to others through an oral will[17] [all the provisions of his wife's *ketubah* must be met]. [The rationale is] that the transfer of property through an oral will does not take effect until after death, as will be explained.[18] Thus, the mandate of the will and the obligations of the estate due to the provisions [of the *ketubah*] take effect simultaneously. Therefore, the widow and [the deceased's] daughters receive support for their sustenance from the estate, and [the deceased's] sons inherit the money due their mother by virtue of her *ketubah* if she dies during her husband's lifetime.[19]

her right to support if she becomes consecrated while she is a minor. This ruling is not universally accepted by the *Rishonim*. The *Maggid Mishneh* quotes Rabbenu Chananel and the Rashba as saying that she does not forfeit this right in such an instance. The *Tur* (*Even HaEzer* 112) mentions a third view: that if she consecrates herself, she forfeits her support, but if her brothers are involved in her consecration, she is still entitled to support. The *Shulchan Aruch* (*Even HaEzer* 112:3) quotes the Rambam's view, while the Ramah mentions the other opinions.

וּבַת הַנִּזּוֹנֶת מִנִּכְסֵי אָבִיהָ לְאַחַר מוֹתוֹ — מַעֲשֵׂה יָדֶיהָ וּמְצִיאָתָהּ לְעַצְמָהּ, לֹא לָאַחִים.

יא פּוֹסְקִין לַבַּת מְזוֹנוֹת וּכְסוּת וּמָדוֹר מִנִּכְסֵי אָבִיהָ, כְּדֶרֶךְ שֶׁפּוֹסְקִין לָאַלְמָנָה.
וּמוֹכְרִין לִמְזוֹן הַבָּנוֹת וּכְסוּתָן בְּלֹא הַכְרָזָה, כְּדֶרֶךְ שֶׁמּוֹכְרִין לִמְזוֹן הָאַלְמָנָה וּכְסוּתָהּ.
אֶלָּא שֶׁהָאִשָּׁה פּוֹסְקִין לָהּ לְפִי כְּבוֹדָהּ וּכְבוֹד הַבַּעַל, וְלַבָּנוֹת פּוֹסְקִין לָהֶן דָּבָר הַמַּסְפִּיק לָהֶן בִּלְבַד.
וְאֵין הַבָּנוֹת נִשְׁבָּעוֹת.

יב אֵין הַבָּנִים יוֹרְשִׁין כְּתֻבַּת אִמָּן וְלֹא הַבָּנוֹת נִזּוֹנוֹת בִּתְנָאִים אֵלּוּ, עַד שֶׁיִּהְיֶה שְׁטַר כְּתֻבָּה יוֹצֵא מִתַּחַת יָדָם.
אֲבָל אִם אֵין שָׁם שְׁטַר כְּתֻבָּה — אֵין לָהֶן כְּלוּם, שֶׁמָּא מָחֲלָה אִמָּן כְּתֻבָּתָהּ.
וְאִם אֵין דַּרְכָּם לִכְתּוֹב כְּתֻבָּה — יֵשׁ לָהֶן כְּפִי הַתְּנָאִים.

יג מִי שֶׁצִּוָּה בִּשְׁעַת מִיתָתוֹ לַעֲקֹר אֶחָד מִתְּנָאֵי הַכְּתֻבָּה,
כְּגוֹן שֶׁאָמַר אַל יִזּוֹנוּ בְנוֹתָיו מִנְּכָסָיו, אוֹ אַל תִּזּוֹן אַלְמָנָתוֹ מִנְּכָסָיו, אוֹ אַל יִירְשׁוּ בָּנָיו כְּתֻבַּת אִמָּן — אֵין שׁוֹמְעִין לוֹ.
נָתַן כָּל נְכָסָיו בְּמַתָּנָה לַאֲחֵרִים — הוֹאִיל וּמַתְּנַת שְׁכִיב מְרַע אֵינָהּ קוֹנָה אֶלָּא לְאַחַר מִיתָה, כְּמוֹ שֶׁיִּתְבָּאֵר, הֲרֵי הַמַּתָּנָה וְחִיּוּב הַנְּכָסִים אֵלּוּ בָּאִין כְּאֶחָד,
וּלְפִיכָךְ אַלְמָנָתוֹ וּבְנוֹתָיו נִזּוֹנוֹת מִנְּכָסָיו, וּבָנָיו יוֹרְשִׁים כְּתֻבַּת אִמָּן שֶׁמֵּתָה בְּחַיֵּי בַּעְלָהּ.

13. Although during his lifetime, her father is entitled to her earnings and the objects she discovers, this right is not given to his sons. The rationale is that the father would prefer for his daughter to receive her own earnings than to have them given to his sons.

14. Although a widow is not required to take an oath when collecting her support, this is because she is required to take an oath when she collects the money due her by virtue of her *ketubah*. Therefore, one might think that a daughter would be required to take such an oath. Indeed, the *Beit Shmuel* 112:15, based on the statements of *Tosafot*, requires that such an oath be taken.

15. The Ra'avad and the *Maggid Mishneh* question the Rambam's ruling with regard to the support the man's daughters receive for their sustenance. They maintain that this support is not dependent on whether the mother receives the money due her by virtue of her *ketubah* (and therefore, the waiver of that payment has no effect). The Rambam's opinion appears to be based on his statements in Chapter 17, Halachah 19, in which he states that a woman who waives payment of her *ketubah* forgoes all the provisions of her *ketubah*. The *Shulchan Aruch* does not mention this issue, and the Ramah (*Even HaEzer* 112:1) cites the opinion of the Ra'avad.

16. The rationale is that the obligation took effect at the time of his marriage, and he is incapable of negating it at a later time.

17. An oral will refers to a person's disposition of his property verbally before his death. As explained in *Hilchot Zechiyah UMatanah*, Chapter 8, our Sages ordain that such a disposition of property is acceptable.

18. *Hilchot Zechiyah UMatanah* 8:8. (See also *Hilchot Nachalot* 8:9.)

19. The Ra'avad differs with the Rambam with regard to the rights of a person's sons and

14. A daughter of a girl who nullifies her marriage through *mi'un* is considered like any other daughter, and she is entitled to support for her sustenance [after her father's death].[20] Nevertheless, the daughter of a *yevamah*,[21] the daughter of a *sh'niyah*,[22] the daughter of one's *arusah,*[23] and the daughter of a woman who has been raped[24] are not entitled to support for their sustenance after their father's death by virtue of this provision. During their father's lifetime, however, he is obligated to support them like any of his other sons and daughters.

15. A man who consecrates a girl who is receiving her sustenance from her brothers is obligated to provide her with support from the time of consecration onward. [Although a husband is ordinarily required to support his wife only after *nisu'in*, an exception is made in this instance, because] the girl is not entitled to support from her brothers after she becomes consecrated. Nor is she past the age of majority, when she is capable of providing for her own sustenance, but rather she is a minor, or a *na'arah*.[25] [Hence, her husband is obligated to support her, because] a manwould not desire that the woman he consecrated be put to shame [by having to] wander and beg [for her support].[26]

16. Should a daughter marry and then leave her husband through the rite of *mi'un*, or be divorced, or be widowed - even if she is obligated to marry a *yavam* - since she returns to her father's home and has not reached the age of *bagrut*, she is entitled to support from her father's estate until she reaches the age of *bagrut* or until she becomes consecrated.[27]

---

daughters. Nevertheless, the *Shulchan Aruch* (*Even HaEzer* 111:17) follows the Rambam's view.
20. This ruling has been contested by other authorities on several grounds. First, the Ra'avad challenges the Rambam, asking: how is it possible for a girl who nullifies her marriage through *mi'un* to have a child? By definition, *mi'un* is possible when a girl is a *k'tanah*, a minor (see Chapter 4, Halachah 7), and while she is a minor it is impossible for her to conceive a child. He explains that *Ketubot* 53b is speaking about a girl who leaves her husband through *mi'un* - she is entitled to return to her deceased father's home and receive support for her sustenance.
    Second, the *Maggid Mishneh* accepts the fact that a girl can conceive a child while a minor, but asks: Since the mother nullifies the marriage through *mi'un*, it is as if her husband had never had any obligations to her at all. Her *ketubah* and all of its provisions are nullified entirely. Why then is his estate liable for the support of his daughter after his death? See the *Beit Shmuel* 112:11 for a possible explanation.
21. When a man dies childless, his brother (the *yavam*) inherits his entire estate, and that estate is responsible for the *ketubah* of the *yevamah* (the widow who is married by the *yavam*). If a *yevamah* bears a girl, the deceased brother's estate is not liable

יד בַּת הַמְמָאֶנֶת — הֲרֵי הִיא כִּשְׁאָר הַבָּנוֹת וְיֵשׁ לָהּ מְזוֹנוֹת.
אֲבָל בַּת הַיְבָמָה וּבַת הַשְּׁנִיָּה וּבַת הָאֲרוּסָה וּבַת הָאֲנוּסָה — אֵין לָהֶן מְזוֹנוֹת אַחַר מִיתַת אֲבִיהֶן בִּתְנַאי זֶה.
אֲבָל בְּחַיֵּי אֲבִיהֶן — הוּא חַיָּב בִּמְזוֹנוֹתָן, כְּדִין שְׁאָר הַבָּנִים וְהַבָּנוֹת בְּחַיֵּי אֲבִיהֶן.

טו הַמְאָרֵס בַּת הַנִּזּוֹנֶת מִן הָאַחִין — חַיָּב בִּמְזוֹנוֹתֶיהָ מִשְּׁעַת הָאֵרוּסִין;
שֶׁהֲרֵי אֵין לָהּ מְזוֹנוֹת מֵאַחֶיהָ אֶלָּא עַד שֶׁתִּתְאָרֵס אוֹ עַד שֶׁתִּתְבַּגֵּר, וְזוֹ אֵינָהּ בּוֹגֶרֶת כְּדֵי שֶׁתָּזוּן עַצְמָהּ, אֶלָּא קְטַנָּה אוֹ נַעֲרָה,
וְאֵין אָדָם רוֹצֶה שֶׁתִּתְבַּזֶּה אֲרוּסָתוֹ וְתֵלֵךְ וְתִשְׁאַל עַל הַפְּתָחִים.

טז נִשֵּׂאת הַבַּת וּמֵאֲנָה אוֹ נִתְגָּרְשָׁה אוֹ נִתְאַלְמְנָה, אֲפִלּוּ הִיא שׁוֹמֶרֶת יָבָם — הוֹאִיל וְחָזְרָה לְבֵית אָבִיהָ וַעֲדַיִן לֹא בָגְרָה, הֲרֵי זוֹ נִזּוֹנֶת מִנִּכְסֵי אָבִיהָ עַד שֶׁתִּתְבַּגֵּר אוֹ עַד שֶׁתִּתְאָרֵס.

---

for the girl's support after her father's (the *yavam's*) death, for she is not the daughter of the deceased brother. Nor is the *yavam's* estate responsible for her support, for he never gave a *ketubah* to the *yevamah*.

Note, however, the *Shulchan Aruch* (*Even HaEzer* 112:5), which states that if the deceased brother did not leave an estate, the *yavam* must give the *yevamah* a *ketubah* from his own property. Hence, in this instance, his estate becomes liable for the support of his daughters.

22. Since the mother's marriage is forbidden, our Sages did not grant her a *ketubah*. *Ketubot* 54a questions whether they also did not grant her the rights stemming from the *ketubah's* provisions, including her daughter's right to support in this instance. Since the question is left unresolved, her daughter is not granted this privilege.

23. Who was born before the couple entered the phase of *nisu'in* (*Shulchan Aruch, loc. cit.*). Since the *ketubah* takes effect only after *nisu'in*, this daughter is not entitled to support.

24. The term *anusah* refers to a virgin who was raped. The rapist is required to marry her and is forbidden to divorce her (Deuteronomy 22:28). Since he is forbidden to divorce her, she is not granted a *ketubah*. Our Sages (*ibid.*) question whether or not she was not granted the provisions of a *ketubah*. This question is also left unresolved, and her daughter is not granted the privilege of deriving her livelihood from her father's estate. Similarly, the daughter of a woman who was raped and never married by the rapist is not entitled to support from her father's estate.

25. The *Beit Shmuel* 112:6 interprets the Rambam's wording as implying that after the girl reaches the age of *bagrut*, she is required to support herself.

The *Beit Shmuel* also mentions that other *Rishonim* interpret *Ketubot* 53b, the source for this halachah, differently. According to their interpretation, the husband is not liable for the girl's support. If the husband desires, continues the *Beit Shmuel*, he may rely on this opinion.

26. It is as if he had made a commitment to support her when he consecrated her.

27. The *Shulchan Aruch* (*Even HaEzer* 112:4) cites the Rambam's view. The Ramah differs, however, citing the opinion of Rabbenu Asher, who maintains that from the time a girl becomes consecrated after her father's death, and onward, she is not entitled to support from his estate.

17. When a mandies leaving both sons and daughters, the sons inherit his estate,[28] and it is their responsibility to provide their sisters with support until they reach the age of *bagrut*, or until they become consecrated.

When does this apply? When the estate is large enough to provide both the sons and the daughters with their sustenance until the daughters reach the age of *bagrut*. This is called an ample estate.

If, however, the estate contains only a lesser amount, the funds necessary to support the daughters until they reach the age of *bagrut* are set aside,[29] and the remainder is given to the sons. If the estate contains only enough to provide for the support of the daughters, the daughters are entitled to their sustenance until they reach *bagrut* or until they become consecrated, and the sons should beg for their support.[30]

18. When does the above apply? When the estate contains landed property. If, however, the estate contains movable property, since it is only by virtue of the ordinance of the *geonim* that the daughters are entitled to derive their support from the movable property, the sons and the daughters should receive their support equally from this meager estate. For with regard to movable property, [the daughters] were given the right to be considered like the sons, but not superior to them. The *geonim* have ruled in this manner.[31]

19. If [a man] left an ample estate of landed property, and afterwards [the value of the estate decreased until] it became meager, the heirs have already acquired [the property].[32]

If [the estate was deemed] meager [in value] at the time of the man's death, and [the value increased afterwards][33] to the point that it is considered ample, the heirs are given the right to inherit it. Even if the value did not increase, if the sons sold an estate that was considered meager, the sale is binding.[34]

20. If the estate was ample but a debt was owed, or [the man] had made a provision with his wife, [promising] to support her daughter [from a previous

---

28. The estate is given to them, and they may use it as they see fit. They are, however, forbidden to sell the property except in an extreme situation - e.g., to use the proceeds to redeem captives (Ramah, *Even HaEzer* 112:11). Moreover, if the court sees that the sons are spending lavishly and abusing the resources of the estate, they should set aside the daughters' portion.

29. They are entrusted to a guardian appointed by the court.

30. For it is more common for males to beg for alms than for females to do so (*Ketubot* 67a). This principle is also followed with regard to the distribution of charity. If there is a needy male and a needy female, and the communal fund cannot provide both of them with their needs, the female is given priority (*Hilchot Matnot Aniyim* 8:15).

יז מִי שֶׁמֵּת וְהִנִּיחַ בָּנִים וּבָנוֹת — יִירְשׁוּ הַבָּנִים כָּל הַנְּכָסִים, וְהֵם זָנִין אֶת אַחְיוֹתֵיהֶם עַד שֶׁיִּבְגְּרוּ אוֹ עַד שֶׁיִּתְאָרְסוּ.

בַּמֶּה דְּבָרִים אֲמוּרִים? בְּשֶׁהִנִּיחַ נְכָסִים שֶׁאֶפְשָׁר שֶׁיִּזּוֹנוּ מֵהֶם הַבָּנִים וְהַבָּנוֹת כְּאַחַת עַד שֶׁיִּבְגְּרוּ הַבָּנוֹת. וְאֵלּוּ הֵן הַנִּקְרָאִין נְכָסִים מְרֻבִּין.

אֲבָל אִם אֵין בַּנְּכָסִים שֶׁהִנִּיחַ אֶלָּא פָּחוֹת מִזֶּה — מוֹצִיאִין מֵהֶם מְזוֹנוֹת לַבָּנוֹת עַד שֶׁיִּבְגְּרוּ, וְנוֹתְנִין הַשְּׁאָר לַבָּנִים.

וְאִם אֵין שָׁם אֶלָּא כְּדֵי מְזוֹן הַבָּנוֹת בִּלְבַד — הַבָּנוֹת נִזּוֹנוֹת מֵהֶן עַד שֶׁיִּבְגְּרוּ אוֹ עַד שֶׁיִּתְאָרְסוּ, וְהַבָּנִים יִשְׁאֲלוּ עַל הַפְּתָחִים.

יח בַּמֶּה דְּבָרִים אֲמוּרִים? בְּשֶׁהִנִּיחַ קַרְקַע; אֲבָל אִם לֹא הִנִּיחַ אֶלָּא מִטַּלְטְלִין — הוֹאִיל וּבְתַקָּנַת הַגְּאוֹנִים הוּא שֶׁיִּזּוֹנוּ הַבָּנוֹת מִן הַמִּטַּלְטְלִין, הֲרֵי הַבָּנִים וְהַבָּנוֹת נִזּוֹנוֹת כְּאֶחָד מִן הַנְּכָסִים הָאֵלּוּ הַמּוּעָטִין,

שֶׁלֹּא תִקְּנוּ לָהֶם בְּמִטַּלְטְלִין אֶלָּא שֶׁיִּהְיוּ כַּבָּנִים.

וְכָזֶה הוֹרוּ הַגְּאוֹנִים.

יט הִנִּיחַ קַרְקַע, וְהָיוּ הַנְּכָסִים מְרֻבִּין, וְנִתְמַעֲטוּ אַחַר כֵּן — כְּבָר זָכוּ בָּהֶן יוֹרְשִׁים. הָיוּ מוּעָטִין בִּשְׁעַת מִיתָה, וְנִתְרַבּוּ אַחַר כָּךְ — הַבָּנִים יוֹרְשִׁין אוֹתָן. וַאֲפִלּוּ לֹא נִתְרַבּוּ, אִם קָדְמוּ הַבָּנִים וּמָכְרוּ נְכָסִים מוּעָטִין — מִכְרָן קַיָּם.

כ הָיוּ הַנְּכָסִים מְרֻבִּין וְיֵשׁ עָלָיו חוֹב, אוֹ שֶׁהִתְנָה עִם אִשְׁתּוֹ שֶׁיָּזוּן אֶת בִּתָּהּ — אֵין הַחוֹב

---

31. The Ramah (*Even HaEzer* 112:12) states that according to the custom to include within the *ketubah* a clause stating that the obligations of the estate are binding on movable property as well, the estate is considered to be meager and the support for the daughters is set aside.

32. I.e., the property should remain in the possession of the sons, and they must continue to provide for their sisters' sustenance. It is not expropriated from the sons and given to a guardian.

33. The *Maggid Mishneh* mentions a difference of opinion with regard to the interpretation of the word "afterwards." Rashi (*Ketubot* 91a) maintains that this means "after the man's death, but before the matter is brought to the court and a guardian appointed." Others (Rabbenu Yitzchak Alfasi and the Rashba) maintain that even after a guardian is appointed, the property can be given to the heirs if its value increases.

The *Shulchan Aruch* (*Even HaEzer* 112:14) quotes the Rambam's wording without relating to this issue. The Ramah mentions the latter view.

34. The opinion of *Tosafot, et al.* is that even if the property has been entrusted to a guardian, if it is sold by the heirs the sale is binding. The Ramah (*loc. cit.*), however, appears to follow the view that the sale is binding only before the property has been entrusted to a guardian.

According to Rabbenu Asher, the daughters have no lien on the money received from the sale. Although Rav Hai Gaon differs, it appears that Rabbenu Asher's view is favored (*Chelkat Mechokek* 112:30).

marriage], the debt or [the obligation to] support the widow's daughter[35] does not prevent the estate from being considered ample.[36] Instead, the sons inherit the entire estate. [It is their responsibility] to pay the creditor his debt, to support the widow's daughter for the time stipulated and to support their sisters until they reach majority, or until they become consecrated and leave their domain.[37]

21. [The following rules apply when a man] left a widow and a daughter, either from her or from another wife, and his estate is not large enough to provide support for both of them. The widow should derive her support from the estate, and the daughter should beg [for alms].[38]

Similarly, I maintain that support for [a man's] daughter takes precedence over [his] sons' inheritance of their mother's *ketubah* if she died in her husband's lifetime, although both [rights] are provisions of the *ketubah*. [This can be derived by making] an inference from a more serious responsibility to a less serious one: If the inheritance [of a man's estate to which the sons are entitled] by virtue of Scriptural law is superseded by [the obligation to provide] the daughter with her support, how much more so should [the sons'] inheritance of [their mother's] *ketubah*, which is only a Rabbinic ordinance, be superseded by [the obligation to provide] the daughter with her support.

22. When a man dies and leaves older daughters and younger daughters, without leaving a son, we do not say that the younger daughters should be granted their sustenance until they reach the age of *bagrut*, and then the entire estate should be divided equally. Instead, the entire estate should be divided equally [immediately].

CHAPTER TWENTY

1. Our Sages decreed that a man give a certain portion of his holdings to his daughter as a dowry.[1] This is referred to as *parnasah*. When [a man] marries off his daughter, he should provide her with at least the wardrobe that is given to the wife of a poor Jewish man, as we have explained.[2]

When does the above apply? When [the bride's] father is poor. If he is wealthy, he should provide for his daughter according to his standards.

---

35. See Chapter 23, Halachah 17.
36. The *Shulchan Aruch* (*Even HaEzer* 112:15) states that the payment of the money due the widow by virtue of her *ketubah* is, however, considered in determining whether the estate is ample or not.
37. This ruling entitles the sons to derive their sustenance from the estate together with the daughters until the funds are depleted.
38. According to the Rambam, the property set aside for the widow's support should be

וְלֹא מְזוֹנוֹת בַּת אִשְׁתּוֹ מְמַעֲטִין בַּנְּכָסִים;

אֶלָּא יִרְשׁוּ הַבָּנִים הַכֹּל, וְיִתְּנוּ לְבַעַל חוֹב חוֹבוֹ, וְיָזוּנוּ בַּת אִשְׁתּוֹ עַד זְמַן שֶׁפָּסַק, וְיָזוּנוּ אַחְיוֹתֵיהֶן עַד שֶׁיִּבָּגְרוּ אוֹ עַד שֶׁיִּתְאָרְסוּ וְיֵצְאוּ מִתַּחַת יְדֵיהֶם.

כא הִנִּיחַ אַלְמָנָה וּבַת, מִמֶּנָּה אוֹ מֵאִשָּׁה אַחֶרֶת, וְאֵין בַּנְּכָסִים כְּדֵי שֶׁיִּזּוֹנוּ שְׁתֵּיהֶן — הָאַלְמָנָה נִזּוֹנֶת, וְהַבַּת תִּשְׁאַל עַל הַפְּתָחִים.

וְכֵן אֲנִי אוֹמֵר, שֶׁמְּזוֹנוֹת הַבַּת קוֹדְמִין לִירֻשַּׁת הַבֵּן אֶת כְּתֻבַּת אִמּוֹ שֶׁמֵּתָה בְּחַיֵּי אָבִיו, וְאַף-עַל-פִּי שֶׁשְּׁנֵיהֶם מִתְּנָאֵי הַכְּתֻבָּה.

וְקַל וָחֹמֶר הַדְּבָרִים: אִם נִדְחַת יְרֻשָּׁה שֶׁל תּוֹרָה מִפְּנֵי מְזוֹנוֹת הַבַּת, לֹא תִּדָּחֶה יְרֻשַּׁת הַכְּתֻבָּה, שֶׁהִיא תְּנָאֵי בֵּית דִּין, מִפְּנֵי מְזוֹנוֹת הַבַּת?!

כב מִי שֶׁמֵּת וְהִנִּיחַ בָּנוֹת גְּדוֹלוֹת וּקְטַנּוֹת, וְלֹא הִנִּיחַ בֵּן — אֵין אוֹמְרִים: יִזּוֹנוּ הַקְּטַנּוֹת עַד שֶׁיִּבָּגְרוּ וְיַחְלְקוּ שְׁאָר הַנְּכָסִים בְּשָׁוֶה, אֶלָּא כֻּלָּן חוֹלְקוֹת בְּשָׁוֶה.

פֶּרֶק עֶשְׂרִים

א צִוּוּ חֲכָמִים, שֶׁיִּתֵּן אָדָם מִנְּכָסָיו מְעַט לְבִתּוֹ כְּדֵי שֶׁתִּנָּשֵׂא בּוֹ. וְזֶה הוּא הַנִּקְרָא פַּרְנָסָה.

הַמַּשִּׂיא אֶת בִּתּוֹ סְתָם — לֹא יִפְחֹת לָהּ מִכְּסוּת שֶׁפּוֹסְקִין לְאֵשֶׁת עָנִי שֶׁבְּיִשְׂרָאֵל, כְּמוֹ שֶׁבֵּאַרְנוּ.

בַּמֶּה דְּבָרִים אֲמוּרִים? בְּשֶׁהָיָה הָאָב עָנִי; אֲבָל אִם הָיָה עָשִׁיר — הֲרֵי זֶה רָאוּי לִתֵּן לָהּ כְּפִי עָשְׁרוֹ.

given to a third party, and he should follow the guidelines set in Chapter 18, Halachah 21 (*Maggid Mishneh*).

There are opinions that maintain that property is set aside for the widow's support only when there is a son and a daughter, and the estate is too meager to support both of them. In that instance, since property is being set aside for the daughters' support, and the widow takes precedence over the daughters, property is also set aside for her. When property is not required to be set aside for the daughters, it is not set aside for the widow's support either. Instead, she, the daughters and the sons, all derive their sustenance from the estate together.

The *Shulchan Aruch* (*Even HaEzer* 93:4) mentions both opinions, and the *Beit Shmuel* 93:9 states that the latter view is favored by most authorities. This difference of opinion also leads to another (*Shulchan Aruch, Even HaEzer* 112:15): Does the obligation to support the widow cause the estate to be considered meager or not? According to the Rambam it does, but according to the other authorities it does not.

1. *Ketubot* 52b states that an allusion to this concept can be found in Jeremiah 29:6: "Give your daughters to men." "Is it possible for a father to initiate marriage proceedings?" our Sages ask. And they explain that the intent of the verse is that a man should provide his daughter with a dowry attractive enough for a man to desire her.

2. I.e., 50 *zuz*, as stated in Chapter 13, Halachah 1.

2. If a father explicitly tells the prospective husband that his daughter does not possess anything, and that [his intent is that] he marry her although she does not possess a wardrobe, [the bride] is not entitled to anything of her father's.

[In such a situation, the prospective] husband should not say: "When she comes to my home, I will provide her with a wardrobe." Instead, he should provide her with a wardrobe while she is living in her father's home.

3. When a father dies and leaves [at least one son and] a daughter [she is provided with a dowry from his estate]. We estimate what the father would have desired to give the daughter as a dowry, and she is given [that sum].

How is it possible to arrive at such an estimate? [We survey the habits of] his friends and acquaintances, his business affairs and his standard of living. If he married off a daughter during his lifetime, we base our estimate [on what she was given]. If the court is unable to determine what he would have desired [to give his daughter], she is given a tenth of his estate as a dowry.[3]

4. When a man leaves [a son and] many daughters, the first [daughter] who desires to marry[4] is given a tenth of the estate. The second [daughter to marry] receives a tenth of what was left after providing the first [daughter with her dowry]. And the third daughter receives a tenth of what was left after providing the second [daughter].

If all [a man's] daughters come to marry at the same time, [money is set aside for them according to the above pattern,] even if there are ten daughters [or more]. Afterwards, [all the allotments are pooled], and then divided equally among the daughters. The remainder of the estate is given to the sons.

5. The allotment of a tenth [of the estate] as a dowry is not one of the provisions of the *ketubah*. Therefore, even according to the enactment of the later Sages,[5] it is only to be collected from landed property.[6] It may, however, be collected from rent due for landed property.[7] If, however, [a girl's] brothers desire to give her money in lieu of a tenth of the landed property, they have that right.

6. With regard to this allotment of a tenth [of the estate], the daughter is considered to be a creditor of her brothers. Therefore, she is entitled to collect it from property of intermediate quality. An oath is not required of her.

3. From the Rambam's wording, it appears that one tenth is the average, but that if a man is known to be generous, his daughter may be given more than a tenth. The Ramah (*Even HaEzer* 113:1) mentions the opinion of certain authorities who maintain that a girl should

ב פֵּרֵשׁ עַל הַבַּעַל שֶׁאֵין לָהּ כְּלוּם וְשֶׁיַּכְנִיסֶנָּה עֲרֻמָּה — אֵין לָהּ כְּלוּם.
וְלֹא יֹאמַר הַבַּעַל: כְּשֶׁתָּבוֹא לְבֵיתִי אֲכַסֶּנָה, אֶלָּא מְכַסֶּנָה וְהִיא בְּבֵית אָבִיהָ.

ג הָאָב שֶׁמֵּת וְהִנִּיחַ בַּת — אוֹמְדִין דַּעְתּוֹ כַּמָּה הָיָה בְּלִבּוֹ לִתֵּן לָהּ לְפַרְנָסָה וְנוֹתְנִין לָהּ.
וּמִנַּיִן יוֹדְעִין אֹמֶד דַּעְתּוֹ? מֵרָעָיו וּמִיְּדָעָיו וּמַשָּׂאוֹ וּמַתָּנוֹ וּכְבוֹדוֹ.
וְכֵן אִם הִשִּׂיא בַּת בְּחַיָּיו — אוֹמְדִין בָּהּ.
וְאִם לֹא יָדְעוּ לוֹ בֵּית דִּין אֹמֶד דַּעַת — נוֹתְנִין לָהּ מִנְּכָסָיו עֲשׂוֹר לְפַרְנָסָתָהּ.

ד הִנִּיחַ בָּנוֹת רַבּוֹת — כֹּל שֶׁתָּבוֹא לְהִנָּשֵׂא, נוֹתְנִין לָהּ עֲשׂוֹר הַנְּכָסִים.
וְשֶׁלְּאַחֲרֶיהָ — עֲשׂוֹר מַה שֶּׁיְּיָרָה רִאשׁוֹנָה.
וְשֶׁל אַחֲרֶיהָ — עֲשׂוֹר מַה שֶּׁיְּיָרָה שְׁנִיָּה.
וְאִם בָּאוּ כֻּלָּן לְהִנָּשֵׂא כְּאַחַת — רִאשׁוֹנָה נוֹטֶלֶת עֲשׂוֹר,
וְהַשְּׁנִיָּה — עֲשׂוֹר מַה שֶּׁיְּיָרָה רִאשׁוֹנָה,
וְהַשְּׁלִישִׁית — עֲשׂוֹר מַה שֶּׁיְּיָרָה שְׁנִיָּה,
וְכֵן אֲפִלּוּ הֵן עֶשֶׂר, וְחוֹזְרוֹת וְחוֹלְקוֹת כָּל הָעֲשׂוּרִים בְּשָׁוֶה, וּשְׁאָר הַנְּכָסִים לָאַחִים.

ה עֲשׂוֹר זֶה שֶׁהוּא לְפַרְנָסָה אֵינוֹ מִתְּנָאֵי כְתֻבָּה.
לְפִיכָךְ, אֲפִלּוּ לְפִי תַּקָּנַת חֲכָמִים אַחֲרוֹנִים, אֵינָהּ נוֹטֶלֶת אֶלָּא מִן הַקַּרְקַע.
וְיֵשׁ לָהּ לִגְבּוֹת עֲשׂוֹר זֶה מִשְּׂכִירוּת הַקַּרְקַע.
וְאִם רָצוּ הָאַחִין לִתֵּן לָהּ מָעוֹת כְּנֶגֶד עֲשׂוֹר הַקַּרְקַע — נוֹתְנִין.

ו הַבַּת בְּעֲשׂוֹר זֶה כְּבַעַל חוֹב שֶׁל אַחִין הִיא,
לְפִיכָךְ נוֹטֶלֶת אוֹתוֹ מִן הַבֵּינוֹנִית בְּלֹא שְׁבוּעָה.

never be given more than a tenth of the estate, but states that the common practice is not to follow this view.
4. The dowry is given to the daughter only when she prepares to marry, not beforehand. Nevertheless, she is given a tenth of the value of the estate at the time of her father's death, regardless of its present value (*Maggid Mishneh*; Ramah, *Even HaEzer* 113:4).
5. I.e., even according to the Sages who ordained that the payment of the money due a woman by virtue of her *ketubah* may come from movable property (Chapter 16, Halachah 8), the payment of the dowry is from landed property alone. Note, however, the opinion of *Tosafot* (*Ketubot* 51a), who differ and maintain that this allotment may also be collected from movable property.
6. Based on the wording of Halachah 12, the *Maggid Mishneh* states that the Rambam's opinion is that the movable property in the estate is not included in the calculation of the size of the estate on which the amount of the dowry is based. Rav Moshe HaCohen and Rabbenu Asher differ, emphasizing that although the dowry allotment is not collected from movable property, the movable property is included in this appraisal. Both authorities agree, however, that if an assessment is made of the amount that the father would have given his daughter, that assessment includes the movable property in the estate.
7. This refers to rent due the father for landed property that was uncollected at the time of

If her brothers die, she is entitled to collect it from their sons, [expropriating] property of inferior quality, and an oath[8] is required of her. For she is collecting property from heirs, and [it is an accepted principle that] a person who comes to collect property from heirs may collect only from that of inferior quality and is required to take an oath [before doing so], as will be explained in the laws of loans.[9]

7. Should her brothers have sold the landed property of their father's estate, or given it as collateral, the daughter may collect her dowry from the purchasers,[10] just as other creditors are entitled to collect from the purchasers, as will be explained in the laws of loans.[11]

8. When a man has [several daughters, but] no sons, [his estate] is divided equally [among his daughters at the time of his death]. Although he married off the older daughters during his lifetime [and provided them with dowries], we do not grant dowries to the younger daughters and then divide the estate.

9. [The following rules apply when a man] has died, leaving two daughters and a son. The older daughter received a tenth of the estate as a dowry, but before the younger daughter had collected her dowry, the son died [without leaving any heirs], and [the two sisters] inherited the entire estate. [In this situation,] the younger sister is not entitled to her tenth of the estate.[12] Instead, the entire estate is divided equally. [In addition,] the older sister retains the tenth [she had received previously].[13]

10. When a man gives an order at the time of his death: "Do not give my daughters a dowry from my estate," his words are heeded. [The rationale is that a dowry] is not one of the provisions of a *ketubah*.[14]

11. [The following rules apply when] a man dies, leaving a widow and a daughter. It has already been explained[15] that the support of a man's widow[16] takes precedence over the support of his daughter. Similarly, if the daughter marries, she is not entitled to collect her tenth [of the estate], because of [the obligation to] support the widow.[17]

---

his death. The Ramah (*loc. cit.*) states that if the heirs have already collected the rental fee, they are not obligated to give it to their sister.
8. That she has not received any of the estate.
9. *Hilchot Malveh V'Loveh* 14:1, 19:1.
10. The rationale is that it is known that a girl is entitled to receive a dowry, and the purchasers of the property of the estate should have taken precautions before buying the property.

וְאִם מֵתוּ הָאַחִין — נוֹטֶלֶת אוֹתוֹ מִן בְּנֵיהֶם מִזְּבוּרִית וּבִשְׁבוּעָה;
שֶׁהֲרֵי הִיא נִפְרַעַת מִנִּכְסֵי יְתוֹמִים, וְהַבָּא לִפָּרַע מִנִּכְסֵי יְתוֹמִים — לֹא יִפָּרַע אֶלָּא מִזְּבוּרִית
וּבִשְׁבוּעָה, כְּמוֹ שֶׁיִּתְבָּאֵר בְּהִלְכוֹת הַלְּוָאָה.

ז וְהָאַחִים שֶׁמָּכְרוּ אוֹ מִשְׁכְּנוּ קַרְקַע אֲבִיהֶם — הַבַּת טוֹרֶפֶת מִן הַלָּקוֹחוֹת פַּרְנָסָתָהּ, כְּדֶרֶךְ
שֶׁטּוֹרְפִים כָּל בַּעֲלֵי חוֹבוֹת מִן הַלָּקוֹחוֹת, כְּמוֹ שֶׁיִּתְבָּאֵר בְּהִלְכוֹת הַלְּוָאָה.

ח מִי שֶׁהִשִּׂיא בָּנוֹת גְּדוֹלוֹת וְנִשְׁאֲרוּ קְטַנּוֹת וּמֵת בְּלֹא בֵן —
אֵין נוֹטְלִין פַּרְנָסָה לַקְּטַנּוֹת וְאַחַר כָּךְ חוֹלְקוֹת הַנְּכָסִים, אֶלָּא חוֹלְקוֹת כֻּלָּן בְּשָׁוֶה.

ט מִי שֶׁמֵּת וְהִנִּיחַ שְׁתֵּי בָנוֹת וָבֵן, וְקָדְמָה רִאשׁוֹנָה וְנָטְלָה עִשּׂוּר נְכָסִים, וְלֹא הִסְפִּיקָה הַשְּׁנִית
לִגְבּוֹת עַד שֶׁמֵּת הַבֵּן וְנָפְלוּ כָּל הַנְּכָסִים לִשְׁתֵּיהֶן —
אֵין הַשְּׁנִיָּה נוֹטֶלֶת עִשּׂוּר, אֶלָּא חוֹלְקוֹת בְּשָׁוֶה, וְזָכְתָה הָרִאשׁוֹנָה בָּעִשּׂוּר שֶׁלָּהּ.

י מִי שֶׁצִּוָּה בִשְׁעַת מִיתָה: אַל תִּפָּרְנְסוּ בְּנוֹתַי מִנְּכָסַי — שׁוֹמְעִים לוֹ, שֶׁאֵין זֶה מִתְּנָאֵי כְתֻבָּה.

יא מִי שֶׁמֵּת וְהִנִּיחַ אַלְמָנָה וּבַת — כְּבָר בֵּאַרְנוּ שֶׁמְּזוֹנוֹת הָאַלְמָנָה קוֹדְמִין לִמְזוֹנוֹת הַבַּת.
וְכֵן אִם נִשֵּׂאת הַבַּת — אֵינָהּ נוֹטֶלֶת עִשּׂוּר נְכָסִים מִפְּנֵי מְזוֹנוֹת הָאַלְמָנָה.

---

11. *Hilchot Malveh V'Loveh* 18:1.

12. *Ketubot* 69a explains that the rationale for this ruling is that the daughter has received a far larger portion of the estate than she could have hoped for.

13. The Rambam's opinion is quoted by the *Shulchan Aruch* (*Even HaEzer* 113:8). The Ramah quotes the opinion of Rabbenu Asher, who maintains that the second daughter is given her dowry and then the estate is divided.

14. The provisions of the *ketubah* - e.g., the support of the daughters - become binding at the time of the marriage, and the man's statements have no effect regarding them (Chapter 19, Halachah 13). The dowry, by contrast, is a gift that we assume a man would make. Therefore if he explicitly states that he does not desire that it be made, his wishes are heeded.

15. Chapter 19, Halachah 21.

16. The *Chelkat Mechokek* 113:17 and the *Beit Shmuel* 113:16 state that the same ruling applies with regard to the daughters. I.e., if there are older daughters who wish to collect their dowry and marry, and younger daughters who still have to receive support from the estate, the younger daughters are entitled to object to the property's being given to their sisters. The rationale is that the support for the widow and for the daughters is considered to be a debt owed by the estate, while their dowry is considered to be a debt owed by the heirs.

17. Once the widow has remarried or received payment for her *ketubah*, the daughter is entitled to inherit the tenth of the estate that should have been given to her. Even when she has already married, her brothers are required to give her these funds from the remainder of the estate.

Even if the daughter dies after she marries, her husband is not entitled to inherit the dowry that should have been given her.[18] For the entire estate is considered to be in the possession of the widow so that she can derive her sustenance.

12. When an orphan girl is married off by her brothers or her mother as a child with her consent, and she is given 50 or 100 *zuz* as a dowry, she is entitled to collect the dowry that is due her - according to the estimation of her father's desires or one tenth of the landed property[19] [of his estate] - from them after she attains the age of majority.

[This applies] even if her brothers did not provide her with sustenance,[20] and even if she did not object at the time of the wedding. For a minor is not capable of making an objection [in court].[21]

13. When a daughter marries after she reaches majority - whether as a *na'arah* or as a *bogeret* - and does not demand her dowry, she forfeits her dowry. If, however, she protested at the time of her marriage, she may collect her due whenever she desires.

[A further point must be considered when] she reaches the age of *bagrut* and remains in her father's house - regardless of whether she reaches *bagrut* after his death, or [he died] when she had already reached the age of *bagrut*.[22] If her brothers have already ceased providing her with her sustenance, which is their prerogative, as we have explained,[23] and [the girl] remained silent and did not demand her dowry, she forfeits her dowry. If she protests, she does not forfeit her dowry.

If, however, her brothers had not ceased providing her with her sustenance [although] she reached *bagrut*, she is not considered to have forfeited her dowry as long as they continue to provide her with her sustenance, even though she did not protest. For she can claim that she did not demand her dowry because [her brothers] are supporting her although they are not obligated to do so,[24] and she has not yet married.[25]

14. [The following rules apply when a man] stated - whether while making an oral will before death or while healthy - that his daughter should be given a specific sum of money as a dowry, and that this sum should be used to purchase landed property, and [then] died [afterwards].

When the money is in the possession of a third party and the daughter states: "Give the money to my husband and let him do with it as he

18. At times a woman's husband is considered to be a purchaser of the property he inherits from his wife, and at times an heir. If he were considered to be a purchaser, he would be entitled to take possession of the dowry due his wife, for a widow is not entitled to collect her support from property that has been sold. Nevertheless, in this instance, out

וַאֲפִלּוּ מֵתָה מֵחֲמַת הַבַּת שֶׁנִּשֵּׂאת — אֵין הַבַּעַל יוֹרֵשׁ פַּרְנָסָה הָרְאוּיָה לְהִנָּתֵן לָהּ;
שֶׁהֲרֵי הַנְּכָסִים כֻּלָּן בְּחֶזְקַת הָאַלְמָנָה שֶׁתְּהֵא נִזּוֹנֶת מֵהֶן.

יב קְטַנָּה יְתוֹמָה שֶׁהִשִּׂיאַתָּה אִמָּהּ אוֹ אַחֶיהָ לְדַעְתָּהּ, וְנָתְנוּ לָהּ מֵאָה אוֹ חֲמִשִּׁים זוּז
— יְכוֹלָה הִיא מִשֶּׁתִּגְדִּיל לְהוֹצִיא מִיָּדָם פַּרְנָסָה הָרְאוּיָה לָהּ,
אוֹ בְּאֹמְדַּן דַּעַת הָאָב אוֹ בְּעִשּׂוּר הַקַּרְקָעוֹת.
וַאֲפִלּוּ לֹא הָיוּ הָאַחִין זָנִין אוֹתָהּ, וְאַף־עַל־פִּי שֶׁלֹּא מִחֲתָה בִּשְׁעַת נִשּׂוּאִין, מִפְּנֵי שֶׁהַקְּטַנָּה
אֵינָהּ בַּת מֶחָאָה.

יג נִשֵּׂאת הַבַּת אַחַר שֶׁגָּדְלָה, בֵּין נַעֲרָה בֵּין בּוֹגֶרֶת, וְלֹא תָּבְעָה פַּרְנָסָתָהּ — אִבְּדָה פַּרְנָסָתָהּ.
וְאִם מִחֲתָה בְּעֵת נִשּׂוּאֶיהָ — הֲרֵי זוֹ מוֹצִיאָה אֶת הָרָאוּי לָהּ כָּל זְמַן שֶׁתִּרְצֶה.
בָּגְרָה וְעוֹדָהּ בְּבֵית אָבִיהָ, בֵּין שֶׁבָּגְרָה אַחַר מוֹתוֹ בֵּין שֶׁהִנִּיחָהּ בּוֹגֶרֶת:

אִם פָּסְקוּ הָאַחִין מִלָּתֵת מְזוֹנוֹתֶיהָ, שֶׁהֲרֵי אֵין לָהּ מְזוֹנוֹת כְּמוֹ שֶׁבֵּאַרְנוּ, וְשָׁתְקָה וְלֹא תָּבְעָה
פַּרְנָסָתָהּ — אִבְּדָה פַּרְנָסָתָהּ;
וְאִם מִחֲתָה — לֹא אִבְּדָה פַּרְנָסָתָהּ.
לֹא פָּסְקוּ הָאַחִים מְזוֹנוֹתֶיהָ וְזָנוּ אוֹתָהּ בְּבֶגֶר — אַף־עַל־פִּי שֶׁלֹּא מִחֲתָה, לֹא אִבְּדָה פַּרְנָסָתָהּ
כָּל זְמַן שֶׁהֵן זָנִין אוֹתָהּ;
שֶׁיֵּשׁ לָהּ לִטְעֹן: מִפְּנֵי שֶׁהֵן זָנִין אוֹתָהּ אַף־עַל־פִּי שֶׁאֵינָן חַיָּבִין, וְהִיא עֲדַיִן לֹא נִשֵּׂאת, מִפְּנֵי
זֶה לֹא תָּבְעָה פַּרְנָסָתָהּ.

יד מִי שֶׁצִּוָּה לָתֵת לְבִתּוֹ כָּךְ וְכָךְ מָעוֹת לְפַרְנָסָתָהּ לָקַח בָּהֶן קַרְקַע, בֵּין שֶׁהָיָה שְׁכִיב
מְרַע בֵּין שֶׁהָיָה בָּרִיא, וָמֵת, וַהֲרֵי הַמָּעוֹת בְּיַד הַשָּׁלִישׁ, וְאָמְרָה הַבַּת: תְּנוּ אוֹתָם לְבַעְלִי,
כָּל מַה שֶּׁיִּרְצֶה יַעֲשֶׂה בָּהֶן —

of consideration for the widow, our Sages considered him like an heir, and thus enabled
the widow to continue receiving her sustenance (*Bava Batra* 139b).
19. The *Maggid Mishneh* cites this phrase as proof that the tenth of the estate set aside as
a dowry is expropriated from landed property alone.
20. See the following halachah.
21. And thus the fact that she did not object at the time of the marriage is not significant.
The *Maggid Mishneh* adds that even if the girl did not object immediately at the time she
reached majority, she is entitled to object afterwards. This decision is quoted by the
Ramah (*Even HaEzer* 113:7).
22. Rabbenu Asher writes that a girl who reached the age of *bagrut* in her father's lifetime
is not entitled to a dowry from her brothers. The later Ashkenazic authorities (see *Beit
Shmuel* 113:19) state, however, that this ruling is not applied.
23. Chapter 19, Halachah 10.
24. Hence, she is ashamed to come to them with this request (*Ketubot* 68b).
25. Implied is that once a *bogeret* marries without demanding her dowry, she has forfeited
it even though her brothers continue to provide her with her sustenance (*Maggid Mishneh*).

desires," [the third party should do as follows]. If [the daughter] has reached the age of majority and has married, she is granted this prerogative.[26] If she is [past majority, but merely] consecrated, the third party should follow the instructions he was given.[27] And if she is a minor, even if she is already married, her request is not heeded.[28] Instead, the third party should carry out her father's instructions.[29]

CHAPTER TWENTY-ONE

1. A husband is entitled to [any ownerless objects] discovered by [his] wife,[1] and the proceeds of her labor.[2] What [type of work] must she perform on his behalf? Everything follows the custom of the country. In a place where it is customary for women to weave, she should weave. [In a place where they] embroider, she should embroider. [In a place where they] spin wool or flax, she should spin.

If it is not customary for women in that place to perform these labors, he may compel her only to spin wool; [wool, but not flax,] because flax damages [a woman's] mouth and lips. [This occupation is chosen because] spinning is a task designated for women, as [implied by Exodus 35:25]: "And all the skilled women put their hands to spinning...."

2. If a woman exerts herself and produces more than would be expected of her,[3] her husband is entitled to the extra amount.[4]

Even when her husband[5] is very wealthy and even when the woman has several maids, she may not sit idle, without work. For idleness leads to lewdness. [Her husband] may not, however, compel her to work for the entire day. Instead, according to the extent of his wealth, her obligation to work is minimized.

In his *Kessef Mishneh*, Rav Yosef Karo writes that if the brothers of a *na'arah* continue to provide her with her sustenance after marriage, she does not forfeit her dowry, even if she does not protest. Although his wording in the *Shulchan Aruch* (*Even HaEzer* 113:7) is slightly problematic, the later authorities explain that this is his intent. A source for both the statements of the *Maggid Mishneh* and the *Kessef Mishneh* can be seen in the Rambam's Commentary on the Mishnah (*Ketubot* 6:6).

26. We assume that the father's intent was that the money should be entrusted to a third party only until after her marriage (Rashi, *Ketubot* 69b).

27. For it is a mitzvah to carry out the directives of a person who dies, even if he was healthy at the time he gave these directives (*Hilchot Zechiyah UMatanah* 4:5).

28. We assume that the father's intent was to safeguard his daughter and her husband against wasting the funds intended for them.

29. The *Shulchan Aruch* (*Even HaEzer* 54:1) quotes the Rambam's ruling. The Ramah

אִם הָיְתָה גְדוֹלָה וְנִשֵׂאת — הָרְשׁוּת בְּיָדָהּ,

וְאִם עֲדַיִן מְאֹרֶסֶת הִיא — יַעֲשֶׂה שָׁלִישׁ מַה שֶׁהַשָּׁלִישׁ בְּיָדוֹ,

וְאִם עֲדַיִן קְטַנָּה הִיא — אֲפִלּוּ נִשֵׂאת, אֵין שׁוֹמְעִין לָהּ, אֶלָּא יַעֲשֶׂה שָׁלִישׁ כְּמוֹ שֶׁצִּוָּה הָאָב.

פֶּרֶק אֶחָד וְעֶשְׂרִים

א מְצִיאַת הָאִשָּׁה וּמַעֲשֵׂה יָדֶיהָ לְבַעְלָהּ.

וּמַה הִיא עוֹשָׂה לּוֹ? הַכֹּל כְּמִנְהַג הַמְּדִינָה.

מְקוֹם שֶׁדַּרְכָּן לֶאֱרֹג — אוֹרֶגֶת, לִרְקֹם — רוֹקֶמֶת, לִטְווֹת צֶמֶר אוֹ פִּשְׁתִּים — טוֹוָה.

וְאִם לֹא הָיָה דֶרֶךְ נְשֵׁי הָעִיר לַעֲשׂוֹת כָּל הַמְּלָאכוֹת הָאֵלּוּ — אֵינוֹ כּוֹפָה אֶלָּא לִטְווֹת הַצֶּמֶר בִּלְבַד, שֶׁהַפִּשְׁתָּן מַזִּיק אֶת הַפֶּה וְאֶת הַשְׂפָתַיִם.

וְהַטְּוִיָּה הִיא הַמְּלָאכָה הַמְיֻחֶדֶת לְנָשִׁים, שֶׁנֶּאֱמַר: וְכָל אִשָּׁה חַכְמַת לֵב בְּיָדֶיהָ טָווּ.

ב דָּחֲקָה עַצְמָהּ וְעָשְׂתָה יוֹתֵר מִן הָרָאוּי לָהּ — הַמּוֹתָר לַבַּעַל.

הָיָה לוֹ מָמוֹן הַרְבֵּה, אֲפִלּוּ הָיָה לָהּ כַּמָּה שְׁפָחוֹת — אֵינָהּ יוֹשֶׁבֶת לְבַטָּלָה בְּלֹא מְלָאכָה, שֶׁהַבַּטָּלָה מְבִיאָה לִידֵי זִמָּה.

אֲבָל אֵין כּוֹפִין אוֹתָהּ לַעֲשׂוֹת מְלָאכָה כָּל הַיּוֹם כֻּלּוֹ, אֶלָּא לְפִי רֹב הַמָּמוֹן מְמַעֶטֶת בִּמְלָאכָה.

---

refers to this ruling in *Choshen HaMishpat* 252:2, which states that this applies only if the funds were specifically entrusted to the third party for this purpose by the deceased at the time he made this statement. If they came into his possession afterwards, the concept that it is a mitzvah to carry out the directives of a person who dies does not apply.

1. *Ketubot* 47a states that since a woman's husband supports her, he might object if she were granted ownership over the items that she discovers. The Jerusalem Talmud (*Ketubot* 6:1) offers a slightly different explanation: that if women were entitled to the objects that they discover, a woman might conceal her earnings and later claim that the funds came to her for ownerless objects that she discovered.
2. As mentioned in Chapter 12, Halachah 4, in exchange for the obligation incumbent on the man to support his wife, our Sages granted him the right to the income she generates.
3. There are two interpretations of "more than would be expected of her": a) that she worked overtime, more hours than common custom requires, b) that she performed several tasks at one time.
4. There are authorities who differ with the Rambam and maintain that a woman is entitled to keep the additional amount she earns. The *Bayit Chadash* (*Even HaEzer* 80) states that it is not Ashkenazic custom to require a woman to give her husband any of her additional earnings.
5. Literally, "he is." Many manuscript copies and early printings of the *Mishneh Torah* state "he and she are," instead of "he is."

3. When a man takes a vow that prevents his wife from doing any work at all, he is obligated to divorce her and pay her [the money due her by virtue of her] *ketubah*. [The rationale is that] idleness leads to lewdness.[6]

Every wife is obligated [to perform the following household tasks] on behalf of her husband: to wash his face, feet and hands, to pour him beverages, to make his bed,[7] and to do his bidding - e.g., to bring him water or a utensil, to remove an article from his presence, or to perform similar tasks. She is not, however, required to do the bidding of his father or his son.

4. These tasks should be performed only by a man's wife alone.[8] Even if she possesses several maids, these tasks are performed for a man only by his wife.

5. There are other tasks that a woman performs for her husband when they are poor; they are: to bake bread in an oven[9] - Ezra ordained that a woman get up early and bake bread so that there will be bread available to give the poor.

She should cook food, wash clothes, nurse her child, place straw before her husband's beast[10] - but not before his cattle - and grind [flour].

What does grinding [flour] involve? [Not that the woman actually operates the mill herself,] but that she stays at the mill, sifts[11] the flour and prods the animal [who turns the mill], so that [the operation of] the mill will not be hampered. If it is the [local] custom, for women to grind [flour] using a hand mill, [a woman] should grind [flour in this manner].

6. When does the above apply? With regard to a poor [couple]. If, however, a woman brings a maid to [the household] or property with which a maid could be purchased, or if the man possesses a maid or funds with which a maid could be purchased, the wife is not required to grind [flour], to bake, to do laundry or to place straw before her husband's beast.

If the wife brings two maids to [the household] or property with which two maids could be purchased, or if the man possesses two maids or is [wealthy] enough to purchase two maids, the wife is not required to cook or to nurse her child. Instead, she gives him to a maid to nurse.[12]

6. Hence, rather than compel a woman to follow a course of conduct that will lead to wanton behavior, *Ketubot* 59b requires the husband to divorce his wife.
7. The commentaries discuss whether the intent is to make her husband's bed or to make all the beds in the house. The difference is with regard to a rich woman, who could have maids perform household services. She is, nevertheless, obligated to make her husband's bed as a reflection of their personal closeness. The question is whether this applies to making the other beds in the house. *Ketubot* 61a uses the expression "makes the bed for him," indicating that the emphasis is on the husband's bed.

ג הַמַּדִּיר אֶת אִשְׁתּוֹ שֶׁלֹּא תַעֲשֶׂה מְלָאכָה כְּלָל — יוֹצִיא וְיִתֵּן כְּתֻבָּה, שֶׁהַבַּטָּלָה מְבִיאָה לִידֵי זִמָּה.

וְכֵן כָּל אִשָּׁה רוֹחֶצֶת לְבַעְלָהּ פָּנָיו יָדָיו וְרַגְלָיו, וּמוֹזֶגֶת לוֹ אֶת הַכּוֹס, וּמַצַּעַת לוֹ אֶת הַמִּטָּה, וְעוֹמֶדֶת וּמְשַׁמֶּשֶׁת בִּפְנֵי בַעְלָהּ, כְּגוֹן שֶׁתִּתֵּן לוֹ מַיִם אוֹ כְּלִי אוֹ תִטֹּל מִלְּפָנָיו וְכַיּוֹצֵא בִּדְבָרִים אֵלּוּ.

אֲבָל אֵינָהּ עוֹמֶדֶת וּמְשַׁמֶּשֶׁת בִּפְנֵי אָבִיו אוֹ בִּפְנֵי בְּנוֹ.

ד וּמְלָאכוֹת אֵלּוּ עוֹשָׂה אוֹתָן הִיא בְּעַצְמָהּ. וַאֲפִלּוּ הָיוּ לָהּ כַּמָּה שְׁפָחוֹת — אֵין עוֹשִׂין מְלָאכוֹת אֵלּוּ לַבַּעַל אֶלָּא אִשְׁתּוֹ.

ה יֵשׁ מְלָאכוֹת אֲחֵרוֹת שֶׁהָאִשָּׁה עוֹשָׂה לְבַעְלָהּ בִּזְמַן שֶׁהֵן עֲנִיִּים, וְאֵלּוּ הֵן: אוֹפָה הַפַּת בַּתַּנּוּר. וְעֶזְרָא תִּקֵּן, שֶׁתִּהְיֶה אִשָּׁה מַשְׁכֶּמֶת וְאוֹפָה, כְּדֵי שֶׁתִּהְיֶה הַפַּת מְצוּיָה לָעֲנִיִּים.

וּמְבַשֶּׁלֶת אֶת הַתַּבְשִׁילִין. וּמְכַבֶּסֶת אֶת הַבְּגָדִים. וּמַנִיקָה אֶת בְּנָהּ. וְנוֹתֶנֶת תֶּבֶן לִפְנֵי בְּהֶמְתּוֹ, אֲבָל לֹא לִפְנֵי בְּקָרוֹ.

וּמַטְחֶנֶת. כֵּיצַד מַטְחֶנֶת? יוֹשֶׁבֶת בָּרֵחַיִם וּמְשַׁמֶּרֶת הַקֶּמַח, וְאֵינָהּ טוֹחֶנֶת. אוֹ מְחַמֶּרֶת אַחַר הַבְּהֵמָה, כְּדֵי שֶׁלֹּא יִבָּטְלוּ הָרֵחַיִם. וְאִם הָיָה דַרְכָּן לִטְחֹן בְּרֵחַיִם שֶׁל יָד — טוֹחֶנֶת.

ו בַּמֶּה דְּבָרִים אֲמוּרִים? בַּעֲנִיִּים;

אֲבָל אִם הִכְנִיסָה לוֹ שִׁפְחָה אַחַת אוֹ נְכָסִים שֶׁרְאוּיִים לִקְנוֹת מֵהֶן שִׁפְחָה אַחַת, אוֹ שֶׁהָיְתָה לוֹ שִׁפְחָה אַחַת אוֹ שֶׁהָיָה לוֹ מָמוֹן כְּדֵי לִקְנוֹת מִמֶּנּוּ שִׁפְחָה אַחַת — אֵינָהּ מַטְחֶנֶת, וְלֹא אוֹפָה, וְלֹא מְכַבֶּסֶת, וְלֹא נוֹתֶנֶת תֶּבֶן לִפְנֵי בְּהֶמְתּוֹ.

הִכְנִיסָה לוֹ שְׁתֵּי שְׁפָחוֹת אוֹ נְכָסִים הָרְאוּיִין לִקְנוֹת מֵהֶן שְׁתֵּי שְׁפָחוֹת, אוֹ שֶׁהָיוּ לוֹ שְׁתֵּי שְׁפָחוֹת אוֹ שֶׁהָיָה רָאוּי לִקְנוֹת שְׁתֵּי שְׁפָחוֹת — אֵינָהּ מְבַשֶּׁלֶת, וְאֵינָהּ מַנִיקָה אֶת בְּנָהּ, אֶלָּא נוֹתֶנֶת אוֹתוֹ לַשִּׁפְחָה לְהָנִיק.

---

8. I.e., they are a reflection of their personal closeness.

9. In contrast to bread baked in a pan or over coals - i.e., the woman must bake in an ordinary manner (*Ma'aseh Rokeach*).

10. I.e., the animal on which she rides. This reflects the version of *Ketubot* 61b possessed by the Sephardic authorities. The *Shitah Mekubetzet* explains that this is included in a woman's household duties, because those duties involve tasks that affect her husband's person. The standard printed text of that Talmudic passage reverses the decisions regarding his beast and cattle. (See the rationale offered by Rashi.)

11. Alternatively, guards the flour (*Tur, Even HaEzer* 80).

12. The commentaries mention the importance of selecting a Jewish nursemaid. For milk that comes from non-kosher food will breed undesirable tendencies in the son's character.

7. Thus, there are five tasks that every woman must perform on behalf of her husband: to spin [thread], to wash his face, hands and feet, to pour beverages for him, to make his bed and to do his bidding. And there are six tasks that some women perform and some women do not perform. They are: to grind [flour], to cook, to bake, to do laundry, to nurse, and to place straw before her husband's beast.

8. All the tasks that a woman must perform on behalf of her husband must also be performed by a woman while she is in the *niddah* state, with the exception of pouring beverages, making his bed and washing his face, hands and feet. [The rationale for the exceptions is that] this is a decree, [enacted] lest [sexual] thoughts arise, and the husband be prompted to engage in relations.

Therefore, when she is in the *niddah* state, she should make his bed when he is not present. When pouring a beverage for him, she should not place it in his hand as is her usual practice, but rather leave it on the ground, on a utensil or on a table, and he will take it.[13]

9. When a woman breaks utensils while performing household tasks,[14] she is not held liable. This ruling does not reflect the dictates of the law, but is instead an enactment [of our Sages]. For if this were not the case, there would never be peace in a household. For a woman would be overly cautious and would refrain from performing many tasks, and there would thus be strife between [the couple].[15]

10. Whenever a woman refrains from performing any of the tasks that she is obligated to perform, she may be compelled to do so, even with a rod.[16] When a husband complains that [his wife] does not perform [her required tasks], and [the wife] claims that she does, [the dispute should be clarified by having] a [neutral] woman dwell with them or [by asking] the neighbors.[17] The judges should clarify the matter in the best way they see fit.

11. During the time a woman nurses her child, she is not compelled to perform as many tasks [as usual], and wine and foods that are beneficial to nursing are added to her support.

13. The Rambam does not mention washing her husband, because his wife is forbidden to touch him while in the *niddah* state. (See *Hilchot Issurei Bi'ah* 11:18-19.)
14. The *Chelkat Mechokek* 80:29 states that based on the Jerusalem Talmud, this law applies even when she breaks household articles while she is not in the midst of her household chores.
15. While he accepts the Rambam's ruling, the Ra'avad offers a different rationale. The commentaries, however, justify the Rambam's view.

ז נִמְצְאוּ כָּל הַמְּלָאכוֹת שֶׁכָּל אִשָּׁה עוֹשָׂה אוֹתָן לְבַעְלָהּ — חָמֵשׁ מְלָאכוֹת:
טוֹוָה, וְרוֹחֶצֶת פָּנָיו יָדָיו וְרַגְלָיו, וּמוֹזֶגֶת אֶת הַכּוֹס, וּמַצַּעַת אֶת הַמִּטָּה, וְעוֹמֶדֶת וּמְשַׁמֶּשֶׁת
בְּפָנָיו.
וְהַמְּלָאכוֹת שֶׁמִּקְצָת הַנָּשִׁים עוֹשׂוֹת אוֹתָן וּמִקְצָתָן אֵינָן עוֹשׂוֹת — שֵׁשׁ מְלָאכוֹת:
מַטְחֶנֶת, וּמְבַשֶּׁלֶת, וְאוֹפָה, וּמְכַבֶּסֶת, וּמְנִיקָה, וְנוֹתֶנֶת תֶּבֶן לִפְנֵי בְּהֶמְתּוֹ.

ח כָּל מְלָאכוֹת שֶׁהָאִשָּׁה עוֹשָׂה לְבַעְלָהּ — נִדָּה עוֹשָׂה לְבַעְלָהּ. חוּץ מִמְּזִיגַת הַכּוֹס, וְהַצָּעַת
הַמִּטָּה, וְהַרְחָצַת פָּנָיו יָדָיו וְרַגְלָיו; גְּזֵרָה מִשּׁוּם הִרְהוּר, שֶׁמָּא יָבוֹא לִבְעֹל.
לְפִיכָךְ מַצַּעַת מִטָּתוֹ כְּשֶׁהִיא נִדָּה שֶׁלֹּא בְּפָנָיו,
וּמוֹזֶגֶת אֶת הַכּוֹס וְאֵינָהּ נוֹתֶנֶת אוֹתוֹ בְּיָדוֹ כְּדַרְכָּהּ תָּמִיד,
אֶלָּא מַנַּחַת אוֹתוֹ עַל הָאָרֶץ אוֹ עַל הַכְּלִי אוֹ עַל הַשֻּׁלְחָן וְהוּא נוֹטְלוֹ.

ט הָאִשָּׁה שֶׁשָּׁבְרָה כֵּלִים בְּעֵת שֶׁעָשְׂתָה מַלְאֲכוֹתֶיהָ בְּתוֹךְ בֵּיתָהּ — פְּטוּרָה.
וְאֵין זֶה מִן הַדִּין, אֶלָּא תַּקָּנָה.
שֶׁאִם אֵין אַתָּה אוֹמֵר כֵּן — אֵין שָׁלוֹם בְּתוֹךְ הַבַּיִת לְעוֹלָם, אֶלָּא נִמְצֵאת נִזְהֶרֶת וְנִמְנַעַת
מֵרֹב הַמְּלָאכוֹת, וְנִמְצֵאת קְטָטָה בֵּינֵיהֶם.

י כָּל אִשָּׁה שֶׁתִּמָּנַע מִלַּעֲשׂוֹת מְלָאכָה מִן הַמְּלָאכוֹת שֶׁהִיא חַיֶּבֶת לַעֲשׂוֹתָן — כּוֹפִין אוֹתָהּ
וְעוֹשָׂה, אֲפִלּוּ בְּשׁוֹט.
טָעֵן הוּא שֶׁאֵינָהּ עוֹשָׂה, וְהִיא אוֹמֶרֶת שֶׁאֵינָהּ נִמְנַעַת מִלַּעֲשׂוֹת — מוֹשִׁיבִין אִשָּׁה בֵּינֵיהֶן אוֹ
שְׁכֵנִים.
וְדָבָר זֶה כְּפִי מַה שֶּׁיִּרְאֶה הַדַּיָּן שֶׁאֶפְשָׁר בַּדָּבָר.

יא הָאִשָּׁה כָּל זְמַן שֶׁהִיא מְנִיקָה אֶת בְּנָהּ — פּוֹחֲתִין לָהּ מִמַּעֲשֵׂה יָדֶיהָ, וּמוֹסִיפִין לָהּ עַל
מְזוֹנוֹתֶיהָ יַיִן וּדְבָרִים שֶׁיָּפִין לֶחָלָב.

---

16. Rav Kapach emphasizes that the Rambam's intent is not that the husband should
beat his wife himself, but that he should bring her to the court, which should administer
corporal punishment if they see fit.

The Ra'avad objects to this ruling, explaining that it is unheard of to compel a
woman by corporal punishment. Instead, her support should be cut back until she
accepts her household duties. The Rashba offers other options - to place her under a ban
of ostracism or to sell her *ketubah* and use the proceeds to hire a maid.

When quoting this law, the *Shulchan Aruch* (*Even HaEzer* 80:15) mentions that the
woman is compelled to perform her tasks, but omits reference to the means of compulsion
employed. The Ramah quotes the opinion of the Rambam together with that of the
Ra'avad and the Rashba, but appears to favor the latter views.

17. The woman is not required to support her claim with an oath, because a pattern
of the husband's complaining and the woman's being compelled to take an oath would
arise, and peace would not reign within the household (*Chelkat Mechokek* 80:28).

If, despite the fact that she was allotted the foods appropriate for her, she desires to eat more or desires to eat other foods, because of the craving in her stomach, she is entitled to eat everything she desires [provided she pays for the additional food] from her own funds. The husband cannot prevent her, saying: "Perhaps she will overeat or eat harmful foods[18] and the child will die." [The rationale is] that the physical pain the woman feels takes priority.

12. When a woman bears twins, she cannot be compelled to nurse both of them. Instead, she is required to nurse one, while the husband is required to hire a nursemaid for the second child.[19]

If a woman desires to nurse another woman's child together with her own, her husband may object and restrict her to nursing only her own child.[20]

13. Although a woman takes a vow not to nurse her child, she may be compelled to do so until the child - whether a boy or a girl - is 24 months old.[21]

If a woman desires to nurse her child, but her husband objects, claiming that this will mar her beauty, she is given this prerogative, for it is painful for her to part from her child.[22] [This law applies] even if she owns several maids.

14. If she is poor and would thus be obligated to nurse her child, but her husband is rich, and it is appropriate that his wife not be obligated to nurse his child - if his wife does not desire to nurse, he must hire a nursemaid or buy a maid, even if he did not possess any maidservants beforehand. [The rationale is] that the woman's social standing rises together with that of her husband and does not descend with his.

15. If a woman claims that [her husband] is of [a social standing that] requires him to hire or purchase a maid, and he claims that he is not, the burden of proof is on the woman. [The husband] is not [required] to take an oath.

16. When a woman is divorced, she cannot be compelled to nurse [her child]. If she desires to nurse the child, [her ex-husband] must pay her a wage.[23] If she does not desire [to nurse], she should give the son to his father, and he should care for him.[24]

18. Although a woman is enjoined not to eat foods that would harm her milk supply, she is allowed to do so if she feels physical pain, because her needs take priority over those of the child. In his *Kessef Mishneh*, Rav Yosef Karo objects to the Rambam's ruling; in the *Shulchan Aruch* (*Even HaEzer* 80:11), he quotes dissenting views together with that of the Rambam, without favoring either view.

Note the *Chelkat Mechokek* 80:22, who emphasizes that when there is a real danger to

פָּסְקוּ לָהּ מְזוֹנוֹת הָרְאוּיוֹת לָהּ, וַהֲרֵי הִיא מִתְאַוָּה לֶאֱכֹל יוֹתֵר אוֹ לֶאֱכֹל מַאֲכָלוֹת אֲחֵרוֹת מִפְּנֵי חֳלִי הַתַּאֲוָה שֶׁיֵּשׁ לָהּ בְּבִטְנָהּ — הֲרֵי זוֹ אוֹכֶלֶת מִשֶּׁלָּהּ כָּל מַה שֶׁתִּרְצֶה.

וְאֵין הַבַּעַל יָכוֹל לְעַכֵּב וְלוֹמַר, שֶׁאִם תֹּאכַל יוֹתֵר מִדַּי אוֹ תֹּאכַל מַאֲכָלִים רָעִים — יָמוּת הַוָּלָד, מִפְּנֵי שֶׁצַּעַר גּוּפָהּ קוֹדֵם.

יב יָלְדָה תְאוֹמִים — אֵין כּוֹפִין אוֹתָהּ לְהָנִיק שְׁנֵיהֶם, אֶלָּא מְנִיקָה אֶחָד וְשׂוֹכֵר הַבַּעַל מְנִיקָה לַשֵּׁנִי.

הֲרֵי שֶׁרָצְתָה הָאִשָּׁה לְהָנִיק בֶּן חֲבֶרְתָּהּ עִם בְּנָהּ — הַבַּעַל מְעַכֵּב, וְאֵינוֹ מַנִּיחָהּ אֶלָּא לְהָנִיק בְּנוֹ בִּלְבַד.

יג נָדְרָה שֶׁלֹּא לְהָנִיק אֶת בְּנָהּ — כּוֹפֶה אוֹתָהּ וּמְנִיקָתוֹ עַד שֶׁיִּהְיֶה בֶּן אַרְבָּעָה וְעֶשְׂרִים חֹדֶשׁ, אֶחָד הַזָּכָר וְאֶחָד הַנְּקֵבָה.

הִיא אוֹמֶרֶת: אֲנִי אָנִיק אֶת בְּנִי, וְהוּא אֵינוֹ רוֹצֶה שֶׁתָּנִיק אִשְׁתּוֹ כְּדֵי שֶׁלֹּא תִּתְנַוֵּל — אַף־עַל־פִּי שֶׁיֵּשׁ לָהּ כַּמָּה שְׁפָחוֹת, שׁוֹמְעִין לָהּ; שֶׁצַּעַר הוּא לָהּ לִפְרשׁ מִבְּנָהּ.

יד הָיְתָה עֲנִיָּה שֶׁהִיא חַיֶּבֶת לְהָנִיק אֶת בְּנָהּ, וַהֲרֵי הוּא עָשִׁיר שֶׁרָאוּי לוֹ שֶׁלֹּא תָנִיק אִשְׁתּוֹ, אַף־עַל־פִּי שֶׁאֵין לוֹ שְׁפָחוֹת, אִם לֹא רָצְתָה לְהָנִיק — שׂוֹכֵר מְנִיקָה אוֹ קוֹנֶה שִׁפְחָה;

מִפְּנֵי שֶׁהָאִשָּׁה עוֹלָה עִם בַּעְלָהּ, וְאֵינָהּ יוֹרֶדֶת.

טו הִיא אוֹמֶרֶת: רָאוּי הוּא לִשְׂכֹּר אוֹ לִקְנוֹת שִׁפְחָה, וְהוּא אוֹמֵר אֵינוֹ רָאוּי — עָלֶיהָ לְהָבִיא רְאָיָה, וְאֵין כָּאן מָקוֹם לִשְׁבוּעָה.

טז הָאִשָּׁה שֶׁנִּתְגָּרְשָׁה — אֵין כּוֹפִין אוֹתָהּ לְהָנִיק.

אֶלָּא: אִם רָצְתָה — נוֹתֵן לָהּ שְׂכָרָהּ וּמְנִיקָתוֹ, וְאִם לֹא רָצְתָה — נוֹתֶנֶת לוֹ אֶת בְּנוֹ וְהוּא מְטַפֵּל בּוֹ.

---

the child's life, and no danger to the mother, the woman must adjust her diet to help the child.

19. Rabbenu Asher states that she is required to nurse both children, but this view is not accepted by the later authorities.

20. The Ramah (*Even HaEzer* 80:14) quotes the *Tur*, which states that a husband may even prevent a woman from nursing her own child who was born to her from a previous husband.

21. Implied in the marital contract is that the woman will nurse her children. Hence, she may not object.

22. Rashi (*Ketubot* 61a) mentions another rationale: having milk without nursing causes pain.

23. For a father is obligated to pay for his child's sustenance until the age of six, as stated in Chapter 12, Halachah 14.

24. The husband cannot, however, be compelled to pay for a nursemaid if the mother is given custody.

When does the above apply? When she did not nurse the child long enough for him to recognize her. If, however, [the child is able] to recognize his mother, even if [the child] is blind,[25] he should not be separated from his mother because of the [possible] danger [the separation will cause] the child.[26] Instead, the woman is compelled to nurse the child for a wage until he reaches the age of 24 months.

17. [A husband] is not [obligated to] support his divorcee, even when she is nursing his child. In addition to the wage she receives [as a nursemaid], he must, however, provide her with those things that the child needs for clothing, food, drink, salves and the like. A woman who is pregnant is not entitled to any [payment] at all [from her ex-husband].

[The following rules apply after the 24] months have been completed, and the child has been weaned. If the divorcee desires that her son remain in her custody, he is not separated from her until he completes his sixth year [of life].[27] Instead, his father is compelled to provide him with his sustenance while he lives with his mother.

After the child completes his sixth year, the father has the right to say: "If [my son] is in my custody, I will support him. If, however, he continues to live with his mother,[28] I will not give him anything."[29]

A mother, by contrast, is given custody of her daughter forever, even after [she passes] the age of six.[30]

18. What is implied? If the father is [wealthy enough] to be obligated to give charity, the money necessary for his daughter's support should be expropriated from him and used to support the daughter, while she is in her mother's custody.

Even if the mother marries another [man], her daughter remains in her custody, and the father is obligated to provide for her sustenance until his death, as an act of charity. [Moreover, even if the girl's] father dies, she is entitled to receive her sustenance from his estate, as a provision of [her mother's] *ketubah*, although she remains in his mother's custody.

If a mother does not want her children - either males or females - to remain in her custody after she weans them, she has this prerogative, and she can give their father their custody, or make them wards of the community if there is no father, and [the community] must care for them.[31]

25. For even a blind child can recognize his mother from her smell and the flavor of her milk.
26. The pain of separation from his mother could cause the child to undergo travail that might lead to weakness. Rashi (*Ketubot* 59b) states that it is possible that the infant might reject another nursemaid and hence starve to death.
27. The Ra'avad objects to the Rambam's decision, explaining that a father is obligated to begin educating his child at an early age, and this is impossible when the child is in

בַּמֶּה דְּבָרִים אֲמוּרִים ? שֶׁלֹּא הֻכִּירָה אוֹתוֹ עַד שֶׁהִכִּירָהּ;

אֲבָל אִם הִכִּירָהּ, וַאֲפִלּוּ הוּא סוּמָא — אֵין מַפְרִישִׁין אוֹתוֹ מֵאִמּוֹ, מִפְּנֵי סַכָּנַת הַוָּלָד,

אֶלָּא כּוֹפִין אוֹתָהּ וּמְנִיקָה אוֹתוֹ בְּשָׂכָר עַד אַרְבָּעָה וְעֶשְׂרִים חֹדֶשׁ.

יז הַגְּרוּשָׁה אֵין לָהּ מְזוֹנוֹת אַף-עַל-פִּי שֶׁהִיא מְנִיקָה אֶת בְּנָהּ,

אֲבָל נוֹתֵן לָהּ יוֹתֵר עַל שְׂכָרָהּ דְּבָרִים שֶׁהַקָּטָן צָרִיךְ לָהֶן מִכְּסוּת וּמַאֲכָל וּמַשְׁקֶה וְסִיכָה וְכַיּוֹצֵא בָּזֶה.

אֲבָל הַמְעֻבֶּרֶת — אֵין לָהּ כְּלוּם.

שְׁלָמוּ חֳדָשָׁיו וּגְמָלַתּוּ, אִם רָצְתָה הַמְגֹרֶשֶׁת שֶׁיִּהְיֶה בְּנָהּ אֶצְלָהּ — אֵין מַפְרִישִׁין אוֹתוֹ מִמֶּנָּה עַד שֶׁיִּהְיֶה בֶּן שֵׁשׁ שָׁנִים גְּמוּרוֹת,

אֶלָּא כּוֹפִין אֶת אָבִיו וְנוֹתֵן לוֹ מְזוֹנוֹת וְהוּא אֵצֶל אִמּוֹ.

וְאַחַר שֵׁשׁ שָׁנִים, יֵשׁ לָאָב לוֹמַר: אִם הוּא אֶצְלִי — אֶתֵּן לוֹ מְזוֹנוֹת, וְאִם הוּא אֵצֶל אִמּוֹ — לֹא אֶתֵּן לוֹ מְזוֹנוֹת.

וְהַבַּת אֵצֶל אִמָּהּ לְעוֹלָם, וַאֲפִלּוּ לְאַחַר שֵׁשׁ.

יח כֵּיצַד ? הָיָה הָאָב רָאוּי לִצְדָקָה — מוֹצִיאִין מִמֶּנּוּ הָרָאוּי לוֹ בְּעַל כָּרְחוֹ וְזָנִין אוֹתָהּ וְהִיא אֵצֶל אִמָּהּ.

וַאֲפִלּוּ נִשֵּׂאת הָאֵם לְאַחֵר — בִּתָּהּ אֶצְלָהּ, וְאָבִיהָ זָן אוֹתָהּ מִשּׁוּם צְדָקָה עַד שֶׁיָּמוּת הָאָב.

וְתִזּוֹן מִנְּכָסָיו אַחַר מוֹתוֹ בִּתְנַאי כְּתֻבָּה וְהִיא אֵצֶל אִמָּהּ.

וְאִם לֹא רָצְתָה הָאֵם שֶׁיִּהְיוּ בָּנֶיהָ אֶצְלָהּ אַחַר שֶׁגְּמָלָתַן, אֶחָד זְכָרִים וְאֶחָד נְקֵבוֹת — הָרְשׁוּת בְּיָדָהּ.

וְנוֹתֶנֶת אוֹתָן לַאֲבִיהֶן, אוֹ מַשְׁלֶכֶת אוֹתָן לַקָּהָל — אִם אֵין לָהֶן אָב — וְהֵן מְטַפְּלִין בָּהֶן.

the mother's custody. The *Maggid Mishneh* refutes that argument, explaining that the amount of teaching that the father is obligated to give the child can be communicated at visits.

It must be emphasized, however, that the Rambam is referring to a situation in which the mother shares the same standards of observance as the father. If that is not the case, and the mother's observance is lacking, the father should be given the right to custody.

28. From the Rambam's wording, it appears that if a son desires to stay in his mother's custody, and the mother is willing to support him, he is entitled to do so. (See *Chelkat Mechokek* 82:9.)

29. At present, there are many courts that require the father to continue supporting his son, even if he desires to remain with his mother.

30. For her mother is more prepared to train her to grow up as a woman.

The Ramah (*Even HaEzer* 82:7) states that this law applies only when the court feels that it is in the daughter's best interests to remain in her mother's custody. If, however, it appears that the daughter's interests will be served better when she is in her father's custody, he is awarded that privilege.

31. The *Maggid Mishneh* states that this implies that a woman does not have any

CHAPTER TWENTY-TWO

1. The husband takes precedence over any other person with regard to the inheritance of his wife's estate.[1]

When does the husband acquire this right? When his wife leaves her father's domain, even though she has not entered the *chuppah*.[2] Since the woman has entered her husband's domain, he [has the right] to inherit [her estate].

2. What is implied? When a woman has been consecrated and her father hands her over to her husband or to his agents, or the agents of the woman's father hand her over to her husband or to his agents, and the woman dies on the way, before she enters the *chuppah*, her husband inherits her estate, even though her dowry is still in her father's home.[3]

Similarly, if the father or his agents went together with the husband, and the husband entered into privacy in a courtyard together with [his bride] with the intent of marriage,[4] and afterwards she dies, her husband inherits [her estate].

If, however, [the woman and] her husband or his agents are still accompanied by her father or his agents on their journey to the husband's house, her father inherits [her estate] if she dies, even if her dowry is already in her husband's home. [This law applies even if the woman] and her husband entered a courtyard together to spend the night, as travelers lodge together in one inn.[5] [The rationale is that] she is accompanied by her father or his agents, and [her husband] has not entered into privacy with her for the sake of marriage.

3. Similarly, when a *bogeret*, an orphan, or a widow[6] goes from her father's house to her husband's home on her own initiative without being accompanied by her husband or his agents, and dies on the way, her husband does not inherit [her estate].[7]

4. Although a man marries a woman with whom he is forbidden [to have relations], if she dies [during his lifetime], he inherits her estate when his

responsibility to raise her children. The *Ma'aseh Rokeach* maintains that if the mother has means, she is required to provide for her children's support and cannot cast the burden on the community. She need not, however, raise them in her home, lest this deter other men from desiring to marry her. This latter opinion is not, however, mentioned in the *Shulchan Aruch* (*Even HaEzer* 82:8) or its commentaries when dealing with this situation.

1. As explained in Chapter 12, Halachah 3 and notes, this is one of the four privileges our Sages granted a husband as part of the marriage contract. (See also *Hilchot Nachalot* 1:8.)

פֶּרֶק שְׁנַיִם וְעֶשְׂרִים

א הַבַּעַל קוֹדֵם לְכָל אָדָם בִּירֻשַּׁת אִשְׁתּוֹ.

וּמֵאֵימָתַי יִזְכֶּה בִּירֻשָּׁתָהּ? מִשֶּׁתֵּצֵא מֵרְשׁוּת הָאָב, וְאַף־עַל־פִּי שֶׁעֲדַיִן לֹא נִכְנְסָה לְחֻפָּה. הוֹאִיל וְנַעֲשֵׂת בִּרְשׁוּת בַּעְלָהּ — יִירָשֶׁנָּה.

ב כֵּיצַד? הָאִשָּׁה שֶׁנִּתְאָרְסָה, וּמְסָרָהּ אָבִיהָ לְבַעְלָהּ אוֹ לִשְׁלוּחֵי בַעְלָהּ,

אוֹ מְסָרוּהָ שְׁלוּחֵי הָאָב לְבַעְלָהּ אוֹ לִשְׁלוּחָיו, וּמֵתָה בַּדֶּרֶךְ קֹדֶם שֶׁתִּכָּנֵס לְחֻפָּה — אַף־עַל־פִּי שֶׁכְּתֻבָּתָהּ עֲדַיִן בְּבֵית אָבִיהָ, בַּעְלָהּ יוֹרְשָׁהּ.

וְכֵן אִם הָלַךְ הָאָב אוֹ שְׁלוּחֵי הָאָב עִם הַבַּעַל, וְנִכְנָס עִמָּהּ בַּעְלָהּ בַּדֶּרֶךְ לְחָצֵר וְנִתְיַחֵד עִמָּהּ שָׁם לְשֵׁם נִשּׂוּאִין, וָמֵתָה — הֲרֵי זֶה יִירָשֶׁנָּה בַּעְלָהּ.

אֲבָל אִם עֲדַיִן הָאָב עִם הַבַּעַל לְהוֹלִיכָהּ לְבֵית בַּעְלָהּ, אוֹ שֶׁהָלְכוּ שְׁלוּחֵי הָאָב עִם שְׁלוּחֵי הַבַּעַל אוֹ עִם הַבַּעַל,

אֲפִלּוּ נִכְנָס הַבַּעַל עִמָּהּ לְחָצֵר לָלוּן כְּדֶרֶךְ שֶׁלָּנִין עוֹבְרֵי דְרָכִים בְּפֻנְדָּק אֶחָד — הוֹאִיל וְהָאָב אוֹ שְׁלוּחָיו עִמָּהּ, וַעֲדַיִן לֹא נִתְיַחֵד עִמָּהּ לְשֵׁם נִשּׂוּאִין, אִם מֵתָה — יִירָשֶׁנָּה אָבִיהָ, אַף־עַל־פִּי שֶׁכְּתֻבָּתָהּ בְּבֵית בַּעְלָהּ.

ג וְכֵן אִם הָיְתָה בּוֹגֶרֶת אוֹ יְתוֹמָה אוֹ אַלְמָנָה, וְהָלְכָה הִיא בְּעַצְמָהּ מִבֵּית אָבִיהָ לְבֵית בַּעְלָהּ, וְאֵין עִמָּהּ לֹא בַּעְלָהּ וְלֹא שְׁלוּחָיו, וּמֵתָה בַּדֶּרֶךְ — אֵין הַבַּעַל יוֹרֵשׁ אוֹתָהּ.

ד הַנּוֹשֵׂא אִשָּׁה שֶׁהִיא אֲסוּרָה לוֹ — הוֹאִיל וְיֵשׁ לוֹ בָּהּ קִדּוּשִׁין, אִם מֵתָה תַּחְתָּיו — יִירָשֶׁנָּה.

---

2. The second phase of marriage, *nisu'in*, does not start until the woman enters the *chuppah*, and it is only at that time that the marriage contract takes effect. Nevertheless, an exception is made in this instance, as explained in the following halachot and notes.

3. The Ramah (*Even HaEzer* 57:1) cites the opinion of the *Tur* and other Ashkenazic authorities, which is that the husband does not have a right to inherit his wife's dowry until it enters his possession.

4. Moreover, if the courtyard belongs to the husband, it is assumed that the couple entered for the sake of marriage, even when they do not explicitly state so. This is the view of all authorities, and the *Maggid Mishneh* explains that it is also shared by the Rambam.

5. If the courtyard belongs to the woman, this intent is understood even when it is not explicitly stated.

6. This law applies even if the widow is still a minor, for she is no longer subject to her father's authority, as reflected in Chapter 3, Halachah 12.

7. In such a situation, once an *arusah* is met by her husband or his agents, however, he is entitled to inherit her estate.

consecration of her is binding.[8] Similarly, a man who marries a *k'tanah* [after her father's death][9] inherits her estate if she dies in his lifetime, even though his consecration of her is not binding entirely.

When, by contrast, a mentally capable man marries a deaf mute, he is not entitled to inherit her estate when she dies.[10] When, however, a deaf mute marries a mentally capable woman and dies, he should inherit her estate. For she is capable of understanding and married him voluntarily. [In doing so,] she gave him a right to her property.[11]

5. When a *k'tanah* was consecrated with her father's consent, but married without his consent - whether in his presence or outside his presence - her father has a right to object, as we have explained.[12] [In such a situation,] if the girl dies, her husband should not inherit her estate, even if the father remains silent, unless he expressed his consent to her marriage.

6. The *geonim* ruled that when a woman falls sick and asks her husband to divorce her so that he will not inherit her estate, her words are of no consequence, [even if] she [agrees to] forfeit her *ketubah*. Even if she says: "I hate him and no longer desire to live with him," her words are not heeded, and she is not judged as a woman who rebels against her husband.[13] This is a desirable ruling.

7. During a woman s lifetime, her husband enjoys the benefits of all the property she owns, regardless of whether it is classified as *nichsei tzon barzel* or *nichsei m'log*. If she dies in her husband's lifetime, her husband inherits everything.

Therefore, if the woman sold property classified as *nichsei m'log* after she married, even if she became the owner of that property before she became consecrated, her husband may expropriate the income from that property from the purchasers throughout his wife's lifetime. He may not, however, expropriate the land itself, for he has no right to the land itself, if it is classified as *nichsei m'log*, until his wife dies.[14]

If she dies in his lifetime, he may expropriate the land from the purchasers[15] without paying them for it.[16] If the actual money that [the

8. See Chapter 1, Halachot 6 and 7; Chapter 4, Halachah 14.
9. Or after she becomes divorced or widowed in her father's lifetime (Chapter 4, Halachot 7 and 8).
10. The rationale is that she is not entitled to a *ketubah* (Chapter 11, Halachah 4). Moreover, since she is not responsible for her actions, she has no right to transfer her property.
11. Although the Ra'avad objects to this ruling, the *Shulchan Aruch* (*Even HaEzer* 90:3) quotes the Rambam's view.
12. Chapter 3, Halachah 13.

וְכֵן הַנּוֹשֵׂא אֶת הַקְּטַנָּה, אַף־עַל־פִּי שֶׁאֵין קִדּוּשֶׁיהָ קִדּוּשִׁין גְּמוּרִים, אִם מֵתָה תַחְתָּיו — יִירָשֶׁנָּה.

אֲבָל הַפִּקֵּחַ שֶׁנָּשָׂא חֵרֶשֶׁת, אִם מֵתָה — לֹא יִירָשֶׁנָּה.

וְהַחֵרֵשׁ שֶׁנָּשָׂא פִּקַּחַת וָמֵתָה — יִירָשֶׁנָּה;

שֶׁהֲרֵי הִיא בַת דַּעַת, וּלְדַעְתָּהּ נִשֵּׂאת, וְזִכְּתָה לוֹ מָמוֹנָהּ.

ה קְטַנָּה שֶׁנִּתְקַדְּשָׁה לְדַעַת אָבִיהָ, וְנִשֵּׂאת שֶׁלֹּא לְדַעַת אָבִיהָ, בֵּין בְּפָנָיו בֵּין שֶׁלֹּא בְּפָנָיו — יָכוֹל הָאָב לְמָחוֹת, כְּמוֹ שֶׁבֵּאַרְנוּ.

וַאֲפִלּוּ שָׁתַק הָאָב, אִם מֵתָה — אֵין הַבַּעַל יוֹרְשָׁהּ, אֶלָּא אִם כֵּן רָצָה הָאָב בְּנִשּׂוּאֶיהָ.

ו הוֹרוּ הַגְּאוֹנִים, שֶׁהָאִשָּׁה שֶׁחָלְתָה וּבִקְשָׁה מִבַּעְלָהּ שֶׁיְּגָרְשֶׁנָּה וְתֵצֵא בְּלֹא כְתֻבָּה, כְּדֵי שֶׁלֹּא יִירָשֶׁנָּה — אֵין שׁוֹמְעִין לָהּ.

וַאֲפִלּוּ אָמְרָה: אֲנִי שׂוֹנְאָה אוֹתוֹ וְאֵינִי רוֹצָה לַעֲמֹד עִמּוֹ — אֵין שׁוֹמְעִין לָהּ. וְאֵין דָּנִין אוֹתָהּ כְּדִין מוֹרֶדֶת.

וְדִין יָפֶה הוּא זֶה.

ז כָּל נְכָסִים שֶׁיֵּשׁ לָאִשָּׁה, בֵּין נִכְסֵי צֹאן בַּרְזֶל בֵּין נִכְסֵי מְלוֹג — הַבַּעַל אוֹכֵל כָּל פֵּרוֹתֵיהֶן בְּחַיֶּיהָ.

וְאִם מֵתָה בְּחַיֵּי בַּעְלָהּ — יוֹרֵשׁ בַּעְלָהּ הַכֹּל.

לְפִיכָךְ, אִם מָכְרָה הָאִשָּׁה נִכְסֵי מְלוֹג אַחַר שֶׁנִּשֵּׂאת, אַף־עַל־פִּי שֶׁאוֹתָן הַנְּכָסִים נָפְלוּ לָהּ קֹדֶם שֶׁתִּתְאָרֵס —

הַבַּעַל מוֹצִיא הַפֵּרוֹת מִיַּד הַלָּקוֹחוֹת כָּל יְמֵי חַיֶּיהָ, אֲבָל לֹא גוּף הַקַּרְקַע; שֶׁאֵין לוֹ כְלוּם בְּגוּף נִכְסֵי מְלוֹג עַד שֶׁתָּמוּת.

מֵתָה בְּחַיָּיו — מוֹצִיא הַגּוּף מִיַּד הַלָּקוֹחוֹת בְּלֹא דָמִים.

---

13. See Chapter 14, Halachah 8.

14. The advantage in the purchaser's continuing to own the land itself is that if the husband dies before his wife, her sale is binding, and the land becomes the purchaser's property. From this time onward, he is entitled to benefit from the land as well.

Rabbenu Asher differs with the Rambam on this issue and maintains that the husband has the right to take the property from the purchaser, even during his wife's lifetime. The *Shulchan Aruch* (*Even HaEzer* 90:9) follows the Rambam's view, while the Ramah quotes that of Rabbenu Asher.

15. Even the Ramah and Rabbenu Asher accept this ruling.

16. There is a difference of opinion with regard to this matter among the *geonim*, but all the later authorities accept this view. The rationale is that the husband's right to the land supersedes that of the purchaser. The money that the purchaser paid is considered to have become a debt owed him by the woman's estate, and the husband is not required to pay his wife's debts.

woman] took from the purchasers still exists, however, it must be returned to the purchasers. The husband cannot say: "Perhaps this money was found [by my wife]," [and on that basis take it as his own].[17]

8. When does the above apply? With regard to property about which the husband knew.[18] When, however, a woman inherits property in another country without her husband's knowledge and sells it, the sale is binding.[19]

Similarly, if a woman sells [property][20] between her consecration and the consummation of the marriage bond, the sale is binding. For the husband has no right to his wife's property until their marriage is consummated.

9. When a woman signs over all[21] of her property to another person - regardless of whether or not that person is a relative - before she marries, even when there is a provision that if she is divorced or if she becomes a widow, this present is nullified - as will be explained in *Hilchot Matanah*[22] - her husband is not entitled to benefit from the income of this property. And if she dies in his lifetime, he does not inherit it.

[The rationale is] that she gave this property away before she married. When she dies during her husband's lifetime, the recipient of the present acquires full title to it.

Moreover, [the same laws apply] even if she gave away a portion of her property - or all her holdings - before she married and wrote [in the deed of transfer] to the recipient: "Acquire the property from this time onward, [dependent] on my consent."[23] [Although] the recipient does not acquire complete ownership until the woman expresses her consent,[24] her husband is not entitled to benefit from the income of this property. And if she dies in his lifetime, he does not inherit it.[25]

17. A husband is entitled to any ownerless object discovered by his wife. His claim is not accepted, however, if he states that money that appears to have come from the sale of property came from the discovery of a lost object. There is no need for witnesses to testify that this is the money from the sale. It is sufficient that it appears to be so. If, however, the money has been changed into a different coinage or currency, the husband is not required to return it (*Maggid Mishneh*).
18. In his Commentary on the Mishnah (*Ketubot* 8:2), the Rambam states that this refers to property located in the bride and groom's city or the surrounding locale, as opposed to property owned by her in more distant locales. It is questionable, however, if the same geographic restrictions apply in today's global village.
19. The *Shulchan Aruch* (*Even HaEzer* 90:11) states that preferably, a woman should not sell this property, because her husband is entitled to inherit it.

The commentaries explain that when the husband knows of his wife's financial holdings, it is an implicit part of the marriage contract - and perhaps part of his intent in entering into the marriage relationship - that he will inherit this property. When, however, he is unaware of her ownership of property, this motive cannot be given as the reason for his desire to enter this relationship.

וְאִם הַדָּמִים שֶׁלָּקְחָה מִיַּד הַלָּקוֹחוֹת קַיָּמִין בְּעַצְמָן — מַחֲזִירָן לַלָּקוֹחוֹת,
וְאֵינוֹ יָכוֹל לוֹמַר: שֶׁמָּא מְצִיאָה הֵן.

ח בַּמֶּה דְבָרִים אֲמוּרִים? בִּנְכָסִים הַיְדוּעִין לַבַּעַל;
אֲבָל אִם נָפְלוּ לָהּ נְכָסִים בִּמְדִינָה אַחֶרֶת, וְלֹא יָדַע בָּהֶן הַבַּעַל, וּמְכָרָה אוֹתָן — מִכְרָהּ קַיָּם.
וְכֵן אֲרוּסָה שֶׁמָּכְרָה קֹדֶם הַנִּשּׂוּאִין — מִכְרָהּ קַיָּם;
שֶׁאֵין לַבַּעַל בְּנִכְסֵי אֲרוּסָתוֹ כְּלוּם עַד שֶׁיִּכְנֹס.

ט הָאִשָּׁה שֶׁכָּתְבָה כָּל נְכָסֶיהָ לְאַחֵר, בֵּין קָרוֹב בֵּין רָחוֹק, קֹדֶם שֶׁתִּנָּשֵׂא —
אַף־עַל־פִּי שֶׁאִם נִתְגָּרְשָׁה אוֹ נִתְאַלְמָנָה תְּבַטֵּל הַמַּתָּנָה, כְּמוֹ שֶׁיִּתְבָּאֵר בְּהִלְכוֹת מַתָּנָה, אֵין
הַבַּעַל אוֹכֵל פֵּרוֹתֵיהֶן, וְאִם מֵתָה בְּחַיָּיו — אֵינוֹ יוֹרְשָׁן; שֶׁהֲרֵי נָתְנָה אוֹתָן קֹדֶם שֶׁתִּנָּשֵׂא.
וּכְשֶׁתָּמוּת בְּחַיֵּי בַּעְלָהּ, יִקְנֶה מְקַבֵּל הַמַּתָּנָה מַתְּנָתוֹ קִנְיָן גָּמוּר.
וְלֹא עוֹד, אֶלָּא אֲפִלּוּ נָתְנָה מִקְצָת נְכָסֶיהָ אוֹ כֻלָּם קֹדֶם נִשּׂוּאֶיהָ, וְכָתְבָה לַמְקַבֵּל: קְנֵה
מֵהַיּוֹם וְלִכְשֶׁאֶרְצֶה, שֶׁהֲרֵי לֹא קָנָה קִנְיָן גָּמוּר עַד שֶׁתִּרְצֶה — אֵין הַבַּעַל אוֹכֵל פֵּרוֹת אוֹתָהּ
הַמַּתָּנָה,
וְאִם מֵתָה — אֵינוֹ יוֹרְשָׁהּ.

It must be added that as soon as the husband becomes aware of this property, it is considered to be part of the woman's *nichsei m'log* and is bound by all the laws pertaining to such property (*Shulchan Aruch, loc. cit.*:12). Moreover, if the woman dies without selling this property, her husband is entitled to inherit it, although he was never aware of his wife's ownership of it during her lifetime.

20. The *Tur* (*Even HaEzer* 90) states that the woman has the full right to sell any property that she owned before she was consecrated. With regard to property that she acquired after she was consecrated, it is preferable that she not sell it - but if she sells it, the husband has no claim to it.

21. As explained in *Hilchot Zechiyah UMatanah*, slightly different rules apply if the woman signed over only a portion of her property.

22. *Hilchot Zechiyah UMatanah* 6:12. It is clearly obvious that the woman's intent in giving the present is to protect her holdings from being inherited by her husband.

23. In his gloss on *Ketubot* 79a, Rabbenu Nissim explains that the Rambam equates this provision with the one mentioned in the previous clause. The only difference between the two is one of tact. The provision in this clause is more gently worded, so that the intent to free the woman's holdings from her husband is less obvious.

24. Unlike the Rambam, Rabbenu Asher and other authorities maintain that the woman need not explicitly mention her consent to the present. All that is necessary is that she refrain from nullifying it.

25. Rabbenu Nissim asks, according to the approach of the Rambam (in contrast to the approach of Rabbenu Asher mentioned in the previous note): If the woman did not explicitly mention her consent to the present before her death, why does her husband have no right to inherit her property? The provision on which the present was based was never fulfilled.

Seemingly, this property can be compared to a woman's property of which her husband

10. While a woman is waiting for her *yavam* [to marry her according to the rite of *yibbum*], she may sell or give as a present property that she acquires during the time she is in this status.[26] Until he marries the *yevamah*, the *yavam* has no right to benefit from the property, even the *nichsei tzon barzel*,[27] that she brought to his [deceased] brother's household.

If the *yevamah* dies in this status, her heirs from her father's household inherit her *nichsei m'log*[28] and half of her *nichsei tzon barzel*.[29] Her husband's heirs inherit [the money due her by virtue of] her *ketubah*[30] and the remaining half of her *nichsei tzon barzel*, and they are responsible for her burial.[31]

11. The money due a *yevamah* by virtue of her *ketubah* is considered to be a lien on her [late] husband's estate. Therefore, a *yavam* is not entitled to sell any of his brother's property[32] - neither before *yibbum* nor after *yibbum*.

If he sells the deceased's property, gives it away as a present, divides it with his brothers - whether before *yibbum* or after *yibbum* - his actions are of no consequence. For it is already obligatory to make this property available to the widow so that she can collect [the money due her by virtue of] her *ketubah* from it.

was unaware. As mentioned in the notes on the previous halachah, the husband has the right to inherit such property, and thus he should also inherit the property mentioned in this clause.

Rabbenu Nissim explains that since the Rambam maintains that a husband's right to inherit his wife's property is a Rabbinical ordinance, there is room for leniency when, as in the present case, it is obvious that the woman did not desire her husband to inherit her estate. Obviously motivated by the same question, but unwilling to offer such a resolution, Rav David Arameah explains that the Rambam's ruling applies in an instance when the woman in fact expressed her consent to the present before her death.

26. As mentioned in the notes on Halachah 8, preferably a woman should not sell property she acquires after her consecration. One might think that the same principle applies to a *yevamah*, for she also shares a bond to her *yavam*. There is, however, a distinction between the two: a woman who is consecrated will most likely be married, while a *yevamah* may be freed from her obligation through *chalitzah*. Hence, there are no restrictions placed upon her with regard to the sale of her holdings.

27. The difference between *nichsei m'log* and *nichsei tzon barzel* is that with regard to *nichsei m'log*, the object itself belongs to the woman, while the property regarded as *nichsei tzon barzel* is considered to belong to her late husband. He was, however, obligated to pay his wife for the value designated for the property at the time of marriage (Chapter 16, Halachah 1).

Since the *nichsei tzon barzel* are considered to belong to the *yevamah's* late husband's estate, one might think that the *yavam* would have a right to them. Hence, it is necessary to clarify that he is given this right only after marriage.

י שׁוֹמֶרֶת יָבָם יֵשׁ לָהּ לִמְכֹּר וְלִתֵּן בְּמַתָּנָה נְכָסִים שֶׁנָּפְלוּ לָהּ כְּשֶׁהִיא שׁוֹמֶרֶת יָבָם.
וְאֵין לַיָּבָם פֵּרוֹת, אֲפִלּוּ בְּנִכְסֵי צֹאן בַּרְזֶל שֶׁהִכְנִיסָה לְאָחִיו, עַד שֶׁיִּכְנֹס.
מֵתָה כְּשֶׁהִיא שׁוֹמֶרֶת יָבָם — יוֹרְשֶׁיהָ מֵאָבִיהָ יוֹרְשִׁין בְּנִכְסֵי מְלוֹג שֶׁלָּהּ וַחֲצִי נִכְסֵי צֹאן
בַּרְזֶל,
וְיוֹרְשֵׁי הַבַּעַל יוֹרְשִׁים כְּתֻבָּתָהּ וַחֲצִי נִכְסֵי צֹאן בַּרְזֶל.
וְיוֹרְשֵׁי הַבַּעַל חַיָּבִין בִּקְבוּרָתָהּ.

יא שׁוֹמֶרֶת יָבָם — כְּתֻבָּתָהּ עַל כָּל נִכְסֵי בַּעְלָהּ.
לְפִיכָךְ אֵין הַיָּבָם יָכוֹל לִמְכֹּר בְּנִכְסֵי אָחִיו, בֵּין קֹדֶם יִבּוּם בֵּין אַחַר יִבּוּם.
וְאִם מָכַר אוֹ נָתַן מַתָּנָה אוֹ חָלַק עִם אָחָיו בְּנִכְסֵי הַמֵּת, בֵּין קֹדֶם יִבּוּם בֵּין אַחַר יִבּוּם
— לֹא עָשָׂה כְּלוּם;
שֶׁכְּבָר נִתְחַיְּבוּ נְכָסִים אֵלּוּ לָאַלְמָנָה לִגְבּוֹת מֵהֶן כְּתֻבָּתָהּ.

As mentioned by the Ra'avad and the *Maggid Mishneh*, most authorities differ with the Rambam on this point. The *Maggid Mishneh* maintains that the *yavam* is entitled to half of the benefit that accrues from the *nichsei tzon barzel*. This opinion is quoted by the *Shulchan Aruch* (*Even HaEzer* 160:6). (The Rambam's opinion is also quoted, but it appears that the other opinion is favored.) The Ramah mentions the opinion of the Ra'avad which goes even further and gives the *yavam* rights to half the benefits of *nichsei m'log* that the *yevamah* acquired while she was married to her deceased husband.

28. For this property belongs to her outright.

29. A division is necessary because this property is considered to belong to the *yevamah's* late husband, as explained above. Therefore, his heirs have a claim to it. Nevertheless, since he died in his wife's lifetime, and she did not receive payment for this property, her own heirs also have a claim.

This ruling is also disputed by other authorities, who maintain that all the *nichsei tzon barzel* are considered the property of the husband's heirs, together with the woman's *ketubah*. The *Shulchan Aruch* (*loc. cit.*:7) quotes the Rambam's view, while the Ramah quotes that of the other authorities.

The Ramah also adds that these laws do not apply in the Ashkenazic community in the present era - or in other communities - where the rite of *yibbum* is not practiced, and instead, the *yevamah* is freed from her obligation through the rite of *chalitzah*. Since the *yevamah* will not marry the *yavam*, he has no rights with regard to her property.

30. I.e., both the essential requirement of the *ketubah* and any additional amount added by her deceased husband.

31. For our Sages associated a woman's burial with the inheritance of her *ketubah* (Chapter 12, Halachah 14).

32. Even if the value of the property left by the deceased brother is many times the value of the woman's *ketubah*, none of the property may be sold, lest the remaining property be destroyed and the woman have difficulty collecting the money due her by virtue of her *ketubah* from the purchasers (*Ketubot* 81b).

12. When a man marries his *yevamah* at a time when there is produce growing on the land left by her husband, this produce should be sold,[33] and the proceeds used to purchase land from which the *yavam* will derive the benefit that accrues.

13. When, [by contrast, the deceased] left produce that was already harvested, money or movable property, it becomes the property of the *yavam*. He may use it as he sees fit, and [the *yevamah's*] objections are of no consequence.

[The rationale is that the woman's right] to collect [the money due her by virtue of] her *ketubah* from movable property stems only from an enactment of the *geonim*, and this enactment does not have the power to prevent [the *yavam* from taking possession] of his brother's property,[34] and cause him to be restrained from dealing with them because of this lien.

14. [The following rules apply when] a *yevamah's* [first husband was not obligated to] grant her a *ketubah*[35] or [when] she waived her *ketubah* in his favor. The *yavam* acquires his brother's estate and may sell [portions of it] or give them away as he desires. When he marries his *yevamah*, he is obligated to compose a *ketubah* for 100 [*zuz*]. All of his property will be considered as being on lien for the *ketubah*, [i.e., the same laws apply to her] as apply to other women who have a *ketubah*.[36]

15. When a woman sells *nichsei tzon barzel* - whether to her husband or to others - after she marries, her act is of no consequence.[37]

Similarly, if her husband sells landed property belonging to his wife - whether it be *nichsei tzon barzel* or *nichsei m'log* - his act is of no consequence.[38]

16. [Should the husband] sell movable property that is classified as *nichsei tzon barzel*[39] - although he is not allowed to make such a sale - the sale is binding.[40]

---

33. I.e., since the produce requires the land, it is considered as if it were landed property, and the money received from the sale has the same status as the landed property mentioned in the previous halachah.

34. The *Maggid Mishneh*, the Rivash (Responsa 365 and 366), and the *Shulchan Aruch* (*Even HaEzer* 168:5) emphasize that the law stated by the Rambam applies only when the husband did not follow the suggestion (Chapter 16, Halachah 8) of stating explicitly in the *ketubah* that the woman may collect from movable property the money due her by virtue of her *ketubah*. (There are other authorities who differ with the Rambam and maintain that even if the provision is not stated explicitly in the woman's *ketubah*, the movable property should be sold and land purchased.)

35. E.g., he died after he consecrated her, but before he consummated the marriage - in which instance, the woman is obligated to undergo either *yibbum* or *chalitzah*, and yet her deceased husband was not obligated to grant her a *ketubah*.

יב כָּנַס אֶת יְבִמְתּוֹ וְהִנִּיחַ אָחִיו פֵּרוֹת מְחֻבָּרִין לַקַּרְקַע — יִמָּכְרוּ, וְיִלָּקַח בָּהֶן קַרְקַע, וְהַיָּבָם אוֹכֵל פֵּרוֹתֵיהֶן.

יג הִנִּיחַ פֵּרוֹת תְּלוּשִׁין מִן הַקַּרְקַע, וְכֵן אִם הִנִּיחַ מָעוֹת וּמִטַּלְטְלִין — הַכֹּל שֶׁל יָבָם, וּמִשְׁתַּמֵּשׁ בָּהֶן כְּמוֹ שֶׁיִּרְצֶה, וְאֵינָהּ יְכוֹלָה לְעַכֵּב. שֶׁהַמִּטַּלְטְלִין אֵין הַכְּתֻבָּה נִגְבֵּית מֵהֶן אֶלָּא בְּתַקָּנַת הַגְּאוֹנִים, וְאֵין כֹּחַ בְּתַקָּנָה זוֹ לְמָנְעוֹ מִנִּכְסֵי אָחִיו וּלְאָסְרָן עָלָיו בְּאַחֲרָיוּת זוֹ שֶׁלֹּא יִשָּׂא וְיִתֵּן בָּהֶם.

יד יְבָמָה שֶׁלֹּא הָיְתָה לָהּ כְּתֻבָּה, אוֹ שֶׁמָּחֲלָה כְּתֻבָּתָהּ — זָכָה בְּנִכְסֵי אָחִיו, וּמוֹכֵר וְנוֹתֵן כְּחֶפְצוֹ. וּכְשֶׁיִּכְנֹס אֶת יְבִמְתּוֹ, יִכְתֹּב לָהּ כְּתֻבָּה מֵאָה, וְיִהְיוּ כָּל נְכָסָיו אַחֲרָאִין לִכְתֻבָּתָהּ, כִּשְׁאָר כָּל הַנָּשִׁים שֶׁיֵּשׁ לָהֶן כְּתֻבָּה.

טו הָאִשָּׁה שֶׁמָּכְרָה אוֹ שֶׁנָּתְנָה אַחַר שֶׁנִּשֵּׂאת בְּנִכְסֵי צֹאן בַּרְזֶל, בֵּין לְבַעְלָהּ בֵּין לַאֲחֵרִים — לֹא עָשְׂתָה כְּלוּם. וְכֵן בַּעַל שֶׁמָּכַר קַרְקַע בְּנִכְסֵי אִשְׁתּוֹ, בֵּין נִכְסֵי צֹאן בַּרְזֶל בֵּין נִכְסֵי מְלוֹג — לֹא עָשָׂה כְּלוּם.

טז מָכַר מִטַּלְטְלִין שֶׁל נִכְסֵי צֹאן בַּרְזֶל, אַף-עַל-פִּי שֶׁאֵינוֹ רַשַּׁאי, אִם מָכַר — מִמְכָּרוֹ מִמְכָּר.

36. Since she has no claim to her deceased husband's property, she is not judged by the laws pertaining to a *yevamah*, but rather by those pertaining to other women.

37. If she sells the land to her husband, the sale is rescinded because she can claim that she did not sell it willingly; she did so only to appease her husband (*Bava Batra* 49b). If she sells the land to others, the sale is rescinded because her husband has a right to benefit from her property, and she cannot take away this right from him without his consent. If, however, the husband agrees to her sale, it is binding, as stated in *Hilchot Mechirah* 30:3).

Note the ruling of the Ramah (*Even HaEzer* 90:13), who writes that if the husband dies, the sale made by the woman is effective retroactively. (But see also the gloss of the *Beit Shmuel* 90:46.)

38. With regard to *nichsei m'log*, it is obvious that the husband's sale is of no consequence, for the woman owns this type of property. With regard to *nichsei tzon barzel*, which are considered to be the husband's property, there are authorities (e.g., the Ra'avad) who differ with the Rambam and maintain that the sale is valid until the time comes when the woman desires to collect the money due her by virtue of her *ketubah*.

The commentaries support the Rambam's opinion, explaining that even though the woman has the potential to expropriate the property afterwards by force of law, the sale should be nullified. For women are not comfortable presenting claims in court. If the sale were allowed to remain binding, the only way the woman could receive her due would be by lodging a legal claim. The *Shulchan Aruch* (*Even HaEzer* 90:13) quotes the Rambam's view.

39. If the woman is divorced, she is entitled to this property. Hence, the husband does not have the prerogative of selling it.

40. The husband is allowed to destroy this property through frequent use. Therefore, the

If both [the husband and the wife] sell [a property classified as] *nichsei m'log*, the sale is binding,[41] regardless of whether the purchaser purchased the property from the husband first and then from the wife, or if he first purchased it from the wife and then from the husband.

17. Similarly, when a woman sells her *nichsei m'log* to her husband or gives them to him as a present, the sale or the gift is binding. She cannot rationalize her actions by saying, "[This was not my true intent.] I did it [only] to appease my husband."[42] With regard to other property, however, she may offer such a rationalization.

18. What is implied? When a woman sells her *nichsei tzon barzel* to her husband or gives them to him as a present, her husband does not acquire this property. [This applies to] landed property and movable property [in this category], to a field that was designated for her from which [she could collect the money due her by virtue of] her *ketubah*, a field belonging to her that was specifically mentioned in her *ketubah* or a field that [her husband mentioned in her *ketubah*] as his present to her [to be included in her dowry].[43]

[In all the above instances,] even though [the husband] formalized the transaction with his wife through an act of contract that she voluntarily agreed to, she has the prerogative of recanting whenever she desires.[44] [We assume that] she gave the present or made the sale only for the sake of maintaining peace in her home.[45]

Accordingly, a husband has no way of substantiating his claim to his wife's property[46] except with regard to *nichsei m'log*, as explained [in the previous halachah].[47]

19. It appears to me that a woman is not entitled [to nullify her statements, based on the rationale]: "I did it [only] to appease my husband," when her *nichsei tzon barzel* were lost or stolen, and she waived the debt in favor of her husband. [This applies even when the commitment] is formalized in the presence of witnesses.[48]

To what can this be compared? To a man and a woman who formalized an agreement in which she forgoes the responsibility [he had taken for property that had been classified as *nichsei tzon barzel*] and considers it instead *nichsei*

woman does not rely on receiving this property, and thus if he sells it the sale is binding (*Maggid Mishneh*, gloss on *Hilchot Mechirah* 30:5; *Chelkat Mechokek* 90:45).

This is the opinion of the Rambam and Rabbenu Tam, and is quoted by the *Shulchan Aruch* (*Even HaEzer* 90:14). Rabbenu Asher, the Rashba and others differ and maintain that the sale is of no consequence. Their view is quoted by the Ramah.

מָכְרוּ שְׁנֵיהֶם בְּנִכְסֵי מְלוֹג — בֵּין שֶׁלָּקַח מִן הָאִישׁ תְּחִלָּה וְחָזַר וְלָקַח מִן הָאִשָּׁה, בֵּין שֶׁלָּקַח מִן הָאִשָּׁה וְחָזַר וְלָקַח מִן הָאִישׁ — מִכְרָן קַיָּם.

יז וְכֵן הָאִשָּׁה שֶׁמָּכְרָה אוֹ נָתְנָה נִכְסֵי מְלוֹג לְבַעְלָהּ — מִמְכָּרָהּ וּמַתְּנָתָהּ קַיָּמִין; וְאֵינָהּ יְכוֹלָה לוֹמַר בְּנִכְסֵי מְלוֹג: נַחַת רוּחַ עָשִׂיתִי לְבַעְלִי.
אֲבָל בִּשְׁאָר נְכָסִים — יֵשׁ לָהּ לוֹמַר.

יח כֵּיצַד? הָאִשָּׁה שֶׁמָּכְרָה אוֹ נָתְנָה לְבַעְלָהּ מִנִּכְסֵי צֹאן בַּרְזֶל, בֵּין קַרְקַע בֵּין מִטַּלְטְלִין, אוֹ שָׂדֶה שֶׁיִּחֵד לָהּ בִּכְתֻבָּתָהּ, אוֹ שָׂדֶה שֶׁכָּתַב לָהּ בִּכְתֻבָּתָהּ, אוֹ שָׂדֶה שֶׁהִכְנִיס לָהּ שׁוּם מִשֶּׁלּוֹ — לֹא קָנָה בַּעְלָהּ.
וְאַף־עַל־פִּי שֶׁקָּנוּ מִיַּד הָאִשָּׁה בִּרְצוֹנָהּ — חוֹזֶרֶת בְּכָל עֵת שֶׁתִּרְצֶה.
שֶׁלֹּא נָתְנָה וְלֹא מָכְרָה אֶלָּא מִפְּנֵי שְׁלוֹם בֵּיתָהּ.
לְפִיכָךְ אֵין לַבַּעַל רְאָיָה בְּנִכְסֵי אִשְׁתּוֹ כְּלָל חוּץ מִנִּכְסֵי מְלוֹג, כְּמוֹ שֶׁבֵּאַרְנוּ.

יט נִכְסֵי צֹאן בַּרְזֶל שֶׁאָבְדוּ אוֹ שֶׁנִּגְנְבוּ, וּמָחֲלָה הָאִשָּׁה אוֹתָם לְבַעְלָהּ, וְקָנוּ מִמֶּנָּה בְּעֵדִים — יֵרָאֶה לִי, שֶׁאֵינָהּ יְכוֹלָה לוֹמַר: נַחַת רוּחַ עָשִׂיתִי לְבַעְלִי.
הָא לְמָה זֶה דוֹמֶה? לְמִי שֶׁקָּנוּ מִיָּדָהּ שֶׁאֵין לָהּ אַחֲרָיוּת, שֶׁהֶחֱזִירָהּ נְכָסִים אֵלּוּ נִכְסֵי מְלוֹג.

---

41. Although both the husband and his wife have a share in the property, since the purchaser dealt with both of them, the sale is binding.
42. Since this property itself belongs to her, there is no reason for her husband to become upset if she does not desire to sell it to him.
43. See Chapter 23, Halachah 11; *Hilchot Mechirah* 30:3.
   There is a difference of opinion among the Rabbis if similar laws apply when a woman waives her claim to property mentioned in her *ketubah* in favor of her husband. The Ra'avad and Rabbenu Asher maintain that her deed is of consequence, while the Rashba and the Ramban state that it is not. The *Maggid Mishneh* maintains that the Rambam subscribes to the latter view.
44. The *Kessef Mishneh* emphasizes that until the woman recants, the transaction is binding. The *Beit Meir*, however, objects, explaining that the Rambam's wording in *Hilchot Mechirah* 30:3 does not indicate such a distinction.
45. Her husband will pressure her by saying, "You are either planning my death or considering a divorce. Otherwise, you would not hesitate to sell this property to me" (*Bava Batra* 49b, 50a).
46. Even if he has a deed or witnesses that testify to the claim, his wife may also negate his claim based on the above rationale.
47. The *Shulchan Aruch* (*Even HaEzer* 90:16) states that if the woman explicitly accepts responsibility for the field if expropriated from the husband, then the transaction is binding.
48. Based on the Rambam's statements in Chapter 17, Halachah 19, it is questionable why witnesses are necessary. See *Chelkat Mechokek* 90:1, *Beit Shmuel* 90:6.

m'log.[49] For the husband is not bringing a proof for the sake of taking possession or maintaining possession of property, merely to free himself of the obligation to pay a claim [his wife will issue].[50]

If, by contrast, she gives him movable property that exists and was considered to be *nichsei tzon barzel*, the husband does not acquire it. For the wife may rationalize her conduct saying: "I did this to appease my husband."

20. When a husband sells [the right to] the benefits from landed property [that belongs to his wife, to another person, while the legal owner of the property remains his wife, the sale] is of no consequence. [The rationale is that] the reason our Sages granted a man [the right to] the benefit that accrues from his wife's property is [to afford him additional income] so that he will spend more generously on the household expenses.[51]

[Based on that rationale,] if he sells the benefit to be derived [from the landed property to another person] and takes the money and invests it in a business [which offers profit], he is given that prerogative.

21. [The following laws apply if] the woman possesses financial resources [that she brings to the household]. If they are *nichsei tzon barzel*, her husband may use them for commercial enterprises.[52]

If they are *nichsei m'log* - regardless of whether she brought them to the household at the time of marriage or she inherited them or received them as a present[53] [- landed property should be purchased with them, from which her husband is entitled to the benefit that accrues].[54] [Similarly,] if she inherited or was given movable property, it should be sold, and the proceeds of the sale should be used to purchase landed property, from which her husband is entitled to the benefit that accrues.

22. Similarly, if a woman was injured by others,[55] all the money that is ordained to be given to her should be used to purchase land, from which her husband is entitled to the benefit that accrues, as stated in *Hilchot Chovel.*[56]

23. [The following law applies when] a woman inherits servants [while she is married]. Even if they are old, they should not be sold, because they bring honor to her family's household.

---

49. A husband is not obligated to pay for *nichsei m'log* that have been destroyed, lost or stolen, while in such situations, he is obligated to pay the original value for *nichsei tzon barzel*. Thus, by changing the status of her property, the woman is in effect waiving a financial obligation due her from her husband.

There is reason to say that just as a woman can say that she was forced to give or sell this property to her husband to appease him, she could also say that she was

שֶׁהֲרֵי אֵין הַבַּעַל מֵבִיא רְאָיָה לִטֹּל כְּלוּם וְלֹא לְהַחֲזִיק בַּנְּכָסִים, אֶלָּא לְהִפָּטֵר מִתְּבִיעָתָהּ מִלְשַׁלֵּם.

אֲבָל אִם נָתְנָה לוֹ מַתָּנָה מְטַלְטְלֵי צֹאן בַּרְזֶל הַקַּיָּמִין — לֹא קָנָה, מִפְּנֵי שֶׁיֵּשׁ לָהּ לוֹמַר: נַחַת רוּחַ עָשִׂיתִי לְבַעְלִי.

כ בַּעַל שֶׁמָּכַר קַרְקַע לְפֵרוֹת — לֹא עָשָׂה כְּלוּם;

מִפְּנֵי שֶׁלֹּא הִתְקִינוּ פֵּרוֹת לָאִישׁ אֶלָּא כְּדֵי לְהַרְוִיחַ בְּהוֹצָאַת הַבַּיִת. לְפִיכָךְ, אִם מָכַר לְפֵרוֹת וְלָקַח אוֹתָן הַמָּעוֹת לִסְחוֹרָה — שׁוֹמְעִין לוֹ.

כא הָיוּ לָאִשָּׁה כְּסָפִים: אִם נִכְסֵי צֹאן בַּרְזֶל הֵן — הֲרֵי זֶה נוֹשֵׂא וְנוֹתֵן בָּהֶן; וְאִם נִכְסֵי מְלוֹג הֵן — בֵּין שֶׁהִכְנִיסָה אוֹתָן לוֹ, בֵּין שֶׁנָּפְלוּ לָהּ בִּירֻשָּׁה אוֹ נָתְנוּ לָהּ בְּמַתָּנָה, אוֹ נָפְלוּ לָהּ מְטַלְטְלִין אוֹ נָתְנוּ לָהּ — הֲרֵי אֵלּוּ יִמָּכְרוּ, וְיִלָּקַח בָּהֶן קַרְקַע, וְהוּא אוֹכֵל פֵּרוֹתֵיהֶן.

כב וְכֵן הָאִשָּׁה שֶׁחָבְלוּ בָּהּ אֲחֵרִים — כָּל הַמָּעוֹת הָרְאוּיוֹת לָתֵת לָהּ יִלָּקַח בָּהֶן קַרְקַע, וְהַבַּעַל אוֹכֵל פֵּרוֹתֵיהֶן, כְּמוֹ שֶׁיִּתְבָּאֵר בְּהִלְכוֹת חוֹבֵל.

כג נָפְלוּ לָהּ עֲבָדִים, אַף־עַל־פִּי שֶׁהֵן זְקֵנִים — לֹא יִמָּכְרוּ, מִפְּנֵי שֶׁבַח בֵּית אָבִיהָ.

---

also forced to waive her husband's obligation in the loss or theft of this property. The Rambam, however, does not accept this rationale. Since this obligation is due only after the husband's death or divorce, there is nothing pressuring her husband to pay it. If he demands that his wife waive this obligation, she may refuse, asking him: "Is it because you want to divorce me that you are asking me to waive this obligation?" (*Maggid Mishneh*).

50. The Ra'avad objects to the Rambam's ruling. Nevertheless, it is the Rambam's decision which is accepted by the *Shulchan Aruch* (*Even HaEzer* 90:18).

51. If, at the outset, the husband sold the rights to benefit from the property for a lump sum, it is possible that all that money would be spent in a short period of time and that afterwards, there would be nothing left for household expenses (*Chelkat Mechokek* 85:41).

52. For their value is explicitly stated in the woman's *ketubah* and will be returned to her in the event of divorce or her husband's death.

53. For money that a woman acquires while married is automatically considered to be *nichsei m'log*.

54. In this way, the woman is assured that the principal will remain hers. If the husband desires to use the money for commercial enterprises, he may afterwards sell the right to benefit from the property, as mentioned in the previous halachah.

55. E.g., people other than her husband. If her husband himself injures her, he is not entitled to benefit from the proceeds of her property, as mentioned in Halachah 28.

56. *Hilchot Chovel UMazik* 4:15. As stated in that source, the husband also has a right to receive a certain portion of the damages as his own funds to which his wife has no right.

[The following law applies when] she inherits olive trees or vines, but did not [inherit] the land on which these trees were planted. If they produce enough to pay for their upkeep, they should not be sold, because they bring honor to her family's household. If they do not, they should be sold as firewood, land should be purchased with the proceeds, from which the husband is entitled to the benefit that accrues.

24. When [a married woman] inherits produce that is still attached to the land [on which it is growing], it becomes her husband's [property].[57] When the produce has been uprooted from the land, it should be sold and used to purchase landed property, from which her husband is entitled to the benefit that accrues.

When, however, a husband divorces his wife, and there was produce that was still attached to the ground, it belongs to the woman. If it has already been reaped, it belongs to the man.[58]

25. A husband is obligated to provide for the sustenance and all the needs of the servants[59] and livestock that belong to his wife and are classified as *nichsei m'log*. They must work for him, and he is entitled to the benefit that accrues. Therefore, a baby born to a maid classified as *nichsei m'log* belongs to the husband. And a calf born to a cow that is classified as *nichsei m'log* belongs to the husband.

If, however, the husband divorces his wife and she desires to pay the worth of a child born from a maidservant who is classified as *nichsei m'log* and take the child as her property because this brings honor to her family's household, she is given that prerogative.[60]

26. [The following laws apply when] a woman brings two utensils or two maidservants to the household and has them classified as *nichsei tzon barzel*. They were [originally] evaluated at 1000 *zuz*; afterwards, their value increased and they were evaluated at 2000 *zuz*. If the woman's husband divorces her, she is entitled to one [utensil or maidservant] for the 1000 *zuz* that she is owed. With regard to the other - if she desires to pay its value and take it because of the honor it brings to her father's household, she has that prerogative.

27. When a man gives a present to his wife - regardless of whether he gave her landed property, or he gave her money and she bought landed property - her husband is not entitled to the benefits that accrue from the present [that was given].[61]

Similarly, when a man gives a woman a present on the condition that her husband not be entitled to derive the benefits from it, but rather the benefits that accrue will belong to the wife to be used for whatever she desires,[62] [the provision is binding, and] the husband is not entitled to the benefits that accrue from this present.

נָפְלוּ לָהּ זֵיתִים וּגְפָנִים, וְלֹא הָיָה לָהּ בְּגוּף הַקַּרְקַע שֶׁהָאִילָנוֹת בָּהּ כְּלוּם:

אִם עוֹשִׂין כְּדֵי טִפּוּלָן — לֹא יִמָּכְרוּ, מִפְּנֵי שֶׁבַח בֵּית אָבִיהָ;

וְאִם לָאו — הֲרֵי אֵלּוּ יִמָּכְרוּ לְעֵצִים, וְיִלָּקַח בָּהֶן קַרְקַע, וְהוּא אוֹכֵל פֵּרוֹת.

כד נָפְלוּ לָהּ פֵּרוֹת מְחֻבָּרִין לַקַּרְקַע — הֲרֵי אֵלּוּ שֶׁל בַּעַל;

תְּלוּשִׁין מִן הַקַּרְקַע — שֶׁלָּהּ, וְיִמָּכְרוּ, וְיִלָּקַח בָּהֶן קַרְקַע, וְהוּא אוֹכֵל פֵּרוֹת.

אֲבָל הַמְגָרֵשׁ אֶת אִשְׁתּוֹ וְהָיוּ לָהּ פֵּרוֹת מְחֻבָּרִין לַקַּרְקַע בִּשְׁעַת גֵּרוּשִׁין — הֲרֵי אֵלּוּ שֶׁלָּהּ;

וְאִם הָיוּ תְּלוּשִׁין — הֲרֵי אֵלּוּ שֶׁלּוֹ.

כה עַבְדֵי נִכְסֵי מְלוֹג וּבֶהֱמַת נִכְסֵי מְלוֹג — הַבַּעַל חַיָּב בִּמְזוֹנוֹת שֶׁלָּהֶן וּבְכָל צָרְכֵיהֶם, וְהֵן עוֹשִׂין לוֹ, וְהוּא אוֹכֵל פֵּרוֹתֵיהֶם.

לְפִיכָךְ: וְלַד שִׁפְחַת מְלוֹג — לַבַּעַל, וְלַד בֶּהֱמַת מְלוֹג — לַבַּעַל.

וְאִם גֵּרְשָׁהּ, וְרָצְתָה הָאִשָּׁה לִתֵּן דָּמִים וְלִטֹּל וְלַד הַשִּׁפְחָה מִפְּנֵי שֶׁבַח בֵּית אָבִיהָ — שׁוֹמְעִין לָהּ.

כו הִכְנִיסָה לוֹ שְׁנֵי כֵלִים אוֹ שְׁתֵּי שְׁפָחוֹת בְּתוֹרַת נִכְסֵי צֹאן בַּרְזֶל, וְשָׁמוּ אוֹתָן עָלָיו בְּאֶלֶף זוּז, וְהוּקְרוּ וְעָמְדוּ בְּאַלְפַּיִם, וְגֵרְשָׁהּ — נוֹטֶלֶת אֶחָד בְּאֶלֶף שֶׁלָּהּ.

וְהַשֵּׁנִי, אִם רָצְתָה שֶׁתִּתֵּן דָּמָיו וְתִטֹּל מִשּׁוּם שֶׁבַח בֵּית אָבִיהָ — שׁוֹמְעִין לָהּ.

כז הַנּוֹתֵן מַתָּנָה לְאִשְׁתּוֹ, בֵּין שֶׁנָּתַן לָהּ קַרְקַע בֵּין שֶׁנָּתַן לָהּ מָעוֹת, וְלָקְחָה בָּהֶן קַרְקַע — אֵין לַבַּעַל פֵּרוֹת בְּמַתָּנָה זוֹ.

וְכֵן הַנּוֹתֵן מַתָּנָה לְאִשָּׁה עַל מְנָת שֶׁלֹּא יִהְיֶה הַבַּעַל אוֹכֵל פֵּרוֹתֶיהָ, אֶלָּא יִהְיוּ פֵּרוֹתֶיהָ לָאִשָּׁה לְמַה שֶּׁתִּרְצֶה — אֵין הַבַּעַל אוֹכֵל פֵּרוֹת מַתָּנָה זוֹ.

57. Although in most instances, produce that is still attached to land is considered equivalent to landed property, an exception is made in this case, because the husband is entitled to the benefit that accrues from his wife's property.
58. For he is entitled to receive all the benefit from her property throughout the duration of their marriage.
59. See *Hilchot Avadim* 9:7, which states that a husband does not have the prerogative of telling a servant: "Work for me, but I will not provide for your sustenance."
60. The Rambam's wording implies that the concept of maintaining the honor of one's household applies only with regard to the children of one's servants, and not to the offspring of one's livestock. See the *Beit Shmuel* 85:38, which quotes a difference of opinion among the Rabbis on this issue.
61. *Bava Batra* 51b states that a person who gives a present gives with a generous spirit. Therefore, we may assume that the husband gives the gift to his wife without wanting to restrict her in any way.
62. The specific wording of the provision that the giver must make is discussed in *Hilchot Zechiyah UMatanah* 3:13.

Similarly, if a woman sells the rights to her *ketubah* [in the event of her divorce or her husband's death],[63] the money she receives belongs to her, and her husband is not entitled to derive the benefit that accrues from it.

28. When a calf born from cattle that was classified as *nichsei m'log* is stolen, and the thief is apprehended and forced to pay twice the amount, the woman receives the extra payment. [The rationale is that] this is not the benefit that our Sages granted [the husband].[64]

When a man injures his wife, the entire [amount he must pay] - the damages and the restitution for the pain and the embarrassment - belongs to the woman,[65] and the husband is not entitled to the benefits that accrue from [property purchased with this money], as explained in *Hilchot Chovel*.[66]

29. [The following rules apply when] a husband sells landed property [that he owns] to his wife. If the husband knew about the funds with which she purchased the land previously, the sale is binding,[67] and the husband is entitled to the benefit that accrues from that land.

If, however, [the existence of] these funds was concealed, she does not acquire the land. For the husband may [explain that he did not really intend to complete the sale]. [His intent was] to reveal the existence of funds that his wife had hidden. The funds that were revealed should be used to purchase landed property,[68] from which the husband is entitled to the benefits that accrue.[69]

30. When funds or movable property are discovered in a woman's possession, and she claims that they were given her as a present, while her husband claims that they stem from the fruits of her labor and hence belong to him, it is the woman's claim that is accepted.[70] [The husband] may, however, have a ban of ostracism [conditionally] issued against anyone who makes false statements.[71] [The funds should be used] to purchase landed property, from which [the husband] is entitled to the benefit that accrues.[72]

If the woman claims that the funds were given to her with the provision that her husband have no control over them, but rather that they be used for

63. The person purchasing the rights to the woman's *ketubah* is taking a risk, because it is possible that she will die in her husband's lifetime and then he will not receive anything.
64. Our Sages entitled a husband to derive the benefit that would ordinarily accrue from property belonging to his wife - e.g., produce that grows on a field, rent from a home, labor from a servant. They did not grant him rights to benefits that arise from abnormal circumstances.
65. The Rambam does not mention two other payments that a person who inflicts an injury would ordinarily pay: *shevet* - reimbursement for the wages that were not earned during the period of convalescence, because the husband is entitled to his wife's wages -

וְכֵן הַמּוֹכֶרֶת כְּתֻבָּתָהּ בְּטוֹבַת הֲנָאָה — אוֹתָן הַדָּמִים לָאִשָּׁה, וְאֵין הַבַּעַל אוֹכֵל פֵּרוֹתֵיהֶן.

כח וְלַד בֶּהֱמַת מְלוֹג שֶׁנִּגְנַב, וְנִמְצָא הַגַּנָּב וְשִׁלֵּם שְׁנַיִם — הַכֶּפֶל לָאִשָּׁה; שֶׁאֵין זֶה פְּרִי שֶׁהִתְקִינוּ לוֹ חֲכָמִים. הַחוֹבֵל בְּאִשְׁתּוֹ — כָּל הַנֶּזֶק וְהַצַּעַר וְהַבֹּשֶׁת שֶׁלָּהּ, וְאֵין הַבַּעַל אוֹכֵל פֵּרוֹת, כְּמוֹ שֶׁיִּתְבָּאֵר בְּהִלְכוֹת חוֹבֵל.

כט הַמּוֹכֵר קַרְקַע לְאִשְׁתּוֹ: אִם הָיוּ הַמָּעוֹת שֶׁלָּקְחָה בָּהֶן אֶת הַקַּרְקַע מִבַּעְלָהּ גְּלוּיִין וִידוּעִין לַבַּעַל — קָנְתָה, וְהַבַּעַל אוֹכֵל פֵּרוֹת אוֹתָהּ הַקַּרְקַע; וְאִם הָיוּ מָעוֹת טְמוּנִין — לֹא קָנְתָה, שֶׁהַבַּעַל אוֹמֵר: לֹא מָכַרְתִּי אֶלָּא כְּדֵי לְהַרְאוֹת הַמָּעוֹת שֶׁטְּמָנָה. וְאוֹתָן הַמָּעוֹת שֶׁנִּרְאוּ — יִלְקַח בָּהֶן קַרְקַע, וְהַבַּעַל אוֹכֵל פֵּרוֹת.

ל הֲרֵי שֶׁנִּמְצְאוּ מָעוֹת אוֹ מִטַּלְטְלִין בְּיַד הָאִשָּׁה, הִיא אוֹמֶרֶת: בְּמַתָּנָה נָתְנוּ לִי, וְהוּא אוֹמֵר: מִמַּעֲשֵׂה יָדַיִךְ הֵם שֶׁהֵם שֶׁלִּי — הֲרֵי זוֹ נֶאֱמֶנֶת. וְיֵשׁ לוֹ לְהַחֲרִים עַל מִי שֶׁטּוֹעֶנֶת דָּבָר שֶׁאֵינוֹ כֵן. וְיִלְקַח בָּהֶן קַרְקַע, וְהוּא אוֹכֵל פֵּרוֹת. וְאִם אָמְרָה: עַל מְנָת כֵּן נָתְנוּ לִי, עַל מְנָת שֶׁלֹּא יִהְיֶה לְבַעְלִי רְשׁוּת בָּהֶן, אֶלָּא אֶעֱשֶׂה בָּהֶן

and *ripui* - payment for the medical treatment required, because a husband is always required to pay for his wife's medical care.

66. *Hilchot Chovel UMazik* 4:16. This differs from instances in which the injury is inflicted by other parties, in which case the husband also has a right to receive a certain portion of the damages as his own funds, to which his wife has no right.

67. The husband cannot claim that the funds belonged to him, but since he could not take them from his wife in any other way, he sold the property to her as a ruse. This applies even if he makes a definite claim (*ta'anat bari*) that the funds belong to him (*Chelkat Mechokek* 85:22,24).

68. This ruling depends on the halachah to follow, which states that a woman's claim is accepted with regard to money found in her possession.

69. The Rambam's ruling is cited by the *Shulchan Aruch* (*Even HaEzer* 85:9). The Ramah mentions the opinion of Rabbenu Asher, who states that if the husband makes a definite claim that the hidden funds belong to him, his claim is accepted.

70. The Jerusalem Talmud (*Ketubot* 6:1) states that a present will be spoken about. Therefore, the woman will be afraid to claim that she was given a present unless the claim was true.

71. He cannot, however, require his wife to take an oath unless he lodges a definite claim against her (*Maggid Mishneh*).

72. If, however, a woman was given responsibility to deal freely with the property belonging to her husband's household, and she claims that funds discovered in her possession belong to her privately, her claim is not accepted (*Bava Batra* 52b; Ramah, *Even HaEzer* 85:12).

whatever purpose she desires, she must bring proof [that such a provision was made].[73] [The rationale is that] the prevailing assumption is that a husband has the right to the benefits from all the funds found in a woman's possession, unless she brings proof otherwise.

31. If [a wife] tells [her husband]: "You gave me [these funds] as a present," she is required to take a Rabbinic oath that her husband gave her [the funds]. [After she takes that oath,] her husband is not entitled to the benefit [from the property purchased with these funds].[74]

32. One should not accept an article for safekeeping that was given by a wife, a servant or a minor.[75] If one transgressed and accepted [an article given by] a woman, one should return it to the woman.[76] If she dies, one should return it to her husband.[77]

If one accepted [an article given by] a servant, one should return it to the servant. If he dies, one should return it to his master. If one accepted [an article given by] a minor, one should purchase a Torah scroll with the proceeds or an article that will provide [the minor] with benefit.[78]

[The following rules apply] with regard to all [the abovementioned individuals], if at the time of their death, they say: "The article I gave for safekeeping belongs to so and so." If the person caring for the article operates under the presumption that the person who entrusted it to him is true to his word, he should carry out the command he was given. If not, he should give [the article] to the person's heirs.

33. [The following rules apply when] a woman has financial resources sufficient [to purchase property] from which the husband would derive the benefits [but they disagree with regard to the property fit to purchase]; he suggests that this type of property be purchased, and she desires that another type be purchased. A property should be purchased that brings a large revenue and requires little upkeep,[79] regardless of whether this is the article desired by [the husband] or by [the wife]. We do not purchase any article that does not renew itself,[80] lest the entire property be used and the principal lost.

34. [The following rule applies when] a woman brings to her husband's household a goat [that she is entitled] to milk, a sheep [that she is entitled] to shear or a date palm whose fruit [she is entitled to take], although she is entitled only to these benefits [and not to the principal]. [Her husband] is entitled to [these benefits] although the principal is dwindling.[81]

73. Although the giving of a present will become public knowledge, the details of the present might not. Therefore, the woman is required to substantiate her statements. Otherwise, we assume that this present was given without any extraordinary conditions (*Ma'aseh Rokeach*).

כָּל מַה שֶּׁאֶרְצֶה — עָלֶיהָ לְהָבִיא רְאָיָה;
שֶׁכָּל מָמוֹן שֶׁנִּמְצָא בְּיַד הָאִשָּׁה — בְּחֶזְקַת הַבַּעַל הוּא שֶׁיֹּאכַל פֵּרוֹתָיו, עַד שֶׁתָּבִיא רְאָיָה.

לא אָמְרָה לוֹ: אַתָּה נָתַתָּ לִי בְּמַתָּנָה — נִשְׁבַּעַת שְׁבוּעַת הֶסֵּת שֶׁנָּתַן לָהּ הַבַּעַל, וְאֵינוֹ אוֹכֵל פֵּרוֹתֵיהֶן.

לב אֵין מְקַבְּלִין פִּקְדוֹנוֹת לֹא מִן הַנָּשִׁים וְלֹא מִן הָעֲבָדִים וְלֹא מִן הַקְּטַנִּים.
וְאִם עָבַר וְקִבֵּל מִן הָאִשָּׁה — יַחֲזִיר לָאִשָּׁה. מֵתָה — יַחֲזִיר לְבַעְלָהּ.
קִבֵּל מִן הָעֶבֶד — יַחֲזִיר לָעֶבֶד. וְאִם מֵת — יַחֲזִיר לְרַבּוֹ.
קִבֵּל מִן הַקָּטָן — יִקְנֶה לוֹ בּוֹ סֵפֶר תּוֹרָה אוֹ דָבָר שֶׁאוֹכֵל פֵּרוֹתֵיהֶם.
וְכֻלָּם שֶׁאָמְרוּ בִּשְׁעַת מִיתָתָן: פִּקָּדוֹן זֶה שֶׁל פְּלוֹנִי הוּא —
אִם הָיוּ בְּחֶזְקַת נֶאֱמָנִין אֵצֶל זֶה שֶׁהַפִּקָּדוֹן אֶצְלוֹ — יַעֲשֶׂה כְּמוֹ שֶׁצִּוּוּ, וְאִם לָאו — יִתֵּן לְיוֹרְשֵׁיהֶם.

לג הָאִשָּׁה שֶׁהָיוּ לָהּ כְּסָפִים הָרְאוּיוֹת לַבַּעַל לֶאֱכֹל פֵּרוֹתֵיהֶם, הוּא אוֹמֵר: כָּךְ וְכָךְ יִלְקַח בָּהֶם,
וְהִיא אוֹמֶרֶת: אֵינִי לוֹקַחַת בָּהֶן אֶלָּא כָּךְ וְכָךְ —
לוֹקְחִים דָּבָר שֶׁפֵּרוֹתָיו מְרֻבִּים וִיצִיאָתוֹ מְעוּטָה, בֵּין שֶׁהָיָה הַדָּבָר כִּרְצוֹנוֹ אוֹ שֶׁהָיָה כִּרְצוֹנָהּ.
וְאֵין לוֹקְחִין אֶלָּא דָבָר שֶׁגִּזְעוֹ מַחֲלִיף, שֶׁמָּא יֹאכַל הַכֹּל וְנִמְצָא הַקֶּרֶן אָבַד.

לד הָאִשָּׁה שֶׁהִכְנִיסָה לְבַעְלָהּ עֵז לַחֲלָבָהּ, וְרָחֵל לְגִזָּתָהּ, וְדֶקֶל לְפֵרוֹתָיו — אַף-עַל-פִּי שֶׁאֵין לָהּ אֶלָּא פֵרוֹת אֵלּוּ בִּלְבַד, הֲרֵי זֶה אוֹכֵל וְהוֹלֵךְ עַד שֶׁתִּכְלֶה הַקֶּרֶן.

The *Maggid Mishneh* mentions the opinion of the Rashba, who differs and maintains that the woman's claim is also accepted in this instance as well. This opinion is mentioned by the later authorities.

74. The rationale is that a woman will not be brazen enough to make false statements in her husband's presence with regard to a matter that he knows to be true (*Maggid Mishneh*).

75. For the likelihood is that the article belongs to the husband, master or father, respectively. It is forbidden to assist a person who takes property that is not his or her own. Moreover, if no one accepts the article for safekeeping, it is likely that it will be returned (*Bava Batra* 51b).

76. For there is no proof that the article was stolen.

77. For even if the article is rightfully hers, he inherits her property.

78. The entrusted article should not be given to the minor, for it is possible that he will not care for it properly and it will be destroyed (Rashbam, *Bava Batra* 52a).

79. In every society, the nature of the type of article purchased depends on the conditions prevalent at that time (*Chelkat Mechokek* 85:33).

80. The Hebrew literally means "whose bark is renewed" - i.e., reaping the benefits one year will not prevent them from being reaped in the future.

81. I.e., in this instance, the goat's milk is not sold and the money used to purchase property that produces benefit, but rather the goat's milk is used for the household.

Similarly, if she brought utensils or articles of clothing to his household that were classified as *nichsei m'log*, he may use them, wearing them or using them as spreads or as covers until the articles themselves are destroyed. If he divorces [his wife], he is not required to pay for any *nichsei m'log* that became worn out.

35. The *geonim* [issued the following] ruling. A husband takes responsibility for the diminished value of *nichsei tzon barzel*. Nevertheless, if [such property] exists [at the time a woman's *ketubah* is due for payment,] and still serves its initial purpose, the woman must take it regardless of its condition at that time.[82]

If they are no longer fit to serve their initial purpose, it is as if they were stolen or lost, and the husband is obligated to pay the value appraised originally at the time of the marriage.

This is the common custom. Whenever a man marries, he accepts responsibility for [the woman's] dowry as contingent on this custom.[83] On the basis of this custom, just as the husband does not pay for the depreciation of the article, so too, he does not take the appreciation of the property if it increases in value.

A husband has the right to compel some of the servants and maidservants who belong to his wife to serve him[84] in the home of another woman he has married.[85] [This applies] regardless of whether the servants are classified as *nichsei m'log* or *nichsei tzon barzel*. The husband may not, however, take these servants to another city without his wife's consent.

CHAPTER TWENTY-THREE

1. [The following rules apply when] a woman makes a provision with her husband in which he agrees to forgo one of the privileges that a husband is granted. If he wrote down [this provision] for her after she was consecrated, but before *nisu'in*, there is no need to formalize the matter with an act of contract; everything he wrote to her is binding.[1] If he wrote down [this provision] for her after *nisu'in*, he must formalize the matter with an act of contract.[2]

2. If, [after *nisu'in*,] the husband stipulates that he will have no say with regard to [his wife's] property, and she sells it or gives it away as a present, the sale or the present is binding.[3] Nevertheless, [the husband] is entitled to the benefits [that accrue from the property] during the time it is in her possession.[4]

---

82. Even if they are worth substantially less than they were originally.
83. As the *Kessef Mishneh* emphasizes, at different times and in different countries, other customs have prevailed. It is the prevalent custom in one's own locale that is binding.

וְכֵן אִם הִכְנִיסָה לוֹ כְּלֵי תַשְׁמִישׁ בְּתוֹרַת נִכְסֵי מְלוֹג — הֲרֵי זֶה מִשְׁתַּמֵּשׁ בָּהֶן וְלוֹבֵשׁ וּמַצִּיעַ וּמְכַסֶּה עַד שֶׁיִּכְלֶה הַקֶּרֶן.

וּכְשֶׁיְּגָרֵשׁ — אֵינוֹ חַיָּב לְשַׁלֵּם הַבְּלָאוֹת שֶׁל נִכְסֵי מְלוֹג.

לה הוֹרוּ הַגְּאוֹנִים, שֶׁנִּכְסֵי צֹאן בַּרְזֶל, אַף־עַל־פִּי שֶׁפְּחִיתָתָן עַל הַבַּעַל, אִם הָיוּ הַבְּלָאוֹת קַיָּמִין וְהָיוּ עוֹשִׂין מֵעֵין מְלַאכְתָּן — נוֹטֶלֶת כֵּלֶיהָ כְּמָה שֶׁהֵן;

וְאִם לֹא הָיוּ עוֹשִׂין מֵעֵין מְלַאכְתָּן — הֲרֵי הֵן כְּמוֹ שֶׁנִּגְנְבוּ אוֹ אָבְדוּ, שֶׁהוּא חַיָּב לְשַׁלֵּם בִּדְמֵיהֶם שֶׁשָּׁמוּ אוֹתָן עָלָיו בִּשְׁעַת נִשּׂוּאִין.

וּמִנְהָג פָּשׁוּט הוּא זֶה, וְכָל הַנּוֹשֵׂא — עַל מִנְהָג זֶה קִבֵּל עָלָיו אַחֲרָיוּת הַנְּדוּנְיָא.

וּכְשֶׁם שֶׁאֵינוֹ מְשַׁלֵּם הַפְּחָת, כָּךְ אֵינוֹ נוֹטֵל אֶת הַשֶּׁבַח, אִם הוֹתִירוּ דְמֵיהֶן, לְפִי מִנְהָג זֶה.

יֵשׁ לַבַּעַל לְכֹף מִקְצָת עַבְדֵי אִשְׁתּוֹ וְאַמְהוֹתֶיהָ שֶׁיִּהְיוּ מְשַׁמְּשִׁין אוֹתוֹ בְּבֵית אִשָּׁה אַחֶרֶת שֶׁנָּשָׂא, בֵּין שֶׁהָיוּ עַבְדֵי מְלוֹג בֵּין שֶׁהָיוּ עַבְדֵי צֹאן בַּרְזֶל.

אֲבָל אֵינוֹ יָכוֹל לְהוֹלִיכָן לְעִיר אַחֶרֶת שֶׁלֹּא מִדַּעַת אִשְׁתּוֹ.

פֶּרֶק שְׁלֹשָׁה וְעֶשְׂרִים

א הָאִשָּׁה שֶׁהִתְנַת עַל בַּעְלָהּ לְבַטֵּל זְכוּת מִדְּבָרִים שֶׁזּוֹכֶה בָּהֶן הַבַּעַל:

אִם כָּתַב לָהּ וְעוֹדָהּ אֲרוּסָה קֹדֶם הַנִּשּׂוּאִין — אֵינוֹ צָרִיךְ לִקְנוֹת מִיָּדוֹ, אֶלָּא כָּל מַה שֶּׁכָּתַב לָהּ קַיָּם;

וְאִם כָּתַב לָהּ אַחַר הַנִּשּׂוּאִין — צָרִיךְ לִקְנוֹת מִיָּדוֹ.

ב הִתְנָה עִמָּהּ שֶׁלֹּא יִהְיוּ לוֹ דִּין וּדְבָרִים בִּנְכָסֶיהָ,

אִם מָכְרָה וְנָתְנָה — מִכְרָהּ וּמַתְּנָתָהּ קַיָּם, אֲבָל אוֹכֵל פֵּרוֹתֵיהֶן כָּל זְמַן שֶׁהֵן בִּרְשׁוּתָהּ.

---

84. The servants may be compelled to serve the husband; they may not, however, be compelled to serve his second wife (*Beit Yosef, Even HaEzer* 85).
85. For having the woman's servants serve her husband in his other wife's home, also elevates the woman's own standard of living (*Ketubot* 80b).

1. Since the man has already established a connection with this woman, but has not acquired the rights due him by virtue of the *ketubah*, any provision that he makes regarding those rights is binding.
2. Since the bond of marriage has already been consummated, the husband has already acquired all the rights to which he is entitled. Therefore, a verbal statement is not sufficient, and an official act of contract is necessary to forgo those rights. (See *Ketubot* 83a, which compares this to the absolution of a partnership agreement.)
3. Moreover, the husband is not entitled to any benefit that accrues from the money his wife receives from the sale (Ramah, *Even HaEzer* 92:1).
4. A husband has three rights with regard to his wife's property: to receive the benefits

If he affirmed these statements with an act of contract between consecration [and *nisu'in*], he is considered to have waived his rights to the land itself, and he no longer has any rights to the benefits that accrue from her property.[5]

His words are not heeded if he protests this action, saying: "I did not realize that this act of contract formalized my waiver of all rights to benefit from the property. [I thought that it only entitled my wife] to make a binding sale. [This interpretation is justified,] for no one will marry a woman without property." Instead, he is considered to have waived [all] rights to the land itself.

3. If [the husband] made a provision with [his wife] not to receive the benefit that accrues from her property, he is not entitled to this benefit. Nevertheless, the benefit that accrues should be converted to financial resources, landed property should be purchased, and [the husband] is entitled to the benefits from that property.[6] For he waived only the rights to the property [she owned originally].

4. If [the husband] made a provision with [his wife] not to receive the benefit that accrues from her property, nor to receive the benefit that results from property purchased with the income from her original property, the proceeds from that property should be used to purchase other property, from which [the husband] is entitled to the benefits that accrue. These are called "the fruit of the fruit's fruit."

This pattern continues until the husband makes a provision that he has no right to any by-product of the proceeds from [his wife's property]. [If he makes such a provision,] he has no right to any benefit during her lifetime, but if she dies, he inherits her entire estate.

5. If he makes a provision that he will not inherit [his wife's] property, the provision is binding. He is, however, entitled to receive the benefits that accrue [from this property] during her lifetime.

Similarly, [his word] is binding if he stipulates that he will inherit [only] a portion of her estate, or if he stipulates that if she dies without bearing children, her estate will return to her father's household.

6. When does the above apply? When he made this provision before *nisu'in*.[7] For a man has the prerogative to forgo an inheritance that comes

---

that accrue from it, to veto any sales or presents, and to inherit it in the event of his wife's death. Since the wording of the provision in the document the husband gave his wife is not specific, he is given the benefit of the doubt and is considered to have waived the least valuable of the rights he has: the veto power over his wife's sales and gifts (Rashi, *Ketubot* 83b).

וְאִם קָנוּ מִיָּדוֹ כְּשֶׁהִיא אֲרוּסָה שֶׁאֵין לוֹ דִּין וּדְבָרִים בִּנְכָסֶיהָ — הֲרֵי סָלֵק עַצְמוֹ מִגּוּף הַקַּרְקַע, וְאֵין לוֹ בִּנְכָסֶיהָ פֵּרוֹת לְעוֹלָם.

וַאֲפִלּוּ עִרְעֵר עַל קִנְיָנוֹ וְאָמַר: לֹא עָלָה בְּדַעְתִּי שֶׁאֵין לִי פֵּרוֹת מִפְּנֵי קִנְיָן זֶה, אֶלָּא שֶׁאִם מָכְרָה — מִכְרָהּ קַיָּם, שֶׁאֵין אָדָם נוֹשֵׂא אִשָּׁה בְּלֹא נְכָסִים — אֵין שׁוֹמְעִין לוֹ, אֶלָּא כְּבָר סָלֵק עַצְמוֹ מִגּוּף הַקַּרְקַע.

ג הִתְנָה עִמָּהּ שֶׁלֹּא יֹאכַל פֵּרוֹת נְכָסֶיהָ — הֲרֵי זֶה אֵינוֹ אוֹכֵל פֵּרוֹתֵיהֶן, אֲבָל מוֹכְרִין אֶת הַפֵּרוֹת, וְלוֹקְחִין בָּהֶן קַרְקַע, וְהוּא אוֹכֵל פֵּרוֹתֶיהָ; שֶׁלֹּא סָלֵק עַצְמוֹ אֶלָּא מִפֵּרוֹת נְכָסִים אֵלּוּ בִּלְבַד.

ד הִתְנָה עִמָּהּ שֶׁלֹּא יֹאכַל פֵּרוֹת נְכָסֶיהָ וְלֹא פֵּרֵי פֵּרוֹתֵיהֶן — לוֹקְחִין הַפֵּרוֹת וְקוֹנִין בָּהֶם קַרְקַע, וְלוֹקְחִין פֵּרוֹת קַרְקַע זוֹ וְקוֹנִין בָּהֶם קַרְקַע שְׁנִיָּה, וְהוּא אוֹכֵל פֵּרוֹת אֵלּוּ שֶׁהֵן פֵּרֵי פֵּרֵי פֵּרוֹת.

וְכֵן הַדָּבָר תָּמִיד, עַד שֶׁיִּתְּנֶה עִמָּהּ שֶׁלֹּא יִהְיוּ לוֹ לֹא פֵּרוֹת וְלֹא פֵּרֵי פֵּרוֹתֵיהֶן עַד לְעוֹלָם. וְאַחַר כָּךְ לֹא יִהְיוּ לוֹ פֵּרוֹת בְּחַיֶּיהָ, אֲבָל אִם מֵתָה — יִירַשׁ הַכֹּל.

ה הִתְנָה עִמָּהּ שֶׁלֹּא יִירָשֶׁנָּה — הֲרֵי זֶה לֹא יִירָשֶׁנָּה, אֲבָל אוֹכֵל פֵּרוֹת בְּחַיֶּיהָ. וְכֵן אִם הִתְנָה עִמָּהּ שֶׁיִּירַשׁ מִקְצָת נְכָסִים, וְכֵן אִם הִתְנָה עִמָּהּ שֶׁאִם מֵתָה בְּלֹא בָּנִים יַחְזְרוּ נְכָסִין לְבֵית אָבִיהָ — הַכֹּל קַיָּם.

ו בַּמֶּה דְּבָרִים אֲמוּרִים? שֶׁהִתְנָה עִמָּהּ קֹדֶם שֶׁתִּנָּשֵׂא, שֶׁהַנַּחֲלָה הַבָּאָה לוֹ לְאָדָם שֶׁלֹּא

5. The rationale is that before *nisu'in*, a deed of contract is not necessary to uphold any sale or gift that a woman may make. Since the husband took an additional step and carried out an act of contract, we assume that he did so with the intent of enhancing his wife's position and waiving all rights he has to her property (*Kessef Mishneh*).

This is the Rambam's interpretation of the above passage. The Ra'avad and Rabbenu Asher advance a different interpretation. The *Shulchan Aruch* (*Even HaEzer* 92:3) quotes both opinions, but appears to favor that of the Rambam.

6. From the Rambam's wording, it appears that it is imperative that the benefits from the land be converted into financial resources and be used to purchase other property. Rabbenu Asher and others do not accept this position and maintain that the woman has the right to use the benefits that accrue from the land as she desires. If, however, she decides to use them to purchase property, her husband is entitled to the benefits that accrue from that property. The *Shulchan Aruch* (*Even HaEzer* 94:4) quotes the Rambam's view, while the Ramah follows that of Rabbenu Asher.

7. If, however, the provision is made before the woman is consecrated, it is also of no consequence. For until a connection between the man and the woman is established, his statements regarding her property are of no consequence whatsoever.

to him from a source outside his family before he acquires the rights to it. If, however, he made the provision after *nisu'in*, his provision is not binding, and he inherits her estate as we explained.[8]

7. When, after *nisu'in*, [a husband] stipulates[9] that he has no say with regard to his wife's property - not with regard to the benefits from that property nor any eventual byproducts from them during her lifetime - then after her death he is not entitled to any benefit from this property at all.[10] If she dies, however, he inherits her estate, as explained [above].

8. [The following rules apply] when a husband spends money [to improve property belonging to his wife that is classified as] *nichsei m'log*. Whether he spent a small amount and derived much benefit, or spent a large amount and derived little benefit [he is not required to pay anything, nor may he collect anything]; what he spent, he spent, and the benefit that he enjoyed, he enjoyed.

[The above applies] even if he ate only one dried fig in a respectful manner,[11] if he ate a *dinar's* worth of produce in a haphazard manner, or if he did not even take produce [from the field on which he spent money] and took merely a bundle of twigs.[12]

9. Similar [laws apply] if a woman inherited funds in a distant place, and the husband undertook expenses in order to bring them [to their home], or [expenses were required] to take them from the person who was holding them. If [the husband] purchased land [with these funds] and ate the measure of fruit [mentioned above, he is not required to pay anything, nor may he collect anything]; what he spent, he spent, and the benefit that he enjoyed, he enjoyed.

[The following procedure is adhered to if] a husband incurred expenses [on behalf of his wife's property] and did not derive any benefit or derived less benefit than the above measure. We evaluate the increment to the property, and we ask him the extent of his expenses.

If the increment is greater than the expenses, the husband must take an oath holding a sacred object, stating how much he spent. He is then reimbursed for those expenses.[13] If the increment is less than the expenses, he receives only the amount of the expenses that is justified by the increment, and he must take an oath [with regard to the extent of those expenses].

10. When does the above apply? When a husband divorces his wife [under ordinary circumstances]. [Different rules apply regarding] a woman who rebels against her husband [and denies him intimacy].[14] Even if he derived much benefit, the benefit that he derives should be evaluated and subtracted from the amount fit to be given him for the expenses he undertook.[15] After

מִמִּשְׁפַּחְתּוֹ מַתְנֶה עָלֶיהָ שֶׁלֹּא יִירָשֶׁנָּה קֹדֶם שֶׁתְּהֵא רְאוּיָה לוֹ;

אֲבָל אִם הִתְנָה עִמָּהּ אַחַר שֶׁנִּשֵּׂאת — תְּנָאוֹ בָּטֵל וְיִירָשֶׁנָּה, כְּמוֹ שֶׁבֵּאַרְנוּ.

ז הִתְנָה עִמָּהּ אַחַר נִשּׂוּאִין שֶׁלֹּא יִהְיוּ לוֹ דִין וּדְבָרִים בִּנְכָסֶיהָ, וְלֹא בְּפֵרֵי פֵרוֹתֶיהָ עַד עוֹלָם, בְּחַיֶּיהָ וּבְמוֹתָהּ — הֲרֵי זֶה אֵינוֹ אוֹכֵל פֵּרוֹת כְּלָל;

אֲבָל אִם מֵתָה — יִירָשֶׁנָּה, כְּמוֹ שֶׁבֵּאַרְנוּ.

ח הַבַּעַל שֶׁהוֹצִיא הוֹצָאוֹת עַל נִכְסֵי מְלוֹג — בֵּין שֶׁהוֹצִיא מְעַט וְאָכַל פֵּרוֹת הַרְבֵּה, בֵּין שֶׁהוֹצִיא הַרְבֵּה וְאָכַל פֵּרוֹת מְעַט,

וַאֲפִלּוּ אָכַל גְּרוֹגֶרֶת אַחַת דֶּרֶךְ כָּבוֹד, אוֹ שֶׁאָכַל דִּינָר אֶחָד אֲפִלּוּ שֶׁלֹּא דֶרֶךְ כָּבוֹד,

וַאֲפִלּוּ לֹא לָקַח בַּפֵּרוֹת מִמַּה שֶׁהוֹצִיא אֶלָּא חֲבִילָה אַחַת שֶׁל זְמוֹרוֹת — מַה שֶׁהוֹצִיא הוֹצִיא, וּמַה שֶׁאָכַל אָכַל.

ט וְכֵן אִם נָפְלוּ לָהּ כְּסָפִים בְּמָקוֹם רָחוֹק, וְהוֹצִיא עֲלֵיהֶן הוֹצָאוֹת עַד שֶׁהֱבִיאָן אוֹ עַד שֶׁהוֹצִיאָן מִיַּד מִי שֶׁהָיוּ אֶצְלוֹ, וְלָקַח בָּהֶן קַרְקַע וְאָכַל פֵּרוֹתֶיהָ כַּשִּׁעוּר — מַה שֶׁהוֹצִיא הוֹצִיא, וּמַה שֶׁאָכַל אָכַל.

הוֹצִיא וְלֹא אָכַל, אוֹ שֶׁאָכַל פָּחוֹת מִכַּשִּׁעוּר — שָׁמִין כַּמָּה שֶׁהִשְׁבִּיחוֹ, וְשׁוֹאֲלִין אוֹתוֹ כַּמָּה הוֹצִיא.

אִם הַשֶּׁבַח יָתֵר עַל הַהוֹצָאָה — יִשָּׁבַע בִּנְקִיטַת חֵפֶץ כַּמָּה הוֹצִיא, וְנוֹטֵל הַהוֹצָאָה;

וְאִם הַהוֹצָאָה יְתֵרָה עַל הַשֶּׁבַח — אֵין לוֹ מִן הַהוֹצָאָה אֶלָּא כְּשִׁעוּר הַשֶּׁבַח, וּבִשְׁבוּעָה.

י בַּמֶּה דְבָרִים אֲמוּרִים? בִּמְגָרֵשׁ; אֲבָל הָאִשָּׁה שֶׁמָּרְדָה עַל בַּעְלָהּ — אֲפִלּוּ אָכַל הַרְבֵּה, שָׁמִין לוֹ כַּמָּה אָכַל, וּפוֹחֵת אוֹתוֹ מִמַּה שֶׁרָאוּי לִתֵּן לוֹ מִן הַהוֹצָאָה אַחַר שֶׁיִּשָּׁבַע

---

8. See Chapter 12, Halachah 9.

9. And affirms his provision with an act of contract (*Maggid Mishneh*).

10. Nor does he have the right to veto a sale (*Chelkat Mechokek* 92:17).

11. I.e., at home, on his table.

12. This bundle must be worth at least a *dinar* (*Chelkat Mechokek* 88:12).

13. If the wife denies his claim and states that she is sure that he spent less, her claim is accepted provided she supports it with an oath (Ramah, *Even HaEzer* 88:7, *Beit Shmuel* 88:17).

14. See Chapter 14, Halachah 8.

15. As reflected by the Rambam's Commentary on the Mishnah (*Ketubot* 8:6), this applies only when the increment to the property exceeds the expenses. If the expenses exceed the increment, all he receives is the increment. (See *Beit Shmuel* 88:18, who quotes other authorities who differ.)

he takes an oath [affirming his claim], he is entitled to collect it. For he did not [incur these expenses on behalf of his wife] so that she would take them and leave him on her own accord.

Similarly, [different rules apply when] a man undertakes expenses [to develop] property belonging to his wife who is below the age of majority, and she dissolves the marriage through the right of *mi'un*.16 We evaluate the amount of benefit he received, the amount of his expenses, the extent of the property's increment - and then he is given the share usually allocated to a sharecropper.17 [This consideration is taken] because he had permission to work [his wife's property].18

11. There are various customs regarding [a woman's] dowry. In certain places it is customary to [state a higher figure] in the *ketubah* [with regard to the value of the dowry], increasing by a third, a fifth or a half. For example, if the dowry was 100 [*zuz*], it is written [in the *ketubah*] that the woman brought 150 [to the household], in order to appear more generous in the eyes of the people. [Therefore,] when the woman comes to collect her dowry, she collects only 100.

Conversely, there are places where it is customary to write a lesser amount. If it is agreed that she will bring utensils worth 100 [*zuz* to the household], she must bring a value of 120 or 150, and yet, [in the *ketubah*,] it is written that she brought only [a value of] 100.19 And there are other places where it is customary to write a value of 100 [*zuz*] as 100.

There are places where it is customary for a man to give a set amount of money proportionate to the dowry, for the bride to adorn herself and purchase perfume and the like. There are places where [it is customary for] the man to add an additional sum of his own for his wife and add it to her dowry, for her to appear attractive.

12. When a man marries a woman without specifying any conditions, he should write her a *ketubah*, giving her a sum that is customarily given in that locale. Similarly, if she makes a commitment to bring [utensils to the household], she must bring what is customarily brought in that locale. And when she comes to collect [the money due her by virtue of] her *ketubah*, she collects as is customary in that locale.

In this and in all similar matters, local custom is a fundamental principle, and it is used as a basis for judgment, provided that the custom is commonly accepted in the locale.

13. [The following rules apply when a man and a woman were engaged to each other. When he asks her, "What is the value [of the utensils] you are bringing [to the household]?", and she answers him with an amount, and she asks him, "How much will you give me [for my *ketubah*]?", and

וְנוֹטְלוֹ;

שֶׁלֹּא הִקְנָה לָהּ כְּדֵי שֶׁתִּטֹּל וְתֵצֵא מֵעַצְמָהּ.

וְכֵן הַמּוֹצִיא הוֹצָאוֹת עַל נִכְסֵי אִשְׁתּוֹ קְטַנָּה, וּמֵאָנָה בּוֹ — רוֹאִין כַּמָּה אָכַל וְכַמָּה הוֹצִיא
וְכַמָּה הִשְׁבִּיחַ, וְשָׁמִין לוֹ כְּאָרִיס; שֶׁהֲרֵי בִּרְשׁוּת יָרַד.

יא מִנְהָגוֹת רַבּוֹת יֵשׁ בַּנְּדוּנְיָא.

יֵשׁ מְקוֹמוֹת שֶׁנָּהֲגוּ, שֶׁיִּכְתְּבוּ בְּכָתְבוֹת הַנְּדוּנְיָא יָתֵר עַל דָּמֶיהָ בִּשְׁלִישׁ אוֹ בְּחֹמֶשׁ אוֹ בְּמֶחֱצָה,
כְּגוֹן שֶׁתִּהְיֶה הַנְּדוּנְיָא מֵאָה וְכוֹתְבִים שֶׁהִכְנִיסָה מֵאָה וַחֲמִשִּׁים, כְּדֵי לְהַרְבּוֹת בִּפְנֵי הָעָם.
וּכְשֶׁתָּבוֹא לִגְבּוֹת — לֹא תִגְבֶּה אֶלָּא הַמֵּאָה.

וְיֵשׁ מְקוֹמוֹת שֶׁנָּהֲגוּ לִכְתֹּב פָּחוֹת,

וְאִם פָּסְקָה לְהָבִיא לוֹ בְּמֵאָה כֵּלִים — נוֹתֶנֶת שָׁוֶה מֵאָה וְעֶשְׂרִים אוֹ מֵאָה וַחֲמִשִּׁים, וְכוֹתְבִין
שֶׁהִכְנִיסָה לוֹ מֵאָה.

וְיֵשׁ מְקוֹמוֹת שֶׁנָּהֲגוּ לִכְתֹּב שָׁוֶה מָנֶה בְּמָנֶה.

וְיֵשׁ מְקוֹמוֹת שֶׁנָּהֲגוּ, שֶׁיִּתֵּן הָאִישׁ מָעוֹת לְפִי הַנְּדוּנְיָא דָּבָר קָצוּב, שֶׁתִּתְקַשֵּׁט בּוֹ הַכַּלָּה וְתִקָּנֶה
בּוֹ בְּשָׂמִים וְכַיּוֹצֵא בָּהֶן.

וְיֵשׁ מְקוֹמוֹת שֶׁיַּכְנִיס הָאִישׁ שׁוּם מִשֶּׁלּוֹ לָאִשָּׁה וְיִצְטָרֵף לַנְּדוּנְיָתָהּ לְהִתְנָאוֹת בּוֹ.

יב הַנּוֹשֵׂא סְתָם — כּוֹתֵב וְנוֹתֵן כְּמִנְהַג הַמְּדִינָה.

וְכֵן הִיא שֶׁפָּסְקָה לְהַכְנִיס — נוֹתֶנֶת כְּמִנְהַג הַמְּדִינָה. וּכְשֶׁתָּבוֹא לִגְבּוֹת כְּתֻבָּתָהּ — מַגְבִּין
לָהּ מַה שֶּׁבִּכְתֻבָּתָהּ כְּמִנְהַג הַמְּדִינָה.

וּבְכָל הַדְּבָרִים הָאֵלּוּ וְכַיּוֹצֵא בָּהֶן, מִנְהַג הַמְּדִינָה עִקָּר גָּדוֹל הוּא וְעַל פִּיו דָּנִין.
וְהוּא, שֶׁיִּהְיֶה אוֹתוֹ מִנְהָג פָּשׁוּט בְּכָל הַמְּדִינָה.

יג אִישׁ וְאִשָּׁה שֶׁהָיוּ בֵּינֵיהֶם שִׁדּוּכִין, וְאָמַר לָהּ: כַּמָּה אַתְּ מַכְנֶסֶת לִי? כָּךְ וָכָךְ! וְאָמְרָה לוֹ:
וְכַמָּה אַתָּה נוֹתֵן לִי אוֹ כּוֹתֵב לִי? כָּךְ וָכָךְ!

---

16. See Chapter 4, Halachah 8.

17. If the husband were not given consideration for his expenses and the increment he brought to the woman's property, he would seek only his own benefit and would deplete the property's value by failing to fertilize it and constantly sowing crops. This is unlikely to happen if he is given a sharecropper's allocation. In such an instance, he is likely to say: "It is possible that the marriage will continue, and so it is to my benefit to maintain the field's value. Even if the marriage does not continue, I will be justly reimbursed for my work."

18. The *Shulchan Aruch* (*Even HaEzer* 88:10) explains that the option is the husband's. He may choose to receive a sharecropper's allocation, or he may desire to leave the property without making a reckoning, as is done in the case when his wife is past the age of majority.

19. In this instance, the woman collects the greater sum when she collects her due.

he answers with an amount, and afterwards he arises and consecrates her, the commitments are binding even though they were not formalized with an act of contract.[20]

Similarly, a commitment made by a father on behalf of his son or daughter [is binding]. For example, if he is asked, "How much will you give on behalf of your son?", and he specifies an amount, or he is asked "How much will you give on behalf of your daughter?", and he specifies an amount, [his commitment is binding].

These are commitments that are established through speech alone.[21]

14. When does the above apply? When a father made a commitment on behalf of his daughter, whether she is a minor or past majority, or on behalf of his son, for their first marriage. For a man feels an inner connection to his son, and because of his happiness at his first marriage, he makes a definite commitment, and designates [the sum] for him with a verbal statement [alone].

[Different rules apply when], by contrast, a brother makes a commitment on behalf of his sister, a woman makes a commitment on behalf of her daughter, [when a commitment is made by] other relatives, and similarly, when a father makes a commitment on behalf of his son or daughter for a second marriage.[22] The commitment is not binding until the person making it formalizes it with an act of contract and states the amount he will give.

15. When a father makes a commitment for his daughter, the daughter does not acquire that present until her husband consummates the marriage with her.[23] Similarly, a son does not acquire [the present that he was promised] until he consummates his marriage. For whenever one makes [such] a commitment, his intent is that [it be fulfilled when] the marriage is consummated.

Therefore, when a man makes a commitment to his [prospective] son-in-law, but the son-in-law dies [after *erusin*, but] before the marriage is consummated, and the woman is bound to his brother, [if he desires to perform the rite of] *yibbum*, [the woman's] father may [retract his commitment], saying: "I desired to give your brother; I do not desire to give you." [This applies] even if the first husband was an unlearned man and the second is a Torah scholar, and even if the woman desires [to marry] the second man.[24]

16. When a man makes a financial commitment to his son-in-law and then moves to another country [without fulfilling his commitment], the woman has the prerogative of telling her [prospective] husband: "I did not make

20. In *Hilchot Zechiyah UMatanah* 6:17, the Rambam adds several dimensions to this statement: a) The person making the commitment must own the items he promises. If

וְכֵן הָאָב שֶׁפָּסַק עַל יְדֵי בְּנוֹ וּבִתּוֹ: כַּמָּה אַתָּה נוֹתֵן לְבִנְךָ? כָּךְ וָכָךְ! וְכַמָּה אַתָּה נוֹתֵן לְבִתְּךָ? כָּךְ וָכָךְ!

עָמְדוּ וְקִדְּשׁוּ — קָנוּ אוֹתָן הַדְּבָרִים, וְאַף-עַל-פִּי שֶׁלֹּא הָיָה בֵּינֵיהֶן קִנְיָן. וְאֵלּוּ הֵן הַדְּבָרִים הַנִּקְנִים בַּאֲמִירָה.

יד בַּמֶּה דְּבָרִים אֲמוּרִים? בְּשֶׁפָּסַק הָאָב לְבִתּוֹ, בֵּין קְטַנָּה וּבֵין גְּדוֹלָה, וּפָסַק הָאָב לִבְנוֹ, וּבְנִשּׂוּאִין רִאשׁוֹנִים;

שֶׁדַּעְתּוֹ שֶׁל אָדָם קְרוֹבָה אֵצֶל בְּנוֹ, וּמֵרֹב שִׂמְחָתוֹ בַּנִּשּׂוּאִין הָרִאשׁוֹנִים גָּמַר וּמַקְנֶה לוֹ בַּאֲמִירָה.

אֲבָל אָח שֶׁפָּסַק לַאֲחוֹתוֹ אוֹ אִשָּׁה שֶׁפָּסְקָה לְבִתָּהּ וְכֵן שְׁאָר קְרוֹבִים,

וְכֵן הָאָב שֶׁפָּסַק לִבְנוֹ אוֹ לְבִתּוֹ בְּנִשּׂוּאִין שְׁנִיִּים —

לֹא קָנוּ אוֹתָן הַדְּבָרִים עַד שֶׁיִּקְנוּ מִידֵי הַפּוֹסֵק שֶׁיִּתֵּן כָּךְ וָכָךְ.

טו הָאָב שֶׁפָּסַק עַל יַד בִּתּוֹ — לֹא קָנְתָה הַבַּת אוֹתָהּ הַמַּתָּנָה עַד שֶׁיִּכְנֹס אוֹתָהּ בַּעֲלָהּ.

וְכֵן הַבֵּן לֹא קָנָה עַד שֶׁיִּכְנֹס. שֶׁכָּל הַפּוֹסֵק אֵינוֹ פוֹסֵק אֶלָּא עַל מְנָת לִכְנֹס.

לְפִיכָךְ, הַפּוֹסֵק מָעוֹת לַחֲתָנוֹ, וּמֵת קֹדֶם שֶׁיִּכְנֹס, וְנָפְלָה לִפְנֵי אָחִיו לְיִבּוּם — יָכוֹל הָאָב לוֹמַר לַיָּבָם: לְאָחִיךָ הָיִיתִי רוֹצֶה לִתֵּן, וּלְךָ אֵינִי רוֹצֶה לִתֵּן.

וַאֲפִלּוּ הָיָה הָרִאשׁוֹן עַם הָאָרֶץ וְהַשֵּׁנִי חָכָם, וְאַף-עַל-פִּי שֶׁהַבַּת רוֹצָה בּוֹ.

טז הַפּוֹסֵק מָעוֹת לַחֲתָנוֹ, וְהָלַךְ הָאָב לִמְדִינָה אַחֶרֶת — יְכוֹלָה הִיא לוֹמַר לַבַּעַל:

---

he does not own them, his commitment is not binding, for a person cannot transfer an entity that does not yet exist.

b) The commitment is not binding on property that has been sold. For only transactions that are formalized by a written deed are binding on the purchasers of property. Moreover, since this commitment can be formalized by the spoken word alone, even if it is later recorded in a written document, it is not binding on the purchasers. If, however, a formal deed of transfer is composed, it must be honored by the purchasers (*Maggid Mishneh, Hilchot Zechiyah UMatanah*). (See also Halachah 18.)

c) The transaction is not effective until the marriage takes place.

21. In general, a business agreement must be formalized by a contractual act (a *kinyan*), and a verbal commitment is not sufficient. An exception is made in this instance because of the happiness and closeness engendered by the marriage relationship (*Ketubot* 102b).

22. If, by contrast, a man or a woman makes a commitment for his or her own marriage, the commitment is binding without a contractual act, even if it is a second marriage that is involved.

23. I.e., *nisu'in*, the second stage of marriage, as well as *erusin*, the first stage, must be completed before the present is binding.

24. For it is her father who is making the financial commitment, not she.

this commitment myself. What can I do? Either consummate the marriage without a dowry or divorce me."25

If, however, she made such a commitment herself, and she was not able to muster the funds, she must remain [in this intermediate state] until she accumulates the sum to which she committed herself or until she dies.

Why does she not release herself from her obligation by becoming a *moredet*26 against her husband? [Because there is a difference between these two instances.] With regard to a *moredet* who has [merely] been consecrated, the husband desires to consummate the marriage; it is she who does not desire. In this instance, by contrast, the husband does not want [to consummate his marriage with] her until she gives the dowry to which she committed herself. She, however, desires him, [as reflected by] her request: "Either consummate [the marriage] or divorce me."

When does the above apply? To a woman past majority. If, however, a woman makes a financial commitment while she is still a minor, we compel [her prospective husband] either to divorce her or to consummate the marriage without a dowry.

17. When a man marries a woman and makes a commitment to support her daughter for [an explicit number of] years, he is obligated to support her for [all] the years to which he committed himself, provided he made this commitment at the time of the woman's consecration.27

If, however, he made the commitment [after] the *kiddushin* [were given], the commitment is not binding until he affirms it with an act of contract or composes a document to that effect, as will be explained in the laws of business transactions.28

[The following rules apply when] a woman is divorced within the time that her husband committed himself to support her daughter, and she married another man who also committed himself to support her daughter for a particular number of years. The first husband does not have the prerogative to say: "If she comes to my house, I will support her."29 Instead, he must bring her support to the place where she is staying together with her mother. Similarly, both husbands do not have the prerogative of saying: "We will together provide for her support." Instead, one of the husbands must provide for her support, and the other must give her the financial value of her support.

18. [The following rules apply when the woman's] daughter marries during the time [in which her mother's husbands] obligated themselves to supply her with her sustenance. Her own husband is obligated to provide her with her sustenance, and both of her mother's husbands are obligated to give her the financial value of her support.

אֲנִי לֹא פָּסַקְתִּי עַל עַצְמִי, מָה אֲנִי יְכוֹלָה לַעֲשׂוֹת? אוֹ כְּנֹס בְּלֹא נְדוּנְיָא אוֹ פָּטְרֵנִי בְּגֵט.

אֲבָל אִם פָּסְקָה הִיא עַל עַצְמָהּ וְלֹא הִגִּיעָה יָדָהּ — הֲרֵי זוֹ יוֹשֶׁבֶת עַד שֶׁתִּמְצָא עַד שֶׁפָּסְקָה אוֹ עַד שֶׁתָּמוּת.

וְלָמָּה לֹא תִּפְטֹר עַצְמָהּ בְּמַרְדּוּת?

שֶׁהַמּוֹרֶדֶת וְהִיא אֲרוּסָה — הַבַּעַל רוֹצֶה לְכָנְסָהּ וְהִיא אֵינָהּ רוֹצָה;

אֲבָל זוֹ — אֵין הַבַּעַל רוֹצֶה בָהּ עַד שֶׁתִּתֵּן הַנְּדוּנְיָא שֶׁפָּסְקָה, וְהִיא רוֹצָה בּוֹ, שֶׁהֲרֵי אוֹמֶרֶת לוֹ: אוֹ כְּנֹס אוֹ פְּטֹר.

בַּמֶּה דְּבָרִים אֲמוּרִים? בִּגְדוֹלָה; אֲבָל בִּקְטַנָּה שֶׁפָּסְקָה עַל עַצְמָהּ — כּוֹפִין אוֹתוֹ לְתֵן גֵּט, אוֹ יִכְנֹס בְּלֹא נְדוּנְיָא.

יז הַנּוֹשֵׂא אִשָּׁה וּפָסְקָה עִמּוֹ שֶׁיִּהְיֶה זָן אֶת בִּתָּהּ כָּךְ וְכָךְ שָׁנִים — חַיָּב לָזוּן אוֹתָם שָׁנִים שֶׁקִּבֵּל עַל עַצְמוֹ.

וְהוּא, שֶׁיִּתְנוּ עַל דָּבָר זֶה בִּשְׁעַת הַקִּדּוּשִׁין;

אֲבָל שֶׁלֹּא בִּשְׁעַת הַקִּדּוּשִׁין — עַד שֶׁיִּקְנוּ מִיָּדוֹ אוֹ עַד שֶׁיִּכָּתֵב בִּשְׁטָר וְכַיּוֹצֵא בּוֹ, כְּמוֹ שֶׁיִּתְבָּאֵר בְּהִלְכוֹת מֶקַּח וּמִמְכָּר.

נִתְגָּרְשָׁה בְּתוֹךְ הַשָּׁנִים שֶׁקִּבֵּל עַל עַצְמוֹ לָזוּן אֶת בִּתָּהּ, וְנִשֵּׂאת לְאַחֵר וּפָסְקָה גַם עִמּוֹ שֶׁיִּהְיֶה זָן אוֹתָהּ הַבַּת כָּךְ וְכָךְ שָׁנִים —

לֹא יֹאמַר רִאשׁוֹן: אִם תָּבוֹא לְבֵיתִי אֲזוּנֶהָ, אֶלָּא מוֹלִיךְ מְזוֹנוֹתֶיהָ לַמָּקוֹם שֶׁהִיא שָׁם אִמָּהּ. וְכֵן לֹא יֹאמְרוּ שְׁנֵיהֶם: הֲרֵי אָנוּ זָנִין אוֹתָהּ כְּאַחַת, אֶלָּא אֶחָד זָנָהּ וְאֶחָד נוֹתֵן לָהּ דְּמֵי מְזוֹנוֹת.

יח נִשֵּׂאת הַבַּת בְּתוֹךְ זְמַן זֶה — הַבַּעַל חַיָּב בִּמְזוֹנוֹתֶיהָ, וּבַעֲלֵי אִמָּהּ שְׁנֵיהֶם כָּל אֶחָד וְאֶחָד נוֹתֵן לָהּ דְּמֵי מְזוֹנוֹת.

---

25. I.e., the husband must take one of these two options. He cannot leave the woman consecrated (in which case she cannot marry someone else), but not married.

This ruling is quoted by the *Shulchan Aruch* (*Even HaEzer* 52:1). The Ramah states that if the woman has the financial means to meet the commitment, she must do so.

26. See Chapter 14, Halachot 8 and 12.

27. Generally, such commitments are not binding, for the commitment does not have a specific scope. In most situations, only when a definite sum is mentioned is the commitment obligatory. (See *Shulchan Aruch*, *Even HaEzer* 114.)

28. *Hilchot Mechirah* 11:15-17.

29. Needless to say, he is obligated to support his divorcee's daughter if his divorcee does not remarry. There is a difference of opinion among the Rabbis if the husband is required to provide his divorcee's daughter with the full measure of support she requires, or he is

[Even when the men] who obligated themselves to support her die, if they affirmed their commitment to her mother with an act of contract or they composed a formal document recording their obligation, [the daughter] is considered to be a creditor whose claim is supported by a deed, and she has the prerogative of collecting her due from property that has been sold until the conclusion of the time period for which he committed himself.

If the commitment was made at the time of the *kiddushin*, and was not affirmed by an act of contract, it is a commitment that was not to be recorded in a contract,[30] and [the daughter] does not have the prerogative of expropriating property [from purchasers] for her support.

CHAPTER TWENTY-FOUR

1. When a man who marries an *aylonit*[1] is childless and does not have another wife with whom he will father children, he is compelled to divorce her.[2] Nevertheless, [during and after the marriage], the financial arrangements that [govern] other women [govern] her. She is entitled to the fundamental requirement of the *ketubah* and [all] the provisions of the *ketubah*. Similarly, her husband acquires the same financial privileges with regard to her as he would with regard to another woman.

2. If, however, a man married a woman without recognizing her condition, and later it was discovered that she was an *aylonit*, or forbidden to him by virtue of a negative commandment [for which he is not liable to death - neither by the hand of God nor by an earthly court] she is not entitled to the fundamental requirement of the *ketubah,* nor to any of the provisions of the *ketubah.* She is, however, entitled to the extra amount that the husband added to the fundamental requirement of the *ketubah.* She is not entitled to receive her sustenance, [neither during her husband's lifetime,] nor even after his death.[3]

The couple [should be] forced to separate.[4] When that is done, the value of the produce of which the husband partook is not expropriated from him.[5]

The same laws apply when a man marries a *sh'niyah*,[6] regardless of whether or not [the husband] was aware of the prohibition.

merely obligated to give her the amount of money it would cost for him to support her in his own home. (See *Shulchan Aruch* and Ramah, *Even HaEzer* 114:6.)

30. As mentioned in the notes on Halachah 13, even if this commitment was recorded in a document, as long as a formal deed is not composed, the purchasers are not under any obligation.

מֵתוּ אֵלּוּ שֶׁפָּסְקוּ לָזוּן אוֹתָהּ: אִם קָנוּ מִיָּדָן אוֹ שֶׁחַיֵּב עַצְמוֹ בִּשְׁטָר — הֲרֵי זוֹ כְּבַעַל חוֹב בִּשְׁטָר, וְטוֹרֶפֶת מְזוֹנוֹתֶיהָ מִנִּכְסֵיהֶן הַמְשֻׁעְבָּדִים עַד סוֹף הַזְּמַן שֶׁפָּסְקוּ; וְאִם פָּסְקוּ בִּשְׁעַת הַקִּדּוּשִׁין וְלֹא הָיָה שָׁם קִנְיָן — הֲרֵי הֵם דְּבָרִים שֶׁלֹּא נִתְּנוּ לִכָּתֵב, וְאֵינָהּ טוֹרֶפֶת בִּמְזוֹנוֹתֶיהָ.

פֶּרֶק אַרְבָּעָה וְעֶשְׂרִים

א הַנּוֹשֵׂא אֶת הָאַיְלוֹנִית, וְלֹא הָיוּ לוֹ בָּנִים וְלֹא אִשָּׁה אַחֶרֶת לִפְרוֹת וְלִרְבּוֹת מִמֶּנָּה — אַף־עַל־פִּי שֶׁכּוֹפִין אוֹתוֹ וּמוֹצִיא, הֲרֵי הִיא כְּכָל הַנָּשִׁים, וְיֵשׁ לָהּ כְּתֻבָּה וּשְׁאָר תְּנָאֵי כְּתֻבָּה.

וְכֵן זוֹכֶה הַבַּעַל בְּמַה שֶּׁזָּכָה בִּשְׁאָר הַנָּשִׁים.

ב אֲבָל הַנּוֹשֵׂא אִשָּׁה וְלֹא הִכִּיר בָּהּ, וְנִמְצֵאת אַיְלוֹנִית אוֹ מְחַיְּבֵי לָאוִין, וְכֵן הַנּוֹשֵׂא שְׁנִיָּה, בֵּין הִכִּיר בָּהּ בֵּין לֹא הִכִּיר בָּהּ — אֵין לָהּ עִקָּר כְּתֻבָּה וְלֹא תְּנַאי מִתְּנָאֵי כְּתֻבָּה, אֲבָל תּוֹסֶפֶת יֵשׁ לָהּ. וְאֵין לָהּ מְזוֹנוֹת, וַאֲפִלּוּ לְאַחַר מוֹתוֹ. וּכְשֶׁכּוֹפִין אוֹתוֹ וּמַפְרִישִׁין בֵּינֵיהֶם — אֵין מוֹצִיאִין מִן הַבַּעַל פֵּרוֹת שֶׁאָכַל.

1. A woman who does not have female physical characteristics and cannot conceive children, as mentioned in Chapter 2, Halachah 6. This halachah is speaking about an instance in which the husband was aware of his wife's condition.
2. See Chapter 15, Halachah 7.
3. The Rambam does not explicitly mention that the woman is not entitled to receive her sustenance during her husband's lifetime. This is taken for granted. Since their marriage is forbidden, our Sages did not bind their relationship by any of the guidelines they instituted to preserve harmony and peace in marriage. Even after his lifetime, she is not entitled to receive her sustenance.
4. In contrast to the previous and subsequent halachot, the Rambam does not mention divorce in this instance. The *Noda BiY'hudah* (*Even HaEzer*, Vol. II, Responsum 80) explains that the Rambam's wording leads to the following hypothesis: Since the husband was not aware of the woman's physical condition (if she was an *aylonit*), or the prohibition forbidding relations (if she was forbidden to him), he entered the marriage under mistaken premises. Hence, the marriage is not binding at all and no divorce is necessary. The couple must, however, be forced to separate.

The *Noda BiY'hudah*, however, rejects this hypothesis and maintains that the *kiddushin* are binding in such instances and a divorce is required.
5. Even though her husband is not obligated to redeem her from captivity - and the right to benefit from the produce is associated with that obligation - he is not required to return the produce. This is a penalty that our Sages imposed upon the woman (*Shulchan Aruch, Even HaEzer* 115:1).
6. A woman with whom he is forbidden to engage in relations because of Rabbinic decree. (See Chapter 1, Halachah 6.)

3. Why are these women not granted the essential requirement of the *ketubah*, when they are granted the extra sum added [by the husband]? The fundamental requirement of the *ketubah* was instituted by our Sages so that [a man] should not think that the divorce [of his wife] is a light matter. Since he was not aware [of the prohibition or of his wife's condition], she is not granted the essential requirement of the *ketubah*.[7]

With regard to the extra amount for which he obligated himself: as long as she desired to maintain their relationship, she kept her part of the agreement. She granted him [marital] satisfaction,[8] and is willing to continue their relationship; it is the Torah that deems her to be forbidden. What then can she do? Therefore, she is granted this extra amount, for it is not her deeds that cause her to be forbidden after marriage;[9] she was forbidden beforehand.

4. Why did [our Sages] not distinguish between a *sh'niyah* [whom her husband] recognized, and one that he did not recognize, but rather said that in all instances she is not entitled to the fundamental requirement of the *ketubah*? Because [the prohibition involving these relations] is Rabbinic [in origin], they reinforced it.

If, by contrast, a man married a woman [whom he was forbidden to marry because of] a negative prohibition of the Torah [that was not punishable by death, neither by the hand of God nor by an earthly court] and he was aware of the prohibition, [his wife] is entitled to [the money due her by virtue of her] *ketubah*.[Similarly, if he marries] a woman whom he was forbidden to marry because of a positive commandment, whether he was aware of the prohibition or not, [his wife is entitled to a *ketubah*].

[The rationale is] that if he recognized that a woman was forbidden by a negative prohibition, he willingly undertook to damage his resources. And with regard to [relations which are forbidden] because of a positive commandment, the prohibition is light.

In both these instances, the women are entitled to support [from their husband's estate] after his death.[10] Similarly, if [during his absence,] they borrowed money for their sustenance, [the husband] is liable to pay.[11] And when the husband is forced to divorce [a woman in either of these situations], he is forced to reimburse her for all the benefit that he received from her property.[12]

5. A woman who dissolves a marriage through the rite of *mi'un* is not entitled to a *ketubah*.[13] She is, however, entitled to the extra amount [added by the husband to the *ketubah*].[14] The husband is not required to reimburse her

7. For the relationship is undesirable, and our Sages wish that it be terminated.
8. This extra amount is granted by the husband on his own volition because of the satisfaction generated by physical intimacy. It is not a requirement of the Sages (Rashi, *Ketubot* 101a).

ג וְלָמָּה אֵין לָהֶם עִקָּר וְיֵשׁ לָהֶן תּוֹסֶפֶת?

הָעִקָּר, שֶׁהִיא תַּקָּנַת חֲכָמִים כְּדֵי שֶׁלֹּא תִּהְיֶה קַלָּה בְּעֵינָיו לְהוֹצִיאָהּ — הוֹאִיל וְלֹא הִכִּיר בָּהּ, אֵין לָהּ עִקָּר;

אֲבָל תּוֹסֶפֶת, שֶׁהוּא חַיָּב עַצְמוֹ בָּהּ כָּל זְמַן שֶׁתִּרְצֶה וְתַעֲמֹד לְפָנָיו — הֲרֵי עָמְדָה בַּתְּנַאי שֶׁלָּהּ,

וַהֲרֵי הִקְנֵת לוֹ הֲנָאָתָהּ, וַהֲרֵי הִיא עוֹמֶדֶת [לְפָנָיו], אֲבָל הַתּוֹרָה אָסְרָה אוֹתָהּ עָלָיו, וּמַה הִיא יְכוֹלָה לַעֲשׂוֹת?

לְפִיכָךְ יֵשׁ לָהּ תּוֹסֶפֶת, שֶׁאֵין מַעֲשֶׂיהָ הֵן הַגּוֹרְמִין לָהּ לְהֵאָסֵר אַחַר הַנִּשּׂוּאִין, אֶלָּא אֲסוּרָה הָיְתָה מִקֹּדֶם.

ד וְלָמָּה לֹא חִלְּקוּ בִּשְׁנִיָּה בֵּין שֶׁהִכִּיר בָּהּ בֵּין שֶׁלֹּא הִכִּיר בָּהּ, אֶלָּא אָמְרוּ: אֵין לָהּ עִקָּר כְּתֻבָּה בְּכָל מָקוֹם? מִפְּנֵי שֶׁהִיא מִדִּבְרֵי סוֹפְרִים, עָשׂוּ בָּהּ חִזּוּק.

אֲבָל אִם נָשָׂא אַחַת מֵחַיָּבֵי לָאוִין וְהִכִּיר בָּהּ,

אוֹ אַחַת מֵחַיָּבֵי עֲשֵׂה, בֵּין הִכִּיר בָּהּ בֵּין שֶׁלֹּא הִכִּיר בָּהּ — יֵשׁ לָהּ כְּתֻבָּה;

שֶׁחַיָּבֵי לָאוִין שֶׁהִכִּיר בָּהּ — רָצָה לָזוּן בִּנְכָסָיו, וְחַיָּבֵי עֲשֵׂה — אִסּוּרָן קַל. וְיֵשׁ לִשְׁתֵּיהֶן מְזוֹנוֹת לְאַחַר מוֹתוֹ.

וְכֵן אִם לָוְתָה וְאָכְלָה — חַיָּב לְשַׁלֵּם.

וּכְשֶׁכּוֹפִין אוֹתָן לְהוֹצִיא — מוֹצִיאִין מִן הַבַּעַל כָּל פֵּרוֹת שֶׁאָכַל מִכָּל נְכָסֶיהָ.

ה הַמְמָאֶנֶת — אֵין לָהּ כְּתֻבָּה, אֲבָל תּוֹסֶפֶת יֵשׁ לָהּ. וְאֵין מוֹצִיאִין מִן הַבַּעַל פֵּרוֹת שֶׁאָכַל.

---

9. Note the contrast to Halachah 6.

10. During the husband's lifetime, however, they are not entitled to support, for the court desires that the relationship be terminated (*Maggid Mishneh*).

11. The Rambam's rationale is that although the husband is not liable for his wife's support while the couple are living together, this is only because the Sages desired to rend apart the couple's relationship. In principle, he should be liable, for she is entitled to a *ketubah* and the conditions of the *ketubah*. Therefore, in an instance where the couple are separating, and the woman demands payment for her support while her husband was abroad, he should be held liable.

Other authorities differ and free the husband from liability in this instance. It is their opinion that is cited by the *Shulchan Aruch* (*Even HaEzer* 116:1).

12. This point is also the subject of a difference of opinion among the Rabbis, and the *Shulchan Aruch* (*loc. cit.*) follows the view of the authorities who differ with the Rambam and do not hold the husband liable.

13. Our Sages instituted the marriage of a minor for her own benefit. If she does not desire to continue the marriage, it is she who suffers the consequences.

14. This additional amount was granted to the woman in consideration of the physical pleasure she gives her husband. Since he received that pleasure and knew that the woman had the right to terminate the relationship, he is liable for this amount.

for the benefit that he received from her property.[15] If she borrowed money for her sustenance while she was still his wife, and afterwards terminated the marriage through the rite of *mi'un*, that money is not expropriated from the husband.

6. When a woman commits adultery [her husband is obligated to divorce her]. She is not entitled to a *ketubah* - neither the fundamental requirement nor the additional amount. Nor is she entitled to any of the conditions of the *ketubah*. [The rationale is that] it is her own deeds that cause her to become forbidden to her husband.

7. What is the law with regard to the rights these women have to their dowries? Whenever a woman's dowry endures, she is entitled to take her property when she leaves [her husband's household after divorce].[16] This applies even when she commits adultery.

[If the property is not intact, the following laws apply.] If the woman was a *sh'niyah* or forbidden as a result of a positive commandment - whether or not her husband was aware of the prohibition - the same laws that apply to other women with regard to their dowries apply to her. Similarly, if the woman was an *aylonit* or was forbidden because of a negative prohibition of the Torah [that was not punishable by death - neither by the hand of God nor by an earthly court], the same laws that apply to other women with regard to their dowries apply to her.[17]

[What are those laws?] The husband is liable for *nichsei tzon barzel*. With regard to *nichsei m'log*, if anything was lost or stolen, she suffers the loss. [The husband] is not liable to pay.

8. [Different rules apply when] a woman is either an *aylonit* or prohibited because of a negative commandment, and [the husband] did not recognize her status. Whatever was lost, stolen, destroyed or damaged from *nichsei tzon barzel*, her husband is not liable to pay. For she gave him permission to use them.[18]

With regard to *nichsei m'log*, by contrast, whatever was lost or stolen, he is liable to pay. This is the opposite of all other women. Since the marriage bond is not of a binding nature, he did not acquire [rights to use] the *nichsei m'log*.[19]

9. A woman who dissolves a marriage through the rite of *mi'un* is not entitled to any compensation at all for property that was destroyed. Nothing is expropriated from her husband in payment for what was lost or stolen, with regard to both *nichsei m'log* and *nichsei tzon barzel*.[20] Instead, she takes whatever property is intact and departs.

10. A woman who committed adultery is not entitled to a *ketubah* - neither

וְאִם לָוְתָה כְּשֶׁהָיְתָה תַּחְתָּיו וְאָכְלָה, וְאַחַר כָּךְ מֵאֲנָה — אֵין מוֹצִיאִין אוֹתָן מְזוֹנוֹת מִן הַבַּעַל.

ו מִי שֶׁזִּנְתָה תַחַת בַּעְלָהּ — אֵין לָהּ כְּתֻבָּה, לֹא עִקָּר וְלֹא תּוֹסֶפֶת וְלֹא אֶחָד מִתְּנָאֵי כְּתֻבָּה; שֶׁהֲרֵי מַעֲשֶׂיהָ גָּרְמוּ לָהּ לְהֵאָסֵר עַל בַּעְלָהּ.

ז וְהֵיאַךְ דִּין נָשִׁים אֵלּוּ בַּנְּדוּנְיָא שֶׁלָּהֶם?
כָּל אִשָּׁה שֶׁנְּדוּנְיָתָהּ קַיֶּמֶת — אֲפִלּוּ זִנְתָה, נוֹטֶלֶת שֶׁלָּהּ וְהוֹלֶכֶת.
וְאִם הָיְתָה שְׁנִיָּה אוֹ אֶחָד מֵחַיָּבֵי עֲשֵׂה, בֵּין הִכִּיר בָּהּ בֵּין שֶׁלֹּא הִכִּיר בָּהּ, אוֹ שֶׁהָיְתָה אַיְלוֹנִית אוֹ מֵחַיָּבֵי לָאוִין וְהִכִּיר בָּהּ — הֲרֵי הִיא בִּנְדוּנְיָתָהּ כְּכָל הַנָּשִׁים. נִכְסֵי צֹאן בַּרְזֶל, חַיָּב בְּאַחֲרָיוּתָן;
וּבְנִכְסֵי מְלוֹג, מַה שֶּׁנִּגְנַב אוֹ שֶׁאָבַד — אָבַד לָהּ, וְאֵינוּ חַיָּב לְשַׁלֵּם.

ח הָיְתָה אַיְלוֹנִית אוֹ מֵחַיָּבֵי לָאוִין וְלֹא הִכִּיר בָּהּ: כָּל מַה שֶּׁאָבַד אוֹ נִגְנַב אוֹ בָּלָה אוֹ שֶׁנִּשְׁחַק מִנִּכְסֵי צֹאן בַּרְזֶל — אֵין הַבַּעַל חַיָּב לְשַׁלֵּם,
שֶׁהֲרֵי הִיא נָתְנָה לוֹ רְשׁוּת לִהְיוֹתָן אֶצְלוֹ;
וְכָל מַה שֶּׁאָבַד אוֹ נִגְנַב מִנִּכְסֵי מְלוֹג — חַיָּב לְשַׁלֵּם.
הֵפֶךְ מִכָּל הַנָּשִׁים. מִפְּנֵי שֶׁאֵין שָׁם אִישׁוּת גְּמוּרָה, לֹא זָכָה בְּנִכְסֵי מְלוֹג.

ט וְהַמְמָאֶנֶת — אֵין לָהּ בְּלָיוֹת כְּלָל. שֶׁאֵין מוֹצִיאִין מִן הַבַּעַל דָּבָר מִמַּה שֶּׁאָבַד אוֹ נִגְנַב מִנְּכָסֶיהָ, בֵּין מִנִּכְסֵי מְלוֹג בֵּין מִנִּכְסֵי צֹאן בַּרְזֶל, אֶלָּא נוֹטֶלֶת הַנִּמְצָא לָהּ וְיוֹצְאָה.

י מִי שֶׁזִּנְתָה תַּחַת בַּעְלָהּ — אֵין לָהּ כְּתֻבָּה, לֹא עִקָּר וְלֹא תּוֹסֶפֶת.

15. For at the time, he had permission to use her property and benefit from it.
16. Even if the entire dowry is not intact, the woman takes the part that is intact. The remaining laws apply only to that portion of the dowry that no longer exists or that is unfit for use.
17. As the Rambam explains in his Commentary on the Mishnah (*Yevamot* 9:3), the rationale for this ruling is that, with the exception of the *sh'niyot*, the women mentioned in this halachah are all entitled to a *ketubah*. As a result, the same laws that apply to other women with regard to their dowries apply to them as well. With regard to a *sh'niyah*, even though she is not entitled to a *ketubah*, our Sages imposed penalties on both her and her husband and required them to suffer a loss.
   With the exception of the case of a *sh'niyah*, the *Shulchan Aruch* (*Even HaEzer* 116:1-4) does not accept the distinction made by the Rambam and applies the laws mentioned in the following halachah to all these instances.
18. Although he accepted responsibility for them, his acceptance was made under false premises. Hence, just as the marriage contract is not binding, so too, his acceptance of responsibility is not binding.
19. Therefore, he is held responsible for any loss that took place.
20. The rationale is that the court gave him the right to use this property, and according to the conditions they established, he is liable only if he divorces her.

the fundamental requirement nor the extra amount. Nor is the husband held responsible for any of her *nichsei tzon barzel* that were lost or stolen.[21] Needless to say, this ruling also applies with regard to her *nichsei m'log*.

[The above does not apply] only to an adulteress, but also to a woman who violates the faith of Moses,[22] one who violates the Jewish faith,[23] or one who is divorced because of a scandalous report.[24] These women are not entitled to a *ketubah* - neither the fundamental requirement nor the extra amount - nor are they granted any of the conditions of the *ketubah*.

When these [women are divorced], each one should take what remains from her dowry and depart. Her husband is not liable to pay anything, neither what was reduced in value nor what was lost.

11. The following are the actions for which a woman is considered to have "violated the faith of Moses":
a) going out to the marketplace with her hair uncovered;[25]
b) taking vows or oaths that she does not keep;
c) engaging in sexual relations [with her husband] while in the *niddah* state;
d) failing to separate *challah* or feeding her husband food that is forbidden to eat - needless to say, this applies to forbidden crawling animals and animals that were not ritually slaughtered; it applies even to produce that was not tithed.[26]

How can the latter [two] matters be known? For example, she said: "So and so, the priest, [separated tithes] from this produce for me," "So and so separated *challah* [from this dough]," "So and so, the Sage, said this stain does not render me a *niddah*" - and after eating the food or engaging in sexual relations with her, the husband asked the person whose name was mentioned and he denied the occurrence of the incident. Another example: a woman's [conduct caused] it to be established in her neighborhood that she was in the *niddah* state,[27] but she told her husband that she was ritually pure. He engaged in relations with her [and afterwards discovered the truth].

12. What is meant by "the Jewish faith"? The customs of modesty that Jewish women practice. When a woman performs any of the following acts, she is considered to have violated the Jewish faith:
a) she goes to the marketplace or a lane with openings at both ends without having her head [fully] covered - i.e., her hair is covered by a handkerchief, but not with a veil like all other women,[28]

---

21. Even if an object was lost because of the husband's negligence, he is not held liable (*Chelkat Mechokek* 115:20).
22. See the following halachah for a definition of this term.
23. See Halachah 12 for a definition of this term.
24. See Halachah 15 for a definition of this term.
25. Numbers 5:18 states that as part of the process of causing a *sotah* distress, her hair is

וְאֵין מוֹצִיאִין מֵהַבַּעַל דָּבָר מִמַּה שֶׁאָבַד אוֹ נִגְנַב מִנִּכְסֵי צֹאן בַּרְזֶל שֶׁלָּהּ, וְאֵין צָרִיךְ לוֹמַר נִכְסֵי מְלוֹג.

וְלֹא הַמְזֻנָּה בִּלְבַד, אֶלָּא אַף הָעוֹבֶרֶת עַל דַּת מֹשֶׁה אוֹ עַל דַּת יְהוּדִית, אוֹ הַיּוֹצֵאת מִשּׁוּם שֵׁם רָע — אֵין לָהּ כְּתֻבָּה, לֹא עִקָּר וְלֹא תּוֹסֶפֶת וְלֹא תְּנַאי מִתְּנָאֵי כְּתֻבָּה.

וְכָל אַחַת מֵהֶן נוֹטֶלֶת הַנִּמְצָא לָהּ מִנְּדוּנְיָתָהּ וְיוֹצְאָה, וְאֵין הַבַּעַל חַיָּב לְשַׁלֵּם כְּלוּם, לֹא מַה שֶּׁפָּחַת וְלֹא מַה שֶּׁאָבַד.

יא וְאֵלּוּ הֵן הַדְּבָרִים שֶׁאִם עָשְׂתָה אַחַת מֵהֶן עָבְרָה עַל דַּת מֹשֶׁה:

יוֹצְאָה בַּשּׁוּק וּשְׂעַר רֹאשָׁהּ גָּלוּי.

אוֹ שֶׁנּוֹדֶרֶת אוֹ שֶׁנִּשְׁבַּעַת וְאֵינָהּ מְקַיֶּמֶת.

אוֹ שֶׁשִּׁמְּשָׁה מִטָּתָהּ וְהִיא נִדָּה.

אוֹ שֶׁאֵינָהּ קוֹצָה לָהּ חַלָּה.

אוֹ שֶׁהֶאֱכִילָה אֶת בַּעְלָהּ דְּבָרִים אֲסוּרִים. אֵין צָרִיךְ לוֹמַר שְׁקָצִים וּרְמָשִׂים וּנְבֵלוֹת, אֶלָּא דְּבָרִים שֶׁאֵינָן מְעֻשָּׂרִין.

וְהֵיאַךְ יוֹדֵעַ דָּבָר זֶה? כְּגוֹן שֶׁאָמְרָה לוֹ: פֵּרוֹת אֵלּוּ פְּלוֹנִי כֹּהֵן תִּקְּנָם לִי, וְעָשָׂה זוֹ פְלוֹנִית הַפְּרִישָׁה לִי חַלָּתָהּ, וּפְלוֹנִי הֶחָכָם טִהֵר לִי אֶת הַכֶּתֶם;

וְאַחַר שֶׁאָכַל אוֹ בָּא עָלֶיהָ שָׁאַל אוֹתוֹ פְּלוֹנִי, וְאָמַר: לֹא הָיוּ דְּבָרִים מֵעוֹלָם.

וְכֵן אִם הֻחְזְקָה נִדָּה בִּשְׁכֵנוֹתֶיהָ וְאָמְרָה לְבַעְלָהּ: טְהוֹרָה אֲנִי, וּבָא עָלֶיהָ.

יב וְאֵי זוֹ הִיא דַּת יְהוּדִית? הוּא מִנְהַג הַצְּנִיעוּת שֶׁנָּהֲגוּ בְּנוֹת יִשְׂרָאֵל.

וְאֵלּוּ הֵן הַדְּבָרִים שֶׁאִם עָשְׂתָה אַחַת מֵהֶן עָבְרָה עַל דַּת יְהוּדִית:

יוֹצְאָה לַשּׁוּק אוֹ לְמָבוֹי מְפֻלָּשׁ וְרֹאשָׁהּ פָּרוּעַ וְאֵין עָלֶיהָ רְדִיד כְּכָל הַנָּשִׁים, אַף-עַל-פִּי שֶׁשְּׂעָרָהּ מְכֻסֶּה בְּמִטְפַּחַת.

אוֹ שֶׁהָיְתָה טוֹוָה בַּשּׁוּק וְוֶרֶד וְכַיּוֹצֵא בּוֹ כְּנֶגֶד פָּנֶיהָ, עַל פַּדַּחְתָּהּ אוֹ עַל לֶחְיֶיהָ, כְּדֶרֶךְ שֶׁעוֹשׂוֹת הָעַכּוּ"ם הַפְּרוּצוֹת.

---

uncovered. From this, *Ketubot* 72a derives the concept that a married Jewish woman's hair should always be covered. Similarly, the *Shulchan Aruch* (*Even HaEzer* 21:2) prohibits a married woman from walking in the public domain with uncovered hair.

Although this custom was not practiced conscientiously in many European communities even within the religious population, our Torah authorities have always called for its observance. The failure of a woman to cover her hair is considered adequate grounds for divorce. It must, however, be emphasized that a husband who married a woman who he knew would not cover her hair cannot later divorce her on the grounds that she fails to do so, without making full settlement of his obligations according to the marriage contract.

26. I.e., prohibitions of Rabbinic origin as well as those explicit in the Torah.

27. E.g., she wore clothes customarily worn when she was a *niddah*. In the present age, it is not customary for women to wear special clothes while they are in the *niddah* state.

28. The previous halachah spoke of her going out to a public place with her hair totally

b) she spins [flax or wool] with a rose on her face[29] - on her forehead or on her cheek - like immodest gentile women,

c) she spins in the marketplace and shows her forearms to men;[30]

d) she plays frivolously with young lads,

e) she demands sexual intimacy from her husband in a loud voice until her neighbors hear her talking about their intimate affairs, or

f) she curses her husband's father in her husband's presence.[31]

13. Ezra ordained that a woman should wear a belt[32] in her home at all times, as an expression of modesty. If a woman does not wear [such a belt], however, she is not considered to have violated the faith of Moses, nor does she forfeit her *ketubah*.

Similarly, if she goes from courtyard to courtyard without having her hair [fully] covered - as long as it is covered with a handkerchief, she is not considered to have violated the [Jewish] faith.

14. A woman who violates the faith must have had a warning issued to her [prior to her having performed the act] and [the warning and her improper conduct must be observed by] witnesses before she forfeits her *ketubah*.

[The following rule applies when a woman] transgresses privately, her husband knows that she violated the faith and [therefore] gives her a warning, [but the warning] was not observed by witnesses, and then she transgresses again. Should the husband claim that she violated [the faith] after receiving a warning,[33] and the woman claims not to have transgressed, or not to have received a warning, the husband must pay her [the money due her by virtue of her] *ketubah* if he desires[34] to divorce her, after she takes an oath that she has not transgressed. [This oath is required because] she would not be entitled to any payment if she admitted to having transgressed after having received this warning.

15. What is meant by "a woman who is divorced because of a scandalous report"? For example, there were witnesses that she performed a very indecent act that indicates that a sin was committed, but there is no definitive testimony [that she committed adultery].

What is implied? She was alone in her courtyard, and they saw a perfume salesman leaving. They entered immediately afterwards and saw her getting up from bed and putting on her underwear or tying her belt, or they found wet spittle on the canopy above the bed.[35] Alternatively, they saw them coming out of a dark place [together], or one helping the other up from a trench or the like, or they saw him kissing the opening of her cloak, or saw them kissing each other, or embracing each other, or they entered a

uncovered. This halachah mentioned the covering of her hair, but not according to the accepted norms of modesty.

אוֹ שֶׁטּוֹוָה בַּשּׁוּק וּמַרְאֵית זְרוֹעוֹתֶיהָ לִבְנֵי אָדָם.

אוֹ שֶׁהָיְתָה מְשַׂחֶקֶת עִם הַבַּחוּרִים.

אוֹ שֶׁהָיְתָה תּוֹבַעַת הַתַּשְׁמִישׁ בְּקוֹל רָם מִבַּעְלָהּ, עַד שֶׁשְּׁכֵנוֹתֶיהָ שׁוֹמְעוֹת אוֹתָהּ מְדַבֶּרֶת עַל עִסְקֵי תַּשְׁמִישׁ.

אוֹ שֶׁהָיְתָה מְקַלֶּלֶת אֲבִי בַעְלָהּ בִּפְנֵי בַעְלָהּ.

יג עֶזְרָא תִּקֵּן שֶׁתִּהְיֶה אִשָּׁה חוֹגֶרֶת בְּסָנָּר תָּמִיד בְּתוֹךְ בֵּיתָהּ, מִשּׁוּם צְנִיעוּת. וְאִם לֹא חָגְרָה — אֵינָהּ עוֹבֶרֶת עַל דַּת מֹשֶׁה, וְלֹא הִפְסִידָה כְּתֻבָּתָהּ.

וְכֵן אִם יָצְאָה וְרֹאשָׁהּ פָּרוּעַ מֵחָצֵר לְחָצֵר בְּתוֹךְ הַמָּבוֹי — הוֹאִיל וּשְׂעָרָהּ מְכֻסֶּה בְּמִטְפַּחַת, אֵינָהּ עוֹבֶרֶת עַל דָּת.

יד הָעוֹבֶרֶת עַל דָּת — צְרִיכָה הַתְרָאָה וְעֵדִים, וְאַחַר כָּךְ תַּפְסִיד כְּתֻבָּתָהּ.

עָבְרָה בֵּינוֹ לְבֵינָהּ, וְיָדַע שֶׁהִיא עוֹבֶרֶת עַל דָּת, וְהִתְרָה בָּהּ בְּלֹא עֵדִים, וְחָזְרָה וְעָבְרָה, הוּא טוֹעֵן וְאוֹמֵר: אַחַר הַתְרָאָה עָבְרָה, וְהִיא אוֹמֶרֶת: לֹא עָבַרְתִּי כְּלָל, אוֹ: לֹא הִתְרָה בִּי, אִם רָצָה לְהוֹצִיא — הֲרֵי זֶה נוֹתֵן כְּתֻבָּה אַחַר שֶׁתִּשָּׁבַע שֶׁלֹּא עָבְרָה; שֶׁאִם תּוֹדֶה שֶׁעָבְרָה אַחַר הַתְרָאָה זוֹ — אֵין לָהּ כְּלוּם.

טו כֵּיצַד הִיא יוֹצְאָה מִשּׁוּם שֵׁם רַע? כְּגוֹן שֶׁהָיוּ שָׁם עֵדִים שֶׁעָשְׂתָה דָּבָר מְכֹעָר בְּיוֹתֵר, שֶׁהַדְּבָרִים מַרְאִין שֶׁהָיְתָה שָׁם עֲבֵרָה, אַף־עַל־פִּי שֶׁאֵין שָׁם עֵדוּת בְּרוּרָה בִּזְנוּת.

כֵּיצַד? כְּגוֹן שֶׁהָיְתָה בְּחָצֵר לְבַדָּהּ, וְרָאוּ רוֹכֵל יוֹצֵא, וְנִכְנְסוּ מִיָּד בְּשַׁעַת יְצִיאָתוֹ. וּמָצְאוּ אוֹתָהּ עוֹמֶדֶת מֵעַל הַמִּטָּה וְהִיא לוֹבֶשֶׁת הַמִּכְנָסַיִם אוֹ חוֹגֶרֶת אֲזוֹרָהּ, אוֹ שֶׁמְּצָאוּ רֹק לַח לְמַעְלָה מִן הַכִּלָּה.

אוֹ שֶׁהָיוּ יוֹצְאִים מִמָּקוֹם אָפֵל, אוֹ מַעֲלִין זֶה אֶת זֶה מִן הַבּוֹר וְכַיּוֹצֵא בּוֹ.

אוֹ שֶׁרָאוּהוּ מְנַשֵּׁק עַל פִּי חֲלוּקָהּ, אוֹ שֶׁרָאוּ אוֹתָן מְנַשְּׁקִין זֶה אֶת זֶה אוֹ מְגַפְּפִין זֶה אֶת זֶה.

---

29. In his Commentary on the Mishnah (*Ketubot* 7:4), the Rambam mentions wearing a rose or perfume in the same manner as worn by wanton gentile women.

30. The Ramah (*Even HaEzer* 115:4) states that this applies when she does so frequently, implying that if she did so on one particular occasion, she is not placed in this category. (See *Beit Shmuel* 115:11.)

31. The Ramah (*loc. cit.*) follows more stringent opinions that state that even if she curses his father outside her husband's presence, or if she curses her husband himself to his face, she is placed in this category.

32. Our translation is based on the Rambam's Commentary on the Mishnah (*Shabbat* 10:4). Rashi (*Bava Kama* 72b) interprets this term as referring to underwear. Based on the Jerusalem Talmud (*Megillah* 4:1), which explains that this practice was instituted after a woman was raped by a monkey, it would appear that the intent is a chastity belt.

33. And he is therefore not required to pay her *ketubah*.

34. See Halachah 16.

35. Why would wet spittle be found on the canopy? Obviously, someone was lying face

room one after the other and locked the doors,[36] or any similar act [that would arouse suspicion].

[In all these instances,] if her husband desires to divorce her, she is not entitled to receive [the money due her by virtue of] her *ketubah*. There is no necessity for a warning [in this instance].[37]

16. [When a woman] violates the faith of Moses or the Jewish faith, and similarly, one about whom is issued a scandalous report, her husband is not compelled to divorce her. If he desires [to remain married], he need not divorce her.[38]

Nevertheless, even when her husband does not divorce her, she is not entitled to a *ketubah*.[39] [The rationale is that] a *ketubah* was ordained by our Sages so that a husband should not consider the divorce [of his wife as] a light matter. Our Sages were concerned only with modest Jewish women. This institution was not enacted for women [who act] wantonly. On the contrary, let their husbands think that divorcing them is a light matter.

17. When a man sees his wife commit adultery, or he was informed of this by one of his relatives or her relatives - whether male or female - whom he trusts and whose statements he believes, he is obligated to divorce her and is forbidden to engage in relations with her,[40] for he relies on their word as true.

He must [however] pay her [the money due her by virtue of her] *ketubah*,[41] [unless] she admits that she has committed adultery, in which case she should be divorced without receiving her *ketubah*. Therefore, if [her husband saw her commit adultery himself], he can require her to take an oath, while she holds a sacred object, that she did not commit adultery while married to him.[42] [Only afterwards] can she collect the money [due her by virtue of] her *ketubah*. With regard to other matters,[43] he cannot require her to take an oath, except through the convention of *gilgul [sh'vuah]*.[44]

---

up on the bed and could not turn to either side. This indicates that the woman had just been involved in sexual relations (Rashi, *Yevamot* 24b).

36. Our translation is based on the additions of the Ramah (*Even HaEzer* 11:1).

37. A woman who acts in this manner is considered to have committed adultery, and there is no need for a warning in such an instance.

38. As mentioned in Halachah 18, the court does not compel a man to divorce his wife unless two witnesses testify that she willingly committed adultery. Nevertheless, in the situations mentioned above, it is clear that our Sages desired that the woman be divorced. Moreover, the *Shulchan Aruch* (*Even HaEzer* 115:4) states that it is a mitzvah to divorce such a woman.

The Ramah adds that even though in most cases we follow the enactment of Rabbenu Gershom, who forbade divorcing a woman against her will, in this instance an exception is made. Even if the woman does not consent to the divorce, her husband may divorce her.

אוֹ שֶׁנִּכְנְסוּ זֶה אַחַר זֶה וְהִגִּיפוּ דְלָתוֹת. וְכַיּוֹצֵא בִּדְבָרִים אֵלּוּ.
אִם רָצָה הַבַּעַל לְהוֹצִיאָהּ — תֵּצֵא בְּלֹא כְתֻבָּה.
וְאֵין זוֹ צְרִיכָה הַתְרָאָה.

טז עוֹבֶרֶת עַל דַּת מֹשֶׁה אוֹ עַל דַּת יְהוּדִית, וְכֵן זֹאת שֶׁעָשְׂתָה דָּבָר מְכֹעָר — אֵין כּוֹפִין אֶת
הַבַּעַל לְהוֹצִיא, אֶלָּא אִם רָצָה — לֹא יוֹצִיא.
וְאַף־עַל־פִּי שֶׁלֹּא הוֹצִיא — אֵין לָהֶן כְּתֻבָּה.
שֶׁהַכְּתֻבָּה תַּקָּנַת חֲכָמִים הִיא כְּדֵי שֶׁלֹּא תְּהֵא קַלָּה בְּעֵינָיו לְהוֹצִיאָהּ, וְלֹא הִקְפִּידוּ אֶלָּא עַל
בְּנוֹת יִשְׂרָאֵל הַצְּנוּעוֹת;
אֲבָל אֵלּוּ הַפְּרוּצוֹת אֵין לָהֶן תַּקָּנָה [זוֹ], אֶלָּא תְּהֵא קַלָּה בְּעֵינָיו לְהוֹצִיאָהּ.

יז מִי שֶׁרָאָה אִשְׁתּוֹ שֶׁזִּנְּתָה, אוֹ שֶׁאָמְרָה לוֹ אַחַת מִקְרוֹבוֹתָיו אוֹ מִקְרוֹבוֹתֶיהָ, שֶׁהוּא מַאֲמִינָם
וְסוֹמֶכֶת דַּעְתּוֹ עֲלֵיהֶם, שֶׁזִּנְּתָה אִשְׁתּוֹ,
בֵּין שֶׁהָיָה הָאוֹמֵר אִישׁ אוֹ בֵּין שֶׁהָיְתָה אִשָּׁה — הוֹאִיל וְסָמְכָה דַּעְתּוֹ לְדָבָר זֶה שֶׁהוּא אֱמֶת,
הֲרֵי זֶה חַיָּב לְהוֹצִיא, וְאָסוּר לוֹ לָבוֹא עָלֶיהָ, וְיִתֵּן כְּתֻבָּה.
וְאִם הוֹדָת לוֹ שֶׁזִּנְּתָה — תֵּצֵא בְּלֹא כְתֻבָּה.
לְפִיכָךְ מַשְׁבִּיעָהּ מַשְׁבִּיעָהּ בִּנְקִיטַת חֵפֶץ שֶׁלֹּא זִנְּתָה תַּחְתָּיו, אִם רָאָה אוֹתָהּ בְּעַצְמוֹ, וְאַחַר כָּךְ תִּגְבֶּה
כְּתֻבָּתָהּ.
אֲבָל בִּדְבָר אַחֵר — אֵינוֹ יָכוֹל לְהַשְׁבִּיעָהּ אֶלָּא עַל יְדֵי גִלְגּוּל.

39. Nor is she entitled to any of the provisions of the *ketubah* while they remain married, as stated above (Halachah 10). Note, however, the *Chelkat Mechokek* 115:18, who states that if the couple remain married, and afterwards the woman repents and begins conducting herself modestly, her husband is obligated to write a new *ketubah* for her.

40. When a married woman has committed adultery, she is forbidden to engage in sexual relations with her husband in the future. (Similarly, she is forbidden to engage in relations with the adulterer.) Since her husband either saw the matter himself or heard it from a person upon whom he relies, he is bound by this prohibition.

41. Since he has no binding evidence that she committed adultery that will be accepted by a court, she cannot be forced to forgo her claim for the money he is obligated to pay her.

42. The Rambam compares this to a situation in which a creditor desires to collect a debt supported by a promissory note, and the debtor states: "I have paid the note." Although the creditor is allowed to collect the debt, he must take an oath first.

43. Our translation follows the standard published text of the *Mishneh Torah*. According to this version, the intent is difficult to comprehend, as reflected in the questions raised by the *Maggid Mishneh*.

The *Kessef Mishneh* explains that the proper version is בדברי אחר. The intent is that if the husband saw his wife commit adultery himself, he may require her to take an oath, because his claim is definite. If, by contrast, his claim is based on the statements of another person, his claim is not definite and he does not have the right to require her to take an oath.

44. I.e., if she is obligated to take another oath before collecting the money due her by

18. When a woman tells her husband that she willingly committed adultery, no attention is paid to her words. [We suspect] that she is attracted to another man [and wants to be released from marriage to her husband so that she can marry him].[45] She does, however, lose the rights to her *ketubah* - both the fundamental requirement and any extra amount - and [her right to any of her property] that was destroyed, for she admitted that she has committed adultery.[46] If he believes her and considers her word to be true, he is obligated to divorce her.

A court, however, does not obligate a man to divorce his wife through any means, unless two witnesses come forth and testify that the person's wife willingly committed adultery in their presence. [In such a situation,] he is compelled to divorce her.

19. A woman who committed adultery unknowingly[47] or who was raped is permitted to [continue marital relations with] her husband, as [implied the Numbers 5:13, which describes adultery:] "and she was not raped," indicating that if she was raped, she is permitted. [This applies whether] she was raped by a gentile or by a Jew.

Whenever [a woman] was forced into relations at the outset, she is permitted [to her husband], even if she ultimately consented - even if she says: "Let him continue, if he had not raped me, I would have hired him." For [her] natural inclination has overcome her; originally, she was forced against her will.

20. When women have been abducted by robbers, they are considered as though they have been taken captive and were raped; they are permitted to their husbands.[48] If, however, they were left alone and they went to the robbers on their own initiative, they are considered to have acted willingly and they are forbidden to their husbands.

The laws applying to a woman who acted unwittingly and to one who was raped are the same. For acting unwittingly is comparable to a deed committed under coercion.

21. When does the above apply? When the woman's husband was an Israelite. If, however, a priest's wife [committed adultery] unwittingly or under duress, she is forbidden to her husband. For these relations cause her to be deemed a *zonah* at all times, and he is forbidden to have relations with a *zonah*, as will be explained in *Hilchot Issurei Bi'ah*.[49]

---

virtue of her *ketubah*, her husband may also require her to take the oath concerning adultery.
45. The husband need not divorce her, and he may continue engaging in marital relations with her without worrying that he is transgressing the prohibition mentioned in the previous halachah.

יח אָמְרָה לוֹ אִשְׁתּוֹ שֶׁזִּנְתָה תַּחְתָּיו בִּרְצוֹנָה — אֵין מַשְׁגִּיחִין לִדְבָרֶיהָ, שֶׁמָּא עֵינֶיהָ נָתְנָה בְּאַחֵר.

אֲבָל אִבְּדָה כְּתֻבָּתָהּ, עִקָּר וְתוֹסֶפֶת, וְאִבְּדָה הַבְּלָאוֹת; שֶׁהֲרֵי הוֹדָת בִּזְנוּת.

וְאִם הָיָה מַאֲמִינָהּ וְסוֹמֵךְ דַּעְתּוֹ עַל דְּבָרֶיהָ — הֲרֵי זֶה חַיָּב לְהוֹצִיאָהּ.

וְאֵין בֵּית דִּין כּוֹפִין אֶת הָאִישׁ לְגָרֵשׁ אֶת אִשְׁתּוֹ בְּדָבָר מִדְּבָרִים אֵלּוּ, עַד שֶׁיָּבוֹאוּ שְׁנֵי עֵדִים וְיָעִידוּ שֶׁזִּנְתָה אִשְׁתּוֹ זֹאת בִּפְנֵיהֶם בִּרְצוֹנָהּ, וְאַחַר כָּךְ כּוֹפִין אוֹתוֹ לְהוֹצִיא.

יט הָאִשָּׁה שֶׁזִּנְתָה תַּחַת בַּעְלָהּ בִּשְׁגָגָה אוֹ בְּאֹנֶס — הֲרֵי זוֹ מֻתֶּרֶת לְבַעְלָהּ. שֶׁנֶּאֱמַר: וְהִיא לֹא נִתְפָּשָׂה; הָא נִתְפָּשָׂה — מֻתֶּרֶת.

בֵּין שֶׁאֲנָסָהּ עַכּוּ"ם בֵּין שֶׁאֲנָסָהּ יִשְׂרָאֵל.

וְכֹל שֶׁתְּחִלַּת בִּיאָתָהּ בְּאֹנֶס, אַף־עַל־פִּי שֶׁסּוֹפָהּ בְּרָצוֹן, וַאֲפִלּוּ אָמְרָה: הַנִּיחוּ לוֹ, שֶׁאִלְמָלֵי לֹא אֲנָס אוֹתִי הָיִיתִי שׂוֹכַרְתּוֹ — הֲרֵי זוֹ מֻתֶּרֶת; שֶׁהַיֵּצֶר לְבָשָׁהּ, וּמִתְּחִלָּה [הָיְתָה] בְּאֹנֶס.

כ נָשִׁים שֶׁגִּנְּבוּ אוֹתָן לִסְטִים — הֲרֵי הֵן כִּשְׁבוּיוֹת, שֶׁהֵן אֲנוּסוֹת, וּמֻתָּרוֹת לְבַעְלֵיהֶן.

וְאִם הִנִּיחוּם, וְהָלְכוּ לַלִּסְטִים מֵעַצְמָן — הֲרֵי אֵלּוּ בְּרָצוֹן, וַאֲסוּרוֹת לְבַעְלֵיהֶן.

וְדִין הַשּׁוֹגֶגֶת וְדִין הַנֶּאֱנֶסֶת אֶחָד הוּא, שֶׁהַשְּׁגָגָה צַד אֹנֶס יֵשׁ בָּהּ.

כא בַּמֶּה דְּבָרִים אֲמוּרִים? בְּשֶׁהָיָה בַּעְלָהּ יִשְׂרָאֵל;

אֲבָל אֵשֶׁת כֹּהֵן שֶׁשָּׁגְגָה אוֹ שֶׁנֶּאֶנְסָה — אֲסוּרָה לְבַעְלָהּ,

שֶׁהֲרֵי נַעֲשָׂת זוֹנָה מִכָּל מָקוֹם, וְהוּא אָסוּר בְּזוֹנָה, כְּמוֹ שֶׁיִּתְבָּאֵר בְּהִלְכוֹת אִסּוּרֵי בִּיאָה.

46. In cases of monetary law, we follow the principle that the statements of the principal himself are equal to those of 100 witnesses. Since she admitted committing adultery, she must suffer the financial consequences.

In his Commentary on the Mishnah (*Nedarim* 11:12), the Rambam explains that when the husband says, "I do not believe her," he is still permitted to engage in relations with her. We do not, however, say: "If you believe her, pay her the money due her by virtue of her *ketubah*," for we divide his statements (*palginin dibburo*), and apply them in one context, but not in another. This explanation has, however, aroused questions in certain commentaries.

47. E.g., two couples were married at the same time and the women unwittingly went into the wrong marriage chambers, and each thought that she was with her own spouse (*Yevamot* 33b). When, however, a woman commits adultery under the impression that she is allowed to do so, she is considered to have acted willfully, and she is forbidden to enter into relations with her husband (Ramah, *Even HaEzer* 178:3).

48. *Ketubot* 51b relates that in Babylonia there was a time when robber bands would frequently abduct women from their homes.

49. Chapter 17, Halachot 1 and 7; Chapter 18, Halachah 1. This prohibition is a result of the extra dimension of sanctity conveyed upon a priest and is not a reflection of the woman's lack of virtue.

22. With regard to both an Israelite's wife and a priest's wife who have been raped, they are entitled to their *ketubah* - both the fundamental requirement and the additional amount. She does not lose anything in this regard. We compel[50] the priest to pay [her the money due her by virtue of] her *ketubah* and then to divorce her.

23. When a priest's wife tells her husband: "I was raped," or "I unwittingly had relations with another man," he should not pay any attention to her words. [We suspect that perhaps] she was attracted to another man.

If he believes her, or he was told about it by a person upon whose word he relies, he should divorce her and pay her [the money due her by virtue of her] *ketubah*.[51]

24. [The following rules apply when] a man tells his wife in the presence of witnesses: "Do not enter into privacy with so and so." If two witnesses observed her entering into privacy with the said person, and she and he remained there sufficient time for relations to have taken place,[52] she is forbidden to engage in relations with her husband until he causes her to drink "the bitter waters",[53] as will be explained in *Hilchot Sotah*.[54]

If he dies before he has caused her to drink [these waters], she is not entitled to her *ketubah*. Although witnesses did not see any [blatant] wanton act, there is no more wanton behavior than [disobeying her husband's words in] this [manner].

In the present age, when the waters [to test a] *sotah* are not available to us, the woman becomes forbidden to her husband forever. She must be divorced without receiving [the money due her by virtue of] her *ketubah*, neither the fundamental requirement nor the additional amount, for it is her evil deeds that caused her to become forbidden.[55]

25. [The following laws apply when a husband] tells [his wife] in private: "Do not enter into seclusion with so and so." If he observed her enter into seclusion with the said person, and she and he remained there sufficient time for relations to have taken place - in the present age,[56] when the waters [to test a] *sotah* are not available to us - the woman becomes forbidden to her husband. He is obligated to divorce her and pay [her the money due her by virtue of] her *ketubah*.

If she admits entering into seclusion with the said person after having received the warning, she must be divorced without receiving [the money due her by virtue of] her *ketubah*. Therefore, she is required to take an oath in this regard.[57] Only afterwards must he pay [her the money due her by virtue of] her *ketubah*.

50. Leviticus 21:8 states: "And you shall make him holy." *Yevamot* 88b infers that the intent is that a priest should be forced to make himself holy and avoid relations with such women, even if that involves compelling him against his will.

כב אֶחָד אֵשֶׁת יִשְׂרָאֵל אוֹ אֵשֶׁת כֹּהֵן שֶׁנֶּאֶנְסָה — כְּתֻבָּתָהּ קַיֶּמֶת, הָעִקָּר וְהַתּוֹסֶפֶת, וְלֹא הִפְסִידָה מִכְּתֻבָּתָהּ כְּלוּם.

וְכוֹפִין אֶת הַכֹּהֵן לִתֵּן לָהּ כְּתֻבָּתָהּ וּלְגָרְשָׁהּ.

כג אֵשֶׁת כֹּהֵן שֶׁאָמְרָה לְבַעְלָהּ: נֶאֱנַסְתִּי, אוֹ שָׁגַגְתִּי וְנִבְעַלְתִּי לְאַחֵר — אֵינוֹ חוֹשֵׁשׁ לִדְבָרֶיהָ, שֶׁמָּא עֵינֶיהָ נָתְנָה בְּאַחֵר.

וְאִם הָיְתָה נֶאֱמֶנֶת לוֹ, אוֹ שֶׁאָמַר לוֹ אָדָם שֶׁהוּא סוֹמֵךְ עַל דְּבָרָיו — יוֹצִיא וְיִתֵּן כְּתֻבָּה.

כד הָאוֹמֵר לְאִשְׁתּוֹ בִּפְנֵי שְׁנַיִם: אַל תִּסָּתְרִי עִם אִישׁ פְּלוֹנִי, וְנִכְנְסָה עִמּוֹ לַסֵּתֶר בִּפְנֵי שְׁנֵי עֵדִים, וְשָׁהֲתָה כְּדֵי טֻמְאָה — הֲרֵי זוֹ אֲסוּרָה עַל בַּעְלָהּ עַד שֶׁיַּשְׁקֶנָּה מֵי הַמָּרִים, כְּמוֹ שֶׁיִּתְבָּאֵר בְּהִלְכוֹת סוֹטָה.

וְאִם מֵת קֹדֶם שֶׁיַּשְׁקֶנָּה — אֵין לָהּ כְּתֻבָּה.

וְאַף־עַל־פִּי שֶׁלֹּא מָצְאוּ דָּבָר מְכֹעָר, שֶׁאֵין לְךָ דָּבָר יוֹתֵר מְכֹעָר מִזֶּה.

וְהַיּוֹם שֶׁאֵין שָׁם מֵי סוֹטָה — נֶאֶסְרָה עָלָיו אִסּוּר עוֹלָם.

וְתֵצֵא בְּלֹא כְּתֻבָּה, לֹא עִקָּר וְלֹא תּוֹסֶפֶת, שֶׁהֲרֵי מַעֲשֶׂיהָ הָרָעִים גָּרְמוּ לָהּ לְהֵאָסֵר.

כה אָמַר לָהּ בֵּינוֹ לְבֵינָהּ: אַל תִּסָּתְרִי עִם אִישׁ פְּלוֹנִי, וְרָאָה אוֹתָהּ שֶׁנִּסְתְּרָה עִמּוֹ וְשָׁהֲתָה כְּדֵי טֻמְאָה — הֲרֵי זוֹ אֲסוּרָה עָלָיו בַּזְּמַן הַזֶּה שֶׁאֵין שָׁם מֵי סוֹטָה.

וְחַיָּב לְהוֹצִיא, וְיִתֵּן כְּתֻבָּה.

וְאִם הוֹדֵת שֶׁנִּסְתְּרָה אַחַר שֶׁהִתְרָה בָּהּ — תֵּצֵא בְּלֹא כְּתֻבָּה.

וּלְפִיכָךְ מַשְׁבִּיעָהּ עַל זֶה, וְאַחַר כָּךְ יִתֵּן כְּתֻבָּה.

---

51. See the explanation in Halachah 18. The reason this woman is entitled to the money due her by virtue of her *ketubah* is that she did not commit adultery willingly.

52. *Hilchot Sotah* 1:2 explains this as the amount of time it takes to roast an egg and swallow it. In quantitative terms, the more stringent of the contemporary authorities have estimated this as 35 seconds.

53. This phrase is borrowed from Numbers 5:18. *Hilchot Sotah* 3:10 explains that the term is used because a bitter-flavored substance was added to the water.

54. Chapter 1, Halachah 2. Although there is no evidence that the woman actually committed adultery, since she was warned by her husband and violated his warning, the burden of proof is upon her. It is only through drinking the waters given a *sotah* that she can vindicate herself.

55. The Rambam is explaining why the woman is forced to forfeit her *ketubah*, although there is no conclusive proof of adultery. She knew about the prohibition against entering into privacy with the said individual and violated it willingly. Hence, she is required to suffer the consequences.

56. The *Kessef Mishneh* questions why the Rambam mentions "the present age." Seemingly, in the time of the Temple as well, a similar problem would arise - if the warning was not given in the presence of witnesses, the waters given a *sotah* could not be used to test the woman's faithfulness.

57. See Halachah 17 and notes.

CHAPTER TWENTY-FIVE

1. When a man marries a woman without having made any specifications about that matter, and it is discovered that she is bound by vows, he [may] divorce her without having to pay [her the money due her by virtue of] her *ketubah* - neither the fundamental requirement nor the additional amount.[1]

With regard to which vows does this rule apply? [I.e., a vow] not to eat meat, not to drink wine, or not to adorn herself with colored garments or with other objects with which women of her locale customarily adorn themselves.[2] If, however, she is bound by other vows, she does not forfeit anything.

2. Similar [rules apply when] a man marries a woman without having made any specifications about the matter, and it is discovered that she has one of the blemishes [that mar] a woman's [appeal to her husband], as outlined above.[3] If the husband neither knew nor heard about this blemish, and did not willingly accept it, he [may] divorce [his wife] without having to pay [her the money due her by virtue of] her *ketubah* - neither the fundamental requirement nor the additional amount.

What is implied? If there is a bathhouse in the city, and he has relatives [in the town], he does not have the prerogative of saying: "I did not know about these blemishes." [This applies even if] the blemishes were located in hidden places. For we assume that he checks with his relatives [and asks them about his wife's condition]. [If he marries her nonetheless,] we can assume that he heard [about the blemishes] and accepted them.

If the town does not possess a bathhouse, or if he does not have relatives, he may issue a claim with regard to blemishes that are usually unseen. Regular fits of epilepsy are considered to be a blemish that is unseen.[4]

By contrast, with regard to physical blemishes that are openly seen, the husband cannot claim [not to have known about the blemish]. For they can be seen by everyone, and it may be assumed that he heard about them and accepted [the matter]. This law applies only in those places where it is customary for women to walk in the marketplace with their faces uncovered, and everyone recognizes each other and will say: "This is so and so's daughter," and "This is so and so's sister," as in the European cities of the present era.

In places where, by contrast, women do not go out to the marketplace at all, and if a girl goes out to the bathhouse in the evening she goes out veiled, and no one will see her except her relatives, a claim may be issued with regard to blemishes that can be openly seen as well.

[Such a claim may be issued] when there is no bathhouse in the city, or [the husband] does not have a relative with whom he can check. If, however, there

1. The husband is not required to pay his wife the money due her by virtue of her *ketubah*,

פֶּרֶק חֲמִשָּׁה וְעֶשְׂרִים

א הַנּוֹשֵׂא אִשָּׁה סְתָם, וְנִמְצְאוּ עָלֶיהָ נְדָרִים — תֵּצֵא בְּלֹא כְּתֻבָּה, לֹא עִקָּר וְלֹא תּוֹסֶפֶת. בְּאֵילוּ נְדָרִים אָמְרוּ?

שֶׁלֹּא תֹאכַל בָּשָׂר, אוֹ שֶׁלֹּא תִשְׁתֶּה יַיִן, אוֹ שֶׁלֹּא תִתְקַשֵּׁט בְּמִינֵי צִבְעוֹנִין, וְהוּא הַדִּין לִשְׁאָר הַמִּינִים שֶׁדֶּרֶךְ כָּל נְשֵׁי הַמָּקוֹם לְהִתְקַשֵּׁט בָּהֶן;

אֲבָל נִמְצָא עָלֶיהָ נֶדֶר אַחֵר חוּץ מֵאֵלּוּ — לֹא הִפְסִידָה כְּלוּם.

ב וְכֵן הַכּוֹנֵס אִשָּׁה סְתָם, וְנִמְצָא בָהּ מוּם מִמּוּמֵי הַנָּשִׁים שֶׁכְּבָר בֵּאַרְנוּם, וְלֹא יָדַע הַבַּעַל בְּמוּם זֶה וְלֹא שָׁמַע בּוֹ וְרָצָה — הֲרֵי זוֹ תֵּצֵא בְּלֹא כְּתֻבָּה, לֹא עִקָּר וְלֹא תּוֹסֶפֶת.

כֵּיצַד? הָיָה מֶרְחָץ בָּעִיר וְהָיוּ לוֹ קְרוֹבִים — אֵינוֹ יָכוֹל לוֹמַר: לֹא יָדַעְתִּי מוּמִין אֵלּוּ, וַאֲפִלּוּ מוּמִין שֶׁבַּסֵּתֶר; מִפְּנֵי שֶׁהוּא בּוֹדֵק בִּקְרוֹבוֹתָיו, וַחֲזָקָה שֶׁשָּׁמַע וְרָצָה.

וְאִם אֵין שָׁם מֶרְחָץ אוֹ שֶׁלֹּא הָיוּ לוֹ קְרוֹבִים — טוֹעֵן בְּמוּמִין שֶׁבַּסֵּתֶר. וְנִכְפָּה בְּעִתִּים יְדוּעִים — הֲרֵי הוּא מִמּוּמֵי סֵתֶר.

אֲבָל בְּמוּמִין שֶׁבַּגָּלוּי — אֵינוֹ יָכוֹל לִטְעוֹן; שֶׁהֲרֵי הַכֹּל רוֹאִין אוֹתָן וְאוֹמְרִין לוֹ, וְחֶזְקָתוֹ שֶׁשָּׁמַע וְנִתְפַּיֵּס.

דָּבָר יָדוּעַ הוּא, שֶׁאֵין זֶה דִין זֶה אֶלָּא בְּאוֹתָן הַמְּקוֹמוֹת שֶׁהָיָה מִנְהַג הַנָּשִׁים שָׁם לְהַלֵּךְ בַּשּׁוּק וּפְנֵיהֶן גְּלוּיוֹת, וְהַכֹּל יוֹדְעִין אוֹתָן וְאוֹמְרִין: זוֹ הִיא בִּתּוֹ שֶׁל פְּלוֹנִי, וְזוֹ הִיא אֲחוֹתוֹ שֶׁל פְּלוֹנִי, כְּמוֹ עָרֵי אֱדוֹם בַּזְּמַן הַזֶּה.

אֲבָל מְקוֹמוֹת שֶׁאֵין דֶּרֶךְ הַבָּנוֹת שָׁם לָצֵאת לַשּׁוּק כְּלָל, וְאִם תֵּצֵא הַבַּת לַמֶּרְחָץ — בַּנֶּשֶׁף תֵּצֵא, מִתְכַּסָּה, וְלֹא יִרְאֶה אוֹתָהּ אָדָם חוּץ מִקְּרוֹבוֹתֶיהָ — הֲרֵי זֶה טוֹעֵן אַף בְּמוּמִין שֶׁבַּגָּלוּי.

וְהוּא, שֶׁלֹּא הָיָה שָׁם מֶרְחָץ וְשֶׁלֹּא הָיְתָה לוֹ קְרוֹבָה לִבְדֹּק בָּהּ;

---

because their marriage agreement is considered to be a *mekach ta'ut,* an agreement entered into under false premises. For he did not expect to marry a woman bound by such vows. Nevertheless, in contrast to the law stated in Chapter 7, Halachah 6, in this instance - since the husband did not make an explicit statement to this effect when he consecrated the woman - he is required to divorce her formally.

2. These vows are considered by *Ketubot* 72b to cause *innui nefesh,* "the oppression of the soul." When a woman is bound by these restrictions, she will be depressed, and she will not be pleasant company for her husband. Hence, he is entitled to divorce her.

3. See Chapter 7, Halachah 7. In the instance described in the present halachah, a divorce is necessary because the husband did not make an explicit statement of intent.

4. The intent is epileptic fits that follow a set pattern. At these times the woman will not go out in public, and her affliction will therefore not be known.

is a bathhouse in the city, [even] when it is not customary for women to go out with their faces uncovered, if [the husband] has a relative in the city he may not issue such a claim, for everyone sees her naked in the bathhouse.

If the woman's habit is to cover herself and to hide even in the bathhouse, or she washes at night, or in a small private room in the bathhouse, so she will not be seen, and no one will know of her, [her husband] may issue a claim, even with regard to blemishes that can be seen openly.

These matters are concepts that reason dictates; they are not decrees of the Torah [to be accepted on faith].

3. Some of the *geonim* have ruled that our Sages' statement that a husband can check [concerning his wife's appearance] with his relatives does not apply only to his relatives, but also to his friends. [According to their thesis,] even if a man lives in a city in which he does not have any relatives at all, if there is a bathhouse in the city he does not have the right to issue a claim, for it is impossible that he will not have friends, and he can tell one of his friends to have his wife or sister check the appearance of so and so [i.e., the woman he thinks of marrying]. Therefore, we assume that he had heard of [any blemishes she had] and accepted them.

I do not agree with this conclusion.[5] For a man will not reveal all the concerns he has regarding matters such as these to anyone other than his relatives. Moreover, he will rely only on the word of his relatives.

4. What is meant by a claim issued because of physical blemishes? If the blemishes that were found were such that it is certain that they existed before she was consecrated - e.g., an extra finger or the like - the burden of proof is on the father. He must prove that the husband knew about them and accepted them, or that they were such that we may assume that he knew.[6] If he cannot bring proof, the woman may be divorced without receiving any [of the money due her by virtue] of her *ketubah* at all.[7]

[The following rules apply when] the blemishes were such that they could have come about after she was consecrated. If the blemishes were discovered after the woman entered her husband's home, the burden of proof is on the husband. He must show that she possessed these blemishes before she was consecrated, and that he entered into the relationship under false premises. If the blemishes were discovered while she still was in her father's home, the burden of proof is on [the father]. He must show that the blemishes came about after the consecration, and the husband suffered the loss.[8]

5. If the husband brought proof that [the woman] had [the blemishes] before she was consecrated, or she admitted that fact, and the father brought proof that the husband had seen the blemishes and accepted them in silence, or that one could assume that he knew about them and accepted them, [the husband] is obligated with regard to the *ketubah*.

אֲבָל הָיָה שָׁם מֶרְחָץ בְּעִיר זוֹ שֶׁאֵין דֶּרֶךְ הַנָּשִׁים לָצֵאת בָּהּ וּפְנֵיהֶם מְגֻלּוֹת, אִם יֵשׁ לוֹ קְרוֹבָה — אֵינוֹ יָכוֹל לִטְעֹן, שֶׁהֲרֵי הַכֹּל רוֹאִין אוֹתָהּ עֲרֻמָּה בַּמֶּרְחָץ.

וְאִם דַּרְכָּן לְהִתְכַּבֵּר וּלְהִתְחַבֵּא אַף בַּמֶּרְחָץ, וְשֶׁתִּהְיֶה הַבַּת רוֹחֶצֶת בַּלַּיְלָה אוֹ בְּבַיִת קָטָן בַּמֶּרְחָץ לְבַדָּהּ, עַד שֶׁלֹּא תֵּרָאֶה וְלֹא תִּוָּדַע — הֲרֵי זֶה טוֹעֵן אַף בְּמוּמִין שֶׁבַּגָּלוּי. וְהַדְּבָרִים הָאֵלּוּ דְּבָרִים שֶׁל טַעַם הֵם, וְאֵינָם גְּזֵרַת הַכָּתוּב.

ג הוֹרוּ מִקְצָת הַגְּאוֹנִים, שֶׁזֶּה שֶׁאָמְרוּ חֲכָמִים 'מִפְּנֵי שֶׁהוּא בּוֹדֵק בִּקְרוֹבוֹתָיו', אֵינוֹ קְרוֹבוֹתָיו בִּלְבַד, אֶלָּא אֲפִלּוּ מְיֻדָּעָיו.

וַאֲפִלּוּ הָיָה גֵּר בְּעִיר שֶׁאֵין לוֹ קָרוֹב כְּלָל, אִם יֵשׁ שָׁם מֶרְחָץ — אֵינוֹ יָכוֹל לִטְעֹן; שֶׁאִי אֶפְשָׁר שֶׁלֹּא יִהְיוּ לוֹ רֵעִים, וְאוֹמֵר לְאֶחָד מֵרֵעָיו שֶׁתִּבָּדֵק לוֹ אִשְׁתּוֹ אוֹ אֲחוֹתוֹ עַל פְּלוֹנִית, וּלְפִיכָךְ חֶזְקָתוֹ שֶׁשָּׁמַע וְנִתְפַּיֵּס.

וְלֹא יֵרָאֶה לִי דִּין זֶה. שֶׁאֵין כָּל אָדָם מוֹצִיא כָּל מַה שֶּׁיֵּשׁ בְּלִבּוֹ מִדְּבָרִים אֵלּוּ לַכֹּל, אֶלָּא לִקְרוֹבָיו.

וְעוֹד, שֶׁאֵין דַּעְתּוֹ סוֹמֶכֶת אֶלָּא לְדִבְרֵי קְרוֹבָיו בְּיוֹתֵר.

ד כֵּיצַד הִיא טַעֲנַת הַמּוּמִין?

אִם הָיוּ הַמּוּמִין שֶׁנִּמְצְאוּ בָּהּ מוּמִין שֶׁוַּדַּאי הָיוּ בָּהּ קֹדֶם שֶׁתִּתְאָרֵס, כְּגוֹן אֶצְבַּע יְתֵרָה וְכַיּוֹצֵא בּוֹ — עַל הָאָב לְהָבִיא רְאָיָה שֶׁיָּדַע בָּהֶן הַבַּעַל וְרָצָה, אוֹ שֶׁחֶזְקָתוֹ שֶׁיָּדַע; וְאִם לֹא הֵבִיא רְאָיָה — תֵּצֵא בְּלֹא כְּתֻבָּה כְּלָל.

הָיוּ מוּמִים שֶׁאֶפְשָׁר שֶׁנּוֹלְדוּ בָּהּ אַחַר הָאֵרוּסִין:

אִם נִמְצְאוּ בָּהּ אַחַר שֶׁנִּכְנְסָה לְבֵית הַבַּעַל — עַל הַבַּעַל לְהָבִיא רְאָיָה שֶׁעַד שֶׁלֹּא נִתְאָרְסָה הָיוּ בָּהּ, וְהָיָה מִקָּחוֹ מִקַּח טָעוּת;

וְאִם נִמְצְאוּ בָּהּ וְהִיא בְּבֵית אָבִיהָ — עַל הָאָב לְהָבִיא רְאָיָה שֶׁאַחַר הָאֵרוּסִין נוֹלְדוּ, וְנִסְתַּחֲפָה שָׂדֵהוּ.

ה הֵבִיא הַבַּעַל רְאָיָה שֶׁעַד שֶׁלֹּא תִּתְאָרֵס הָיוּ בָּהּ, אוֹ שֶׁהוֹדָה לוֹ בְּכָךְ, וְהֵבִיא הָאָב רְאָיָה שֶׁרָאָה וְשָׁתַק וְנִתְפַּיֵּס, אוֹ שֶׁחֶזְקָתוֹ שֶׁיָּדַע בָּהֶן וְנִתְפַּיֵּס — הֲרֵי זֶה חַיָּב בִּכְתֻבָּה.

---

5. The *Shulchan Aruch* (*Even HaEzer* 117:5) follows the Rambam's rulings. Rabbenu Asher follows the other opinion that the Rambam mentioned. It is also cited by the Ramah (*loc. cit.*).

6. E.g., a blemish on her face that her prospective husband obviously must have seen.

7. The Ramah (*Even HaEzer* 117:8) quotes opinions that maintain that if the father issues a definite claim, the burden of proof is on the husband.

8. The Rambam's wording literally means "his field became flooded." The intent is that the woman had already become his wife, and her suffering the blemish is his loss.

6. If [a husband] had relations with his wife and waited several days,[9] and [afterwards,] claimed that he discovered a blemish only then, his words are disregarded. [This applies] even if [the blemish] is in the folds [of the woman's skin] or on the sole of her foot. [The rationale is that] we presume that a man will not drink from a cup unless he checks it well first.[10] [Therefore,] we assume that he knew [of the blemish] and accepted it.[11]

7. [The following rules apply when a man] marries a woman and it is discovered that she does not have a fixed time for the onset of her menstrual period, but rather she does not feel anything until she begins to menstruate. She may engage in sexual relations only if she uses two cloths with which she checks herself, one before relations and one afterwards. In addition, her husband must also check himself with a cloth, as will be explained in *Hilchot Issurei Bi'ah*.[12]

8. Even though this is a great blemish, it does not cause the woman to forfeit anything [with regard to her *ketubah*], for she can inspect herself and engage in relations.

[The following rules apply if] she inspected herself and then engaged in relations, and when she and her husband cleaned themselves afterwards, blood was found on either his cloth or her cloth.[13] If this phenomenon recurred on three consecutive occasions, she is forbidden to remain married to her husband. Instead, she must be divorced, and she is not entitled to the money due [her by virtue of] her *ketubah* - neither the fundamental requirement nor the additional amount.[14] Nor do any of the provisions of the *ketubah* apply to her. [She suffers these losses] because she is not fit to engage in sexual relations.[15]

When he divorces her, he may never remarry her. [This restriction was instituted,] lest her condition heal, in which instance his decision to divorce her would not have been final.[16]

She is permitted to marry another man,[17] as will be explained with regard to [the laws of] *niddah*.[18]

---

9. The *Kessef Mishneh* emphasizes that, as evident from the rationale the Rambam gives, what is important is that the couple engage in relations. For then we may assume that the husband looked at his wife's body first. The Rambam mentions waiting several days only to show that even if he waited - and thus it would appear that there is some basis to his claim - his words are disregarded.

10. The Rambam is obviously using a euphemism. The intent is that a husband will not enter into relations until he has looked at his wife's body.

11. The *Maggid Mishneh* notes the similarity to the laws regarding a husband's claim that his wife was not a virgin, as mentioned in Chapter 11, Halachah 15.

12. In that source (Chapter 4, Halachah 16), the Rambam states that the woman must insert a cloth into her vagina before relations and inspect it to make sure that there

ו בָּא עַל אִשְׁתּוֹ, וְשָׁהָה כַּמָּה יָמִים, וְטָעַן שָׁמוּם זֶה לֹא נִרְאָה לִי עַד עַתָּה — אֲפִלּוּ הָיָה בְּתוֹךְ הַקְּמָטִים אוֹ בְּכַף הָרֶגֶל, אֵין שׁוֹמְעִין לוֹ. חֲזָקָה שֶׁאֵין אָדָם שׁוֹתֶה בְּכוֹס אֶלָּא אִם כֵּן בּוֹדְקוֹ יָפֶה, וְחֶזְקָתוֹ שֶׁיָּדַע וְרָצָה.

ז הַנּוֹשֵׂא אִשָּׁה וְנִמְצָא שֶׁאֵין לָהּ וֶסֶת קָבוּעַ לְנִדָּתָהּ, אֶלָּא לֹא תַּרְגִּישׁ בְּעַצְמָהּ עַד שֶׁתֵּרֵד דַּם נִדָּה — הֲרֵי זוֹ לֹא תְּשַׁמֵּשׁ אֶלָּא בִּשְׁנֵי עֵדִים, שֶׁבּוֹדֶקֶת בָּהֶן עַצְמָהּ: אֶחָד לִפְנֵי תַשְׁמִישׁ, וְאֶחָד לְאַחַר תַּשְׁמִישׁ. חוּץ מִן הָעֵד שֶׁל אִישׁ, שֶׁמְּקַנֵּחַ בּוֹ עַצְמוֹ, כְּמוֹ שֶׁיִּתְבָּאֵר בְּהִלְכוֹת אִסּוּרֵי בִיאָה.

ח וְאַף־עַל־פִּי שָׁמוּם גָּדוֹל הוּא זֶה — לֹא הִפְסִידָה כְּלוּם, שֶׁהֲרֵי בּוֹדֶקֶת עַצְמָהּ תְּחִלָּה וּמְשַׁמֶּשֶׁת.
הֲרֵי שֶׁבָּדְקָה עַצְמָהּ וְנִבְעֲלָה, וּבְעֵת שֶׁקִּנְּחָה עַצְמָהּ הִיא וָהוּא נִמְצָא דָם עַל עֵד שֶׁלָּהּ אוֹ עַל עֵד שֶׁלּוֹ,
אִם אֵרַע זֶה פַּעַם אַחַר פַּעַם שָׁלֹשׁ פְּעָמִים סְמוּכוֹת זוֹ לָזוֹ — הֲרֵי זוֹ אֲסוּרָה לֵישֵׁב עִם בַּעְלָהּ.
וְתֵצֵא בְּלֹא כְּתֻבָּה, לֹא עִקָּר וְלֹא תּוֹסֶפֶת, וְאֵין לָהּ תְּנַאי מִתְּנָאֵי כְּתֻבָּה; שֶׁהֲרֵי אֵינָהּ רְאוּיָה לְתַשְׁמִישׁ.
וְיוֹצֵא וְלֹא יַחֲזִיר לְעוֹלָם; שֶׁמָּא תִּתְרַפֵּא, וְנִמְצָא שֶׁלֹּא גָמַר לְגָרְשָׁהּ בִּשְׁעַת גֵּרוּשִׁין. וּמֻתֶּרֶת לְהִנָּשֵׂא לְאַחֵר, כְּמוֹ שֶׁיִּתְבָּאֵר בְּעִנְיַן הַנִּדָּה.

is no sign of bleeding. Similarly, after relations, both she and her husband must wipe themselves with cloths and check whether there is any sign of bleeding.

The Rambam's opinion is not accepted by all other authorities. Although his view is mentioned in the *Shulchan Aruch* (*Yoreh De'ah* 186:2), the *Shulchan Aruch* favors the view that requires such an inspection only on the first three occasions of intercourse after marriage.

13. Since the inspection was made directly after relations, we assume that she menstruated in the midst of the relations. It is forbidden to continue relations in such a situation.

14. Although there are authorities who maintain that she is entitled to the additional amount, the Rambam (and similarly, the *Shulchan Aruch, Even HaEzer* 117:1) frees the husband of the obligation. The rationale is that in contrast to an *aylonit*, he is forbidden to have relations with her. And in contrast to a *sh'niyah*, he could not have known that this condition existed beforehand. Hence, he is not obligated at all.

15. The recurrence of this phenomenon on three consecutive occasions is considered to be a *chazakah*, causing us to presume that the woman will continue to experience menstrual bleeding in the midst of relations. Hence, these relations are forbidden.

16. I.e., the husband might consider his divorce as if it were made conditionally - i.e., that if her condition heals, it is not effective. For this reason, it is made clear that he may never marry her again.

17. For the sexual experience is different with each man, and it is possible that she will not menstruate in the midst of relations with another man. If, however, this occurs three times, with three different men, she is no longer permitted to marry.

18. *Hilchot Issurei Bi'ah* 4:21.

9. When does the above apply? When the woman had this condition from the beginning of her marriage, and on the first occasion that she engaged in relations she menstruated.

If, however, this ailment occurred after she married, it is the husband who suffers the loss.[19] Therefore, if [the couple] engaged in relations once and the woman did not menstruate, and afterwards she began to menstruate whenever they engaged in relations, he must divorce her and pay her all [the money due her by virtue of] her *ketubah*. He may never remarry her, as explained above.

10. Similarly, if a woman suffers blemishes after marriage, even if she becomes a leper [the loss is her husband's]. If he desires to remain married to her, he may. If he desires to divorce her, he must pay [her the money due her by virtue of] her *ketubah*.

11. [The following rules apply when] a husband suffers blemishes after he marries. Even if his hand or foot is cut off, or he becomes blinded in one eye,[20] and his wife no longer desires to live with him, he is not forced to divorce her and pay [her the money due her by virtue of] her *ketubah*. Instead, if she desires to remain married, she may. If she does not desire this, she may obtain a divorce without receiving [the money due her by virtue of] her *ketubah*, as is the law concerning any woman who rebels against her husband.[21]

If, however, he becomes[22] afflicted by [constant] bad breath or a smell from his nose, or becomes a collector of dog feces, a miner of copper, or a tanner,[23] he is forced to divorce his wife and pay [her the money due her by virtue of] her *ketubah* [if she desires to terminate the marriage].[24] If she desires, she may remained married to her husband.

12. If a man becomes a leper,[25] he is compelled to divorce his wife and pay [her the money due her by virtue of] her *ketubah*. Even if she desires to remain married to him, her request is not heeded. Instead, they are compelled to separate, because [having relations with] her will cause his flesh to be consumed. If she says: "I will remain married to him, [and we will live in the presence of] witnesses, so that we will not engage in relations," her request is heeded.

13. [The following rules apply when] a woman's husband had [constant] bad breath or a smell from his nose, or he was a collector of dog feces, or the like, and he died [childless, causing his wife to be obligated to fulfill the mitzvah of either *yibbum* or *chalitzah*]. If [the *yavam*] possesses the same difficulty that his brother, [the late husband,] had, she has the right to say: "I was

ט בַּמֶּה דְּבָרִים אֲמוּרִים? כְּשֶׁהָיְתָה כָּךְ מִתְּחִלַּת נְשׂוּאֶיהָ, וּמִבְּעִילָה רִאשׁוֹנָה רָאֲתָה דָם; אֲבָל אִם אֵרַע לָהּ חֵלִי זֶה אַחַר שֶׁנִּשֵּׂאת — נִסְתַּחֲפָה שָׂדֵהוּ. לְפִיכָךְ, אִם בָּעַל פַּעַם אַחַת וְלֹא נִמְצָא דָם, וְאַחַר כָּךְ חָזְרָה לִהְיוֹת רוֹאָה דָם בְּכָל עֵת תַּשְׁמִישׁ — יוֹצִיא וְיִתֵּן כְּתֻבָּה כֻּלָּהּ. וְלֹא יַחֲזִיר עוֹלָמִית, כְּמוֹ שֶׁבֵּאַרְנוּ.

י וְכֵן אִשָּׁה שֶׁנּוֹלְדוּ בָהּ מוּמִין אַחַר שֶׁנִּשֵּׂאת, אֲפִלּוּ נַעֲשֵׂת מֻכַּת שְׁחִין: אִם רָצָה לְקַיֵּם — יְקַיֵּם, וְאִם רָצָה לְהוֹצִיא — יִתֵּן כְּתֻבָּה.

יא הָאִישׁ שֶׁנּוֹלְדוּ בּוֹ מוּמִין אַחַר שֶׁנִּשָּׂא, אֲפִלּוּ נִקְטְעָה יָדוֹ אוֹ רַגְלוֹ אוֹ נִסְמֵית עֵינוֹ, וְלֹא רָצְתָה אִשְׁתּוֹ לֵישֵׁב עִמּוֹ — אֵין כּוֹפִין אוֹתוֹ לְהוֹצִיא וְלִתֵּן כְּתֻבָּה. אֶלָּא: אִם רָצְתָה — תֵּשֵׁב, וְאִם לֹא רָצְתָה — תֵּצֵא בְּלֹא כְּתֻבָּה, כְּדִין כָּל מוֹרֶדֶת. אֲבָל אִם נוֹלַד לוֹ רֵיחַ הַפֶּה אוֹ רֵיחַ הַחֹטֶם, אוֹ שֶׁחָזַר לִלְקֹט צוֹאַת כְּלָבִים אוֹ לַחְצֹב נְחֹשֶׁת מֵעִקָּרוֹ אוֹ לְעַבֵּד עוֹרוֹת — כּוֹפִין אוֹתוֹ לְהוֹצִיא וְלִתֵּן כְּתֻבָּה. וְאִם רָצְתָה — תֵּשֵׁב עִם בַּעְלָהּ.

יב נַעֲשָׂה הָאִישׁ מֻכֵּה שְׁחִין — כּוֹפִין אוֹתוֹ לְהוֹצִיא וְלִתֵּן כְּתֻבָּה. וְאַף־עַל־פִּי שֶׁהִיא רוֹצָה לֵישֵׁב — אֵין שׁוֹמְעִין לָהּ, אֶלָּא שֶׁמַּפְרִישִׁין אוֹתָן בְּעַל כָּרְחָן, מִפְּנֵי שֶׁהִיא מְמִקָתוּ. וְאִם אָמְרָה: אֵשֵׁב עִמּוֹ בְּעֵדִים כְּדֵי שֶׁלֹּא יָבוֹא עָלֶיהָ — שׁוֹמְעִין לָהּ.

יג מִי שֶׁהָיָה בַּעְלָהּ בַּעַל רֵיחַ הַפֶּה אוֹ רֵיחַ הַחֹטֶם אוֹ מְלַקֵּט צוֹאַת כְּלָבִים וְכַיּוֹצֵא בָּהֶן, וָמֵת, וְנָפְלָה לִפְנֵי אָחִיו, וְיֵשׁ בּוֹ אוֹתוֹ מוּם שֶׁהָיָה בְּבַעְלָהּ —

19. Since there was no difficulty at the time of marriage, it is the husband who bears the burden of the loss. (See Halachah 4.)

20. If, however, he becomes blinded in both eyes, or both his hands are cut off, he is compelled to divorce his wife (Ramah, *Even HaEzer* 154:4).

21. As explained in Chapter 14, Halachah 8, above.

22. If, before marriage, his prospective bride knew that he had these difficulties, or was involved in these professions and married him nevertheless, they are not considered to be grounds for divorce (Ramah, *Even HaEzer* 154:1).

23. All these professions cause a man to have a foul odor.

24. Although divorce proceedings must be commenced by the man, in these and certain other situations the court compels a man to commence these proceedings.

25. Here, the intent is not leprosy as described in the Torah (*tzara'at*), but rather the illness that is referred to as leprosy in contemporary terms.

willing to accept this difficulty with regard to your brother. I am not willing to accept it with regard to you." He should perform the rite of *chalitzah* and pay [her the money due her by virtue of] her *ketubah*.[26]

"May you see your children [father] children, and may there be peace over Israel."[27]

---

26. I.e., pay this money from her deceased husband's estate.

27. This verse is lacking in all manuscript copies and early printings of the *Mishneh Torah*. It appears to be a printer's addition so that the text will conclude on a positive note. (The connection to the previous subject is based on the exegesis of the verse in *Ketubot* 50a.)

יְכוֹלָה הִיא לוֹמַר: לְאָחִיךָ הָיִיתִי יְכוֹלָה לְקַבֵּל, וּלְךָ אֵינִי יְכוֹלָה לְקַבֵּל. וְיַחֲלֹץ וְיִתֵּן כְּתֻבָּה.

וּרְאֵה בָנִים לְבָנֶיךָ, שָׁלוֹם עַל יִשְׂרָאֵל.

סָלְקוּ הִלְכוֹת אִישׁוּת.

We find several halachot of the *Mishneh Torah* in which the Rambam concludes with a thought whose relevance goes beyond that of the laws that he outlined in that work, and others like this text, that conclude with the final relevant law without adding such thoughts.

Dedicated to the
Lubavitcher Rebbe

Rabbi MENACHEM MENDEL SCHNEERSON

who opened the study of the Rambam's
works to the general public.
May his teachings and example
continue to serve as a never-ending
source of life for all mankind.